Military Lives

Selected by **Hew Strachan**

OXFORD
UNIVERSITY PRESS

OXFORD
UNIVERSITY PRESS

Great Clarendon Street, Oxford OX2 6DP

Oxford University Press is a department of the University of Oxford.
It furthers the University's objective of excellence in research, scholarship,
and education by publishing worldwide in

Oxford New York

Auckland Bangkok Buenos Aires Cape Town Chennai
Dar es Salaam Delhi Hong Kong Istanbul Karachi Kolkata
Kuala Lumpur Madrid Melbourne Mexico City Mumbai Nairobi
São Paulo Shanghai Singapore Taipei Tokyo Toronto

Oxford is a registered trade mark of Oxford University Press
in the UK and in certain other countries

Published in the United States
by Oxford University Press Inc., New York

© Oxford University Press 2002

Database right Oxford University Press (maker)

First published 2002

British Library Cataloguing in Publication Data
Data available

Library of Congress Cataloging in Publication Data
Data available

ISBN 0-19-860532-3

10 9 8 7 6 5 4 3 2 1

Typeset in DanteMT
by Alliance Interactive Technology, Pondicherry, India
Printed in Great Britain
by T. J. International, Padstow, Cornwall

Preface

'The best record of a nation's past that any civilization has produced': G. M. Trevelyan's view in 1944 of the *Dictionary of National Biography* highlights the achievement of its first editor Leslie Stephen. Between 1885 and 1900 quarterly volumes rolled out from the presses in alphabetical order by subject. A national institution had come into existence, making its distinctive contribution to the national aptitude for the art of biography.

In his initial prospectus for the *DNB*, Stephen emphasized the need to express 'the greatest possible amount of information in a thoroughly business-like form'. Dates and facts, he said, 'should be given abundantly and precisely', and he had no patience with the sort of 'style' that meant 'superfluous ornament'. But he knew well enough that for 'lucid and condensed narrative', style in the best sense is essential. Nor did he content himself, in the many longer memoirs he himself contributed to the *DNB*, with mere dates and facts: a pioneer in the sociology of literature, he was not at all prone to exaggerate the individual's impact on events, and skilfully 'placed' people in context.

Stephen's powerful machine was carried on by his work-horse of a successor Sidney Lee, who edited the first of the ten supplements (usually decennial) which added people who died between 1901 and 1990. It was in these supplements that all of the memoirs published in this volume first appeared, so they were often written soon after the subject died; their authors were frequently able to cite 'personal knowledge' and 'private information'. In such cases there is always a balance to be struck between waiting for written sources to appear and drawing upon living memory while still abundant and fresh. Stephen had no doubts where he stood: he published book-length biographies of his Cambridge friend Henry Fawcett and of his brother Fitzjames within a year of their deaths, and cited Boswell's *Johnson* and Lockhart's *Scott* as proof that the earliest biographies are often the best. Furthermore, memoirs of the recently dead were included in the *DNB* right up to the last possible moment, the press often

Preface

being stopped for the purpose. Roundell Palmer, for example, died on 4 May 1895 and got into the 43rd volume published at the end of June.

So the memoirs published in this series are fully in line with what was *DNB* policy from the outset. Furthermore, all have the virtue of reflecting the attitudes to their subjects that were taken up during their lifetimes. They may not always reflect what is now the latest scholarship, but as G. M. Young insisted, 'the real, central theme of history is not what happened, but what people felt about it when it was happening'. So they will never be superseded, and many are classics of their kind—essential raw material for the most up-to-date of historians. They have been selected by acknowledged experts, some of them prominent in helping to produce the new *Oxford Dictionary of National Biography*, which will appear in 2004. All are rightly keen that this ambitious revision will not cause these gems of the *DNB* to be lost. So here they are, still sparkling for posterity.

Brian Harrison
Editor, *Oxford Dictionary of National Biography*

Military Lives—selections from the DNB

Introduction

In 1900 the Royal Navy was both the greatest navy in the world and the pre-eminent armed service in Britain. It was the country's principal weapon in the event of hostilities against a major power and—not least because it stood at the cutting edge of technological innovation—it appropriated a far larger share of the defence budget than did the Army. Indeed, so costly was the price of maritime supremacy that Britain spent more per capita on its armed forces than did any other nation in the world. None of these points remained true in 1990, the year by which subjects for inclusion in this volume had to have died.

In the First World War, contrary to the expectations of many in 1914, the country adopted conscription. This was done partly to ensure a sensible division of manpower between the services and industry. But the service which needed conscription was the Army, which was manpower-dependent in a way that the Navy was not. Conscription was a wartime expedient, and it was once again abandoned after the war ended. However, conscription was reintroduced in 1939 and this time it did last beyond the end of the war, not being phased out until 1960. The fact that the two world wars produced most of the military leaders who inhabit the pages that follow will surprise nobody; the fact that in the twentieth century military service was—unusually for Britain—so widespread a male experience had three consequences which have affected the editing of this volume.

First, the armed services became much more obviously public possessions than had been the case in the nineteenth century. Then the business of soldiering or seafaring was conducted by a minority of the population, more often than not at some distance from Britain itself. The empire, much of which was conquered and held by the sword, was the principal field of military activity. But in the first half of the twentieth century Britain's military leaders were engaged directly in the business of national defence. They were responsible for the safety of loved ones, and their strengths and weaknesses became subjects for public debate and controversy. Successful commanders, particularly those like Montgomery who understood the role of the media in a democracy, became national heroes as Nelson and Wellington had done. But many more, pre-eminently Douglas Haig, found their reputations less secure and more hotly contested.

Secondly, as a result of conscription, a great many of those who distinguished themselves in public life in Britain between 1900 and 1990 had served in the military. Indeed, a 'good war' was often a passport to subsequent success. Nobody in this category is included here—for by definition such individuals became leaders in walks of life other than the military. But the result of the two world wars was that some became career servicemen who had not previously been able to do so or had not originally intended to do so. The normal curriculum for the acquisition of professional competence—the Royal Naval College at Dartmouth, the Royal Military Academy at Woolwich, or the Royal Military College at Sandhurst—was elbowed out. Combat in the world wars was the ultimate 'professionalizing' experience. Those who had been uncertain about their careers on leaving school found themselves converted to the profession of arms. Two soldiers whose army careers only became possible because of the First World War went all the way to the top—Bill Slim and 'John' Harding. The result was a leavening both socially and technically, which made the services much less inward-looking and much more open to talent.

Thirdly, conscription elevated the Army over the Royal Navy, at least in terms of numbers. Pro rata it had more senior officers. By the second half of the twentieth century the former had produced more candidates for inclusion in this volume than had the latter. Whether all of them were qualified on the grounds of merit was more controversial, as the reference to Haig has already suggested. But the generals of the First World War were undoubtedly on the winning side and Haig, not least, can take the credit for that. It is in some respects strange that the British image of military incompetence in the First World War should be mired on the western front when the two unequivocal defeats of that war represented in this volume—Gallipoli (for which see Ian Hamilton) and Kut (where Charles Townshend was in command)—occurred in other theatres. Moreover, however questionable some aspects of the Army's performance in the First World War, it was unequivocally superior to that delivered in 1940–2. Individually the defeats in Norway, France, Greece, Singapore, and North Africa could be attributed to other, external, factors. But the collective impact suggests a level of military ineptitude rarely, if ever, equalled in the history of the British Army. Richard O'Connor's brilliant campaign against the Italians in Libya in 1941 was in some respects the exception that proved the rule. If he could do it, why could not others? The public face of the successes which followed after the battle of El Alamein in October 1942 is fully represented in this volume—not only by Montgomery and Slim but also by Alexander and Alan Brooke. However, the origins of those victories were also to be found in the rear, and above all in the personnel policies of the Adjutant General, Sir Ronald Adam. Adam recognized the democratizing effects of conscription for the British Army, and harnessed them for its betterment. He is not here because—staggeringly—he was not included in the *DNB*.

The Army's failure in the early years of the Second World War was the Royal Air Force's opportunity. The formation of the third armed service in 1918 created a displacement in military elites unparalleled in the armed forces of other nations in the first half of the twentieth century. Italy apart, no other state established an independent air force so soon in the evolution of flight. In 1918 the ambitions for aircraft far outstripped their ability to deliver: many of the designers responsible for transforming aspiration into reality figure in the *DNB*, but they—like other scientists working in defence-related industries—have been omitted from this volume. Given the as yet unfulfilled promise of the aircraft, the independence of the Royal Air Force had to be buttressed instead by strategic argument. Assertions regarding the efficacy of independent air action challenged the primacy of the Royal Navy in European war and of the Army in colonial policing. The Navy's pre-eminence was restated through the belief that final victory in the First World War had been the product of blockade, a policy which hit the enemy's civilian population rather than its front-line fighting capacity. But if the targets were cities and their populations, the long-range bomber promised to be both more direct and more speedy in its effects than the warship. Hugh Trenchard, chief of the air staff for ten years, from 1919 until 1929, became the public spokesman of this philosophy. Many of those who would implement it in practice—notably Arthur Harris, head of Bomber Command between 1942 and 1945—reinforced its message by the experience they had gained in the use of aircraft in the colonies in the inter-war period. The Army's monopoly in this, its primary and long-standing area of expertise, was thus challenged. In 1929, the Royal Air Force, according to one airman who served on the north-west frontier, John Slessor, argued that five or six squadrons of aircraft could do the job of thirty infantry battalions and ten artillery batteries in the policing of India for a saving of £2 million a year.

Senior air officers, including Slessor himself, had a key role in shaping British defence policy in the early years of the Cold War. The advent of the atomic bomb seemed to clinch the arguments of the air-power theorists, and in 1957 Duncan Sandys, as Minister of Defence, announced that nuclear weapons and their accompanying ideas of deterrence would be the basis of future planning. Sandys was one of a number of reforming service ministers who might have fought their battles in Westminster and Whitehall but who have good title to be incorporated in a volume devoted to military leaders: Richard Burdon Haldane, the Secretary of State for War between 1905 and 1912, is another. But both have other claims to fame, and they and their ilk, politicians and statesmen, have been left to one side.

The eventual outcome of the 1957 defence review frustrated the Royal Air Force on two counts. First, Sandys reckoned that the missile, not the manned aircraft, would be the means of delivering nuclear warheads. Secondly, in 1962 Britain decided to buy the Polaris system from the United States: this was carried in a submarine, not in an aeroplane.

Polaris threw the Royal Navy a lifeline, which the First Sea Lord, Lord Louis Mountbatten, seized. Mountbatten was both a throwback and a pointer to the future. He was immersed in the traditions of the Royal Navy, his father having been First Sea Lord when war broke out in 1914. He was not alone in being a son who followed his father, not only into the service but also, as a result, into the pages of the *DNB*. Such military families—the Goughs are another represented in these pages—are evidence of a form of military professionalism which is easily overlooked because it is now unfashionable. Mountbatten was the Queen's cousin. He therefore gave outward confirmation that the close link between the royal family and the armed services—of immense political importance to them both—was far more persistent than is often acknowledged. Both the Duke of Cambridge, the commander-in chief of the Army from 1856 until 1895, and the Duke of Connaught, whom Queen Victoria hoped would in due course fill her cousin's boots at the War Office and who was inspector-general of the forces between 1904 and 1907, qualify for entry to this book. They have not been included because the decision has been taken to incorporate only those military leaders from the pre-1914 period who shaped the armed forces for the future: Garnet Wolseley and Frederick Roberts for the Army and Jackie Fisher and Lord Charles Beresford for the Royal Navy.

Also included from this pre-1914 generation is the sole civilian administrator to grace these pages, Reginald Brett, Lord Esher. Esher never led forces in war, but his contribution to the reform of the army and to the reconfiguration of the machinery for the formation of defence planning was so immense that his omission would have left a gaping hole in the story of Britain's armed services in the twentieth century. Esher's ultimate

objective was the co-ordination of the (then) two services and their integration with civilian ministers in the development of national strategy.
The Royal Navy, not the Army, was the central pillar in his thinking; he
was also an ardent royalist. It was therefore entirely appropriate that
Mountbatten—and this was his claim to be forward thinking—should have
been a key figure in carrying such thoughts to fulfilment. In 1959
Mountbatten became the second holder of the office of chief of the defence staff. He was twice renewed in office, holding the appointment for
six years in all. From him can be traced the comparative harmony which
subsisted between the three services by 1990, and which enabled them to
claim that all operations were inherently joint.

The twin themes of nuclear deterrence and of bureaucratic infighting in
Whitehall do not exhaust post-1945 definitions of military leadership. In
practice the armed forces, and especially the Army, found themselves
engaged in almost continuous fighting—mostly as a result of colonial
withdrawal. The campaigns in Malaya and in Cyprus are dealt with in the
lives of those responsible for their overall conduct—Gerald Templer and
Harding. Hugh Stockwell commanded at Suez, the operation which
provided the catalyst for the Sandys defence review. Not represented here
are the Army's peacekeeping efforts in Northern Ireland or the war in the
Falklands. The reputation for excellence which the Army in particular
enjoyed by 1990 rested on these more limited actions, not on the two
world wars. The impression created by then, however apparently long
established, would have seemed strange in 1900, when the Army was being
battered by the Boers, not least by Christiaan de Wet, the only one of
Britain's enemies in the pages that follow.

The absence of more recent campaigns from this book is a tribute to the
longevity of their senior commanders as well as to the comparatively low
casualties which they have caused. Colonel 'H.' Jones, who was awarded a
posthumous Victoria Cross in the Falklands War, did not find his way into
the *DNB*. And yet the paradox for the compilers of the *DNB*, as well as for
armies everywhere, has been that in major war in the twentieth-century
military leadership in a heroic and traditional sense has been exercised at
lower and lower levels of command. Jones was leading his battalion from
the front. Senior commanders in modern war were to the rear—for very
good administrative and practical reasons. They were easily tied to their
desks and their situation maps—even to their chateaux in the demonology
of the First World War. The Royal Navy alone took senior officers into
action, fusing operational responsibility with tactical immediacy. John
Jellicoe, the commander of the Grand Fleet, was himself under fire at
Jutland in 1916. Tom Phillips went down with his command, the *Prince of
Wales* and the *Repulse*, on 10 December 1941.

Introduction

To represent military leadership at the sharp end of war in this volume has not been easy. The only soldiers whom the *DNB* recognized who fall into this category were the founders of the Chindits, Orde Wingate, and the Special Air Service, David Stirling. Successive editors were however more indulgent towards the Royal Air Force, despite the fact that most senior Air Force commanders have been even more removed from the action than generals (although Basil Embry was a noteworthy exception). Heroic leadership in the air is represented by the First World War aces Albert Ball and James McCudden, and by Douglas Bader, Richard Hillary, and Guy Gibson for the Second World War.

In general the *DNB* has been as remiss in its acknowledgement of the role of military theory as an aspect of military leadership. Julian Corbett is second only to the American A.T. Mahan in the history of the development of naval strategy—and yet the *DNB* discussed him primarily as a historian. But he is here, as are two other writers on naval matters, Herbert Richmond and Stephen Roskill, as well as J. F. C. Fuller and Basil Liddell Hart for the Army. Unlike Corbett, who was a lawyer by profession, all of them saw action.

Changing priorities in biography are also evident in the representation accorded to intelligence, itself largely the result of the *DNB*'s *Missing Persons* volume. The inability to reveal the Ultra secret, the fact that the British were cracking the German codes in the Second World War, meant that Alan Turing, who died in 1954 and whose computing skills were critical to that success, is not included because his *DNB* entry says simply of his wartime service that he was in the communications department of the Foreign Office. By contrast Mansfield Cumming and Reginald Hall, who masterminded intelligence in the First World War, are here, as are A. G. Denniston, whose career in naval intelligence spanned both wars, and 'Dilly' Knox, who carried on working at Bletchley while racked with cancer.

The covert operations of the Special Operations Executive in the Second World War were run in London by Colin Gubbins, and were co-ordinated with the resistance in France by Forest Yeo-Thomas. One of their agents was Violette Szabo, who died in a concentration camp in 1945. Szabo is not the only woman represented in what was largely a man's world. One doctor and two nurses figure. Elsie Inglis served in Serbia between 1915 and 1917. Maud McCarthy, as matron-in-chief for the Army in the First World War, was a leader in the mould of Florence Nightingale (who herself lived on until 1910 and is therefore technically eligible for inclusion). Edith Cavell, executed by the Germans in 1915, became a leader in the manner of her death—both a *cause célèbre* in international law and a vehicle for British propaganda. That too was the fate of Captain Charles Fryatt, the only representative of the Merchant Navy here, but indubitably a leader in war.

In sum the lives chosen for inclusion in this book aim to do more than round up the usual suspects—the names of Britain's principal commanders in both world wars (although it does do that). The volume sets out to give a flavour of the principal campaigns in which Britain was engaged in the years 1900–90, and it is driven by a broad definition of what constitutes military leadership. Thus administrative, political, and cerebral qualities are as evident as are fighting attributes. What unites most of those whose careers and achievements are chronicled here is extraordinary courage, if not physical then certainly moral.

HEW STRACHAN

April 2002

Contents

Alexander, Harold Rupert Leofric George (1891–1969)　　　　I
DAVID HUNT

Allenby, Edmund Henry Hynman (1861–1936)　　　　10
CYRIL FALLS

Auchinleck, Sir Claude John Eyre (1884–1981)　　　　19
BRIAN BOND

Bacon, Sir Reginald Hugh Spencer (1863–1947)　　　　25
VINCENT W. BADDELEY

Bader, Sir Douglas Robert Steuart (1910–1982)　　　　29
P. B. LUCAS

Ball, Albert (1896–1917)　　　　31
HENRY ALBERT JONES

Beatty, David (1871–1936)　　　　33
W. S. CHALMERS

Beresford, Lord Charles William de la Poer (1846–1919)　　　　46
VINCENT W. BADDELEY

Brett, Reginald Baliol (Lord Esher) (1852–1930)　　　　50
C. HARRIS

Brooke, Alan Francis (1883–1963)　　　　55
D. W. FRASER

Cameron, Neil (1920–1985)　　　　67
HENRY A. PROBERT

Carton de Wiart, Sir Adrian (1880–1963)　　　　69
E. T. WILLIAMS

Cavell, Edith (1865–1915)　　　　71
BENEDICT WILLIAM GINSBURG

xiii

Contents

Coningham, Sir Arthur (1895–1948) 74
T. W. ELMHIRST

Corbett, Sir Julian Stafford (1854–1922) 77
G. A. R. CALLENDER

Cumming, Sir Mansfield George Smith (1859–1923) 80
CHRISTOPHER ANDREW

Cunningham, Andrew Browne (1883–1963) 82
S. W. C. PACK

de Guingand, Sir Francis Wilfred (1900–1979) 90
MICHAEL CARVER

Denniston, Alexander Guthrie (Alistair) (1881–1961) 94
F. H. HINSLEY

De Wet, Christiaan Rudolph (1854–1922) 96
D. REITZ

Dill, Sir John Greer (1881–1944) 100
CYRIL FALLS

Douglas, William Sholto (1893–1969) 106
PETER WYKEHAM

Dowding, Hugh Caswall Tremenheere (1882–1970) 111
E. B. HASLAM

Edmonds, Sir James Edward (1861–1956) 116
CYRIL FALLS

Embry, Sir Basil Edward (1902–1977) 119
PETER WYKEHAM

Evans, Edward Ratcliffe Garth Russell (Lord Mountevans)
(1880–1957) 122
H. G. THURSFIELD

Fergusson, Bernard Edward (Lord Ballantrae) (1911–1980) 125
RONALD LEWIN

Fisher, John Arbuthnot (1841–1920) 128
VINCENT W. BADDELEY

Fraser, Bruce Austin (1888–1981) 137
MAX HASTINGS

Contents

French, John Denton Pinkstone (1852–1925) 142
H. DE WATTEVILLE

Freyberg, Bernard Cyril (1889–1963) 151
D. M. DAVIN

Fryatt, Charles Algernon (1872–1916) 159
BENEDICT WILLIAM GINSBURG

Fuller, John Frederick Charles (1878–1966) 161
MICHAEL CARVER

Gibson, Guy Penrose (1918–1944) 165
RALPH A. COCHRANE

Glubb, Sir John Bagot (1897–1986) 168
JAMES LUNT

Gough, Sir Hubert de la Poer (1870–1963) 170
BRIAN BOND

Gubbins, Sir Colin McVean (1896–1976) 176
PETER WILKINSON

Haig, Douglas (1861–1928) 179
FREDERICK MAURICE

Hall, Sir (William) Reginald (1870–1943) 190
W. M. JAMES

Hamilton, Sir Ian Standish Monteith (1853–1947) 195
C. F. ASPINALL-OGLANDER

Harding, Allan Francis ('John') (1896–1989) 201
DAVID HUNT

Harris, Sir Arthur Travers (1892–1984) 206
DENIS RICHARDS

Hart, Sir Basil Henry Liddell (1895–1970) 211
RONALD LEWIN

Hasler, Herbert George ('Blondie') (1914–1987) 214
EWEN SOUTHBY-TAILYOUR

Hillary, Richard Hope (1919–1943) 217
DENIS RICHARDS

Holland, John Charles Francis (1897–1956) 219
M. R. D. FOOT

Contents

Horrocks, Sir Brian Gwynne (1895–1985)   220
RICHARD LAMB

Hull, Sir Richard Amyatt (1907–1989)   222
JOHN KEEGAN

Inglis, Elsie Maud (1864–1917)   225
EDITH PALLISER

Ironside, William Edmund (1880–1959)   229
R. MACLEOD

Ismay, Hastings Lionel (1887–1965)   232
RONALD LEWIN

Jackson, Sir Henry Bradwardine (1855–1929)   236
F. E. SMITH

Jellicoe, John Rushworth (1859–1935)   240
GEOFFREY CALLENDER

John, Sir Caspar (1903–1984)   254
DAVID WILLIAMS

Joubert de la Ferté, Sir Philip Bennet (1887–1965)   257
EDWARD CHILTON

Keyes, Roger John Brownlow (1872–1945)   262
W. M. JAMES

Kitchener, Horatio Herbert (1850–1916)   267
FREDERICK MAURICE

Knox, (Alfred) Dillwyn (1884–1943)   279
MAVIS BATEY

Lawrence, Thomas Edward ('Lawrence of Arabia') (1888–1935)   281
RONALD STORRS

Leigh-Mallory, Sir Trafford Leigh (1892–1944)   287
W. B. CALLAWAY

Ludlow-Hewitt, Sir Edgar Rainey (1886–1973)   289
MAX HASTINGS

McCarthy, Dame (Emma) Maud (1858–1949)   292
HELEN S. GILLESPIE

McCudden, James Thomas Byford (1895–1918)   293
HENRY ALBERT JONES

Contents

Maitland, Edward Maitland (1880–1921)   295
DENIS RICHARDS

Martel, Sir Giffard Le Quesne (1889–1958)   297
B. H. LIDDELL HART

Maurice, Sir Frederick Barton (1871–1951)   301
JOHN KENNEDY

Monash, Sir John (1865–1931)   306
C. V. OWEN

Montgomery, Bernard Law (1887–1976)   309
E. T. WILLIAMS

Mountbatten, Louis Francis Albert Victor Nicholas (1900–1979)   324
PHILIP ZIEGLER

Newall, Cyril Louis Norton (1886–1963)   347
M. J. DEAN

O'Connor, Sir Richard Nugent (1889–1981)   350
MICHAEL CARVER

Park, Sir Keith Rodney (1892–1975)   352
D. M. DAVIN

Peake, Frederick Gerard (1886–1970)   356
JOHN BAGOT GLUBB

Phillips, Sir Tom Spencer Vaughan (1888–1941)   360
H. G. THURSFIELD

Plumer, Herbert Charles Onslow (1857–1932)   363
GEORGE MACMUNN

Portal, Charles Frederick Algernon (1893–1971)   369
DENIS RICHARDS

Pound, Sir (Alfred) Dudley (Pickman Rogers) (1877–1943)   382
R. V. BROCKMAN

Ramsay, Sir Bertram Home (1883–1945)   387
G. E. CREASY

Rawlinson, Sir Henry Seymour (1864–1925)   394
FREDERICK MAURICE

Richmond, Sir Herbert William (1871–1946)   399
H. G. THURSFIELD

Contents

Roberts, Frederick Sleigh (1832–1914)   403
FREDERICK MAURICE

Robertson, Sir William Robert (1860–1933)   413
FREDERICK MAURICE

Roskill, Stephen Wentworth (1903–1982)   421
CORRELLI BARNETT

Salmond, Sir (William) Geoffrey (Hanson) (1878–1933)   423
E. COLSTON SHEPHERD

Scott, Sir Percy Moreton (1853–1924)   425
VINCENT W. BADDELEY

Slessor, Sir John Cotesworth (1897–1979)   429
MAX HASTINGS

Slim, William Joseph (1891–1970)   433
M. R. ROBERTS

Stirling, Sir (Archibald) David (1915–1990)   439
FITZROY MACLEAN

Stockwell, Sir Hugh Charles (1903–1986)   441
ANTHONY FARRAR-HOCKLEY

Studdert Kennedy, Geoffrey Anketell (1883–1929)   444
D. G. ROWELL

Sueter, Sir Murray Frazer (1872–1960)   446
P. K. KEMP

Sykes, Sir Frederick Hugh (1877–1954)   448
ROBERT BLAKE

Szabo, Violette Reine Elizabeth (1921–1945)   452
M. R. D. FOOT

Tedder, Arthur William (1890–1967)   453
PETER WYKEHAM

Templer, Sir Gerald Walter Robert (1898–1979)   458
MICHAEL CARVER

Townshend, Sir Charles Vere Ferrers (1861–1924)   463
H. DE WATTEVILLE

Trenchard, Hugh Montague (1873–1956)   468
PETER WYKEHAM

Contents

Tyrwhitt, Sir Reginald Yorke (1870–1951)   474
P. K. KEMP

Vereker, John Standish Surtees Prendergast (Lord Gort)
  (1886–1946)   477
CYRIL FALLS

Warburton, Adrian (1918–1944)   483
CONSTANCE BABINGTON SMITH

Wavell, Archibald Percival (1883–1950)   484
BERNARD FERGUSSON

Wemyss, Rosslyn Erskine (Lord Wester Wemyss) (1864–1933)   490
VINCENT W. BADDELEY

Wilson, Sir Henry Hughes (1864–1922)   496
H. DE WATTEVILLE

Wilson, Henry Maitland (1881–1964)   503
J. W. HACKETT

Wingate, Orde Charles (1903–1944)   509
LORD WAVELL

Wolseley, Garnet Joseph (1833–1913)   513
FREDERICK MAURICE

Yeo-Thomas, Forest Frederic Edward (1902–1964)   522
JAMES HUTCHISON

ALEXANDER Harold Rupert Leofric George

(1891–1969)

First Earl Alexander of Tunis

Field-marshal, was born in London 10 December 1891, the third son of James Alexander, fourth Earl of Caledon, and his wife, Lady Elizabeth Graham-Toler, daughter of the third Earl of Norbury. His youth was spent at the family estate, Caledon Castle, in the county Tyrone. His father, who had served briefly in the Life Guards but was better known as an adventurous deep-water yachtsman, died when Alexander was six; his mother, eccentric and imperious, held aloof from her children; but their four sons were perfectly happy in their own company. It was in Northern Ireland that Alexander developed both the athletic and the aesthetic sides of his character; he trained himself as a runner and enjoyed all the usual country sports, but he also taught himself to carve in wood and stone and began what was to prove one of the main passions of his life, painting. After reading Reynolds's *Discourses on Art* he decided that the thing he wanted most in the world was to be president of the Royal Academy. At Harrow he worked well enough to rise smoothly up the school. His games were cricket, athletics, rackets, rugger, boxing, fencing, and gymnastics and he won distinction at all of them; he is best remembered as nearly saving the game for Harrow in what *Wisden* called the most extraordinary cricket match ever played, at Lord's in 1910. He also won a school prize for drawing.

He went on to the Royal Military College, Sandhurst, and was commissioned in the Irish Guards in 1911. Although he was pleased at the idea of spending a few years in a Guards battalion, he intended to retire before long and make a living as an artist. These plans were upset by the outbreak of war in 1914. Alexander's battalion went to France in August and he served there continuously until early 1919, being in action throughout except when recovering from wounds or on courses. He was twice wounded, awarded the MC (1915), and appointed to the DSO (1916). Promotion was rapid. A lieutenant when he arrived, he became a captain in February 1915, a major, one of the youngest in the army, eight months later, with the acting command of the 1st battalion of his own regiment, and a lieutenant-colonel, commanding the 2nd battalion, in October 1917. During the retreat from Arras in March 1918 he was acting brigadier-general in command of the 4th Guards brigade.

The war was a turning-point in Alexander's character and career. He had painted in the trenches, and he continued to paint throughout his life, reaching at times a standard only just short of the professional; but in the course of the war he had come to realize the fascination of the profession of arms, and had proved to himself, and demonstrated to others, that he was outstandingly competent at it. His reputation stood very high for courage but also for a cheerful imperturbability in all circumstances. For four years he lived the life of a regimental officer, without any staff service; he later criticized senior commanders of that war for never seeking personal experience of the conditions of the fighting troops.

Not wishing to go back to barracks or to the army of occupation in Germany, he applied in 1919 for an appointment to one of the many military missions in Eastern Europe. He was first posted as a member of the Allied Relief Commission in Poland under (Sir) Stephen Tallents and later went with Tallents to Latvia which was in danger of falling either to Russia or to Germany. The Allies had no troops in the Baltic and only a small naval detachment under Sir Walter Cowan. Tallents placed the *Landwehr*, composed of Baltic Germans, under Alexander's command. At the age of twenty-seven he found himself at the head of a brigade-sized formation with mainly German officers. He was good at languages and had taught himself German and Russian; his authority derived from his charm and sincerity and his obvious professionalism. He kept his men steady and resistant to the attractions of the German expeditionary force under von der Goltz and led them to victory in the campaign which drove the Red Army from Latvia.

Alexander retained all his life a keen interest in Russia. During the war of 1914–18 he designed a new uniform cap for himself with a high visor and flat peak, on the model of one he had seen a Russian officer wearing. He always wore the Order of St. Anne with swords which Yudenitch awarded him in 1919; when he met Rokossovsky in 1945 the Russian general muttered to him in an aside that he had once had it too. In the second war, like Churchill, he admired Stalin and was enthusiastic about the Soviet Army.

After the Soviet Union recognized the independence of Latvia in 1920 Alexander returned to England to become second-in-command of his regiment. In 1922 he was given command and took it to Constantinople as part of the army of occupation. In 1923, after the treaty of Lausanne, the regiment went to Gibraltar and thence in 1924 to England. In 1926–7 he was at the Staff College. He was very senior in rank, a full colonel, but for the duration of the course he was temporarily reduced to the rank of major. After commanding the regiment and regimental district of the Irish Guards (1928–30), he attended the Imperial Defence College. This was followed by the only two staff appointments in his career, as GSO 2 at the War Office (1931–2) and as GSO 1 at Northern Command (1932–4). He was

already widely regarded as likely to make the outstanding fighting commander of a future war; the other name mentioned, from the Indian
Army, was that of (Sir) Claude Auchinleck.

In 1934 Alexander was appointed to command the Nowshera brigade on
the North-West Frontier, one of the most coveted in India. Auchinleck
commanded the next brigade, in Peshawar. Alexander surprised and delighted his Indian troops by learning Urdu as rapidly and fluently as he had
Russian and German. Next year he commanded the brigade in the Loc
Agra campaign (called after a small village north of the Malakand pass)
against invading tribesmen; and not long after, under Auchinleck's command as the senior brigadier, in the Mohmand campaign. Both operations
were successful; roads were built, large regions pacified; Alexander was
appointed CSI (1936). It was noted not only that he had mastered the
difficult techniques of fighting in mountainous country but also that he
was always to be seen with the foremost troops. This was both a revulsion
from the behaviour he had condemned in his senior commanders in
France and a natural result of his personal courage; it remained to the end
a characteristic of his style of leadership.

His promotion to major-general in 1937, at the age of forty-five, made
him the youngest general in the British Army; in 1938 he was given
command of the 1st division at Aldershot. In 1939 he took the division to
France as one of the two in I Corps under Sir John Dill. In the retreat to
Dunkirk his division only once fought a serious if brief battle, when he
successfully defended the Scheldt for two days, throwing back all German
penetrations; for the rest of the time he was obliged to fall back to conform
to the movement of other divisions. It was Dunkirk which first brought his
name prominently before the public notice. I Corps was to form the final
rearguard and Lord Gort superseded the corps commander and put
Alexander in command. His orders were definite: to withdraw all the
British troops who could be saved. A different interpretation of the military
necessities of the moment was held by the French commander, Admiral
Abrial, and Alexander confessed that to carry out his orders while leaving
the French still fighting made him feel that he 'had never been in such a
terrible situation'. During the three days in which he commanded, 20,000
British and 98,000 French were evacuated: Alexander left on the last motor
launch in which he toured the beaches to see that there were no British
troops remaining.

On his return to England he was confirmed in command of I Corps
which was responsible for the defence of the east coast from Scarborough
to the Wash. Promoted lieutenant-general, in December 1940 he succeeded
Auchinleck at Southern Command. He showed himself an admirable
trainer of troops and was the first to introduce the realistic 'battle-schools'

which became so prominent a feature of military life from 1940 to 1944. He was also put in command of a nominal 'Force 110' which was to be used for amphibious operations; he and his staff planned a number which never came off, such as the invasion of the Canaries and of Sicily.

In February 1942 Alexander was suddenly informed that he was to take command of the army in Burma where the situation was already desperate. The key battle had been lost before Alexander arrived; the Japanese were across the Sittang river, in a position to encircle and capture Rangoon. It was by the greatest good fortune, and the oversight of a Japanese divisional commander in leaving open one narrow escape route, that Alexander himself and the bulk of his forces were able to escape from Rangoon which, in obedience to ill-considered orders from Sir A. P. (later Earl) Wavell, he had tried to hold almost beyond the last reasonable moment. After its fall Burma had no future military value except as a glacis for the defence of India. Alexander decided that the only success he could snatch from the jaws of unmitigated defeat was to rescue the army under his command by withdrawing it to India. It was a campaign of which he always spoke with compunction and distaste, except for his admiration for General (later Viscount) Slim. Left entirely without guidance after the fall of Rangoon—not that the guidance he had received previously had been of any value—Alexander did the best he could. As a further sign of the gifts he was to display as an Allied commander, it should be recorded that he got on the best of terms not only with Chiang Kai Chek but also with General J. W. Stilwell.

It might be thought that two defeats in succession would have meant the end to Alexander's hopes of high command. Churchill had shown no mercy to Gort or Wavell and was to show none to Auchinleck. But as he wrote in *The Hinge of Fate* (1951), in sending Alexander to Burma 'never have I taken the responsibility for sending a general on a more forlorn hope'. He had formed so high an appreciation of Alexander's ability that he immediately confirmed his designation as commander-in-chief of the First Army which was to invade North Africa, under Eisenhower's command, in November 1942 when the Allies for the first time seized the strategic initiative. But before that could take effect, Churchill felt impelled in early August to visit Egypt. Auchinleck was more impressive in the field than in conversation in his caravan; Churchill decided to replace him with Alexander. It is ironical that one of the main reasons why Auchinleck was replaced was that he declared himself unable to take the offensive until September: Churchill was to accept from Alexander, with but little remonstrance, a postponement until late October.

Alexander took over as commander-in-chief, Middle East, on 15 August 1942. For the first time he found himself in a position which was not only not desperate but full of promise. He had a numerical superiority, and at last equality of equipment, against an army fighting at the end of a long and precarious line of communication with its bases and debilitated by sickness. General Gott, who was to have been his army commander, was killed; but he was replaced immediately by General Montgomery (later Viscount Montgomery of Alamein) who had been one of Alexander's corps commanders in Southern Command and whose capacities as a trainer and inspirer of men were well known to him. He had a sound defensive position, strongly manned, and plans had been prepared for the expected enemy assault; they were based on a partial refusal of the left flank while holding the strong position of Alam Halfa, fortified and prepared by Auchinleck to block an advance on Alexandria. Reinforcements in men and tanks continued to arrive. Nevertheless there was a problem of morale, since the Eighth Army had been fighting in retreat since May and had lost one position after another; it was natural for the troops to wonder whether they might not find themselves retreating once more. The first step towards victory in Egypt was when Alexander made it known, as soon as he assumed command, that there was to be no further retreat; the decisive battle was to be fought on the Alamein line.

The defensive battle of Alam Halfa and the offensive battle of Alamein were, as Alexander always insisted, Montgomery's victories. He had always had the gift of delegating and no one was more generous in acknowledging the merits of his subordinates. There is reason for argument whether, after the failure of the first plan at Alamein, *Lightfoot*, part of the credit for *Supercharge*, the modified version, should go to suggestions from Alexander. In truth the two generals, the commander-in-chief and the army commander, were aptly suited to their respective roles and played them well. The successful campaign in Egypt, won at almost the lowest point in the Allied fortunes, marked the beginning of a period in which British and Allied armies knew scarcely anything but success.

The invasion of North Africa in November meant that after two months a British Army, the First, with a French and an American corps, was fighting in northern and central Tunisia against a mixed German-Italian army and meanwhile the German-Italian Armoured Army of Africa, defeated at Alamein, was withdrawing towards southern Tunisia pursued by the Eighth Army. It was evident that a headquarters was required to command and co-ordinate the two Allied armies. Alexander was summoned to the Casablanca conference of January 1943. He made a great impression on President Roosevelt, General Marshall, and the United States chiefs of staff; his reputation at home had never been higher. The conference decided to appoint him deputy commander-in-chief to General Eisenhower with command over all the forces actually fighting the enemy.

He set up a very small headquarters, called the 18th Army Group from the numbers of the two British armies which made up the bulk of his command; this was originally located in the town of Constantine, but as soon as he could Alexander moved out into the field and operated from a tented camp, moved frequently.

The Tunisian campaign provides a convincing proof of Alexander's capacity as a strategist. It also demonstrates his great gift of inspiring and elevating the morale of the troops he commanded, as well as his skill in welding together the efforts of different nationalities. At the beginning he faced a difficult task. The southern flank of his western front had been driven in by a bold enemy thrust which threatened to come in upon the communications of the whole deployment. Alexander was on the spot, even before the date at which he was officially to assume command (20 February 1943); he was seen directing the siting of gun positions at the approaches to the Kasserine pass. This was a flash of his old style but it was not long before he took a firm grip on higher things and reorganized the whole direction of the campaign. He sorted out the confusion into which the First Army had been thrown by the rapid vicissitudes of the past, brought into play the ponderous but skilful thrust of the Eighth Army, and directed the efforts of both in the final victory of Tunis. In this last battle in Africa he employed an elaborate and successful plan of deception, based on an accurate knowledge of enemy dispositions and intentions, and broke through their strong defensive front with a powerful and well-concealed offensive blow. In two days all was over. A quarter of a million enemy were captured. On 13 May he was able to make his historic signal to the prime minister: 'Sir, it is my duty to report that the Tunisian campaign is over. All enemy resistance has ceased. We are masters of the North African shores.'

Sicily was the next objective on which the Casablanca conference had decided. The forces commanded by Alexander, as commander-in-chief 15th Army Group, consisted of the United States Seventh and British Eighth armies. The principal interest in the campaign lies in the immense size of the amphibious effort required, larger in the assault phase even than for the invasion of Normandy, and in the elaborate planning which preceded it. It fell to Alexander to decide on the final form of the plan, a concentrated assault on the south-eastern corner of the island, rather than, as originally proposed by the planning staff, two separate attacks in the south-east and the north-west. In this decision he was vindicated, mainly because of his correct assessment of the new possibilities of beach maintenance produced by recently acquired amphibious equipment. In the course of the first few days, however, he made one of his few strategic errors in yielding to Montgomery's insistence that the Eighth Army could finish off the campaign by itself if the United States Seventh Army were kept out of its way; admittedly Alexander was deceived by inaccurate reports of the progress that the Eighth Army was making. As a result the reduction of the island took rather longer than expected and a high proportion of the German defenders managed to withdraw into Calabria. Nevertheless, the capture of Sicily in thirty-eight days was not only a notable strategic gain but also brought encouraging confirmation of the validity of the methods of amphibious warfare of which so much was expected in the next year's invasion of France.

That invasion was the principal factor affecting the last two years of Alexander's career as a commander in the field, during which he was engaged on the mainland of Italy. His troops were now no longer the spearhead of the Allied military effort in Europe. He was required to give up, for the benefit of the western front, many divisions of his best troops on three occasions and his task was defined as to eliminate Italy from the war and to contain the maximum number of German divisions. The first part of this directive was rapidly achieved. In his second task also, which from September 1943 onwards represented the sole object of the campaign, he was strikingly successful. So far from diverting troops from Italy to the decisive front, the Germans continuously reinforced it, not only robbing the Russion front but even sending divisions from the west. To obtain this success, however, in a terrain always favouring the defence, Alexander was obliged to maintain the offensive and to compensate for the lack of superior force by using all the arts of generalship.

'The campaign in Italy was a great holding attack', Alexander states in his dispatch. As is the nature of holding attacks, it was directed against a secondary theatre. Nevertheless it gave scope for daring strategic planning in spite of the odds and of the forbidding and mountainous nature of the ground. The initial assault at Salerno, simultaneous with the announcement of the Italian surrender, was a good example; a force of only three divisions, all that could be carried in the landing craft allotted to the theatre, was thrown on shore at the extreme limit of air cover. The landing at Anzio was a masterpiece of deception which caught the enemy off balance and forced him to send reinforcements to Italy. It made a vital contribution to the offensive of May and June 1944 in which the Germans were driven north of Rome, with disproportionately heavy losses in men and equipment. For this offensive Alexander made a secret redeployment of his two armies and mounted a most ingenious plan of deception; his opponent, Field-Marshal Kesselring, was unable to react in time, for all that his defensive positions were strong both by nature and artificially. The capture of Rome just before the landing in Normandy was a fillip to Allied morale. A more important result from the point of view of Allied grand strategy was that this crushing defeat obliged the Germans to reinforce

Italy with eight fresh divisions, some taken from their western garrisons; a month later, in contrast, Alexander was ordered to surrender seven of his divisions for the campaign in France. The final battle, in April 1945, was another example of Alexander's skill in deployment and in deception; by 2 May he had routed the most coherent enemy group of armies still resisting; all Italy had been overrun and a million Germans had laid down their arms in the first big surrender of the war.

The Italian campaign showed Alexander at the height of his powers. These included besides the skill of a strategist a thorough grasp of the principles of administration. As an Allied commander he was supreme; there were no instances of friction anywhere in his command in spite of its varied composition, including at one time or another troops from Britain, the United States, India, Canada, New Zealand, South Africa, France, Poland, Italy, Brazil, and Greece. For the greater part of the campaign, as commander-in-chief of 15th Army Group, later renamed Allied Armies in Italy, he acted as an independent commander, since it had been agreed that the commander-in-chief, Mediterranean, Sir Maitland (later Lord) Wilson, should concern himself primarily with the general maintenance of the Italian campaign and with the security of the other areas of the command.

On 12 December 1944 Alexander succeeded Wilson. He was appointed to the rank of field-marshal to date from 4 June 1944, on which day the Allied armies entered Rome. But for all his high rank and heavy responsibilities he remembered his criticism of the commanders in the war of 1914–18. He always spent more time with the forward troops than in his headquarters. His popularity was immense, and his strategic planning benefited because he knew what the war was like at the point that counted.

After the war it was expected by some that Alexander would become chief of the imperial general staff. But W. L. Mackenzie King invited him to be governor-general of Canada, and Churchill pressed him to accept. His sense of duty was reinforced by a strong attraction to the idea of serving Canada. His extended tenure of office ran from 1946 to 1952. He was the last British governor-general and his popularity was as great as that of any of his predecessors. He was comparatively young and brought a young family with him; he toured the whole country, played games, skied, and painted. To his dignity as the representative of the King of Canada and his reputation as a war leader he added an informal friendliness and charm. While in Canada he produced his official dispatches on his campaigns published in the *London Gazette*; they have been described by his biographer as 'among the great state papers of our military history'.

In January 1952 Churchill visited Ottawa and offered Alexander the post of minister of defence in his Government. When a friend remonstrated he replied: 'Of course I accepted. It's my duty.' To another friend he said, 'I simply can't refuse Winston.' As he entered on his first political post in that frame of mind it is not surprising that he did not much enjoy his period of office. He was not temperamentally suited to political life and in any case he had few real powers to exercise. Churchill continued to behave as though it was he who was the minister of defence and Alexander his spokesman in the Lords. Nevertheless, Alexander had the assets of his great personal popularity, his charm, and the fact that he numbered so many personal friends among foreign statesmen and military men, especially in the United States, and especially after the election of President Eisenhower. He made no particular mark as minister of defence because he preferred to rely on discreet persuasion and guidance; but he led a good team and suffered no diminution of his reputation. After two and a half years he resigned at his own request, in the autumn of 1954.

In the last fifteen years of his life he accepted a number of directorates. He was most active as director of Alcan and also served on the boards of Barclay's Bank and Phoenix Assurance. He travelled extensively on business for Alcan. He continued to paint and devoted more and more time to it. In 1960 he was persuaded by the *Sunday Times* to allow his memoirs to be ghosted. They were edited by John North and published in 1962, but were not very favourably received because of the curiously disorganized and anecdotal form. His motive in agreeing to publication was the desire to see that justice was done to the armies in Italy; for himself he preferred to be judged on the basis of his dispatches. For the rest he devoted himself to his garden and to reunions with old comrades. He died suddenly after a heart attack on 16 July 1969, in hospital in Slough. His funeral service was held in St. George's Chapel, Windsor, and he was buried in the churchyard of Ridge, near Tyttenhanger, his family's Hertfordshire home. The headstone of his grave bears at the top the single word ALEX, the name by which he was known to his friends and his soldiers.

He married in 1931 Lady Margaret Diana Bingham (died 1977), younger daughter of the fifth earl of Lucan; she was appointed GBE in 1954. They had two sons, one daughter, and an adopted daughter. He was succeeded by his elder son, Shane William Desmond (born 1935).

Alexander was created a viscount in 1946 and an earl in 1952 on his return from Canada. He was appointed CB (1938), KCB and GCB (1942), GCMG on his appointment to Canada, and in the same year (1946) KG. He was sworn of the Privy Council in 1952 and also of the Canadian Privy Council. In 1959 he was admitted to the Order of Merit. He was colonel of the Irish Guards from 1946 to his death, constable of the Tower of London from 1960 to 1965. From 1957 to 1965 he was lieutenant of the county of London, and for a further year of Greater London. He was chancellor and then grand master of the Order of St. Michael and St. George, an elder brother of Trinity House, and in 1955 president of the MCC. He was a freeman of the City of London and of many other cities. His numerous foreign decorations included the grand cross of the Legion of Honour and the Legion of Merit and Distinguished Service Medal of the United States.

Alexander was 5 feet 10 inches tall, slim, muscular, and handsome. His features were regular in the style which when he was young was regarded as typical of the army officer; he wore a trim Guardsman's moustache all his life. He dressed with careful and unaffected elegance on all occasions; his Russian-style cap was only the precursor of a number of variations on uniform regulations whereas in plain clothes he favoured neatness, fashion, and the avoidance of the elaborate.

There are two portraits of him at the National Portrait Gallery, by Edward Seago (a close personal friend) and by Maurice Codner; and two at the Imperial War Museum, by R. G. Eves and Harry Carr. The Irish Guards have two, by John Gilroy and Richard Jack; another version of the Gilroy portrait is in McGill University, Montreal. White's Club has a portrait by Sir Oswald Birley. The National Portrait Gallery has a sculptured bust by Donald Gilbert. A bronze bust by Oscar Nemon, in the Old Radcliffe Observatory at Oxford, was unveiled by Queen Elizabeth the Queen Mother in 1973 to mark the endowment of a chair of cardio-vascular medicine at the university in Alexander's memory. In the possession of the family is a bronze bust by Anthony Gray.

[Nigel Nicolson, *Alex*, 1973; dispatches in *London Gazette*, 5 and 12 February 1948, 12 June 1950; I. S. O. Playfair and C. J. C. Molony, and others, (Official) *History of the Second World War. The Mediterranean and Middle East*, vol. iv, 1966, and C. J. C. Molony and others, vol. v, 1973; personal knowledge.]

DAVID HUNT

published 1981

ALLENBY Edmund Henry Hynman

(1861–1936)

First Viscount Allenby of Megiddo

Field-marshal, was born 23 April 1861 on the estate of his maternal grandfather, Brackenhurst, near Southwell, Nottinghamshire. He was the eldest son and second child of Hynman Allenby, a country gentleman, by his wife, Catherine Anne, daughter of the Rev. Thomas Coats Cane. From the year of their marriage (1859) until that of Edmund's birth his parents had lived at Dartmouth. Soon afterwards they purchased Felixstowe House, in Suffolk, and West Bilney Lodge, with a considerable estate, in Norfolk. The family thenceforth spent spring and summer at Felixstowe, autumn and winter at West Bilney. Young Allenby grew up in close contact with the life and sport of the countryside. He rode, shot, fished, and sailed, and he early acquired the ornithological and botanical interests which were to remain with him all his life.

Allenby was educated at Haileybury, a new public school founded the year after his birth, and at the Royal Military College, Sandhurst. It had been his original intention to enter the Indian civil service, but he failed to pass the entrance examinations in 1879 and 1880, when there were vacancies for only about one-seventh of the candidates. His next choice was the army. He was not particularly distinguished at work or sport at Haileybury but he passed well into and out of Sandhurst, where he was an under-officer in his last term. In May 1882 he was gazetted to a commission in the Inniskillings (6th Dragoons). He was then a big, strong, good-looking young man, somewhat clumsy in build, although his weight did not increase unduly to his dying day. His eye had been trained for observation of country, and he possessed a strong and dominating character, physical and moral courage, and presence of mind, so that he had good prospects in his career.

The Inniskillings were stationed in South Africa, and Allenby gained invaluable experience in two little expeditions, both bloodless, or nearly so, into Bechuanaland (1884–1885) and Zululand (1888), as well as knowledge of people and country which were to serve him well later on. In 1886 he went home for two years' service at the cavalry depot at Canterbury. He was promoted captain early in 1888, the year of his return, and appointed adjutant next year. It was noted by his brother officers that the new responsibility not only made him take his profession much more seriously but also induced a certain grimness of disposition.

The regiment returned to England in 1890, and in 1896 Allenby passed into the Staff College, by competition, at a time when few cavalrymen entered except by nomination. He made no outstanding mark in his military studies but was popular with his fellow students, and was elected master of the drag hounds in preference to Douglas (afterwards Earl) Haig, a better horseman than himself. He passed out with a good report. While at Camberley he had been promoted major in May 1897, and qualified as an army interpreter in French. He had also married, in 1896, Adelaide Mabel, daughter of Horace Edward Chapman, of Donhead House, Salisbury. In March 1898 he became what would now be termed brigade-major but was then termed adjutant to the 3rd Cavalry brigade at the Curragh, in

Ireland. While he was holding this appointment his only child, a son, was born.

Allenby rejoined his regiment the following year on the outbreak of the South African war. Shrewd and cautious, with knowledge of the character and qualities of his adversary, he fell into none of the traps laid by the Boers, and it was due to his good work in the operations round Colesberg that his squadron was chosen as part of the cavalry division formed under General French for the relief of Kimberley in the early part of 1900. In the numerous small actions or marches with convoys his losses were small.

Early in 1900 Allenby assumed temporary command of his regiment at Bloemfontein and with it took part in the main advance to Pretoria. His great chance came with the final period between January 1901 and May of the following year, when the Boers remaining under arms had been reduced to a handful of picked men, not exceeding 50,000 even at the outset, yet brilliantly manœuvred against the numerous columns sent out to round them up and to clear the country. In these trying operations he commanded a column, generally of two regiments of cavalry, artillery, and half a battalion of infantry. He suffered no reverse and never lost a convoy, and at the end of the war had established a sound if not a spectacular reputation. He received brevet promotion to colonel and was appointed C.B.

Allenby began his home service, which was to last until the outbreak of war twelve years later, in command of the 5th Royal Irish Lancers at Colchester. In October 1905, as a brigadier-general, he took over command of the 4th Cavalry brigade. In September 1909 he was promoted major-general, and after some six months on half-pay, during which he visited South Africa, was appointed inspector-general of cavalry. So far he had been generally popular in the army and with his subordinates, but his always high temper was now becoming even less under control and his roughness of manner was unwelcome to the staffs and regimental officers. On the outbreak of war in 1914 he was appointed to the command of the unwieldy cavalry division, of which the brigades had seldom trained together, to accompany the British Expeditionary Force to France.

Allenby's conduct of his command in the retreat from Mons is a matter which has aroused controversy. By some he is held to have displayed weakness in losing control of a large proportion of it, while others consider that circumstances would have been too much for any commander in his position. It is universally acknowledged, however, that he showed coolness and resolution throughout and that the rear and flanks of the retreating British infantry corps were effectively protected from a superior force of German cavalry. In the advance to the Aisne the cavalry was handled with a prudence approaching timidity, but that was in part founded on orders from British headquarters and in part upon reactions from previous over-confidence, in which, however, Allenby himself had never shared.

Five British cavalry brigades were now formed into two divisions of more manageable size, and after the transfer of the Expeditionary Force from the Aisne to Flanders these became the Cavalry Corps, to the command of which Allenby was appointed. In the first battle of Ypres (19 October–22 November) the cavalry performed magnificent service. One of the decisive elements in the British defence proved to be the skill of the dismounted trooper with the rifle, for which the former inspector-general must be given at least part of the credit. In fighting of this nature there was little that a corps commander could effect beyond maintaining a reserve for the ugliest situations, and this Allenby contrived to do. On 6 May 1915 he took over command of the V Corps in the midst of the second battle of Ypres, which had opened with the German gas attack. Later in the year he carried out local operations in support of offensives farther south, but his efforts were rendered abortive by superior German observation and equipment.

In October 1915 Allenby was appointed to the command of the newly formed Third Army north of the Somme. He was not, however, destined to take part in the battle, as in the following March his army side-slipped northward to relieve the French in front of Arras. He was by this time identified with the costly and somewhat unimaginative methods on which the offensives and counter-attacks had been conducted, but it should be recognized that his loyalty to his superiors was so complete that he always fulfilled his orders to the letter and allowed no criticism even in the bosom of his own military family, his staff. His nickname of 'the Bull', dating from days of peace, had by now become universal.

The outstanding episode in Allenby's military career in Europe was the battle of Arras in 1917. The plan had been to a certain extent compromised by the German retreat to the Hindenburg Line, which extended on its northern flank to the front of his right corps and necessitated an improvisation of dispositions prejudicial to its chances of success. In an effort to obtain a measure of surprise Allenby had decided to cut down the length of the preliminary bombardment, at the same time intensifying it by increasing the rate of fire. This project met with objections from general headquarters resulting in a compromise by which the bombardment was to cover four days instead of the forty-eight hours proposed by him. As the attack was postponed by one day to suit the French, the bombardment was in fact increased to five days. The object of the Third Army's offensive was to break the German defences between Arras and Cambrai while the First Army on the left captured the Vimy ridge. The attack was launched on

Allenby

Easter Monday, 9 April, a day punctuated by squalls of snow and sleet, which, however, blew in the faces of the enemy. Although the right-hand corps made only limited progress, the main attack on the first day was remarkably successful. The maximum advance, just north of the Scarpe, was three and a half miles, believed to be the longest carried out by any belligerent on the western front since trench warfare had set in. As so often in that war, however, the success was not exploited. The complete breach through which it had been hoped to pass the Cavalry Corps was never fully opened or cleared of wire. The Germans made a partial recovery and brought up some reinforcements. The fighting degenerated into costly local actions, until Field-Marshal Sir Douglas Haig, the commander-in-chief, ordered a pause on the 14th to reorganize for a further co-ordinated attack. This, known officially as the second battle of the Scarpe, was launched on 23 April and achieved only limited success after very heavy fighting. A third attempt, on 3 May (the third battle of the Scarpe), was disastrous. Against Allenby's will the assault was carried out in darkness, and the half-trained reinforcements with which the ranks of the divisions had been filled fell into confusion.

Meanwhile a new commander was wanted in Palestine, where the British had suffered a sharp check in April in front of Gaza. Allenby was known as a man of abounding energy and it was considered that he would be more likely to give of his best outside the orbit of Haig. The two men were uncongenial to each other and Allenby always felt himself tongue-tied in the presence of the commander-in-chief. He assumed command of the Egyptian Expeditionary Force at the end of June 1917, and, as soon as the move could be carried out, transferred general headquarters to the Palestine border, close behind the front. He came like a fresh breeze to the somewhat dispirited troops. As he drove from camp to camp for brief visits of inspection he contrived to impress his personality upon them. The independently minded Australians took to him at once and gave him their full confidence. It was a promising beginning to his command. He received most of the reinforcements which he demanded, bringing his army to a strength of seven infantry and three mounted divisions.

Allenby's plan, largely based upon an appreciation put forward by Lieutenant-General Sir Philip Chetwode, and the work of his staff officer, Brigadier-General Guy Payan Dawnay, was to capture Beersheba, on the Turkish left, then roll up the enemy's centre and net the largest possible proportion of the forces between it and the coast by a sweep with his three mounted divisions. It was a difficult operation in which every move depended upon the capture of water supplies for men, horses, and camels. The attack on Beersheba began on 31 October. The opening stages of the offensive were brilliantly successful, but, as so often happens in a campaign of this type, there were some delays and the cavalry became more dispersed than was desirable. As a consequence, although the Turks suffered heavily, their main body escaped envelopment. Meanwhile, however, Allenby's left had broken through at Gaza. He immediately transferred all available transport to this flank, leaving much of the rest of the force temporarily immobilized round the railhead, and drove the enemy northward up the Philistine plain, beyond Jaffa, to the Nahr el Auja.

Allenby then decided to wheel a strong force into the hills and capture Jerusalem—which for religious and political reasons it was important not to harm—by envelopment between this force and another advancing northward from Beersheba up the road through Hebron. He penetrated without excessive difficulty almost to the Nablus road, but then his XXI Corps and Yeomanry mounted division became involved in fierce and bloody fighting. To the east progress was blocked; to the north the thinly held British flank was fiercely counter-attacked by the able and energetic hostile commander-in-chief, General (Marshal in the Turkish army) von Falkenhayn. Floods in the plain delayed the movement of supplies. But the flank held and the supply situation gradually improved. Allenby brought up the XX Corps. Another assault proved successful, and on 9 December Jerusalem was surrendered intact to Allenby, who made his impressive ceremonial entry on foot into the holy city on 11 December. During the following days a counter-offensive was defeated and the front advanced to a distance sufficiently far north and east of the city to ensure its safety. The Turks had suffered some 28,000 casualties, almost half as many again as those of the British.

Allenby was called upon by the government to exploit his success to the extent of driving Turkey right out of the war, but his attitude was cautious. Storms prevented the unloading of supplies on the coast. Railway construction was required. While it was in progress he proposed to operate against the enemy beyond Jordan, on the Hejaz railway. His plans were finally approved, but all hope of a major offensive early in 1918 was removed by the success of the German offensives of March and April in France. Heavy demands fell upon the Egyptian Expeditionary Force for reinforcements. Two whole divisions, nine yeomanry regiments, twenty-three infantry battalions, heavy artillery, machine-gun battalions, etc., were withdrawn. Their place was taken by two Indian divisions, and by Indian cavalry regiments and infantry battalions, the latter being in many cases raw and without experienced officers or specialists. The spring and summer were occupied in reorganization and training, and it was not until mid-September that Allenby was ready for his next main stroke. His operations beyond Jordan were not particularly successful, but they caused acute anxiety to the new Turkish commander-in-chief, the German Liman von Sanders. Allenby accentuated this by keeping a strong force in the low-lying Jordan valley despite its torrid heat and other discomforts.

On his arrival Allenby had taken over from his predecessor and strengthened the policy of assisting the Arabs in the Hejaz and Trans-Jordan in revolt against the Turks. He worked through a body of able officers, of whom the most outstanding was Colonel T. E. Lawrence. Much had already been effected in breaching the Hejaz railway and locking up garrisons at Medina, Ma'an, and elsewhere along the line. In his final offensive he called upon the Arabs, now partly organized as semi-regular forces, to keep the Turks engaged round the vital station of Der'a, the junction of the Hejaz and Palestinian systems, to interrupt the traffic in any case, and if possible to block it altogether. It was the one key objective which he could not reach quickly himself. Arab activity also increased Turkish fears of a British thrust on this flank, and they were strengthened by a number of skilful ruses.

It was actually Allenby's intention to attack on the left, in the coastal plain, massing the bulk of his forces of all arms in that sector, carrying out with the infantry of the XXI Corps a huge right wheel to drive the enemy into the hills and open a gateway for three cavalry divisions concentrated immediately in the rear. These were to cross the Samarian ridge which ends with Mount Carmel above the Bay of Acre, sweep down into the Plain of Esdraelon (or Megiddo), and pass through the Valley of Jezreel down to the Jordan near Beisan, thus throwing a net round the Turkish armies. Allenby possessed a superiority of four to one in cavalry, about six to four—the exact figures on the Turkish side are still a matter of dispute—in infantry, and nearly three to two in artillery. He had complete command of the air, so that his concentration could be carried out unobserved. His troops were fit and well found, whereas the Turks were ill supplied and ragged.

The assault was launched at 4.30 a.m. on 19 September with complete success. The two leading cavalry divisions entered the gateway before 9 a.m. They carried out their great drive against only scattered opposition. The hostile commander-in-chief was surprised in his headquarters at Nazareth and narrowly escaped capture in person. The 4th Cavalry division reached Beisan after covering over seventy miles in thirty-four hours. The Turkish forces west of Jordan were almost completely destroyed. Their transport was smashed by the Royal Air Force in defiles. Those down the Hejaz railway were trapped at Amman, and those east of Jordan harried and hunted by the Arabs. The remnant streamed north towards Damascus. Allenby ordered the cavalry to push on to that city, the Arabs moving parallel to its right flank. Damascus was entered on 1 October. Already malaria was taking a heavy toll, as Allenby had known would be the case when he left an area in which precautions had been taken for country in which there had been none. A wave of influenza followed. Allenby sent on his fittest cavalry division, the 5th, which captured Homs and Tripoli and entered Aleppo on 26 October. Almost immediately afterwards an armistice was signed with Turkey in Mudros harbour on 30 October. Allenby had captured 75,000 prisoners, 360 guns, and taken or destroyed all the enemy's transport. His own casualties were 5,666.

It was the last great campaign of cavalry employed in strategic mass in the annals of war, and one of the most notable. That fact alone would suffice to render Allenby's name immortal. The distances covered were enormous. The 5th Cavalry division marched 550 miles in 38 days, fighting four considerable actions and losing only 21 per cent. of its horses from all causes—there never have been better horse-masters than Allenby's Indians, British yeomanry, Australians, and New Zealanders. And throughout the offensive his inspiration, thrustfulness, and the confidence which he inspired were priceless assets.

Many problems, chief among them the rivalry between French and Arab claims in Syria and the withdrawal of the Turks, were still to be solved, but Allenby was not left to deal with them for long. In March 1919 he was appointed special high commissioner for Egypt, where his former corps commander in Palestine, Lieutenant-General Sir E. S. Bulfin, was engaged in stamping out a dangerous revolt. It was a difficult post because Egypt felt herself conscious of nationhood and had found a national champion in the person of the violent Saad Zaghlul. Allenby began with a disputed measure, for which he obtained the rather reluctant approval of the Foreign Office, the release of Zaghlul and three colleagues who had been arrested and deported to Malta. In September of that year he went on leave to England, which he had not seen since June 1917. He was fêted as one of the great victors of the war. He had already been promoted field-marshal (July 1919); he was now created a viscount (October 1919), received the thanks of parliament, and was given a grant of £50,000, while during the war he had been appointed K.C.B. (1915), G.C.M.G. (1917), and G.C.B. (1918). The allied countries had bestowed upon him their principal decorations. Among the universities which conferred honorary degrees upon him were Oxford, Cambridge, Edinburgh, and Aberdeen. In 1920 he was made colonel of the 1st Life Guards, which included the court appointment of Gold Stick in Waiting.

Back in Egypt, Allenby carried through his task grimly and in face of difficulties in the country and differences of opinion with the Foreign Office. He produced, and persuaded the British government to accept, a declaration abolishing the protectorate and recognizing Egypt as a sovereign state in February 1922. The end of his tenure of office was clouded by the murder of Sir Lee Stack, the sirdar, and his indifferent relations with the then foreign secretary, Mr. (afterwards Sir) Austen Chamberlain, which brought about his resignation. He left Egypt in June 1925. There may still be discussion as to the value of his work there and by some he is considered to have committed grave mistakes, but on balance the view must be favourable. His moral courage and integrity and his grip of the essence of the Egyptian problem cannot be questioned.

As a field-marshal Allenby remained theoretically on the active list, but the remainder of his life was spent in retirement. His chief public work was done as president (1930) of the British National Cadet Association, which owes him a deep debt. He was able to indulge to the full his hobby of bird-watching, and established an aviary in the small garden of his London home. He fished enthusiastically and travelled extensively. He died very suddenly in London, through the bursting of a blood-vessel in his brain, 14 May 1936. His ashes are buried in Westminster Abbey. His son Michael, a young man of the greatest promise, had been killed in action in France in 1917. His viscountcy passed by special remainder to his nephew, Dudley Jaffray Hynman Allenby (born 1903).

Allenby's worst foe was his violent temper, but he rarely punished except with his tongue, and, like Napoleon, constantly continued to employ men whom he had forcibly abused. It is also true to say that, although he never apologized for fits of unjustified anger, he often made amends for them. He was grateful for good service and generous in rewarding it, and in many respects kindly and thoughtful. Like some other famous soldiers he was devoted to children. The men who knew him best and were brought most closely in touch with him either in the army or during his six years in Egypt were his warmest admirers, and on them he left the impression of a great man. The worst error that can be made about him is to look upon him as an unimaginative, heavy-handed soldier on the western front and a brilliant and inspired soldier in Palestine. Doubtless he expanded and gained confidence in independent command, but essentially he remained the same. The difference was in the conditions. This is not to say that his plan and performance in Palestine, especially in the final offensive, were not masterly. As a man he was ever animated by the highest sense of duty, simple and sincere, thorough in everything. The strength of his character may be exemplified by the fact that he imposed upon himself restraint in indulgence in the pleasures of the table, to which he was at one time addicted, because he feared they were injuring his health, just as he gave up smoking because he thought the habit might affect his remarkable eyesight, which he considered a professional asset. Although he had never been a scholar he was a man of considerable cultivation, widely read, and a passable Grecian and Latinist. But the most significant thing to be said of him is that he stands in the tradition of the great cavalrymen and, if the term be confined to horsemen, that he is the last of the line.

A portrait of Allenby is included in J. S. Sargent's picture, 'Some General Officers of the Great War', painted in 1922. There is also a chalk drawing (likewise in the National Portrait Gallery) by Eric Kennington.

[*The Times*, 15 May 1936; Viscount Wavell, *Allenby: a Study in Greatness*, 2 vols., 1940–1943; Cyril Falls, (Official) *History of the Great War. Military Operations. France and Belgium, 1917*, 1940, and *Egypt and Palestine*, vol. ii, 1930; private information.]

CYRIL FALLS

published 1949

AUCHINLECK Claude John Eyre

(1884–1981)

Sir

Field-marshal, was born at Aldershot 21 June 1884, the elder son and eldest of four children of Colonel John Claude Alexander Auchinleck, of the Royal Artillery, who died when Claude was eight, and his wife, Mary Eleanor, daughter of John Eyre. As the son of a deceased officer he qualified for a foundation place at Wellington College but his mother was hard pressed to pay even the reduced fee of £10 a year. Accustomed to hardship at home or with his mother's relations in Ireland, Auchinleck acquired a lifelong indifference to personal comfort. He passed into Sandhurst just high enough on the list to secure a posting to the Indian Army where in 1904 he was commissioned into the 62nd Punjabis. He displayed a marked aptitude for learning local languages and soon developed a close rapport with the ordinary soldiers of the Indian Army.

On the outbreak of World War I Auchinleck as a captain accompanied his regiment to Egypt where he first saw action in repelling the Turkish attack on the Suez canal in February 1915. From 1916 to the end of the war he served in Mesopotamia, taking part in the desperate attempts to relieve Kut-el-amara and at one point commanding his depleted battalion. Promoted brigade-major to the 52nd brigade, he took part in the victorious advance to Baghdad in operations characterized by appalling conditions, defective medical supplies, and faulty tactics. Though appointed to the DSO (1917) and thrice mentioned in dispatches, his promotion after 1918 was slow. In 1921 he married Jessie, daughter of Alexander Stewart, civil engineer, of Kinloch Rannoch, Perthshire.

He passed at the Staff College, Quetta, in 1919, attended the inaugural course at the Imperial Defence College in 1927, and, as a full colonel, returned to Quetta as an instructor from 1930 to 1932. In 1933 he took over command of the Peshawar brigade which was immediately involved in operations against the upper Mohmands, followed by another campaign in 1935. Auchinleck displayed professional competence and skill in improvization in one of the most difficult forms of warfare; in consequence he was promoted major-general and in 1936 became deputy chief of the general staff in India. In 1938–9 he was a key member of the Chatfield committee on the modernization of the Indian Army. Here he evinced his progressive belief in the feasibility of replacing British officers by Indians.

Early in 1940 he was posted to England to prepare IV Corps for eventual dispatch to France but, as an expert in mountain warfare, was precipitately sent to Norway, after the disastrous opening of the campaign, to take command of the land forces in the Narvik area. Auchinleck's insistence on the provision of essential supplies, artillery, and air cover irritated (Sir) Winston Churchill, then first lord of the Admiralty, and was symptomatic of their relations. The general's forebodings were justified in that underequipping and tragi-comic mismanagement continued to dog operations which were overshadowed from the outset by the German attack in the west on 10 May. Narvik was duly retaken, only to be speedily abandoned. Auchinleck's report to the war cabinet, stating that the French contingent had impressed him more than the British, was not well received.

Nevertheless he was at once instructed to form V Corps for the defence of southern England against invasion, and in July 1940 he was promoted GOC Southern Command where he experienced considerable friction with his successor at V Corps, Lieutenant-General B. L. Montgomery (later Viscount Montgomery of Alamein). In November, when the immediate threat of invasion had passed, Auchinleck was promoted to full general and appointed commander-in-chief in India. This was perhaps a surprising transfer from an active to a secondary, support theatre, but India's military importance was increasing. It was the potential source of many divisions equipped from local manufacturing resources which were badly needed in the Middle East and the Far East; it might become a target for Japanese aggression; and its internal unrest needed handling by a respected Indian Army veteran. Auchinleck won Churchill's approval by his prompt dispatch of a force to help put down the rebellion of Rashid Ali in Iraq. The prime minister decided 'the Auk' had the necessary drive after all, as well as the other professional and personal attributes which he admired, and that he must take over as C-in-C Middle East where Sir A. P.

(later Earl) Wavell, in his opinion, was too exhausted to achieve the desperately needed victory. Consequently, when Operation Battleaxe failed in June 1941, Churchill ordered Wavell and Auchinleck to change places.

Auchinleck had been warned by successive CIGSs, Sir John Dill and Sir Alan Brooke (later Viscount Alanbrooke), that Churchill would expect an early offensive and quick results, and if he could not provide them he must explain why very diplomatically. Unfortunately Auchinleck was a bluff, uncompromising soldier, unable or unwilling to learn diplomatic finesse. After a brisk exchange of signals he bluntly told Churchill: 'I must repeat that to launch an offensive with the inadequate means at present at our disposal is not, in my opinion, a justifiable operation of war.' To all Churchill's relentless pressure and cajolery he returned a bleak factual explanation of the desert army's unreadiness for battle. From London, the reinforcements in troops, tanks, and guns seemed more than adequate (particularly in the light of the enemy's deficiencies as revealed by Ultra Intelligence); but in Auchinleck's judgement the troops required training and acclimatization, while the tanks and guns were inferior to the enemy's.

On this occasion Auchinleck got his way. Only on 18 November did Eighth Army open Operation Crusader by advancing round the southern flank of the Axis forces' position on the Italian frontier. General Sir Alan Cunningham intended to drive towards the besieged Tobruk so forcing Rommel to defend his communications on ground not of his own choosing whereupon he would be defeated by the superior numbers of the British armour. An extraordinarily confused situation developed in which tanks and armoured cars milled about the desert desperately trying to retain cohesion and restore order in an unusually dense 'fog of war'. Units of the Axis forces and Eighth Army became interspersed and layered upon one another in a remarkable fashion. As the battle appeared to swing against him with Rommel's bold dash towards the Egyptian frontier, Cunningham lost his nerve and began to talk of retreat. Warned of this situation, Auchinleck flew up to the front, restored confidence, and ordered the offensive to be renewed. Shortly afterwards he relieved Cunningham, replacing him with his deputy chief of staff from Cairo, (Sir) Neil Ritchie, initially as a temporary measure to avoid changing the Corps commanders.

The immediate outcome was an impressive victory. Tobruk was relieved and Rommel forced to retreat into Cyrenaica with the loss of 20,000 prisoners and masses of *matériel*. In February 1942 however, Rommel, having received reinforcements, unexpectedly counterattacked, driving the Eighth Army out of Benghazi and back to the Gazala line with its right flank on the sea about thirty-five miles west of Tobruk.

Auchinleck

As in the previous year, Auchinleck was placed under increasing pressure from Churchill to mount a new offensive, now with the urgent need to contribute to the relief of Malta by seizing Axis-held airfields. In these circumstances Auchinleck's adamant refusal to fly to London to explain his case that offensive operations before 1 June might risk defeat and the loss of Egypt was unwise. Churchill and the war cabinet were unsympathetic: Auchinleck was instructed to attack before 1 June only to be pre-empted by Rommel on 26 May.

Auchinleck offered another hostage to fortune in his retention of Ritchie as Eighth Army commander despite private warnings that he lacked the quality and experience to stand up to Rommel, and also lacked the confidence of his Corps commanders, W. H. E. Gott and C. W. M. N. (later Lord) Norrie, both senior to him and more experienced in command. Auchinleck in effect got the worst of both worlds: he expressed confidence in Ritchie yet tried to control him at long distance by feeding him detailed advice before and during the Gazala battle. More serious still, as conclusively shown by Field-Marshal Lord Carver, Ritchie was correct in his diagnosis of Rommel's intended line of attack round the south of the British defences, and Auchinleck wrong, despite his access to Ultra. As a consequence of Auchinleck's misjudgement, Norrie's armoured brigades were not concentrated to check and defeat Rommel's initial attack as they might otherwise have been. Auchinleck's Ultra intelligence, which revealed Rommel's severe logistic problems and shortage of tanks and fuel, also caused him to urge Ritchie to seize the initiative for which he was later to be blamed as over-optimistic.

The outcome of the Gazala battle was a clear-cut defeat. Tobruk surrendered and the Eighth Army was driven all the way back to the line of El Alamein. Auchinleck at this late stage in the battle (25 June) removed Ritchie and assumed command himself. Despite Auchinleck's excellent intelligence of Rommel's weaknesses, dispositions, and intentions, there is little evidence that he displayed exceptional skill in his execution of counterattacks, which all petered out ineffectually. Nevertheless his resolution and calm contributed to the defensive success. By mid-July Rommel's advance had been decisively halted and his diaries reveal that he had come close to total defeat. By early August Churchill had decided to remove Auchinleck, replacing him with Montgomery, news which Auchinleck heard on 8 August.

Montgomery's sweeping criticisms of his predecessor sought to deny Auchinleck any credit either for checking Rommel or bequeathing a feasible defensive plan. By the end of July the defensive layout of minefields and field fortifications was indeed well in hand. Montgomery was certainly unjust in telling Churchill a few days after he had taken command that Auchinleck had no plan and in the event of a heavy attack intended to retreat to the Nile delta.

On the other hand Montgomery's buoyant personality did inject new confidence into a tired army, and he did make significant changes to the plans he inherited. In particular he realized immediately that if all available reserves were called up from the delta he would be able to man a continuous line of defence as far south as Alam Halfa. On that ridge he would reinforce his left flank and threaten any enemy attempt to turn it by a counterattack. All contingency plans for insuring against failure were cancelled. Ironically, Auchinleck was dismissed by Churchill for refusing to be pressured into a premature offensive, whereas Montgomery took several additional weeks to prepare his offensive which began on 23 October.

Auchinleck was hurt by the manner of his removal and refused relegation to the command in Persia and Iraq. Consequently he spent nearly a year idle in India before again becoming commander-in-chief there on Wavell's promotion to viceroy in June 1943.

Though deprived of responsibility for the conduct of operations against the Japanese, Auchinleck bore the burden of the vast expansion of the Indian Army and its war industry. He had to provide bases, troops, and supplies for the Burma campaign, and also assist the Chinese and American forces in that theatre. His immense prestige in the Indian Army was a great asset in this task. He was one of the few British generals to gain the respect of the American 'Vinegar Joe' Stilwell but, unlike Wavell, was too conventional a soldier to be sympathetic to the unorthodox methods and exorbitant demands on Indian resources, of Orde Wingate.

In 1945 Auchinleck was appointed GCB, and the following year he was promoted field-marshal, but these honours were overshadowed by a personal tragedy. His wife left him for another senior officer at GHQ and they were divorced in 1946. They had no children. Jessie had found her husband's long office hours and dedication to work tiresome and ultimately intolerable. Her departure left a void in the field-marshal's life which he filled by working harder than ever. His last phase in India proved tragic in an even deeper sense. Auchinleck had hoped that India, and hence his cherished Indian Army, would remain united, but he quickly realized that partition of the country and the army were inevitable. He knew that considerable time would be needed for the peaceful reconstitution of two dominion armies without the steadying influence of British officers, the great majority of whom would wish to retire. Partition in 1948 would have been difficult enough, but the sudden decision of the new viceroy, Viscount (later Earl) Mountbatten of Burma to bring forward independence to 15 August 1947, made Auchinleck's task impossible. The Indian Army itself was deeply affected by religious conflict and rapidly disintegrated as an organized force. The meagre British military and police forces were powerless to prevent the massacres that accompanied the partition of the Punjab.

After independence Auchinleck decided to stay on as supreme commander of the Indian and Pakistan forces. He was openly criticized by some Indian leaders as being too favourable to Pakistan, and beneath a polite façade his relations with Mountbatten were increasingly strained. In September 1947 Mountbatten asked him to resign and he left India on 1 December in a mood of bitterness and despair after forty-four years' service. He refused a peerage lest the honour be associated with the events that he considered to be dishonourable.

After retiring from the army, Auchinleck led an active life, frequently revisiting India on business. His numerous appointments included being a governor of Wellington College (1946–59), president of the London Federation of Boys' Clubs (1949–55), vice-president of the Forces Help Society and Lord Roberts's Workshops, and chairman of the Armed Forces Art Society (1950–67). He characteristically refused to join in the battle of the memoirs, but in 1967 presented his personal papers to Manchester University, convinced that history would eventually do him justice.

Auchinleck had a most attractive personality; he detested all forms of pomp, display, and self-advertisement; but his simple tastes in personal matters did not inhibit him as a generous and entertaining host. His former private secretary, Major-General Shahid Hamid, has described Auchinleck in his element among his Indian soldiers: 'There is nothing dominating or overbearing in his character at all ... His mental energy, enthusiasm, good temper and driving power are immense ... He has become a legend in his lifetime.'

In 1968, when over eighty, Auchinleck left England to live in an unpretentious flat in Marrakesh. There he received visitors and spent his time painting, fishing, and walking. He had received honorary LLDs from Aberdeen and St Andrews universities in 1948 and from Manchester in 1970. He had many other honours, among which were OBE (1919), CB (1934), CSI (1936), GCIE (1940), and GCB (1945). He was among the ten field-marshals of World War II honoured by a memorial in the crypt of St Paul's in November 1976. He died in his Marrakesh home 23 March 1981.

[*The Times* and *Daily Telegraph*, 25 March 1981; *Listener*, 4 July 1974 and 16 April 1981; John Connell (John Henry Robertson), *Auchinleck*, 1959; Roger Parkinson, *The Auk*, 1977; Philip Warner, *Auchinleck: the Lonely Soldier*, 1981; Michael Carver, *Dilemmas of the Desert War*, 1986; Shahid Hamid, *Disastrous Twilight*, 1986.]

BRIAN BOND

published 1990

Reginald Hugh Spencer

(1863–1947)

Sir

Admiral, was born 6 September 1863 at Wiggonholt rectory, Sussex, the youngest of the eight children of the rector, the Rev. Thomas Bacon, and his wife, Emma Lavinia, daughter of George Shaw, of Teignmouth.

He entered the *Britannia* in January 1877 and was joined there by the Princes Edward and George. Success in the final examinations won him rating as midshipman on leaving, and he was appointed (January 1879) to the *Alexandra*, flagship in the Mediterranean of Sir Geoffrey Hornby and later of Sir Beauchamp Seymour (later Lord Alcester). A shooting accident at Corfu in 1882 sent him to hospital, but in 1883 he became acting sub-lieutenant in February and lieutenant in August, after complete success in his examinations at Greenwich.

He next went to sea in the sailing training ship *Cruiser*, and then, having decided to specialize in torpedo, went to the *Vernon* torpedo school. As torpedo lieutenant, in 1888 he joined the *Northumberland*, flagship of the Channel squadron which was relieved by the *Camperdown* next year. He served on the staff of the *Vernon* from August 1891 until May 1893, and with the *Vesuvius*, attached to the *Vernon*, as lieutenant and commander, until in June 1895 he was promoted commander. He was appointed in 1896 to the cruiser *Theseus* of the special service squadron which in January 1897 was suddenly withdrawn from the Mediterranean to join the squadron of Sir Harry Rawson on the west coast of Africa in order to deal with the critical situation in Benin where an English visiting party had been massacred. Bacon accompanied the land expedition from the coast to Benin city as intelligence officer and was mentioned in dispatches and appointed to the D.S.O.

In June 1897, having in the meantime written a spirited account of the expedition, *Benin, The City of Blood* (1897), he was transferred to the *Empress of India* which, after taking part in the jubilee review, joined the Mediterranean Fleet. In October 1898 she was ordered to Crete to take part in the punitive operations conducted by Sir Gerard Henry Uctred Noel after a massacre of Christians including the British vice-consul and his family.

At the end of 1899 Sir John (later Lord) Fisher, fresh from the first Hague conference, took command of the Mediterranean Fleet. Bacon was one of the first officers to comply with his request for suggestions for torpedo-boat manoeuvres. During his time in the *Vernon* he had in several annual naval manœuvres been in charge of torpedo craft. Fisher was so much pleased with the scheme which Bacon produced that he employed him frequently in strategic problems and on Fisher's recommendation Bacon was promoted captain in June 1900.

As a recognized torpedo and electricity expert he was at once sent to Paris to report on the electrical part of the 1900 Paris Exhibition, and then attended one of the first war courses at Greenwich. Thereafter he was given the duty of superintending the introduction and construction of submarine boats for the navy. Just before G. J. (later Viscount) Goschen had left office as first lord he had decided to order five submarine boats of the American (Holland) type to be built experimentally by Vickers Sons and Maxim. Bacon was placed in charge of this project, with the appointment of inspecting captain of submarines, and retained the post until October 1904. He thus became the father of the submarine service: both in the boats' construction and trial, and in training the crews.

Fisher, on becoming first sea lord in October 1904, asked Bacon to join him for a year as naval assistant. Bacon was chiefly occupied with the work of the famous Designs committee of which he was a member. It produced the designs of the *Dreadnought* and the first battle cruisers. In December 1905 he was given command of the *Irresistible* in the Mediterranean. His tenure was short, for in July 1906 he was transferred to be the first captain of the *Dreadnought*, but during it he wrote a private letter to Fisher in which he referred to conversations he had recently had with the King in the Mediterranean and which contained the remark 'Lord Charles and Admiral Lambton have been getting at the King' (on the subject of naval reforms to which they were opposed). The letter was printed by Fisher for private circulation; it was one to which no reasonable exception could be taken as coming from his former naval assistant, but some years later its existence became public; the mention of the King made it impossible for Fisher to publish the text, and Bacon received a good deal of odium which affected his career in the Service on the assumption that as an officer of the fleet he had been sending confidential reports on his superior officers direct to the Admiralty.

When Sir Francis Bridgeman hoisted his flag in the *Dreadnought* as admiral of the Home (Reserve) Fleet, Bacon became his chief of staff. In 1907 he was appointed to succeed Sir John (later Earl) Jellicoe as director of naval ordnance and torpedoes. Bacon was promoted rear-admiral 12 July 1909. Reginald McKenna then invited him to join the Board as controller in succession to Jellicoe after a short period afloat. But at the same time he was offered the post of managing director of the Coventry Ordnance Works, and he decided to obtain leave to retire from the navy in order to accept it, having come to the conclusion that, after serving the usual term of years as controller, he was unlikely, owing to his short sea experience, to obtain any important command afloat.

He was accordingly placed on the retired list in November 1909 and went to Coventry to undertake the new duties for which his experience as director of naval ordnance fully equipped him. On the outbreak of war in 1914 he designed and produced at Coventry some new 15-inch howitzer guns for use in Flanders and was sent in charge of them to France in January 1915 with the temporary rank of colonel 2nd commandant Royal Marines. (Sir) Winston Churchill, however, recalled him in April to become rear-admiral, Dover Patrol, and senior naval officer, Dover, which had become one of the most important war appointments. He was promoted vice-admiral later in the year. On the efficiency of the Dover Patrol depended not only the military sea routes across the Channel, sustaining our armies in France, but also the security of the shipping passing through the Straits, assembling in the Downs, and bringing supplies to the port of London. The forces at Bacon's command, which he set to work with characteristic zeal to organize for the duties involved, were at first meagre in the extreme, and although they were later strengthened, the strategic situation was always such that the enemy was in a position to bring superior force to bear before reinforcement could arrive. The measure of Bacon's success during his period of command is that the patrol stood firm, despite enemy attack, and our shipping moved in safety in this dangerous area both behind the mine barrage and on its way to the Thames estuary. The Dover Patrol took an active part in supporting the sea flank of the armies in France. This support, which Bacon always provided on demand, involved naval operations in waters of great difficulty navigationally, and in face of formidable enemy defences. An outstanding incident amongst many actions with the enemy occurred in April 1917 when the *Swift* and the *Broke* defeated a division of German destroyers in a night action. Throughout his tenure of the command Bacon's work and conduct had the complete approval of his chiefs in Whitehall; and he enjoyed the trust and enthusiastic admiration of the numerous officers under his command, notably of Commander Edward Evans of the *Broke* (later Lord Mountevans) who became his chief of staff. But when Sir Eric Geddes was sent by Lloyd George to take charge of the Admiralty there was a marked change, and at the end of 1917 Bacon shared the fate of his illustrious friend and leader, Jellicoe, and was abruptly dismissed from his command.

Bacon's public services were, however, far too valuable to be lost, and (Sir) Winston Churchill, then minister of munitions, at once appointed him controller of the department of munitions inventions. His advisory panel included the most distinguished scientists in the country. On 31

March 1919 Bacon finally retired into private life, having been advanced to the rank of admiral in September 1918. He received the official appreciation of the Ministry for 'valuable assistance given while holding his responsible and important post'.

Bacon had from boyhood been devoted to shooting game, and recognizing that his public career was over he retired to his home in Hampshire and during the winter months spent many days shooting with his neighbours and friends. He records that in one season he met 149 different guns. He also became chairman of the Romsey bench. In the summer he lived on a property near Lerici in Italy where he had built a house. Apart from country pursuits he soon found opportunities for showing his merit as a writer. He wrote his autobiography in two volumes, *A Naval Scrap-Book, 1877–1900* (1925) and *From 1900 Onward* (1940); two books on the Dover Patrol; *The Jutland Scandal* (1924), an able and trenchant justification of Jellicoe's conduct of the battle, the title of which was, however, much resented in some naval circles; and the standard biographies of Fisher (1929) and Jellicoe (1936).

King Edward VII had appointed Bacon C.V.O. on his inspection of the Home Fleet in 1907. In 1916 he was appointed K.C.B. in recognition of his work in the Dover Patrol, and also promoted K.C.V.O. He held several foreign decorations. Bacon was a man of brilliant professional attainments with a most original mind. He was perhaps the cleverest of the many able young naval officers of his time, and Fisher picked him out as his principal lieutenant in promoting drastic reforms in naval education, strategy, and ship construction. He won early promotion by sheer merit, and his early work on submarines as well as his command of the Dover Patrol was of inestimable service to his country during the critical years of the war of 1914–18.

Bacon married in 1894 Cicely Isabel (died 1955), daughter of Henry Edward Surtees, M.P., M.F.H., of Redworth Hall, county Durham; they had one daughter and two sons, the elder of whom died on active service in the battle of Loos, and the younger while a naval cadet. Bacon died at his home, Braishfield Lodge, near Romsey, 9 June 1947. A portrait by Lance Calkin is in the possession of the family, and a drawing by Francis Dodd is in the Imperial War Museum.

[Bacon's own writings; Admiralty records; private information; personal knowledge.]

VINCENT W. BADDELEY

published 1959

Douglas Robert Steuart

(1910–1982)

Sir

Royal Air Force officer, was born at St John's Wood, London, 21 February 1910, the younger child and younger son of Frederick Roberts Bader, a civil engineer working in India, and his wife, Jessie McKenzie. He was educated at St Edward's School, Oxford, where he was a scholar, and at the Royal Air Force College, Cranwell, where he was a prize cadet. He finished second in the contest for the sword of honour at Cranwell and his confidential report described him as 'plucky, capable, headstrong'.

Bader was commissioned in August 1930 and was then posted as a pilot officer to No. 23 Fighter Squadron at RAF station, Kenley. He was an exceptional pilot and was selected, with another officer from the squadron, to fly the pair for the RAF at the Hendon air display in 1931 before a crowd of 175,000. As a young officer, he was good looking and charming. He was also determined and dogmatic, and could be thoroughly 'difficult'. He was, however, a natural leader, fearless and always eager for a challenge. While he could be brusque and impatient, he was socially at ease in any company. He was intensely loyal to the causes he cared about and to his friends.

Bader was twenty-one when on 14 December 1931 he crashed on Woodley airfield, near Reading. Both legs had to be amputated in the Royal Berkshire Hospital where his life was saved. He was later transferred to the RAF Hospital at Uxbridge. Six months after his operations, he was walking unaided on his artificial legs. 'I will never use a stick', he said.

He was discharged from the RAF in the spring of 1933. That summer he became a clerk in the Asiatic Petroleum Company (later Shell Petroleum) in the City and on 5 October 1933 married Olive Thelma Exley, daughter of Lieutenant-Colonel Ivo Arthyr Exley Edwards, RAF (retired), and Olive Maud Amy Addison (née Donaldson), secretly at Hampstead register office. Four years later, on 5 October 1937, the two were formally married at St Mary Abbots church, Kensington. There were no children of the marriage.

Bader was re-engaged by the RAF in November 1939, two months after the outbreak of World War II and on 7 February 1940 he was posted to No. 19 Fighter Squadron at Duxford, near Cambridge, as a flying officer. Within six weeks he was appointed to command 'A' Flight in No. 222 Squadron. As a flight lieutenant, he saw action with the squadron at Dunkirk. Promotion continued and on 24 June 1940 he was posted to command No. 242

(Canadian) Squadron at Coltishall, in Norfolk. He led the nearby Duxford wing with this unit with signal success throughout the Battle of Britain, being appointed to the DSO on 13 September and awarded the DFC a month later.

Bader's advocacy of his much misunderstood 'Big Wing' tactics served to fuel the controversy which existed between the air officers commanding Nos. 11 and 12 Groups of Fighter Command—(Sir) Keith Park and (Sir) Trafford Leigh-Mallory—and between the C-in-C, Sir Hugh (later Lord) Dowding, and the deputy chief of the air staff, Sholto Douglas (later Lord Douglas of Kirtleside). The controversy was further inflamed by Leigh-Mallory's decision to ask Bader to accompany him to the high-level, tactical conference held at the Air Ministry on 17 October 1940 with Sholto Douglas in the chair. In March 1941 Bader became the first wing commander flying at Tangmere, in Sussex, leading his three Spitfire squadrons with notable success in the frequent offensive operations over northern France. His aggressive leadership was recognized with the award of a bar both to the DSO and the DFC. The French croix de guerre and the Legion of Honour followed. There were three mentions in dispatches. With his official score of twenty-three enemy aircraft destroyed, Bader was shot down on 9 August 1941 near St Omer in the Pas de Calais and became a prisoner of war until he was released from Colditz in April 1945. He made repeated attempts to escape, refusing repatriation on the grounds that he expected to return to combat.

After the armistice, the 'legless ace' was promoted to group captain and posted to command the North Weald sector in Essex. From here he led the victory fly-past over London on 15 September 1945. He retired from the RAF six months later and in July 1946 rejoined the Shell Company, eventually to become managing director of Shell Aircraft Ltd (1958–69). He flew himself to many parts of the world, often taking his wife with him. An outstanding games player before his accident, he played golf on his tin legs to a handicap of four.

Paul Brickhill's biography of Bader, *Reach for the Sky* (1954) was followed by the film bearing the same title with Kenneth More playing Bader (1956). This brought the Battle of Britain pilot world-wide fame. Notwithstanding this, his unsung work for the disabled continued apace and in 1956 he was appointed CBE.

Bader, who lived mainly in London, retired from Shell in 1969 and from 1972 to 1978 was a member of the Civil Aviation Authority. He accepted several non-executive directorships, maintained his long-established connections with Fleet Street, and continued with his numerous public speaking engagements. Latterly, his principal business base was as a consultant to Aircraft Equipment International at Ascot.

Bader's wife died in London 24 January 1971 after a long illness. Two years later, on 3 January 1973, he married Mrs Joan Eileen Murray, daughter of Horace Hipkiss, steel mill owner. In the same year was published *Fight for the Sky* (1973), his story of the Hurricane and the Spitfire. Knighted in 1976 for service to the public and the disabled, Bader died in London 4 September 1982, while being driven home through Chiswick after speaking at a dinner in Guildhall. He was FRAeS (1976), an honorary D.Sc. of the Queen's University, Belfast (1976), and DL of Greater London (1977).

[P. B. ('Laddie') Lucas, *Flying Colours* (biography), 1981; private information; personal knowledge.]

P. B. Lucas

published 1990

BALL Albert

(1896–1917)

Airman, was born at Nottingham 21 August 1896, the elder son of Sir Albert Ball, estate agent, sometime mayor of the city, by his wife, Harriet Mary Page, of Derby. He was educated at Trent College, Long Eaton, Derbyshire, where he showed himself a sensitive, conscientious boy, with a disturbing passion for collecting pistols. He left school in December 1913, and bought an interest in two engineering companies at Nottingham. On the outbreak of the European War in August 1914 he volunteered for the Nottinghamshire and Derby regiment, Territorial Force, and within two weeks of joining was promoted sergeant. He was granted his commission in October, and spent the winter in training. Chafing at the delay in getting to France, he transferred to a cyclists' corps near Ealing, but aviation caught his fancy, and he entered at Hendon for a course of training. He had to do his flying at dawn in order to be back in camp at Ealing for the 6.0 a.m. parade. He passed out in October 1915, and went to Norwich for training as a flying officer. He was a careful rather than a brilliant pilot. He survived some serious crashes, and having completed his training at the Central Flying School, Upavon, Wiltshire, was seconded to the Royal Flying Corps in January 1916, when he was sent to Gosport as instructor.

Ball flew overseas on 18 February 1916 in order to join No. 13 squadron, and spent his early days chiefly in artillery reconnaissance, which he described as 'great sport'; but he felt the responsibility for his observer's life. Although he was by temperament a single-seater pilot, his two-seater

31

machine drove down, during April, two enemy aeroplanes and destroyed one. In May he was given a single-seater, from which on the 15th he destroyed his first German aeroplane. By the end of the month he was attracting notice. After a short leave in England he returned to France and joined his squadron, No. 11, ten days before the opening of the Somme battle (1 July). Before the battle ended the British air service had established an ascendancy over the enemy which was never afterwards lost, and Ball was the spearhead of this achievement. But the strain told on him, and on 17 July he was wisely transferred to a two-seater squadron, No. 8. On 1 August he was promoted lieutenant, and on the 15th of the same month he was back with No. 11; the next day, on his Nieuport machine, he attacked five enemy aeroplanes, destroying one and forcing two down. On 22 August, his last day with No. 11 squadron, he flew into an enemy formation of twelve machines, crashed two of them, set fire to another, returned for ammunition, attacked fourteen more, ran out of petrol, landed just clear of the trenches, slept by his machine, and flew next morning to No. 60, his new squadron. His audacity and skill were remarkable. By the end of the month he was the leading Allied pilot, and on 1 September he destroyed four more enemy machines. He was promoted captain on 13 September.

Ball's extraordinary success had a heartening effect on the British infantry. When the Somme campaign ended, he was sent home to infuse his spirit and methods into flying officers in training. He was in England from 4 October 1916 until 7 April 1917, when he flew out with No. 56 squadron, arriving for the Arras offensive which opened on 9 April. His method now was to lead his patrol on S.E. 5 (scout experimental) machines and, in addition, to go out alone on his Nieuport. On 3 May he had destroyed thirty-eight enemy machines, one more than the record of the leading French airman, Georges Guynemer. On 5 May, after shooting down two Albatross scouts, he wrote home, describing his spare time, 'I dig in the garden and sing.' Two days later, 7 May 1917, Ball made his last flight. The reports are conflicting. He flew into a formation led by the German airman, Manfred Freiherr von Richthofen, fought three of the enemy, and, it would seem, sent two down before he himself was hit. He was buried at Annoeullin, east of La Bassée. His posthumous Victoria cross award (June 1917) credited him with a record of forty-three aeroplanes and one balloon destroyed and a large number sent down out of control. Ball was awarded the military cross (1916), the distinguished service order with two bars (1916), the croix de guerre and legion of honour (1917), and the Russian order of St. George, fourth class (1917).

Ball was a cheerful young soldier, of gentle manners and vigilant conscience. 'I hate this killing business,' he wrote; but he fought with an almost religious fervour. When he was flying his aeroplane was as much a part of him as were his sensitive hands. He was the greatest fighting pilot of the air service, and his personality has contributed much to its traditions of efficiency and self-sacrifice.

[W. A. Briscoe and H. R. Stannard, *Captain Ball, V.C.*, 1918; official records; personal knowledge.]

HENRY ALBERT JONES

published 1927

BEATTY David

(1871–1936)

First Earl Beatty

Admiral of the fleet, was born at Howbeck Lodge, Stapeley, near Nantwich, Cheshire, 17 January 1871, the second son in a family of four sons and one daughter of Captain David Longfield Beatty, of the 4th Hussars, by his first wife, Katherine Edith, daughter of Nicholas Sadleir, of Dunboyne Castle, co. Meath, a remarkable woman who more than once prophesied that England would ring with David's name. The Beattys were of old Irish stock; the admiral's grandfather was long master of the Wexford hounds, and his parents, when they settled in Cheshire, devoted themselves to hunting and training the horses sent over from the family estates at Borodale in county Wexford. It is not therefore surprising that Beatty's favourite sport was hunting, or that he wrote to his sister about the battle of Jutland as if it had been a hunt. 'I describe the battle to you thus because only in this way would you understand it.'

Sea and ships had always greatly fascinated young Beatty, and there was never any doubt that he was destined for the navy. At thirteen years of age he passed into the *Britannia*, and on passing out two years later he was posted to the *Alexandra*, flagship of Prince Alfred, Duke of Edinburgh, commander-in-chief of the Mediterranean Fleet, and he served practically the whole of his time as midshipman in this ship. During the period from 1890 to 1892 he was under training ashore at Portsmouth and at the Royal Naval College, Greenwich, as acting sub-lieutenant, emerging with a first-class certificate in torpedo, a second class in seamanship, gunnery, and pilotage, and a third class in navigation. He was promoted lieutenant in August 1892, and spent his watch-keeping days in the training corvette

Ruby, and the battleships *Camperdown* and *Trafalgar*, for the most part in the Mediterranean.

Beatty's early enthusiasm for the navy was damped at this time by the monotony of service routine; but his opportunity came in 1896, when Kitchener asked for a small force of gunboats to operate on the Nile in support of his expedition for the recovery of the Sudan. (Sir) Stanley Colville, commander of the *Trafalgar*, chose his shipmate Beatty as second-in-command of this little expedition in stern-wheel gunboats. Only three of these boats, one of which was Beatty's, passed the Third Cataract, and immediately above it they were hotly engaged by the Dervishes, not without artillery. Colville, severely wounded, handed over the command to Beatty who immediately decided to attempt the daring manœuvre of leading the flotilla upstream beyond the Arab position. He was assisted in this by the army, which, thanks to the action of the gunboats, had been able to establish artillery and infantry within close range. Beatty, however, pressed on at full speed to Dongola, and after another stiff fight won for the navy the honour of being the first to occupy the town. The enemy were by now in full retreat, but Beatty continued to harass them and did not give up the pursuit until he reached the Fourth Cataract. This gallant piece of leadership was highly praised by Kitchener, Beatty was appointed to the D.S.O., and his name was noted for early promotion.

After a brief spell at home, Beatty, at Kitchener's special request, was again lent, in 1897, to the Egyptian government for operations on the Nile in a flotilla reinforced by specially designed gunboats. He had a narrow escape when, on 4 August, his ship, the *Hafir*, capsized at the Fourth Cataract. During the advance on Omdurman in 1898 he was constantly in action, and commanded a rocket battery ashore at the battle of the Atbara (8 April). After the battle of Omdurman (2 September) Beatty was in one of the gunboats that escorted the sirdar to Fashoda, on his return from whence he received special promotion to commander (November) at the early age of twenty-seven, over the heads of 395 senior officers on the lieutenants' list.

After a winter spent at home in the hunting field, Beatty was appointed (April 1899) to the China station as commander of the battleship *Barfleur*, commanded by Colville. In spite of his youth, Beatty won the respect of both officers and men. After twelve months of normal duty he found himself again on active service in the Boxer rebellion. Sir Edward Seymour, the British naval commander-in-chief, made a gallant attempt to reach Pekin with an international force but was compelled to return to Hsiku, where he was completely surrounded. The foreign settlement at Tientsin, six miles to the south, was also besieged, and Beatty landed from the *Barfleur* to reinforce the garrison. In this he succeeded and was continuously employed in sorties; in one across the river he was ambushed. Wounded and in severe pain, he nevertheless brought his men back in good order, remaining with the rearguard until all the wounded had been embarked. While still suffering from his wounds, he accepted the command of a naval detachment which eventually assisted in extricating Seymour from Hsiku. For his services in this campaign he was promoted captain (November 1900). The average age of a captain being then forty-three, his promotion at twenty-nine caused considerable stir.

As captain, Beatty commanded (1902–1910) the cruisers *Juno*, *Arrogant*, *Diana*, and *Suffolk*, and the battleship *Queen*. His marriage had made him independent of the service and his rapid promotion brought him to the head of the list of captains before he had completed the six years' service at sea required for promotion to flag rank. Nevertheless, in view of the time lost on account of the wounds which he had received in China and his war services, he was promoted rear-admiral by order in council on 1 January 1910, the youngest flag-officer for over a hundred years, being just under thirty-nine years of age, whereas Nelson on his promotion was a few months over thirty-eight. This promotion created even greater stir than the previous one, and with perhaps more justification in view of the length of time during which he had been on half-pay.

Beatty was far more interested in the proper employment of the fleet in war than in its technicalities, and soon after Mr. Churchill, with his 'mind full of the dangers of war', became first lord of the Admiralty in October 1911, he chose Beatty, in spite of naval advice to the contrary, for his naval secretary (1912). They were admirably suited to each other; and, probably in order to confound the critics of Beatty and to test his capacity as a flag-officer, the first lord gave him the command of a cruiser squadron in the important manœuvres of 1912. Clearly Beatty fulfilled Mr. Churchill's expectations, for in the spring of 1913 he appointed Beatty 'over the heads of all' to command the battle-cruiser squadron. Beatty hoisted his flag in the *Lion* in March 1913, and when war broke out on 4 August 1914 he was in northern waters in command of the scouting forces of the Grand Fleet based at Scapa Flow under Sir John (later Earl) Jellicoe.

When, on 22 September 1914, the three cruisers *Cressy*, *Hogue*, and *Aboukir* were torpedoed with great loss of life off the Dutch coast, the shock to a fleet which had not wholly appreciated the potentialities of the submarine was such that the commander-in-chief, apprehensive about the security of the Grand Fleet at Scapa Flow, decided to take the fleet to ports on the west coast of Scotland and Ireland until Scapa could be properly defended. Although Beatty recognized the need for this decision, the result of government improvidence was more than he could bear, and he lost no time in pressing his views in the strongest terms by private letter to

Mr. Churchill. Believing Scapa to be too distant from the enemy, he urged that Cromarty and Rosyth should also be equipped and defended as operational bases, and these defences were completed by the end of the year.

It has been a matter for wonder why the Germans did not take fuller advantage of the awkward predicament in which the Grand Fleet found itself at this time. The answer is supplied by the success of the offensive movement into the Heligoland Bight, carried out by Beatty, (Sir) Reginald Yorke Tyrwhitt, and Roger John Brownlow (later Lord) Keyes, during the first month of the war. The plan designed by the Admiralty was, briefly, that Tyrwhitt with his destroyers should penetrate deeply into the Bight under cover of darkness and sweep out at dawn from east to west with the object of destroying all enemy ships encountered, while Keyes with his submarines lay off the mouths of the German rivers in suitable positions to attack enemy heavy ships if they came out. Two older battle-cruisers from the Humber under Rear-Admiral Sir Archibald Gordon Henry Wilson Moore were to act in support. Jellicoe, uneasy as to the adequacy of this support, directed Beatty to proceed to Heligoland with the battle-cruisers *Lion*, *Queen Mary*, *Princess Royal*, and Commodore (Sir) William Edmund Goodenough's six light cruisers. The weather was calm, but visibility was bad. Beatty's first move was to make contact with the Humber battle-cruiser force, which he did at daylight on 28 August, and he was thus able to obtain detailed information of the movements of the other units. The presence of British forces in the Bight having become known, the enemy sent out cruisers and destroyers to reinforce their patrols. In the thick weather, the British flotillas lost touch with one another, the situation became confused, and it was difficult to distinguish friend from foe. In several fleeting actions, the German cruiser *Mainz* and a destroyer were sunk. Just before noon, Tyrwhitt's flagship *Arethusa*, which had been badly damaged a short time previously, was attacked by four enemy cruisers. Captain W. F. Blunt in the *Fearless*, with a division of destroyers, came to her support, but could do little against such a superior force. At this critical moment, to the north-westward out of the mist, Beatty appeared with his battle-cruisers steaming at high speed to the rescue. Sundry other British forces rallied towards the battle-cruisers, and in a hot pursuit of the enemy into the Bight, the *Köln* and *Ariadne* were sunk. The two remaining German cruisers, *Strassburg* and *Stralsund*, made their escape. At 1.10 p.m. Beatty made the general signal 'Retire'.

There is no doubt that by his prompt action Beatty turned what would certainly have been a disaster into an important success. It is interesting to note how he arrived at his decision, which was no easy one in view of the risks involved in the face of mines, submarines, and enemy heavy ships. At 10 a.m., realizing that the whole position was confused, Beatty broke wireless silence and informed all concerned where he was and what he was doing. He became very uneasy, and on receipt of various signals for assistance he decided to disregard the dangers and proceed at high speed in support of the *Arethusa*. His reasons for this are given in his own dispatch: 'The situation appeared to me to be extremely critical ... there was the possibility of a grave disaster. At 11.30 I therefore decided that the only course possible was to take the battle-cruiser squadron at full speed to the eastward ... I had not lost sight of the danger to my squadron.' Here he enumerates the risks and discounts them methodically one by one, a good example of Beatty's power of tempering boldness with caution but, once the situation had been weighed, acting with vigour and determination. No British ship was lost in an action which, although a marked success, disclosed grave deficiencies in staff work and system of command. Nevertheless, the moral effect was profound: the German navy in particular was severely shaken, and the inactivity of the enemy from August to September enabled the defences of the British bases to be completed and the position of the Grand Fleet in the North Sea was consolidated.

December 1914 was an anxious month for the British command. Owing to the commitments in other seas, only three battle-cruisers were available. There were signs of German naval activity and on 14 December the Admiralty reported that the enemy battle-cruisers were about to carry out a 'tip and run' raid on the east coast of England. As it was impossible to ascertain where the enemy would choose to attack, a strong British force, including the second battle squadron under Admiral Sir George Warrender and the first battle-cruiser squadron under Beatty, were dispatched to a point between Heligoland and Flamborough Head, where they would be in a good position to intercept the enemy on his return.

At dawn on 16 December, when the British forces were in process of concentrating, news was received that Scarborough, Whitby, and Hartlepool were being bombarded. The weather was thick and the situation was complicated by the fact that a German mine-field lay between the British fleet and the five bombarding battle-cruisers. Aided by mist and the mine-field, the enemy slipped through the British forces and escaped. It was an exasperating day for the British admirals who were frustrated because there was no scientific means of locating the enemy or of synchronizing the movements of the four British squadrons groping blindly for their prey. The success of the raid emphasized the need for basing strong British forces farther south. Accordingly Beatty's battle-cruisers were stationed at Rosyth, and they had not long been there before Beatty found himself speeding across the North Sea to intercept Admiral Hipper, who, according to Admiralty intelligence, was expected to be near the Dogger Bank with four battle-cruisers, accompanied by cruisers and destroyers, on the morning of 24 January. So accurate was this intelligence that the British scouting forces sighted the enemy, as if at a pre-arranged rendezvous, at 7.30 a.m. on that day.

Beatty pressed forward at full speed to attack with the *Lion*, *Tiger*, and *Princess Royal*. Rear-Admiral Moore with the older and slower *Indomitable* and the *New Zealand* began to fall astern. Hipper turned to run for home but Beatty was overhauling him and had a good chance to destroy the enemy ships before they could reach their base. But it was not to be. At 9 a.m. the British ships opened fire, the *Seydlitz* was severely damaged, and the *Blücher*, the rear ship of the enemy, very soon fell out of line and was abandoned to her fate. On the other hand, Beatty's flagship *Lion* became the target for the concentrated fire of the German squadron and after two hours' fighting received a blow which stopped one engine and caused her to list heavily to port. The other ships swept past her, and Beatty, who could no longer lead his squadron, was obliged to issue instructions by flag signals.

The British squadron had now lost some distance on account of a turn to avoid a reported submarine. Beatty has been criticized for having ordered this turn, but he was no doubt influenced by the fate which had befallen the three cruisers in September. In order to continue the pursuit and get his guns to bear on the fleeing enemy, Beatty gave the order to his signal officer: 'Course north-east—attack the rear of the enemy.' But the *Lion* had only two signal halyards left, and the arrangement of the signals as hoisted conveyed the meaning 'Attack the rear of the enemy bearing north-east', and so it was interpreted by Moore, the second-in-command. The effect was tragic, for by coincidence the *Blücher*, now well separated from her consorts, bore north-east: consequently the whole of the British squadron attacked and destroyed her. The *Lion* by now had dropped well astern, and Beatty was at a loss to know why his squadron was not continuing the pursuit of the main German force. He accordingly gave the order to use Nelson's signal 'Engage the enemy more closely', but was told that it had been omitted from the signal book. The modern substitute 'Keep nearer to the enemy' was then hoisted, but by this time the *Lion* was so far away that the signal could not be read. He transferred to a destroyer and gave chase; but it was too late: the enemy had escaped. So ended an action, which, although acclaimed as a British victory, was not so satisfactory as it might have been had Beatty been able to retain his leadership.

In December 1915 Beatty, now promoted to vice-admiral, had under his command ten battle-cruisers organized into three squadrons, three light cruiser squadrons, and the thirteenth destroyer flotilla, with the *Lion* as fleet flagship. As that year wore on it was clear that the Germans had no intention of challenging British sea power in the North Sea, and no major action took place, but in January 1916 Admiral Scheer, the new commander-in-chief of the German fleet, announced his intention of coming to 'close grips with England'. He implemented his threat by carrying out some ineffective 'tip and run' raids at scattered points on the east coast, hoping that public indignation would cause dispersal of the British fleet. He was disappointed; so he planned a more ambitious operation in which his light forces were to attack trade off the Norwegian coast and in the Skagerrak while the High Sea Fleet remained fifty miles to the south ready to pounce on any British detachment which might be sent to deal with the raiders. Before putting this plan into action, he placed strong forces of submarines in positions where they could intercept British units coming out from Rosyth, Cromarty, and Scapa.

The date selected was 31 May, and by an extraordinary coincidence Jellicoe had also prepared for 2 June an operation which was in essence the same as Scheer's, namely, to draw the German forces into the Skagerrak and destroy them with the Grand Fleet. Towards the end of May the fleet had taken up its disposition for the impending operation, and as the third battle-cruiser squadron under Rear-Admiral (Sir) H. L. A. Hood happened to be at Scapa for routine gunnery practice, Jellicoe sent Rear-Admiral (Sir) H. Evan-Thomas with the fifth battle squadron to replace it in Beatty's fleet at Rosyth.

On 30 May the Admiralty warned Jellicoe that the enemy intended to go to sea by way of Horn's Reef on 31 May; on the evening of the 30th the Grand Fleet sailed from Scapa, and Beatty left Rosyth with six battle-cruisers and the fifth battle squadron. Jellicoe's plan was that the Grand Fleet should pass through a position 200 miles east of Kinnaird Head on a southerly course. Beatty was to take his force to a point seventy miles south of this, and, if nothing was sighted, to turn north and take up his position ahead of the Grand Fleet. The whole fleet would then sweep south towards Horn's Reef with the cruiser screen ahead covering a wide front.

Scheer left the Jade the same night, but neither Beatty nor Jellicoe had any definite information that the enemy was at sea. About noon on the 31st, the Admiralty incorrectly informed Jellicoe and Beatty that the German flagship was still in the Jade. Beatty reached his rendezvous at 2 p.m., and having sighted nothing he turned his whole force to the north to meet Jellicoe. He stationed the fifth battle squadron five miles to the northward of him so that it could be conveniently situated to drop into its normal position ten miles north of the battle-cruisers when the whole fleet had finally concentrated, and was proceeding to the southward in accordance with Jellicoe's plan. A few minutes later Commodore (Sir) Edwyn Sinclair Alexander-Sinclair in the *Galatea*, scouting to the eastward,

reported the presence of enemy cruisers and destroyers. Beatty immediately turned to south-south-east to place himself between the enemy and
his base. Evan-Thomas with the fifth battle squadron did not turn to
follow Beatty until six minutes later, partly because he had not at the
moment received the report of the enemy, and partly because smoke had
prevented him from seeing the turning signal. This, opening the distance
between the two squadrons, caused Beatty to go into action without the
support of the four battle-ships. It has been suggested that he should have
waited for Evan-Thomas, but his primary duty was to locate the enemy,
and, if in superior force, to destroy him. In view of the Admiralty intelligence received two hours previously, he had every reason to believe that
he would be in superior force, and he had six battle-cruisers against
Hipper's five.

At 3.25 p.m. Beatty sighted the German battle-cruisers and reported
their position to Jellicoe, at this time about sixty miles to the northward.
The two squadrons closed, and at 3.48 p.m. a fierce battle began on a
southerly course at high speed. The British were unfavourably placed for
wind and light, and the Germans quickly found the range. The *Lion* was
repeatedly hit, and twenty minutes after the battle was joined the *Indefatigable*, which was struck by two plunging salvoes, blew up. Twenty
minutes later the *Queen Mary* blew up, which caused Beatty to remark to
his flag-captain: 'There seems to be something wrong with our bloody
ships to-day, Chatfield.' In spite of these two disasters, Beatty kept at close
action range; meanwhile Evan-Thomas, by cutting corners and cramming
on maximum speed, had skilfully managed to bring his squadron into
action against the rear of the enemy. At this critical moment, Beatty threw
his destroyers into the attack. Hipper did the same, and a brisk destroyer
battle took place between the lines in which the British attack was the
more successful, for a torpedo struck the *Seydlitz* and Hipper was forced to
turn away. The German attack failed completely, and this gave the British a
slight breathing space and from now onwards their fire began to tell.
'Nothing', reported Hipper, 'but the poor quality of the British bursting
charges saved us from disaster.'

At 4.40 p.m. with dramatic suddenness the scene changed. A forest of
masts appeared on the southern horizon where for the moment visibility
was good. This was the High Sea Fleet, reported for the first time seven
minutes previously by Commodore Goodenough, who had been scouting
ahead of the battle-cruisers. Beatty's duty was clear. He must retire to the
northward at once and endeavour to lead Scheer into Jellicoe's clutches.
Accordingly he reversed his course and after another hour and a half of
dogged fighting, in which the fifth battle squadron bore the brunt, he
sighted the Grand Fleet. During this time the two British squadrons

inflicted very heavy damage on the German battle-cruisers, all the turrets of the *Von der Tann* being put out of action.

At 5.35 p.m. Beatty, realizing that Jellicoe was not far off, turned sharply to the eastward in order to bend back Hipper's van and prevent him from sighting the main British battle-fleet. This manœuvre gave Beatty improved visibility and after a sharp encounter the enemy withdrew from the action behind a smoke screen. Of this action, the German official account says: 'Hard pressed and unable to return the fire, the position of the German battle-cruisers soon became unbearable.'

And now the battleships of the Grand Fleet appeared out of the mist in six columns to the northward, and Beatty found himself streaking across their front. In spite of conflicting reports as to the position of the enemy battle fleet, Jellicoe deployed into line of battle in the nick of time on an easterly course, with the object of getting between the enemy and his base, and Beatty was able to take up his position in the van while Evan-Thomas proceeded to his alternative battle-station in the rear. By 6.30 p.m. the main battle fleets were in action, and Beatty was joined a little later by the two remaining battle-cruisers out of the three that composed the third battle squadron under Hood, who at 6.34 had been lost in the *Invincible*. At 8.25 p.m., Beatty, who was conforming as arranged with the movements of the Grand Fleet, got a sight of the German battle-cruisers and one of their battle squadrons. He immediately closed and opened fire; but the Germans, having no spirit for further fighting, turned away and were lost in the mist.

Although Beatty's force had sustained heavy losses, he had by nightfall under his command, ready for action next day, six battle-cruisers, whereas Hipper had only one. To Evan-Thomas Beatty gave full credit in his dispatch for the part played by the fifth battle squadron in achieving this result.

Professional investigations at the Royal Naval War College and Staff College over many years confirm the view expressed in Jellicoe's dispatch that Beatty carried out the duties assigned to him with conspicuous success. Despite heavy losses, he located the enemy battle fleet and led it to a position where the Grand Fleet could engage it. He also, at the critical moment, prevented Hipper from sighting the British main fleet and so enabled Jellicoe to complete his deployment unobserved in the right direction while Beatty himself took up his position in the van of the British line of battle in accordance with the commander-in-chief's plan. It is true that reports of the enemy's positions coming in from Beatty and his cruisers were misleading to Jellicoe. The main reason for this (apart from bad visibility) was that each ship's position was based upon her own individual calculations, and no means then existed for synchronizing these estimates on a common basis. Errors of omission can be accounted for by the fact that Beatty was hotly engaged most of the time, and the *Lion's* wireless was inoperative. It was only natural, therefore, that there should have been recriminations, arising mainly from the fact that in the conditions of visibility prevailing, no two commanders got the same view of the action, and that, although 250 ships took part, there were never more than three or four enemy ships in sight at the same time from any point in our line of battle. It must always be remembered that a complete bird's-eye view of the battle was denied to those who took part, and particularly to the commander-in-chief, who that day bore on his shoulders the responsibility for possibly losing the war in an afternoon.

At the end of 1916 Jellicoe became first sea lord, and Beatty, at the age of forty-five, when most of his contemporaries were still on the captains' list, was appointed with the acting rank of admiral to command the most powerful fleet in history. Early in 1917 he chose the *Queen Elizabeth* as his flagship because she had the speed to enable him to get to the most favourable position for exercising supreme command in battle. He immediately set to work to enforce the lessons of Jutland. To make his system of leadership clear to all, he changed the title 'Battle Orders' to 'Battle Instructions', thereby implying that senior officers could use their own initiative to the fullest extent in translating into action the general intentions of the commander-in-chief. Being determined that the confusion in information experienced at Jutland should not recur, he introduced a system of plotting the positions of British and enemy units upon a synchronized basis. He always believed in aircraft and arranged for kite balloons to be flown by various selected units. Ships were taken in hand by the dockyards to improve their magazine protection, and meanwhile the Admiralty had designed a really effective projectile and was hastening its supply to the fleet.

The anti-submarine campaign of 1917 aroused Beatty's hunting instincts. While keeping a sharp look-out for a sortie by the German fleet—there was indeed one abortive attempt—he used every means in his power to combat the menace. He was a firm believer in the convoy system, and, growing impatient with the Admiralty slowness in organizing it, asked and obtained permission to run convoys under his own direction to and from Norway. Over 4,000 ships sailed in convoy in the North Sea with negligible loss in six months. But it was only a question of time before one of the Norwegian convoys would be located by fast enemy surface ships, using the hours of darkness to evade the British patrols. This happened on two occasions in the autumn of 1917 and the following winter. Fortunately neither convoy was large and the total loss was sixteen merchant ships, four destroyers, and four armed trawlers. It was, nevertheless, only to be expected that the enemy would try again, so Beatty decided to send larger convoys at longer intervals, but escorted by a division of battleships. The inherent hope that this would entice the enemy to send out still stronger forces to attack the convoys was nearly fulfilled, for Scheer, in April 1918, did make one more sortie, but he miscalculated the date and dared not prolong his stay in waters where Beatty might be met.

The advent of a squadron of United States battleships under Admiral Hugh Rodman diminished the strain on the Grand Fleet. Beatty and Rodman worked in perfect harmony and in a very short time the American squadron became an integral part of Beatty's battle fleet. In 1918 the added strength of the United States navy enabled more effective measures to be brought against enemy submarines, and the patrols round the coasts of Great Britain became so effective that the enemy was compelled to look for targets far out at sea, only to be frustrated by the convoy system. By midsummer the submarine danger was definitely mastered, but in October there were indications that Scheer might take a 'death-ride' with his fleet. Beatty countered the German move of concentrating all their submarines in the North Sea in positions where they could attack the Grand Fleet on its way to battle, by massing all available anti-submarine vessels at the threatened points. Then he dispatched Rear-Admiral (Sir) Arthur Cavenagh Leveson with the second battle-cruiser squadron and a strong destroyer force on a high-speed sweep through the submarine-infested waters towards the Skagerrak. When Leveson reported on his return that only one torpedo had been fired at his force, it was evident that the morale of the German navy was broken, and this opinion was confirmed by the news that the High Sea Fleet had mutinied and refused to obey orders to sail.

Two days after the signing of the armistice on 11 November, the German cruiser *Königsberg* arrived at Rosyth, having on board Rear-Admiral Meurer and a 'soldiers' and workmen's council' which claimed to have plenipotentiary powers. Beatty made it clear that he would only negotiate with a naval officer of flag rank. The delegates could not but agree, and Meurer, while thanking Beatty at the conference table, stated that this was the first time that his rank had been recognized during the last two months. The necessary arrangements were made on 15 and 16 November, and on 21 November the Grand Fleet escorted the High Sea Fleet to its anchorage in the Firth of Forth. A service of thanksgiving was held in every ship, and that evening Beatty made the famous signal: 'The German flag will be hauled down at sunset, and will not be hoisted again without permission.' On 1 January 1919 Beatty was promoted admiral and on 3 April admiral of the fleet: four days later he hauled down his union flag and the Grand Fleet ceased to exist.

Beatty

On 1 November 1919 Beatty succeeded Admiral of the Fleet Sir R. Wemyss (later Lord Wester Wemyss) as first sea lord, and was immediately confronted with the problem of reducing the navy in order to reconcile the demands of economy with the maintenance of sea power adequate for national security. The presentation of the freedom of many cities gave him a fine opportunity of impressing on the public the need for a strong navy. At the Washington Conference, which assembled in November 1921, although he agreed generally with the principle of parity with the United States, he insisted upon Great Britain retaining the right to have the number of cruisers necessary for her own peculiar needs. He succeeded in getting the British case accepted, and it was not until he had left the Admiralty that the minimum of seventy cruisers for Britain was abandoned. Wrapped up with this problem was that of overseas bases, and Beatty, with his eye on Japan, succeeded in convincing the Cabinet that if the fleet was to operate in Far Eastern waters a strongly defended base with full docking facilities must be established at Singapore. There were some warm controversies with the Air Ministry over this and other problems, including that of the status of the Fleet Air Arm which the Air Ministry considered should be retained within its own organization, including responsibility for providing material and training air personnel, but which the Admiralty maintained must be an integral part of the navy. The dispute was ended by the government decision of 1937 by which the administration, operating, and training of the Fleet Air Arm were put almost wholly under naval control. Experience in the war of 1939–1945 proved that Beatty's view was correct.

Beatty's experience of naval warfare convinced him of the value, which he had learned under Mr. Churchill, of a trained body of staff officers to assist admirals in all the ramifications of war. He approved and encouraged the Naval Staff College, and re-established the war course for senior officers only. To ensure common doctrine both were established at Greenwich. At the Admiralty he made the naval staff responsible for seeing that construction and armaments were designed to meet fighting requirements, in which he was ably assisted by Rear-Admiral (Lord) Chatfield. He confirmed the creation of the Department of Scientific Research advocated by Rear-Admiral (Sir) William Coldingham Masters Nicholson and established the Admiralty experimental laboratory at Teddington. He played a leading part in the inauguration of the Chiefs of Staffs Committee which has since proved to be a most efficient instrument for the conduct of war under the prime minister. He was first sea lord for seven and a half years, a longer period than any of his predecessors, and all the time he had to resist continual assaults aimed at reducing British naval strength. Yet he left the Admiralty in July 1927, not only with the goodwill and admiration of the navy, but with the thanks of the government for invaluable assistance 'during a period of exceptional difficulty'.

On retirement Beatty went back to the hunting field, where he had a serious accident which necessitated his lying for three months with a broken jaw tightly screwed. Some years afterwards, while suffering from a severe attack of influenza, he rose from a sick bed against all medical advice, to attend Jellicoe's funeral in November 1935. During a halt in Fleet Street a member of the staff of a newspaper office, noticing how ill he looked, kindly revived him with a glass of brandy, and he marched on with the procession. Barely four months later he died in London 11 March 1936, and was buried in St. Paul's Cathedral on the 16th.

Beatty took a deep interest in the welfare and recreation of the ships' companies and devoted much time and energy to improving their domestic and service conditions. An increase of pay being long overdue, he created two committees under Rear-Admiral Sir Lionel Halsey and Admiral Sir T. H. M. Jerram to investigate the question, and as a result of their report the pay of officers and men was substantially raised in 1919 for the first time for many years. This well-timed measure did much to alleviate distress and successfully checked any discontent which might have arisen during the dangerous period of transition from war to peace. Of the many honours done to him none pleased him more than the invitation issued to him in 1919 by the men of the fleet to be their guest at a banquet at Portsmouth, where amid a vociferous reception, gun teams dragged his car through the streets. Ordinary honours were legion. He was appointed M.V.O. in 1905, C.B. in 1911, K.C.B. in 1914, K.C.V.O. and G.C.B. in 1916, and G.C.V.O. in 1917. In 1919 he was appointed to the Order of Merit and later in that year he was raised to the peerage as Earl Beatty, at the same time receiving the thanks of both Houses of Parliament and a grant of £100,000. In 1927 he was sworn of the Privy Council. He received honorary degrees from the universities of Oxford and Aberdeen and was lord rector of Edinburgh University from 1917 until his death. His foreign decorations included that of grand officer of the Legion of Honour.

Beatty married in 1901 Ethel (died 1932), only daughter of Marshall Field, of Chicago, and formerly wife of Arthur Magic Tree, of the United States of America. They had two sons, the elder of whom, David Field (born 1905), succeeded as second earl.

In the course of his naval career, Beatty was sometimes the target of ill-informed criticism, but he never spoke a word in reply, being content to abide by the verdict of his countrymen and of history. He was neither impetuous nor rash; his judgement was sound and his decisions were the result of careful reflection and forethought. During the war he never took any leave, and, although his wife and family lived close to Rosyth, he slept in his flagship every night. He landed every afternoon while in harbour for physical exercise and maintained perfect health throughout, nor did he ever show the slightest sign of the strain imposed upon him. In moments of crisis his brain worked with absolute clarity and he never had cause to reverse an important decision. Above all was his dauntless courage, both moral and physical.

A portrait of Beatty is included in Sir A. S. Cope's picture 'Some Sea Officers of the Great War', painted in 1921, in the National Portrait Gallery. Another portrait is that in Sir John Lavery's 'Surrender of the German Fleet' in the Imperial War Museum. Other portraits include a full-length in captain's uniform, by Hugh Riviere (1909), a full-length in evening dress by Cowan Dobson (1930), and a head (black and white), by J. S. Sargent (1919), all in the possession of the second Earl Beatty; a head, by P. A. de László, owned by the Hon. Peter Beatty; and a painting in admiral's uniform (unknown artist) at the Naval and Military Club, Pall Mall. There is a bust, by Feredah Forbes, at Brooksby Hall, near Leicester.

[Official dispatches; Staff College records; Admiralty office memoranda, The German official account of the Battle of Jutland; Winston Churchill, *The World Crisis*, 1923; Sir E. H. Seymour, *My Naval Career and Travels*, 1911; Geoffrey Rawson, *Beatty*, 1930; private information; personal knowledge.]

W. S. CHALMERS

published 1949

<hr>

BERESFORD Lord Charles William de la Poer

(1846–1919)

Baron Beresford

Admiral, was born at Philipstown, King's county, 10 February 1846, the second son of the Rev. John de la Poer Beresford, fourth Marquess of Waterford, by his wife, Christiana, fourth daughter of Charles Powell Leslie, M.P., of Glaslough, county Monaghan. He was educated at Bayford School, Hertfordshire, and at Stubbington House, near Fareham. He entered the *Britannia* as a naval cadet in December 1859, and in March 1861 was appointed to the *Marlborough*, flagship in the Mediterranean and one of the finest of the old wooden line of battleships. He was rated midshipman in June 1862. He was transferred in July 1863 to the *Defence*, a new ironclad, and after less than a year was appointed as senior midshipman to the *Clio*, corvette, in which he made a voyage to the Falkland Islands and round Cape Horn to Honolulu and Vancouver. In December 1865 he was transferred to the *Tribune* at Vancouver, promoted sub-lieutenant 1866, and in the following February transferred to the *Sutlej*, flagship on the Pacific station. In the following June he returned home in her and joined the *Excellent*, gunnery school ship. After eight months in the royal yacht *Victoria and Albert*, which gave him his promotion to lieutenant in October 1868, he was appointed to the *Galatea*, frigate (captain, Prince Alfred, Duke of Edinburgh), in which he made a voyage of two and a half years, visiting the Cape, Australia, New Zealand, Japan, China, India, and the Falkland Islands. In November 1872 he was appointed flag lieutenant to Sir Henry Keppel, commander-in-chief at Plymouth, and remained there till August 1874, when he was sent for a few months to the *Bellerophon*, flagship of the North American station. At the general election of 1874 Lord Charles was returned to parliament for Waterford in the conservative interest, and retained the seat until 1880. In September 1875 he went as aide-de-camp to the Prince of Wales on his tour in India and was promoted commander in November of that year. In May 1877, after a short period in the *Vernon* for torpedo instruction, he was appointed commander to the *Thunderer*, Channel squadron, till June 1878. A year later he was appointed to the command of the royal yacht *Osborne*, a post which he retained till November 1881. During these years, 1874–1881, he was chiefly known as a dashing sportsman, a personal friend of the Prince of Wales, and a prominent popular figure in smart society.

At the beginning of 1882 Lord Charles took command of the *Condor*, gunboat, under Sir Beauchamp Seymour (afterwards Lord Alcester), commander-in-chief of the fleet that bombarded Alexandria (11 July) during the Egyptian crisis; he took the leading part in engaging and silencing Fort Marabout in that operation. After the bombardment he was sent ashore under Captain John (afterwards Lord) Fisher and appointed provost-marshal and chief of police, and restored order with admirable efficiency, nerve, and tact. He was promoted captain and mentioned in dispatches for gallantry for these services. He was offered an appointment on the staff of the khedive and also that of war correspondent of the *New York Herald*, but Sir Garnet (afterwards Viscount) Wolseley refused to release him. He then returned home and remained on half-pay till August 1884, when he was appointed to the *Alexandra*, to act on the staff of Lord Wolseley during the Nile expedition for the relief of Khartoum. He was afterwards placed in command of the naval brigade on the Nile, with which he took part in the battle of Abu Klea on 17 January 1885. He also commanded the expedition which went to the rescue of (Sir) Charles

William Wilson in the *Safieh*, when he kept his ship steadily engaged under heavy fire while his engineer, Mr. Benbow, repaired her disabled boiler (4 February). He was commended in the House of Commons, and described by Lord Wolseley in his dispatch as 'an officer whose readiness and resource and ability as a leader are only equalled by his daring'. For these services he was made C.B.

Lord Charles came home in July 1885, and was returned to parliament for East Marylebone, and re-elected in 1886. The Prince of Wales, with whom he had become very intimate, urged Lord Salisbury, on the formation of the conservative government, to give him political office, but the prime minister preferred to appoint him fourth naval lord of the Admiralty under Lord George Hamilton. He proved a difficult colleague and early showed himself hostile to the policy of the Board. He found fault with the shipbuilding programme and with the organization and pay of the intelligence department, and objected to the supreme authority of the first lord in naval administration. At length he resigned in January 1888. For the next two years he was a constant and outspoken critic of naval affairs in the House of Commons, until, in December 1889, he was appointed to the command of the *Undaunted*, armoured cruiser, on the Mediterranean station, resigning his seat in parliament. He returned to England in June 1893, to take command of the Medway dockyard reserve till March 1896. In 1897 he was appointed aide-de-camp to Queen Victoria, and in September of that year was promoted to flag rank and won for his party, at a by-election at York, a seat which he retained till January 1900, when he was sent to the Mediterranean as second in command under Sir John Fisher. In the meantime, in 1898–1899, he had gone to China on a special mission on behalf of the Associated Chambers of Commerce, and had published his report in a spirited volume entitled *The Break-up of China* (1899). In the Mediterranean he worked in general harmony with his chief, whose reforming zeal he shared and at that time approved; but he earned a rebuke from the Admiralty for allowing the publication in the press of a letter highly critical of Admiralty policy. In February 1902, on returning to England, he was returned to parliament for Woolwich. He was promoted vice-admiral in October 1902, and early in 1903 he again left the House of Commons in order to take up the chief command of the Channel squadron, being promoted K.C.B. in the following June. In March 1905 he hauled down his flag, and two months later went to the Mediterranean as commander-in-chief, with the acting rank of admiral, to which he was promoted in November 1906.

After two years in the Mediterranean Lord Charles was made commander-in-chief of the Channel fleet, then the principal fleet of the navy, including as it did fourteen battleships. It was a time when, in order to meet the growing German danger, the naval forces in home waters were being gradually but radically reorganized by Sir John Fisher, then first sea lord. Beresford was out of sympathy with many of the changes, and relations between him and Whitehall became exceedingly strained: the gradual development of the home fleet, comprising some fully-manned vessels and some reserve ships with nucleus crews, as an independent command in peace time caused him great irritation; and at last, in March 1909, he was ordered to haul down his flag and come on shore, the Channel fleet being abolished as a separate command and absorbed into the greatly enlarged home fleet. Beresford at once challenged the whole policy of the Board of Admiralty and its organization of the fleets in a long polemical document addressed to the prime minister, Mr. Asquith. This was referred to a sub-committee of the Committee of Imperial Defence, composed of the prime minister and four secretaries of state. The report of this committee was published in August 1909, and on the whole vindicated the action and policy of the Admiralty, though in certain respects its wording seemed to justify some of Beresford's criticisms. Beresford published an account of his views in 1912 in a book called *The Betrayal*. He was again returned to parliament, as a member for Portsmouth, in 1910, and held the seat till January 1916, when he was raised to the peerage as Baron Beresford, of Metemmeh and of Curraghmore. He was placed on the retired list in February 1911, and received the G.C.B. He died of apoplexy while staying at Langwell, Caithness, 6 September 1919, and was honoured with a state funeral in St. Paul's Cathedral.

Beresford was one of the most remarkable personalities of his generation: brave, high-spirited, an enthusiastic sportsman, of noble birth, and possessed of ample private means, he touched life at many points, and to the general public was the best-known sailor of his day. He had some of the faults as well as many of the virtues of his Irish ancestry, and although he was passionately devoted to the navy and to his country, his love of publicity and impatience of control sometimes led him into conduct that was alien from the strict traditions of the service. In parliament and on the platform, while not strong in argument, he was an attractive and forceful speaker and was popular with all parties, confining himself as a rule to naval topics in which he was especially interested. Owing partly to his variety of interests and partly to his quarrels with authority, he had until late in life comparatively little actual sea experience; but from the day in January 1900 on which he hoisted his flag in the Mediterranean, when nearly fifty-four, he was for the greater part of nine years continuously afloat. He soon showed himself an able and active flag officer; and he commanded the most important of the fleets of the country during a period of great naval development, when the position of foreign affairs was often critical, with an energy and ability that won general recognition from the service. He maintained and enhanced the fighting efficiency of the squadrons and flotillas placed in his charge, and devoted immense personal care to the welfare of the great body of men under his orders. He fully understood and practised the art of delegating authority, and he won the devoted loyalty of all ranks by his frank recognition of merit and his readiness to overlook minor faults when the intention of the action was good and sound. He was ambitious to reach the highest position in his profession, and it was unfortunate that the last years of his command were clouded by what came to be a personal antagonism between himself and that other great sailor, Lord Fisher, with whom, until 1903, he had been on terms of amity and in full agreement on naval policy. But a man of his geniality and good humour could not long nurse resentment; and in his entertaining autobiography, *Memories*, published in 1914, all traces of this regrettable dispute have practically disappeared. An admirable host, in London and general society he enjoyed a well-deserved and universal popularity.

Beresford married in 1878 Mina, daughter of Richard Gardner, M.P. for Leicester, and left two daughters.

There is a portrait of Beresford by C. W. Furse in the National Portrait Gallery.

[Admiralty records; Lord Charles Beresford, *Memories*, 1914.]

VINCENT W. BADDELEY

published 1927

BRETT Reginald Baliol

(1852–1930)

Second Viscount Esher

Government official, was born in London 30 June 1852, the elder son of William Baliol Brett, afterwards first Viscount Esher, master of the Rolls, by his wife, Eugénie, daughter of Louis Mayer, an Alsatian. His mother, a step-daughter of Colonel John Gurwood, the editor of Wellington's dispatches, belonged to the D'Orsay-Blessington circle and also had influential friends in Paris. Reginald Brett was educated at Eton, where A. C. Ainger was his tutor, and where he came under the influence of William Johnson Cory, and at Trinity College, Cambridge. At both he made important friendships and developed social as well as political and literary interests. In 1879 he married Eleanor, third daughter of Sylvain Van de Weyer, the Belgian minister in London, who was a close friend of Queen Victoria.

As private secretary to the Marquess of Hartington for seven years (1878–1885), the last three of them spent at the War Office, Brett lived in a society which still retained something of the Disraeli atmosphere; knowing 'everybody', handling confidential affairs touching great men, freely suggesting ideas and actions to ministers, generals, viceroys, and in touch also with literature and the stage. In 1880 he was elected to parliament in the liberal interest as one of the members for Penryn and Falmouth, but at the general election of 1885 he unsuccessfully contested Plymouth and never stood again. Maintaining his friendships, Brett withdrew to Orchard Lea near Windsor Forest, where he was admitted to the queen's private circle; entertained, wrote some minor books, mainly biographical, kept for a time a small racing stable and breeding stud, shot, and fished. But sport was never his passion, and after ten rather aimless years the civil service attracted him. In 1895 his school friend Lord Rosebery, then prime minister, after Brett had refused to enter diplomacy, made him secretary of the Office of Works. He showed such practical talents in improving the domestic arrangements of the royal residences and in superintending the diamond jubilee of 1897 (in which year he was made C.B.) that the queen held him to his post when he succeeded his father as second viscount in 1899, and again, when, in 1900, he was offered the permanent under-secretaryship at the War Office. Esher had already (1899) refused the same post at the Colonial Office under Mr. Chamberlain, and the governorship of Cape Colony, declining to work in leading-strings. The queen created him K.C.V.O. in December 1900 just before her death. After so long a reign, memories of a sovereign's funeral and coronation were dim; he mastered the precedents, and took charge of both ceremonies with complete success.

Queen Victoria had made Esher one of her intimate friends, and she often visited Orchard Lea informally. King Edward VII gave him close friendship and wider scope, in connexion with the new civil list, as secretary of the committee of the Queen Victoria Memorial fund, as deputy constable and lieutenant-governor of Windsor Castle (1901), and as editor, in collaboration with Arthur Christopher Benson, of *Selections from the Correspondence of Queen Victoria* (1907). Esher also published *The Girlhood of Queen Victoria* in 1912. Whatever he touched succeeded, and the king's confidence seemed boundless.

In the universal anxiety about the state of the army, its reform became with Esher an obsession. He saw that the key to it lay in the rejected proposals of the Hartington commission of 1890: viz. no commander-in-chief, a War-Office council on the Admiralty model, and an inspector-general; and he at once sought the ear of the king. He retired from the Office of Works and was created K.C.B. in 1902. In the same year he was made a member of the royal commission appointed, under the chairmanship of the ninth Earl of Elgin, to inquire into the military preparations for and conduct of the South African War. Esher commented on the commission's proceedings in daily letters to the king, who by the end of the year had accepted his views. Although general War Office reform was outside the commission's reference, Esher appended to its report (July 1903) a note formulating his proposals. The prime minister, Mr. Balfour, Esher's lifelong friend, assured of the king's support, definitely approved the policy without further debate, and asked Esher to become secretary of state for war in order to carry it through. Esher would not re-enter politics, but proposed to do the work as chairman of a prime minister's committee, independent of the secretary of state about to be appointed, Mr. Arnold-Forster. The War Office Reconstruction Committee, generally known as the Esher Committee, was set up accordingly, with Admiral Sir John (afterwards Baron) Fisher and Colonel Sir George Clarke (formerly secretary of the Hartington commission, and afterwards Baron Sydenham) as members and Lieutenant-Colonel (afterwards Lieutenant-General Sir) Gerald Ellison as secretary. On 11 January 1904, a fortnight after Clarke's return from the governorship of Victoria, Part I of the Report proposed in outline the creation of an Army Council on Admiralty lines, and an inspector-general of the forces. The Committee would go no further until this had been accepted. That done, and the Council formally constituted (6 February), it produced in quick succession Parts II (26 February) and III (9 March), containing detailed proposals, claiming that they followed logically from the action already taken, and insisting that the Report should be accepted as an organic whole, without any alteration. It was, in fact, approved as it stood. It made two important improvements on Esher's note, namely, the provision of a permanent naval and military secretariat for Mr. Balfour's Committee of Imperial Defence, on which political and service chiefs sat together under the prime minister, and the creation of a General Staff for the army. With the internal working of the War Office (of which Esher's experience was out of date and the other members had none) the Committee dealt less successfully, and many of its recommendations, designed to remove financial control, were founded on errors of fact, and after due trial abandoned within five years. Esher's note had put the adjutant-general first of the military members of the newly-formed Army Council, and the director-general of military intelligence, head of an incomplete thinking department, last. The Committee created a chief of the general staff, ranking first, charged with everything pertaining to operations of war and to training, and furnishing to commanders, in war and peace, staffs trained in such duties. This all-important change was a complete reversal of recent War Office evolution, in which peace and personal considerations had destroyed system. Under the Duke of Cambridge (who commanded in chief 1856–1895) the adjutant-general, as his chief staff officer, had been allowed to swallow whole the surveyor-general (Lord Cardwell's business head) and to eat the quartermaster-general (Wellington's right-hand man) leaf by leaf, that empty title being transferred to a soldier purveyor of transport and supplies. Operations had dropped out of sight. In the field, similarly, there had been a factotum chief staff officer; no clear line had been drawn between command and the business of supply; and no organized operations staff had existed. Accustomed in India to a quartermaster-general, in Wellington's sense of the term, at the head of the operations staff, and to an adjutant-general dealing with personnel and discipline, Lord Roberts had been shocked to find this state of things prevailing in South Africa. At the War Office, therefore, on becoming commander-in-chief (1901), he had overruled opposition and ordered the preparation of a staff manual on Wellingtonian lines. Colonel Ellison, who had worked out the ground-plan of this under Roberts's orders before being appointed secretary to the Esher Committee, produced it to the Committee, which adopted it entire and distributed War Office duties accordingly, only changing the title of Roberts's quartermaster-general to that of chief of the general staff. Thus Esher's uncompromising dictatorship combined with Roberts's initiative to produce a true General Staff which, expanded later by Lord Haldane into the Imperial General Staff, embracing India and the Dominions, built up the armies of the British Empire during the European War of 1914–1918.

His committee dissolved, Esher joined the Committee of Imperial Defence in its search for an improved army system, becoming a permanent member of it in 1905, just before political changes transferred the secretaryship of state for war to Lord Haldane. His support of Lord Fisher's case for a stronger navy brought upon him a personal attack by Kaiser Wilhelm II. A conscriptionist, Esher yet saw that the voluntary system must have full trial, and he gave Haldane invaluable support in his army reforms, commending them to the king as the best work accomplished since Cardwell's secretaryship (1868–1874); and he became the very active chairman (1909–1913) and later (1912–1921) president of the London County Territorial Force Association. His position at this period is perhaps best described as *liaison* between king and ministers. He gave advice freely, but all action was taken constitutionally by the responsible minister.

Neither Sir Henry Campbell-Bannerman's succession as prime minister in December 1905 nor the accession of King George V in May 1910 caused any interruption of this relation.

An admirable committee man, Esher was in great demand for boards such as those of the British Museum (of which he was a king's trustee), the Imperial College of Science (of which he was governor), and the Wallace Collection; but after two years' trial of *haute finance* in the City he abandoned it as uncongenial (1904). He was created G.C.V.O. (1905) and G.C.B. (1908), sworn a privy councillor (1922), and appointed keeper of the king's archives (1910) and governor and constable of Windsor Castle (1928); but he refused the viceroyship of India in 1908 and an earldom at some date not known to his family. From September 1914 onwards he was in France on a confidential mission, at the request of Lord Kitchener, subsequently renewed by Mr. Asquith and by Mr. Lloyd George. The documents relating to it remain under seal in the British Museum until 1981 together with Esher's diaries for the first half of the War and other papers, but it is known that in 1917–1918 he was present at conferences with French ministers on military matters.

After the return of peace in 1919, Esher devoted much time to literature and published some more biographical books, including *Ionicus* (1923), an informal biography of William Johnson Cory. He died suddenly 22 January 1930 at his London house, leaving a widow, two sons, and two daughters. His family life was peculiarly happy, and, in particular, his relations with his younger son, Maurice, even while at Eton, as revealed in Esher's published *Journals and Letters*, were rather those of a brother than a father. He was succeeded as third viscount by his elder son, Oliver Sylvain Baliol (born 1881).

Inheriting marked ability, great social gifts, and influential connexions, Esher possessed all the qualifications for success in public life except the conviction that it was worth while. The first Viscount Esher had been spurred, by love and by lack of independent means, to set his foot on the path that led him to professional eminence; the second, whose dislike of the dust of the arena outweighed his liking for power, might have returned to the earlier Brett tradition of enjoying life as it came, without effort, had not his association with the royal family pointed a way to the power without the dust, and justified him in recording, when refusing the viceroyalty, that, with his opportunity of influencing vital decisions at the centre, India for him 'would be (it sounds vain, but it isn't) parochial'. This influence he exercised behind a curtain, seeking neither personal advancement nor the interests of a political party, but only the public good as he saw it—and his vision was acute. His work on the committee which goes by his name and his effective backing of Lord Haldane's army reforms at a critical juncture made no mean contribution to the Allied victory of 1918.

There are three portraits of Lord Esher at Watlington Park, Oxfordshire, painted by Julian Storey, Edmund Brock, and Glyn Philpot in or about 1885, 1905, and 1925 respectively.

[Maurice V. Brett, *Journals and Letters of Reginald Viscount Esher* (to 1910), 2 vols., 1934; C. H. Dudley Ward, *A Romance of the Nineteenth Century*, 1923; Sir Gerald Ellison, *Lord Roberts and the General Staff*, in the *Nineteenth Century*, December 1932; private information; personal knowledge.]

C. HARRIS

published 1937

BROOKE Alan Francis

(1883–1963)

First Viscount Alanbrooke

Field-marshal, was born at Bagnères de Bigorre, France, 23 July 1883, the ninth and youngest child and sixth son of Sir Victor Alexander Brooke, third baronet, of Colebrooke in county Fermanagh, and his wife, Alice Sophia Bellingham, second daughter of Sir Alan Edward Bellingham, third baronet, of Castle Bellingham in county Louth. On both sides of the family his roots lay deep in the Irish Protestant ascendancy. The first Brooke of Colebrooke, Sir Henry Brooke of Donegal, was the son of an Elizabethan captain of Cheshire origin, and had been rewarded for his part in suppressing the native rising of 1641 by the grant of Colebrooke and 30,000 acres of Fermanagh. From that time until Alan Brooke's the natural tastes and aptitudes of the men of the family were for the soldier's life. They fought campaign after campaign, often achieving high rank and distinction in the service of the Crown. Twenty-six Brookes of Colebrooke served in the war of 1914–18; twenty-seven in that of 1939–45.

Alan Brooke was born and brought up at or near Pau in the south of France where his family owned a villa and periodically took a small house in the neighbouring hills in the heat of summer. His mother preferred life at Pau, where there was a flourishing and fashionable English society, excellent hunting and shooting, and an agreeable climate, to the rigours of Colebrooke; one consequence was that Alan Brooke spoke French—and German—before he spoke English, never underwent a conventional English schooling, and, although he was an excellent horseman, shot, and

55

fisherman, he first entered communal British life on joining the Royal Military Academy at Woolwich at the age of eighteen, largely ignorant of the team games and the usual *mores* of the English schoolboy. From so comparatively solitary an upbringing—he had been to a small local school in Pau, was by some years the youngest of the family, and his father had died when he was eight—he was, by his own account, shy and unsure of himself. He was also delicate and introspective. Nevertheless, he passed out of Woolwich well—not high enough to become a Royal Engineer, but sufficiently well to join a battery of Royal Field Artillery in Ireland and to be earmarked early as a likely candidate for the coveted jacket of the Royal Horse Artillery.

Brooke's first four years of army life were spent in Ireland; then, from 1906, in India where he entered with enthusiasm into every aspect of his profession, caring for his men and his horses and his guns with a meticulous throughness and an eye for detail which were his abiding hallmark. He was a noted big-game hunter in India, just as he was a noted race rider there and in Ireland. If early he had thought of himself as uncertain and hesitant, diffidence dissolved in the warmth of regimental life. He became the best of companions, quick-witted and amusing, an excellent draughtsman and caricaturist, and a skilled mimic. He early showed, however, a deep vein of seriousness about both life and his profession which found expression in long letters to the mother he adored. He was highly efficient and incisive, and received outstanding reports at every step. In 1909 he joined N battery, Royal Horse Artillery, in India, and in 1914 found himself commanding the Artillery brigade ammunition column in France.

The 1914–18 war saw Brooke's progress from lieutenant to lieutenant-colonel, at all times on the western front and in artillery appointments. In each he shone, and his name as an intelligent, thoughtful, and, in some respects, innovatory, gunner came to stand very high. He was brigade major, Royal Artillery, in the 18th division (Ivor Maxse) during the Somme battle, and was credited with the production of the first 'creeping barrage' to ensure that the ground between the enemy's trench lines was covered and the exposure of our advancing infantry to unsilenced machine-gun fire was minimized. He himself attributed the idea to the French; whatever its provenance, it was highly successful and both in the 18th division battles and in the great Canadian attacks of 1917—he was posted as chief artillery staff officer to the Canadian Corps (Julian Byng) in 1917—ground was gained with fewer casualties than in other engagements in the same period. The artillery support in all formations in which Brooke served and where his ideas accordingly prevailed was widely praised and trusted absolutely.

It was natural that he should be selected for the first post-war course at the Staff College at Camberley where he met the best of his contemporaries in the army, men like Gort, Dill, Freyberg, Fuller, and others whose careers or ideas were to coincide with or cross his own. He was an outstanding student and after a few years on the staff of a Northumbrian division of the Territorial Army he was brought back to Camberley as an instructor in 1923. There he distilled his experience of artillery in the recent war and drew lessons which found expression in a series of lectures and published articles. He believed, unequivocally, that firepower dominated movement, which was itself impossible in modern war without the production of massive and effective supporting fire. He also believed that the effect of firepower tended to be underestimated in peacetime, because of the difficulties of simulation and therefore to be extruded from men's calculations; whereas movements, because they could actually be performed, were practised with inadequate regard to the dominant effect of fire. This was the period when the British prophets of armoured warfare were singing different songs—that mechanization would restore mobility to the battlefield in a way which even the major tank battles of the recent war had not demonstrated because of inadequate comprehension and therefore inadequate exploitation of opportunity; and that deep penetration and great operational movements would again become possible, the tactical stalemate apparently imposed by machine-gun, cannon, and barbed wire having been potentially nullified by the tank. Nevertheless, the tank was not yet reliable and its limited operational effectiveness had probably owed as much to mechanical factors as to unimaginative handling. Brooke pondered the matter deeply. He was initially unconvinced and he was certainly not one of the pioneers of armoured warfare such as Hobart, Lindsay, and Martel, who looked to Fuller as in some ways their most original mind and to Liddell Hart as their most articulate spokesman. Nevertheless, Brooke's ideas moved a great deal between 1926 when he left the Staff College as instructor and 1937 when, to the surprise of some and the displeasure of those who felt that the appointment should go to a tank expert rather than to a gunner, he became the first commander of the Mobile division—prototype of the later armoured divisions—on Salisbury Plain.

Meanwhile, however, Brooke went in 1927 as one of the first students to the new Imperial Defence College, to which he returned in 1932 for two years as an instructor. There he first studied in depth questions of imperial strategy, joint service co-operation, and the higher politico-military direction of war—and of preparations for or prevention of war—with which his life was to be so intimately concerned. He was, by now, a man who inspired no little awe. As at the Staff College he made a profound impact through the speed and incisiveness of his mind, the clarity and brevity of his speech, and—not least—the gift of friendship all the more profound because never lightly given. He was a generous and delightful companion to those who got to know him. He was invariably thoughtful and a good listener. He retained his wide interests, his capacity to amuse and for repartee, and his immense knowledge and love of all things connected with nature. Sport, at which he was invariably skilful, had to some extent yielded to ornithology among his loves. He was passionately interested in all sorts of birds, particularly waders; loved photographing them at which he made himself an expert; and started to collect books and pictures connected therewith. As an ornithologist he has been placed by the highest experts as 'of the very first rank of non-professionals'. Brooke retained this enthusiasm to the end, and it provided solace in many dark hours of the war which was to come.

Before his time as instructor at the IDC, Brooke, now a brigadier, commanded the School of Artillery at Larkhill between 1929 and 1932. He made his usual mark as a meticulous and absolutely determined superior, a man of clear and original ideas, and a dedicated gunner. He commanded an infantry brigade from 1934—a widening experience he greatly enjoyed and was the first to say found highly educative. After a short spell as inspector, Royal Artillery, in the rank of major-general in 1935, he had an equally brief tour as director of military training. It was from that post that he was selected to command the Mobile division.

Two contentious issues lay at the heart of policy. First was the principle and the pace of mechanization and the whole future of horsed cavalry. Second was the proper operational employment—and thus the size and shape—of armoured formations. This second question contained another, whether such formations should be virtually 'all tank' or whether the needs of the tactical battle, whatever the scale of the operational movement, would require the combination—and therefore the mobility and the protection—of all arms. Brooke was by now a convinced supporter of rapid mechanization, and his tact and understanding did much to reconcile the sentiment of the dedicated cavalrymen to the stubborn facts of technology. On the operational and tactical issues he stood four-square behind those who believed that future battle would, as before, demand the co-operation of all arms and that therefore all arms must have appropriate equipments in the armoured formations of the future.

From 1938 until shortly before the outbreak of World War II Brooke was moved to a completely different but no less vital sphere. He was taken from the Mobile division, promoted to lieutenant-general, and placed in command first of a newly reshaped Anti-Aircraft Corps and then of the whole Anti-Aircraft command. Our air defences were in a state of inadequacy which the European situation and the rate of growth of the Luftwaffe forced upon the Government's tardy attention. The first necessity was a sufficiency of fighter aircraft, a requirement supervised by the chief of Fighter Command, Air Marshal Sir Hugh (later Lord) Dowding, alongside whose headquarters Brooke established his own and with whom he developed a warm rapport. Next was the need for a great increase in the number of searchlights and anti-aircraft guns—and the volunteers to man them. A huge expansion was under way, and it fell to Brooke to organize this, to ensure that manning kept pace with production and that organization and operational requirements matched the need of the hour. This was in harmony with RAF doctrine and pursued as expeditiously as the familiar constraints of finance and bureaucracy permitted. Brooke achieved much and laid foundations on which others successfully built for the test to come.

In August 1939 Brooke was made commander-in-chief, Southern Command, and nominated to command the II Corps of a British expeditionary force on mobilization. It was not long delayed. In September he moved with his largely untrained and ill-equipped corps to France, taking over a part of the line on the Franco-Belgian frontier and profiting by the unexpected pause before the Germans attacked in the west to get his corps into as good shape as conditions permitted. After much debate it had been agreed (plan 'D') that in case of German attack through Belgium and Holland—the repetition of Schlieffen's 'giant wheel' of 1914 which the Allies anticipated albeit at a mechanized rate—the Allied left wing, including the British Expeditionary Force under Gort, would advance into Belgium and prolong the French Maginot line defences northwards on the line of the Meuse and thence from Namur, Wavre, to Antwerp, meeting and following the river Dyle.

From the first Brooke disliked the concept of moving from prepared positions and meeting the German Army in open warfare for which he believed neither the Allied left wing's equipment nor its tactical expertise to be adequate. He had two further doubts. He knew the French well and had not only seen much of them in the war of 1914–18 but had grown up among them and loved them. He saw enough of them in 1939 now to have profound misgivings about their quality and morale. Secondly, although he deeply respected the courage and energetic character which Gort as a leader radiated throughout the army, Brooke did not believe he had the strategic vision required in a commander-in-chief. For his part Gort regarded Brooke as showing pessimism where duty demanded the reverse whether or not it was justified. The two men were too different to do justice to each other, and throughout the war after Dunkirk Gort felt that Brooke was unfair in his apparent determination to keep him from another field command. Others, including Alexander but not Montgomery (and both were protégés of Brooke) were disposed to feel with Gort on that issue. Brooke was sharp and ruthless in judgements: however, he had what he certainly believed was a sound nose for success.

When the German attack came in May 1940 Brooke's corps took part in the series of withdrawals forced on the BEF by the disintegration of the front in the French sector around Sedan and the rapid advance of the German spearheads. The surrender of the Belgian Army soon left his left wing in the air—a gap which he closed by a series of hazardous manœuvres of great ingenuity and boldness—while in the south the deep flank of the British Army had already been bypassed by the virtually unopposed westward advance of the German armoured forces. Gort, on his own initiative and (at the time) contrary to the instructions of the British Government, cancelled a joint counter-attack with the French which he rightly saw would be futile and withdrew his army and as many French troops as possible to Dunkirk whence the majority were safely embarked. On 29 May Brooke himself was recalled to England and after a few days' rest was sent to Cherbourg to make contact with General Weygand who had assumed the Supreme Command from General Gamelin, and to build a new British Army in France on the foundations of the numerous line-of-communication troops between Normandy and the Loire.

Brooke soon saw that any plan to hold an Allied bridgehead in Brittany, as was the declared intention, was impracticable for lack of troops. He was also certain that French will to continue fighting was exhausted. He therefore urgently persuaded the British authorities to cancel plans for sending new formations to the Continent. Meanwhile he organized the evacuation of the many remaining troops from the various northern and western ports still available. On his second return to England on 19 June he reverted to his previous post at Southern Command. After a brief interval there, organizing his sector of the English coast against invasion, he became commander-in-chief, Home Forces.

Invasion was expected daily, and throughout the last two months of 1940 and the early part of 1941, counter-invasion measures and the reorganization and re-equipment of the army were pursued with the greatest energy. Brooke believed that invasion should meet light beach defences, then be dealt with by the strongest and most concentrated counter-attack by mobile troops which could be mounted. Meanwhile, however, the battle for air supremacy, the winning of which Hitler had laid down as a prerequisite for invasion, was won by the Royal Air Force. Operation 'Sea Lion'—the German invasion project—was postponed, and finally abandoned. In June 1941 the German Army invaded Russia. British isolation was over.

Thereafter it was clear that the function of the British Army would be to prepare for overseas operations, a task upon which Brooke had directed increasing emphasis through the early months of 1941. He was untiring in his visits and unsparing in his scrutiny of every part of the expanding army which would soon again, it became clear, be able to go over to the offensive. In December the Japanese attacked Pearl Harbor. The Axis Powers thereafter declared war on America. Japanese forces invaded British possessions or treaty states in Hong Kong and Malaya, and the war became global. In December 1941, also, Brooke assumed the appointment of chief of the imperial general staff in place of Dill who had been no match for Winston Churchill. Soon thereafter Brooke became, in addition, chairman of the chiefs of staff committee and effectively the principal strategic adviser to the War Cabinet as well as the professional head of the army.

The issue which dominated the early part of Brooke's tenure of office was to obtain agreement on an Allied strategy—co-ordinated between very disparate allies—one of which (the Soviet Union) was unconcealedly hostile and about whose ultimate intentions he had few illusions. The Red Army had been very nearly extinguished by the brilliance and rapidity of the initial German operations and great sacrifices by Britain were regarded as imperative to keep Russia combatant. These sacrifices took the form of huge quantities of British and American war *materiel,* and a series of hazardous convoys in northern waters, expensive in ships and casualties with no gratitude from the recipient, Stalin's sole concern being to procure the earliest possible offensive against Germany in the west to take the pressure off Russia—and later to ensure that no western Allied theatre of operations would be opened in the Balkans where the advance of Allied armies might interfere with long-term Soviet plans when the German tide ultimately ebbed.

With the United States—and in the early years of Brooke's chairmanship the United States had comparatively small forces engaged and the Americans were not yet the senior partners—the first issue was to agree over-all priorities: it was determined that the war against Germany would be treated as paramount. Next the question of theatres of engagement. Against Germany and Italy the Americans, with some reluctance, were persuaded to co-operate in a Mediterranean campaign, including landings in North Africa, linking up with the British Eighth Army which would take the offensive and advance westwards along the North African coast, and a subsequent invasion of Italy. This strategy inevitably postponed the cross-Channel invasion of France which the Americans regarded as the most expeditious route to Germany and to victory. They were persuaded that it could be successfully contemplated only after German strength had been drawn off by a Mediterranean campaign with consequent release of shipping resources, and after the further prosecution of an intensive strategic air offensive.

In the event this strategy was carried out. North Africa was cleared, Italy was invaded and made independent peace, the Anglo-American armies invaded France in June 1944, and Germany capitulated unconditionally eleven months later. Meanwhile the campaign against Japan was conducted by a successful defence of India followed by a counter-offensive in Burma; and by a maritime and 'island-hopping' Pacific strategy progressively reconquering territory taken by Japanese armies, culminating in the surrender of Japan in August 1945 after the dropping of two atomic bombs. All this was accompanied by a savage Russian war of attrition on Germany's eastern front which ultimately bled her white.

If the course of events appeared rational, if not inevitable, in retrospect, at the time they were highly debatable. 1942, Brooke's first year as CIGS, started with Allied fortunes at a low ebb. The key to strategy lay in shipping resources and their provision and protection were necessary in support of every existing or projected Anglo-American front. Because of their shortage offensive plans were inevitably delayed and preliminary steps had to be taken to lessen the strain on and threat to shipping without which even direct defence on land would be inadequate. Meanwhile the British Empire overseas, with the entry of Japan into the war, was increasingly menaced. Hong Kong and Singapore fell, the latter the greatest single blow to the British arms and prestige for centuries. India was directly threatened by land and sea, communications with Asia equally threatened by Japanese maritime concentration in the Indian Ocean. In North Africa there were serious and profoundly disappointing reverses. Promising Allied offensives would peter out and be turned by the ever-resourceful German command into what too easily appeared triumphs of German boldness and professionalism over British infirmity of purpose and uncertain grasp of the principles of war. In June Tobruk fell to Rommel's forces. In Russia the Germans advanced to the Volga and invaded the Caucasus. Throughout all this the amount of work Brooke got through astonished his staff, yet he always found time to think, and think ahead.

Ahead the tide would undoubtedly turn, since the material resources of the Western Allies and the geographic extent of Russia would, after the first shocks and reverses, lead to overstretch by the Axis Powers. In the summer of 1942 Brooke agreed with Churchill to certain changes in the high command in Egypt which brought Alexander and Montgomery to the direction of affairs in the desert and which immediately preceded the great victory of El Alamein in November. In North Africa in the same month took place the Allied landings under General Eisenhower which were to culminate in the surrender of the German forces in Africa, the invasion of Sicily and Italy, and Italian capitulation in 1943. In February 1943, the German Sixth Army surrendered at Stalingrad, the Germans began to extricate their army from the Caucasus and seek to shorten their front. The long withdrawal in the east began.

Brooke had himself been offered high command instead of Alexander. The temptation was sore but he believed, certainly with justice, that he could best serve his country and the Allied cause as CIGS and that he must remain in Whitehall.

Meanwhile the battle of the Atlantic was still the overwhelming anxiety of the British Government and chiefs of staff. At the conference held with the Americans at Casablanca in February 1943 defeat of the German submarine offensive was agreed as the first Allied operational priority, followed by the invasion of Sicily, the clearance of the Mediterranean, and any step which might bring Turkey into the war. Yet another priority was to be the remorseless bombing of Germany, creating a new front in a third dimension.

The first six months of 1943 were probably the most critical in the battle of the Atlantic. By the second half of the year the menace had been largely mastered by a brilliant combination of maritime and aerial operations. By the end of the year everywhere the enemy was withdrawing. For Brooke the year was dominated by inter-Allied conferences. Casablanca, Washington in May, Quebec in August, Moscow in October, and Cairo followed by Teheran at the end of the year. At each of these hard talking and hard bargaining took place, and at each Brooke's business was to ensure that, from the British point of view, plans were realistic in scope and in timing, that resources matched aspirations, and—not least, and with increasing difficulty—that British strategic and military interests were safeguarded. In all this, and by universal consent, no military man at Churchill's elbow could have been more intelligent, more robust, more zealous, or more loyal.

In 1944 the Allied triumphs began which were to end in the total rout of those who had attacked them in 1939 and 1941. France was successfully invaded in June, and by September had been completely liberated. From that point the only serious setbacks were the remarkably (albeit temporarily) successful German offensive in the Ardennes in December 1944, and the Allied airborne operation at Arnhem. In May 1945 the German armed forces surrendered unconditionally, and in August so did those of Japan.

In his chairmanship of the chiefs of staff committee and in his dealings therein with his naval and RAF colleagues, Brooke combined personal charm and sufficient tact with the vigorous conviction that on no account should there be compromise on essentials unless as the result of genuine conviction. If the chiefs could not agree—and he spent long and patient hours seeking honest agreement on the many contentious issues which arose from simultaneous demands on scarce resources—then he was invariably sure that the matter could be resolved only at the political level and by the prime minister himself who should hear all the arguments in the case. He never wavered in this belief and practice, just as he never wavered in his certainty that no 'neutral' military chairman should preside over the chiefs of staff committee, and that the votes should be those and only those of the men personally and individually responsible for the Armed Services whose chiefs they were (although he supported the concept of a joint commander-in-chief of an operational theatre). Brooke's colleagues during this time as chairman were first Dudley Pound (who died in October 1943), then Andrew (Lord) Cunningham, first sea lords, and 'Peter' (later Lord) Portal, chief of the air staff; and the system worked the better for the fact that, sharp though professional disagreement often was, these men had deep personal affection for each other. They shared many tastes as well as qualities. Portal like Brooke was a dedicated or- nithologist and like both Brooke and Cunningham, a keen and skilful fisherman.

Brooke's chief concerns throughout were to procure and maintain (but only at the appropriate price) sufficient Allied harmony to achieve the great design; to ensure that the British Army in its various war theatres— Far Eastern, North African, Italian, and Northwest European—was properly organized, equipped, reinforced, and, above all, commanded; to achieve consensus in the chiefs of staff committee between the three British Services about the right operational policy to follow, particularly over such matters as the appropriate application of air power; and, often above all, to contrive that the indispensable and magnificent energies of the prime minister were not misdirected towards unsound and erratic strategic schemes for which, at least in the view of his professional ad- visers, he had a pronounced and idiosyncratic penchant.

In his dealings with the War Cabinet, and with Churchill in particular, Brooke succeeded magnificently, although not without many sharp ex- changes and a good deal of passing acrimony. He always said exactly what he thought, and, in the face of even the most unremitting determination by Churchill to hear something palatable rather than true, he stuck to his guns. Brooke, as chairman of the committee, was its spokesman on joint matters and it fell to him to enforce in stubborn argument the compulsion of strategic facts upon Churchill's restless genius without sacrifice of its astonishing impetus and fertility. Churchill never overruled the chiefs of staff, when united, on a professional matter. He goaded them and girded at their constraints but he respected their robust integrity. Neither Churchill or Brooke could have done so much without the other—yet each found the other abrasive as well as stimulating and indispensable. That they were able to work together—Brooke wrote of the prime minister as someone whom he 'would not have missed working with for anything on earth', Churchill firmly rejected the idea that he ever contemplated replacing Brooke—was a tribute at once to Churchill's perspicacity as to Brooke's strength of mind, character, and physique. It was a high-spirited, high-tempered, exhausting, and astonishingly successful partnership. An indispensable figure in all this was 'Pug' Ismay, chief staff officer to the minister of defence, capable as few have been of softening obduracy and interpreting strong men to each other.

Brooke was not an easy man—his brain moved too fast for him to suffer fools gladly and he was impatient, sometimes to a fault, with slower wits than his own. In his dealings with ministers, with colleagues and with subordinates alike he could appear intolerant. Junior officers were always struck by the considerable awe in which their seniors held the CIGS—the man, not just the office. Clearly they recognized 'Brookie' as the best soldier of them all, straight as a die, uncompromising and unambiguous and entirely devoid of pomposity or self-seeking. In his demanding and abrupt efficiency he knew when to scold, when to encourage, when to protect. He was admired, feared, and liked: perhaps in that order. He became, in particular, the conscience of the army: a dark, incisive, round-shouldered Irish eagle. To those who worked for him he was a tower of strength, a man whose own inner power radiated confidence. All were grateful he was where he was. Only to his diary, intended for the eyes of his wife alone, did he confide the irritations, anxieties, self-questionings, and uncertainties of a deeply sensitive mind and heart. To all others he was calm, energetic, and indomitable. Those who knew the man rather than just the soldier were to discover an almost unexpected gentleness within the undoubted authority. He had unfailing power to interest and amuse and he was intensely sympathetic to those with whom he had real affinity.

At first Brooke's rapidity of thought and speech, his abrupt, staccato, and very positive method of expression led the Americans to regard him with some reserve, in succession to the exceptionally popular and courteous Dill. Soon, however, they appreciated Brooke's worth for what it was—that of a first-class and utterly professional mind. Even the redoubtable Admiral King came to recognize that he was biting on granite. The British and American Combined Chiefs of Staff became a remarkable, indeed unique, example of Allied co-operation. With the Russians it was inevitably different. As the war drew closer to its obvious end Russian intransigence grew as their fears receded and their ambitions loomed more naked. Churchill and Brooke saw with unwilling clarity what

President Roosevelt and the American chiefs of staff chose to ignore or treat as a distraction—the shape of post-war Europe and the new tyranny by which Allied victory would be succeeded.

In his second responsibility, the professional leadership of the British Army, Brooke's influence and effectiveness lay largely in his selection of commanders; he delegated to Sir Archibald Nye, vice-chief, much of the running of the general staff in the War Office, concentrating only on major issues and on senior personalities. He trusted, and brought to high positions, Alexander, Montgomery, and Slim, amongst others. They, in turn, respected him as one whose opinion was almost invariably justified in the event and whose word, once given, was law.

After the war Brooke handed over office as soon as could be arranged, only ensuring that Montgomery did not appoint his own favourites. He had been promoted field-marshal in 1944. Now additional honours were conferred upon him. He became master gunner of St. James's Park in 1946, an exacting chancellor of Queen's University, Belfast, in 1949, lord lieutenant of the county of London and constable of the Tower in 1950. At the coronation of Queen Elizabeth II in 1953 he was nominated lord high constable of England and commander of the Parade. He was created Baron Alanbrooke, of Brookeborough, in September 1945 and Viscount Alanbrooke in January 1946. In 1946 too he received the freedom of Belfast and of London.

Alanbrooke had been appointed to the DSO and had received the bar and six mentions in dispatches in the war of 1914–18. Appointed KCB in 1940, he later received the grand cross of both the Bath (1942) and the Victorian Order (1953). In 1946 he was created KG and admitted to the Order of Merit. After giving up active service he became a director of the Midland Bank and numerous companies, engaged in a number of philanthropic activities, and pursued his beloved ornithology. From 1950 to 1954 he was president of the Zoological Society. He died 17 June 1963 at his Hampshire home, Ferney Close, Hartley Wintney, shortly before his eightieth birthday.

Alanbrooke was twice married: first, in 1914, to Jane Mary (died 1925), the daughter of Colonel John Mercyn Ashdall Carleton Richardson, of Rossfad in Fermanagh. They had a daughter and a son, the second viscount, who died without issue. The first Mrs Brooke died tragically after a car accident in which her husband was driving. In 1929 he married, secondly, Benita Blanche (died 1968), daughter of Sir Harold Pelly, fourth baronet of Gillingham in Dorset, and widow of Sir Thomas Evan Keith Lees, second baronet, of Lytchet Manor. There were born to them a daughter, who died as a result of a riding accident in 1961, and a son Victor, who became the third Viscount Alanbrooke in 1972.

Portraits of Alanbrooke by Sir Oswald Birley, Anthony Devas, and (Sir) James Gunn (1957) are held by the Royal Regiment, and an unfinished portrait by R. G. Eves is in the possession of the Honourable Artillery Company. There is also a small portrait, by R. G. Eves (1941), at the Staff College, Camberley. A stained-glass memorial window by Lawrence Lee was unveiled at the Royal Military Academy, Sandhurst, in 1965. There is a portrait chalk drawing by Juliet Pannett (1961–3) in the National Portrait Gallery.

[The Alanbrooke Papers in the Liddell Hart Centre, King's College, London; Arthur Bryant, *The Turn of the Tide*, 1957, and *Triumph in the West*, 1959, both of which include edited extracts from Alanbrooke's wartime diaries; *The Economist*, 23 February 1957; private information; personal knowledge.]

D. W. FRASER

published 1981

CAMERON Neil

(1920–1985)

Baron Cameron of Balhousie

Marshal of the Royal Air Force, was born in Perth 8 July 1920, the only son and younger child of Neil Cameron, an inspector of the poor, and his wife, Isabella Stewart. His father died in the year he was born and he and his sister were brought up by his mother and grandfather in Perth. Having attended Perth Academy he worked in the Royal Bank of Scotland. After joining the RAF Volunteer Reserve in May 1939 he was called up on the outbreak of war and qualified as a pilot. He joined No. 17 Squadron towards the end of the Battle of Britain, was commissioned in 1941, flew in Russia with No. 151 Wing, and in 1942–3 served with the Desert Air Force in No. 213 Squadron. In 1944–5, now a squadron leader, he commanded No. 258 Squadron and flew Hurricanes and Thunderbolts in Burma, earning the DFC (1944) and DSO (1945) for his outstanding leadership.

Awarded a permanent commission after the war, he instructed at the School of Air Support, Old Sarum, attended the Staff College, and in 1949 went to the Air Ministry, where he became seriously ill with sub-acute bacterial endocarditis. He was never again allowed a full flying category, making his eventual rise to the top of the RAF particularly remarkable. A spell instructing at the Staff College (1953–6) enabled him to deepen his thinking and begin writing about air power, and he saw something of the academic world while commanding London University Air Squadron (1956–8). He then served as personal staff officer to the chief of the air staff (1958–60), commanded RAF Abingdon (1960–2), attended the Imperial Defence College (1963), went to the Supreme Headquarters Allied Powers in Europe (1964), and in 1965—now an air commodore—became assistant commandant at Cranwell. There ensued four years in the Ministry of Defence working in Denis Healey's programme evaluation group and as assistant chief of staff (policy), when he showed the ability to take an overall defence view but in the process aroused suspicions among his single-service contemporaries, and he subsequently saw little chance of further advancement. Nevertheless after serving at Headquarters Air Support Command and RAF Germany he was promoted to air marshal in 1973 to become AOC No. 46 Group. Ten months later he became air member for personnel, where—at a time of major cuts in RAF strength—he combined his essential humanity with the ability to take hard decisions, notably in the matter of redundancy.

He became chief of the air staff in 1976 but had hardly had time to make much impression before the sudden death of Sir Andrew Humphrey led to his becoming chief of the defence staff (1977–9) and marshal of the Royal Air Force (1977). As CAS he had already emphasized the need for better communication within the RAF and deeper thinking about air power, and as CDS he was determined to argue the defence case in public debate; he held strong views on what he saw as a dangerous growth in Soviet military power and his much publicized reference in China to the Russians as 'an enemy' led to their calling him 'a drunken hare' and to a minor political storm at home. Of the domestic issues he faced the most difficult was service pay, where he led his colleagues in confronting the government and winning the battle for the military salary.

After handing over as CDS in 1979 he was appointed principal of King's College, London, in August 1980, giving him the opportunity to show his leadership qualities in the academic environment that had eluded him in his youth. Here, despite failing health, he played a major part in the restructuring of London University and in particular the merger between King's, Chelsea, and Queen Elizabeth colleges. He was created a life peer in 1983 and a Knight of the Thistle the same year. He had been appointed CBE (1967), CB (1971), KCB (1975), and GCB (1976). He received an honorary LL D from Dundee in 1981.

His many wider interests included the RAF Rugby Football Union, the RAF Club, the RAF Museum, the Trident Trust, and the British Atlantic Committee, and underlying all else was a deep Christian faith rooted in his experience when ill in the 1950s and quietly but sincerely demonstrated through his support for St Clement Danes and organizations such as the

Officers' Christian Union. A man of great honesty, integrity, and forthrightness, who was widely respected, he saw no difficulty in combining a firm military stance based on a belief in nuclear deterrence with his strongly held Christian convictions.

In 1947 he married Patricia Louise, daughter of Major Edward Asprey, a civil engineer. They had a son and daughter. Cameron died in the Middlesex Hospital 29 January 1985.

[Neil Cameron, *In the Midst of Things*, 1986; official records; personal knowledge.]

HENRY A. PROBERT

published 1990

CARTON DE WIART Adrian

(1880–1963)

Sir

Lieutenant-general, was born in Brussels 5 May 1880, the son of Léon Carton de Wiart, lawyer, who moved to Cairo, and his first wife, who died when the boy was six. He was educated at the Oratory School, Edgbaston, from 1891 and went up to Balliol College, Oxford, in January 1899, having failed 'Smalls' at the first attempt. He proceeded to fail the preliminary examination in law but returned to an indulgent college for Michaelmas term. He ran away and under an assumed name and age joined Paget's Horse, a yeomanry unit off to fight the Boers. He was severely wounded, his identity was revealed, and he returned to Balliol to be treated as the college hero for whom his friend, Auberon Herbert (later eighth Baron Lucas) subsequently coined the description 'genius in courage'. He returned to South Africa and enlisted in the Imperial Light Horse. The war ending, he obtained a regular commission in the 4th Dragoon Guards, then stationed in Rawalpindi. Pigsticking and polo began to pall and he became ADC to Sir Henry Hildyard, C-in-C South Africa. Three years later, in 1908, he rejoined his regiment in England and was seconded as adjutant to the Royal Gloucestershire Hussars. In July 1914 he sailed for Somaliland to join the Camel Corps to fight the 'Mad Mullah'. Shortly after the outbreak of war in Europe, he used an eye injury sustained while storming a fort to get himself back to England. His eye was removed and he was appointed to the DSO.

His heroic career in the war of 1914–18 was spent in the trenches or in hospital. He was severely wounded eight times and lost his left hand. He was awarded the Victoria Cross after the battle of the Somme, in which he led the 8th battalion of the Gloucestershire Regiment in the capture of La Boiselle, in the first week of July 1916. He subsequently commanded a series of infantry brigades—the 12th, and at Arras the 105th and 113th. After the armistice he was appointed second in command to General Louis Botha, who was to lead the British Military Mission to Poland. When Botha died in 1919 Carton de Wiart took over. In 1924 he resigned his commission when Prince Charles Radziwill, who had been his last Polish ADC, lent him a house in the Pripet marshes where he spent the interwar years happily shooting duck. He was summoned back to England and asked to resume his old mission to Poland in July 1939 but he had strong disagreements with Marshal Smigly-Rydz, the Polish C-in-C. When the Germans invaded Poland Carton de Wiart returned to England by way of Romania and was given command of the 61st division, a Midland Territorial formation with its headquarters in Oxford. In the spring he left his division to command a force bound for Namsos in Norway, whose capture was a forlorn hope and from which he skilfully extricated his forces. In April 1941 he was dispatched to form a British military mission in Yugoslavia but his aircraft was shot down in the sea and he became an Italian prisoner. He joined a group of senior officers held prisoner at Sulmona and the Castello di Vincigliati at Fiesole and was at once busy with plans to escape. The Italians eventually found a role for their restless captive as an intermediary, dispatched to Lisbon in August 1943, in the arrangements which led to Italy's withdrawal from the war in September 1943.

Less than a month after his return to England, (Sir) Winston Churchill sent him, as a lieutenant-general, as his personal representative to Generalissimo Chiang Kai-shek in China. The rest of the war he spent in Chungking where he made a great impression. He attended the Cairo conference and in December 1944 made a personal report to the Cabinet, at the prime minister's insistence, on the situation in the Far East. He also managed to be involved in the naval bombardment of Sabang. He was invited by Attlee to continue in his post after the British general election of 1945 and eventually retired to England in 1946, having broken his back in Rangoon *en route*.

In 1908 he had married Countess Frederica, eldest daughter of Prince Fugger Babenhausen, they had two daughters. His wife died in 1949 and two years later he married Mrs. Joan Sutherland. They settled in county Cork where he continued the tireless pursuit of snipe and salmon. There he died 5 June 1963.

With his black eye-patch and empty sleeve, Carton de Wiart looked like an elegant pirate and he became a figure of legend, an 'absolute nonducker', utterly without sentimentality but full of fine-drawn sentiments. His pleasures were simple, his contempts obvious. His *Happy Odyssey* gives something of the flavour. He might have ridden out with Prince Rupert over Magdalen Bridge any May morning in the sunshine. He was unusually quick and so was his temper. He bore himself magnificently, loathed humbug, and detested meanness. He taught himself to manage with one hand—and one eye—more neatly than most ever achieve with two. He was elected an honorary fellow of Balliol in 1947 and held an honorary doctorate from Aberdeen. He was appointed CMG in 1918, CB in 1919, and KBE in 1945, and he held several Belgian, French, and Polish decorations. It was said of him that in the world of action he occupied the sort of niche which Sir Max Beerbohm occupied in the world of letters.

The National Portrait Gallery owns a portrait in oils by Sir William Orpen (1919). A portrait in oils by Simon Elwes was exhibited at the Royal Academy Summer Exhibition in 1972.

[Sir Adrian Carton de Wiart, *Happy Odyssey*, 1950; *The Times*, 6 June 1963; *Balliol Record*, July 1964; personal knowledge.]

E. T. WILLIAMS

published 1981

CAVELL Edith

(1865–1915)

Nurse, was born at Swardeston, Norfolk, 4 December 1865, the eldest daughter of the Rev. Frederick Cavell, vicar of Swardeston, by his wife, Louisa Sophia Walming. She was educated at home, at a school in Somerset, and in Brussels. In 1888, having inherited a small competency, she travelled on the Continent. When visiting Bavaria, she took much interest in a free hospital maintained by a Dr. Wolfenberg, and endowed it with a fund for the purchase of instruments. In 1895 she entered the London Hospital as a probationer. In 1897 she took charge of an emergency typhoid hospital at Maidstone. Having attained the position of staff nurse at the London Hospital, she engaged in poor law nursing, serving in the Highgate and Shoreditch infirmaries. Subsequently she took temporary charge of a Queen's district nursery in Manchester. In 1906 she went to Brussels to co-operate with Dr. Depage in establishing a modern training school for nurses on the English system, the best nurses hitherto obtainable in Belgium having been sisters belonging to Catholic religious orders. Edith Cavell was appointed in 1907 the first matron of Depage's clinic—the Berkendael medical institute—the success of which soon made it of national importance. Shortly before the European War it obtained official recognition, a new and larger building being added to it from state funds. She also organized and managed the hospital of St. Gilles. In August 1914 Dr. Depage went away to organize military hospitals, and Miss Cavell remained in charge. The German authorities gave her permission to continue her work in Brussels, the institute became a Red Cross Hospital, and she and her assistants devoted themselves to the care of the wounded, Germans as well as Allies.

When, in the latter part of 1914, the French and British forces were compelled to retire from Belgium, many soldiers from both these armies were cut off from their units. They hid themselves as best they could, for some, at least, of those who fell into German hands were summarily executed. But many escaped with the aid of the Belgian farmers and peasants. A regular system grew up under which these men were enabled to escape from the country. Miss Cavell was naturally one to whom those who needed aid applied; and she readily responded. Her conduct, careful as it was, aroused suspicion. Suspicion led to espionage. On 5 August 1915 she was arrested and placed in solitary confinement in the prison of St. Gilles. Nine weeks later (7 October) she was brought to trial together with some thirty-five other prisoners. The charges against all were of a similar kind; the tribunal before which these persons, many of them women, were arraigned was a court martial; the proceedings were conducted in German, though a French interpreter was provided.

During the weeks when Miss Cavell lay in prison Mr. Brand Whitlock, the United States minister in Brussels, was active on her behalf. He wrote to Baron von Lancken, the civil governor of Belgium, stating that he had been instructed to take charge of her defence, and he asked that a representative of his legation might see her. This letter elicited no reply. When Mr. Whitlock wrote again he was told that the prisoner had already confessed her guilt, and that a M. Braun had been engaged by her friends to conduct the defence. In fact the defence was handed over to a member of the Brussels bar, M. Sadi Kirschen, who did everything possible under the circumstances. But, as the event showed, the conviction of Miss Cavell was a foregone conclusion. In accordance with the usual procedure of such courts in Germany, the prisoner was not allowed to see her advocate before the trial, nor was he granted access to the documents in the case. The allegation was that she had enabled no less than 130 persons to escape from Belgium. Merely assisting these men to escape to Holland would have constituted no more than an *attempt* to 'conduct soldiers to the enemy'. Under German military law this is not a capital offence. But the confession which Miss Cavell is alleged to have signed on the day previous to the trial stated that she had actually assisted Belgians of military age to go to the front, and that she had also concealed French and English soldiers, providing them with funds and with guides whereby they had been enabled to cross the Dutch frontier.

That such a confession was made by Miss Cavell is probable enough. Nine weeks of solitary confinement, the absence of any adviser who might have insisted that she should put her accusers to the proof of their charges, the conviction that what she had done was morally right, though legally wrong—all these considerations might well have induced her to tell the full story. But for her confessions, however, the capital charge would seem not to have been sustainable. The prosecution appears to have had no evidence that she had succeeded in enabling military refugees to reach England. She stated at the trial, however, that she had received letters of thanks from those whom she had helped to repatriate. In the absence of this admission she could only have been found guilty of an attempt to conduct soldiers to the enemy. Her statement showed that her attempt had been successful. So the penalty was death. The trial ended on Friday, 8 October. At eight o'clock on the evening of the following Monday (11 October) an official of the United States Legation was told unofficially that three hours previously sentence of death had been pronounced on Miss Cavell and that she would be shot at 2 a.m. on the following morning (12 October). Strenuous, but unavailing, efforts were made both by Mr. Whitlock and the Spanish minister to obtain at least a respite. All that they were granted was permission for the chaplain of Christ Church, Brussels, the Rev. H. S. T. Gahan, to visit her before the end, and he brought away her last messages.

Memorials of Miss Cavell have been set up in England and elsewhere. On 15 May 1919 her body was brought to Norwich Cathedral after a memorial service in Westminster Abbey. A statue of her, the work of Sir George Frampton, R.A., stands in St. Martin's Place, London, to record the price which she paid for doing what she conceived to be her duty.

To many English minds the execution of Miss Cavell was a judicial murder. British tribunals throughout the War avoided passing sentence of death upon women, even when found guilty of the most dangerous espionage. There is no evidence that Miss Cavell was in any sense a spy. She did nothing for pecuniary reward. Charity and the desire to aid the distressed were the mainsprings of her life. But the German military code prescribed the penalty of death for the offence of which she was found guilty. The procedure in this case was the same as that in other courts martial. Deference to her sex and some allowance for honourable motives might have been expected from humane judges. Presumably the judges were afraid to be humane and thought that the obedience of the Belgian population must be assured by severe sentences. The execution then was justified according to German standards. But, if legally justifiable, it was assuredly a blunder. Popular opinion in the allied countries considered Nurse Cavell to be a martyr.

[*The Times*, 16 and 22 October 1915; *Correspondence with the United States Ambassador respecting the Execution of Miss Cavell at Brussels*, Cd. 8013, 1915; *La Vie et la Mort de Miss Edith Cavell*, 1915; private information. Portraits, *Royal Academy Pictures*, 1916 and 1917.]

BENEDICT WILLIAM GINSBURG

published 1927

CONINGHAM Arthur

(1895–1948)

Sir

Air marshal, was born at Brisbane, Australia, 19 January 1895, the elder son of Arthur Coningham, chemist and Australian cricketer, by his wife, Alice Stanford. His parents moved to New Zealand where he was educated at Wellington College. On the outbreak of war in 1914 he enlisted as a trooper in the Canterbury Mounted Rifles in which he served first in Samoa and later in the Gallipoli campaign. From this service in a New Zealand regiment came his nickname of 'Maori' (which was distorted through usage to become 'Mary') by which he was thereafter generally known. Coningham transferred to the Royal Flying Corps in August 1916 and in December went to France as a second lieutenant in No. 32 Squadron, in which he served for the first seven months of 1917 until he was wounded. In this short period he was appointed to the D.S.O., awarded the M.C., and promoted to captain for his gallantry as a fighter pilot. The citation for these two decorations mentions his dash and fine offensive spirit, his splendid example of pluck and determination, qualities which were to mark him throughout his career.

After a year in England he returned to France in July 1918 as major commanding No. 92 Squadron with which he remained until war ended. He was awarded the D.F.C. for his services during this period. Early in 1919 he reverted from major to captain and in August was granted a permanent commission in the Royal Air Force as a flight lieutenant.

Between the two wars he commanded No. 55 Squadron in Iraq and, among other appointments, served as a flying instructor at the Royal Air Force College, Cranwell, and as a staff officer at Middle East headquarters in Cairo and likewise at the headquarters of Coastal Area. As a wing commander he commanded the Royal Air Force detachment in the Sudan and as a group captain the flying-boat base at Calshot. When a staff officer at Cairo he was selected in 1925 to command and lead a 'trail-blazing' flight across Central Africa from Cairo to Kano and, after the successful conclusion of the flight, was awarded the A.F.C.

Just before the outbreak of hostilities in 1939 Coningham was promoted to air commodore and given command of No. 4 Group which consisted of the long-range night bombers based in Yorkshire. His group was actively engaged in operations over Germany during the two years he was in command, and in 1941 he was appointed C.B. for his services. In that year he was selected to command the Desert Air Force supporting the Eighth Army in the North African campaign, as part of Air Marshal A. W. (subsequently Lord) Tedder's Middle East Air Force. Coningham remained in command of this force in support of the Eighth Army under its successive commanders throughout the ebb and flow of the desert campaigns of 1941 and 1942, including the El Alamein battle, after which he was promoted K.C.B. After the capture of Tripoli in January 1943 he was switched to the Algerian front to form the 1st Allied (North African) Tactical Air Force. His new command controlled the British and American air forces supporting their respective armies in the campaign for the capture of Tunisia. He set up his headquarters on 17 February 1943 alongside those of the newly formed 18th Army Group under Sir Harold Alexander (subsequently Earl Alexander of Tunis). After Tunis fell Coningham was responsible for command of the Allied Tactical Air Forces employed in the capture of Pantelleria and Sicily and thereafter in support of the British and American armies in southern Italy. In January 1944 he returned to England to take command of the 2nd Tactical Air Force then preparing to go to Europe alongside the 21st Army Group. Coningham moved to Normandy with his force in July 1944 and remained in command until the conclusion of the war in Europe. His appointment for the last year of the war was that of a commander-in-chief, and his force, commanded finally from his headquarters in Germany, consisted of some 1,800 first-line aircraft and 100,000 men, spread from Copenhagen and Bremen in the north to Marseilles in the south, and comprising British, Canadian, Belgian, French, Dutch, Polish, and Norwegian air forces.

Coningham, as air vice-marshal and air marshal, was commanding air forces operating against the Germans from the first day of the war until the last. Although he was highly strung he seemed to have no nerves, and his youthful and gay spirit inspired his whole force and in particular young pilots with whom he was at his best. In command of a force in which he knew the strength and weakness of every subordinate commander he was outstanding, but as his sphere of operations necessarily expanded his personal touch could then be felt less keenly. His most remarkable contribution therefore was made, perhaps, from his small, neat caravan in the Western Desert, a part of North Africa he came to know in exceptional detail even at a time when many claimed to know every ridge and wadi. Coningham was a very handsome man whose fine head had silvered early. He held himself well and his young, springy step gave that impression of alertness which was reinforced by the swift eagerness of his mind and interest. He was exceptionally quick in the uptake; moreover, he talked well, with a fluent and vivid vocabulary which held his hearers, to whom he exhibited a singular capacity to transfer his excitement in being alive and 'on the job'. He was always intensely loyal to his superior commander and he seldom made a mistake in his choice of commanders to serve under him. He took no leave between 1939 and 1945 and concentrated his entire and most remarkable energies on defeating the enemy air force in front of him. Where commendation was due he commended with a singular directness, but he was ruthless where there was inefficiency. A clear thinker and an exciting strategist, he seemed the very personification of the offensive spirit. His directions when commanding Tactical Air Forces had the sole purpose of destroying the enemy air forces opposed to him, on the ground or in the air, and thereafter putting the whole weight of his force onto targets which would assist the advance of the army he was supporting. He was quite clear about his purposes and priorities. Although his air forces in the field were, of course, always independent of the army, he invariably set himself the task of assisting the land forces to the fullest extent, and from the day of his arrival in the desert in 1941 until the end of the war he always set up his headquarters alongside those of the army in order to ensure the closest co-operation. A pioneer in this, he was also the original architect of Tactical Air Forces and the way in which he used them was a model for all who came or may come after him.

For his services in the final 'Liberation' campaign he was appointed K.B.E. in 1946 and awarded a number of foreign decorations. He returned from Germany after the war to take up the appointment of commander-in-chief of the Royal Air Force Flying Training Command but retired at his own request in 1947. He was an active pilot himself throughout his Air Force career but it was as a passenger that he lost his life as a result of an accident to the aeroplane 'Star Tiger' between the Azores and Bermuda 30 January 1948.

Coningham married in 1932 Nancy Muriel, daughter of John Brooks, and widow of Sir Howard George Frank, first baronet, and had one daughter. A portrait of him painted by Raeburn Dobson is in the possession of the family. A drawing by H. A. Freeth is reproduced in Philip Guedalla's *Middle East, 1940–1942* (1944); a drawing was also made by Sir William Rothenstein.

[Private information; personal knowledge.]

T. W. ELMHIRST

published 1959

CORBETT Julian Stafford

(1854–1922)

Sir

Naval historian, was the second son of Charles Joseph Corbett, architect, of Thames Ditton, Surrey, by his wife, Elizabeth, daughter of Philip Henry Byrne, of London. He was born at Imber Court, Thames Ditton, 12 November 1854, and was educated at Marlborough and Trinity College, Cambridge, where he gained a first class in the law tripos in 1875. In 1879 he was called to the bar by the Middle Temple, and continued to practise for five years, although the work from the first appears to have been irksome. In 1882 he abandoned it and, having private means, travelled extensively, visiting among other places India and the United States. In 1886 Corbett found in fiction an outlet for literary ability which in his Cambridge days had occasioned remark. His first novel was *The Fall of Asgard*, and this was quickly followed by *For God and Gold* (1887) and *Kophetua the Thirteenth* (1889). By a natural process he was drawn towards biography, contributing to the 'English Men of Action' series the life of Monk in 1889, and in the following year Drake. It would, however, be a mistake to suppose that these volumes helped to shape his subsequent career. In 1895 he reverted to fiction, his next novel being *A Business in Great Waters*.

During this, the formative period of his life, Corbett continued to travel, visiting Norway frequently, and almost invariably spending the winter in Rome. It was his taste for sport and travel that induced him in 1896 to accompany the Dongola expedition as special correspondent of the *Pall Mall Gazette*. His experiences were much less exciting than he had anticipated, but the campaign undoubtedly set him thinking about the conduct of war as a subject for his pen. In 1898 he produced his first serious contribution to historical literature, *Drake and the Tudor Navy*. Corbett had already written two novels on this theme as well as a biography, and the choice was natural enough; but his experiences as a war correspondent had changed his outlook, and the two volumes may be taken as inaugurating a new chapter in his life. He was not quite sure, however, that he was pursuing the right course, even though his researches had brought him into touch with the Navy Records Society, recently founded by Sir John Knox Laughton, who had persuaded him to edit a volume connected with Drake, *Papers Relating to the Navy during the Spanish War, 1585–1587* (1898). At forty-five Corbett was hesitating whether to follow his own preference and resume the role of the novelist or yield to the counsel of his friends and stand for parliament, when his marriage in 1899 with Edith, only daughter of George Alexander, cotton manufacturer, of Manchester, enabled him to make up his mind. At his wife's request he decided to devote himself to serious historical writing.

The first fruit of this decision was *The Successors of Drake* (1900), which may be regarded as continuing and concluding his work on the Tudor navy, although two years later (1902) he edited for the Navy Records Society Sir William Slyngsbie's contemporary *Relation of the Voyage to Cadiz, 1596*. On the strength of work already completed Corbett was appointed in 1902 lecturer in history to the Royal Naval War College, just established at Greenwich, and in 1903 was selected to deliver the Ford lectures at Oxford. In 1904 he presented the substance of the research which his two new spheres of work had involved in *England in the Mediterranean, 1603–1714*, a comprehensive study of naval strategy. Naval tactics next engaged his attention, and for the centenary of Trafalgar (1905) he prepared for the Navy Records Society a volume which he called *Fighting Instructions, 1530–1816*, a collection of documents illustrating the art of handling battle-fleets in the days of sail. But at the War College it was strategy rather than tactics that his audiences required, and in 1907 he completed another notable contribution to the subject, *England in the Seven Years' War*, a book which, more than any of its precursors, demonstrated the true relationship of naval power and national policy.

In 1908, almost by way of relaxation, Corbett edited for the Navy Records Society volumes dealing with *Views of the Battles of the Third Dutch War* and *Signals and Instructions, 1776–1794*, the latter a supplement to his *Fighting Instructions*. He found time, also, to write numerous articles and pamphlets, one of which, *The Capture of Private Property at Sea*, was reprinted by A. T. Mahan in *Some Neglected Aspects of War* (1907). But at this time Corbett was chiefly engaged upon a new study, *The Campaign of Trafalgar*, published in 1910. This, his most important work so far, disappointed the reviewers, who were expecting a controversial treatment of

Nelson's tactics and received what may be called the first staff history of a naval campaign. The welcome which the book received from naval officers induced Corbett in the following year to present the essence of his doctrine in *Some Principles of Maritime Strategy*; while a paper on 'Staff Histories' which he read to the International Congress of Historical Studies in 1913 was reprinted in *Naval and Military Essays* (1914), the first volume of a series which was interrupted by the War. At this time (1913) he was editing for the Navy Records *Private Papers of George, second Earl Spencer*, which threw a flood of new light on naval administration in Nelson's day; and on the appearance of the second volume he was awarded the Chesney gold medal by the Royal United Service Institution (1914).

When the European War broke out, Corbett offered his services to the Admiralty and, in addition to organizing a bureau for the collection of material for the history of the struggle at sea, wrote pamphlets for the enlightenment of neutrals and supplied tabular statements of historical parallels for the assistance of the naval staff. In 1917 he was knighted.

Shortly before the War Corbett had undertaken to write an official history of the naval campaigns of 1904–1905; this was completed in 1915 under the title *Maritime Operations in the Russo-Japanese War* (for official use). The experience which he gained in the compilation of this work was invaluable. It showed him what was needed in the way of sources, and in conjunction with his labours at the war bureau accelerated the writing of *Naval Operations*, the official history of the European War at sea. The first volume appeared in 1920, and the second, carrying the narrative down to the resignation of Lord Fisher, appeared in the following year. In 1921 Corbett delivered the Creighton lecture at King's College, London, sketching in outline the subject which he had put aside to deal with the Russo-Japanese War and to which he always hoped to return—'Napoleon and the British Navy after Trafalgar' (published in the *Quarterly Review*, April 1922). But his plans were denied fruition; for he died quite suddenly at Stopham, Sussex, 21 September 1922, leaving one son and one daughter. He had just completed a third volume of *Naval Operations*, containing his account of the battle of Jutland, and this was printed posthumously (1923).

Corbett had a natural bent for antiquarian pursuits, collected rare books and manuscripts bearing on his chosen themes, and wrote in a cultured and arresting style; but left to himself, he would hardly have devoted himself so whole-heartedly to naval history. There was as much of the philosopher in him as the historian. It was the good fortune of his country that he had not committed himself to any definite line of inquiry when, at the opening of the new century, the Royal Naval War College was instituted and, finding in him the instrument it needed, inspired the series of monographs and histories which won for his original genius a wide measure of esteem.

[Letters and papers in possession of the family; personal knowledge.]

G. A. R. CALLENDER

published 1937

CUMMING Mansfield George Smith

(1859–1923)

Sir

The first chief of the modern secret service (CSS or C), was born Mansfield George Smith 1 April 1859 in India, the youngest in the family of five sons and eight daughters of Colonel John Thomas Smith, of the Royal Engineers, of Föellalt House, Kent, and his wife Maria Sarah Tyser. After entering the Royal Naval College, Dartmouth, at the age of thirteen, he began his career afloat as acting sub-lieutenant on HMS *Bellerophon*. He served in operations against Malay pirates 1875–6 and in Egypt in 1883. He suffered, however, from severe seasickness and in 1885 he was placed on the retired list.

Cumming (he changed his name in 1889 after marriage) spent the early 1890s largely as a country gentleman on his second wife's Morayshire estate. In 1898, while still on the Royal Navy retired list, Cumming was posted to Nelson's old flagship *Victory* 'for special service at Southampton'. The 'special service' included occasional intelligence work abroad, but his main work for the next decade was the construction and command of the Southampton boom defences.

In 1909 Cumming was appointed head of what became the foreign section of the Secret Service Bureau (the forerunner of the Secret Intelligence Service, better known as SIS or MI6). He described pre-1914 espionage as 'capital sport', but was given few resources with which to pursue it. His early operations were directed almost entirely against Germany. Between 1909 and 1914 he recruited part-time 'casual agents' in the shipping and arms business to keep track of naval construction in German shipyards and acquire other technical intelligence. He also had agents collecting German intelligence in Brussels, Rotterdam, and St Petersburg.

With the outbreak of World War I, Cumming's control of strategic intelligence gathering as head of the wartime MI 1c was challenged by two rival networks run by GHQ. Cumming eventually out-performed his rivals. His most important wartime network, 'La Dame Blanche', had by January 1918 over 400 agents reporting on German troop movements from occupied Belgium and northern France. Cumming was less successful in post-revolutionary Russia. Despite a series of colourful exploits, his agents obtained little Russian intelligence of value.

Like the rest of the British intelligence community, the postwar SIS was drastically cut back. Cumming succeeded, however, in gaining a monopoly of espionage and counter-intelligence outside Britain and the empire. He also established a network of SIS station commanders operating overseas under diplomatic cover. To the end of his life Cumming retained an infectious, if sometimes eccentric, enthusiasm for the tradecraft and mystification of espionage, experimenting personally with disguises, mechanical gadgets, and secret inks in his own laboratory. His practice of writing exclusively in a distinctive green ink was continued by his successors. He was appointed CB in 1914 and KCMG in 1919.

Cumming had a fascination with most forms of transport, driving his Rolls at high speed around the streets of London. In his early fifties he took up flying, gaining both French Aviators' and Royal Aero Club certificates. But his main passion was boating in Southampton Water and other waters calmer than those which had ended his active service career. In addition to owning 'any number' of yachts, Cumming acquired six motor boats. In 1905 he became one of the founders and first rear-commodore of the Royal Motor Yacht Club.

In 1885 Cumming married Dora, daughter of Henry Cloete, esquire, of Great Constantia, Cape of Good Hope, South Africa. After her death he married, in 1889, a Scottish heiress, Leslie Marian ('May'), daughter of Captain Lockhart Muir Valiant (afterwards Cumming), of the 1st Bombay Lancers and Logie, Morayshire. As part of the marriage settlement he changed his surname to Smith-Cumming, later becoming known as Cumming. Their only son, Alastair, a dangerous driver like his father, was killed in October 1914, driving Cumming's Rolls in France. Cumming himself lost the lower part of his right leg in the same accident. He died suddenly at his London headquarters 14 June 1923, shortly before he was due to retire.

[Christopher Andrew, *Secret Service: the Making of the British Intelligence Community*, 1985; Nicholas Hiley, 'The Failure of British Espionage Against Germany, 1907–1914', *Historical Journal*, vol. xxvi, 1983, pp. 867–89; family information.]

CHRISTOPHER ANDREW

published 1993

CUNNINGHAM Andrew Browne

(1883–1963)

Viscount Cunningham of Hyndhope

Admiral of the fleet, was born in Dublin 7 January 1883, the third of the five children—three sons and two daughters—of Daniel John Cunningham, then professor of anatomy at Trinity College, Dublin, by his wife, Elizabeth Cumming, daughter of the Revd Andrew Browne, of Beith, Ayrshire. 'A. B. C.', as he was generally known, was not related to Sir John Henry Dacres Cunningham, who succeeded him in 1943 in the Mediterranean command and again in 1946 as first sea lord. Andrew Cunningham's elder brother, John, had reached the rank of lieutenant-colonel by 1924 as a doctor in the Indian Medical Service, and later practised in Edinburgh. His younger brother became General Sir Alan Cunningham during a long and striking career as a professional soldier.

Although none of his forebears had served at sea, Cunningham was always interested in boats, and throughout his life he took more interest in sailing than in any other sport. He was educated first at Edinburgh Academy, followed by three years at Stubbington House, Fareham, preparing for the Royal Navy; in January 1897 he entered the *Britannia* fourteenth in order of merit among sixty-five cadets and was tenth upon passing out in May 1898 when he earned first class passes in mathematics and seamanship.

Having stated a preference for service on the Cape station, Cunningham was serving there as midshipman in the *Doris* when the South African war broke out in 1899; by February 1900 he had winkled his way into the Naval Brigade which promised opportunities for brave deeds and distinction in action. Lord Roberts, who knew his father, used his influence to get Cunningham to the front line, to the annoyance of his commanding officer who resented such nepotism. Thus in spite of front line service with mobile naval guns, Cunningham was the only midshipman to be omitted from a list of those 'noted for early promotion'. This upset him, but he bore it philosophically. About the same time he met and was impressed by (Sir) Walter Cowan, then a lieutenant and naval aide-de-camp to Lord Kitchener and who at twenty-nine had seen more action than many admirals.

In 1902–3 Cunningham took sub-lieutenant courses at Portsmouth and Greenwich, obtaining first class passes in seamanship and torpedo. As a sub-lieutenant, Cunningham's first six months were in the battleship *Implacable* in the Mediterranean; but his most rewarding time took place when he was transferred to the destroyer *Locust*, September 1903, to serve as second-in-command under a young lieutenant, a 'taut hand' renowned for efficiency and ability, with the reputation for getting rid of sub-lieutenants who failed to come up to his requirements. Cunningham passed the test well and developed a great fondness for destroyers. He was promoted lieutenant in 1904, but it was not until 1908, after service in the cruisers *Northampton*, *Hawke*, and *Suffolk*, and as a result of repeated requests, that he found himself back in his beloved 'boats', in command of torpedo-boat no. 14.

His persistent importuning, together with the advent of war, and the increasing number of vessels becoming available, were responsible for keeping Cunningham in the 'boats'. He was given command of the destroyer *Scorpion* in 1911 and was destined to serve in her until 1918. At the Dardanelles the *Scorpion* seemed to be always at the forefront of action; he witnessed the tragic losses of British capital ships and the failure of naval bombardment undertaken without the follow-up of troops, until too late—an experience he never forgot. He was promoted commander in 1915, and was appointed to the DSO in the same year. Meanwhile his reputation as a first-class destroyer commander and man of action was growing, and it was not long before he was regarded as a rising star by various influential senior officers such as (Sir) John De Robeck, Roger (later Lord) Keyes, and Sir Reginald (later Lord) Tyrwhitt with whom he had served. He was known as an effectual leader, aggressive fighter, and highly competent seaman. But beneath that redoubtability lay the sense of fun which in his *Britannia* days had led to records of 'laughing in study', and 'skylarking at muster': a quality which endeared him to those who really knew him, and which during the war of 1939–45 would be responsible for such remarks as 'I hope the old man is coming with us . . . we shall be all right if he is'.

Throughout most of 1918 he took part in numerous engagements in the Dover Patrol under Keyes (including the Zeebrugge raid), for which he was awarded a bar to his DSO the following year; he was promoted captain in December 1919, and a second bar was awarded in 1920 for service the previous year with a force in the Baltic under the command of Cowan (by then a rear-admiral), where Cunningham had taken firm but diplomatic individual action against the encroachment of German troops in Latvia. Post-war international problems and demobilization reduced the number of sea-going appointments: nevertheless, after taking the senior officers' technical course at Portsmouth, Cunningham found himself back in destroyers early in 1922, first as captain (D) of the 6th flotilla, and in January 1923 as captain (D) of the 1st flotilla, then temporarily in the Mediterranean to support British ships based on Istanbul. He gave considerable thought to exercises using destroyers in an offensive role with torpedoes in mass attacks against heavy ships, and also in the underwater detection and destruction of submarines.

After a spell ashore in command of the destroyer base at Port Edgar in the Firth of Forth during 1924–6, Cunningham became flag captain and chief staff officer to Cowan, who had become vice-admiral and commander-in-chief North America and West Indies station: an appointment to gladden any captain's heart, although Cunningham deplored what he called 'the mysteries' of red tape and paperwork involved in administration, and took a certain humorous pride in the fact that he never did a staff course. He admired Cowan's courage and dedication, owning that Cowan had taught him a lot.

In December 1929, at the end of a year at the Imperial Defence College, he was given command of the battleship *Rodney*—an appointment marking him as a captain of great promise. Eighteen months later he was appointed commodore of the Royal Naval Barracks at Chatham. Promotion to flag rank in September 1932, in which year he was also naval aide-de-camp to the King, was followed (December 1933) by his appointment as rear-admiral (destroyers) in the Mediterranean, a job he said he would have chosen above all others. He was appointed CB in 1934. The period was one of increasing naval training, with much attention to night exercises as well as to all-round readiness in case of war with Italy.

On his promotion to vice-admiral in July 1936, prospects for further active employment seemed remote. However, a year later there occurred a vacancy suddenly caused by the illness of Sir Geoffrey Blake and Cunningham assumed his combined appointment of commander of the Battle Cruiser Squadron and second-in-command of the Mediterranean Fleet, hoisting his flag in the *Hood*. This important command he retained until September 1938, when he was appointed to the Admiralty as deputy chief of the naval staff, a post he took up in December. He accepted a shore job with reluctance, maintaining that he was no good at paperwork; but the appointment was clear proof of the Board of Admiralty's high regard for him, and for six months he acted as deputy, on the Committee of Imperial Defence and Admiralty Board, to the first sea lord, Sir Roger Backhouse, during the latter's illness. However, in June 1939 Cunningham was appointed commander-in-chief Mediterranean station with the acting rank of admiral. Hoisting his flag in the battleship *Warspite*, he took over from Sir Dudley Pound (who was to succeed Backhouse). In the same year he was promoted KCB.

Italy's attitude remained uncertain both before and after the outbreak of war until the collapse of France in June 1940, when she threw in her lot with Germany. Cunningham's immediate aim was to restore and maintain

British supremacy in the Mediterranean with the policy of 'seek out and destroy'. He unequivocally deprecated suggestions of withdrawal from the Mediterranean, and insisted that both Alexandria and Malta must be maintained as British naval bases to sustain communications and to provide support for the army and the RAF. When ordered (from London) to seize the French fleet, which under Admiral Godfroy at Alexandria had hitherto co-operated fully against the Axis, Cunningham instead entered into friendly but firm negotiation with Godfroy and obtained a clear agreement whereby the French warships would remain permanently immobilized in Alexandria harbour, safe from misappropriation by the Axis. This was a masterly achievement, especially when viewed against the considerable bloodshed and national hatred engendered by the British naval attack ordered against the French fleet at Oran at the same time. Cunningham no longer had the French as an ally, however, and was also faced with an Italian fleet of considerable strength.

The Italians adopted a policy of maintaining a 'fleet in being', best achieved by withdrawing to harbour whenever their material superiority was threatened. Cunningham's first encounter with the Italian navy occurred 9 July 1940, when a powerful fleet was returning to Italy after covering the passage to North Africa of a large military convoy bound for Libya. Cunningham also was at sea, covering an important convoy from Malta to Alexandria. Neither knew of the other's presence. Upon receiving a submarine report of an enemy fleet at sea, Cunningham aimed to intercept the Italians off Calabria before they could reach port. In numbers of capital ships his fleet was superior to that of the Italians, but in effect the latter were so modern that they could outrun and outrange all his battleships except the modernized *Warspite*. With the *Warspite* were the old battleships *Malaya* and *Royal Sovereign*, both unable to keep up with the fleet at full speed. Moreover, although Cunningham had the benefit of reconnaissance from the carrier *Eagle*, the latter lacked suitable aircraft and experienced crews to provide a strike which would effectively slow down the Italians. The great moment came, however, when the *Warspite* brought the leading enemy battleship, the fast and powerful *Cesare*, within range of her guns. Until that moment, five light British cruisers had been having a rough time from the enemy's six heavy and ten light cruisers firing at a range of thirteen miles. It was at 4.00 p.m. that the *Warspite*, her fifteen-inch guns elevated to maximum range, scored a direct hit on the *Cesare*, causing a heavy explosion and fires. The Italians immediately withdrew for home under a heavy smoke-screen, hoping to lure the British fleet into waters close to Italian shore-based bombers. In the face of heavy attacks from the latter, and the danger also of submarines in the smoke-laden sea, Cunningham was forced to relinquish pursuit.

His audacity in closing the Italian coast at Calabria with three veteran battleships and an old and vulnerable carrier, in the presence of a powerful modern enemy fleet and air force, established a moral ascendancy which set the pattern of aggressive action for the next eighteen months, during times of both triumph and adversity. Cunningham's strategy and daring received support in August 1940 with the arrival of the new carrier *Illustrious* and the old but modernized battleship *Valiant* on the Mediterranean station, together with two anti-aircraft cruisers. Both sides continued the covering of convoys: the British, east–west; the Italian, north–south. But in general the Italian battleships were safely confined in the harbour of Taranto, and although Cunningham's ships never relaxed their offensive role, the prospect of a main fleet action appeared remote. Cunningham, however, scored a dramatic success in November 1940 with a night attack on Taranto harbour, using naval Swordfish aircraft armed with torpedoes. Half the Italian battleships were put out of action, and since the remaining three were promptly removed to Naples for safety, the threat to British convoys bound for Greece and Crete was greatly diminished.

On 3 January 1941 Cunningham was confirmed in the rank of admiral. His reputation was high, for British convoys were now passing both ways through the Mediterranean and his fleet was exacting an increasing toll of the enemy's convoys to Tripoli. There was also no appearance of the Italian battle fleet. He celebrated promotion with a bombardment of Bardia to give support to the inshore squadron which worked in co-operation with the British army in the desert. The presence of the *Illustrious* gave him local control of the air whenever he took his fleet to sea. But already a shadow lay over the scene: Mussolini's fiasco in Greece had provoked German intervention in the Mediterranean, the Luftwaffe arrived in Sicily in January 1941, and Germany's campaigns in Greece and Libya were already in preparation. The *Illustrious* was put out of action when her flight-deck was wrecked by Junkers 87 and 88 on 10 January: Cunningham was once again without fighter defence at sea, and until the new carrier *Formidable* arrived in the Mediterranean two months later, he suffered some loss and damage to his ships.

But that spring Cunningham gained a major victory over the Italian fleet off Cape Matapan—the first large-scale naval action for twenty-five years. He sailed from Alexandria after dark, 27 March, with the battleships *Warspite*, *Valiant*, and *Barham* (all of which had fought at Jutland), the *Formidable*, and nine destroyers, having received a report earlier that day that a force of three Italian cruisers had been sighted heading towards Crete. A light force of four British cruisers which was already operating in the Aegean sea, covering British military convoys proceeding to Greece, was ordered to rendezvous south of Crete with Cunningham at dawn 28 March. Cunningham believed that the Italian battle fleet might be at sea, and at first light reconnaissance aircraft from the *Formidable* reported the presence of two groups of Italian heavy cruisers, eight in all. One of these groups sighted the British light cruiser force and engaged them from 8.12 a.m. to 8.55 a.m. at a range which was beyond that of three of the British light cruisers. The latter began leading the Italian ships to the south-east, where it was hoped they would meet Cunningham's battle fleet head on.

Unknown to Cunningham was the presence of the *Vittorio Veneto*, one of Italy's newest battleships flying the flag of Admiral Iachino, the Italian commander-in-chief. It was the latter, then only a few miles to the west of his own cruisers, who had ordered them to cease fire at 8.55 a.m. and to steam north-west, unwilling as he was that his forces should be drawn further into the unknown. The British light force then turned to shadow the Italian cruisers, and at 10.58 a.m. unexpectedly sighted the *Vittorio Veneto* to the northward. She immediately opened fire on the British light cruisers, whose survival seemed remote as they altered course to the southward at full speed. But at least the presence of the *Vittorio Veneto* was known, and Cunningham immediately increased to full speed in his advance north-westward. Meanwhile Iachino, still unaware of Cunningham's presence only eighty miles to the south-east, experienced no difficulty in keeping up with the British light cruisers and finding the range. Moreover, he had dispersed his fleet so that the division of Italian heavy cruisers which had attacked the British light cruisers earlier should be in a position to supplement the *Vittorio Veneto*'s fire. Annihilation of the four British ships would have certainly followed but for a tactical surprise: the providential torpedo strike at 11.27 a.m. by the *Formidable*'s aircraft, which had been dispatched from the carrier by Cunningham at 9.39 a.m. Their arrival at this critical moment saved the British light cruisers. No hits were scored, however, and the Italians began to hasten home at twenty-eight knots, with Cunningham doing his utmost, only forty-five miles astern, at a speed which would be quite insufficient to catch them unless the Italian fleet could be slowed down. An afternoon strike from the *Formidable* succeeded in hitting the *Vittorio Veneto*, but she was able to maintain a speed of nineteen knots after some repair, and later to increase it.

With the approach of twilight it appeared that the Italians—who had had no effective air protection the whole day—would be able to reach home under cover of darkness. However, a dusk strike from the *Formidable* successfully slowed down the heavy cruiser *Pola*; Iachino thereupon sent back two heavy cruisers, the *Zara* and *Fiume*, together with four destroyers, to stand by her. These were seen on the *Valiant*'s radar screen and reported, and Cunningham decided on a night attack with his battle fleet, despite the risk from enemy torpedoes. At 10.20 p.m. the *Pola* was only four miles away according to the radar screen, and at that very moment the massive shapes of darkened ships could be seen by eye, crossing the path of Cunningham's battle fleet: seven enemy ships, all unsuspecting and unready. Almost simultaneously the *Warspite*, *Valiant*, and *Barham* opened fire with fifteen-inch broadsides at a range of two miles. At 10.31 Cunningham made an emergency turn to avoid possible enemy torpedoes and ordered his destroyers to finish off the enemy. The loss to the Italians was three heavy cruisers and two destroyers, against Cunningham's loss of one aircraft, although Iachino himself had escaped with the remains of his fleet. The results were substantial, but there were to be lean months ahead for Cunningham as for the army, during the withdrawal from Greece and Crete and the reverses in North Africa, while the growing local Axis strength in the air was to create a position calling for the greatest defiance and supreme leadership—qualities in which Cunningham excelled.

The immobilization of the *Formidable* from damage in the attack on Scarpanto, May 1941, and the fall of Crete itself shortly afterwards, left Cunningham virtually without air protection in the 'Narrows' around Malta and in 'Bomb Alley' south of Crete, and the forces under his command suffered increasingly grievous losses right through to the end of 1941. But his inspiring attitude at Crete was typical of his steadfast refusal to give up: 'it takes the navy three years to build a ship but three hundred years to build a tradition', and 'we must not let the army down'.

From June to October 1942, however, Cunningham was with the combined chiefs of staff in Washington, as head of the British Admiralty delegation, where he made a profound impression. His contribution to Allied harmony was considerable, and his selection as 'Allied naval commander Expeditionary Force', under General Eisenhower, was highly acceptable to all, especially to the Americans who admired his integrity and the resolute manner in which he had maintained a presence in the Mediterranean through times of dire shortage and adversity, and who, in fact, were not prepared to accept any other naval commander.

There followed the covering of the successful 'Torch' landings in North Africa, November 1942; the convoying of the Allied armies for the invasion of Sicily, July 1943, and Salerno landings, September 1943; and the Italian collapse which enabled Cunningham to make his historic signal: 'be pleased to inform their lordships that the Italian battle fleet now lies at anchor beneath the guns of the fortress of Malta.' Admiral Iachino generously acknowledged Cunningham's humanity in victory.

In January 1943, resuming his title of commander-in-chief Mediterranean, he was promoted admiral of the fleet, and in October the same year, on the death in harness of Sir Dudley Pound, he was selected for the highest post, that of first sea lord and chief of naval staff, in which he remained for the rest of the war. Apart from his earlier honours and decorations, Cunningham had been promoted GCB in March 1941, and was created a baronet in July 1942; in January 1945 he was created KT, an honour which he prized more than any other. Further laurels followed the conclusion of the war, when he was raised to the peerage in September 1945 as Baron Cunningham of Hyndhope, of Kirkhope, county Selkirk. In 1946 he was advanced to a viscountcy, and in the same year he was appointed to the OM on relinquishing his office as first sea lord. His retirement was quiet but not inactive, for in addition to publishing a lengthy volume of memoirs, *A Sailor's Odyssey* (1951), he was lord high commissioner to the General Assembly of the Church in Scotland in 1950 and 1952, lord rector of Edinburgh University in 1945–8, and president of the Institution of Naval Architects in 1948–51, besides other honorary posts and memberships. He received many foreign orders and decorations, as well as honorary degrees from the universities of Oxford, Cambridge, Birmingham, Leeds, Edinburgh, Glasgow, St. Andrews, and Sheffield. He also received the freedom of the cities of London, Edinburgh, Manchester, and Hove, and was an elder brother of Trinity House from 1943.

Cunningham was of medium stature, compact, and with a rosy, weatherbeaten complexion; his implacable and resolute spirit was expressed in steely blue eyes which could—and frequently did—twinkle with humour and optimism. He was a man of human warmth, sympathy, and generosity, although he did not suffer fools gladly, and had no use for slackers. He drove himself to the limit of excellence and endurance, and expected his men to do the same. Some could not stand up to his thrusting and testing: (Sir) Richard Symonds-Tayler claimed to have been Cunningham's thirteenth first lieutenant in the *Scorpion*—all his predecessors having been 'flung out'. 'The Old Man of the Sea', as soldiers came to call him, was forthright and would truckle to nobody: this sometimes led to strained relationships with authority, notably (Sir) Winston Churchill, who at times attempted—always unsuccessfully—to force him to an action which he considered unsound.

In 1929 Cunningham married Nona Christine (died 1978), third daughter and ninth child of Horace Byatt, schoolmaster, of Midhurst, Sussex, and sister of Sir Horace Byatt, GCMG, then governor of Trinidad and Tobago. The marriage was a very happy one, although there were no children. Cunningham died suddenly in London 12 June 1963 and was buried at sea off Portsmouth.

Lord Alexander of Tunis referred to him as one of 'the great sea commanders of our island race': by holding the Mediterranean with a handful of ships while Britain fought alone, Cunningham prevented the certain disaster which would have followed withdrawal from the Mediterranean, the loss of Malta, and probably also of Egypt and the Suez. It was fitting, therefore, that he should be commemorated close to the Nelson monument in Trafalgar Square, his bust (by Franta Belsky) alongside those of Jellicoe and Beatty, the naval leaders of the war of 1914–18. At his memorial service in St. Paul's Cathedral 12 July 1963, the bishop of Norwich, an old shipmate, thanked God for 'giving our people and nation such a man at such a time'.

There is a portrait in oils of him by (Sir) Oswald Birley (1947) in the Royal Naval College at Greenwich; a copy of it hangs in the Britannia Royal Naval College at Dartmouth, and another is in the Imperial War Museum, together with portraits of him by Henry Carr (1943) and John Worsley (1945); a painting by David S. Ewart was exhibited at the Royal Academy in 1944.

[S. W. C. Pack, *The Battle of Matapan*, 1961, and *Cunningham the Commander*, 1974; *The Times*, 13 June 1963.]

S. W. C. PACK

published 1981

DE GUINGAND Francis Wilfred

(1900–1979)

Sir

Major-general, was born 28 February 1900 at Acton in Middlesex, the second of the four children and eldest of the three sons of Francis Julius de Guingand, a manufacturer of briar-root pipes, and his wife, Mary Monica Priestman. Educated at Ampleforth and the Royal Military College, Sandhurst, he was commissioned into the West Yorkshire Regiment (The Prince of Wales' Own) in December 1919. Two years later his regiment was serving in the 17th Infantry brigade at Cork in southern Ireland. The brigade-major was Captain (Brevet-Major) Bernard Montgomery (later Field Marshal Viscount Montgomery of Alamein). It was as chief of staff to him, when he commanded the Eighth Army and 21st Army Group in World War II, that de Guingand became prominent.

Their paths crossed again when 'Freddie', as de Guingand was universally known, was at his regimental depot at York in 1922. Montgomery, on the staff of the 49th Territorial division, lived in the same officers' mess, and they struck up a friendship. Their paths then diverged; de Guingand, bored with regimental soldiering in England and keen to increase his income—he had expensive tastes: gambling, card-playing, and racing, as well as shooting and fishing—volunteered in 1926 to serve with the King's African Rifles in what was then Nyasaland, now Malawi. He stayed there for five years, acquiring a lifelong affection for Africa.

In 1932 he returned to his regiment as adjutant of its 1st battalion in Egypt, where Montgomery was commanding the 1st battalion of the Royal Warwickshire Regiment. On an important exercise Montgomery was made to act as brigade-commander, with de Guingand as his brigade-major. It was the first of several occasions on which, later in life, de Guingand was to claim that his cooler judgement saved Montgomery from the consequences of his own impetuousness. Montgomery was certainly impressed with his ability, and persuaded him to attempt the Staff College examination, rather than return to Nyasaland. De Guingand had left it late; but, in 1934, when he was in India, pressure from Montgomery obtained a nomination for him to the Staff College at Camberley. On graduation in 1936 he was appointed brigade-major to the Small Arms School at Netheravon, and was still there in June 1939 when he was posted as military assistant to the secretary of state for war, Leslie (later Lord) Hore-Belisha. This appointment gave him an insight both into the conduct of military affairs at the highest level and into its political aspects. His judgement in these matters was to prove sounder than Montgomery's.

When Hore-Belisha was dismissed in January 1940, de Guingand, at his own request, left also, being posted as an instructor, now in the rank of lieutenant-colonel, to the newly formed Middle East Staff College at Haifa, moving on from there at the end of the year to become the army member of the joint planning staff in Cairo. He became highly critical of his C-in-C, accusing Sir A. P. (later Earl) Wavell of taking an over optimistic view of the prospects of British intervention in Greece in May 1941.

He therefore welcomed Wavell's supersession by Sir Claude Auchinleck, whom he warmly admired. The admiration was mutual, Auchinleck appointing him as the director of military intelligence in February 1942, and subsequently, when he had taken direct command of the Eighth Army from General (Sir) Neil Ritchie and halted Rommel on the Alamein line in July of that year, as brigadier general staff at Eighth Army headquarters. De Guingand felt that his experience had qualified him for neither of these appointments. But his clarity and speed of mind, his sense of the possible, his ability to analyse a problem and draw together the different characters at work on it, made him the perfect staff officer.

It was therefore a fortunate chance which brought de Guingand at 7.30 a.m. on 13 August 1942 to the point near Alexandria where the road from

Cairo joined the coastal road which led to El Alamein and eventually Tunis. There he met the newly arrived Montgomery. De Guingand expressed his disquiet at the general malaise of the Eighth Army. This was music to Monty's ears, and the dramatic results have been fully recorded. Montgomery announced that de Guingand was to be accepted as his chief of staff with full authority over all branches, logistic as well as operational. It was therefore something of a shock to be warned by his master a few days later that he had asked the War Office to replace him by Brigadier (Sir) Frank Simpson, his principal staff officer in a succession of his commands. Fortunately for both de Guingand and Montgomery, Sir Alan Brooke (later Viscount Alanbrooke) refused; 'Freddie' stayed with 'Monty' until the war's end.

But then the intimate relationship, which had been established and which lasted until VE-Day, began to fall apart on the issue of where the credit lay for the decisions on which Montgomery's claim to fame rested. De Guingand never ceased to express the highest admiration for Montgomery, while acknowledging that he had defects of judgement and character which led him into error from time to time. In later years de Guingand claimed credit for the important change of plan in the later stages of the Battle of El Alamein, which led to the final breakthrough: for the change of plan at Mareth to switch the main effort far out to the left and for devising, with (Sir) Harry Broadhurst, the exceptional air support for it: for recognizing that the initial plans for the invasion both of Sicily and Normandy were unsound, and recommending the changes on which Montgomery insisted: all of these decisions Montgomery made much of as being his own. While fully supporting Montgomery against the criticisms levelled at him by Sir Arthur (later Lord) Tedder and others over the Normandy campaign, he never concealed his disagreement with his chief in the protracted argument with Eisenhower over the subsequent strategy and the need for an overall land force commander. De Guingand admitted failing to see the importance of an early clearance of the Scheldt estuary in order to open Antwerp as the Allies' main supply port, but took no responsibility for Arnhem, as he was away sick at the time.

Sickness, in the form of stomach trouble, which long after the war was diagnosed as due to a gallstone, removed de Guingand from the scene at several crucial periods, the first being after El Alamein. If the doctors then had had their way, his period as chief of staff to Montgomery would have been short; but Montgomery overruled them, and de Guingand used the opportunity to marry (in 1942) Arlie Roebuck Stewart, the beautiful Australian widow of a brother officer, Major H. D. Stewart, and daughter of Charles Woodhead, director of companies, of Brisbane. There was one daughter of the marriage, which was dissolved in 1957.

The disagreement between Montgomery and Eisenhower festered throughout the last winter of the war, and came to a head as a result of the former's tactless briefing of the press during the Ardennes campaign. His remarks were taken as an insult to the American generals, Bradley and Patton, and Eisenhower had drafted a signal to General Marshall protesting that he could stand it no longer. Fortunately his chief of staff, Bedell Smith, was on excellent terms with de Guingand who, in very hazardous weather, flew to see Eisenhower and flew back to persuade Montgomery to dispatch an apologetic signal. Eisenhower tore up his draft. De Guingand believed that he had saved his master from dismissal, and resented Montgomery's pretence in his memoirs that he had himself taken the initiative to send de Guingand to see Eisenhower.

He never forgave his chief for that and three other actions. The first was the brusque refusal to let de Guingand be present at the formal surrender of the Germans on Lüneburg Heath: the second, the failure to give him any part in the victory parade; and the final blow, the abandonment of his pledge to make de Guingand vice-chief of the imperial general staff, when he became the chief. The last blow was especially hard, not only because Simpson received the post, but because it was delivered in an offhand manner, and de Guingand, against medical advice and his own wishes, had taken up the post of director of military intelligence at the War Office in 1945 to prepare himself for it. He never knew that it was Alanbrooke who had insisted that Montgomery could not import his favourites from 21st Army Group into all the important posts in the War Office. He became major-general and left the army in 1946.

This bitter blow was almost certainly a blessing in disguise, since it forced him to turn his hand to business, at which, through the influence of friends and his own natural ability, he was successful, gaining an income which allowed him to indulge in his favourite activities, as bon viveur, gambler, and sportsman. His first venture was in Southern Rhodesia at the end of 1946 and he moved later to Johannesburg, becoming deputy chairman of Tube Investments Ltd. He left in 1960 to join the tobacco firm of Rothmans, as chairman of their subsidiary group in Britain. His first book, *Operation Victory*, published in 1947, was one of the first authoritative accounts of the war and ran into seven editions in hardback and three impressions in paperback. His other publications, *African Assignment* (1953), *Generals at War* (1964), and *From Brass Hat to Bowler Hat* (1979), were not of the same standard.

In addition to his clear and agile mind and his grasp of detail, one of his principal gifts was his ability to bring people of different views and interests together. He himself had an open mind and by nature was inclined to welcome strangers. All who worked with him regarded him with admiration and affection in equal proportions. He was the perfect foil to Montgomery. His imaginative and widely ranging mind, fertile with ideas, was subjected to his master's passion for simplification and concentration on one fundamental issue. He was to Montgomery what Berthier was to Napoleon, and perhaps more.

He was appointed OBE in 1942, CBE in 1943, KBE in 1944; CB in 1943, and to the DSO in 1942. He died in Cannes 29 June 1979.

[*The Times*, 19 November 1979; private information; personal knowledge.]

MICHAEL CARVER

published 1986

DENNISTON Alexander Guthrie (Alastair)

(1881–1961)

Public servant (intelligence), was born 1 December 1881 at Greenock, the eldest child of James Denniston, a medical practitioner, and his wife, Agnes Guthrie. He was educated at Bowdon College, Cheshire, and at the universities of Bonn and Paris.

From 1906 to 1909 Denniston taught at Merchiston Castle School. He then went to teach foreign languages at Osborne, the pre-Dartmouth naval college. A considerable athlete, he played hockey for Scotland in the pre-war Olympic Games. When war broke out in 1914, as one of the few men in the service of the Admiralty who were fluent in German, he played a leading part in the hasty establishment of Room 40 OB. Taking its name from the office in which it operated (Room 40, Old Buildings, Admiralty), this organization intercepted, decrypted, and interpreted, on behalf of the naval staff, German and other enemy wireless and cable communications. For its wartime exploits—and most of all, perhaps, for its success in decrypting the notorious Zimmermann telegram—Room 40 OB subsequently became internationally known. The fame did not extend to Denniston, nor (though he was at the centre of the cryptanalytical process) did he contribute to the publicity on which it rested: he was by nature reticent, and in 1919 he had been selected to lead the country's peacetime cryptanalytical effort as head of the Government Code and Cypher School (GC and CS).

In this capacity he served from 1919 to February 1942. He supervised the formation of GC and CS as a small interdepartmental organization of twenty-five people recruited from Room 40 OB and its equivalent section in the War Office. It included defectors from Russia, linguists, and talented amateurs of all kinds. Denniston, appointed CBE in 1933, presided over its slow expansion during the inter-war years—a period in which it had to cope with the continuously increasing sophistication of cipher security and a decline in wireless communications, as well as against a shortage of funds, but nevertheless succeeded in the important task of preserving a continuity of expertise and experience—and also over its rapid expansion and transfer to Bletchley Park on the outbreak of World War II in 1939. In the first half of 1940 he had the satisfaction of knowing that, reinforced by wartime staff which he had recruited (many having served with him in Room 40 OB), and assisted by the change to wartime conditions, it was beginning to solve the problem which had most stubbornly defied all its efforts, the problem posed by the adoption by Germany since the late 1920s, for the secret communications of the armed forces, the railways, the secret service, the police, and other government organizations, of the Enigma cipher machine.

GC and CS achieved virtually complete mastery of the Enigma machine in the second half of 1941, reading from then till the end of the war most of the many ciphers based on it. In the course of doing so, it increased its staff further to some 5,000, it encountered new administrative requirements, and to an ever greater extent it came to rely for its operation on specialized apparatus and machinery. Although Denniston recognized that these developments called for a major reorganization, he was not himself the man to carry it out: he had always been a reluctant administrator, preferring to concentrate on technical matters. The reorganization adopted in February 1942 divided GC and CS into a military, and a civil, and much smaller, wing. As head of the military division Denniston was succeeded by Commander (Sir) Edward W. Travis; he himself, having been appointed CMG in 1941, remained the head of the civil division, moving to London (to Madame Riché, couturier des dames in Berkeley St.) where, on seven floors, he and his team worked on intercepts dealing with German diplomatic and Abwehr activity. The department worked eighteen hours a day, seven days a week, and achieved many successes. Although Denniston was bitterly disappointed at what had occurred, he headed the Berkeley St. section most effectively. He retired in 1945 and thereafter taught French and Latin at a Leatherhead preparatory school.

Throughout his long period of office as head of an undivided GC and CS, directly responsible to the chief of the Secret Service, Denniston brought unusual distinction and expertise, as well as devotion, to his work. If he had little liking for questions of administration, he had even less for the ways of bureaucracy and the demands of hierarchy. By his willingness to delegate, his trust in subordinates, his informality and his charm he set his stamp on the character of the place, particularly in the early war years in Bletchley Park. More than any other man, he helped it to maintain both the creative atmosphere which underlay its great contribution to British intelligence during World War II, and the complete security which was a no less important precondition of its achievement.

In 1917 Denniston married Dorothy Mary, who worked at the time with him in Room 40 OB. She was the daughter of Arthur Gilliat, a business man; they had one son and one daughter. Their son, Robin, made his career in publishing, and became the academic publisher at the Oxford University Press. Alastair Denniston was a small man, with a strong, craggy-featured face—indeed, he was known to his colleagues as 'the little man'. With his athletic figure, he was always very neatly turned out. Denniston died at Lymington Hospital 1 January 1961.

[F. H. Hinsley, with others, *British Intelligence in the Second World War*, vol. i, 1979 (official history); Patrick Seale and Maureen McConville, *Philby: The Long Road to Moscow*, 1973.]

F. H. HINSLEY

published 1981

DE WET Christiaan Rudolph

(1854–1922)

Boer general and politician, was born at Leeuwkop, Smithfield district, in the former Orange Free State republic 7 October 1854. He was the sixth son of Jacobus Ignatius De Wet, of De Wetsdorp, by his wife, Aletta Susanna Margaretha, daughter of Gert Cornelis Strijdom. Of his early years little is known save that he was privately educated and lived the roving life common to the nomad Boers of the period. During the Transvaal War of 1880–1881 De Wet served with the republican forces, taking part in the various engagements which culminated in the British disaster on Majuba Hill (27 February 1881). After the retrocession of the Transvaal he remained in that country farming for some years, in the course of which he was elected (1885) to represent Lydenburg in the republican Volksraad. But ordered routine did not suit him. He resigned his seat and took to his old life once more, ultimately returning to the Free State.

In 1889 De Wet achieved some local notoriety by collecting an armed force and riding with it to Bloemfontein, the seat of government, to protest against the building of a railway line from the coast, for he and his followers looked upon this as a dangerous innovation calculated to throw the country open to foreign invasion. His vigorous political methods were so much in keeping with the times that, in consequence of his exploit, he became a member of the Free State Volksraad; but after an unsuccessful attempt to prohibit the use of mail-coaches and other vehicles on Sunday, he left law-making to others and although he remained a member of the Raad until 1898 he returned to his former roving.

On the outbreak of the South African War in October 1899 De Wet was called up for service as an ordinary burgher and sent to the Natal frontier, where he participated in various preliminary encounters with the British troops. Then came his great chance in life. A British force had marched out of Ladysmith at night, intending to strike at the rear of the Boer army, but plans miscarried and daylight (30 October) found the troops isolated on the flat-topped summit of Nicholson's Nek. Here De Wet attacked them with a few hundred men whom he had hurriedly collected, and so determined was the assault that he captured the whole force, taking over a thousand prisoners and scoring the first important success of the campaign. This exploit was his making. There was a dearth of leaders among the Boers, and he was immediately promoted to the rank of general and sent to the western borders of the Free State, where British troops were massing for the relief of Kimberley.

General Piet Cronje was in supreme command of this front, and De Wet made strenuous but unsuccessful efforts to prevent him from committing the series of blunders that led to his capture by Lord Roberts at Paardeberg on 27 February 1900. De Wet had further distinguished himself by his capture of Roberts's convoy at Waterval on 13 February, so that it is not surprising that when he escaped from the *débâcle* of Paardeberg he found himself appointed commander-in-chief of the Free State forces. His post was a thorny one. The effects of Cronje's surrender, coinciding as it did with the Boer defeats in Natal, proved disastrous to the republican cause. The commandos were melting away, and on every hand were discouragement and wholesale desertions.

De Wet, however, rose superior to these misfortunes. Ably seconded by Martinus Steyn, president of the Orange Free State, a man as indomitable as himself, he set to work to rally his demoralized army. On 31 March he ambushed Colonel R. G. Broadwood's mounted brigade at Sanna's Post, outside Bloemfontein, and on 4 April defeated a British detachment at Reddersburg. As the tide of war rolled northwards to the Transvaal, he remained in the rear of the invading British forces and by immense efforts succeeded in re-establishing the fighting spirit of his men. Realizing that the Boers could no longer resist in the open field, he now decided, in conjunction with the Boer leaders in the Transvaal, to resort to guerrilla tactics. Of this form of warfare he became one of the greatest exponents in modern times. With a few thousand hard-bitten followers he kept the field for the next two years against tremendous odds, to the despair and admiration of his opponents. No detailed account can be given here of his innumerable exploits, his hairbreadth escapes, and his many successes and failures. Suffice it to say that when the long drawn-out contest came at last to an end in June 1902, De Wet was still holding his own. By that time he had won an international reputation for his daring and courage, a reputation generously endorsed by his former enemies.

After the war De Wet, who had taken part in the peace negotiations, visited Europe with the other Boer generals. On the granting of responsible government to South Africa, he entered the political arena. He was elected a member of the first parliament of the Orange River Colony (1907) and appointed minister of agriculture. He was a delegate to the Union Convention of 1908–1909 and a member of the Union Defence council under General Louis Botha.

For a time there was peace and material progress in South Africa; but in 1911 there sprang up a bitter feud between the followers of General Botha on the one side and those of General J. B. M. Hertzog on the other. De Wet flung himself into the fray with characteristic energy on the side of Hertzog. He became a strong supporter of a movement that was set on foot which aimed at secession from the British Empire and the re-establishment of the republics of the Orange Free State and Transvaal.

The outbreak of the European War in August 1914 found De Wet in the midst of this agitation, and when, immediately afterwards, Botha announced his intention of invading German South-West African territory with South African troops, De Wet expressed great hostility to the expedition. On 15 September there followed the accidental shooting of General J. H. De la Rey by the police during the operation of rounding up a gang of desperadoes which had been terrorizing the suburbs of Johannesburg. This event profoundly influenced De Wet's subsequent conduct. General De la Rey and he had both played a great part during the Boer War, and they were close personal friends. He mistakenly assumed that De la Rey had been killed by order of Botha's government, and this goaded him into action.

In conjunction with General C. F. Beyers, the leader of the Transvaal malcontents, De Wet planned an armed revolt. On 24 October Beyers raised the standard of rebellion in the north, and two days later De Wet followed suit in the Free State. Both men speedily collected thousands of adherents, and the insurrection assumed formidable proportions. Botha, however, took prompt action against his former companions-in-arms. Summoning his supporters, he took the field in person, and within a week he fell on Beyers and signally defeated him (27 October). Then he turned upon De Wet. He found him at Mushroom valley in the central Free State at the head of 6,000 men, and in a pitched battle drove him in headlong rout (12 November). De Wet now attempted to resort to the old guerrilla tactics that had served him so well in former days, but he had met his master. Botha understood the art of mobile warfare even better than De Wet himself, and, in addition, the era of the motor-car had set in, which made it impossible for the mounted commandos of the Boers to play hide-and-seek across the veld as they had done in the past. Botha was the first to demonstrate this. By the skilful use of motor detachments he harried and hustled the rebels, giving them and their horses no rest. So hot was the pursuit that within ten days De Wet was a mere fugitive fleeing westward with less than a dozen men for the sanctuary of the Kalahari desert, whence he hoped to escape into German territory. But Botha's men were hot on his trail, and on 2 December the old *condottiere* was run to earth and captured on the farm Waterberg in the Kuruman district. A week before, Beyers had met his death while trying to cross the Vaal river, and with both its leaders accounted for the rebellion was soon stamped out.

De Wet was arraigned before a special tribunal at Bloemfontein on 9 June 1915, and tried for high treason. On 21 June he was found guilty on eight of the ten counts against him, and sentenced to six years' imprisonment and a fine of £2,000. In the following December, however, he was released on parole by Botha and allowed to return to his farm in the Free State. Here he lived quietly until his death which took place on the farm Klipfontein, district De Wetsdorp, 3 February 1922. He was buried at the Women's monument at Bloemfontein beside his old leader President Steyn.

De Wet married in 1873 Cornelia Margaretta, daughter of Isaak Johannes Christian Kruger, of Bloemfontein. They had five sons and one daughter. He wrote an account of his campaigns of 1899–1902 which appeared in an English version as *Three Years' War* (1902).

A cartoon of De Wet appeared in *Vanity Fair* 31 July 1902.

['The Times' History of the War in South Africa, 1900–1909; Sir Arthur Conan Doyle, The Great Boer War, 1900; Sir J. F. Maurice and M. H. Grant, (Official) History of the War in South Africa, 1899–1902, 1906–1910; F. H. E. Cunliffe, History of the Boer War, 2 vols., 1901–1904; Louis Creswicke, South Africa and the Transvaal War, 6 vols., 1900–1902.]

D. Reitz

published 1937

(1881–1944)

Sir

Field-marshal, only son and second child of John Dill, by his wife, Jane, daughter of George Greer, of Woodville, near Lurgan, county Armagh, was born 25 December 1881 at Lurgan, where his father was then manager of the local branch of the Ulster Bank. He was educated at Cheltenham College and the Royal Military College, Sandhurst. Having been gazetted to the Leinster Regiment, he left England in May 1901 to join its 1st battalion, then on active service in South Africa. The war had then only a year to run. Dill served in the field until the conclusion of peace.

In 1907 Dill married Ada Maud, daughter of Colonel William Albert Le Mottée, late of the 18th Regiment of Foot. He was promoted to the rank of captain in 1911, and was a student at the Staff College, Camberley, at the outbreak of war with Germany in August 1914. At this early stage of his career several of those who knew him well marked him out as destined for a distinguished future—one prophesied in that year that he would eventually become chief of the imperial general staff. He was not what is commonly called an intellectual, but his talent for military affairs, sense of duty, and strength of mind were strongly marked. They were combined with a purity of character which made it impossible to conceive that he would ever be involved in or even contemplate an unworthy action. Good looks and personal charm contributed to his prospects.

In October 1914 Dill was appointed brigade-major of the 25th brigade (8th division), with which he went to France in the following month. He was present at the battles of Neuve Chapelle and Aubers Ridge and the action of Bois Grenier. In 1916 he was appointed G.S.O.2 to the Canadian Corps and promoted to the rank of major. Early in 1917 he became G.S.O.1 to the 37th division, which was heavily engaged that Easter at Arras and in the summer at Ypres. It was already apparent that he was a staff officer of exceptional ability and possessed a wide vision. These qualities were recognized when he was transferred to G.H.Q. as G.S.O.1 in the operations branch. In March 1918, the month of the first great German offensive, he was appointed chief of that branch, with the temporary rank of brigadier-general. In the course of the war he was wounded and awarded the D.S.O. (1915), the C.M.G. (1918), as well as French and Belgian decorations, and was eight times mentioned in dispatches. His reputation in the army was assured. He was, it is believed, the only officer of the British Army who held a post as high as that which he reached in the war of 1914–18 and also held the highest military appointments almost to the end of that of 1939–45.

In 1919 Dill's first post-war appointment was as chief assistant to the commandant of the Staff College, on its reopening. Next year he was promoted colonel. In 1922, after a brief period on half-pay, he took over command of the Welsh Border brigade, Territorial Army. In November 1923 he was transferred to the command of the 2nd, a regular brigade, at Aldershot. His training methods were thorough and effective, so that the esteem in which he was held continued to grow. Late in 1926 he was appointed army instructor—the first commandant being a naval officer, Sir Herbert Richmond—at the new Imperial Defence College. In 1929 he went to India as chief general staff officer to the Western Command, where he remained two years. He was given accelerated promotion to the rank of major-general (1930), and in January 1931 became commandant of the Staff College, where he was thus stationed for the third time. As a consequence he acquired an almost unexampled knowledge of the officers of the army destined to reach high command or to hold senior staff appointments. He proved a successful and popular commandant, practical, painstaking, and inspiring. In January 1934 he became director of military operations and intelligence at the War Office, again adding to his reputation. He remained at the War Office until 1936, in which year he was promoted lieutenant-general and took part in the important Anglo-French staff talks in April.

That September Dill was sent to the Middle East in command of the forces in Palestine and Trans-Jordan. An Arab campaign of violence was then in progress, and to combat it the decision had been taken to end the system of Royal Air Force control and place an army officer in command. Dill acted with a combination of determination and patience, but he was not allowed to remain long enough in the country to bring about the restoration of law and order. A year later, in October 1937, he was transferred to the Aldershot Command. Aldershot was at that time on the down-grade as a training-centre and about to yield pride of place to the Southern Command, with its more extensive facilities on Salisbury Plain, but when Dill arrived there it was still the principal command in the United Kingdom. His immediate predecessors had been farther advanced in seniority than he, who had been promoted to the rank of lieutenant-general only the year before. He returned to the task of training troops enriched with experience and observation. Always carefully watching the character and talents of subordinates, he now noted a number who subsequently distinguished themselves, the senior of whom was the commander of the 3rd division, Major-General Henry Maitland (subsequently

Lord) Wilson, a man a few months older than himself, to whom promotion had come more slowly.

Hitherto Dill had climbed the ladder steadily and without a check, and all his ambitions had been fulfilled. Now, however, he suffered a set-back. He had looked forward with every justification to becoming the next chief of the imperial general staff, an appointment which might be expected to involve the reversion of the command of the expeditionary force, if one should be sent to the continent in the event of war. However, when Leslie (later Lord) Hore-Belisha, the secretary of state for war, decided to rejuvenate the general staff at the War Office, his choice for chief of the imperial general staff fell upon Major-General Lord Gort, Dill's junior in seniority and in rank. When war broke out in 1939 and Gort was in fact appointed to command the Expeditionary Force, Sir Edmund (subsequently Lord) Ironside was chosen as his successor. Dill was appointed to command the I Corps, which was transported to France with all possible speed. There can be no doubt that he experienced deep disappointment, although he took pains to conceal it.

Dill's corps was stationed on the frontier of Belgium, then neutral, and its commander had no major tasks other than those of supervising its training and improving the skeleton frontier defences. In training he was in his element. The troops were kept fully occupied lest the period of waiting, out of contact with the enemy, should exercise an adverse moral effect. On 1 October Dill was promoted to the rank of general, with seniority from December 1937. He was not destined to see active service in command in this war. It was decided to create a new appointment at the War Office, that of vice-chief of the imperial general staff, to relieve the chief of some of his burdens. Dill came back to England to assume this post in April 1940, thus missing the great German offensive, although his visits across the Channel at the height of the crisis between 20 and 25 May served the Government well by affording it a clearer view of the desperate situation. On 27 May he succeeded General Ironside as chief of the imperial general staff.

It was an ideal appointment, since the holder held the confidence of the army as a whole and was well and favourably known to the chiefs of the sister Services. The legacy was, however, a sorry one. The fall of France appeared to have brought about the collapse of the whole military structure, in view of the German possession of the west coast of Europe from Trondheim to Bayonne, the strengthening of Axis prospects in the Middle East, and the terrible strategic effects of the footing which Japan speedily demanded and obtained in French Indo-China. There was little enough that Dill could effect positively at this period. More often than not, indeed, he felt himself compelled to advocate restraint and even inaction rather than accept risks which he considered might involve ruin. To throw cold water upon schemes for the offensive is never a welcome task for a soldier in a position such as Dill's, and when the head of the Government is at once as ardent, courageous, inventive, impetuous, and impatient of warning as was (Sir) Winston Churchill, the role may become very difficult and ungrateful. This happened in Dill's case, although his taste for the offensive was shown by his support of the Commandos, if indeed they did not originate with him.

One difference with the prime minister and minister of defence followed another. Churchill gradually came to believe that Dill was over-cautious, obstructive, and unimaginative. Dill became haunted by anxiety lest the nation should be rushed into undertakings which in his view would not only fail in themselves but which would at best heavily discount future prospects (by using up resources he believed ought to be husbanded for more favourable occasions), and which at worst would bring about irretrievable disaster. In matters of high strategy the main weight fell upon him. His colleagues on the chiefs of staff committee were able heads of their own Services, but tended to confine themselves to problems which affected these. Under this strain, increased by intolerably long hours of work and conferences which often lasted into the small hours of the day, Dill's health weakened. The long illness of his wife depressed him. She died in 1940, leaving a son, an officer in the Royal Artillery.

Between February and April 1941, Dill visited the eastern Mediterranean. Affairs in that quarter had become complex. The winter offensive had resulted in brilliant successes against the Italians, a great part of whose forces in North Africa had been destroyed. Meanwhile the Greeks also had inflicted heavy defeat on the Italians, who had wantonly attacked them at the end of October 1940. Germany at first regarded this conflict as a minor episode, but early in 1941 the likelihood of her intervention increased. It was hoped, although with little confidence, that Yugoslavia and Turkey would intervene in favour of Greece. Britain had already assisted Greece against the Italians, chiefly in the air. Now it had to be decided whether British land forces should be sent to the Greek mainland.

The general staff, including Dill, had opposed this course, and he had held that forces sent to Greece would be lost. It was argued that such strength as could be assembled, mostly from the Middle East, would not provide equality with the Germans if they attacked, and that withdrawal of forces from Cyrenaica would ruin the prospects of success there. If all available resources were employed in the task it seemed possible that the North African coast up to the Tunisian frontier might be occupied, which would be of incalculable benefit. Ironically enough, the Greeks at first advocated this course as the correct British strategy, whereas they considered that the landing of small British forces in Greece would bring the Germans down upon that country in overwhelming force. The earlier argument in favour of reinforcing Greece was mainly moral, but it may fairly be said that in the end it was decided to do so on military considerations even though these may have been mistaken. Dill was much occupied in negotiations with the Turks and Yugoslavs—he visited both Ankara and Belgrade—but the Greek problem also engaged him. He changed his mind in favour of the landing of British troops in Greece, but was bitterly disappointed in the extent and efficacy of aid from allies on the spot. The affair ended in a disaster, on the mainland mercifully mitigated by courage and good fortune, and in a more complete disaster in Crete. Another consequence was the heavy defeat of the depleted British forces in North Africa.

In October 1941 Dill married again. His second wife was Nancy, daughter of Henry Charrington, brewer, of London, and widow of Brigadier Dennis Walter Furlong. Dill became manifestly a happier man, but he did not recover his full powers. Churchill therefore decided to make a change. On 18 November it was announced that, on attaining the age of sixty on Christmas Day, Dill would relinquish his appointment as chief of the imperial general staff and would be succeeded by Sir Alan Francis Brooke (subsequently Viscount Alanbrooke). It was also stated that the King had conferred the rank of field-marshal upon Dill and approved of his appointment as governor-designate of Bombay. Dill was saddened by the prospect of leaving the army, but it is probable that he could not in any case have continued at his post much longer.

Feeling that his influence must necessarily be weakened during the next five weeks, he prevailed upon General Brooke to assume the heavy responsibilities at the War Office as quickly as possible and did not continue his work there until the nominal end of his appointment. After the entry of Japan into the war he accompanied the prime minister to the United States, and there he stayed. The decision was taken to set up in Washington a body of representatives of the British chiefs of staff who would form with the American counterpart a joint staff. Dill was the senior member of this body and in a special position, since under him there was a British representative of the Army as well as representatives of the Royal Navy and Royal Air Force. He was thus concerned mainly with matters of high moment and was commonly called in only when difficulties in the way of agreement about plans or about the performance of those upon which agreement had been reached threatened to become insuperable. Freed of the burden of unending office work at high pressure, he appeared to make a great improvement in health. In May 1942 the tenure of the office of the governor of Bombay was extended for six months and at the end of the year a new governor was appointed, with the announcement that Dill's post in the United States was no longer to be considered as temporary.

In January 1943 he attended the Casablanca conference, where his tact and persuasiveness proved invaluable in reconciling conflicting opinions, and afterwards he flew to India and China to confer with Sir Archibald (later Earl) Wavell and General Chiang Kai-shek. That year he did a great deal more travelling, visiting Brazil, returning in July to England, attending the Quebec conference in August, visiting Canada again in October, and attending the Teheran conference at the end of November.

In the United States Dill won the trust and even the affection of the President and became the personal friend of the chief of staff of the army and the commander-in-chief of the fleet, General Marshall and Admiral King. His prestige became extraordinarily high. Few Britons have established themselves more firmly in the confidence of the official and military world of the United States, although he was little known to the public, at least outside Washington. However, in 1944 he received the exceptional honour of the Howland memorial prize from Yale University and an honorary doctorate of laws from the College of William and Mary at Williamsburg. He also received honorary degrees from Princeton and Toronto. Late in 1944 his health again broke down, and on 4 November he died in hospital in Washington. He was buried in Arlington cemetery.

The supreme American honour accorded to him was posthumous, that of the D.S.M., conferred by President Roosevelt, who spoke of him as 'the most important figure in the remarkable accord which has been developed in the combined operations of our two countries.' If his appointment as chief of the imperial general staff had ended unhappily, that as senior British representative on the combined chiefs of staff committee in Washington had been completely successful and fulfilled his highest promise. From his own country, apart from the field-marshal's baton, the only honour bestowed on him took the form of promotion in the Order of the Bath. He had been appointed C.B. in 1928 and promoted to K.C.B. in 1937; in 1942 he was advanced to G.C.B. The Leinster Regiment having been disbanded, he became colonel of the East Lancashire Regiment in 1932 and colonel commandant of the Parachute Regiment, Army Air Corps, in 1942.

Dill was not a genius, but he will rank as one of the most capable of a generation of able soldiers. He was thorough in mental processes and in action. Mental and physical fatigue were the only weaknesses he showed as chief of the imperial general staff. Although even-tempered, he could not contrive to the same extent as his successor strong defences against assaults on his energy and patience. In personality he was most attractive, kindly and considerate, with a pleasant sense of humour. All who came in contact with him were left with the impression of a charming as well as of a high-minded man.

A portrait painted in Washington by the American artist Edward Murray is on long loan from Dill's son to Cheltenham College. There is a copy in the Imperial War Museum in London. A statue has been erected to his memory in Washington.

[L. F. Ellis, (Official) *History of the Second World War. France and Flanders, 1939–40*, 1953; I. S. O. Playfair and others, (Official) *History of the Second World War. The Mediterranean and Middle East*, vols. i and ii, 1954–6; official announcements; private information; personal knowledge.]

Cyril Falls

[Sir Arthur Bryant, *The Turn of the Tide, 1939–1943; a study based on the diaries and autobiographical notes of Field Marshal the Viscount Alanbrooke*, 1957; Sir John Kennedy, *The Business of War*, edited by Bernard Fergusson, 1957.]
published 1959

DOUGLAS William Sholto

(1893–1969)

Baron Douglas of Kirtleside

Marshal of the Royal Air Force, was born in Oxford 23 December 1893, the second son of the Revd Robert Langton Douglas, secretary of the Church of England Temperance Society, and his first wife, Margaret Jane, daughter of Percival Cannon, printer. Descended from the Red and Black Douglases of ancient Scottish history, his father was a man of great intelligence and diverse interests, who relinquished his orders and later became director of the National Gallery of Ireland. Douglas's domestic background changed with bewildering speed from that of the Anglican Church to the home base of a widely travelling art critic and historian, and finally, when his parents were divorced shortly after his seventh birthday, to a maternal establishment in London where he lived with his mother and two younger brothers in considerably straitened circumstances. His father, fast acquiring a new family, continued to increase his accomplishments and reputation, ending his life as an American citizen, a Roman Catholic, and an acknowledged authority on the history of Italian art.

Despite the commitments of a second and later a third family, his father managed to see that Douglas had a good education, and after due preparation at local schools he went to Tonbridge, then in 1913 to Lincoln

College, Oxford, where he won a classical scholarship and sang in the Bach Choir. Before he could take a degree, or show any inclination for a career, all choice was brutally resolved by the outbreak of war. He immediately joined the Royal Field Artillery, and within a few months he was in France. He found land warfare dull, and with the impulsive energy which was to mark him throughout his life he responded to a call for volunteers to join the Royal Flying Corps. By the beginning of 1915 he was training as an observer, and within a few days he was flying reconnaissance patrols. The back seat of an aeroplane still did not satisfy him, and he quickly won a pilot's course. After training he was sent to No. 8 Squadron on the western front, where he rapidly proved himself an aggressive and intelligent airman. He was heavily engaged throughout the fierce fighting of 1915. In 1916 he returned to England, then spent much of the year in Scotland forming and training 43 Squadron; he so proved his quality that in 1917 he led it back to France as commander. He was again involved in continual and bitter air combat, and his squadron suffered heavy losses at the hands of the Richthofen Staffel. His period of command ended when a take-off crash dispatched him to hospital in England.

His naturally assertive nature turned him away from reconnaissance and bombing roles to the fighter or scout type of unit which the air war had then developed, and he was happy to gain command of No. 84 Squadron, flying SE5s, and to lead it into further heavy fighting in France. He finally completed four tours of operations on the western front, and he was credited with six victories in combat. Among those he met in battle was the German fighter pilot Hermann Goering, whose death warrant he was to sign thirty years later. By the end of the war Douglas was a very seasoned and hardened major in the fighter arm of the Royal Flying Corps, awarded the MC (1916) and the DFC (1919), and three times mentioned in dispatches. In circumstances where a pilot's life was measured in days he had lasted nearly four years, and he was still fighting in the last week of the war. Despite the offer of a permanent commission, the tremendous re-action of the war's end separated him from the Service, and caused him to reject the possibility of returning to Oxford for his degree. Handley-Page Aircraft Company was forming an air transport section, and wanted pilots. Douglas applied for a civil commercial pilot's licence and was issued with No. 4, landing a job with Handley-Page, and became one of the first of the airline captains, working the British and cross-Channel services. But post-war malaise still gripped him. He was discontented with the routine of civil flying. He thought of following in his brilliant if erratic father's footsteps as an art critic, but the pull of aviation was too strong. Finally, after a chance meeting with Sir Hugh (later Viscount) Trenchard, he rejoined the air force, in 1920, with a permanent commission in the rank of squadron-leader. He was now launched upon his career. Universally known as 'Sholto', he was a burly man of middle height, giving an impression of great strength and power, occasionally approaching that of a tiger about to pounce. He claimed to be acutely shy with people, but concealed it so well as to instil fear into nervous subordinates, while his manner sometimes came dangerously close to pomposity.

From 1920 until 1936 he served in flying schools, staff appointments, and the Imperial Defence College; with one foreign post, when he was senior RAF officer in the Sudan—and sang in the cathedral choir in Khartoum. He built up a solid reputation as a professional officer who looked and talked like one of the bulldog breed, but who proved on closer inspection to be disconcertingly intelligent without the drawback of over-sensitivity. By 1938 he was an air vice-marshal, once more on the Air Ministry staff. Chance, and particularly timing, play a great part in the military man's career. They served him well; he was the right man at the right place at the right time. He was given the new post of assistant (in 1940 deputy) chief of air staff, responsible for training and for specifying new equipment; in short for the future performance of a Service once more on the brink of war. In this capacity he was compelled to force some very unpalatable truths upon senior officers and politicians, a task from which he did not shrink. At the outbreak of war, which he greeted in a mood of 'sombre anger', he was striving to force the new aircraft types through the factories and into service, pushing the first developments of radar, and attempting to convince the army and navy of the importance of air operations to their own survival. He found some difficulty in keeping his energies solely focused on his own task. At his Air Ministry desk he had to endure the agonizing months of the Norwegian and French campaigns, and watch the RAF's growing power cut down again by its losses in those disasters, followed by the almost unbearable tension of the Battle of Britain. In this struggle he resisted, with indifferent success, an overpowering impulse to urge a change of tactics on Sir Hugh (later Lord) Dowding, commander-in-chief of Fighter Command. Dowding elected to meet the enemy as and when he could intercept them; Douglas favoured the assembly of a large defensive force in the air to do the maximum damage to the bombers, so that, even if allowed to drop their bombs first, enemy striking power would be steadily depleted. As the only fighter pilot among the senior officers of the air staff his views carried great weight, and when Dowding left Fighter Command in November 1940 he succeeded him, with the rank of air marshal, and a KCB (1941).

His immediate task was to fight the German night air offensive known to history as 'the blitz', with all its problems of radar detection and control. His second, which he tackled with particular relish, was to exploit the daylight victories of the Battle of Britain into an air offensive across the Channel, to engage and destroy the Luftwaffe, and to demonstrate British resistance to the rest of the world. At the same time he built Fighter Command from its dangerously weak condition in 1940 to the formidable strength it achieved two years later. When he was appointed commander-in-chief Middle East, at the end of 1942, by now an air chief marshal, the entry of Russia and the United States had transformed the war. He arrived in Cairo shortly after the battle of El Alamein, and was plunged at once into the wide diversity of operational and diplomatic problems which always distinguished that area. He took part in the Cairo conference on the future conduct of the war in November 1943. Among his greatest problems was the ill-fated Allied campaign in the Aegean sea, for which he carried a share of the responsibility, and which brought him into some conflict with Eisenhower and Sir Arthur (later Lord) Tedder at Supreme Allied Command Mediterranean, but before he left the Middle East the Axis forces in Africa had been eliminated, Sicily and Italy invaded, and Italy knocked out of the war. None the less it had been a difficult time, and it was with relief that he returned, at the beginning of 1944, to be commander-in-chief of Coastal Command.

His third major command appointment came at a time when the most desperate engagements of the Battle of the Atlantic had been fought, and the naval-air combinations of the Allies had won a large degree of control. The last danger with which he had to contend was the German use of the schnorkel submarine. Nominally under the direction of the Admiralty, Douglas was left in practice to work out his operations with his fellow naval commanders. He was able to extend and strengthen the Allied control of the seas by the application of all the new techniques and aircraft now available, culminating in the supremacy necessary to the Anglo-American invasion of France in June 1944. This provided the last great flurry of activity in the strike and reconnaissance squadrons of his command, and as the enemy was forced back into Germany he was able, for the first time in nearly four years, to feel some lightening of the weight of command responsibility. His great experience with other nations and Services was needed, however, in the difficult situation existing in defeated Germany, and in July 1945 he was appointed commander-in-chief British Air Forces of Occupation, under General Montgomery (later Viscount Montgomery of Alamein). Beginning with problems involving the re-patriation of nationals whose countries were now under Russian occupation he became increasingly involved, to his intense dismay, with the differences which heralded the cold war. He detested his job, hated the atmosphere of despair inherent in a ruined and defeated country, and determined to retire from the Service. But while in the process of doing so in January 1946, he was promoted GCB and marshal of the Royal Air Force, becoming one of the only two officers ever to reach that rank without being chief of air staff. At the same time he was nominated to succeed Montgomery as commander-in-chief British Forces in Germany and military governor of the British zone, and under pressure from the Cabinet, he accepted the appointment. The very aspect of command in Germany which he had most disliked was now intensified, for he was the British member of the four-power Allied Control Council, with all its difficulties and tensions. He was doubtful of the propriety of the Nuremberg trials, and to his distress found that he had to confirm sentences passed on the German leaders following their trials for war crimes. Although he dreaded the responsibility he was forced to resist attempts by the British Cabinet to judge the issue for him in London, and the strain of all these tensions culminated when he signed the document confirming the executions. This was but one of many such judgements, and he welcomed the end of his appointment, when it came in November 1947. He subsequently cited it as the unhappiest period of his life.

After his return to England he retired in 1948 from active duty, and was awarded a peerage. He was then able to declare, without the inhibitions normal to a serving officer, that his political views had always been those of a moderate socialist, and he took his seat in the House of Lords on the Labour benches. This alone made him a somewhat unusual member of the higher military hierarchy. In 1948 his wide experience in aviation brought him a directorship in the British Overseas Airways Corporation, and in 1949, not without some opposition from political anti-militarists, he was appointed chairman of British European Airways. With relish he proceeded to prove that he was no figurehead, by forceful and shrewd management of that company during the emergence of the jet airliner, and he continued to lead BEA, with outstanding success, until 1964. Once more he was doing work which he loved. When he left BEA in 1964 the jet revolution was complete, and it had grown into a large profit-making national airline. He became chairman of Horizon Travel Ltd. in the same year. During the last four years of his life he had to endure increasingly arduous ill health and he died in hospital in Northampton 29 October 1969. His great abilities, persistence, and capacity for sustained hard work had kept him intensively engaged until his seventieth year, and he had filled posts of the highest responsibility for twenty-three consecutive years. He commanded loyalty and affection in those who worked for him, and a guarded respect from his opponents. In 1941 he had been elected an honorary fellow of his college, in 1950 he was made an honorary companion of the Royal Aeronautical Society, and in 1956 he was president of the International Air Transport Association.

In 1919 Douglas married Mary Howard; the marriage was dissolved in 1932 and in 1933 he married Joan Leslie, daughter of Colonel Henry Cuthbert Denny. With the dissolution of this marriage, he married in 1955 Hazel, daughter of George Eric Maas Walker and widow of Captain W. E. R. Walker; they had one daughter.

There is a portrait of Douglas by Eric Kennington and another by Sir James Gunn, both in the Imperial War Museum. A drawing by H. A. Freeth is the property of the Ministry of Defence.

[Lord Douglas of Kirtleside, *Years of Combat*, 1963, and *Years of Command*, 1966; Air Historical Branch (RAF); private information; personal knowledge.]

PETER WYKEHAM

published 1981

DOWDING Hugh Caswall Tremenheere

(1882–1970)

First Baron Dowding

Air chief marshal, was born at Moffat, Dumfriesshire, 24 April 1882, the eldest in a family of three boys and one girl of Arthur John Caswall Dowding, a schoolmaster of Wiltshire stock, and his wife, Maud Caroline, daughter of Major-General Charles William Tremenheere, chief engineer in the Public Works Department in Bombay.

During his early schooldays at St. Ninian's, Moffat, he lived at home enjoying the combination of kindly parents who were also the respected headmaster and his wife. He entered Winchester, his father's old school, in 1895, where he spent four not entirely happy years. His lack of facility with the classics led him to join the army class, thence to choose an army career.

By way of the Royal Military Academy, Woolwich, he became a gunner in the Royal Garrison Artillery, following the advice of his family. His subaltern's life in Gibraltar, Ceylon, and Hong Kong was that of a typical young gunner officer. After transfer to a mountain battery in 1904, he spent six years in India, half the time with a native battery. He relished the strenuous, solitary, and often dangerous life on manœuvres in the Himalayan foothills. Subsequently (1912–13), two years at the Staff College, Camberley, coincided with his developing interest in aviation. In his own time he learned to fly at Brooklands, the flying school run by the firm of Vickers, and obtained his Royal Aero Club pilot's certificate No. 711 early in the morning of the same day as he passed out from Camberley, 20

Dowding

December 1913. He then took a three-month course at the Central Flying School at Upavon, where his flying instructor was (Sir) John Salmond and his assistant commandant H. M. (later Viscount) Trenchard. Dowding returned to the Garrison Artillery in the Isle of Wight as a Royal Flying Corps Reserve officer.

When war was declared in 1914 he was appointed commandant of the RFC Dover camp whence the squadrons left for France. Thereafter he served at home and in France with Nos. 7 and 6 Squadrons, both as observer and pilot and then as flight commander with No. 9 Squadron. He specialized in early experiments in wireless telegraphy. Appointed to command No. 16 Squadron at Merville in 1915, Dowding in many ways found it a testing time. His nickname from Camberley days of 'Stuffy' appeared to younger aircrew to suit his older, more withdrawn, and austere approach to flying duties. His general reputation was not advanced by a brush with Trenchard over a supply of propellers, although Dowding proved that he himself had the better technical knowledge. Promotion followed regularly until by 1917 he was a brigadier-general; however, another brush with Trenchard in 1916, when Dowding commanded the headquarters wing of HQ, Royal Flying Corps, probably denied him field command for the rest of the war.

Becoming, not without difficulty, a permanent officer in the newly created Royal Air Force in 1919, Dowding was group commander at Kenley and then chief of staff at Headquarters, Inland Area. His name became prominent as the organizer of the second and some subsequent Hendon pageants. A posting as chief staff officer to Air Headquarters, Iraq, in 1924 provided further opportunities for active flying. In 1926 he became director of training at the Air Ministry and achieved a much-needed rapport with Trenchard, who was now at the height of power as the chief of air staff. So far did Dowding gain Trenchard's confidence that he was sent in 1929 to Palestine to report on the need for Service reinforcements when an Arab rising seemed imminent. His balanced reports won favour with Trenchard.

After a brief spell in command of the Fighting Area on return from Palestine, Dowding joined the Air Council in 1930 as air member for supply and research. His period of office saw continuous revolutionary changes in the design and construction of aircraft. It saw the development of all-metal monoplanes like the Hurricane and Spitfire, early work on the Stirling and other heavy bombers, and the development of eight-gun armament and especially of radar. Dowding's practical bent, his insistence on experimentation and trials, and his imaginative grasp of aircrew requirements often led him into conflict with colleagues or other holders of received orthodox opinions. Although Dowding was willing to listen to his scientific advisers, it was clear that he formed his own opinions. His title changed to air member for research and development when in 1935 supply became another member's responsibility.

It was fitting that Dowding was appointed AOC-in-C of the new Fighter Command in 1936. The fifty-four-year-old widower moved to Stanmore where his sister Hilda was hostess for him. (Dowding had married in 1918 and his wife died suddenly in 1920.) For the next four years in Fighter Command he dedicated himself to preparing the air defences of the United Kingdom. The introduction of efficient land-line communications, operations rooms, improved VHF R/T, and above all the completion of the chain of radar stations round the east and south coasts were his concern. Together with these went the creation of new squadrons of Spitfires and Hurricanes. The announcement that Sir Cyril (later Lord) Newall was to be appointed chief of air staff in 1937 must have been a blow to any hopes Dowding may have had of achieving that office. He bore this just as stoically as he endured the five separate indications between August 1938 and August 1940 of Air Ministry intention to terminate his active service on grounds of age.

Although a massive Luftwaffe attack did not come, Dowding had to fight a constant paper war to resist diversions of his modern fighters from home defence. Single-mindedly, Dowding sought to retain in readiness the number of squadrons he deemed essential to resist the destruction of his force and the invasion of the country. The loss of fighters in Norway was small compared with the fighter reinforcements demanded by the French premier after the German assault on France. In an appearance at his own request at a Cabinet meeting on 15 May, and in his historic letter to the Air Ministry of 16 May 1940, Dowding set out the stark issues of survival or irremediable defeat. On 20 May the War Cabinet decided that no more fighter squadrons should leave the country. Providing fighter cover at long range during the withdrawal from Dunkirk provided successful combat experience for Dowding's men, but at the cost of further losses of aircraft and pilots. At this time a sympathetic working relationship between Dowding and his AOC No. 11 Group in south-east England, Air Vice-Marshal (later Air Chief Marshal Sir) Keith Park was confirmed and deepened in the summer and autumn of 1940. A similar sympathetic accord was established with his colleague, Lieutenant-General (later General) Sir Frederick Pile, GOC-in-C Anti-Aircraft Command.

The Battle of Britain was fought tactically at Group and Sector Operations Room level. But it is to Dowding that praise must go for his overall mastery of the air weapon. The deployment of his forces, his rotation of squadrons which had been heavily engaged, his constant regard for reserves of aircraft and personnel, indicated skill of a high order. In addition to commanding the struggle by day for air superiority over south-east

England, Dowding spent most nights in monitoring the development of airborne radar and other techniques to meet the threat of the night bomber. His complete personal commitment partly explains his failure to control the clash of tactics and personalities which developed between Park and Air Vice-Marshal Leigh-Mallory (AOC No. 12 Group) over the use of squadrons in big wing formation. Dowding was replaced at Fighter Command on 25 November 1940 by the deputy chief of air staff, Air Marshal Sholto Douglas (later Lord Douglas of Kirtleside). Dowding was undoubtedly very tired. He was also a victorious airman and an embarrassingly senior officer.

To many, Dowding's replacement so soon after his victory in Britain's first great air battle appeared ungrateful. Some unusual mark of recognition might have tempered the eventually inevitable decision to appoint a new commander for Fighter Command in its more offensive role. Dowding was persuaded by the prime minister to visit the United States on behalf of the Ministry of Aircraft Production. The trip was not successful. Dowding was inclined to put forward his own views which were not always in accord with those of Britain's permanent representatives there. On his return in June 1941 he was asked to prepare a dispatch on the Battle of Britain. This was ready before October, the date of his retirement as indicated to him by the Air Ministry.

The prime minister expressed 'indignation' when he learned of this intention and virtually commanded Dowding to accept an appointment in the Air Ministry involving the scrutiny of RAF establishments. At the same time he took possession of a book *Twelve Legions of Angels* which Dowding had submitted for clearance. The new appointment was not to Dowding's taste and before long the old arguments with the Air Ministry reappeared. At his own request he eventually retired in July 1942 but his book was suppressed under the wartime regulations until 1946.

In his retirement Dowding devoted himself to a study of spiritualism and theosophy. His nature had always been contemplative and philosophical. He published several books—*Many Mansions* (1943), *Lychgate* (1945), *God's Magic* (1946), and *The Dark Star* (1951). He wrote articles for newspapers and gave lectures on occult subjects. His second marriage in 1951 brought him a wife and companion who shared his beliefs. He gave up shooting and became a vegetarian.

As a young officer Dowding seemed set for an honourable but conventional soldier's life. Aviation opened new possibilities for his devoted spirit and inquiring mind. He became a dedicated airman, rising almost to the top of his profession. His stern sense of duty, added to his well-founded competence in practical flying matters, made him a formidable advocate for views strongly held. No easy compromiser or politician, he often aroused hostility, sometimes unwittingly. His vision was intense but narrow. His high moment was in the Battle of Britain. Few served their country more selflessly and courageously. His life had many bleak and lonely periods but his old age was mellow, surrounded, as he was, by the affection of family and friends. After the war Dowding became a legendary figure to the Battle of Britain pilots and one of his proudest moments was to receive a standing ovation from his so-called 'chicks' at the première of the film *Battle of Britain* in 1969. In his later years as a senior officer Dowding had an erect lean figure. He was dour in aspect with an almost expressionless face. This appearance coupled with his sparing use of speech had a daunting effect on some who met him for the first time. But a twinkle in the eye and a slight pursing of the lips showed his inner kindliness and humour to those of whom he approved. He died at his home in Kent 15 February 1970. His ashes are interred in Westminster Abbey. Dowding was appointed CMG in 1919, CB in 1928, KCB in 1933, GCVO in 1937, and GCB during the Battle of Britain in 1940. In 1943 a barony was conferred on him and he took the style of his old headquarters, Bentley Priory.

His first marriage was in 1918 to Clarice Maud Vancourt, daughter of Captain John Williams of the Indian Army and the widow of an army officer, who had one daughter by her first marriage; in January 1919 she gave birth to a son. She died suddenly in 1920. Dowding's second marriage was in 1951 to Muriel, widow of Pilot Officer Maxwell Whiting, RAF, and daughter of John Albino. Dowding was succeeded by his only child, Wing Commander Derek Hugh Tremenheere Dowding.

There is a pastel drawing (1939) by Sir W. Rothenstein in the Imperial War Museum, a portrait (1942) by Sir W. Russell at Bentley Priory, and one by F. Kenworthy-Browne in the possession of the family. A bronze by David Wynne was exhibited in 1968 at the National Portrait Gallery.

[*The Times*, 16 February 1970; Basil Collier, *Leader of the Few*, 1957; Robert Wright, *Dowding and the Battle of Britain*, 1969; private information.]

E. B. HASLAM

published 1981

EDMONDS James Edward

(1861–1956)

Sir

Military historian, was born in Baker Street, London, 25 December 1861, the son of James Edmonds, master jeweller, and his wife, Frances Amelia Bowler. He went as a day boy to King's College School, then still in the east wing of Somerset House, and astonished masters by the extent, maturity, and exactitude of his knowledge. He was wont to relate that he learnt languages at the breakfast table at home. In after life he could extract what he wanted from any European language and a number of Eastern, although he could not write an idiomatic letter in any language save German.

He passed first into the Royal Military Academy, Woolwich, the most experienced examiners being unable to recall any year in which he would not have done so. As a matter of course he passed out first after winning the sword awarded for the best gentleman cadet, the Pollock medal, and other prizes. In 1881 he was gazetted to the Royal Engineers, specializing in submarine mining, then treated as a task which the Royal Navy could not be expected to undertake.

In 1885, after long anxiety about the possibility that Russia might walk into Hong Kong without warning, it was decided to reinforce the colony with two companies of engineers of which one, the 33rd, was Edmonds's. His criticism of the situation was blistering. The reinforcement of two companies reached the scene in one case eight strong, in the other about thirty. The non-starters were either sick, permanent invalids, or on attachment from which they had not been liberated in time to catch the boat. Edmonds found that the numerous rock pillars just below the surface in Hong Kong harbour were uncharted and consequently often grazed by ships, once in a while causing a serious accident. He set about demolition by trailing a rail between two longboats and lowering a diver to fix a guncotton necklace on the peak.

Three months' sick leave in Japan was followed by a leisurely return home in 1888 by way of the United States. In 1890 he became instructor in fortification at the Royal Military Academy, where he spent six happy years and made use of the long vacations to travel and learn more languages, including Russian. In 1895 he entered the Staff College, once again first. His conversation became more stimulating and impressive than ever. Among those who enjoyed it were Douglas (later Earl) Haig, of whom he heard an instructor predict that he could become commander-in-chief, (Sir) Aylmer

Haldane, and E. H. H. (later Viscount) Allenby. His verdict on Allenby was that it was impossible to hammer anything into his head, an error typical of Edmonds's worst side.

In 1899 Edmonds was appointed to the intelligence division under Sir John Ardagh with whom in 1901 he went to South Africa, at the request of the Foreign Office, to advise Lord Kitchener on questions of international law. Lord Milner next borrowed him (1902–4) in the task of establishing peace. Back at home in 1904, Edmonds resumed work at the War Office in the intelligence division and was put in charge of a section formed to follow the Russo-Japanese war. He was promoted in 1907 to take charge of M.O.5 (counter-espionage, later known as M.I.5). It was Edmonds who in 1908 definitely convinced the secretary of state for war, R. B. (later Viscount) Haldane, of the size, efficiency, and complexity of the German espionage network in Britain.

In 1911 Edmonds, who had reached the rank of colonel in 1909, was appointed G.S.O. 1 of the 4th division. His divisional commander, (Sir) Thomas Snow, a formidable and irascible man, gave him his complete confidence and at an early stage said to him 'I provide the ginger and you provide the brains'. This was very much to Edmonds's taste, and if ever he spoke with excessive pride it was of his achievement in the training of the 4th division for the war, the summit of his career, although fatal to his personal ambitions. During the retreat from Mons he broke down from insufficient food, lack of sleep, and strain. The engineer-in-chief stretched out an arm to him from G.H.Q. where he remained for the rest of the war, in the latter part of it as deputy engineer-in-chief. He was regularly consulted by Haig and regarded as a mentor on the general staff side and every branch of his own corps, which in its turn could afford him greater knowledge of transportation problems than those who had to undertake the tasks.

In 1919 Edmonds retired with the honorary rank of brigadier-general and was appointed director of the historical section, military branch, Committee of Imperial Defence. His task was to direct; all narratives were to be written by historians; but finding the first choice unsatisfactory, Edmonds himself took over the main field, the western front, and sowed and reaped it to the end. He was altogether too patient with failures, although delighted to be able to say that he sacked three lieutenant-generals in quick succession. He has been blamed for tardiness in producing the history, but his resources were minimal by comparison with those accorded to the historians of the second world war. The first virtue of his style was compression, the second lucidity; but it was attractive to a minority only and came to be regarded as dull. A feature of the method, not new, but brought to perfection, was the combination of material from British records with those of foes and allies with equal care, whereas many famous predecessors had left the second and third as pale as ghosts. He was allowed to establish liaison with his German opposite number and treated him with complete candour. He found Berlin equally reliable and disinclined to make propaganda; a practice which only began after Hitler's ascent to power. It may indeed be said that Edmonds revolutionized the very principles on which the history of campaigns and battles had hitherto been compiled in this country. His humour as chief was mordant, but when he denounced one man as a crook, another as a drunkard, and a third as utterly incompetent, he was nine-tenths of the time playing an elaborate game. Part of the vast stock of *boutades* took the form of letters which were treasured by recipients. Some turned up finally as evidence for theories which he would have repudiated: for instance, the belittlement of Haig.

Edmonds was gifted with a prodigious memory. He never forgot the sciences learnt in youth and kept up with them throughout his life. The originality of his reflections and his skill in engineering earned for him the sobriquet of 'Archimedes', which amused him and with which he frequently signed letters to the press. Between the two wars he made further contributions to knowledge in innumerable book reviews. A history of the American civil war (1905), in collaboration with his brother-in-law, W. B. Wood, ran through a number of editions and became an official textbook in the United States. He collaborated also with L. F. L. Oppenheim in the official manual *Land Warfare* (1912), an exposition of the laws and usages of war on land. After his retirement in 1949 he wrote *A Short History of World War I* (1951). Coming from an author almost ninety years of age it naturally showed signs of wear and tear, but it is none the less a highly useful and creditable vade-mecum.

Edmonds was the happiest of men and never felt the slightest regret that he had not risen to a rank befitting his talents. As a soldier he was intellectually brilliant and in both theory and technical knowledge the outstanding figure of his generation; yet he could not be regarded as complete master of his profession or as having to reproach fortune for failure in attaining that status. He was over-sensitive, shy, inclined to be uncertain in emergency, and lacking in that sustained energy, carried almost to the point of harshness and sometimes beyond it, which has marked great soldiers and without which powers of command are generally limited.

Edmonds was appointed C.B. in 1911, C.M.G. in 1916, and knighted in 1928. He received the honorary degree of D.Litt. from the university of Oxford in 1935. In 1895 he married Hilda Margaret Ion (died 1921), daughter of the Rev. Matthew Wood; they had one daughter. He died at Sherborne, Dorset, 2 August 1956.

[*Royal Engineers Journal*, December 1956; private information; personal knowledge.]

CYRIL FALLS

published 1971

EMBRY Basil Edward

(1902–1977)

Sir

Air chief marshal, was born in Longford, Gloucestershire, 28 February 1902, the youngest of the three children and second son of the Revd James Embry, an Anglican clergyman, and his wife, Florence Ada Troughton. In conversation he always claimed to be Irish, though only his paternal grandfather is traceable to Ireland.

His early years were uneventful, and he attended Bromsgrove School without scholastic distinction but showing athletic prowess coupled with a precocious longing, from his tenth year onwards, to fly aeroplanes. The main part of his schooling coincided with World War I, and when it ended he thought that his chance of flying was gone. However, in spite of strong opposition from his parents, who wanted him to go to Cambridge, he managed to join the Royal Air Force as a short service officer, and was commissioned on 29 March 1921.

After flying training he joined No. 4 Bomber Squadron, but found the immediately post-war home service scene too tame for his taste, and applied for service in Iraq. This was the first of his many initiatives to 'march towards the sound of the guns'. In Iraq he was able to pioneer the airmail route across the desert and join in the development of new techniques of 'air control', devised by Sir H. M. (later Lord) Trenchard, to keep the peace in the Kurdish border districts. This, and his work with the first air ambulance service, won him an AFC in 1926, and the award of a permanent commission. In 1927 he returned to England and qualified as a flying instructor, commanded a training flight, and specialized in the development of instrument flying. He remained an instructor until he took the RAF Staff College course in 1933.

For Embry this was more than enough of training and home service, so he applied for a posting to India. He arrived in 1934, and after suffering staff and training appointments was promoted to squadron leader in 1936 and given his first command, No. 20 Squadron at Peshawar. This was far more to his taste, and in the hazardous flying on the North-West Frontier, during the various campaigns of 1937 and 1938, he was appointed to the DSO (1938), and established a lifelong reputation for courage and leadership.

He was therefore discontented to find himself, at the outbreak of war in 1939, in the directorate of operations in Whitehall. It took him eight days to get out, to the command of No. 107 Day Bomber Squadron, and to the opportunity to continue to apply his principles of leadership in operational practice. The air service's greatest morale problem had always been the confinement of commanders to the ground, due usually to their age and lack of flying practice, so that while their men endured the greatest dangers of any combatant they themselves were safer than many civilians. It might be deplorable, but it was accepted. Embry would have none of this. His own Blenheim was riddled with bullets on his first sortie over Germany, but he continued to lead the squadron on missions of great danger, bringing home a damaged aircraft fifteen times and even flying in the air-gunner's position, the better to understand his problems. It would be hard to exaggerate the affection he inspired in the members of his squadron. His extreme personal recklessness made them feel protective to him.

His luck could not last. On the day he was promoted and posted from his squadron he was wounded and shot down over France. Captured and marched towards a prison he passed a signpost labelled 'Embry', and taking this as a portent he slipped away from the column and hid in a French farm. He was recaptured and escaped again by belabouring his guards with an iron bar, finally arriving safely in Gibraltar.

Back in England he was promoted to group captain, and commanded a night fighter wing and a fighter sector. During this period at home he was received into the Roman Catholic faith. He was sent to North Africa in 1941, at the request of Sir A. W. (later Lord) Tedder to advise on tactics. He then had two staff appointments in England, until in May 1943 he was given command of No. 2 Bomber Group, with the rank of air vice-marshal. His task was to prepare this tactical group for the Overlord invasion, and thereafter to support the Allied armies in Europe. In these operations he continued to use his individual style of personal leadership, flying with his crews and carrying forged identity documents, for fear of execution if captured. He was awarded the DFC (1945) for these operations, a most unusual decoration for a man of his rank. In 1945 he was awarded a third bar to his DSO, appointed CB and KBE, and received a number of foreign honours, thus making him one of the most highly decorated officers in the three fighting services.

But the end of the war brought him to Whitehall again as assistant chief of air staff (training). Although he liked training he hated Whitehall; yet through this appointment he was able to supervise the complete overhaul of RAF training that followed the war. In April 1949 he was promoted air marshal and made commander-in-chief Fighter Command, and though there was now nobody to fight he used all his explosive energy to bring the Command to a new peak of efficiency. In 1953 he was appointed KCB, and, in December, air chief marshal. In July 1953 he was posted to France as commander of Allied Air Forces Central Europe, in the new NATO organization. This ponderous multinational organization was little suited to his qualities. Though buttressed by his great reputation he spoke little French, distrusted politicians, suspected diplomats, and was unenthusiastic about foreigners generally. It was not the best use of an outstanding fighting leader, and this miscasting contributed to his early retirement in September 1956, at the age of fifty-four, when he was appointed GCB.

He had long planned to take his whole family to start life anew in New Zealand, and he now put this scheme into practice, though shortly after arriving he moved on to Western Australia. There he bought a tract of bush and worked, helped by his wife and eldest children, to create a farming estate out of the wild. As the years went by the Embry family, now naturalized Australians, gradually conquered all obstacles. Embry built a house with his own hands, and by 1972 he was president of the Farmers Union of Western Australia and founder and first chairman of the Rural Traders Co-operative. He was made first chairman of the world-wide RAF Escaping Society, a freeman of the City of London and of the Cinque Port of Dover, and a liveryman of the Worshipful Company of Glass-sellers. He died at Boyup Brook, Western Australia, 7 December 1977. He bequeathed to the Royal Air Force an example of personal leadership which became an enduring tradition of the service.

Embry was a small spare man, wiry and strong, Celtic in colouring with extremely piercing blue eyes under fierce eyebrows. He had a puckish face, by no means handsome, which could express a wide variety of emotions from demoniac rage to delight, laughter, and goodwill, often within a few seconds. He had a trick of speaking to people from such close range, and with so fixed a blue glare, that even those whom he meant only to please were disconcerted. Though not particularly witty, he had a strong sense of fun, and a great capacity to inspire and charm most people, coupled with a talent to dismay and antagonize some others.

Embry married in 1928 (Margaret Mildred Norfolk) Hope, daughter of Captain Charles Sinclair Elliott, RN, and had three sons and one daughter. There is a portrait by Eric Kennington in the possession of the family, and another by the same artist is held by the Ministry of Defence.

[B. E. Embry, *Mission Completed*, 1956; private information; personal knowledge.]

PETER WYKEHAM

published 1986

EVANS Edward Ratcliffe Garth Russell

(1880–1957)

First Baron Mountevans

Admiral, was born in London 28 October 1880, the second of the three sons and the third child of Frank Evans, barrister, and his wife, Eliza Frances Garth. From the first he was of an adventurous disposition and more than once ran away from home; although not the eldest son, he was always the ringleader. He and his elder brother went in due course to Merchant Taylors' School, whence they were soon expelled for repeatedly playing truant. Evans was then sent to a school for 'troublesome boys' at Kenley where he was very happy. He went on to Warwick House School, Maida Vale, whence he passed into the *Worcester*, mercantile marine training ship. Two years later he obtained a naval cadetship.

His first ship in the Royal Navy was the *Hawke*, in the Mediterranean Fleet, a good ship for one who loved 'clean, well-run ships and well-dressed, smart men-at-arms', for she was famous for those qualities. He was later appointed to the training sloop *Dolphin*, where the experience of handling a ship under sail alone was later of inestimable value to him. In 1900 he was promoted sub-lieutenant and in 1902 he was selected, chiefly on account of his superb physical fitness, to be second officer of the *Morning*, the relief ship sent out by the Royal Geographical Society to the first Antarctic expedition of R. F. Scott. The *Morning* located the *Discovery* fast in the ice; but after revictualling her was obliged to leave her there for a second winter. In January 1904 the *Morning* returned, accompanied by the *Terra Nova*; the *Discovery* broke out of the ice in February, and the three ships came home.

Evans, who had been promoted lieutenant in 1902, returned to naval duty and qualified as a navigating officer. In 1909 he was selected by Scott himself as second-in-command of his second expedition and captain of the *Terra Nova* which left England in June 1910. He accompanied Scott in

January 1912 to within 150 miles of the Pole where he turned back. Struck down by scurvy he was saved only by the devotion of his two companions, Chief Stoker Lashley and Petty Officer Crean. After a brief period of convalescence in England, which he devoted to raising money for the expedition, he returned to take command of the *Terra Nova* in New Zealand and sailed south, only to find on arrival at Cape Evans in January 1913 that Scott had succumbed in an unparalleled period of bad weather when returning from the Pole in March of the previous year. After bringing home the expedition and clearing up its affairs Evans went on half pay and spent some time lecturing in Canada and the United States. He had been promoted commander in 1912.

In the summer of 1914 he resumed naval service in command of the *Mohawk*, destroyer, in the Dover Patrol. He went on to command various ships in the Patrol, the one for which he was best known being the *Broke*. In April 1917 the *Swift*, under Commander Ambrose Peck, and the *Broke* were sent out to counter-attack six German destroyers which had just bombarded Dover harbour. They met the enemy on opposite courses and at once fired torpedoes and turned to ram. The *Swift* was unsuccessful, passing through the enemy line, but the *Broke* rammed the G.42 and sustained forty casualties while the ships were locked together. There were no more German raids on Dover. This action struck the public imagination as the first in which ships came to close quarters in the old style, and he was always thereafter known as 'Evans of the *Broke*'. Peck and he were both appointed to the D.S.O. and promoted captain. He became chief of staff to the admiral of the Dover Patrol, Sir Reginald Bacon. When Roger (later Lord) Keyes took over the command Evans was eventually relieved, and until the end of the war, in the scout *Active*, was employed on escorting convoys to and from Gibraltar.

He paid off the *Active*, without orders, after the armistice, and following a period on half pay which he spent in Norway, he was for some months senior naval officer at Ostend, leaving only when all the mines had been swept up and the scars of war removed. He went next (1920–22) to the small cruiser *Carlisle* on the China station where he distinguished himself by swimming with a line to rescue the survivors on the steamer *Hong Moh*, ashore near Swatow, an exploit which again brought him before the public. After another leave in Norway he became in 1923 captain of the auxiliary patrol, later renamed the fishery and minesweeping flotilla, in the sloop *Harebell*. It was an appointment after his own heart, for he was his own master and was able to visit many out-of-the-way places, a rare privilege at that period. In 1926 he received one of the plums for a captain, the command of the battle cruiser *Repulse* which he held until shortly before his promotion to rear-admiral in February 1928.

His first flag command was the Australian squadron (1929), with his flag in the cruiser *Australia*. He was immensely popular in the Commonwealth, where his unconventional ways were fully appreciated. When he left in 1931, instead of inspecting each ship 'in all the dingle-dangle of braid', he entertained some 2,000 ratings and their wives at a cinema. He was promoted vice-admiral in 1932 and in the following year became commander-in-chief on the Africa station, where again he was immensely popular. But he was much criticized when acting in 1933 as high commissioner in the absence of Sir Herbert Stanley, for his handling of the case of Tshekedi, the regent of the Bamangwato tribe in Bechuanaland, who had ordered the flogging of a European accused of assault and known to be seducing African women in tribal territory. Evans travelled to Bechuanaland in state, accompanied by a strong force of armed sailors, suspended Tshekedi, and expelled the European. Tshekedi was recognized as, on the whole, an enlightened and capable chieftain and after a few weeks Evans reinstated him. It was thought that the case would have been better handled with less ostentation; but that was not Evans's way. While on the Africa station he attempted to renew his acquaintance with the Antarctic, shifting his flag in 1934 to the sloop *Milford* and visiting Bouvet Island to check its position on the charts; but he was unable to continue to the south as the *Milford*'s coal supply had been depleted by heavy weather.

Evans next served as commander-in-chief at the Nore (1935–9), an appointment which provided little scope for his special talents; but during his tenure he was promoted admiral (1936) and received the freedom of Dover (1938) and Chatham (1939), and many other distinctions. In the spring of 1939 he was made a regional commissioner for London under the civil defence scheme. After the German invasion of Norway in 1940 he was sent there to establish liaison with the King. On his return he was at first employed in organizing the defence of aircraft factories and only when that was completed did he resume his duties as regional commissioner. His energy and fearlessness through the blitz on London were an inspiration to all who served under him. He retired from the navy in 1941 but continued to hold his post in civil defence until the end of the war. In 1945 he was one of the seven selected for peerages, ostensibly to strengthen the Labour Party in the House of Lords, taking the title of Baron Mountevans. He had been appointed C.B. (civil, 1913, military, 1932) and K.C.B. (1935).

Evans was not a typical naval officer, except in his skill as a seaman. He revelled in publicity and was never happier than when in the public eye. That trait, which in a lesser man would have provoked severe criticism, was recognized as being part of his make-up and excused; for he was as universally popular with those brother officers who knew him personally as he was with the lower deck.

Evans was elected rector of Aberdeen University in 1936, a very unusual distinction for a serving officer; and he was re-elected in 1939. He wrote a number of books, one of the first being *South with Scott* (1921) which he wrote to beguile the tedium of his voyage to China to take command of the *Carlisle*. Exploration was the theme of most of his books, but he also had a flair for writing for boys. He was twice married: first, in 1904, to Hilda Beatrice (died 1913), daughter of Thomas Gregory Russell, barrister, of Christchurch, New Zealand. There were no children. Secondly, in 1916, to Elsa (died 1963), daughter of Richard Andvord, *statshauptman* of Oslo, by whom he had two sons.

Mountevans died at Golaa in his beloved Norway 20 August 1957, and was succeeded by his elder son, Richard Andvord (born 1918). There are two portraits of Mountevans in the possession of the family, by W. A. Bowring and Mario Grixoni; one by S. Morse Brown is in the National Museum of Wales, Cardiff.

[Lord Mountevans, *Adventurous Life*, 1946, and *Happy Adventurer*, 1951; Reginald Pound, *Evans of the Broke*, 1963; private information; personal knowledge.]

H. G. THURSFIELD

published 1971

Bernard Edward

(1911–1980)

First Baron Ballantrae

Soldier, author, and public servant, was born in London 6 May 1911, the third son in the family of four sons and a daughter of (General) Sir Charles Fergusson, seventh baronet, of Kilkerran, and his wife, Lady Alice Mary Boyle, second daughter of the seventh Earl of Glasgow. Educated at Eton and the Royal Military College, Sandhurst, in 1931 he was commissioned into the Black Watch: during a life of many loyalties and varied achievement, perhaps nothing gave him greater satisfaction than his appointment (1969–76) as colonel of the Black Watch (Royal Highland Regiment). In 1935 he became aide-de-camp to the regiment's most distinguished representative, Major-General (later Field-Marshal Earl) Wavell, whom he later served as staff officer in North Africa and India and recalled in *Wavell: Portrait of a Soldier* (1961). He published, in 1950, *The Black Watch and the King's Enemies*.

Fergusson

But Fergusson was never the typical regimental soldier. Though 'a bonny fechter', he was ardently unorthodox. Apart from a brief spell with his battalion outside Tobruk, preceded by service in Palestine (1937) and an instructorship at Sandhurst, he was selected for wartime duties of the most diverse character. In 1941 he was staff officer to General Sir James Marshall-Cornwall during his mission of liaison with the Turkish Army. For a while in 1942 he was GSO 1 Joint Plans, India. In 1945–6 he was director of Combined Operations (Military) and from 1946 to 1947 assistant inspector-general, Palestine Police. But it is for the part he played under Orde Wingate in operations behind the Japanese lines in Burma that he will be chiefly remembered.

Fergusson joined Wingate's embryonic Chindit group in October 1942 and trained with it for the first long-range penetration experiment (as it was assessed by the C-in-C, Wavell). Early in 1943 a number of independent columns, one under Fergusson's command, made their way by foot into Japanese territory, crossing both the Chindwin and the Irrawaddy. After much suffering and severe losses the remnants withdrew, having proved the viability of some of Wingate's techniques, particularly air supply, but achieved little beyond a boost to British morale. From Fergusson's column of 318 only 95 returned.

Nevertheless, when a special force of six brigades was assembled under Wingate for operations in 1944, Fergusson accepted command of the 16th brigade and with it a formidable commitment. Whereas other brigades in Operation Thursday were to be flown into the heart of Burma, Fergusson's task was to march southwards from General Stilwell's territory around Ledo on the Chinese border, over mountain ranges 8,500 ft. high and through some of the heaviest rainfall in the world. With extraordinary tenacity and ingenuity the brigade reached the edge of its objective, the airfields at Indaw in central Burma. But now, largely due to Wingate's unpredictable orders and counter-orders, everything fell apart. After a futile assault at Indaw 16th brigade was soon flown out to India: its sacrificial efforts were denied their due reward. Strongly though Fergusson always defended Wingate's military virtues, he was too clear-sighted to join the band of his unqualified hero-worshippers. The ghosts of those who had died unnecessarily kept him company. He described his experiences in *Beyond the Chindwin* (1945) and *The Wild Green Earth* (1946).

There is an extensive analysis of Wingate in Fergusson's engaging autobiography, *The Trumpet in the Hall* (1970), which also describes frankly another near-disaster. Post-war Palestine was a maelstrom: these were the days of the Hagana, the Stern Gang, and the Irgun Zwai Leumi. To further his counter-terrorist role within the police Fergusson recruited a small group of officers whose wartime experiences fitted the situation: including

Roy Farran who, before he was twenty-three, had won two DSOs and three MCs. A young Jew mysteriously disappeared and Farran, accused of his murder, bolted. There was international uproar and Fergusson's neck was on the block. After anxious months he survived the courts martial and other enquiries, but he knew that his professional career had been within a hair's breadth of ruin. Instead, he was put in command of the 1st battalion, the Black Watch, in Germany. A period as colonel (Intelligence) at SHAPE in Paris, a brief appointment as director of psychological warfare during the Suez venture of 1956, and command of the 29th Infantry brigade at Dover completed an idiosyncratic record. Brigadier was perhaps his peacetime 'ceiling'.

After he had hung up his 'trumpet in the hall' Fergusson sailed calmer waters. Like his father, he was an outstanding governor-general of New Zealand (1962–7), where both his grandfathers had been governor. Since childhood, indeed, he had loved and known New Zealand intimately as the braes of Ayrshire. As lord high commissioner to the general assembly of the Church of Scotland he was equally at home: relishing ritual and ceremony, he was also a Christian of sure and tranquil faith. Chairman of the British Council from 1972 to 1976, he interpreted his responsibilities as global, travelling assiduously and revelling in his scope. A productive writer, he lived during his last years largely by his pen, excelling (like Wavell) in the tricky art of light verse.

Except for those moved by envy, or who mistook brio for froth, Fergusson's charm was irresistible. He and W. J. (later Viscount) Slim were the only 'limeys' accepted by the acidulous Stilwell. Bumptious, perhaps, in his youth—and with a proper ambition—he still lacked all the unattractive trimmings of the 'Scotsman on the make' of Sir James Barrie. As a friend he was sword-true. The New Zealanders—the Maori in particular—showed at his death that time and distance had not diminished their affection. He was the hero-figure John Buchan always just failed to capture in his novels, and he lived to the last on the principle of 'homo sum: humani nil a me alienum puto' ... except the enemies of the realm.

Ballantrae died in London 28 November 1980, from a cancer whose earlier onset he had mastered with a cool, indifferent fortitude which, like his faith, enabled him also to absorb the tragic loss of his wife who, during a gale on their estate in 1979, was killed in a car accident as she sat beside him. He had married in 1950 Laura Margaret, younger daughter of Lieutenant-Colonel Arthur Morton Grenfell, DSO. They had one son.

Ballantrae was appointed OBE (1950), to the DSO (1943), GCMG (1962), and GCVO (1963). He was created KT (1974) and a life peer (1972). He was made honorary DCL of Canterbury (1965), D.Univ. of Waikato (1967), honorary LL D of Strathclyde (1971) and Dundee (1973), and honorary

D.Litt. of St. Andrews (1974), of which university he became chancellor in 1973.

A portrait by Ruskin Spear is in the Black Watch headquarters and museum in Balhousie Castle, Perth. A presentation portrait of Ballantrae as governor-general is now in the possession of the New Zealand government.

[Bernard Fergusson, *The Trumpet in the Hall*, 1970; personal knowledge.]

RONALD LEWIN

published 1986

FISHER John Arbuthnot

(1841–1920)

First Baron Fisher, of Kilverstone

Admiral of the fleet, born 25 January 1841 in Ceylon, was the elder son of Captain William Fisher, of the 78th Highlanders and 95th Foot, by his wife, Sophia, daughter of Alfred Lambe, of New Bond Street, London. Fisher entered the royal navy on 13 July 1854, on a nomination from Admiral Sir William Parker. He was appointed as naval cadet to the *Calcutta* and served in the Baltic fleet during the Crimean War. Two years later he joined the *Highflyer* as midshipman and served in China during the war of 1859–1860, being present at the capture of Canton and the attack on the Peiho forts. He was transferred to the *Furious*, promoted acting lieutenant early in 1860, and confirmed in November of that year, after winning the Beaufort testimonial, while still on the China station. Having qualified in the gunnery school *Excellent* he joined the *Warrior*, the first 'ironclad', in 1863, and a year later was appointed to the staff of the *Excellent*, where he remained till November 1869; he was promoted commander in August of that year. Then came another three-year commission in the flagship on the China station, and in 1872 he was again appointed to the *Excellent*, this time for experimental work on the torpedo, a new weapon then being tested. He remained on instructional and experimental work at Portsmouth for the next four years, and devoted himself to the development of the torpedo. He was chiefly responsible for establishing a separate torpedo school which was developed out of the gunnery school and finally placed in the *Vernon*. In 1874 he was promoted captain at the age of thirty-three, and at the end of 1876 he came for the first time to the Admiralty to serve on a torpedo committee and to go out to Fiume to study experiments with the

Whitehead torpedo. He was then at sea for six years—in command of the *Pallas*, under Sir Geoffrey Hornby, in the Mediterranean; as flag captain to Sir Cooper Key in the *Bellerophon* and *Hercules* in the North America and particular service squadron; then again commanding the *Pallas* in the Mediterranean; and from September 1879 to January 1881 in the *Northampton* as flag captain to Sir Leopold McClintock on the North America and West Indies station; finally being brought home specially to fit out and command the *Inflexible*, the greatest battleship of the day. In her he was present at the attack on the Alexandria forts (July 1882), under Sir Beauchamp Seymour (afterwards Lord Alcester), and did signal service in fitting out an armoured train and commanding it in action against Arabi Pasha. For this he was awarded the C.B. He returned from Egypt with fever and was ill for nine months.

Fisher now began a period of fourteen years' service ashore, only broken by a few weeks in command of the *Minotaur* in the evolutionary squadron of the summer of 1885. He was for three years captain of the gunnery school at Portsmouth, for four years director of ordnance and torpedoes at the Admiralty, being promoted rear-admiral in 1890; for one year superintendent of Portsmouth dockyard; and for three years third sea lord and controller of the navy. In the ordnance department he secured, after a long fight with the War Office, in which Lord Salisbury as prime minister was called in to arbitrate, the transfer of the control of naval guns from the army to the Admiralty. At Portsmouth dockyard he superintended the building of the new battleship *Royal Sovereign*. As controller he was responsible for the execution of the great programme of shipbuilding authorized by the Naval Defence Act (1889), and carried the adoption of the water-tube boiler in the face of great opposition. He had long been a marked man, noticed for his outstanding ability and originality by all first lords from Mr. Ward Hunt to Earl Spencer. He was promoted K.C.B. in 1894.

Mr. (afterwards Viscount) Goschen, on coming to Whitehall as first lord for the second time in 1895, found Fisher a member of the board, and appointed him commander-in-chief, North America and West Indies station, in 1897, after he had been promoted vice-admiral in May 1896. On that station Fisher showed his diplomatic quality by his friendly relations with the American Admiral Sampson during the Cuban War. As British naval delegate he attended the first Hague Conference in 1899, and was one of the outstanding figures in that gathering of diplomatists, international lawyers, seamen, and soldiers of the principal nations of the world. His grasp of realities and of the essential principles of modern warfare did much to keep the conference on reasonably sound lines. He was then transferred to the Mediterranean with his flagship *Renown* to take command of the greatest fleet England then possessed. His tenure of that command was remarkable for his determination to ensure in every department and detail complete naval efficiency and the instant readiness of the fleet for war. He encouraged his officers of all ranks to study for themselves the problems of modern warfare. He visited every part of his station with his mind alert to seize every opportunity of making his fleet ready for any emergency that might arise. He introduced longer ranges for firing, and insisted on the need for constant training and practice in gunnery and in testing and developing every new device, from the control of firing to the newly invented wireless telegraphy, for making his ships and squadrons more effective in action. It was typical of him that, whereas other commanders-in-chief had given cups for boat-pulling and sailing, he offered one for tactical essays. He was immensely popular on the lower deck and was an inspiration to the younger officers, who admired his dislike of routine and contempt for any customs and precedents which were not warranted by sound reason. He inspired officers to enthusiasm by personal lectures on all manner of subjects connected with the future development of their profession, couched in a language as fresh and as invigorating as it was unconventional. The preparation of these lectures was the starting-point in his own mind of a great scheme of administrative reform to fit the navy for defending the Empire, under the new conditions of modern science and the changing aspect of foreign relations. The Earl of Selborne, who had become first lord of the Admiralty at the end of 1900, paid a visit to Malta and the Mediterranean fleet in the summer of 1901. Fisher laid before him an outline of his projected reforms; and after returning home Lord Selborne invited Fisher to rejoin the Admiralty board in the following summer as second sea lord with charge of the personnel of the fleet. This post had usually been filled by the appointment of a rear-admiral, and the fact that Fisher reached the rank of full admiral in November 1901 served in itself to indicate that an unusual task was expected of him.

Fisher, who was promoted G.C.B. at King Edward's coronation (August 1902), lost no time on his arrival in Whitehall in formulating the first, and in some ways the most striking, of his proposed changes. This was the new scheme of entry in training of officers, under which executive officers, engineers, and marines were all to be entered at the early age of twelve and trained together under one common system for four years in colleges on shore before going to sea, specializing later in the particular branch of the service they were to adopt. The scheme was promulgated in a memorandum published on Christmas Day 1902. Both the naval and the civil members of the board were unanimous in its favour, and Lord Selborne, who took a personal hand in framing it, secured the sanction of the

Cabinet for its issue. The novelty of training all officers in engineering for four years on shore aroused considerable hostility among many naval officers, especially of the older school, and there was abundant criticism in detail. Fisher devoted the next nine months, with a buoyant enthusiasm and indomitable energy, to carrying the reforms into immediate effect. The sudden drop of three years in the age of entry made it necessary to carry on the old scheme of entry for three years so as to prevent a gap in the flow of new officers to the fleet. A college at Dartmouth was already under construction to replace the old *Britannia* training ship; but a second college was wanted at once to accommodate the larger number of officers of the new entry system for the longer course of four years. As the navy was undertaking the entire education of the boys from the early age of twelve, a staff of masters on the public-school system, as well as of officers responsible for instilling naval training and traditions, was necessary. To prevent the evils of competitive examination for lads of such tender years, a new system of selection, after interview, was adopted; and a new college, constructed and completely equipped in nine months, was opened in September 1903 in the grounds of the Osborne House property belonging to the King. This device of selection after interview, tempered by a qualifying examination, has by its proved merit lived down much initial criticism, has been permanently adopted, and has since been imitated, with suitable modifications, in other branches of the public service. The scheme of common entry has been subjected to certain changes; the inclusion of officers intended for the Royal Marines has been abandoned, and the age of entry has been slightly raised to correspond with the normal age at which boys leave preparatory schools for public schools: but in all the main essentials it has so far stood the test of time, and seems likely to be a permanent feature of the royal navy. Alterations in the organization and training of all branches of the lower ranks in the service occupied Fisher's attention during this *annus mirabilis*. At the end of it, in September 1903, he went to Portsmouth as commander-in-chief, where he was able to superintend the birth and early growth of the college at Osborne. Before the end of the year, while still at Portsmouth, he was appointed by Mr. Arnold Forster, the secretary of state for war, to be a member of a committee, with Viscount Esher and Sir George Clarke (afterwards Baron Sydenham), which was instructed to recommend reforms in the organization of the War Office. Sir George Clarke was thousands of miles away when the committee was appointed, and Fisher, with characteristic energy, had written out the first draft of the report before the three members could meet. The chief points of Fisher's draft were adopted by the committee, and, as a result, the organization of the Army Council on the lines of the Admiralty Board, in place of the former dual control of secretary of state and commander-in-chief, was approved by the government. Fisher knew that Lord Selborne and the prime minister (Mr. Balfour) intended him to return to the Admiralty on the retirement of Lord Walter Kerr in the following October (1904), and he devoted part of his untiring energy during his remaining months at Portsmouth to working out in draft the second part of his great scheme of reforms: the redistribution of the fleet on the new alignment required by the substitution of Germany for France as England's leading naval rival, and a reconstruction of the *matériel* of the navy itself to meet the most modern fighting conditions.

Fisher took a pride in the selection of Trafalgar day, 21 October, for his entry upon the office of first sea lord, though in fact he joined the board a day earlier. Throughout his life Nelson was his hero and model. Reference to the great sailor's sayings and actions was never long absent from his conversation and writings. By the end of 1904 Lord Selborne published his memorandum on the redistribution of the fleet. Fisher had realized that the country was growing restless under increased expenditure on armaments, and that severe economies in all non-essentials would be required if the construction of new fighting weapons, the necessity for which he foresaw, was not to be hindered. During the long peace since the Crimean War the types of ships of the royal navy had completely changed; but the naval stations and dockyards throughout the world had been little altered, and many of the ships, particularly on foreign stations, would have been of little fighting value against a well-equipped and determined foe. The principles of the redistribution of the fleet were the concentration of the main fighting strength of the navy in the North Sea, the ruthless abolition of small ships of little fighting value, and the closing down of various small foreign dockyards. Halifax, Jamaica, Esquimalt, and Trincomalee were closed down; Ascension and Bermuda were reduced; and 150 of the older ships were, as Mr. Balfour said, with one stroke of the pen struck off the list of the navy. The personnel set free from these ships enabled Fisher to carry out another cherished scheme which enormously increased the efficiency of the war fleet without increasing the number of men voted by parliament. Hitherto ships not in commission had been paid off and lay in the dockyards and harbours with small care and maintenance parties. Fisher devised and carried out a nucleus crew system under which the more important ships in reserve that would be required to join the fleet on the outbreak of war had the active service part of their crews permanently on board, the balance being provided from the naval reserves when these were called up. By these measures the strength, both actual and potential, of the navy in home waters *vis à vis* the growing menace from Germany was vastly enhanced.

Fisher had long been meditating the creation of an 'all big gun' fast battleship and the use of the turbine engine, and early in 1905, at his request, Lord Selborne appointed a new designs committee to advise the board on new types of ships of war. The result was the production of the design of the famous *Dreadnought* type of battleship and battle cruiser, which, by combining great speed, produced by powerful turbine engines, with immensely increased gun power, made a revolution in warship construction throughout the world. Fisher at the same time encouraged the building of destroyers of greatly increased speed and power as well as the development of the submarine, with its torpedo weapon, particularly for coast defence purposes. At the same time a committee was appointed to examine the organization of the dockyards and the reserve of stores of all kinds kept in them, in order that all non-essentials, many of which had accumulated on principles unrevised for many years, might be got rid of.

In April 1905, when Lord Selborne left the Admiralty to become governor-general of South Africa, Fisher found in Earl Cawdor a new chief no less enthusiastic in support of his reforms. These changes had proceeded with great rapidity for such a conservative service as the royal navy, and a storm of criticism arose both in parliament and in the press. Nothing daunted, Fisher determined that, before the conservative government, which was visibly tottering to its fall, went out of office, a general statement of the Admiralty's naval policy in the many fields of its operation should be published. Lord Cawdor readily agreed, and after a wise revision by that able statesman's hand, a statement of Admiralty policy, commonly called the Cawdor memorandum, was issued to parliament, with Cabinet approval, in November 1905, just before the fall of Mr. Balfour's government. The reforms and economies introduced at Fisher's instigation made it possible to reduce the navy estimates by £3,500,000 in 1904–1905 and by £1,500,000 in 1905–1906, while the fleet under his creative hand was becoming a more powerful weapon than it had been for generations. The *Dreadnought* was laid down in October 1905, launched in February 1906, and completed in December 1906, a triumph of rapid work and organization.

In the new and not very friendly atmosphere of the liberal government of 1906, Fisher thought it prudent to consent to a diminution of the programme of four capital ships a year which had been laid down in the Cawdor memorandum, and to postponing the construction of the proposed new great dockyard at Rosyth. At this time he had to meet the unabated hostility of the critics of his reforms and the insistent demands of a considerable 'little England' party in the House of Commons. He found in Lord Tweedmouth, his new chief, as loyal, if not so enthusiastic, a supporter of the principles he advocated as Lord Selborne and Lord Cawdor. The development on sound lines of the numerous schemes and reforms he had inaugurated required his unremitting attention. He never gained the sympathy of the new prime minister (Sir Henry Campbell-Bannerman) in the same degree as he possessed that of Mr. Balfour and later of Mr. Asquith; but he was encouraged by the constant sympathy and close personal friendship of King Edward, to whom he was first and principal naval A.D.C. from 1904 to 1910. He felt that he was fighting not only for his official career but for the life of the new navy that he was building up. It was an anxious time, and feeling himself with his back to the wall, he began to show towards his opponents, particularly those who belonged to his own profession, a vindictiveness which tended to foster personal rancour and division among the personnel of the great sea service, hitherto singularly free from these evils. In 1907 Lord Charles Beresford was appointed commander-in-chief of the Channel fleet. That great and popular commander had been on cordial terms with Fisher, when his second in command in the Mediterranean, and had at first been an enthusiastic supporter of the common entry scheme of 1902; but from the date of his taking command of the Channel fleet he found himself continually at variance with the Admiralty on points both of detail and principle. Fisher was in no mood to welcome criticisms from the principal admiral afloat, and an unfortunate estrangement began which continued until Fisher's retirement. In April 1908 Lord Tweedmouth was succeeded at the Admiralty by Mr. Reginald McKenna, who soon made up his mind that Fisher's naval policy was in essentials right, and determined to give him the fullest support. Early in the following year, they both reluctantly became convinced that Germany, so far from responding to the slowing down of the shipbuilding programme decided on by Sir H. Campbell-Bannerman's government, was secretly accelerating her own to an extent which would soon place the naval supremacy of this country in jeopardy. The result, after a bitter contest in the Cabinet, was the famous programme of eight battleships of 1909–1910 and the hastening of the deferred construction of the Rosyth dockyard. Lord Charles Beresford's continued differences with the Admiralty resulted in the termination of his command of the Channel fleet in January 1909. He subsequently addressed a communication to the prime minister criticizing the Admiralty policy in various directions. These criticisms were examined at great length by a committee of the Cabinet, whose conclusions, though expressing anxiety at the differences of opinion revealed, were generally favourable to Mr. McKenna's and Lord Fisher's policy. At the end of the year Fisher, on whom King Edward had conferred the order of merit in 1904 and the G.C.V.O. in 1908, was raised to the peerage with the title of Baron Fisher, of Kilverstone, a Norfolk estate which had been bequeathed to his son Cecil by his old friend, Mr. Joseph Vavasseur.

In January 1910 Fisher resigned office and was succeeded as first sea lord by his old friend, Sir Arthur Knyvet Wilson, who had followed him as controller in 1897, and was in general sympathy with his naval policy. In 1912 Fisher became chairman of the royal commission on oil fuel, the importance of which, both in saving of personnel and in rapidity of re-fuelling, he had been urging for the past ten years. The commission's report resulted in the adoption of oil-fuel for all new ships. For the next four years Fisher maintained an unabated interest in naval affairs and was in constant communication with Mr. McKenna and with Mr. Winston Churchill who became first lord in October 1911.

In October 1914, after the outbreak of the War, Mr. Churchill invited Fisher to return to the Admiralty as first sea lord, on the resignation of Prince Louis of Battenberg. Fisher obeyed the call with alacrity, and a period of intense activity ensued in Whitehall. At first all went well. Fisher had for years past been urging that Sir John Jellicoe was the officer to command the fleet when the threatened war with Germany broke out. The officer of his own choosing held the command, and in Mr. Churchill he found an enthusiastic chief with an activity of mind and fertility of imagination not inferior to his own. Fisher's first work was to redress the loss of Sir Christopher Cradock and his squadron at Coronel by sending Sir Doveton Sturdee with two battle cruisers from the grand fleet to intercept Admiral von Spee, whose squadron was met and destroyed at the Falkland Islands. The complete success of this operation was made possible by Fisher's instant grasp of the situation and his insistence on the hastened preparations which brought Sturdee's squadron on the scene of action just in time with only a few hours to spare. The battle cruiser—his own conception—was more than justified. He then devoted his energies to the building on a great scale of all types of vessels in which the navy was deficient, especially submarines and monitors, and to his long-projected scheme for securing the command of the Baltic and landing a military force on the German flank in Pomerania. A large number of specially constructed barges were ordered for immediate building, but before they were completed the attention of the government was diverted to the Dardanelles, and Fisher saw his cherished design gradually excluded in favour of an operation in which he never believed. In deference, however, to the wishes of his chief and of the Cabinet he assented to the naval attempt to force the passage of the Dardanelles and to the allocation of a considerable portion of the fleet for this purpose, although he had no faith in a purely naval attack upon fortifications which was not combined with military operations. As the operations of the spring of 1915 at the

Dardanelles proceeded, Fisher grew more and more discontented, until at last, becoming convinced that the Cabinet's policy of persisting in the attack upon the Dardanelles despite the naval losses suffered and the further risks incurred, jeopardized the success of the major naval strategy of the war, he resigned office as first sea lord. The fall of the government followed almost immediately, and Mr. Balfour became first lord in the new coalition ministry. Fisher, however, was not invited to return to the Admiralty. He became chairman of the Admiralty inventions board, but his career as a naval administrator was finished. His wife, Frances, only daughter of the Rev. Thomas Delves Broughton, his devoted companion for fifty-two years, died in July 1918. After the armistice at the end of that year he diverted himself by publishing two volumes of reminiscences: compilations of a most informal character consisting chiefly of copies of letters and documents and notes dictated to a shorthand writer. His continued interest in public affairs was shown in a series of letters to *The Times* urging the necessity of cutting down expenditure on the services once the War was won. He died 10 July 1920, and was accorded a public naval funeral in London at Westminster Abbey; he was buried at Kilverstone.

Fisher was one of the most remarkable personalities of his time, and one of the greatest administrators in the history of the royal navy. Belonging to a traditionally conservative service, he offended many susceptibilities by his absence of reverence for tradition and custom; but he had a singular clarity of vision and grasp of essentials, combined with a burning patriotism and belief in the destinies of the English race. He was quick to recognize ability in every grade of the service or department of life, and he won the enthusiastic support and co-operation of most of those whose help he invited by treating them as his personal friends. In later years, when his policy aroused serious opposition, he tended to treat those who did not respond to his advances, or found themselves in direct antagonism, with a hostility that left bitter feelings behind. He accepted help from every conceivable quarter whence he thought the end in view could be promoted. He possessed a daemonic energy combined with a gaiety and charm which few of his associates could resist. His conversation was sparkling, and his voluminous correspondence was full of pithy sayings and arresting phrases couched in vigorous English, and pointed by frequent quotations, particularly from the Bible, of which he was a devoted reader. Behind all lay his constantly quoted motto: 'The fighting efficiency of the fleet and its instant readiness for war.' Fate never allowed him to command a fleet in action, but it was his creative genius that reformed the ships and personnel of the royal navy and forged the weapon which finally brought Germany to her knees in the War, the date of which he had predicted with the instinct of genius.

Fisher was succeeded in the peerage by his only son, Cecil Vavasseur, who was born in 1868, and married in 1910 Jane, daughter of Randal Morgan, of Philadelphia. His three daughters, Beatrix, Dorothy, and Pamela, all married naval officers, viz., Rear-Admiral R. R. Neeld, Captain Eric Fullerton, and Captain Henry Blackett.

Fisher's portrait was painted by Sir A. S. Cope in 1903 (*Royal Academy Pictures*, 1903).

[Lord Fisher's *Memories*, 1919, and *Records*, 1919; private information; personal knowledge.]

VINCENT W. BADDELEY

published 1927

FRASER Bruce Austin

(1888–1981)

First Baron Fraser of North Cape

Admiral of the fleet, was born in Acton, London, 5 February 1888, the younger son (there were no daughters) of General Alexander Fraser, CB, of the Royal Engineers, and his wife, Monica Stores Smith. He was educated at Bradfield College before passing into HMS *Britannia* in September 1902. He completed his cadetship with distinction, and was appointed a midshipman in HMS *Hannibal*, a battleship with the Channel Fleet, in January 1904.

In the years that followed, Fraser served in a succession of battleships and destroyers in home waters, being promoted sub-lieutenant in September 1907. In 1911, having determined to become a gunnery specialist, he was posted to HMS *Excellent* at Whale Island. Fraser passed out top of the course. He acted as gunnery officer in the cruiser *Minerva* (1914–16), and saw action in the Dardanelles. He spent some months of 1916 on the senior staff of HMS *Excellent*, thus missing Jutland. At the end of the year, he was posted to the new battleship *Resolution*, in which he became commander in 1919. Ironically, for an officer who had shown exceptional leadership and technical capabilities, Fraser was obliged to end the war without experiencing a major action in a modern warship.

In April 1920 he suffered a bizarre misfortune. Because he was on poor terms with his captain in *Resolution*, he sought escape by responding to a call for Mediterranean Fleet volunteers to travel to Baku and assist the White Russian fleet against the Bolsheviks. He arrived in command of his

137

detachment of thirty-one men, just in time to be caught up in a local Bolshevik coup. The British party was imprisoned in wretched conditions until freed in November, when Fraser came home to spend a further two years on the staff of *Excellent*.

Despite favourable reports and widespread acceptance as a popular and able officer, Fraser's career thus far had been sluggish. But from 1922 onwards he was plainly marked for high rank, earning the commendation of the Admiralty Board in 1924 for his work on a new fire control installation. As fleet gunnery officer in the Mediterranean (1925–6) and as a captain in the Admiralty tactical division (1926–9), he worked close to the heart of the navy's gunnery development. From 1929 to 1932 he held his first seagoing command in the cruiser *Effingham* in the East Indies. As director of naval ordnance (1933–5), he devised the armament for Britain's last generation of battleships, the 14-inch King George V class.

In 1936–7 Fraser commanded the aircraft carrier *Glorious*. In January 1938, just short of his fiftieth birthday, he was appointed rear-admiral, and chief of staff to Sir A. Dudley Pound, C-in-C Mediterranean. It was in this role that he forged the close relationship with Pound that continued in World War II, when Pound was first sea lord.

In March 1939 Fraser became controller of the navy and third sea lord. In this role, for three testing years he bore responsibility for the navy's construction and repair programme, perhaps above all for the creation of the corvette, the mainstay of the Atlantic convoy escort system. He also played an important part in the development of warship radar. In May 1940 he became vice-admiral.

Fraser won the confidence of (Sir) Winston Churchill in this period at the Admiralty, and never lost it for the remainder of the war, despite periodic differences of opinion, for instance when the controller opposed Churchill's enthusiasm to build a new battleship. In June 1942 Fraser was sent to sea once more, as second-in-command of the Home Fleet under Sir John (later Lord) Tovey. He arrived just before the tragedy of convoy PQ17, one of the darkest naval episodes of the war.

By 8 May 1943, when Fraser was appointed to succeed Tovey as C-in-C Home Fleet, he could claim wide experience of both naval operations at sea, and their strategic direction ashore. A bluff, cheerful, straightforward officer with much shrewdness and technical knowledge but no pretensions to intellectualism, he was committed throughout his career to making inter-service co-operation a reality. He had shown remarkable gifts for winning the confidence of his peers and political masters at home, while commanding the affection and loyalty of subordinates afloat. Essentially a simple man who used to declare without embarrassment that he had never read a novel in his life, a bachelor who had made the Royal Navy his life-work, he was acknowledged as one of the outstanding naval professionals of his generation. His elevation was widely welcomed.

Yet in the strategic situation in the summer of 1943, it seemed unlikely that Fraser would be granted the opportunity to conduct a major fleet action. The Russian victory at Stalingrad, and the consequent shift in the balance of advantage against the Germans, diminished the importance of the western Allies' Arctic convoys. These now offered a lure to the three German capital ships based in Norwegian waters—*Tirpitz*, *Scharnhorst*, and *Lützow*—but it seemed unlikely that the Germans would consider the bait worth the hazard to their remaining fleet. Correspondingly, the British Home Fleet had been weakened by the transfer of ships to the Mediterranean. *Anson* and *Duke of York*—in which Fraser flew his flag—were now the only British battleships at Scapa.

Yet in September, to the surprise of the British, *Tirpitz* and *Scharnhorst* sortied for two days to bombard Spitsbergen. This was a negligible feat, yet sharply reminded the Royal Navy of the difficulties of keeping effective watch on the German ships. A fortnight later, a substantial British success was gained, when midget submarines successfully crippled *Tirpitz* in Kaafiord. She was rendered unfit for active operations for six months. Four days afterwards, *Lützow* escaped into the Baltic. *Scharnhorst* was now alone.

As a succession of Allied convoys sailed to Russia that autumn, almost unmolested but shadowed by units of the Home Fleet, Fraser, having declined an offer by Churchill to become first sea lord, continued to believe that *Scharnhorst* would sooner or later come out. Earlier in the war, the German battle cruiser had inflicted major damage upon British shipping. On 19 December British Ultra decrypts revealed that *Scharnhorst* had been brought to three hours' readiness for sea. Fraser's Force 2, led by the cruiser *Jamaica* and the *Duke of York*—the only British ship with the armament to match that of *Scharnhorst*—sailed from Icelandic waters at 23.00 hours on 23 December. Fraser had carefully briefed his captains, and carried out repeated exercises in identifying and engaging hostile ships by radar, given the almost permanent Arctic darkness.

On the afternoon of 24 December 1943, in atrocious weather, the British convoy JW55B was ordered to slow to eight knots because Force 2 was 400 miles behind, too distant for comfort when the convoy was only the same distance from *Scharnhorst* in Altenfiord. *Scharnhorst* sailed to attack JW55B at 19.00 on 25 December, commanded by Rear-Admiral Erich Bey.

Eight hours later, this news was passed to Fraser, whose ships were still struggling through mountainous seas to close the gap with the convoy. Fraser accepted the risk that *Scharnhorst* would turn away if he broke wireless silence, and ordered JW55B to turn northwards, away from the

Germans. Bey was still searching in vain for the convoy at 07.30 on 26 December, when the 8-inch cruiser *Norfolk*, a unit of Force I, led by Vice-Admiral (Sir) R. L. Burnett, located *Scharnhorst* on radar at 33,000 yards. The British ship, with her 6-inch consorts *Belfast* and *Sheffield*, opened fire at 09.29. They strove to close the range speedily, and avoid the sort of mauling *Graf Spee* had inflicted upon a British cruiser squadron four years earlier. At this early stage, *Norfolk* damaged *Scharnhorst*'s radar. Bey, as the British had expected, at once withdrew at 30 knots.

The British now suffered almost three hours of acute apprehension, having lost touch with *Scharnhorst*, and being fearful that she might break away into the Atlantic. Only at 12.20 did *Belfast* triumphantly report the battle cruiser once more in sight. Bey had turned north, still searching for JW55B. Burnett's cruisers and destroyers lay between the Germans and the convoy.

In the second twenty-one minute cruiser action, the British ships suffered significant damage before *Scharnhorst* broke away unscathed. Yet Bey now hesitated fatally. He knew that a British battle group was at sea. But he believed it was too distant to harm him. Only at 14.18 did he abandon the attempt to engage the convoy and turn for home, independent of his destroyer escort.

Fraser was now racing to cut across *Scharnhorst*'s southward track. At 16.17, *Duke of York*'s 14-inch guns opened fire at 12,000 yards, and straddled their target—clearly illuminated by starshell—with the first broadside. Critics subsequently suggested that *Scharnhorst* might have been destroyed at this stage of the battle, had Fraser not delayed ordering in his destroyers. He was fearful that a premature torpedo attack would drive the German ship away north-eastwards, beyond his grasp.

Under fire from *Duke of York*, *Scharnhorst* turned away at full speed first north, then east. By 17.13, when at last Fraser loosed his destroyers, he had left it too late. The enemy was outrunning both the British cruisers and destroyers. Only *Duke of York*'s guns were still within range. At 18.20, an 11-inch shell from *Scharnhorst* temporarily severed the flagship's radar cables, blinding her gunners. For a few terrible minutes, Fraser believed that victory had been snatched from him.

Yet just before the British ship was hit, although *Scharnhorst* had succeeded in opening the range to 20,000 yards, a shell from *Duke of York* burst in her number 1 boiler room, abruptly cutting the ship's speed to eight knots. Power was restored soon afterwards. But the brief crisis allowed three of Fraser's destroyers to close. Four of the twenty-eight torpedoes which they launched hit *Scharnhorst*, drastically reducing her power and ensuring her destruction. At 19.45, after enduring concentrated gunfire and torpedo attacks for almost three hours more, *Scharnhorst* sank. Her guns continued firing almost to the last. Out of her complement of 1,803, thirty-six survivors were plucked from the Arctic darkness.

Duke of York's gunnery had plainly been the decisive factor in the victory. For all the undoubted British advantage of strength, the entrapment and destruction of *Scharnhorst* had been a considerable achievement, ensuring Fraser's perpetual celebrity in the annals of the Royal Navy, alongside that of the Norwegian North Cape beyond which the battle was fought.

Fraser's remaining service with the Home Fleet was dominated by the conduct of further Russian convoys. But with the shift of strategic attention from the Mediterranean to north-west Europe, force was now available to provide massive escorts, and Allied losses declined steeply. On 16 June 1944 Fraser relinquished command. He was now assigned to become commander-in-chief, Eastern Fleet. In November he became C-in-C Pacific Fleet.

Fraser's task in the Pacific was delicate. The US navy dominated the theatre, and the Royal Navy's contribution seemed not merely modest, but even unwelcome. The Americans were deeply suspicious of British imperial motives in the eastern hemisphere. It is a tribute to Fraser's competence and transparent good nature that he achieved an amicable working relationship with the Americans. He believed passionately in the need to develop—and to perpetuate post-war—Anglo-American co-operation. Such gestures as volunteering to adopt US navy signalling procedures went far to encourage trust.

His command continued to suffer from lack of resources, and it was only in the last weeks of the war that its forces achieved real weight. The British were hampered by the acute discomfort of their ships in tropical conditions. But the fleet made a useful contribution to the last stages of the Pacific war. It was Fraser who signed the Japanese surrender document for Britain, aboard the battleship *Missouri* in Tokyo Bay on 2 September 1945.

On his return home in 1946, Fraser was saddened to be denied the succession as first sea lord. He was appointed C-in-C Portsmouth in May 1947, and at last gained the first sea lordship in September 1948, together with promotion to admiral of the fleet a month later.

Fraser's tenure at the Admiralty embraced a series of cold war crises, and finally responsibility for British naval participation in the Korean war. For all the affection and respect that he commanded as an old 'sea-dog', Fraser was considered by some critics to possess too limited an intellect to distinguish himself at the summits of power. He retired from the Royal Navy in April 1952, and passed the next twenty-eight years in almost uneventful retirement.

A barony was conferred upon him in 1946. He was appointed GCB in 1944 (KCB 1943, CB 1939); KBE in 1941 (OBE 1919). He was first and principal naval ADC to the King (1946–8), and held honorary degrees from the universities of Oxford (DCL 1947), Edinburgh (LLD 1953) and Wales (LLD 1955). He held the American DSM. He was a member of the Russian Order of Suvarov and of the Grand Order of Orange Nassau (Netherlands); was a chevalier of the Legion of Honour and holder of the croix de guerre with palm (France); and held the grand cross, Order of St Olav (Norway).

A lifelong bachelor, he died in London 12 February 1981. The barony became extinct. A portrait of him by Sir Oswald Birley hangs in the Royal Naval College, Greenwich.

[Richard Humble, *Fraser of North Cape*, 1983; Stephen Roskill, *The War at Sea 1939–1945* (official history), 3 vols., 1954–61; F. H. Hinsley and others, *British Intelligence in the Second World War*, vol. III, pt. i, 1984; John Winton (John Pratt), *The Forgotten Fleet*, 1969; Stephen Roskill, *Churchill and the Admirals*, 1977.]

MAX HASTINGS

published 1990

FRENCH John Denton Pinkstone

(1852–1925)

First Earl of Ypres

Field-marshal, was born 28 September 1852 at Ripple, Kent. He was the only son and the youngest of the seven children of Commander John Tracy William French, R.N., J.P. and D.L. for the county of Kent, by his wife, Margaret, daughter of William Eccles, of Glasgow. Both his parents died while John French was still a child, so that he was brought up by his sisters, who intended him to enter his father's profession. To that end he was educated at Eastman's Naval Academy, Portsmouth, and entered H.M.S. *Britannia* in 1866, whence he passed out as a midshipman in 1868. But he never took kindly to the sea, and hankered after a military career. In 1870 he therefore left the navy to join the Suffolk Artillery Militia, serving with that regiment until he succeeded in passing into the regular army. In 1874 he was gazetted to the 8th Hussars, being transferred to the 19th Hussars a few weeks later.

French's advancement proved rapid. After serving as adjutant for a few months he was promoted captain in October 1880, and obtained his majority in April 1883. His career during these years differed in no wise from that of many of his colleagues. He learnt to ride well, played polo, and took great interest in the training of his men. In addition he developed a taste for books and showed anxiety to acquire some knowledge of the science of war. This was the more noteworthy in that he subsequently never displayed any bent for abstract knowledge nor even aspired to pass into the Staff College. In 1881 he had been appointed adjutant of the Northumberland Hussars (yeomanry), but relinquished that post in September 1884 when offered the opportunity of going to Egypt, where Lord Wolseley was organizing an expedition for the relief of General Gordon, then besieged in Khartoum. On arrival, French assumed command of the detachment of the 19th Hussars which was allotted to the column of Sir Herbert Stewart. This column crossed the Bayuda desert from Korti to Metemmeh. But long before coming within sight of Khartoum Stewart learnt that the place had been captured and Gordon killed. Thereupon he decided to retreat by the way he had advanced. Throughout this withdrawal French displayed courage and resource, covering every movement with success. During this campaign he was present at the actions of Abu Klea, Gubat, and Metemmeh, and on one occasion was all but cut off by the pursuing enemy. On return home, after being specially commended for his work, he was awarded a brevet lieutenant-colonelcy in February 1885.

After three years' home service, in September 1888 French was promoted to the command of the 19th Hussars. As he was then thirty-six years of age and had only fourteen years service to his credit he had every prospect of rising high in a profession where seniority counted for so much. His Egyptian experience, together with a practical grasp of minor tactics, stood him in good stead. In February 1889 he was advanced to the rank of brevet-colonel, and shortly afterwards took his regiment to India, where it gained a name for efficiency. At the end of his period of command, in the spring of 1893, French was placed on half pay, and, in spite of early promise, there seemed some prospect of his being forgotten. But the adjutant-general, Sir Redvers Buller, mindful of French's work in the Sudan, offered him the appointment of assistant-adjutant-general at the War Office; this post he accepted in August 1895, being simultaneously promoted full colonel. In his new employment French was occupied in the production of a new *Cavalry Manual*, in the formation of cavalry brigades, and in other reforms, long overdue, in the mounted branch. In May 1897 he was transferred from the War Office to Canterbury in order to assume the duty of colonel on the staff, an appointment which carried with it the command of the newly formed 2nd Cavalry brigade with the rank of brigadier-general. Eighteen months later he was again transferred—to the 1st Cavalry brigade at Aldershot, a move which gave him the temporary rank of major-general.

French

The outbreak of the South African War proved the great opportunity of French's career. In September 1899 he was dispatched to Natal to command the mounted troops under Sir George Stuart White. Almost on arrival he was sent forward to assist the retirement of Major-General Penn Symons from Dundee to Ladysmith. After the death of Penn Symons at Talana Hill the command devolved on Major-General Yule, who was greatly assisted in his retreat by French. The latter had succeeded in dislodging the enemy from a strongly held position at Elandslaagte on 21 October. It was French's first opportunity of commanding a force of all arms in the field, and he was highly commended for his share in the operations. Shortly afterwards White's troops were concentrated in Ladysmith, and it became obvious that a siege was inevitable, so that mounted troops would find no employment there. French and his staff accordingly managed to escape in the last train that succeeded in leaving the town.

French was now sent to the Cape, where he was confronted with a menacing situation. Lord Methuen was advancing along the railway towards the Orange Free State in an endeavour to relieve Kimberley, and encountering serious opposition. Further east Major-General Sir William Forbes Gatacre was attempting to prevent the disaffected Dutch from joining the Boer commandos. Between the two British forces lay an invading Boer column whose farther advance must gravely threaten Methuen's communications. French thereupon led all available mounted troops to Naauwpoort junction in order to check any further Boer movements. While he was able to keep the enemy at bay in the region of Colesberg, the general situation was made more difficult by the successive defeats of Methuen and Gatacre in Cape Colony and of Buller in Natal. In spite of these complications French continued to work round his opponents with such success that he virtually cleared Cape Colony of invaders before the arrival of Lord Roberts in South Africa in January 1900.

With his mounted troops French was next ordered by Roberts to turn the Boer left on the River Modder, where Methuen was facing the enemy. By forcing the passage of the River Riet French achieved this object. Then, by launching against the Boers two whole cavalry brigades in open order at the gallop, he cleared the road to Kimberley, and relieved the town on 15 February. His further movements enabled him to seize Koodoesrand Drift on the Orange River, thereby holding up the Boer retreat from Kimberley towards Bloemfontein. This check resulted in the surrender of 4,000 Boers at Paardeberg on 27 February. During the subsequent advance on Pretoria, French, by turning the Boer front at Poplar Grove (7 March) and again at Driefontein (10 March), greatly assisted the advance, and on 13 March Bloemfontein was occupied. But French's next manœuvres at Karee Siding on 29 March and at Thaba Nchu on 28 April were not so conspicuously successful. After the fall of Pretoria on 5 June French followed up the Boers until they retreated over the Portuguese frontier at Koomati Poort. Finally during July he carried out some skilful movements which led to the occupation of Middelburg, and in September he took Barberton as the result of a clever manœuvre. For his noteworthy share in the campaign his rank of major-general was made substantive and he was created K.C.B.

The remainder of French's service in South Africa does not require detailed record. After losing the services of his two brilliant staff officers, Major (later Sir) Herbert Lawrence and Major (later Field-Marshal Earl) Haig, he assumed command of the Johannesburg district in November 1900. In June 1901 he was transferred to Cape Colony in order to hunt down the last Boer commandos active in that district. His movements during these two years, if sadly lacking the characteristics of his earlier operations, were slowly brought to a satisfactory conclusion. In August 1902 he was promoted lieutenant-general and created K.C.M.G.

Shortly after his return home French was appointed commander-in-chief at Aldershot, and held that post until November 1907. The reform of army-training on the basis of South African experiences was then to the fore, while the troops themselves were being regrouped according to a new plan of divisional organization. French found himself fully occupied with these tasks; but he held very conservative views as to any tactical innovations in his own arm, the cavalry. Before vacating his position he was promoted general in February 1907, and created G.C.V.O. A few months later, on leaving Aldershot, he was appointed inspector-general of the forces. In this capacity he was responsible for a total reform in the conduct of military manœuvres; he visited Canada; and he was engaged in supervising the training of the higher commands of the army generally. In March 1912, when he was close on sixty years of age, he succeeded Field-Marshal Lord Nicholson as chief of the Imperial General Staff. In June 1913 he was promoted field-marshal.

The principal interest in French's tenure of the headship of the general staff centres round what is known as the Curragh incident. This arose out of the declaration made by a number of officers stationed at the Curragh in county Kildare that they would resign their commissions rather than participate in any armed coercion of Ulster into the acceptance of Home Rule for Ireland. A written pledge that they would not be thus employed was handed to the representatives of these officers by the secretary of state for war, Colonel Seely, after the document had been initialed by French in his capacity of chief of the general staff and by Sir Spencer Ewart in that of adjutant-general. The Cabinet, however, repudiated this undertaking, whereupon both French and Ewart resigned their appointments.

French

It had long been an open secret that in the event of a European war French would command any British forces dispatched to the Continent. His appointment as commander-in-chief of the British Expeditionary Force followed the declaration of war against Germany on 4 August 1914. On 14 August he landed at Boulogne at the head of one cavalry and four infantry divisions. On the 21st he met General Lanrezac, commanding the French Fifth Army, which formed the extreme left of the French forces, and he conceived an antipathy for this officer which produced grave results. The British troops, after concentrating round Maubeuge, began moving forward in prolongation of Lanrezac's advance with a view to gaining touch with the Belgian forces. The British came into contact with the Germans near Mons, where French, dissatisfied with the information supplied by his allies, decided to give battle. On the morning of the 23rd the German First Army there attacked the British. The blow fell upon the II Corps under General Sir Horace Lockwood Smith-Dorrien, who was left virtually unsupported by the I Corps under Sir Douglas Haig, which was on the inner flank. The full significance of the German movement then began to dawn upon French. On 24 August, realizing that he was threatened with a total envelopment of his left, he began to retreat, following the similar French movement. In so doing he allowed his army to separate, the II Corps retiring to the west of the forest of Mormal, the I Corps keeping to the east of it. The Germans pressed forward, with the result that on 26 August Smith-Dorrien, in view of the fatigue of his troops, and after consulting Major-General Allenby, then commanding the cavalry, decided to contest the enemy's advance. Smith-Dorrien informed French of this decision and received his written approval. The battle of Le Cateau resulted, and the German advance was effectually checked, though at the cost of severe loss in men and guns. Thereupon French, convinced that the II Corps had met with disaster, motored forty miles back to Noyon, thinking only of saving what he could of his army; accordingly he prevented Haig from going to assist Lanrezac when the latter fought a rearguard action at Guise on the 30th, and finally informed the Cabinet of his intention of retreating south-westwards to St. Nazaire, regardless of his allies' movements. The situation grew so critical that Lord Kitchener, then secretary of state for war, travelled to Paris, met French on 1 September, and enjoined him to conform to the French plan of action. French did so, but after suggesting a stand on the River Marne, on the 3rd, continued to retreat on the 4th and 5th, although he must have learnt from General Gallieni, the governor of Paris, that the French armies were about to turn.

By this time a new French Sixth Army was being formed near Amiens. On 5 September General Joffre, the French commander-in-chief, gave the order for a general attack. On the 6th French thereupon advanced northwards. On the 9th he recrossed the River Marne and entered a gap of thirty miles that had been allowed to form between the German First and Second Armies. This threat, combined with the pressure of the new French Sixth Army, was really instrumental in bringing about the German retreat to the River Aisne, where they held fast to a strongly entrenched position. French, now as optimistic as he had been pessimistic before, and imagining the enemy to be still in retreat, ordered several attacks on the German line that were carried out with great gallantry. In spite of them, by the 15 September a stalemate resulted which led to a succession of attempts made by both armies to outflank each other farther to the north-west; this was the so-called 'race to the sea'.

The British Expeditionary Force was now transferred to Flanders. The first troops left the Aisne on 1 October, and arrived in the region of Bethune a week later; the rest continued to detrain in Flanders until the 19th. On the 14th the II Corps was heavily engaged at La Bassée. On the 20th the Germans began a series of violent attacks on the Allied left that only grew fiercer as they proved to be inconclusive. On the 22nd French reported to Kitchener that the enemy were 'playing their last card'. Two days later, in spite of a grave shortage of munitions, he was writing that the battle was 'practically won'. Yet the crisis was not reached until the 31st in front of Ypres, where the British stood flanked on either side by the French. No commander-in-chief could exercise much influence on the course of such a struggle. The valour of the men in the ranks and the efforts of their direct leaders could alone affect the ebb and flow of the battle, while the French troops, themselves heavily engaged, lent precious aid to their British allies. By the middle of November the fighting died down into the comparative quiet of trench warfare.

Throughout the winter French continued in optimistic mood, maintaining that he could break the German line provided he were given adequate forces and a sufficiency of high-explosive ammunition. Accordingly on 10–13 March he made his attempt at Neuve Chapelle. In spite of an auspicious opening the effort proved fruitless. It had been planned on too small a scale and was inadequately supported. French next combined with the Allies in elaborating a greater project. But before this could be put into effect the Germans again attacked at Ypres on 22 April. The infantry assault was preceded by the first discharge of chlorine gas released in the War, which drove back the French on the British left in wild disorder. Failing to exploit this somewhat unexpected success the Germans yet succeeded in placing the British flank, then commanded by Smith-Dorrien, in jeopardy. French, now swayed by alternate hope and fear, succeeded in holding his own, but subsequently vented his resentment on Smith-Dorrien so strongly that the latter resigned his command on 6 May. The battle of

Frezenberg Ridge followed, involving severe fighting from the 8th to the 13th of May, while there was a final attack on Bellewarde Farm on the 24th.

Meanwhile, in compliance with his allies' plans, French attempted to seize the Aubers Ridge on 9 May, hoping thereby to facilitate the capture of Lille. As the operation failed, renewed attempts were made at Festubert from the 15th to the 27th, and, on the failure of these, yet a third attack was launched at Givenchy on 15 June. In each of these French failed in his purpose. The attacks were delivered with inadequate forces, while on every occasion the enemy, being well prepared to meet the British tactics, parried the assault.

At length a more ambitious plan was put forward by the French—a combined attack against both fronts of the great German salient in France. This time French was not so confident of success. Only with reluctance was he induced, on the grounds of reasons of state, to participate in the operation, the British share of which became the battle of Loos (25–28 September 1915). This opened with a British attempt, under cover of a gas attack, to carry the Lens coal-field, a difficult area strongly fortified by the enemy. On the right the attempt at first made headway. But the gains could not be held. Moreover, French's handling of his general reserves, composed of raw 'new army' divisions, has since given rise to much criticism that may be regarded as justified. No real success was ever attained, and the fighting dragged on in a forlorn manner until 14 October.

Dissatisfaction with the conduct of the operations in France now became more pronounced. French himself was beginning to show signs of strain. Doubts were being freely expressed as to his fitness to cope with the intellectual and physical exigencies imposed by modern warfare on the high command. It is difficult not to sympathize with a leader who for fourteen months had filled a most unenviable position to the best of his ability. At the very outset he had found himself involved in a plan of campaign which was practically unknown to him. The plan failed; whereupon he had been compelled to carry out a retreat difficult and hazardous in the extreme. He did not have a fair opportunity of understanding his allies; they did not even try to understand him; worse still, they underrated the quality of the British troops and of their leaders. Grave difficulties arose in the conduct of the War as a whole. Inadequate provision had been made to meet the needs of such a campaign. Weaknesses became evident even in French's own head-quarters staff. Nevertheless, when all these unforeseen and immense obstacles are taken into account, the fact remains that French revealed defects not only of temperament but also of military aptitude, which must preclude him, in spite of his military qualities, from ever ranking with any of the great generals of the past. In particular, his protracted quarrel with Sir Horace Smith-Dorrien, and its grave sequel, together with the eventual publication of its details in an ill-judged book, *1914* (1919), can only be regarded as deplorable.

On 4 December 1915 French resigned his position as commander-in-chief, being succeeded on 19 December by his former staff-officer, Sir Douglas Haig. He had received the Order of Merit in December 1914; in January 1916 he was created Viscount French of Ypres and of High Lake, county Roscommon, and appointed commander-in-chief of the Home Forces. The constitution of this office was urgently needed, since the high command of all troops in the United Kingdom had so far been vested in the War Office, while the training of troops for overseas required much closer supervision and simplification than was thus possible. In this new capacity French achieved satisfactory results. More difficult was the protection of Great Britain against the air attacks which were threatening to impede the flow of munitions to the armies overseas. This complicated problem was assigned to French in the spring of 1916 and finally solved by the organization of special staffs and troops to deal with the raiders, so that by October 1916 the menace of the enemy's attacks by Zeppelin air-ships had been effectively countered. But during the summer and autumn of 1917 a series of hostile aeroplane raids revived the danger in a more acute form. Thanks to the vigorous efforts of the British aviation and anti-aircraft services these attacks were also overcome and French's task was thus achieved. No other enemy activity, save a few insignificant coastal bombardments, disturbed the United Kingdom down to the close of the War. French's reorganization of the system of home defence, whereby any possible enemy landings were to be resisted on the spot, was consequently never put to the test.

In Ireland, however, a situation of real gravity arose at Easter 1916, when the Sinn Fein party rose in arms in Dublin (24 April), seized certain points of the city, and proclaimed a republic. Fighting ensued, and French dispatched two Territorial divisions to Dublin. He also appointed General Sir John Maxwell to be commander-in-chief in Ireland. Within a short time the Rebellion was crushed and certain of its leaders shot after trial by court-martial. But Ireland remained a hotbed of acute discontent and a source of considerable anxiety until long after the end of the War.

In May 1918 French was appointed lord-lieutenant of Ireland. It was then thought that his Irish extraction and military reputation might win for him both respect and obedience among the Irish. As a result of the Irish Convention, which had just concluded its labours, it was still imagined that Ireland might accept some form of conscription in return for the grant of Home Rule. All such hopes were doomed to speedy disappointment. French next attempted to raise 50,000 voluntary recruits, but scarcely 10,000 could be obtained. Matters went from bad to worse, until the country could only be governed by military authority based on special regulations for the restoration of order. Nevertheless, the troops, supported by the Irish Constabulary and assisted by newly formed auxiliary police units, were hampered by restrictions of every kind. The struggle degenerated into a campaign of aggression and punishment, of outrages and of reprisals. In December 1919 a serious attempt was made on French's life, when a bomb and a volley of shots were aimed at the cortège of cars in which he travelled. French escaped unharmed, but his position only grew more unsatisfactory with the lapse of time. As a soldier there was no opening for him to command; as an administrator he was never able to enforce the law. On 30 April 1921 he resigned his post, after the passing of the Government of Ireland Act, which by its nature entailed a change of viceroy. French thereupon retired into private life, and was created Earl of Ypres for his services in June 1922. Thereafter much of his time was spent in France, mainly in Paris, until in August 1923 he was appointed captain of Deal Castle by the lord warden of the Cinque Ports. There he decided to make his home, and there he died, after a severe operation, on 22 May 1925.

French married in 1880 Eleanora, daughter of Richard William Selby-Lowndes, of Elmers, Bletchley, Buckinghamshire. He had two sons and one daughter; both his sons served in the European War. He was succeeded as second earl by his elder son, John Richard Lowndes (born 1881), who had retired from the Royal Artillery some years before the War, as the result of a hunting accident.

French figures in the picture 'Some General Officers of the Great War' by J. S. Sargent, which is hung in the National Portrait Gallery. A portrait of him by J. St. H. Lander belongs to the Cavalry Club, Piccadilly. A cartoon appeared in *Vanity Fair* 12 July 1900. There is a monument to him in the rebuilt cathedral at Ypres and a memorial tablet in Canterbury Cathedral.

[*The Times*, 23 May 1925; Sir J. E. Edmonds, (Official) *History of the Great War. Military Operations, France and Belgium, 1914–1915, 1922–1928*; Edward Gerald French, *Field-Marshal Lord French*, 1931; Lord French, *1914*, 1919; E. L. Spiers, *Liaison*, 1930; personal knowledge.]

H. DE WATTEVILLE

published 1937

Bernard Cyril

(1889–1963)

First Baron Freyberg

Lieutenant-general, was born 21 March 1889 in Richmond, Surrey, the seventh son of James Freyberg, a surveyor, and the fifth by his second wife, Julia Hamilton. The family emigrated to New Zealand in 1891 and settled in Wellington, where James Freyberg joined the Forestry Department. Bernard Freyberg was educated at Wellington College, New Zealand, where he distinguished himself as a swimmer. After leaving school at the age of nearly sixteen, he took up dentistry, and after qualifying in Otago (1911), practised his profession for a couple of years. He had already formed the ambition of swimming the English Channel, for which he trained assiduously in the Waihou and Waikato rivers, an interest which early began to be rivalled by his soldiering with the local territorials, and by 1912 he had been gazetted in Morrinsville as a second lieutenant. He could not resist the opportunity for change afforded by the dock strike of 1913 and volunteered as a stoker in the *Maunganui* en route to Sydney. On his return he obtained a stoker's certificate and then set off for America.

His adventures from then on are both legendary and obscure but, before the end of August 1914, he had somehow got himself to London where he perhaps contrived to meet (Sir) Winston Churchill. Through Churchill's influence he became a temporary lieutenant in the Royal Naval Volunteer Reserve and was soon given command of A company in the Hood battalion of the Royal Naval Division. He led his company in the Antwerp adventure, Churchill's brain-child, and brought it back via Ostend from the subsequent débacle, the first of Freyberg's four evacuations by sea.

The division was next assigned to Gallipoli. Freyberg sailed with the Hood battalion 28 February 1915. Among the other officers of a brilliant mess were Arthur Asquith (son of the prime minister), (Sir) A. P. Herbert, and Rupert Brooke. When Brooke was buried on Scyros 23 April, Freyberg helped carry his coffin and dig his grave.

The division's role was to cover the landings of the main force by a mock landing in the Gulf of Xeros. Freyberg managed to persuade his superiors to entrust the task of diversion to him rather than risk many lives for a job which a bold and powerful swimmer could achieve alone. After dark, 25 April, he swam ashore and lit a series of flares along the beaches. He then swam back again and was got safely aboard his ship. For this he was appointed to the DSO, the first of his many decorations.

In the later fighting on Gallipoli he was severely wounded in July but recovered rapidly, and by 19 August he was not only back with his battalion but was its commanding officer. He remained with the battalion for the rest of the campaign, and after the evacuation of the Dardanelles in January 1916 he returned to England. The division had gone directly to France and was now reformed as 63rd division, although without losing its anomalous character. Freyberg was confirmed in command of the Hood battalion with the rank of lieutenant-colonel, and left for France with it in May. His first major battle on the new front was in November on the Somme. Within forty-eight hours he was four times wounded but he refused to be evacuated until the advanced position, captured largely because of his leadership and example, had been consolidated against counter-attack. He was awarded the Victoria Cross.

His wounds were severe, and detained him in hospital and on leave until March 1917. In April, as brigadier-general, he was given command of 173rd brigade of 58th division—thus ending his service with the Royal Naval Division and his men of the Hood battalion—and distinguished himself in the May fighting at Bullecourt. In September, during the third battle of Ypres, he suffered multiple wounds and had to spend three months in hospital in England. On his return to the front he was given command of 88th brigade of 29th division, near Passchendaele, a grim name which he never forgot. He was in much of the major fighting of 1918, including the last battle of Ypres, where he won a bar to his DSO. He ended the war, ardent to the last, with a successful dash to forestall the demolition of a bridge at Lessines just before 11.00 hours on Armistice Day, winning a second bar to his DSO. He had already been mentioned in dispatches five times, wounded six times, and the French Government now awarded him the croix de guerre with palms. His eldest brothers, Oscar and Paul, had not been so lucky: Oscar was killed at Gallipoli in 1915 and Paul in France two years later.

In England, although deprecating heroics himself, Freyberg had become a byword for heroism and a friend of many people in positions of influence. In spite of a hankering to go to Balliol where some of his Hood friends had been educated, he had by now recognized his *métier* and resolved to become a professional soldier; his peacetime army career was interrupted briefly in 1922 by an unsuccessful attempt, under Liberal auspices, to win a seat in the House of Commons. He had passed the staff course at Camberley in 1920, and served for a time with the Grenadier Guards until, in 1929, he was given command of the 1st battalion of the Manchester Regiment. But soldiering had not altogether ousted his earlier ambitions, and he made three attempts to swim the Channel—in 1925, when he failed by only 500 yards, and again twice in 1926. In 1931–3 he was assistant adjutant and quartermaster-general of the Southern Command, and by 1934 was a major-general. In 1937, however, his strikingly successful career received its first real check, under the axe of Leslie (later Lord) Hore-Belisha. He was declared medically unfit, and indignantly challenged his examiners to climb Snowdon: they refused—he went, alone; he was retired with the rank of major-general. For the next two years he interested himself in business and industry as a director of the Birmingham Small Arms Company. He also revived his interest in politics and in 1938 was adopted as prospective Conservative candidate for the Spelthorne division of Middlesex.

On the outbreak of war in 1939 he was recalled to the army, and offered his services to the New Zealand Government. With the warm approval of Sir Edmund (later Lord) Ironside, Lord Gort, and Winston Churchill he was appointed general in command of the 2nd New Zealand Expeditionary Force, 23 November. He flew to New Zealand and met the War Cabinet and thereafter obtained from the New Zealand Government a document—his 'charter'—which gave him wide powers of decision over the organization, administration, and employment of the forces under his command, which were to be trained in Egypt and to fight as a single unit.

The 5th brigade, one of the three in the newly formed New Zealand division, was diverted to England in 1940, where it was to remain to strengthen the defences against the threatened invasion, and stayed there until the end of the year when the threat had receded. So it was not until March 1941 that Freyberg had his division together as a whole in Egypt, with all three brigades, under the over-all command of Sir Archibald (later Earl) Wavell and Sir Henry Maitland (later Lord) Wilson. In a matter of days the division embarked for Greece, an enterprise about which Freyberg had considerable but private misgivings: his diary says, 'the situation is a grave one; we shall be fighting against heavy odds on a plan that has been ill-conceived and one that violates every principle of war'.

What had begun as a forlorn hope soon became a fighting withdrawal in the face of an enemy far greater in numbers and vastly superior in all the materials of war. This withdrawal was followed by an evacuation which owed its success to the British Navy as well as to the fighting troops and their commanders. The essential Freyberg was revealed in his refusal to obey Wavell's orders to leave by air, staying with his men to the end.

Two of his brigades had been evacuated to Crete, the third to Egypt. When Freyberg halted in Crete to see his troops he found Wavell who had come to see the situation for himself. Wavell ordered Freyberg to take command of the island and hold it against the expected German invasion by sea and air. With a very few and inefficient tanks, obsolete artillery and little of it, a grave shortage of arms and equipment, virtually no air force, and every kind of supply problem, it was a desperate undertaking. Freyberg performed prodigies in the three weeks before invasion began, 20 May 1941. But the enemy, landing by glider and parachute, gained a foothold on the airfield at Maleme, after fierce fighting. This enabled them to land men and weapons by air. Given this and their total command of the sky, their success was now certain, even though an attempted sea invasion was destroyed by the Royal Navy. The best that Freyberg and his troops could do was to keep an unbroken front, mount counter-attacks whenever possible, avoid encirclement, and withdraw to the southern evacuation beaches. Once again, the Royal Navy brought salvation.

After his return to Egypt an inter-services inquiry fully exonerated Freyberg for the loss of Crete, and indeed praised him warmly for his conduct there and in Greece. He now pressed on with reorganizing the division and training it for desert operations. Both he and the division played a vital part in the battle of November-December ('Crusader') for the relief of Tobruk but, through no fault of its commander, the division suffered heavy losses. Sir Claude Auchinleck had succeeded Wavell as commander-in-chief Middle East, and he and Freyberg differed profoundly in their views about the use of brigade groups and the handling of ar-moured forces. It was with some relief, therefore, that Freyberg received orders to take the division to Syria.

The reverses suffered by the Eighth Army in the summer of 1942 in its battles with Rommel made it necessary for the division to return to the fray. Freyberg brought his men back from Syria in a lightning march which covered 1,200 miles in under eight days and they arrived in time to prevent the withdrawal of the Eighth Army from becoming a rout. The division was surrounded by German armour at Minqar Qaim but broke out in a night battle, Freyberg himself being wounded and coming out on a stretcher. The division withdrew safely to the Alamein line where it played an important part in checking Rommel's further advance.

On 10 August 1942, Freyberg returned from hospital, a tonic to the division which had suffered heavily in ill-advised offensives during his absence. Sir Harold Alexander (later Earl Alexander of Tunis) now suc-ceeded Auchinleck as commander-in-chief Middle East, and Bernard Montgomery (later Viscount Montgomery of Alamein) took command of the Eighth Army. Montgomery and Freyberg held the same views about the role of armour and the use of brigade groups and the two were in close agreement in the operations which followed: the defensive battle of Alam Halfa, when the division held the main southern flank while Rommel's armour ground itself to a standstill; and the decisive battle of Alamein when the Eighth Army at last went over to a victorious offensive. Freyberg and his division were in the thick of the initial fighting, the breakthrough, and the pursuit which followed.

After a bold assault by one of its infantry battalions had cleared the Halfaya Pass and ensured the way into Libya, the division was given a rest until after the fall of Benghazi. When Montgomery felt ready to undertake dislodging Rommel from the El Agheila positions he sent Freyberg and the division, with armour under command, in a left hook round Agheila which narrowly failed to cut off Rommel's retreat. A further attempt at Nofilia went even closer to success. Rommel continued his withdrawal but could not hold Tripoli which was taken 23 January 1943, the division among the leading British forces. During a halt there, Churchill paid a visit and at a parade of the whole division hailed Freyberg as 'the salamander of the British Empire'.

The enemy now took up a strong position on the Mareth Line. Montgomery decided to try and turn the defence by a left hook through the Tebaga Gap and assigned the job to Freyberg and his division which was so strongly reinforced for the operation that it temporarily became the New Zealand Corps. Contact was made with the enemy 21 March, and the course of the subsequent fighting made Montgomery decide to switch (Sir) Brian Horrocks and his X Corps from the frontal attack to the more promising one on the left flank. The move was a success and Rommel was forced to abandon the Mareth Line. Difficult actions in mountainous country followed but the German and Italian forces were now pinned between First and Eighth Armies and the end was inevitable. By 13 May 1943 Tunis had fallen and the war was over in North Africa.

Ever since the entry into Libya the New Zealand Government had been considering whether its division, like the 9th Australian division, should be withdrawn to the Pacific. Freyberg was consulted at that time and, after sounding out the feeling of the division, favoured staying in North Africa. The Government, warmly applauded by Churchill, had then decided in favour of staying. Now that the fighting in North Africa was over, the question came up again. There were strong political and administrative arguments for transfer to the Pacific front. And the New Zealand Government was also concerned lest Freyberg's own professional career should suffer if they exploited his loyalty to keep him with the division: by ability and experience he was well qualified to command a corps, or even an army. In the event, it was again decided by the Government to keep the division in the Mediterranean theatre; and Freyberg, a lieutenant-general since 1942 although only commanding a division, made it clear that he wanted to go on leading his New Zealanders. At least one of those who might have succeeded him, Brigadier (Sir) Howard Kippenberger, had no regrets: 'campaigning without the General seemed unthinkable,' he said.

Indeed, the men of the division were as devoted to Freyberg as he was to them, and in the minds of many they were as inseparable as the two parts of a centaur.

After a period of rest and reorganization, during which 4th brigade was equipped with tanks and reincorporated, Freyberg took the division to join the Eighth Army on the Sangro front in Italy. There they met their old enemies from Crete, the German paratroops, amid conditions very different from the desert. The days of widely flanking left hooks and deep armoured penetration in terrain the mastery of which had earned for the division the description 'ball of fire' were for the time being over. A fierce battle which had opened in great promise settled into a grim winter campaign and by Christmas there was stalemate.

In January 1944 the division was switched to the command of the Fifth Army and the Cassino front. Freyberg became GOC New Zealand Corps once more, this time with two British divisions under command and a regiment of American armour in support. His task was to try to break through at Cassino where two formidable onslaughts by the Fifth Army had already failed. In spite of the controversial destruction of the monastery and the town of Cassino by aerial bombardment, two powerful attacks by the corps failed to get through, although narrowly. Losses were heavier than the New Zealand Government was prepared to go on accepting, and towards the end of March the division was withdrawn to a quieter sector of the front.

Alexander now turned to the planning and execution of the May offensive which took place in the south-west sector of the front and broke through to link up with the Anzio bridgehead and drive through to Rome. The division conformed on the north of the main advance and took part in the pursuit north of Rome; it went on to play a conspicuous forcing role in the advance towards Florence. According to Sir Oliver Leese, in command of the Eighth Army, if it had not been for Freyberg and his division the whole advance of the Eighth Army would have had to be held up for fresh formations to be brought in. Meanwhile, Freyberg's only son, Paul, an officer of the Grenadier Guards in the British 1st division, had been reported missing in Italy on 24 February. It later transpired that he had been taken prisoner, escaped, and made his way to Vatican property at Castel Gandolfo. He was then smuggled into the Vatican City in the boot of a papal car, and was finally collected by his father after the liberation of Rome in June.

The division was transferred in August to the Adriatic front, where Freyberg was injured in an air accident. But his impatient resilience and powerful constitution soon had him out of hospital again and he commanded the division in the difficult advances to the Senio river. When the spring offensive opened 9 April 1945, the division took the front running and raced ahead so fast that, when the Germans in Italy capitulated 2 May, it was already in Trieste and Freyberg had won a third bar to his DSO. Once more at an ending Freyberg had moved with such speed as to gain a vital position before the guns became silent, the armour halted, and the infantry grounded arms.

So ended Freyberg's last campaign and that of the division with which he had become identified. In 1945 he was appointed governor-general of New Zealand, an appointment so successful that it was extended in 1950 at the request of the New Zealand Government. When the extension ended in 1952 he was appointed lieutenant-governor and deputy constable of Windsor Castle.

Freyberg was a large man physically, six feet and one and a half inches tall and very powerfully built. He was large also in other ways: large-minded, lion-hearted, magnanimous, and great of soul. So closely was he identified, in the war of 1939–45, with his New Zealand Division that it was difficult to recall the one without the other. Freyberg moulded the division into a superb fighting machine, but the New Zealanders provided the material and they in turn had their effect on the mature Freyberg, modifying the stiffness of the British-trained regular soldier. The combination of men and commander produced, behind an appearance of casualness, a disciplined camaraderie within all ranks which stood the test of some of the severest fighting and heaviest casualties of the war. When Montgomery first took command of the Eighth Army he remarked that the New Zealanders did not seem to salute much. 'If you wave to them they'll wave back,' Freyberg replied. The great Churchill parade at Tripoli was another sort of reply. When spit-and-polish were required Freyberg knew that his division could be counted on to produce them with the best. The confidence he inspired in his men was founded not only on the standards of courage and endurance and fire that he himself exemplified, but on his respect for them and his tireless solicitude for their welfare in and out of battle. 'You cannot treat a man like a butler and expect him to fight like a lion', was a favourite saying of his. He was known to all his men by sight and was never far from where the fighting was hottest. His imperturbability under fire was the subject of endless anecdote—he was a man who 'did not know the use of fear'. As 'the General' he was a myth, and as 'Tiny' he was a mascot, and he had the sort of fame in the world at large which normally comes only to the commanders of armies.

He had the gift of finding and keeping senior officers of the same toughness and aggressive competence as himself and he controlled them by a natural authority, a formidable presence, a total integrity, which did not need the support of outward forms. He commanded the division for five long years in and out of battle and, in spite of all the changes in men and fortune, the division which fought in the last campaign was recognizably the same and fought with the same *élan* as the division which fought in Greece and Crete and at Sidi Rezegh. This was Freyberg's doing. He was an example not only to his own men but to his equals and superiors in rank. Many a corps commander felt he had to live up to his redoubtable subordinate; and even Montgomery was known to acknowledge the help which Freyberg gave him.

Nor should Freyberg's contribution to the war on the high political level be overlooked. He was in effect a sort of plenipotentiary of the New Zealand Government, although answerable to it and deeply aware also of the problems of the British War Cabinet. Here he had the advantages of the expatriate, an equal understanding of both his countries, and a sense of their common cause. His modesty and his objectivity about himself, and his discretion in dealing with the perplexities of a loyalty both common and divided, evoked and met with corresponding qualities in the members of the New Zealand and the British Governments and produced a relationship which was a model of its kind. In this particular role he is important for constitutional history, for the history of the relations between the United Kingdom and the Dominions and the United States, at a time of great stress. It was not by his decision that the New Zealand Division stayed and contributed so much to victory in North Africa and Europe, but the confidence felt in him by both his Government and his troops had been fully earned and was a vital factor in the ultimate success.

Freyberg received an honorary LLD from St. Andrews in 1922 and a DCL from Oxford in 1945. He was appointed CB in 1936 and KCB as well as KBE in 1942, CMG in 1919 and GCMG in 1946, and was raised to the peerage in 1951. In 1922 he married Barbara, daughter of Sir Herbert Jekyll and widow of a brother-officer, the Hon. Francis Walter Stafford McLaren, MP, killed in 1917. She also made a distinguished contribution by organizing welfare for the troops during the second war and was appointed OBE in 1943. She was as popular as her husband in New Zealand when he was governor-general, and was appointed GBE in 1953. She died in 1973. Their only son, Paul Richard (born 1923), succeeded to the title when his father died at Windsor 4 July 1963.

Two portraits painted by Peter McIntyre are in the possession of the family. There is a portrait in the Imperial War Museum painted by Ambrose McEvoy in 1918; another portrait by Peter McIntyre painted during the second war is in the Wellington Art Gallery; and there is a painting by Edward I. Halliday, executed shortly before Freyberg's death, in the Auckland War Memorial Museum. There is a bronze bust by Oscar Nemon in New Zealand House in London and a replica of it in the Defence

Ministry in Wellington, as well as a posthumous bronze by Nemon in Freyberg's tablet in the Soldiers' Corner of the crypt of St. Paul's Cathedral.

[*Official History of New Zealand in the Second World War 1939–45*, War History Branch, Department of Internal Affairs, Wellington, New Zealand; Douglas Jerrold, *The Royal Naval Division*, 1927; Peter Singleton-Gates, *General Lord Freyberg, V. C.*, 1963; Sir Howard Kippenberger, *Infantry Brigadier*, 1949; private information; personal knowledge.]

D. M. DAVIN

published 1981

FRYATT Charles Algernon

(1872–1916)

Merchant seaman, was born at Southampton 2 December 1872, the second son of Charles Fryatt, merchant seaman, by his wife, Mary Brown Percy. He first attended the Freemantle school in his native town, but was transferred to the corporation school at Harwich when his father removed to that port on entering the service of the Great Eastern Railway Company, in which he eventually rose to be a chief officer. Young Charles Fryatt adopted his father's calling, served his apprenticeship, and worked his way upward in large sailing-vessels till in 1892 he entered the service of the Great Eastern Railway as an able seaman on the paddle-steamer *Colchester*, which was then the company's latest passenger vessel and was engaged on the route between Harwich and Antwerp. This vessel he eventually commanded (1913), it being the practice of the company to select its officers from those in the lower ranks of its own service. The system stood the test of war conditions; in spite of the removal of guiding lights and buoys, under the constant menace of enemy warships, submarines, and mines, the company maintained a service between British and Low Country ports throughout the European War, Captain Fryatt himself making no fewer than 143 trips before he was captured by the enemy.

Fryatt's first encounter with an enemy vessel was on 2 March 1915, when, being in command of the chartered steamer *Wrexham*, he was chased for forty miles by a German submarine but eventually made Rotterdam in safety. His own skill and determination and the exertions of the engine and boiler-room staffs were suitably recognized alike by the directors of the company and by the lords of the Admiralty. Captain Fryatt was now transferred to the Great Eastern Railway Company's s.s. *Brussels*, and on 28 March following was again attacked by a submarine, the u. 33. The enemy was sighted off the Maas light-vessel when four miles distant, and made direct for the mail steamer. Fryatt at once realized that the attacker was far speedier than his own ship. If, therefore, he attempted to get away he would soon be torpedoed; if he stopped in obedience to the enemy's signal he would make his ship an easier mark. He accordingly made up his mind to ram his enemy. He steered straight for the submarine, discharging rockets as he went, in order to call for any aid there might be in the neighbourhood and to make it appear that his ship had been supplied with guns. As the vessels approached, the u-boat submerged, and Captain Fryatt and others aboard the *Brussels* thought that the submarine was struck as they passed over her. In this they were mistaken; but the *Brussels* got safely away. For this exploit Captain Fryatt received from the Admiralty a gold watch 'in recognition of the example set by him when attacked by a German submarine'. In the following month the lords of the Admiralty, in a letter to the Great Eastern Railway Company, stated that the attention of the secretary for foreign affairs had been called to the 'highly courageous and meritorious conduct of the masters of the Company's steamers'. The commander of the *Wrexham* and of the *Brussels* was indicated amongst others, and the letter went on to express the Admiralty's thanks to the officers concerned for conduct 'which reflected credit on British seamanship'.

These well-earned recognitions, which naturally became generally known, seem to have led to Captain Fryatt's undoing. The Germans made long and careful preparations to capture him, intending to make an example which they fondly hoped would strike terror into his comrades under the red ensign. At length on the night of 22 June 1916, when the *Brussels* was homeward bound from the Hook of Holland, she was surrounded and captured by a considerable force of German destroyers, whose action showed that their commanders had obtained full information as to the ship's intended movements, probably from spies in Holland. The prize was taken into Zeebrugge and the master and crew sent on to Ruhleben internment camp, near Berlin. Captain Fryatt, however, was soon taken back to Belgium, where he was put on his trial before a court martial at Bruges on 27 July 1916 and condemned to death. Two days later he was shot, in spite of the protests of the United States minister, who had before the trial vainly attempted to secure adequate legal assistance for the prisoner. The charge laid against Captain Fryatt was that, not being a member of a combatant force, he had attempted to ram the submarine, u. 33. The official report of the trial characterized the prisoner as a *franc-tireur* of the sea, and laid stress on the approval of his conduct by the Admiralty and in the House of Commons as an aggravation of his alleged offence.

The deepest indignation was felt by all maritime peoples. The *franc-tireur* argument was seen to be wholly unfounded. It may be observed that a *franc-tireur* is a civilian who, without being attacked, picks off enemy soldiers unaware. Captain Fryatt was a civilian, but in no other respect comparable with a *franc-tireur*. In the House of Commons two days after the execution, Mr. Asquith, then prime minister, characterized the action of the German court martial as 'murder', and declared that 'His Majesty's government had heard with the utmost indignation of this atrocious crime against the law of nations and the usages of war'. More deliberate judgement in the calmer atmosphere of peace has in no way tended to alter opinion as to the gross illegality of the condemnation of Captain Fryatt.

Charles Fryatt married in 1896 Ethel Townend, who, with one son and six daughters, survived him. On his marriage he settled at Dovercourt, near Harwich. After the conclusion of peace his body was brought from Belgium to England on 7 July 1919 by a British war vessel, and buried at Dovercourt. A memorial service was held in St. Paul's Cathedral on 8 July.

[*The Times*, 9 July 1919; private information.]

BENEDICT WILLIAM GINSBURG

published 1927

FULLER John Frederick Charles

(1878–1966)

Major-general, was born 1 September 1878 at Chichester, son of the Revd Alfred Fuller, rector of the parish of West Itchenor, by his wife, Selma Marie Philippine de la Chevallerie. His father was descended from Roundheads, and his mother from Huguenots, by which Fuller explained his own heretical attitude to accepted dogma, the prime motive of his life. At an early age he developed a dislike of the conventional religious background in which he lived, first at Chichester, then at Lausanne, Switzerland, to which his parents moved when he was eight. Three years later he was sent to a preparatory school in Hampshire, from which he went to Malvern College at the age of fourteen. He stayed there for two years, detesting public-school life, as he said. The wishes of his maternal grandfather directed him towards the army, for which he showed no more enthusiasm than he had for Malvern, for the 'crammer' to which he went at the age of seventeen, or for the Royal Military College, Sandhurst, where he spent a year in 1897–8. He showed little brilliance, was not interested in sport, and took to reading works of history and fiction of his own choice.

Fuller was commissioned in 1898 into the 43rd, the 1st battalion Oxfordshire Light Infantry, and joined them in Ireland where he led the idle life of an infantry subaltern until the battalion was sent just before Christmas 1899 to participate in the South African war; he was promoted lieutenant two months later. Appendicitis removed him from the unit, and after his convalescence and return he spent the final six months of the war as an intelligence officer and for the first time began to take an interest in his profession. This died when he rejoined the battalion in 1902 just before it was sent to India, where he whiled away the boredoms of garrison life in studying Hindu religion and philosophy, including yoga, an interest which was to endure. Illness came to his aid again, this time in the form of a severe attack of enteric fever, and he was sent back to recuperate in England in 1906.

He had obtained his captaincy in 1905, and, in order to avoid a return to India, he applied for and obtained a post as adjutant of a militia battalion, shortly afterwards converted into the 10th Middlesex as a unit of the new Territorial Army. He enjoyed the independence of the job, and the association with keen part-time soldiers. It led to his first attempts at writing, in the form of training pamphlets for his unit. In 1911 the prospect of returning to his regiment loomed, and in order to avoid it he decided to try to enter the Staff College. His first attempt in 1912 failed; 1913 found him successful. By this time, at the age of thirty-five, he was applying himself seriously to his profession and also employing his pen, not only in training pamphlets but also in articles for the *Army Review* and the *Journal* of the Royal United Service Institution. He continued to do this at the Staff College, his principal theme, from which he was never to waver, being that weapons and their intelligent use were of much greater importance than either numbers of men or adherence to the classic dogma evolved from previous campaigns.

This brought him into conflict with the established teaching of the college, and, in retrospect, he considered it fortunate for him that August 1914 struck, the college broke up half-way through the two-year course, and Fuller went off to organize train movements in and out of Southampton docks. He found this interesting at first (and it brought him the temporary rank of major, made substantive in September 1915), but he wished to get nearer the front. After a spell on the staff at Tunbridge Wells, he joined the headquarters of VIII Corps in France in July 1915 as a GSO 3, from which he was promoted (February 1916) as GSO 2 of 37th division.

The division was broken up after the fierce and bloody battles of that summer on the Somme, and Fuller went, as temporary lieutenant-colonel, to a similar post in the Third Army headquarters of Sir Edmund (later Viscount) Allenby, involved to a great extent with training and organization. In these appointments he had time to think about the conduct of the war, write a little about it, and achieve a reputation as an efficient, methodical staff officer of sardonic humour, given to trenchant criticism.

Then came the turning point of his life, his posting as GSO 2 (later GSO 1) to the newly formed headquarters of the Tank Corps—or Heavy Branch, Machine-Gun Corps, as it was first called, commanded by (Sir) Hugh Elles—in late 1916. Although up to this point he had little knowledge of tanks, he was quick to see an opportunity to find fulfilment for all the frustrations which had built up in him: from *tabula rasa* to develop an entirely new arm, new methods of fighting the enemy, new ways of training. This novel and exciting task drew out all that was best in him and the plan for the famous battle of Cambrai (November 1917), for which he was largely responsible, was both his achievement and his reward. Its success led to consideration of more ambitious plans and ideas, and the decision to establish a tank branch of the general staff in the War Office under the leadership of Fuller, in July 1918. In preparation for this he and his colleagues at Tank Corps headquarters had developed 'Plan 1919', based on the performance of an experimental tank which had reached the speed of 20 m.p.h. Its concept was revolutionary: the deployment of fast tanks with a range of 200 miles in mass and depth, changing the whole idea of a tank from a slow trench-crossing fortress, working closely with infantry, to a truly mobile arm replacing cavalry in its historic role, a concept which was to be translated into reality in the war of 1939–45.

The end of the war in 1918 put paid to it, and Fuller, to his intense frustration, found all his plans shelved and the army intent on returning to its pre-war pattern, giving high priority to imperial policing. As an outlet he poured his energy into his pen, the first effusion, perhaps the most significant of all his writings, being the essay with which he won the gold medal of the Royal United Service Institution for 1919 (printed May 1920), in which he set out the blueprint for a new model army based on tanks, wholesale mechanization, and exploitation of wartime scientific and technical developments, notably wireless, aircraft, and gas. It was followed by other articles which provoked much controversy, in the midst of which he left the War Office and in 1923 went as a senior instructor to the Staff College. His mind and pen both now became more active, although the publication of many of his lectures and writings was suppressed for a time. It was in fact a disastrous posting. Hitherto the range of his imagination had been kept in check by the practical responsibilities of his job. But from now on his thoughts and writings became more theoretical, complicated, and less likely to be implemented, as he plunged deeper and wider in his search for theoretical bases for his ideas, making him vulnerable to those critics—and they were many—who were only too ready to point out that this forty-five-year-old colonel (he had been promoted in 1920) had hardly ever commanded any body of men and none at all in action.

In 1925 he published *The Foundations of the Science of War*, and the following year he became military assistant to the new CIGS, Sir George (later Lord) Milne. Fuller, with others, had high hopes that he and Milne together would transform the army into a 'new model', but opposition was too great and Milne too cautious. The breaking point came over Fuller's selection in 1927 to take command of what was intended to be an experimental mechanized force, but which was watered down to a standard infantry brigade and garrison on Salisbury Plain with only temporary *ad hoc* control over a few mechanized units. Fuller refused the command, and sent in his papers, but was persuaded to withdraw his resignation and went off to be GSO 1 to the 2nd division at Aldershot, commanded by Sir Edmund (later Lord) Ironside; in 1929 he was given command, at last, of an infantry brigade, first in the occupation army on the Rhine and then in Catterick, until he was promoted major-general (September 1930) at the age of fifty-two, and placed on half-pay. In 1931 he was offered command of Bombay District, with hardly any soldiers in it; this he refused, and remained on half-pay until retiring at the end of 1933.

Meanwhile he had lectured frequently and his pen had been hard at work. In 1932 he published one of his most authoritative works, *Lectures on F.S.R.*, vol. iii, which showed him both at his best and at his worst. Dealing with general ideas and prognostications, he showed brilliance of imagination, much of it prophetic, on how armoured forces should be organized and employed; but when he began to develop concrete examples of how detailed operations should be executed, he began to disappear into a fairyland of mobile 'anti-tank castles' or 'laagers' from which the tank formations would sally forth like medieval knights to do battle and return, accompanied by 'swarms of motorized guerrillas' and copious clouds of gas, great emphasis being laid on the defensive aspect of a defensive-offensive strategy. The organization of armoured forces and the operations carried out by General Guderian, said to be his pupil, in France and Russia in the war of 1939–45 bore little relation to this pattern, although the development of German armoured forces did owe much to the visionary inspiration of Fuller as well as of (Sir) Basil Liddell Hart.

Free of the cares of office, Fuller devoted the rest of his life to writing, probing deeper and deeper into the past and wider afield in his search for the truth. It led him into curious by-ways, the first being towards an idealized form of Fascism with which he was associated in the thirties; he spent some months in 1935–6 with the Italian forces in Abyssinia. Between his retirement and the outbreak of war in 1939 he published ten books, including his *Memoirs of an Unconventional Soldier* (1936).

Since 1923 he had been delving deeply into military history, and this study was to bear fruit in the two-volume *Decisive Battles* (1939–40), followed by *The Decisive Battles of the U.S.A.* (1942). From an apostle of future armoured warfare he had changed into an historian, although he re-edited his *F.S.R.* vol. iii lectures as *Armoured Warfare* in 1943. A short history of the war of 1939–45 (1948) could be regarded as a pot-boiler; but the major work on which his reputation as a historian must rest was *The Decisive Battles of the Western World, and their Influence upon History* (3 vols., 1954–6). Thenceforward he was able to bask in the sunshine of a prophet restored to honour in his own country, the gadfly which had lost its sting, sharing the limelight with Liddell Hart, engagingly modest in his lack of jealousy towards one who had stolen much of his thunder. At the same ceremony at the Royal United Service Institution both received the Institution's Chesney gold medal, October 1963. Fuller was appointed to the DSO in 1917, appointed CBE in 1926, and CB in 1930. Known to his friends as 'Boney', he was described (about 1918) as 'a little man with a bald head, and a sharp face, and a nose of Napoleonic cast ... a totally unconventional soldier [whose] attacks on the ... hierarchy were viewed in the spirit of a rat hunt; a spirit he responded to with much vivacity, and no little wit.'

In 1906 Fuller married Sonia, daughter of M. Karnatzki, of Warsaw; it was a happy lifetime partnership although they had no children. He died at Falmouth 10 February 1966.

[Fuller's own writings; *The Times*, 11 and 16 February 1966; B. H. Liddell Hart, *The Tanks*, 2 vols., 1959; private information; personal knowledge.]

MICHAEL CARVER

published 1981

GIBSON Guy Penrose

(1918–1944)

Airman, was born in Simla 12 August 1918, the younger son of Mr. Alexander James Gibson, of the Indian Forest Service, and his wife, Nora Mary Strike. He was educated at St. Edward's School, Oxford, where his housemaster, Mr. A. F. Yorke, describes him as 'strong-minded without obstinacy, disarmingly frank and of great charm'. As a prefect, he exerted his authority without apparent effort, whilst at games, although he had no special aptitude, he forced himself into good teams by sheer determination, showing signs of that physical stamina which was later to stand him in such good stead.

Gibson left school somewhat early to join the Royal Air Force. He was granted a short-service commission in November 1936 and ten months later joined No. 83 (Bomber) Squadron as a trained pilot. He took part in the first attack—on the Kiel canal—of the war of 1939–45. In July 1940 he was awarded the D.F.C. and shortly afterwards completed his first full operational tour. This would normally have earned him a rest at a training unit, but within two months his persistence had gained him access to Fighter Command where he carried out a further operational tour on night fighters, shooting down at least four enemy aircraft and gaining a bar to his D.F.C.

In April 1942, at the early age of twenty-three, he was promoted wing commander and returned to Bomber Command in command of No. 106 Squadron. At this time he had reached operational maturity and the quiet forcefulness of his character permeated the whole squadron, although it must be admitted that his relations with his aircrews had a special intimacy which he was never quite able to achieve with the groundcrews. He held command of the squadron for eleven months, an unusually long period and one covering the intensive fighting associated with the early attacks on the Ruhr, culminating in the first 1,000-bomber raid, and the difficult period in the winter of 1942–3. One who knew him well during this period said that he was the best captain he ever flew with and that it would have had to be a very smart night-fighter pilot to catch him out. It was during this period that he was appointed to the D.S.O. and later awarded a bar, a recognition of the pre-eminence which the squadron had attained under his leadership, and his own exceptional contribution of 172 sorties.

By ordinary standards, Gibson should have been more than usually ready for a spell away from operations, but his rest proved short-lived, and after only a week at headquarters No. 5 (Bomber) Group, setting down his thoughts on bomber tactics, he was offered the command of No. 617 Squadron, which was then about to be formed for a special attack on the Möhne and Eder dams. He accepted with alacrity and thus entered a period which was to show the full measure of his leadership, in the intensive, and at times highly dangerous, preliminary training, and in the meticulous planning which alone made the subsequent operations possible. During the attack on the Möhne dam on the night of 16–17 May 1943 Gibson himself released the first weapon at low level in the face of heavy fire, and then flew so as to draw the fire of the defences from each crew as they went into attack. For this gallant act, and for his leadership throughout this highly successful action, he was awarded the Victoria Cross.

During the next twelve months Gibson undertook a variety of staff appointments, including a lecture tour in America, where his modesty, his straightforward approach to all problems, and the aura of operational success, made him a notable figure; but in June 1944 he was back once more in No. 5 (Bomber) Group where he took up the appointment of operations officer in No. 55 Base which included his old squadron, No. 617.

For some weeks Gibson strove hard for permission to fly on operations but met with a firm refusal. However, on the night of 19–20 September 1944, when the main Lancaster force of No. 5 Group was attacking a target involving only slight penetration into enemy-held territory, it was agreed that he should fly in a Mosquito and act as 'master bomber'. Gibson successfully directed the attack, wished the Lancaster force 'good-night' and turned for home in the normal manner. He did not reach base and it was subsequently learned that through some unknown cause his aircraft crashed in Holland. He was buried in the small cemetery at Steenbergen, Bergen-op-Zoom, Holland.

Thus ended a career which has few equals in the history of air warfare—a career of action, of which the mainspring was a wholly phenomenal faith. Given this faith, all things were possible, for if the devil ever temptingly suggested that a project was beyond him, he would unceremoniously order him where he belonged. In this attitude, there was nothing that was foolhardy, for every action which he took was planned in detail and he knew precisely what he would do in every emergency. Throughout, he had the loyal support of all who flew with him.

In 1940 Gibson married Evelyn Mary Moore; there were no children. A portrait by Cuthbert Orde hangs in the R.A.F. officers' mess at Scampton, Lincolnshire. A drawing by Sir William Rothenstein is reproduced in his *Men of the R.A.F.* (1942).

[Guy Gibson, *Enemy Coast Ahead*, 1946; Air Ministry records; private information; personal knowledge.]

RALPH A. COCHRANE

published 1959

(1897–1986)

Sir

Soldier, Arabist, and author, was born 16 April 1897 in Preston, Lancashire, the only son and younger child of (Sir) Frederic Manley Glubb, a major (later major-general) in the Royal Engineers, and his wife, Frances Letitia Bagot. 'Jack' Glubb was educated at Cheltenham College and passed second into the Royal Military Academy, Woolwich, in 1914. He was commissioned in the Royal Engineers on 20 April 1915 and joined a field company of the RE in France in November. He served there throughout World War I, being three times wounded, once nearly fatally in the jaw, and was awarded the MC (1917).

In 1920 he was posted to Mesopotamia, where he later became a ground intelligence officer with the RAF. This was the beginning of his connection with the Arabs, for whom he formed an instant sympathy, so much so that in 1926 he left the army to join the British administration in Iraq. At that time the Iraqi bedouin and shepherd tribes in the southern desert were being terrorized by raids by Ibn Saud's Wahabis (*Al Ikhwan*). Glubb was posted there in 1928 as administrative inspector.

Partly by persuading the bedouin to join his armed police, and partly with RAF support, Glubb had ended the raiding by 1930, when he was invited to join the Arab Legion in Trans-Jordan, with a similar mission. This he accomplished within three years, raising a force of bedouin camel police, which became famous as the Desert Patrol. In 1939 Amir Abdullah appointed him to command the Arab Legion as *Feriq* (lieutenant-general), although he was better known perhaps as *Abu Hunaik* (Father of the Little Jaw), a reference to his 1917 war wound.

Glubb was probably the first man to succeed in turning the bedouin tribesmen into disciplined soldiers. Previously they had been considered untameable. Glubb was, however, careful to train his bedouins in accordance with their age-old customs. In 1941 he led them alongside the British army in Syria and Iraq, and was appointed to the DSO. His contribution to the capture of Baghdad in 1941 and the subsequent capture of the desert fortress of Palmyra in Syria was decisive, for it denied the eastern flank of the Middle East to Hitler. Later he formed a complete mechanized brigade, almost entirely bedouin. He was now known as Glubb Pasha, 'pasha' being an Ottoman honorific title.

On 15 May 1948 Glubb led the Arab Legion across the Jordan to occupy the West Bank, as laid down by the United Nations partition resolution of

November 1947. He did not expect to have to fight for it, which is what actually happened. When the fighting ended with an armistice in March 1949, Glubb had the responsibility for defending the West Bank, but with far too few troops with which to do it. The Arab Legion had to be expanded with British financial support, but with the proviso that the British officers serving in the Arab Legion should be increased in number. They occupied all the important posts, which gave rise to resentment among many Jordanian officers. Glubb shared their disquiet, but the subsidy was vital. He was greatly reliant on King Abdullah's support, which vanished when the king was assassinated on 20 July 1951. His son Talal reigned only a few months before abdicating, and was succeeded by his son, Hussein, still only sixteen and a schoolboy at Harrow. Although Hussein respected Glubb, the gap between their ages proved impossible to bridge and they soon fell out. Military and political developments were rapidly outgrowing Glubb, and the influential foreign adviser to an oriental monarch was becoming an anachronism.

Hussein, who came of age in 1953, particularly disagreed with Glubb's plan for the defence of the West Bank. Glubb sought to gain time by a planned withdrawal until Britain intervened in accordance with her treaty with Jordan. Hussein refused to countenance any withdrawal. The two views were irreconcilable and resulted in Hussein's dismissal of Glubb Pasha on 1 March 1956. The order giving him twenty-four hours to leave the country was intended to forestall any attempt to reinstate him. Glubb had in fact forbidden any bloodshed and had told his British officers to calm the situation. Soon they too were on their way. Glubb's abrupt dismissal caused a furore in Britain, and shocked many in Jordan.

Although Glubb was deeply hurt by the manner of his dismissal he behaved with exemplary dignity. Neither then nor later did he blame the king. He arrived in Britain with only £5, and was not awarded a general's pension by either Britain or Jordan. He was appointed KCB (1956) on his arrival and thereafter the British government washed its hands of him. He had been appointed OBE in 1925 and CMG in 1946. Glubb turned to his pen, and to lecturing, to provide for himself and his family of two sons and two daughters. He had married in 1938 Muriel Rosemary, daughter of James Graham Forbes, physician. They had a son in Jerusalem in 1939, whom they named Godfrey (later Faris), after the Crusader king. In 1944 they adopted a baby bedouin girl, and, after the death of another son who was born prematurely in 1947, adopted another daughter and son, both Palestinian refugees. Glubb was not impressive in appearance and was almost diffident in manner, speaking in rather a high-pitched voice. Yet there was about him an unmistakable air of authority, and when in uniform he wore no fewer than five rows of medal ribbons.

Glubb wrote twenty-two books, mostly on the Arabs, and lectured in Britain and the USA. His best book is perhaps *War in the Desert* (1960), which tells of his Iraq service. He had a soldier's aversion to politics—and to politicians. He had tried hard not to become involved, but as commander of Jordan's security forces some involvement was unavoidable. His dismissal was a political act, supported by Hussein's prime minister, Samir Rifai. Glubb remained nevertheless throughout his life a staunch supporter of Jordan and King Hussein. He was a devout Christian, an Edwardian in both manner and values. A servant of both Britain and Jordan, he was the last in the long line of powerful British proconsuls. He died from aplastic anaemia 17 March 1986 in Mayfield, Sussex.

[Sir John Glubb, *The Changing Scenes of Life* (autobiography), 1983; James Lunt, *Glubb Pasha*, 1984; Trevor Royle, *Glubb Pasha*, 1992; personal knowledge.]

JAMES LUNT

published 1996

GOUGH Hubert de la Poer

(1870–1963)

Sir

General, was born at Gurteen, county Waterford, 12 August 1870, the elder son (there were no daughters) of (General Sir) Charles John Stanley Gough, GCB, VC, and his wife, Harriette Anastasia, daughter of John W. de la Poer, formerly MP for county Waterford. He was educated at Eton and Sandhurst and commissioned in the 16th Lancers in 1889. Regimental service in India in the 1890s provided ample leisure to display his first-class horsemanship in racing and polo, and he also took part in the Tirah Expedition in 1897. The following year he married (Margaret Louisa) Nora, daughter of Major-General H. C. Lewes. In the South African war he displayed characteristic dash and impulsiveness when relieving Ladysmith against orders, but later the same qualities cost his mounted-infantry regiment heavy casualties in an ambush at Blood River. Nevertheless he ended the war with an enhanced reputation. From 1903 to 1906 he was an instructor at the Staff College and subsequently commanded the 16th Lancers. In 1911 he returned to Ireland as a brigadier-general commanding 3rd Cavalry brigade at the Curragh.

By the end of 1913 there was considerable speculation both inside and outside the army about the position of the armed forces should the

Government be obliged to impose the policy of Home Rule for Ireland by force. In December, in an attempt to dispel anxiety, the secretary of state for war, Colonel J. E. B. Seely (later Lord Mottistone), discussed the constitutional position with senior officers, making it clear *inter alia* that officers domiciled in Northern Ireland would not be compelled to take part in possible hostilities there. By mid March 1914 trouble appeared imminent and certain precautionary movements of troops in Ireland (and of naval forces) were agreed upon by a Cabinet committee. Seely summoned Sir Arthur Paget, the commander-in-chief in Ireland, to London and instructed him to brief his officers on the lines agreed upon in December: in event of hostilities in Northern Ireland, Ulster-domiciled officers might 'disappear' but other officers who for conscientious reasons were unwilling to carry out their duty were to say so and be dismissed the Service.

Seely was thus initially to blame for obliging officers to make a fateful choice on hypothetical orders, and for presenting Paget with six possible contingencies rather than definite orders. All might still have been well had Paget possessed a cool head and a clear mind, but he lacked either, apprehending fearfully that a number of officers would refuse to go to Ulster if ordered. By his first confused and emotional harangue to senior officers in Dublin on the morning of Friday 20 March 1914 he created the very dilemma which he feared. Contrary to the Government's opinion that precautionary moves might be carried out without resistance, Paget declared that he expected the country to be ablaze by the following day. He was extremely confused about how the troops should react if hostilities occurred. He then stressed the difficulty he had had in obtaining concessions from the War Office and ordered commanders to put the following terms to their officers: officers actually domiciled in Ulster would be exempted from any operations and would be allowed to 'disappear'; any officers unwilling to serve would immediately be dismissed from the Service. In answer to a question from Gough, Paget replied that 'domiciled in Ulster' was to be strictly interpreted, and he added rudely 'You cannot be held to come under that clause. You need expect no mercy from your old friend in the War Office' (i.e. Sir John French, the CIGS). Gough left the meeting very angry at his personal treatment and under the impression that the army was to be used to coerce Ulster prior to the passing of the Home Rule Bill. He determined to resign, and although he did not attempt to influence the officers of his brigade, the great majority freely opted for the same course. In reporting this outcome to Paget, Gough stressed in writing that while he and his officers were quite prepared to maintain law and order they were not willing to *initiate* active military operations against Ulster.

Gough

Paget addressed all the officers of the Cavalry brigade at the Curragh on the morning of Saturday 21 March. Mixing reassurance with threats he failed to convert Gough and the officers who had decided to resign. He now said that senior officers refusing to do their duty would be court-martialled. He also falsely stated that the terms he had offered derived directly from the King; he would not obey the orders of 'mere politicians' (according to some accounts the phrase he used was 'those dirty swine of politicians'). So the War Office received a signal from Dublin on the evening of 21 March, 'Regret to report brigadier and fifty-seven officers 3rd Cavalry Brigade prefer to accept dismissal if ordered North'.

Gough and his regimental commanding officers were summoned to the War Office to be reprimanded by Seely, but by the time they arrived on the Sunday morning 22 March Asquith had become aware of the muddle which Seely and Paget had between them created and was insisting that order must be promptly restored to avoid a real military mutiny. He made it clear to Seely that there were no grounds for punishing or dismissing Gough and the others who had only taken a choice forced on them by Paget. Meanwhile Lord Roberts had discovered that Seely now repudiated the alternatives presented by Paget and the elderly field-marshal conveyed this information to Gough. The latter therefore reported to the War Office on the Monday morning 23 March fortified in the integrity of his position. He first saw Sir John French who assured him that there had been a misunderstanding and offered his word that the army would not be asked to enforce the current Home Rule Bill upon Ulster. But he felt unable to put his assurance in writing. French then took Gough to see Seely, Paget and the Adjutant-General Sir (John) Spencer Ewart also being present. Seely vainly attempted to browbeat Gough who stubbornly demanded a written assurance. French broke the deadlock by tactfully suggesting that Gough needed documentary proof to convince his own officers. Seely capitulated and left for a Cabinet meeting while Ewart drafted a state-ment. After lunch Seely received the statement as revised by the Cabinet in Asquith's handwriting, but when Gough called to see it only Seely and Lord Morley were present. Undeterred by the confusion caused by his previous instructions, Seely then took the remarkable step, with Lord Morley's assistance, of adding two paragraphs, the latter affirming that (the Government) had 'no intention whatever of taking advantage of the right to crush political opposition to the policy or principles of the Home Rule Bill'. When the statement had been copied French handed it to Gough who requested a quarter of an hour to study it together with his two colonels, his brother 'Johnnie', who was BGS to Sir Douglas Haig at Aldershot, and Sir Henry Wilson, the DMO. They were still not entirely satisfied, so Hubert Gough added the rider 'I understand the meaning of the last paragraph to be that the army will not be used under any circumstances to enforce the present Home Rule Bill on Ulster'. Sir John French added 'That is how I read it. J. F.'

The Government speedily repudiated the two 'peccant paragraphs' and Seely, shortly followed by French and Ewart, resigned. Gough had apparently triumphed, although as he explained to a friend at the time, his obdurate stand had been inspired more by resentment at the War Office and Paget's attempt to bully than by the Ulster issue. But his triumph was not unblemished: officers who had agreed to do their duty in Ireland resented the acclaim accorded him; and there was strong feeling among Liberal and Labour politicians that the Government had stooped to bargain with rebellious group of officers. In fact Gough was innocent of the imputation of political intrigue, but he suffered from his reluctant association with Henry Wilson who was hand-in-glove with the Opposition and crowing over Gough's triumph as his own.

In the short term, however, the brilliant cavalryman's career suffered no ill effects from the Curragh incident. He led his brigade with distinction during the opening weeks of the war in 1914 and was promoted major-general in command of the newly formed 2nd Cavalry division in the first battle of Ypres. Further promotions followed in rapid succession: after the battle of Neuve Chapelle in March 1915 he was given command of 7th division and in July he was promoted lieutenant-general in command of I Corps, which played a prominent part in the battle of Loos, though Gough himself was in no way to blame for the disaster. Jealousy at his rapid rise was offset by his wide reputation for moral as well as physical courage. His chief failings were his hot temper and his tendency to quick, impulsive judgements. A fighting general *par excellence*, Gough discovered that as a Corps commander he was remote from the battle and could not visit the front frequently without arousing the resentment of his divisional commanders. This frustration was intensified before the battle of the Somme in 1916 with his promotion to command of the Reserve (soon to be titled Fifth) Army. 'It was not that he enjoyed pitching men into battle to be killed or wounded,' a biographer remarks, 'simply that he was confident of his ability to lead soldiers successfully in the dreadful tasks to which they were committed.'

In the third Ypres campaign in 1917 Gough's Fifth Army was placed on the left wing and given the major role in the first phase of the offensive. Gough was never sanguine about the prospects of a complete breakthrough into open country, but he differed from GHQ in believing that it was essential to secure all short-range objectives on the first day rather than by a series of short advances. Fifth Army was initially successful on its left but made little progress on the right. When heavy rain and stubborn resistance held up the second and third attacks in mid August, Gough vainly asked Haig to call off the offensive. Second Army took over the major role in September and Fifth Army's reputation declined. Gough's personal relations with his subordinate commanders remained good but his chief of staff, Neill Malcolm, had a brusque manner which caused resentment and uncertainty about his general's real feelings. By the end of the campaign Haig had gained the impression that units had become reluctant to serve in Fifth Army.

In March 1918 the Germans were expected to launch an all-out spring offensive with an army strongly reinforced from the eastern front. The British Fifth Army was holding a vulnerable forty-two mile sector between Gouzeaucourt and La Fère with a fully stretched front line and very meagre reserves. Haig was aware of this weakness but gave the Third Army of Sir Julian Byng (later Viscount Byng of Vimy), which was on Gough's left, priority because of the vital need to protect the Channel ports, and because he assumed that the French would quickly reinforce Gough's sector in a crisis. When on 21 March Ludendorff launched his main blow against Fifth Army's front he enjoyed a local superiority of about eight to one. Gough decided he could not hope to hold out in the forward battle zone but must fight a delaying action to save his army from complete destruction while preserving an intact line until British and French reinforcements arrived in strength. Unfortunately for Gough, Pétain and Foch both proved reluctant to commit reserves to the British sector for several days, and to make matters worse one of his Corps commanders interpreted Gough's orders as permitting disengagement and withdrawal to the Somme. This precipitate action forced the two adjacent Corps to conform and by 24 March leading German units were already across the river. Nevertheless the German offensive was already losing momentum in the face of Fifth Army's stubborn resistance when Gough was informed, on 27 March, that he was to be replaced by Sir Henry Rawlinson and the staff of Fourth Army on the following day. Haig attempted to keep him employed in France but Lloyd George and Lord Derby, the war minister, insisted (3 April) that he be sent home immediately. Gough's brilliant career thus came to an abrupt end and the official inquiry which he had been promised was never held. 'His treatment', Haig admitted to a brother officer of them both in February 1919, 'was harsh and undeserved: but after considerable thought I decided that public opinion at home, whether right or wrong, demanded a scapegoat, and that the only possible ones were Hubert or me. I was conceited enough to think that the army could not spare me.'

In 1919 Gough accepted the thankless appointment of chief of the Allied military mission to the Baltic but he was speedily recalled by Lloyd

George. He was appointed GCMG in 1919. No further employment followed and in October 1922 he was retired with the rank of full general. He had been created KCB in 1916, and KCVO in 1917. In 1922 Gough stood as a Liberal candidate at a by-election at Chertsey but was narrowly defeated. After a few years of farming in Surrey he took up a successful career in business.

However, Gough's chief preoccupation in the long life that remained to him was to vindicate his own and his army's reputation against the slurs cast upon them over the operations in March 1918. In 1924 he was reconciled to Haig and went with Lady Gough to stay with the Haigs at Bemersyde. In 1928 he was a pall bearer at Haig's funeral. In 1931 he published his own dignified and restrained account of the campaign in *Fifth Army*. As the tragic episode began to be viewed more objectively and new evidence appeared Gough's conduct of the retreat tended to be not merely exonerated but praised as a remarkable exercise of generalship in adverse circumstances. This trend in various histories and memoirs culminated in the belated but none the less welcome amends made by Lloyd George in 1936 in the volume of his *War Memoirs* dealing with the episode. No official government action followed, but in awarding Gough the GCB in 1937 King George VI made it clear that Gough's and Fifth Army's honour were fully restored.

In 1939 Gough was still in vigorous health and eager to serve in a military capacity. He formed the Chelsea branch of the Home Guard in 1940 and later commanded a London Zone until he was finally retired in 1942. At the age of eighty he was still an active chairman of numerous companies. Lady Gough, by whom he had a son who died in infancy, and four daughters, died in 1951. Gough then devoted his time to writing his memoirs and published *Soldiering On* in 1954. He survived all other senior commanders of World War I by many years and died at his home at 14 St. Mary Abbots Court, London W14, 18 March 1963.

There is a drawing by Francis Dodd (1917) in private possession. In the National Portrait Gallery are a bust by Patricia Kahn (1961–2) and a chalk drawing by Sir William Rothenstein (1932). A portrait in oils was painted by Frank O. Salisbury.

[A. H. Farrar-Hockley, *Goughie*, 1975; A. P. Ryan, *Mutiny at the Curragh*, 1956; Geoffrey Brooke, *Good Company*, 1954; private information.]

BRIAN BOND

published 1981

GUBBINS Colin McVean

(1896–1976)

Sir

Major-general and leader of Special Operations Executive, was born in Tokyo 2 July 1896, the younger son and third-born in the family of two sons and three daughters of John Harington Gubbins, who was oriental secretary at the British legation, and his wife, Helen Brodie, daughter of Colin Alexander McVean, JP, of Mull. Educated at Cheltenham College and at the Royal Military Academy, Woolwich, he was commissioned in 1914 into the Royal Field Artillery.

In the war of 1914–18 he served as a battery officer on the western front, was wounded, and was awarded the MC. In 1919 he joined the staff of W. E. (later Lord) Ironside in north Russia. It was the Bolshevik revolution no less than his subsequent experience in Ireland in 1920–2 that stimulated his lifelong interest in irregular warfare. After special employment on signals intelligence at GHQ India, he graduated at the Staff College at Quetta in 1928, and was appointed GSO 3 in the Russian section of the War Office in 1931. Promoted to brevet major, in 1935 he joined MT 1, the policy-making branch of the military training directorate. In October 1938, in the aftermath of the Munich agreement, he was sent to the Sudetenland as a military member of the international commission—an experience which left him with a lasting sympathy for the Czechs. Promoted to brevet lieutenant-colonel, he joined G(R)—later known as MI(R)—in April 1939. In this obscure branch of the War Office he prepared training manuals on irregular warfare, translations of which were later to be dropped in thousands over occupied Europe; he also made a rapid visit to Warsaw to exchange views on sabotage and subversion with the Polish general staff.

On mobilization in August 1939 Gubbins was appointed chief of staff to the military mission to Poland, led by (Sir) Adrian Carton de Wiart. Among the first to report on the effectiveness of the German Panzer tactics, Gubbins had no illusions about the Polish capacity to resist. Yet the campaign left him with an enduring sense of obligation to the Poles, whose chivalrous and romantic nature was somewhat akin to his own.

In October 1939, having returned to England, he was sent to Paris as head of a military mission to the Czech and Polish forces under French command. The mission was viewed with suspicion by the French since its main purpose was to keep the War Office in touch with the burgeoning Czech and Polish Resistance movements. Gubbins was recalled from France in March 1940 to raise the 'independent companies'—forerunners of the commandos—which he later commanded in Norway. Although criticized in some quarters for having asked too much of untried troops, he showed himself to be a bold and resourceful commander, and was appointed to the DSO (1940). Back in England, he was charged by GHQ Home Forces with forming a civilian force to operate behind the German lines if Britain were invaded. Stout-hearted but utterly inexperienced, these so-called auxiliary units could not have survived for long; but their secret recruitment, training, and equipment in the summer of 1940 was a remarkable feat of improvisation and personal leadership.

In November 1940 Gubbins became acting brigadier and, at the request of E. H. J. N. (later Lord) Dalton, was seconded to the Special Operations Executive (SOE) which had recently been established 'to co-ordinate all action by way of sabotage and subversion against the enemy overseas'. Besides maintaining his connections with the Poles and Czechs, he was initially given three tasks for which he was admirably qualified: to set up training facilities, to devise operating procedures acceptable to the Admiralty and Air Ministry, and to establish close working relations with the joint planning staff. Inevitably he bore the brunt of the suspicion and disfavour which SOE provoked in Whitehall—partly because of the nature of its operations and partly because of the excessive secrecy which surrounded them. However, Gubbins had no doubt it was his duty to identify with SOE notwithstanding all the risk of misrepresentation of his motives that this entailed.

Despite frustrations and disappointments—and there were many, due mainly to the shortage of aircraft—he persevered with his task of training organizers and dispatching them to the field. The first liaison flight to Poland took place in February 1941, and during 1942 and 1943 European Resistance movements patronized by SOE scored a number of notable successes, including the raid on the heavy water installation in Norway which aborted Hitler's efforts to produce an atom bomb.

At this stage Gubbins had no direct responsibility for SOE's subsidiary headquarters in Cairo whose activities in Yugoslavia and Greece had for some time been raising awkward issues of foreign policy. However, in September 1943 these issues came to a head; Sir Charles Hambro resigned; and Gubbins, now a major-general, became executive head of SOE. He immediately faced a concerted attack on SOE's autonomy, mounted by the Foreign Office, GHQ Middle East, and the joint intelligence committee (JIC). As always he had the steadfast support of his minister, the third Earl of Selborne, but it was not until a meeting on 30 September, presided over by the prime minister, that a *modus operandi* was agreed. Nevertheless Gubbins's position remained precarious and in January 1944 there was a further attempt to dismantle SOE. This followed the disclosure that SOE's operations in Holland had been penetrated by the Germans—for which Gubbins characteristically took the blame. Undaunted he set about co-ordinating the activities of the various Resistance movements, now supported world-wide by SOE, with the operational requirements of individual commanders-in-chief. Although control was decentralized wherever possible, harnessing the force of Resistance to the conventional war effort proved a delicate and controversial task—as often political as military—involving consultation at the highest level with the Foreign Office and the chiefs of staff; as well as with representatives of the patriot organizations, the governments-in-exile, and other allied agencies—in particular the United States Office of Strategic Services (OSS). In the event the effectiveness of organized resistance exceeded Whitehall's expectations. In north-west Europe, where SOE's activities remained under Gubbins's personal control, General Eisenhower later estimated that the contribution of the French Resistance alone had been worth six divisions.

When SOE was wound up in 1946 the War Office could offer Gubbins no suitable employment, and on retirement from the army he became managing director of a large firm of carpet and textile manufacturers. However, he kept in touch with the leading personalities in many of the countries he had helped to liberate; invited by Prince Bernhard of the Netherlands he joined the Bilderberg group; and he was an enthusiastic supporter of the Special Forces Club of which he was a co-founder. A keen shot and fisherman, he spent his last years at his home in the Hebrides. He was appointed CMG in 1944, advanced to KCMG in 1946, and appointed deputy lieutenant of the Islands Area of the Western Isles in 1976. He held fourteen foreign decorations.

Gubbins had a creative spirit that made him a natural leader of the young; and he delegated generously to those he trusted, both men and women. Above all, he was a dedicated professional soldier. With his quick brain, the imagination and energy necessary to transform ideas into action, and his force of will, he might have held high command in the field had his abilities not been confined to special operations. As it was, he left his mark on the history of almost every country which suffered enemy occupation in the war of 1939–45.

In 1919 Gubbins married Norah Creina, daughter of Surgeon-Commander Philip Somerville Warren RN, of Cork; the marriage was dissolved in 1944. In 1950 he married secondly Anna Elise, widow of Lieutenant R. T. Tradin, Royal Norwegian Air Force, and daughter of Hans Didrik Jensen, of Tromsö, Norway. He had two sons by his first marriage, the elder of whom was killed at Anzio in 1944. Gubbins died at Stornoway in the Hebrides 11 February 1976.

There is a portrait by Susan Beadle in the possession of the family.
[*The Times* 12, 17, and 19 February 1976; private information; personal knowledge.]

PETER WILKINSON

published 1986

HAIG Douglas

(1861–1928)

First Earl Haig

Field-marshal, the youngest son of John Haig, of Cameron Bridge, Fife, by his wife, Rachael, daughter and co-heiress of Hugh Veitch, of Stewartfield, Midlothian, was born in Edinburgh 19 June 1861. John Haig belonged to a younger branch of a famous Border family, the Haigs of Bemersyde, Berwickshire. Douglas, after some schooling in Edinburgh and at Mr. Hanbury's preparatory school in Warwickshire, was sent to Clifton, and proceeded in 1880 to Brasenose College, Oxford. In 1883 he passed into the Royal Military College, Sandhurst, which he left in the winter of 1884 as senior under-officer, first in order of merit of his year, with the Anson memorial sword, to be gazetted (February 1885) to the 7th Hussars, then in India.

Devoted to horses, Haig had shown some skill at polo both at Oxford and at Sandhurst, and although the 7th Hussars was then the crack polo team in India, he was soon playing for the regiment. In 1888 he was made adjutant and began to study French and German, spending much of his leave in France and Germany. His knowledge of German and of the German army brought him his first staff appointment, as aide-de-camp to the inspector-general of cavalry in England. While in that position he passed the entrance examination for the Staff College, but was rejected for colour blindness, a decision which was fortunately reversed on appeal. He was promoted captain in 1891.

Haig entered the Staff College in 1896, Edmund (afterwards Viscount) Allenby being amongst his contemporaries there, and came under the influence of Colonel George Francis Robert Henderson, who was on the staff of the college. Henderson prophesied of Haig that he 'one of these days will be commander-in-chief', an indication of the impression which the young cavalry captain made at the college. To that impression he owed his first chance of active service, for (Earl) Kitchener, who was engaged in the reconquest of the Sudan, applied to the college at the end of 1897 for some special service officers, and Haig was one of those chosen. He was employed with the Egyptian cavalry during the advance to Omdurman, and distinguished himself in the reconnaissance before that battle. For his services he received the brevet of major, and on his return home was appointed brigade-major of the 1st Cavalry brigade at Aldershot, then under the command of Major-General French (afterwards Field-Marshal the Earl of Ypres).

Haig was holding that position when, in October 1899, war broke out with the South African republics. French was given command of the cavalry division in the army sent out under Sir Redvers Buller, and Haig accompanied him as his staff officer. Owing to the critical situation in Natal, Buller sent French, who had arrived before his division, to take charge of the mounted troops in that colony, and on 21 October French defeated the Boer force in the battle of Elandslaagte, the plan of which was in the main Haig's. When it became clear that Ladysmith would be invested, French and Haig escaped in the last train to leave the town, and returned to Cape Town to meet the cavalry division, which was arriving. French was then sent to Naauwpoort to cover that railway junction. He established himself in a position on the heights round Colesberg, holding in check a superior force of Boers, and in this successful work at a critical time Haig's ingenuity, enterprise, and brilliant staff work played an important part. On the arrival of Lord Roberts with reinforcements, the cavalry division was secretly moved to the Modder River, and played a leading part in the relief of Kimberley, the battle of Paardeberg, and the occupation of Bloemfontein and Pretoria (February–June 1900). Towards the end of 1900 when the war became almost entirely of the guerrilla type, Haig received his first independent command, that of a column, and he continued to serve with distinction as a column commander until the end of the war (31 May 1902).

For his services in the South African War, Haig received the brevet of colonel and the C.B., and was appointed aide-de-camp to the king; he was also given command of the 17th Lancers, then in South Africa, and brought the regiment home to Edinburgh. Haig's work in the Sudan and South Africa had attracted the notice of Kitchener, who was commander-in-chief in India in 1903, and in that year had Haig appointed as his inspector-general of cavalry. Haig was promoted major-general in 1904 at the age of forty-three. During a short period of leave in 1905, while the guest of King Edward VII at Windsor, he met his future wife, the Hon. Dorothy Vivian, daughter of Hussey Crespigny, third Baron Vivian, one of the queen's ladies in waiting, whom he married in that year, and thus began a family life of unclouded happiness.

A year later (1906) Haig was summoned home by Mr. (afterwards Viscount) Haldane, then secretary of state for war, to aid him, in his military reorganization, as a director on the general staff at the War Office. Haig was responsible for the scheme of the Imperial General Staff, under which the Dominions accepted establishments and methods of training uniform with those of the British regular army, and for the drafting of the first British field service regulations, which defined the principles of military organization and tactics—measures which in the main stood the test of the European War. This experience caused Haig to appreciate, as few soldiers did at the time, how much the country owed to Haldane's courage, ability, and foresight, and one of his first acts on returning home after the European War was to call on Haldane and present him with a copy of his dispatches inscribed 'To Viscount Haldane of Cloan, the greatest Secretary of State for War England has ever had'.

In 1909 Lord Kitchener completed his term of office as commander-in-chief in India. His successor, Sir O'Moore Creagh, was an officer of the Indian army, and custom required that his chief of staff should be of the British service. Haig was offered and eagerly accepted the appointment. His primary object was to complete Kitchener's plan for enabling the Indian army to take part in the great struggle which both predicted. This plan was strenuously opposed by many in high places, who maintained that a European war would not concern India. Haig's energy and ability, however, overcame all obstacles, and it was due to the work which he built upon Kitchener's foundations that India was able to give Great Britain prompt assistance at the time of crisis in 1914.

In the autumn of 1911 Haig, who had been created K.C.V.O. in 1909 and promoted lieutenant-general in 1910, was appointed to the Aldershot command, a post which carried with it the command of the first army corps in the event of the mobilization of a British expeditionary force. Thus in August 1914 Haig (now K.C.B., 1913, and aide-de-camp general, 1914), took to France the I Army Corps, mainly composed of the Aldershot troops which he had been training for nearly three years.

Haig did not share the cheerful optimism which prevailed with Sir John French and many of the head-quarters staff. He had continued the close study which he had begun as a young man of the French and German armies, and one of his first acts was to urge upon Lord Kitchener that the War would last for years, and that Great Britain must set about the creation of a great national army. How far the two men simultaneously and independently arrived at the same conclusion is uncertain; but there is no doubt that Haig held these views, which were not shared by most military authorities either at home or in France, and on the outbreak of war he pressed them on the secretary of state for war, who first gave public expression to them in his call to the nation for men issued in the second week of August. During the battle of Mons (23–24 August) Haig's corps was on the inner flank and was but lightly engaged. Having expected the great German turning movement through Belgium, he was not surprised when the order came for retreat, and having his plans ready he got his corps away without difficulty.

On 25 August the retreating British troops reached the forest of Mormal; this entailed a separation of the I and II Corps, the I Corps making a detour to the east of the forest, which left it in an isolated position that night. Consequently, chance collisions with the Germans at Landrecies and Maroilles created considerable, but as it turned out, unnecessary alarm. On 1 September Haig's rearguards were heavily engaged in the forest of Villars-Cottérêts, but the long retreat came to an end on 5 September without further fighting, and with the morale and efficiency of the I Corps unimpaired.

Turning northwards in pursuit of the retreating Germans on 6 September, the I Corps reached and began to cross the Marne early on the morning of 9 September, well ahead of the French on its right. The corps had struck a gap in the German front, and the opportunity presented itself of separating von Kluck's First Army from von Bulow's Second Army. By an unlucky chance Haig at this moment received an air report that a strong force of the enemy was posted on his right front. The commander-in-chief had cautioned him against getting ahead of the French on his right, and fearful of being attacked in the act of crossing the river, Haig stopped his advance and directed his troops to entrench. The German troops reported to be menacing Haig's flank shortly afterwards moved off to support von Kluck's right, but this was not discovered until too late.

Continuing the advance on 10, 11, and 12 September, the I Corps on the 13th reached and began to cross the Aisne. Once again his corps had struck a gap, and Haig pressed forward with all energy to secure the important Chemin des Dames ridge, but was just anticipated by the arrival of German reinforcements at the critical point. Thus twice the hopes of a resounding success were disappointed, but Haig by his handling of his men had won both their confidence and that of his commander-in-chief. The battle of the Aisne then settled down into trench warfare, in which numerous attempts of the Germans to drive the British forces over the river were defeated.

At the end of September French had arranged with General Joffre that the British army should be relieved on the Aisne and should move round to Flanders in order to attempt to turn the German right. The I Corps was the last to leave the Aisne, and on 19 October was approaching Ypres, where the corps commanded by Sir Henry (afterwards Baron) Rawlinson, after the abortive attempt to relieve Antwerp, had already arrived. Already the British I and II Cavalry Corps were engaged in a fierce struggle extending from La Bassée through Armentières to the Messines ridge, and the Belgian army, retiring from Antwerp, was arriving on the Yser on Haig's left. Then suddenly a new crisis developed with the appearance of four new German army corps, which endeavoured to drive in and turn the Allied left. In the first battle of Ypres (19 October–22 November) Haig's magnificent defence, his imperturbable calm, and tactical skill made him a national figure. Like Wellington at Waterloo he was on the spot at every crisis, during a period of weeks instead of hours, and the successful defence of Ypres was due as much to his personal influence as to the dogged gallantry of his men.

Early in 1915 the arrival of reinforcements in France brought about the organization of the British forces into two armies, and Haig at Ypres had earned the right to the command of the First, which was composed of his own I Corps, the Indian Corps, and the IV Corps. In February the commander-in-chief called for plans for attack from his army commanders, and selected Haig's proposal for the battle of Neuve Chapelle (10–13 March). Haig's plan was original in that it comprised a short and intense bombardment, followed by an infantry assault. In the attack Neuve Chapelle was quickly captured, but the difficulty of getting up reserves and of overcoming the German machine-guns, quickly put a stop to progress. Neuve Chapelle none the less marked the beginning of a new epoch in the War, for the first success gained convinced both the French and British that, given a sufficiency of guns and shells, the German front could be broken.

Joffre had planned an offensive campaign in Artois for the spring of 1915 to be conducted by General Foch, and to assist this effort Haig's First Army was directed to attack the Aubers ridge. The attack on the Aubers ridge, begun on 9 May, failed from lack of heavy guns and high explosive shell, but as the French, on the British right, were making progress and pressed for co-operation, the battle was renewed on the Festubert front (15–25 May). Again, however, owing to lack of the requisite munitions, the gains were small and the losses heavy. During the summer of 1915 the arrival of divisions of the new army created by Kitchener enabled the British to extend their front, and Haig's right was prolonged across the plain of Loos. The French army had then reached its maximum strength, and its supply of guns and munitions had been greatly increased. This decided Joffre to make a great effort to break through the German lines by attacks in Champagne and Artois, the latter again under the direction of Foch. Joffre desired the British army to attack on Foch's left across the plain of Loos, but both French and Haig objected that the ground there was such as to present little prospect of success. Joffre thereupon appealed to his government, with the result that the British Cabinet directed French to fall in with Joffre's plans. Again the attack was entrusted to Haig who, finding that the supply of guns and munitions would still be inadequate, determined to use gas, with which the British had been experimenting ever since the first German gas attack in April 1915. The attack on Loos began on 25 September, and was at first successful, but owing to an unfortunate misunderstanding between French and Haig the general reserve did not arrive in time to improve the first success, while Foch's attack on the Vimy ridge failed. Consequently the battle of Loos resolved itself into bitter trench warfare in which some of the first British gains were lost. The battle dragged on until 14 October.

One of the results of the battle of Loos was to determine the British government to change the commander-in-chief, and on 19 December Haig succeeded French. Meanwhile the British forces in France, now organized in three armies, were steadily increasing in strength, while the evacuation of the Gallipoli Peninsula, completed early in January 1916, made further reinforcements available. Thus, when on 21 February 1916, the Germans began the battle of Verdun, Haig was able to respond at once to Joffre's appeal to extend the British front and set free French reinforcements for Verdun. Gradually during the summer the British front was extended southwards to the Somme, and a Fourth Army was created. At Joffre's request Haig set about preparing for a counter-offensive on the Somme to relieve Verdun. On 23 June the Germans captured Fort Thiaumont and Joffre therefore called upon Haig to make his effort; thus on 1 July began the battle of the Somme, with a combined British and French attack astride that river. Only on the French front and on the British right was the first attack successful, but the situation at Verdun was such that no cessation of effort was possible, and Haig determined to follow up the success gained by his right. In a prolonged struggle which lasted until the middle of November the Germans were slowly driven from the uplands north of the Somme and compelled to concentrate their efforts on resisting British attacks, with the result that before the end of the year the French were able to regain most of the ground which they had lost in the battle of Verdun.

This failure at Verdun and their heavy losses in the Somme fighting alarmed the Germans: General von Falkenhayn was dismissed and replaced by General von Hindenburg with General Ludendorff as his chief of staff. Both Joffre and Haig, realizing the exhaustion of the enemy, wished to continue their efforts, but the French and British governments had been equally alarmed at the cost in life of the Somme battle—the British casualties had amounted to 343,000 of whom about 90,000 were killed.

General Nivelle had in two attacks at Verdun won important successes at comparatively small cost, and it was hoped that his methods could be applied on a larger scale. So Joffre was made a marshal of France, and given an honorific position in Paris, and Nivelle was made commander-in-chief of the French armies. Nivelle's plan involved a further extension of the British front, and considerable delay in order to complete his preparations. At an Allied conference held at Calais at the end of February 1917 Haig was directed to conform to Nivelle's instructions, which comprised, in addition to the extension of the front, a British attack in the neighbourhood of Arras in combination with a secondary French attack on the St. Quentin front, and a main French effort in Champagne. Profiting by the delay which Nivelle's plans involved, the Germans on 14 March began a retreat from the Somme to their 'Hindenburg' lines, a retreat of which, owing to the weakening of their front by extension, the British were unable to take full advantage. Despite this radical change in the situation Nivelle adhered to his plans, and his campaign began on 9 April with a British attack on the Vimy ridge and on the German lines in front of Arras. This attack was successful, and the Vimy ridge, which in two campaigns had resisted Foch's efforts, was captured.

The French attacks failed, however, with heavy loss. Nivelle had rashly held out hopes of speedy and complete success, and the reaction was severe. There followed a series of mutinies in the French armies and general depression in France, and it became essential for the British army to gain time for the French to recover. The fighting in front of Arras was therefore continued until 15 May, several weeks longer than had been projected, and on 7 June Haig began an offensive campaign in Flanders, his Second Army under Sir Herbert Plumer capturing the Messines ridge, thus eliminating the greater part of the Ypres salient, which had been a weakness in the British lines since the winter of 1914. General Pétain, who had taken Nivelle's place as commander-in-chief of the French armies on 15 May, urged Haig to continue his attacks that he might have time to restore the *moral* of the French armies, and Haig therefore on 31 July began an attack on the Ypres front.

Haig's reasons for choosing this front were that this appeared to him to be the only part of the front on which the Germans could not, without great sacrifices, repeat the manœuvre of retreat to the Hindenburg lines, that the Admiralty was pressing for an attempt to capture Ostend and Zeebrugge, which the Germans were using as submarine bases, and lastly that there was a prospect, if the attack progressed, of making effective use of naval co-operation against the Belgian coast. Unfortunately, at the very beginning of August the weather broke, and the country to the east of Ypres became a sea of mud. In view of the state of the French army and of

Pétain's request that there should be no relaxation of pressure on the enemy, it was impossible to change the front of attack, and the British army was committed to an even more exhausting effort than the battle of the Somme. Slowly and painfully it forced its way up the Ypres ridges, and on 6 November captured Passchendaele. It had early become apparent that there was no prospect of driving the Germans from the Belgian coast, but the second purpose of the battle was attained. Pétain was given time to nurse the French army back to health, and on 23 October at Malmaison and on 3 November on the Ailette it signalized its recovery by two successful attacks.

By the middle of October Haig had decided to take advantage of the effect upon the Germans of the long struggle in front of Ypres by delivering a surprise attack with the aid of 'tanks' which, first used in September 1916 in the battle of the Somme, were then available in considerable numbers. This attack was made on the Cambrai front on 20 November, and a considerable initial success was won. But, before it was made, a severe crisis had arisen in Italy owing to the defeat on 24 October of the Italian army at Caporetto. Accordingly, the British and French governments decided that each should send five divisions from France to Italy. This made a serious diminution of the reserves available to follow up the success won at Cambrai, and the Germans were able in a counter-attack to recover a considerable part of the ground which they had lost. The situation in the winter of 1917–1918 was critical for the Allies. The French and British armies were weakened by the detachments sent to Italy, and in both countries man power was approaching exhaustion. It became necessary to reduce in each British division the number of battalions in a brigade from twelve to nine. The United States had joined the Allies in April 1917, but it was improbable that American troops could take the field in strength before the late summer of 1918. On the other side, the collapse of Russia had released the German armies on the Eastern front, and German divisions were arriving in a steady stream in France and Belgium. Under pressure from the French government Haig was compelled reluctantly to agree to a further extension of his front, and his Fifth Army under General Sir Hubert Gough prolonged his right as far south as the Oise. The crisis in Italy had caused the Allied governments to create the Supreme War Council for the better co-ordination of Allied efforts, and at a meeting of this body held at Versailles at the end of January 1918 it was decided to meet the danger of the expected German attack by creating a general reserve to be controlled by an executive committee with Foch as chairman. This committee required Haig to contribute eight British divisions to the reserve, and to this request he at once replied that, in view of the masses of German divisions on his front, he could not provide more than two divisions which were to be returned to him from Italy. At a further meeting of the Supreme War Council in London early in March 1918 Haig's views were upheld, and the proposal to create the general reserve collapsed, Haig being left to concert with Pétain arrangements for mutual support.

The expected German blow fell upon the British Third and Fifth Armies on 21 March. The right of both armies was driven in, and this involved a general retreat which threatened a rupture of the junction of the British and French armies in the neighbourhood of Amiens. Haig's reserves were quickly exhausted, and Pétain was disposed to consider it of greater importance to cover Paris than to maintain connexion with the British. In these circumstances Haig telegraphed to Lord Milner, the secretary of state for war, to come over with the chief of the Imperial General Staff, Sir Henry Wilson, with the object of getting Foch appointed to control operations on the Western front. This object was achieved in a conference at Doullens on 26 March. On coming out of this conference Haig said: 'I can deal with a man, but not with a committee.' Foch set to work energetically to fill the gap in the Allied front which was opening in the neighbourhood of Amiens; but before his efforts could take effect a great German attack on the left of the British Third Army and the right of the British First Army on the Arras front, intended to recapture the Vimy ridge, was shattered—a result which fully justified Haig's policy of keeping the bulk of his reserves north of the Somme, leaving the Fifth Army south of that river to be supported by the French.

Hardly had this first crisis of the year been resolved when a second arose. On 9 April the Germans attacked in Flanders, and broke through a portion of the line near Neuve Chapelle held by a Portuguese division. This opened a dangerous gap and involved another general withdrawal on the British front, which appeared to endanger the security of the Channel ports. As at Ypres in 1914, so in April 1918 with an immeasurably greater burden of responsibility on his shoulders, Haig's calm courage and resolution called forth all that was best in his men. In a memorable order issued on 11 April he told them: 'With our backs to the wall and believing in the justice of our cause, each one of us must fight to the end. The safety of our homes and the freedom of mankind depend upon the conduct of each one of us at this crisis.'

On 29 April the second great German effort petered out; but five weeks of the severest fighting against heavy odds had woefully reduced the British army in France, and no less than twenty divisions had to be broken up. Fortunately the Germans gave Haig a respite, of which he took full advantage. Reinforcements were hurried to France from Palestine and Salonika, and more man power was made available from home. Thus, while in May and June the Germans were seeking to break through the French front, Haig was able to make good most of the losses of the spring. Thrice during this period Foch appealed to Haig for help, and on each occasion the British authorities at home warned Haig of the danger of weakening his front; but each time Haig ignored the warning and loyally supported Foch.

At length the tide turned. Foch's counter-attack begun on 18 July had by the first week of August driven the Germans from the great salient which in their May attack on the Chemin des Dames had brought them a second time to the Marne. By this time the preparations of the American army were well advanced and the Allies were assured of superior power on the Western front. Already, by the middle of July, Haig had become convinced that the German strength was diminishing, and before Foch's counter-attack was delivered he had begun preparations for an attack on the Amiens front. This attack delivered by the British Fourth Army with the help of the French First Army on 8 August was completely successful. Foch, delighted with this success, urged Haig to press forward across the Somme and to capture Péronne; but on 12 August Haig had found that the German resistance was hardening in ground much broken up in earlier battles, and having now sufficient guns and munitions to be able to extend rapidly the front of attack, he refused to risk renewal of the experience of prolonging the fighting on the original front of battle, with the probable result of small gains in return for heavy losses. Instead, on 21 August, he attacked with his Third Army across the Somme battlefield of 1916, and proposed to extend gradually the front of battle right up to Arras. This change proved decisive. It altered Foch's plan of limited attacks, designed to free the Allied lines of railway communications, into a general advance against the enemy. In fact, Haig was the first to envisage the possibility of victory before the end of 1918. In a general order issued to his armies in the third week of August, he told them that the situation had changed decisively, and that the time had come to press the enemy everywhere with the utmost energy. At that time Foch himself was looking for a victory in 1919, and the British government was considering plans for a final effort in 1920.

Under Haig's inspiration the British armies pressed forward, and by the third week in September the Germans had everywhere on their front been driven into the shelter of their great 'Hindenburg' defensive system. The responsibility of assaulting these formidable defences was great, but Haig, confident that his judgement was right, and that the time had come for a supreme effort, unhesitatingly assumed it, despite authoritative warnings from home. By 12 October the British troops had broken clean through the 'Hindenburg' lines, the Germans were in retreat to their last organized system of defence behind Lille, and Hindenburg had advised his government to seek terms of peace. On 11 November, when the enemy accepted terms of armistice which left them militarily helpless, Haig's judgement was triumphantly vindicated. It was his decision that made victory in 1918 possible.

After leading his armies to the Rhine, Haig came home in July 1919 in order to take up the post of commander-in-chief of the Home Forces, to which he had been appointed in the previous April, and to superintend the demobilization of the nation in arms. In the following year he turned to a work which was very near his heart. In the last year of the War he had been perturbed to learn of the grave distress amongst those who had been disabled in the War, and while still commanding in France he had, with the help of Lady Haig, taken steps to provide remedies. After the Armistice he informed the government that he would accept no further honours until parliament had made better provision for those who had served under him. When this was done, he received the thanks of both Houses of Parliament and a grant of £100,000. The king created him Earl Haig and conferred on him the Order of Merit. He had been awarded the G.C.B. in 1915, the G.C.V.O. in 1916, and in 1917 had been made a knight of the Thistle.

On giving up the chief command of the Home Forces in January 1921, Haig devoted himself entirely to the cause of the men who had served under him in the War. In 1921 he succeeded in uniting the various organizations of ex-service men which had been created to deal with their grievances into one body, the British Legion, of which he became president. In this he rendered an inestimable service, not only to those who had fought but to the nation at large, by removing causes of discontent which at one time threatened to become dangerous. He also became chairman of the United Services Fund, created to administer for the benefit of ex-service men and their dependants the large profits made by the canteens during the War. Together the United Services Fund and the British Legion formed the largest benevolent organization ever created in Great Britain, and to its administration Haig gave himself unsparingly.

Always somewhat reserved, and with no gifts of speech, Haig, as a commander in the field, never aroused in his men the enthusiasm and affection inspired by a Marlborough or a Roberts, but his devoted services to their cause won for him from those who had fought for their country a measure of esteem such as few British commanders-in-chief have ever enjoyed. He undoubtedly shortened his life by denying himself rest; and when he died suddenly in London 30 January 1928 and was awarded a national funeral, the most striking tribute to him came from the thousands of ex-service men who lined the route of the procession.

In 1921 Haig was presented with the ancestral home of the Haigs, Bemersyde, purchased by public subscription. He was at his own request buried hard by Bemersyde in Dryburgh Abbey. A statue of him was erected in Edinburgh, and another at his old head-quarters, Montreuil, the cost of which was defrayed by public subscription in France; parliament granted the sum of £5,000 for the erection of a third statue in Whitehall. A national memorial fund provided groups of Haig Homes for disabled ex-service men in various parts of the country. A portrait of Haig is included in J. S. Sargent's picture, 'Some General Officers of the Great War', painted in 1922, in the National Portrait Gallery. There are also portraits of him in the Imperial War Museum, South Kensington, by Sir W. Orpen and Solomon J. Solomon, the Cavalry Club by Oswald Birley, the Royal and Ancient Golf Club of St. Andrews by Sir J. Guthrie, and Brasenose College, Oxford, by Sir William Orpen. In 1916 he had been elected rector of St. Andrews University and two years later he became its chancellor. He received the honorary degree of D.C.L. from the University of Oxford in 1919.

Haig had one son, George Alexander Eugene Douglas (born 1918), who succeeded him as second earl, and two daughters.

[Sir J. F. Maurice and M. H. Grant, (Official) *History of the War in South Africa 1899–1902*, 1906–1910; Sir J. E. Edmonds, (Official) *History of the Great War. Military Operations, France and Belgium, 1914–1916*, 1922–1931; G. A. B. Dewar and J. H. Boraston, *Sir Douglas Haig's Command, 1915–1918*, 1922; *Sir Douglas Haig's Despatches*, ed. J. H. Boraston, 1919; J. Charteris, *Field-Marshal Earl Haig*, 1929; British Legion *Journal*, Earl Haig Memorial Number, 1928. See also Duff Cooper, *Haig*, 2 vols., 1935, 1936.]

FREDERICK MAURICE

published 1937

HALL (William) Reginald

(1870–1943)

Sir

Admiral, was born at The Close, Salisbury, 28 June 1870, the elder son and second child of Lieutenant (later Captain) William Henry Hall, R.N., of Ross, Herefordshire, the first director of naval intelligence and later captain superintendent of Pembroke dockyard, by his wife, Caroline Elizabeth, daughter of the Rev. Henry Thomas Armfield, vicar of the cathedral and the close of Salisbury.

Hall's first sea trip was in his father's ship, the *Flamingo*, gun-vessel, at the age of ten. He entered the *Britannia* as a cadet in 1884 and became a lieutenant in January 1890. Of the two specialist branches (gunnery and torpedo) then open to lieutenants who had passed their examinations with credit, Hall chose the gunnery branch. His forceful personality and driving power were already in evidence and, after serving a commission at sea as gunnery lieutenant, he was appointed a senior staff officer on the books of the *Excellent*, then one of the most coveted appointments in the navy. He was promoted to commander in 1901 and, as executive officer of a battleship, achieved distinction by his methods of enforcing discipline. On one occasion the depot sent all the men of bad character to his ship, confident that he would either reform them or rid the Service of them. But, although a terror to malefactors, he was already implementing views on the welfare of the ship's company and on brightening their lives when afloat which were far in advance of the times. He was promoted to captain in 1905 and, after serving as inspecting captain of the new mechanical training establishments, in 1907 assumed command of the cadet training cruiser, the *Cornwall*. His next ship was the *Natal*, cruiser, where his keen interest in gunnery was reflected by the ship retaining the first place in the navy at the annual gunnery tests. From 1911 to 1913 he was naval assistant to the controller of the navy.

In 1913 Hall assumed command of the new battle cruiser, the *Queen Mary*. He now had the opportunity of introducing a wide range of reforms to which he had given much thought. Convinced of the importance of raising the prestige of the petty officers, in his view the most important link in the chain of command, he had all their messes reconstructed in order to give them greater comfort. At the Admiralty's suggestion he accepted the responsibility of commissioning without the customary staff of ship's police and trusting to the petty officers to undertake police duties. He broke with tradition by introducing a three-watch system for the organization of the ship's company instead of the two-watch system, because he was convinced that a three-watch system was more suitable for wartime. When war broke out, all the larger units followed this lead. The first cinematograph, the first laundry, the first bookstall, the first adequate hot-water system on board were other fruits of his imagination and devoted interest in the welfare of his men. A deeply religious man, he built into the ship the first chapel in a man-of-war; a few years later all big ships were fitted with chapels. In a conservative Service, these reforms inevitably aroused a storm of adverse criticism, but this never deflected Hall from his crusade to improve life on board ship. His monument is to be found in every ship which flies the white ensign.

Hall

Hall was in command of the *Queen Mary* at the battle of Heligoland Bight (28 August 1914), but before the end of the year he was invited to become director of the intelligence division of the Admiralty. He had, in abundant measure, all the qualities for his new post. Officer prisoners from German submarines who had stubbornly refused to respond to ordinary interrogation often became as putty in his hands. There was a hypnotic power about his glance which broke their resistance. On occasions his manner became explosive, and the facial twitch, which gave him his nickname of 'Blinker', became exaggerated; at other times his disarming smile and twinkling eyes looking out from bushy eyebrows overcame opposition to a new scheme for gaining intelligence.

The main source of intelligence of the German fleet was through intercepted signals. On the outbreak of war Sir Alfred Ewing, then director of naval education, formed a small department to study German naval signals. When the German cruiser *Magdeburg* was sunk in the Baltic, a drowned signalman was picked up clasping a signal book in his arms, and as soon as this book reached the Admiralty the deciphering of German signals began to exercise a profound influence on the movements of the British fleet. Wireless stations for the interception of German naval signals on all waves were rapidly erected, and the staff of cryptographers was augmented to deal with the increasing number of signals arriving at the Admiralty. The department could no longer remain a private enterprise under Ewing; naval officers were needed to interpret the deciphered signals; someone vested with authority was required to enrol additional staff and order the erection of new wireless stations. The work was properly a function of the naval intelligence division, and so it was transferred into that division and Hall took control. Under his driving power the new section (called Room 40 O.B.) extended its work until there were over a hundred men and women deciphering signals and issuing intelligence reports to the Admiralty and commanders-in-chief afloat, and fifty wireless stations in direct land-line communication with Room 40. Hall spread his net far and wide to draw into Room 40 a staff who were German scholars and gifted with the type of brain which can unravel ciphers. There came a time when the movements of the British fleets and squadrons were entirely governed by this intelligence, and it was a principal factor in winning the long-drawn-out battle against the German submarines.

Hall also developed the interception of messages between Germany and Spain for onward transmission by cable to Mexico and the United States, and between Germany and Turkey. These messages which frequently contained information of vital importance were properly the concern of the Foreign Office, but the Cabinet trusted Hall implicitly and left to him the responsibility of deciding when the purport of a signal should be shown to ministers. From these messages the trend of German foreign policy and the activities of German diplomatic officials and of German-paid saboteurs could be followed. Hall was able to forewarn the British authorities of a German conspiracy in Persia and Afghanistan, and of plans to destroy the Siberian railway. He was able to follow closely the activities of the Indian revolutionaries in the United States whose efforts to foment a rising in India continued unabated until the end of the war. These messages also enabled him to get on the track of Sir Roger Casement who in the early months of the war was assisting saboteurs in America, and to follow him to Germany where he sought the support of German armed forces for a rebellion in Ireland, and finally to come up with him when he landed from a submarine on the west coast of Ireland.

The most important message handled by Hall was the famous Zimmermann telegram, in which the German foreign minister instructed the German minister in Mexico to propose an offensive alliance with that country should America enter the war on the side of the Allies. Relations between America and Mexico were severely strained and Germany hoped that by offering financial support and an undertaking that Mexico should reconquer her lost territories in Texas, New Mexico, and Arizona, the Mexicans would declare war and strain America's war potential, as yet undeveloped, to such an extent that no military help could be given to the Allies. Hall handled this message most skilfully. He had to convince President Wilson that it was genuine, yet, in order to safeguard Room 40, to arouse no suspicion that it had been deciphered by the British intelligence service. When the Zimmermann telegram was published, and the credit given to the American intelligence service, it did much to influence the American decision to declare war on Germany. At a later stage of the war Hall employed the same safeguards when his staff deciphered a series of messages to Berlin from the German minister in the Argentine in which he recommended that merchant shipping should be sunk without trace. The publication of these messages in America severely strained relations between the South American republics and Germany which had hitherto been friendly.

Throughout the war Hall worked in close accord with (Sir) Basil Thomson, assistant commissioner of the metropolitan police. Information in the intercepted messages considerably helped their joint efforts to counter the activities of spies and agents. Hall employed his own agents in Spain, Morocco, and Mexico to counteract the attempts of German agents to refuel and reprovision their submarines. Among the most successful of these agents was A. E. W. Mason. Hall also devised many ruses to deceive the German high command, such as planting false code-books on German agents in Holland and passing false information to Germany by the same means.

Few men made a greater contribution to winning the war than did Hall. He not only exploited to the full every field of intelligence but made the best use of everything that came to hand. His work was recognized by his appointment as C.B. in 1915 and as K.C.M.G. in 1918. He was promoted rear-admiral in 1917, vice-admiral (retired) in 1922, and admiral in 1926. The university of Oxford conferred upon him the honorary degree of D.C.L. in 1919 and Cambridge that of LL.D. in 1920.

At the end of the war Hall retired and entered the House of Commons as Conservative member for the West Derby division of Liverpool. Ill health hampered his political career, but on the few occasions on which he addressed the House on naval subjects he commanded a respectful hearing through his obvious sincerity and his detailed and inside knowledge of international and imperial affairs. In March 1923 Hall became principal agent of the Conservative Party, an office which he held until after the Conservative losses at the general election of December. The qualities which had stood him in such good stead as director of naval intelligence were other than those required in a principal political agent when his party's fortunes were on the wane, and he was not well suited for the post. He lost his seat at the election but re-entered Parliament in 1925 as member for Eastbourne. Ill health caused his retirement from politics at the general election of 1929. He died in London 22 October 1943.

Hall married in 1894 Ethel Wootton (died 1932), daughter of (Sir) William de Wiveleslie Abney. They had one daughter and two sons, both of whom became naval officers, the elder dying in 1942.

A drawing of Hall by Francis Dodd is in the Imperial War Museum. A crayon drawing by Louis Raemaekers is in the possession of the family. A bust by Lady Kennet is at the Royal Naval College, Dartmouth.

[*The Times*, 23 and 29 October 1943; Sir William James, *The Eyes of the Navy*, 1955; private information; personal knowledge.]

W. M. JAMES

published 1959

(1853–1947)

Sir

General, was born at Corfu 16 January 1853, the elder son of Captain (later Lieutenant-Colonel) Christian Monteith Hamilton of the 92nd Highland Regiment of Foot (2nd battalion Gordon Highlanders), by his wife, Maria Corinna, daughter of John Prendergast Vereker, third Viscount Gort, and granddaughter of Standish O'Grady, first Viscount Guillamore, an Irish judge famous for his wit. Owing to his mother's death when he was three years old Hamilton was brought up at Hafton, the Argyllshire home of his paternal grandparents. There he learnt to shoot with gun and rifle, and developed an eye for country.

Destined for the army, he was sent to R. S. Tabor's school at Cheam, and thence to Wellington College, but neither at work nor play did he show much promise. Nevertheless, in 1870, after six months with a crammer, he made light of the examination for a commission, and was seventy-sixth in a list of 392 successful candidates. He then spent a year in Dresden, receiving tuition from a retired German general, and returned to England in 1871 to attend a special twelve months' course at the Royal Military College, Sandhurst, where, too, his record was disappointing.

Posted to the 12th Foot (Suffolk Regiment) in April 1872, Hamilton served with them in Ireland for eighteen months, and was then transferred to the 92nd Highlanders in India. There he found himself at home, for his father had only recently given up command of the regiment, and his character developed rapidly. Quick, intelligent, and blessed with abundance of charm, 'Johnny' Hamilton had much to recommend him. Intellectually he was far ahead of the majority of his companions. Ambitious to excel, he worked hard at everything he undertook, and he wrote with a fluent and picturesque pen. He was a good sportsman and an unusually fine shot, and, combined with these tastes, he had a flair for painting and a keen appreciation of music and poetry. He loved crowds, but was equally content with solitude. Emergency found him at his best, and he courted the thrill and excitement of personal danger. The drab routine of regimental life could not satisfy his restless spirit for long, and he soon set himself to study Hindustani, with the idea of obtaining early staff employment. Meanwhile, his military interest lay in improving the musketry efficiency of his company, and whenever leave could be had his delight was to spend it alone on a Himalayan hillside, in search of a bigger 'head' than had ever been shot before. This ambition was achieved in 1876 when he

195

bagged the largest markhor head on record. In 1877, while on furlough in England, he attended a course at the Musketry School at Hythe and exhibited marked proficiency. Later he became musketry instructor to his battalion, and made it the best-shooting battalion in India.

Hamilton's first experience of active service was with the Gordons in Afghanistan in 1879. There, in an outpost affair, his plucky initiative changed the course of his life. His general, Sir Frederick (later Earl) Roberts, asking him to describe the incident in detail, was so struck by his personality that he determined to have him as aide-de-camp when opportunity offered. Meanwhile he sent him as orderly officer to W. G. D. Massy commanding the Cavalry brigade. In this, his first campaign, Hamilton was twice mentioned in dispatches.

Early in 1881 the Gordons were ordered to Natal and on 27 February Hamilton was present, with a small detachment of the regiment, at the disastrous engagement of Majuba Hill. There he received a wound which crippled his left arm for life, and he was specially mentioned in dispatches for conspicuous gallantry. Invalided home, he was invited to Osborne by Queen Victoria to tell her his story of the battle. Early in 1882, while studying for the Staff College examination, he was offered and accepted the post of aide-de-camp to Roberts, then serving as commander-in-chief, Madras. Thus began an association and close friendship which lasted twenty years and saw Hamilton rise from captain to lieutenant-general. In the autumn of 1884 he obtained leave from India in the secret hope of getting himself employed with the Gordon relief expedition. When his ship reached Suez he dashed up to Cairo, left for the front next day with the 1st battalion of his regiment, and was present at the action of Kirbekan. He was again mentioned in dispatches and was promoted brevet major. Early in 1886 he returned as aide-de-camp to Roberts, now commander-in-chief in India, and at the end of the year he accompanied him to Burma for three months, in connexion with the final pacification of that country after its annexation. He was again mentioned in dispatches and became brevet lieutenant-colonel in 1887.

In 1890 Hamilton was appointed assistant adjutant-general for musketry, Bengal, and in two and a half years he improved the musketry efficiency of the Indian Army beyond recognition. He became full colonel in 1891, and when Roberts left India in 1893 and was succeeded by Sir George White, Hamilton was brought back to Simla as White's military secretary. In 1895, during the operations in Chitral, he was on the staff of the lines of communication, and six months later, after another mention in dispatches and the appointment of C.B., he returned to Simla as deputy quarter-master-general. In 1897 he was given command of the 3rd brigade of the Tirah Expeditionary Force but broke his leg before the campaign began, and only rejoined his command when the fighting was over.

After twenty-five years of almost continuous service in India, he sailed for England in April 1898, on his appointment to command the Musketry School at Hythe. In September 1899, in view of the threat of war, he was ordered to Natal as assistant adjutant-general to White. A month later he was commanding a column with the temporary rank of major-general. At the battle of Elandslaagte he showed such conspicuous gallantry at a critical moment that he was recommended for the Victoria Cross, but, as it had never previously been awarded to an officer commanding a brigade, the Duke of Cambridge refused to establish a precedent. During the siege of Ladysmith Hamilton again exhibited resolution and valour; after the relief he was called to Bloemfontein by Roberts, who had meanwhile assumed the chief command in South Africa, and given charge of a mounted infantry division, with the rank of lieutenant-general, for the final advance on Pretoria. For this Hamilton was appointed K.C.B., and when Roberts returned to England as commander-in-chief at the War Office, he went with him as military secretary. Some months later, when Lord Kitchener was finding himself increasingly tied to his office, Roberts offered him Hamilton as chief of staff. The offer was accepted and Hamilton returned to Pretoria. But Kitchener was ever inclined to decide everything himself. Hamilton was little more than 'so-called' chief of staff, and four months after his arrival he was sent to the Western Transvaal to take command of four columns whose action was hanging fire for lack of central direction. Thus he suddenly found himself in command of 17,000 men and in charge of the final great 'drive' which brought the war to an end. Promoted substantive lieutenant-general, and with a record surpassed by none of his contemporaries, he returned to England with Kitchener to resume his duties as military secretary at the War Office. Nine months later, in 1903, he became quarter-master-general.

Hamilton, however, could not be long content with any sedentary post, and early in 1904, on the outbreak of the Russo-Japanese war, he was appointed chief of a military mission with the Japanese armies in the field. Although the movements of foreign attachés in the war area were severely restricted, he made the most of his opportunities, and his trenchant diary, *A Staff Officer's Scrap Book* (2 vols., 1905–7), was widely read in England and on the continent. In 1905 he was recalled to the Southern Command and held the appointment for four memorable years. Tidworth House, then the official residence, was admirably suited to the requirements of a commander and his wife who, with no financial cares, had a genius for entertaining. The Government found that the most popular way of entertaining foreign royalties and other distinguished visitors was to send them to Salisbury Plain to see the army at work and enjoy the hospitality of the Hamiltons.

Promoted general in 1907, Hamilton became adjutant-general in 1909. A year later, after being promoted G.C.B. (1910), he was given the Mediterranean Command, recently vacated by the Duke of Connaught, with headquarters at Malta; the importance of the appointment was increased by making him in addition inspector-general of oversea forces. Before leaving England, however, he was asked by R. B. (later Viscount) Haldane, then secretary of state for war, to assist him by writing, for his private information, a memorandum on the highly controversial subject of compulsory service which was being advocated by the National Service League under the powerful leadership of Roberts. The Government was unconvinced of its necessity and Hamilton, despite his long association with Roberts, pointed out in his memorandum that his old chief's proposals were far less suited to British needs than was the existing system of voluntary enlistment. It was decided that the memorandum should be published. Signed by Hamilton, with an introduction by Haldane, and entitled *Compulsory Service*, its publication in the autumn of 1910 caused considerable surprise in military circles; and a few months later its arguments were indignantly answered by Roberts himself in *Fallacies and Facts* (1911). The controversy lasted for years. Roberts was not to live to see the end of it; and it was not until the war of 1914–18 had been raging for two years that conscription was introduced into the British Army.

After four years at Malta, Hamilton returned to England in 1914, and was appointed aide-de-camp general to the King. When war broke out and Kitchener assumed charge at the War Office, one of his first acts was to give Hamilton command of the Central Force, responsible for the defence of England in the event of enemy invasion.

The supreme opportunity of Hamilton's career, and the highest test of his capacity, began on 12 March 1915, when Kitchener summoned him and told him to start next day to assume command of an Anglo-French army which, Kitchener disclosed, was already assembling at Mudros in connexion with the allied resolve to force the Dardanelles. His formal instructions, written on one sheet of paper, were necessarily vague, for no military plans had been made. The navy had undertaken to force the Straits, and apart, perhaps, from some minor military enterprises to occupy areas where hidden guns might be impeding progress, it was expected that the fleet would get through unaided. In this case the army would not be wanted until Constantinople was approached, and it was even hoped that Turkish resistance would collapse with the arrival of allied transports in the Marmora. Yet if the navy failed—and on this point Kitchener's instructions were precise—Hamilton was to throw in his whole force to open the way for the fleet. 'Having entered on the project of forcing the Straits', Kitchener said, 'there can be no idea of abandoning the scheme.'

Hamilton accepted his uncertain task with equanimity. 'Are not the best moments in life', he had written in his *Scrap Book*, 'those in which it is borne in to a poor mortal that some immortal has clearly designated the field of action, wherein he has only to be true to his convictions and himself, and advance confidently by word of command to the accomplishment of some predestined end?' Kitchener's demeanour had fixed Hamilton's attention more firmly on the gleaming minarets of Constantinople than on the rugged precipices of the Peninsula, and when he left London, 13 March, with his hastily collected staff, Hamilton's sanguine temperament was already painting pictures of easy victory. 'If the fleet gets through, Constantinople will fall of itself', Kitchener had told him that morning, 'and you will have won, not a battle, but the war!' But on 18 March, from the deck of a light cruiser, Hamilton was an eye-witness of the fleet's losses in the unsuccessful attempt to force the Dardanelles. Later, when the admiral reported that he could not renew the attack until the army had captured the Peninsula, Hamilton concurred, and on 27 March, after a fruitless effort by (Sir) Winston Churchill to persuade the Government to insist upon a further unaided attack by the navy, the dreaded alternative of military operations was decided upon. Not until after the war did it become clear that Churchill's hopes had perhaps been well founded. The losses which the admiral had attributed to floating mines or shore torpedo-tubes had been due to a small and unsuspected minefield. The Turks on the night of the 18th were weighed down by a premonition of defeat. Most of their ammunition had been shot away, and they expected a renewed attack next morning. In Constantinople a British victory was thought to be inevitable, and the Germans feared a revolt in the capital.

It would be hard to exaggerate the difficulties of Hamilton's problem. His knowledge of the situation on shore was nil, and his maps were out of date. His army, mostly still on the high seas, had been shipped without regard to possible tactical requirements on arrival. There were no quays in the wind-swept harbour of Mudros; the whole force would have to be unpacked and repacked in the glare of publicity at Alexandria; and at least a month must elapse before it could be ready to undertake that most difficult of military tasks—a landing from ships' boats on an open beach, in face of opposition. All chances of secrecy and surprise had gone, and the Turks were digging for their lives. But Hamilton remained confident and infected his command with his own spirit. When the landing took place on 25 April it was within an ace of succeeding. Three times in the next six weeks, with unexampled courage, his troops renewed the battle, and on each occasion it was mainly the want of another fresh brigade, or of more ammunition, which cheated them of victory. But Hamilton himself cannot be absolved of all responsibility for these checks. The enthusiasm, self-confidence, and personal courage demanded of the military commander-in-chief, he possessed in full measure. But he lacked the iron will and dominating personality of a truly great commander. Although the force originally allotted to him bore no relation to his possible requirements, but consisted merely of such numbers as Kitchener had felt able to provide without embarrassment in France, he refused to risk Kitchener's displeasure by asking for one man more than his sanguine temperament hoped would just suffice. When Kitchener learnt, from the Admiralty not from Hamilton, of the crying need for more troops, he immediately ordered them from Egypt, but they arrived just too late. Hamilton's optimism, too, inclined him to over-confidence in battle. He left too much to his subordinates and hesitated to override their plans, even when in his opinion they were missing opportunities.

Later in the summer, when for a short time, in their anxiety to force a decision, the Government made Gallipoli the main British theatre, Hamilton was allotted lavish reinforcements for a new offensive in August. The kernel of the whole plan, which consisted of three independent attacks on three separate fronts, was a surprise landing at Suvla, to be followed by a turning movement. When battle was joined on the night of 6 August, the weak Turkish detachments at Suvla, completely surprised, began to retire. But disastrous delays occurred on the Suvla beaches, and the whole British plan eventually fell to bits. After the initial success on the 6th, Hamilton's habitual optimism and his confidence in an untried leader had allowed him to dismiss the Suvla front from his mind and concentrate his attention elsewhere. Only on the afternoon of the 8th were his suspicions at last aroused, and he hurried to intervene in the Suvla battle, but by then the chance of victory had gone.

Hamilton had now lost the confidence of the Government. In view of the difficulties of sparing him further men, and the vanishing chances of success, the feasibility of evacuating the Peninsula was considered. When, in October, he replied to Kitchener that, at best, an evacuation might cost him half his force, and, at worst, might end in catastrophe, it was decided to replace him by a general who would view the situation with a fresh and unbiased mind.

No further command was offered to Hamilton; he became lieutenant of the Tower in 1918 and in 1919 he was appointed G.C.M.G. He was for many years colonel of his old regiment, the Gordon Highlanders, of which he was ever the firm friend and supporter. After his retirement in 1920 he published *Gallipoli Diary* (2 vols., 1920), a faithful record of his experiences and a revealing self-portrait. He took an active interest in the British Legion and in all organizations for the benefit of servicemen, as also in the Gordon Boys' Home and in Wellington College, of which he became a governor. From 1932 to 1935 he was lord rector of Edinburgh University, and in 1947 he was given the freedom of Inverness. He was a grand officer of the Legion of Honour and received decorations from Germany, Japan, and Spain.

Hamilton married in 1887 Jean Miller (died 1941), the beautiful and gifted daughter of Sir John Muir, first baronet, of Deanston, Perthshire. There were no children of the marriage, but after the war Lady Hamilton adopted a baby boy, Harry, who had been abandoned in the Paddington crèche of which she was president, and who died of wounds received in action in 1941. Hamilton died in London 12 October 1947, and was buried beside his wife at Doune, Perthshire. A portrait of Hamilton by J. S. Sargent is in the Tate Gallery and another in the Scottish National Portrait Gallery. A pencil drawing by Sir William Rothenstein is in the National Portrait Gallery.

[Sir Ian Hamilton, *When I Was a Boy*, 1939, *Jean*, 1942, and *Listening for the Drums*, 1944; C. F. Aspinall-Oglander, (Official) *History of the Great War. Military Operations, Gallipoli*, 2 vols., 1929–32; personal knowledge.]

C. F. ASPINALL-OGLANDER

published 1959

Allan Francis ('John')

(1896–1989)

First Baron Harding of Petherton

Field-marshal, was born 10 February 1896 at Rock House, South Petherton, Somerset, the second child and only son in the family of four children of Francis Ebenezer Harding, solicitor's clerk and local rating officer, and his wife Elizabeth Ellen, daughter of Jethro Anstice, draper, of South Petherton. At the age of ten he was sent as a weekly boarder to Ilminster Grammar School. His headmaster, Robert Davidson, was a sound scholar; in later years, when already a lieutenant-general, Harding would attribute his capacity for hard work to Davidson's example and his gift of logical thinking to hours spent construing Ovid to him.

The family had not enough money to finance a career either in farming, his own preference, or the law, which Davidson recommended; he became at the age of fifteen a boy clerk in the Post Office Savings Bank. After attending night classes at King's College, London, he was promoted and in his new posting he was influenced by his superior in the office to apply for a commission in the Territorial Army. Two regular officers interviewed him and, although he was only eighteen and from a station in life different from that of most regular officers, they showed discernment and lack of prejudice in recognizing his quality. He was gazetted as second lieutenant in the 1/11th battalion of the London Regiment (the 'Finsbury Rifles') in May 1914.

He first saw action on 10 August 1915 in the Dardanelles campaign, where he was wounded after only five days. When Gallipoli was abandoned his battalion went to Egypt. Here he decided to apply for and in March 1917 was granted a regular commission as a lieutenant in his county regiment, the Somerset Light Infantry. By now he was specializing in machine-guns. In the third battle of Gaza he was divisional machine-gun officer, as acting major at the age of twenty-one, and was awarded the MC (1917). In 1918 he was made corps machine-gun officer at XXI Corps headquarters. From experience on the staff he learned, among other things, the value of strategic deception, which was practised with great success in both wars by British commanders in the Middle East.

Between the wars Harding served in India from 1919 to 1927, first with the Machine-Gun Corps and then with his regiment. From 1928 to 1930 he attended the Staff College. In May 1933 he was appointed brigade-major of the 13th Infantry brigade which was chosen as the British contingent in the international force which supervised the Saarland plebiscite. It was a good preparation for the tasks of collaborating with forces of different nationalities which were to fall to him later in the Mediterranean theatre; he also made a special study of the Italian contingent, whose light tanks were to prove so ineffective in the desert. In July 1939, at the age of forty-three, he was given command of the 1st battalion of his regiment, again in India. He earned a mention in dispatches for frontier operations, but his reputation ensured that he would soon be required for more serious service; in autumn 1940 he was posted to Egypt, where staff officers were required.

His first task was to plan Compass, the offensive against the Italian Tenth Army organized by Sir A. P. (later first Earl) Wavell; he went on to become brigadier general staff to (Sir) Richard O'Connor, commanding the Western Desert Force, later XIII Corps. Compass was brilliantly successful, expelling all Italian formations from Cyrenaica and capturing 125,000 prisoners, at little cost in British casualties. Harding's services were rewarded with a CBE (1940) and a second mention in dispatches. When the counter-attack led by Field-marshal Erwin Rommel overwhelmed the British in Cyrenaica, and both O'Connor and his successor, (Sir) Philip

Neame, were taken prisoner it was Harding who took temporary charge, organized the defence of Tobruk, and persuaded Wavell that it could be held. After the first two misdirected German attacks on the fortress had been repulsed he was transferred to be brigadier general staff of a revived Western Desert Force at Matruh and appointed to the DSO (1941).

For Crusader, the operation which saw Rommel's army defeated in the field and the siege of Tobruk relieved, he was BGS to (Sir) A. R. Godwin-Austen, a robustly competent commander whose qualities were harmoniously supplemented by Harding's intellectual grasp of the often perplexing problems created by Rommel's ineffectual precipitancy. He received a bar to his DSO for this victory. In January 1942 he supported Godwin-Austen's correct appreciation of the capabilities of the German counter-offensive and found himself organizing for the second time a hurried withdrawal through western Cyrenaica. The differences between the army and the corps commanders being irreconcilable, Godwin-Austen was replaced. Harding considered he was also honour bound to ask for a transfer; he went to GHQ as director of military training. He was promoted to brigadier and then major-general in 1942.

In Cairo Harding found himself frequently at variance, in practical matters of organization, with the chief of staff and his deputy. It was a relief to be given command, in September, of 7th Armoured division, the original desert armoured formation. In the second battle of Alamein his division was originally employed on the southern flank, its purpose mainly to deceive General Stumme into maintaining the original faulty disposition of his armour; but, with the return of Rommel and the intensification of the struggle in the northern sector, 7th Armoured was transferred there. In the pursuit that followed the successful change of plan, Harding fretted at the constraints imposed on him, but drove hard, always up with the forward troops. In January 1943, when approaching Tripoli, he was severely wounded by a nearby shell burst. He received a second bar to his DSO but was not graded fit to return to duty until ten months had passed.

In November 1943 he took command of VIII Corps, having been promoted to lieutenant-general, but six weeks later, by the personal decision of Sir Alan Brooke (later first Viscount Alanbrooke), chief of the imperial general staff, he was transferred to be chief of staff to Sir Harold Alexander (later first Earl Alexander of Tunis), commander-in-chief, Allied Armies in Italy. This was an inspired appointment. Harding and Alexander not only got on well together but admirably complemented each other. Alexander was both an intellectual and a fighting soldier, combining a tactical grasp of the battlefield with the talent of an imaginative and fertile strategist. In Harding he had someone who could be relied on without reservation to implement his ideas.

Harding

After the capture of Rome Harding was appointed KCB (1944). He chose to be known as Sir John Harding, that being the name he had used in the regiment and the family since 1919. After fifteen months as chief of staff he was at last, in March 1945, given the chance to command a corps in action; he took over XIII Corps, with which he had served in the desert nearly five years earlier. The last battle in Italy was as hard fought as the first. Harding's corps, originally on the British left, changed direction in the closing stages and pursued the retreating enemy up to and across the Po with a speed and effectiveness greater than he had been allowed to achieve after Alamein. That headlong pursuit brought him to Trieste on 2 May, just after the Yugoslavs, and to the centre of a long-lasting dispute with Britain's former ally. The acute stage of the confrontation with the Yugoslavs was overcome when they backed down in June, the first victory, it has been called, in the cold war. For two years Harding ruled with popular acclaim over what became the free city of Trieste in reasonable tranquillity.

In the summer of 1947 he was appointed to Southern Command and two years later became commander-in-chief Far East. He arrived just as what was euphemistically called 'the emergency' was beginning in Malaya; it was destined to last for twelve years. The foundations of the system by which this formidable Chinese communist insurrection was eventually suppressed were laid by Harding. Malcolm MacDonald, the special commissioner for the Far East, paid a firm tribute to the sagacity and tenacity of purpose with which Harding dominated the defence co-ordinating committee.

Promoted to general in 1949 and appointed GCB at the beginning of 1951 Harding was transferred in August 1951 to command the British Army of the Rhine. After the Russian take-over in Czechoslovakia and the Berlin blockade Britain had begun rearming and NATO set up the Supreme Headquarters, Allied Powers in Europe (SHAPE), commanded by Dwight Eisenhower. The British army was being transformed. New defence plans were studied. Harding had to display prodigies of inter-Allied tact, organizational flair, and determination. By contrast his period as chief of the imperial general staff, three years from 1952 to 1955, passed off with little more excitement than the Mau Mau rebellion in Kenya and the beginning of the dissolution of the British base in Egypt. In November 1953 he was promoted field-marshal and presented with his baton by the young queen.

As the end of the three-year term approached and Harding was making plans for his retirement, a proposal was made to him by the new prime minister, Sir Anthony Eden (later the first Earl of Avon), that he should become governor of Cyprus. Eden considered that his experience in Malaya and Kenya would help him to control the demand for union with Greece, which was supported by the majority of Greek Cypriots. He accepted reluctantly, from a sense of duty. He realized at once that the only favourable prospect lay in negotiating with Archbishop Makarios for some acceptable form of self-government. The two men were well matched in quickness of intelligence; Makarios later declared that Harding was both the cleverest and the most straightforward of the governors he had known. Though circumstances denied them the pleasure of a successful agreement, Harding's measures brought greatly improved security in the island, with the Greek Cypriot insurgent leader, George Grivas, reduced to impotent clandestinity. After the two years' term for which he had originally stipulated, Harding was able to hand over in October 1957 to his successor, Sir Hugh Foot (later Baron Caradon), a sound basis for the eventual achievement of Cypriot independence.

In January 1958 he was raised to the peerage in acknowledgement of his service in Cyprus. In retirement he accepted several directorships, including one on the board of Plesseys, a major supplier of telecommunication equipment of which he became chairman in 1967. In 1961 he was invited to become the first chairman of the Horse Race Betting Levy Board. He was colonel of three regiments, the Somerset Light Infantry (from 1960 the Somerset and Cornwall Light Infantry), the 6th Gurkha Rifles, and the Lifeguards. He was awarded an honorary DCL of Durham University (1958).

He was slight in build with a frank and courteous expression, clear blue eyes, and a trim moustache. His manner was open and friendly; throughout a career that could have excited jealousy no one spoke badly of him. Apart from a notable skill in personal relationships, his leading characteristic was a lucidity of intellectual apprehension and strength of reasoning that enabled him to grasp the essence of every problem. Those who served with him were exhilarated by the speed and certainty with which he arrived at the right solution.

He married in 1927 Mary Gertrude Mabel, daughter of Joseph Wilson Rooke, solicitor and JP, of Knutsford, Cheshire, and sister of an officer in his regiment. She died in 1983. They had one son, John Charles (born 1928), who succeeded to the barony. Harding died 20 January 1989 at his home in Sherborne, Dorset.

[Michael Carver, *Harding of Petherton*, 1978; David Hunt, *A Don at War*, revised edn. 1990; I. S. O. Playfair *et al.*, (Official) *History of the Second World War. The Mediterranean and Middle East*, vols. i–vi, 1956–88; personal knowledge.]

DAVID HUNT

published 1996

(1892–1984)

First baronet

Marshal of the Royal Air Force, was born 13 April 1892 at Cheltenham, the second youngest in the family of four sons and two daughters of George Steele Travers Harris, an engineer-architect in the Indian Civil Service, and his wife, Caroline Maria, daughter of William Charles Elliot, a surgeon in the Madras Cavalry. The second son died in 1917 and the youngest son died as an infant. Educated at Gore Court, Sittingbourne, and All Hallows, Honiton, while his parents were in India, he soon became exceptionally self-reliant. At seventeen, against his father's wishes, he went out to farm in Rhodesia.

In October 1914 Harris joined the new 1st Rhodesian Regiment as a bugler—almost the only vacancy. He took part in the successful operations against German South-West Africa, and on the disbanding of the regiment returned to England to enlist. Failing to find a place in the cavalry or artillery, he applied to join the Royal Flying Corps. Half an hour's tuition at Brooklands qualified him as a civilian pilot, and in November 1915 he was commissioned as a second lieutenant.

In the RFC Harris became an 'anti-zeppelin night pilot' and soon commanded No. 38 Squadron. Posted to No. 70 Squadron in France, he was invalided home after a crash, but returned in May 1917 for fighter work with No. 45 Squadron. During 1918 he commanded a night-training and night-fighting squadron (No. 44) in England, and was awarded the AFC.

In August 1919 Harris was offered a permanent commission in the RAF as a squadron leader. Between then and 1925 he commanded No. 2 Flying Training School at home, No. 31 Squadron in India (with operations on the North-West Frontier), and No. 45 Squadron in Iraq, where he successfully adapted his troop-carrying Vernons for day and night bombing. He also invented an electric truck by which these cumbersome aircraft could be moved on the ground by two men instead of sixteen. His spell in Iraq completed, Harris then commanded (1925–7) No. 58 Squadron of Virginia bombers at Worthy Down and made it one of the most efficient in the Service. Again his work involved intensive training by night. In 1927 he was appointed OBE.

Having passed successfully through the Army Staff College (1928–9) and declined an invitation to stay on as an instructor, Harris then served for two years on the air staff in the Middle East. He was next posted home, in 1933, to take a flying-boat pilot's course and briefly command No. 210

(Flying-boat) Squadron. Six months as deputy director of operations and intelligence at the Air Ministry then followed, after which he became deputy director of plans (1934–7). Here, as a member of the chiefs of staff joint planning sub-committee, he was much concerned with national defence policy as a whole. On the RAF side he urged the development of mines for aircraft to lay at sea, and he gave ardent support to the conception of new ultra-heavy (including four-engined) bombers. These were specified in 1936, and used by Harris with devastating effect in 1942–5.

A year's command of the newly formed No. 4 (Bomber) Group, during which Harris became an air commodore (1937), then followed. The squadrons of this group, on Whitleys, were specially trained for night bombing. Before taking up his next post in 1938 Harris was then sent to the United States to study the aircraft and aircraft equipment position there, and make purchases. He and his small staff hit on two winners: the Hudson for general reconnaissance and the Harvard advanced trainer.

Harris took up his next appointment as air officer commanding Palestine and Transjordan (1938–9). In his task of helping to restrain the growing hostility between Jews and Arabs Harris co-operated smoothly with the army and devised what he called the 'air pin'—pinning down villagers by the threat of bombing from patrolling aircraft until the army could get to the scene and root out the trouble-makers. During the course of this posting Harris was promoted air vice-marshal (1939) and mentioned in dispatches. He returned home with a duodenal ulcer which was to give him trouble later.

Shortly after the outbreak of war in 1939 Harris was given command of No. 5 (Bomber) Group. His Hampden aircraft soon proved unsuitable for daylight raids against the German fleet and became largely confined to operating by night. They did useful work against German barge concentrations and airfields during the invasion threat, and began the task which Harris was to develop so greatly later, of mining German waters. In the course of his year's command Harris secured many improvements in these aircraft, initiated operational training under simulated battle conditions, and received recognition in appointment as CB (1940).

In November 1940 Sir Charles Portal (later Viscount Portal of Hungerford) summoned Harris to serve under him at the Air Ministry as deputy CAS. Six months later he sent him out to Washington as head of the RAF delegation there, to speed up the purchase of aircraft and air supplies. Harris brought his characteristic drive to the task, got on well with the Americans, and had secured a marked improvement when in 1942 Portal called him home to become AOC-in-C Bomber Command.

The success of Harris's work at Bomber Command, though it seemed obvious at the time, has been questioned subsequently. Critics have denounced area bombing, his most favoured form of attack, as not only immoral but ineffective compared with precision bombing. Harris, however, did not determine bombing policy, which was a matter for Whitehall. Area bombing had come about because the British bombers of 1940–1 had proved incapable of penetrating Germany by day and of finding and hitting precision targets by night. It was a policy already in operation when Harris took over Bomber Command. Behind it lay the view that Germany had set ample precedents; that the destruction of industrial cities and the homes of the workers would seriously weaken the enemy; and that unless Bomber Command were given a practicable task no offensive action at all could be taken against Germany for years to come.

It was under Harris, who was selflessly supported by an outstanding senior air staff officer, Air Marshal (Sir) Robert Saundby, that Bomber Command developed from a force of modest size and doubtful efficiency into a truly formidable instrument of war. Well versed in technical matters, Harris eagerly grasped at developments which transformed the capabilities of his force: the Lancaster bomber, new bombs (up to 22,000 lb.), the succession of navigational or bombing aids (Gee, H2S, Oboe, GH), new techniques of target-marking and saturation raids under the direction of a master bomber—these are but a few of the best-known examples. By the latter part of 1944 his force had in fact become capable of precision bombing by night over Germany in cloudy weather, and was so employed with decisive results against German oil plants and communications. Area bombing, however, also remained in his directive from the Air Ministry, though in lower priority, until April 1945; and critics have suggested that Harris's own preference for this led him to continue it after precision bombing became regularly possible. But to Harris the retention of area bombing in his directive provided a flexibility he considered essential—the freedom to choose within a diversity of large targets in the light of meteorological conditions and the need to achieve tactical surprise. He was promoted air chief marshal in 1943.

On many occasions Harris strenuously resisted pressure from the Air Ministry; but when his objections were overruled, he prided himself on obeying his orders wholeheartedly. Perhaps the most striking instance was his initial opposition to the idea that Bomber Command should give direct assistance in the invasion of Normandy: he maintained that the best help he could give would be to continue bombing German cities. When overruled, he abundantly fulfilled his orders by attacks on railway and coastal targets in France which greatly facilitated the Allied landings and helped to prevent reinforcement of the forward German troops.

The contribution of Bomber Command under Harris to the Allied victory was in fact outstanding. It took many forms: sea mining, attacking

German warships and U-boat bases, co-operating with the Allied armies, disrupting German V-weapon activity, and waging a strategic offensive against German industry and urban industrial life. It cannot, however, be properly considered in isolation from the work of the Americans, without which it would not have been so effective. It was the combination of the two forces in 'round the clock' bombing from 1943 onwards that pinned down over a million civil workers, hundreds of thousands of German soldiers, and nearly 20,000 guns to the air defence of the Reich. According to Albert Speer, the Anglo-American air offensive 'opened a second front long before the invasion of Europe' and constituted 'the greatest lost battle on the German side'. Without this joint offensive, which among other things crippled the Luftwaffe and its sources of replenishment, it is inconceivable that the Allied armies could have successfully invaded Normandy in 1944.

For his achievements Harris was mentioned in dispatches (1939 and 1941) and appointed KCB (1942). An abundance of foreign honours descended on him: the Russian Order of Suvorov in 1944 and then in 1945 the Order of Polonia Restituta, the Brazilian National Order of the Southern Cross (grand cross), the French Legion of Honour (grand officer) and the croix de guerre with palm. In 1946 came the US DSM.

In Britain, the story was different. In June 1945 Harris accepted the GCB reluctantly—he was pressing at the time for proper recognition for his crews, and had said that if this were denied he wanted nothing for himself. He was omitted from the New Year's honours of 1946, though other commanders received peerages; but in his own Service he was promoted to the highest rank—in 1946 he became a marshal of the RAF. Also in 1946 Liverpool University awarded him an honorary LLD. Later, after (Sir) Winston Churchill's return to power, he was asked if he wished to be recommended for a peerage, but he preferred to retain his familiar style, and accepted a baronetcy (1953).

After the war Harris, in poor health and aggrieved at what he felt was lack of understanding of the magnitude of his Command's efforts, retired and departed for South Africa. Through a friend he started up, as a subsidiary of a larger concern, a shipping firm, the South African Marine Corporation. He ran this until 1953 when he returned to England and settled down amiably at Goring-on-Thames, where his favourite diversions included entertaining, cooking, and carriage-driving. Surprisingly, perhaps, for the commander whose forces destroyed most of the Ruhr, Hamburg, Berlin, and Dresden, he enjoyed the company of children and excelled at making up stories for them.

Until his old age Harris was of heavy build and reddish hair and complexion. A man of combative temperament who could be gruff and dismissive as well as affable, he was nevertheless popular with most of his colleagues, including those from other Services and nations. He was on the best of terms with Dwight D. Eisenhower and Viscount Montgomery of Alamein, and his collaboration with the American air forces based in Britain was virtually perfect. His own crews in Bomber Command rarely, if ever, saw him, but somehow the power of his personality and his utter commitment to his task radiated out from High Wycombe and provided a grim inspiration: his airmen knew he might be sending them to their death, but they also knew that their lives would not be lightly gambled, and that he would fight to his last gasp on their behalf. His nicknames—'Bomber' to most of his crews and the world at large, 'Butcher' to some, 'Bert' to his colleagues (from naval associates, for in the navy all Harrises are Berts), and 'Bud' or 'Buddy' to his second wife and family friends—testify to the varying elements within him. But his main characteristics were throughout clear: drive, efficiency, courage, determination, loyalty, common sense, practicality, humour, and a habit of exaggeration, particularly on paper, which got him into trouble but also resulted in perhaps the most readable official letters ever written by an air marshal.

There is a crayon portrait of Harris by Eric Kennington in the Imperial War Museum; a portrait by Anna Zinkeisen at Strike Command HQ; a picture by Herbert Olivier entitled 'Ops. Room Conference' showing Harris, Saundby, and others, in the RAF Museum; and a portrait with General Fred Anderson, USAAF, by Herbert Olivier in the possession of the family.

In 1916 Harris married Barbara Daisy Kyrle, daughter of Lieutenant-Colonel Ernle William Kyrle Money, of the 85th King's Shropshire Light Infantry. A son and two daughters were born of this marriage, which was dissolved in 1935. In 1938 Harris married Thérèse ('Jill'), daughter of Major Edward Patrick Hearne, of Carlow, Eire. There was one daughter of this marriage, born in 1939. Harris died 5 April 1981 at his home in Goring. He was succeeded in the baronetcy by his only son, Anthony Kyrle Travers (born 1918).

[A. T. Harris, *Bomber Offensive*, 1947; Dudley Saward, *'Bomber' Harris*, 1984; Sir C. Webster and N. Frankland, *The Strategic Air Offensive Against Germany, 1939–1945* (official history), 4 vols., 1961; private information; personal knowledge.]

DENIS RICHARDS

published 1990

(1895–1970)

Sir

Military historian and strategist, was born in Paris 31 October 1895, the younger son of the Revd Henry Bramley Hart, Wesleyan minister in Paris, and his wife, Clara, daughter of Henry Liddell. He was educated at St. Paul's School. In 1913 he went up to Corpus Christi College, Cambridge, to read history, but on the outbreak of war in 1914 he obtained a temporary commission in the King's Own Yorkshire Light Infantry. Posted to France in September 1915, he was invalided home after a shell-burst at Ypres; he returned to the front in the spring of 1916, only to be rendered *hors de combat* by gas on the Somme. Deep thought about his intense experiences on the western front permeated his subsequent military ideas. As adjutant (temporary captain) of training units of the Volunteer Force in 1917–21, he evolved new methods of instruction and an original battle drill. These attracted the attention in 1919 of two generals, Sir Ivor Maxse and Winston (later Lord) Dugan, who were responsible for compiling a post-war *Infantry Training* manual, much of which, although junior in rank, Liddell Hart was to revise or compose. His concepts did not always survive the War Office sieve, but he promulgated them with characteristic assurance in articles and lectures. He transferred to the Army Education Corps in 1921 with a regular commission, but his health wrecked his professional career; he was placed on lieutenant's half-pay in 1924, and retired as captain in 1927 'on account of ill health caused by wounds'. Nevertheless, he was already launched as a military thinker.

Oppressed by the slaughter on the western front, which he ascribed to inflexible generalship and bull-at-a-gate offensives, he sought by intellectual analysis to prevent or ameliorate any recurrence, taking as his slogan 'if one wishes peace one should understand war'. His key concepts were the 'expanding torrent' and the 'indirect approach'. The former, drawing on techniques employed in the German offensive of March 1918, emphasized fluidity, continuous forward motion, and the vital need to reinforce spearheads by immediately available reserves. The latter stressed tactical and strategic outflanking, the paramount virtue of surprise, and the importance of striking not at an opponent's main body but at nerve centres such as headquarters and lines of communication. Between the wars he expounded these principles volubly, and his *Strategy—The Indirect Approach* appeared in different forms in six editions between 1929 and 1967. Some felt that as he elaborated his theories they became more a philosophy of life than a *vade mecum* for the commander, but it is unquestionable that their forceful and lucid reiteration had a seminal and liberating effect on educated soldiers at home and abroad.

With the inter-war pioneers of British armoured development—J. F. C. ('Boney') Fuller, (Sir) Percy Hobart, (Sir) Charles Broad, and (Sir) Giffard Martel—his affinity was two-way. They discussed with him their practical experiments and forward thinking; he stimulated in argument and provided a public forum for the unorthodox group, struggling as it was against conservatism and the 'cavalry spirit'. As military correspondent of the *Daily Telegraph* in 1925–35, and as correspondent and defence adviser of *The Times* in 1935–9, he assiduously charted the efforts of the pioneers of mechanization, while also turning a critical eye on broader aspects of the British military machine, and registering the progress of German rearmament. His intimate contacts with the Service hierarchy, both at unit levels and in Whitehall, gave him an unequalled insight into dead wood and growth points. He was cultivated by the alert, and rejected by closed minds.

Wide reading in military history gave his theories backbone. Over thirty books he wrote included studies of Scipio Africanus (1926), Sherman (1930), Foch (1931), and (1934) of T. E. Lawrence, with whom he had a warm *rapport*. A man of sturdy loyalty, he devoted much time to defending Lawrence against his denigrators, as he did in the case of David Lloyd George, whose war memoirs owed much to his assistance. His Lees Knowles lectures for 1932–3, on 'The Movement of Military Thought from the Eighteenth to the Twentieth Century', were published as *The Ghost of Napoleon* (1933). In 1930 *The Real War* (enlarged and reissued as *A History of the World War*, 1934) made a controversial indictment of the command of Earl Haig. Widely read by military students—indeed, often 'required reading' in military colleges—Liddell Hart's writings advanced his authority.

This seemed at a peak in 1937–8, when the war minister, Leslie (later Lord) Hore-Belisha, enlisted him as unofficial adviser. He gave a creative impulsion to Hore-Belisha's reforms, but when the connection waned in mid 1938 it had damaged him: the reforms (although mainly salutary) were resented and the minister himself was distrusted by the military establishment, where Liddell Hart was felt to have enjoyed an excessive influence—particularly over senior appointments. In November 1939 *The Times* accepted his resignation, tendered in August after mounting frustration over his inability to publish the truth as he saw it. He thus lost both power-bases, and the issue in July of *The Defence of Britain* had even raised doubts about the stability of his judgement. Its stress on the current need for defence rather than offence seemed inconsistent with his ardent advocacy of the 'expanding torrent'.

Throughout the war of 1939–45 he was excluded from positions of influence. This was not surprising, since he advocated a compromise peace and consistently opposed 'total war'. (Sir) Winston Churchill, who had sought his advice in the thirties, made no further overtures. Journalism and private consultation were his lot, and pain as he watched the Germans in 1940, and other belligerents later, apply the ideas he had preached. The latter were not his alone, but he had been an especially perceptive prophet: he had fertilized the British Army—particularly the Royal Tank Corps— and in Germany men like Field-Marshal Reichenau and General Guderian acknowledged his stimulus, although it was perhaps not so directly influential as their post-war confidences suggested.

After 1945 he recovered from his eclipse. *Persona grata* with captive German generals, he recorded his interrogations in *The Other Side of the Hill* (first issued 1948, and enlarged in 1951), for long a source-book on their attitudes, and his edition of *The Rommel Papers* (1953) became an enduring text. *The Tanks* (2 vols., 1959) lifted regimental history on to the highest plane, and years of preparation resulted in his posthumous *History of the Second World War* (1970). Here his strength as a military analyst was qualified by limitations, for in describing a total war he overlooked its totality in terms of sociological, economic, and political consequences.

During the post-Hiroshima years he denounced 'massive retaliation' and denied, in speech and writing, that the existence of nuclear weapons would proscribe warfare at lower levels, in which he was as prescient as in his warning that antidotes must be prepared for the coming plague of guerrilla insurgency. But in his Indian summer it was as a sage that he most happily contributed to military affairs. States House, Medmenham, became a place of multi-national pilgrimage; the gamut ran through chiefs of staff to graduate researchers. His study was lined with photographs of statesmen and soldiers with whom he had shared a dialogue—his 'rogues' gallery'—and a later collection, the 'young rogues', who represented the cream of a new generation of military historians, beneficiaries of his passionate tutorial dissection of their writing and the incessant dialectic of his conversation. His ideas, moreover, were still a weapon: in 1967 the Israelis affirmed that their war that year had been won by 'the true strategy of indirect approach', and Yigal Allon inscribed a photograph to 'the captain who teaches generals'.

Unusually tall, light of frame, with a busy inquisitive air, he struck one as like a secretary-bird. But his eyes were Robin Goodfellow's, puckish and smiling; his laughter effervesced, and an ill-concealed streak of vanity endeared more than it offended. Brocade waistcoats and an indefinably dandiacal pose reflected his eccentric but deeply informed studies of feminine fashion, about which the experts approached him on their own level. As a young officer he had reported for leading newspapers on lawn tennis and rugby, and his lifelong addiction to war games, chess, and croquet (in which he was described as a fiendish opponent) refreshed rather than reduced his competitive spirit.

In 1918 he married Jessie Douglas, daughter of J. J. Stone; they had one son. The marriage was dissolved, and in 1942 he married Kathleen, daughter of Alan Sullivan, of Toronto, and widow of Henry Philbrick Nelson, FRCS. In 1963 he was awarded the Chesney gold medal of the Royal United Service Institution, in 1964 Oxford made him an honorary D.Litt., and in 1965 he was elected an honorary fellow of Corpus Christi College, Cambridge. He was a founder-member of the Institute of Strategic Studies, president of the Military Commentators' Circle in 1953–70, and an honorary member of the United States Marine Corps. In 1965–6 he was visiting distinguished professor at the university of California, and also in 1965 he was presented with a Festschrift, *The Theory and Practice of War*, edited by Michael Howard. He was knighted in 1966. A unique archive, the hundreds of files containing his correspondence and voluminous papers, is lodged in King's College, London.

He died 29 January 1970 at his home at Medmenham. A drawing by Sava Botzaris (1938) and two portraits by Eric Kennington (1943) are in the possession of the family.

[Basil Liddell Hart, *Memoirs*, 2 vols., 1965; *The Times*, 30 January 1970; R. J. Minney, *The Private Papers of Hore-Belisha*, 1960; Kenneth Macksey, *Armoured Crusader: Major-General Sir Percy Hobart*, 1967; Sir Giffard Martel, *An Outspoken Soldier*, 1949; private information; personal knowledge.]

RONALD LEWIN

published 1981

HASLER Herbert George ('Blondie')

(1914–1987)

Inventor, and founder of the Royal Marines Boom Patrol Detachment (the forerunner of the Special Boat Service) and short-handed ocean racing, was born in Dublin 27 February 1914, the younger child and younger son of Lieutenant Arthur Thomas Hasler, quartermaster, of the Royal Army Medical Corps, and his wife, Annie Georgina Andrews. His father was drowned when the troop-ship *Transylvania* was torpedoed on 4 May 1917, leaving his mother to bring up the young boys on her own. She sent Herbert, with a bursary, to Wellington College, where he distinguished himself at cross-country running, rugby football, and as captain of swimming. He also boxed but, according to him, with rather less distinction.

'Blondie' Hasler (as he now became known, except to his family, because of his thinning blond hair and fair moustache) combined remarkable powers of physical endurance with above average strength and fitness (he was about six feet tall). Yet, throughout his subsequent career, he was loath to take advantage of these attributes, although they stood him in good stead in war and peace, preferring a well-reasoned, calm, and quietly conducted discussion to make his case. He also hated punishing men under his command, believing that their failure was the result of his lack of leadership. He had a totally original mind.

Hasler was commissioned into the Royal Marines on 1 September 1932, and by 1935 had already achieved yachting distinction by sailing a twelve-foot dinghy single-handed from Plymouth to Portsmouth and back again. It was then that he began expounding advanced nautical theories through illustrated articles in the international press—a hobby he pursued until his death. After World War II broke out, as fleet landing officer in Scapa Flow in 1940, he was sent to Narvik in support of the French Foreign Legion. In just a few weeks he was appointed OBE, mentioned in dispatches, and awarded the croix de guerre.

On his return he wrote a paper suggesting the use of canoes and underwater swimmers to attack enemy shipping, but this was rejected by Combined Operations as being too radical and impracticable. However, in January 1942 Hasler was appointed to the Combined Operations Development Centre where, after the Italians had severely damaged HMS *Queen Elizabeth* and HMS *Valiant* in Alexandria harbour by the use of 'human torpedoes', his paper was immediately resurrected. He was ordered to form the Royal Marines Boom Patrol Detachment (later to be dubbed the 'Cockleshell Heroes'—an expression of which he disapproved). When the problem of blockade-runners operating out of Bordeaux was identified in September, Hasler had his solution ready the next day. The submarine HMS *Tuna* launched a raid on the night of 7 December 1942. Four men out of the original twelve reached the target in tiny two-man canoes, and only two, including Hasler, returned, having made their way overland to Spain. Hasler was recommended for the VC, but was technically ineligible, having not been fired on. He was appointed to the DSO. The episode was turned into a film, which was only loosely based on fact, *Cockleshell Heroes*, starring José Ferrer and Trevor Howard, in 1955.

Subsequently, Hasler experimented with different methods of attack, employing some of these ideas between 1944 and 1945 while serving as training and development officer with No. 385 Royal Marines detachment in the Small Operations Group (Ceylon), planning submarine-launched raids into Burma.

In 1946 he won the Royal Ocean Racing Club's class iii championships in his unconventional yacht, the thirty-square-metre *Tre Sang*. This was a remarkable achievement for a young officer. Hasler was invalided out of the Royal Marines in 1948 with the wartime rank of lieutenant-colonel. Retirement now allowed him time to concentrate on exploring, writing (in 1957 he wrote a play with Rosamund Pilcher, *The Tulip Major*, which was performed in Dundee), inventing, and developing a wide range of ideas, many of which are still in daily use. They included a floating breakwater and towed dracones (Hasler developed an earlier idea into a feasible design for transporting bulk oil).

In 1952 Hasler published *Harbours and Anchorages of the North Coast of Brittany* (revised 1965), which set the standard for the genre, but his greatest civilian triumphs of invention—and quiet, gentlemanly persuasion—were yet to come. In 1953 he conceived and built *Jester*, based on a modified twenty-six-foot Folkboat design, as a test bed for various sail plans (he eventually settled on the junk rig), and the internationally acclaimed, and first commercially successful, Hasler self-steering gear. *Jester* was a radical advance in British yacht design and she was not the last yacht to come from his drawing-board.

In 1957 he proposed the idea of a quadrennial single-handed transatlantic race for yachts and after many set-backs this was sailed in 1960 by five yachts; Hasler came second in *Jester*. He followed this in 1962 with a search for the Loch Ness monster and in 1966 by the first quadrennial two-handed round Britain and Ireland race, in which Hasler (again, the instigator) was crewed by his wife in the equally radical *Sumner*. These two races have spawned almost all modern, short-handed racing worldwide, with Hasler acknowledged as the founding father: he received a number of international awards. In his later years he moved to the west of Scotland, where he farmed organically and wrote *Practical Junk Rig* with J. K. McLeod (1988). His most important invention had been the self-steering gear, which became standard equipment and revolutionized sailing.

Hasler was married in 1965, when in his early fifties, to Bridget Mary Lindsay Fisher, then in her mid-twenties, the daughter of Rear-Admiral Ralph Lindsay Fisher, and an experienced yachtswoman in her own right. Despite the age difference the marriage brought them immense happiness and a son and a daughter. Hasler died of a heart attack in Glasgow, 5 May 1987.

[Mountbatten archives, Southampton University; C. E. Lucas Phillips, *Cockleshell Heroes*, 1956; Lloyd Foster, *OSTAR*, 1989; Ewen Southby-Tailyour, *Blondie Hasler, a Biography*, 1996; private archives; personal knowledge.]

EWEN SOUTHBY-TAILYOUR

published 1996

HILLARY Richard Hope

(1919–1943)

Battle of Britain pilot and author, was born 20 April 1919 in Sydney, Australia, the only child of Michael Hillary, DSO, OBE, Australian government official, and his wife Edwyna Hope. He came to England at the age of three, when his father received a London posting. From Shrewsbury School Hillary in 1937 went up to Trinity College, Oxford, starting to read philosophy, politics, and economics and then moving to modern history. He stroked the Trinity boat to head of the river, and as a notably good-looking but somewhat challenging undergraduate enjoyed to the full the leisured life of his college. He also joined the University Air Squadron with the motive, he later asserted, not of patriotism but self-realization. World War II began before he took his degree.

After enlistment and commissioning in the RAF and completion of his service flying training Hillary was posted on 6 July 1940 to No. 603 (City of Edinburgh) Fighter Squadron in Dyce. The Battle of Britain was beginning, and on 10 August No. 603 was ordered south to Hornchurch. Hillary's valiant combat career lasted three weeks, during which he was credited with five enemy aircraft. On 3 September 1940, over the North Sea, he was himself shot down. He fell from his Spitfire, but was sustained in the water by his buoyancy jacket and parachute. Horribly burned about the face and hands, he was rescued after three hours by the Margate lifeboat. There followed months in hospital and repeated operations, mostly by (Sir) Archibald McIndoe. His face was miraculously mended—he was given new upper eyelids and a new upper lip—but he was left with very wasted and weakened hands.

During 1941 Hillary persuaded the Air Ministry to send him to the United States on a speaking tour. But when he arrived there the British embassy expressed fears that his scarred features would only reinforce anti-involvement sentiments among American parents. His talks were confined to broadcasts, where he could not be seen. In America Hillary met many prominent people and enjoyed the affection of the film star Merle Oberon.

He also finished a book and secured its publication there (in February 1942) under the title *Falling Through Space.*

Retitled *The Last Enemy* and published in England the following June, this begins with a vivid account of Hillary's final flight. The narrative switches back to Oxford and the RAF, and then forward again to his hospital and surgical experiences. But it is concerned less with the facts of his life than with his feelings and motivation. The self-analysis is sustained and un-flattering. He presents himself as an individualist, who only later and al-most reluctantly becomes aware of the wider aspects of the war as a battle for civilization and humanity. The success of *The Last Enemy* was imme-diate. Hillary was acclaimed not only as a born writer but also as a rep-resentative of the doomed youth of his generation, although in his constant self-analysis he was in fact a most untypical British fighter pilot of 1940.

After returning from the United States in October 1941 Hillary had gone through Staff College, and thence to HQ Fighter Command. But he be-came obsessed with a desire to return to operations—as he saw it, to keep faith with his dead comrades. After repeated pleas he secured a medical board to consider his case. Surprisingly, it passed him fit for operations. On 24 November 1942 Hillary joined No. 54 Operational Training Unit at Charter Hall in Berwickshire for training as a night fighter pilot. On 8 January 1943, in a night of poor weather, he was circling a beacon on an exercise when his Blenheim lost height and crashed nearby, killing both Hillary and his radio operator. The subsequent inquiry, unable to deter-mine a specific cause for the accident, concluded that the pilot had lost control of his aircraft. After Hillary's death a Richard Hillary Trust was instituted and a Hillary archive was accumulated at Trinity College, Oxford.

After Hillary's death a considerable literature developed. Arthur Koestler, Eric Linklater, and John Middleton Murry all wrote about him, the last-named falsely hypothesizing a death-wish and suicide. Lovat Dickson, his publisher, wrote a biography. Much later, in 1988, Michael Burn, in *Mary and Richard*, published a selection of the love letters which had passed in 1942 between Hillary and Mary Booker, an understanding and beautiful woman twenty-two years Hillary's senior, whom Burn later married. Hillary's letters, remorselessly self-analytical as ever, confirm the writing talent of this brave, charming, self-assertive, mocking, and rather uncomfortable young man.

[Richard Hillary, *The Last Enemy*, 1942; Arthur Koestler, 'The Birth of a Myth', *Horizon*, April 1943; Eric Linklater, 'Richard Hillary' in *The Art of Adventure*, 1947, pp. 73–98; R. Lovat Dickson, *Richard Hillary, a Biography*, 1950; Michael Burn, *Mary and Richard*, 1988.]

DENIS RICHARDS

published 1993

HOLLAND John Charles Francis

(1897–1956)

Soldier and secret organizer, was born in India (probably Calcutta) 21 November 1897, the only son and elder child of (Sir) Thomas Henry Holland, geologist, and his wife Frances Maud, daughter of Charles Chapman, deputy commissioner in Oudh. Close friends called him 'Jo'.

He went from Rugby to the Royal Military Academy, Woolwich, whence he was commissioned into the Royal Engineers on 28 July 1915. He was posted to the eastern Mediterranean, arriving too late for the Gallipoli campaign, but serving on the Salonika front for most of the rest of the world war. He was mentioned in dispatches in 1917, and in the summer of 1918 was awarded the DFC for gallantry in action with the Royal Air Force. He was badly wounded in Dublin during the troubles of 1919–21, in which he admired the technical skills of his Irish guerrilla opponents.

In 1922 he reverted from temporary major to lieutenant; he was promoted captain in 1924 and major seven years later. He passed the staff college, and held a staff captain's appointment in northern command in 1934–6. In 1938, again due for promotion but medically unfit, he took an appointment as a second-grade staff officer in the War Office to research on any subject he chose. He chose irregular warfare. His branch, in which he was at first the only officer, was called GS (R).

His Irish experiences led his lively imagination well outside the normal range of military thinking at the time. Early in 1939 his branch was renamed MI R, and placed in the military intelligence directorate, though Holland concentrated rather on operations. Encouraged by A. P. (later first Earl) Wavell, he laid the foundations of several wartime secret services, and was one of the originators of the Commandos. For a few months in the summer of 1939 he worked at 2 Caxton Street, Westminster, alongside L. D. Grand, a Woolwich contemporary who ran the then inadmissible section D of the secret service. On the outbreak of war in September Holland went back to the War Office.

He gathered like-minded officers round him, and dispatched each in turn to run the service for which he seemed fit: N. R. Crockatt, whose prowess he had admired at Rugby, to secure intelligence from prisoners of war; E. R. Coombe to form the inter-services security board, which handled code-names and deception as well as security; (Sir) Gerald Templer to run the security of the expeditionary force; and M. R. Jefferis to invent and exploit secret gadgets. He sent (Sir) Colin Gubbins to the independent companies in Norway, then to command projected stay-behind parties to damage the communications of any invading German forces, and eventually to run the Special Operations Executive.

In July 1940 his staff, and Grand's, and a semi-secret propaganda branch of the Foreign Office, were all amalgamated to form the SOE. Holland thereupon went back to regimental duty, on being offered a regular lieutenant-colonel's command. By July 1943 he was back in the War Office, as deputy chief engineer and a major-general. He was appointed CB in 1945, and received also the American legion of merit and medal of freedom with silver palm. In 1947–8 he was chief of staff, Western Command; in 1949–50 he was again employed, briefly, on secret planning; and he retired in 1951.

He was a shortish, burly man who went bald early; a heavy cigarette smoker; quick-tempered, but recovering fast from anger. He married in 1924 Anne Christabel, daughter of Sir James Bennett Brunyate, KCSI, CIE, of the Indian Civil Service; they had two sons and a daughter. He died at his elder son's house in Wimbledon 17 March 1956.

[*Army Lists*; private information.]

M. R. D. Foot

published 1993

HORROCKS Brian Gwynne

(1895–1985)

Sir

Soldier, was born at Ranniken in India 7 September 1895, the elder child and only son of a doctor of medicine, Colonel Sir William Heaton Horrocks, and his wife, Minna, daughter of the Revd J. C. Moore, of Connor, Antrim, Ireland. Educated at Uppingham and the Royal Military College, Sandhurst, he was commissioned into the Middlesex Regiment on the outbreak of war in 1914. Captured during the battle of Ypres in October 1914, he passed the war as a prisoner of war in Germany, and was a Soviet prisoner for another eighteen months after going to Vladivostok in 1919 as a staff officer in a mission under Major-General Sir Alfred Knox to the White Russian Admiral Alexander Kolchak. He was awarded the MC (1919).

Horrocks spent fifteen years as an infantry captain, but such was his love of the army that he was not dismayed by the poor career prospects. In 1924 he won the British modern pentathlon championship, and took part in the

Olympic Games. Having passed out of the Staff College in 1933 he was well poised to achieve high rank when World War II started in 1939.

Horrocks was something of an actor, tall and good looking with charisma and charm, and a capacity to make friends although he could sometimes quarrel. He became friendly with A. P. (later Earl) Wavell and B. L. Montgomery (later Viscount Montgomery of Alamein) during peacetime exercises when he shared their enthusiasm for mechanized mobile warfare at a time when some senior officers still hankered after horse cavalry. (Sir) Frank Simpson had become a close friend at the Staff College, and during the war as director of military operations (War Office) he helped Horrocks to achieve promotion.

Horrocks went to France in 1939 commanding the 2nd battalion, Middlesex Regiment, and was promoted brigadier during the evacuation of Dunkirk. Soon he was a divisional commander, and in 1942 Montgomery summoned him to the Western Desert to command XIII Corps and later IX and X Corps. At El Alamein and the Mareth line his troops performed magnificently, and Sir C. Denis Hamilton claimed that a combination of Montgomery as army commander and Horrocks as corps commander made 'an unbeatable team'.

Horrocks was seriously wounded at Bizerta in an air raid in August 1943 as he was preparing X Corps for the Italian campaign. Five operations and eighteen months of illness and convalescence at Aldershot followed. However in July 1944, when Montgomery sacked the XXX Corps commander after a lack-lustre tank battle in Normandy, he sent for Horrocks to replace him. Everyone connected with XXX Corps at the time testified to the spectacular way in which he revived the morale of his war-weary troops. Still suffering from recurrent fever, Horrocks led XXX Corps in the dramatic dash from the Seine to Antwerp. Then he made a mistake by ordering his corps to rest for three days at a moment when it was imperative to rush a crossing of the wide Albert canal while the Germans were still in confusion. Hitler used the delay to send up fresh formations and the British drive into Holland was halted.

Both the British and Polish airborne commanders in their autobiographies criticize Horrocks for his failure to link up with them after the Arnhem drop in September 1944. According to some of his colleagues Horrocks was unwell, but he crossed the Nijmegen bridge within a few hours of its capture by the Grenadiers to congratulate them. The truth is Montgomery had set XXX Corps an impossible task.

When Karl von Rundstedt's 1944 Christmas offensive threatened Brussels and Antwerp, Horrocks told Montgomery the German armour should be allowed to cross the Meuse and then his corps would annihilate them on the battlefield of Waterloo. This did not appeal to Montgomery who sent him home on compulsory sick leave. He was quickly back to lead his corps over the Rhine and in the final triumphal drive to the Elbe. Friends of General (Sir) Miles Dempsey, commander of the Second Army, have criticized Horrocks during this period for bypassing Dempsey and taking his instructions direct from Montgomery. The fault lay with Montgomery who was nostalgic for his previous relationship with Horrocks in Africa. Horrocks was appointed CB (1943), to the DSO (1943), KBE (1945), and KCB (1949).

After the war Horrocks became GOC Western Command in February 1946 and then GOC-in-C British Army of the Rhine early in 1948. The problems of defeated Germany put too much of a strain on his health and he was invalided out of the army in 1949, with the rank of lieutenant-general.

Immediately he was offered the post of gentleman usher of the Black Rod in the House of Lords, which he discharged with distinction from 1949 to 1963. He also became a television star, making around forty programmes with (Sir) Huw Weldon. Horrocks loved the bustle and immediacy of television and also the floods of fan mail which in no way affected his character. After fourteen years as Black Rod Horrocks resigned to become a director of Bovis, and to leave himself more time for television, sailing, and charities. He had an honorary LLD from Belfast.

He married in 1928 Nancy, daughter of Brook Taylor Kitchin, architect, of the Local Government Board. They had one daughter who was drowned when swimming in the Thames in 1979. Horrocks died 4 January 1985 in Chichester.

[Brian Horrocks, *A Full Life*, 1960 (2nd edn. 1974); Philip Warner, *Horrocks*, 1984; Richard Lamb, *Montgomery in Europe*, 1983; Sir Frank Simpson's papers in the Imperial War Museum.]

RICHARD LAMB

published 1990

HULL Richard Amyatt

(1907–1989)

Sir

Field-marshal and chief of the defence staff, was born 7 May 1907 in Cosham, Hampshire, the only son and youngest of three children of Major-General Sir Charles Patrick Amyatt Hull, KCB, late of the Royal

Scots Fusiliers, of Beacon Downe, Pinhoe, near Exeter, Devon, and his wife Muriel Helen, daughter of Richard Reid Dobell, businessman, of Beauvoir, Quebec, and Vancouver, Canada. He was educated at Charterhouse and Trinity College, Cambridge, where he took a pass degree. At Cambridge he was a close friend of (Sir) Peter Scott, the naturalist, and it was there that he began to develop his great interest in wildlife and country sports.

He was commissioned as a university entrant into the 17th/21st Lancers in 1928 and went with the regiment to Egypt in 1930. It was then still horsed. Hull, who in any case lacked the money for expensive mounts, was a competent rather than enthusiastic horseman, but acquired a reputation as a polo umpire. His knowledge of the rules and firmness in applying them were paralleled by the attention to detail, energy, and integrity he showed in his professional life, qualities which underlay his successful career and brought him early promotion to captain and appointment as adjutant when the regiment moved to India in 1933.

He was a student at the Staff College, Quetta, in 1938–9, while the regiment was undergoing mechanization, a change which the forward-looking Hull strongly supported, and then supervised the return home of the regimental families in 1939. His efficiency in so doing brought him an appointment in the staff duties branch of the War Office, and promotion to lieutenant-colonel, but he soon chose to drop a rank and return to the 17th/21st as a squadron leader. He became commanding officer in 1941.

In 1942 he was promoted to colonel and given command of Blade Force, an all-arms group based on the 17th/21st, which had the mission during the North African landings of November 1942 of advancing from Algiers to capture Tunis. The force covered the 350 miles in two days but was thwarted fifteen miles from the city when German reinforcements secured it first. For the dash he had shown and his bravery under fire Hull was appointed to the DSO (1943) and promoted to brigadier to command 12th Infantry and then 26th Armoured brigade during the Tunisian campaign.

After another spell at the War Office, he was promoted to major-general and given command of 1st Armoured division in Italy in 1944. Its role was to outflank the Gothic Line on the Adriatic shore and lead a break-out into the plain of the Po. At Coriano on 5 September, however, its armoured brigade met heavy German resistance and was checked. Controversy surrounds this episode; terrain and weather were on the side of the enemy but Hull has also been criticized for his tactical dispositions.

This did not halt his progress. His formidable abilities as a staff officer had been recognized and, after commanding 5th Infantry division, he embarked on a long ascent of all the key staff appointments, interspersed with several important commands. He was commandant of the Staff College, Camberley (1946–8), director of staff duties, War Office (1948–50), chief army instructor, Imperial Defence College (1950–2), and chief of staff, Middle East Land Forces (1953–4). As lieutenant-general he then succeeded to the command of the British troops in Egypt and supervised the difficult evacuation from the canal zone in 1955–6.

On his return he became deputy chief of the imperial general staff (1956–8) and was at once embroiled in the series of defence reductions, imposed by Britain's shrinking world role and financial difficulties, that were to dominate the rest of his service career. He first chaired a committee whose task was to determine the future size of the army and, though he unsuccessfully opposed the army's reduction to a strength of 165,000, his doubts about its ability to meet its commitments with those numbers were proved right and the figure was later fixed at 185,000. He oversaw the abolition of national service in 1957, and the regimental amalgamations that resulted, but succeeded in sparing several threatened regiments. The shape of the army for the next thirty years was largely determined by his guidance.

Promoted to general in 1958, he was commander-in-chief, Far East Land Forces (1958–61), but then returned to the Ministry of Defence as chief of the imperial general staff (1961–5) ('imperial' was dropped in 1964 and so he was the last CIGS), and then chief of the defence staff (1965–7), in succession to the second holder of that office, the first Earl Mountbatten of Burma. As CIGS and CGS he was responsible for the army's part in such operations as the deterrence of the Iraqi attack on Kuwait in 1961, 'confrontation' with Indonesia in Malaysia, the suppression of the East African mutinies, and the defeat of the Nasserist rebellion in the Radfan province of the Aden Protectorate.

His bitterest battles, however, were fought in Whitehall after he became CDS in July 1965. During his term of office Britain withdrew from Singapore and Aden and was challenged by rebellion in Rhodesia. At home, he found the navy and air force locked in conflict over the funding of air power, while Denis (later Baron) Healey, an imperious defence secretary, demanded budgetary sacrifices by all services. Hull, whose professional feelings for Mountbatten had amounted to loathing, was too upright to allow that to influence his arbitration of the dispute between the air marshals and the admirals. He perceived that the large carriers the navy wanted would cost too much and threw his weight behind the decision to spend available funds for the purchase of American aircraft for the Royal Air Force as a means of providing Britain with long-range strike capability. The small carriers that provided the Royal Navy with its later air support were the product of that chiefs of staff committee's decision.

Hull was promoted to field-marshal on appointment as CDS. On retirement in 1967 he became a director of Whitbreads (1967–76) and rationalized business in its western division. He held many state, army, and charitable appointments, including those of constable of the Tower of London (1970–5), deputy lieutenant of Devon (1973–8), high sheriff (1975), and lord-lieutenant (1978–82). He was president of the Army Benevolent Fund (1968–71), and was made an honorary LL.D. by Exeter University in 1965. Appointed CB in 1945, he was advanced to KCB in 1956 and GCB in 1961. He became a knight of the Garter in 1980.

Hull typified a certain sort of regular cavalry officer of his generation. A devout but undemonstrative Christian, a devoted husband and father, whose temperament often prevented him from disclosing his affections, a loyal friend to brother officers who won his favour, a devotee of regimental tradition, he was happiest shooting or fly fishing, two sports at which he excelled, and in his garden, where he knew the Latin, English, and Devon name of every plant. He was tall and of impressive bearing, with grave features.

In 1934 Hull married Antoinette Mary, only child of Francis Labouchère de Rougemont, of the Bank of Egypt. They had two daughters and a son and were a couple noted for their devotion. Hull died 17 September 1989, of cancer, at his home at Beacon Downe, Pinhoe, Exeter, which he had rebuilt after wartime bombing, was given a state funeral at Windsor, and was buried in the graveyard of the local church where he had regularly worshipped.

[Sir William Jackson and Edwin Bramall (as Bill Jackson and Dwin Bramall), *The Chiefs*, 1992; private information.]

JOHN KEEGAN

published 1996

INGLIS Elsie Maud

(1864–1917)

Physician and surgeon, the second daughter of John Inglis, of the East India Company's service, by his wife, Harriet Thompson, was born at Naini Tal, India, 16 August 1864. Her father was a descendant of the Inglis of Kingsmill, Inverness-shire. Her mother was the granddaughter of John Fendall, governor of Java. Elsie Inglis spent her childhood in India until her father retired in 1878, when the family came back to Scotland and settled in Edinburgh. She was educated there at the Charlotte Square Institution, and after a year at Paris returned to Edinburgh shortly before her mother's death in 1885. Between Elsie Inglis and her father there existed a strong bond of friendship. He was a wholehearted advocate of her choice of a medical career, and a wise counsellor in all her undertakings. At the time of her entry upon her medical studies the battle for the admission of women to the medical profession had been fought and won by Sophia Louisa Jex-Blake, although there still remained a considerable amount of opposition. Her studies were begun in Edinburgh and continued at Glasgow, with some months in Dublin for a special course of midwifery. In 1892 she received her medical diploma, and returning to Edinburgh she inaugurated there a second school of medicine for women, a successful venture which became, after the closing of the first medical school founded in Edinburgh in 1886 by Sophia Jex-Blake, the only school of medicine for women, until the doors of Edinburgh University were thrown open to them (1894).

In 1892 Elsie Inglis was appointed house-surgeon to the New Hospital for Women in London (afterwards the Elizabeth Garrett Anderson Hospital), and later received the appointment of joint-surgeon to the Edinburgh Bruntsfield Hospital and Dispensary for women and children. Realizing the serious disabilities imposed on women by their exclusion from resident posts in the chief maternity hospital and Royal Hospital in Edinburgh, she conceived the bold scheme of establishing there a maternity hospital to be staffed by women. This scheme resulted in the foundation of a hospice for women, opened in 1901, which is still the only maternity training centre in Scotland managed by women. Dr. Elsie Inglis began private practice in 1895, first in partnership with Dr. Jessie McGregor, later by herself. In her profession she won the love and esteem of her patients in all classes of life. To the poor patients of the hospital she was more than a doctor, for they found in her a friend full of sympathy with their difficulties, and always ready to help in lightening the burden of their poverty.

In 1900 Elsie Inglis joined the constitutional movement for the political enfranchisement of women, under the leadership of Mrs. Millicent Garrett Fawcett, devoting all her spare time to speaking and lecturing on women's suffrage. She was the founder of the Scottish Women's Suffrage Federation (1906), and it was at a committee meeting of the Federation in August 1914 that the idea was first conceived of forming a Scottish Women's Hospitals committee, to raise hospital units staffed by women for service in the European War. Elsie Inglis was the leading spirit of this venture, travelling all over the kingdom to make public appeals for funds to equip the units. Her enthusiasm roused a quick response from the public, resulting in a steady flow of funds and of offers from women for active service.

The first fully equipped unit left for France in November 1914, a second unit going out to Serbia in January 1915. Elsie Inglis carried on the work of organizing further units until April 1915, when she left for Serbia in order to take the place of Dr. Eleanor Soltau, who had contracted diphtheria. An epidemic of typhus, which had broken out at the end of January 1915, had nearly abated when she arrived, and she immediately proceeded to organize three hospitals in the north of Serbia in readiness for the autumn offensive of the Serbs.

The invasion of Serbia by German, Austrian, and Bulgarian armies in the autumn of 1915 drove the Serbs back, and the hospitals established at Valjevo, Lazarovatz, and Mladanovatz had to be hastily evacuated and moved to Kragujevatz, where Elsie Inglis had started a surgical hospital. The relentless tide of invasion drove the hospitals farther south to Krushevatz. Here she worked at the Czar Lazar hospital, having decided that she could give more effectual help to the Serbs by remaining at her post. This decision was welcomed by the Serbian medical authorities, who had experienced the benefit not only of her surgical aid but also of the moral support given by the Scottish Women's Hospitals units during their retreat. For three months after the entry of the Germans and Austrians into Krushevatz on 7 November 1915, she continued to work at the hospitals, until the great majority of the patients were removed to Hungary. On 11 February she and her unit were sent under a strong Austrian guard first to Belgrade and then to Vienna, where, owing to the intervention of the American embassy, they were released and allowed to return to England.

Elsie Inglis's offer to the War Office of a unit for service in Mesopotamia, where the need for medical aid seemed urgent, was refused; but, after her return from a visit of inspection to the Scottish Women's Hospitals units in Corsica, she received an appeal from the Serbian minister for aid for the Serbian division in Russia. This request met with an immediate response. The London committee of the Scottish Women's Hospitals supplied two units with motor transport attached. On 16 August 1916 Elsie Inglis left for Russia, going to the front at Megidia to join the Serbian division fighting in the Dobrudja. Here the units worked until the retreat of the Russians in October brought her to Braila, where perhaps the hardest task, and what to most would have seemed a hopeless one, was presented to her. Braila was one vast dumping ground for the wounded, who streamed in every day. Only seven doctors were in the town, and no nurses, when she arrived. The units were now attached to the Russian division, until the Serbs, whose losses were very heavy owing to the lack of Russian support, had been reformed. From Braila the units went first to Galatz and then on to Reni.

The revolution in Russia had broken out in the meantime, and the difficulties of the units were increased, but despite the general confusion and the suspicion with which spy-hunters regarded a foreign hospital, they managed to work smoothly until the hospital was evacuated in August 1917 and Elsie Inglis rejoined the Serbs at Hadji-Abdul. Their position, however, became serious, for there was not much hope of the Russians making a stand; and efforts were made to get the Serbs out of Russia. Moreover, Dr. Inglis's health showed grave signs of failure, and her condition was aggravated by the intense cold and the lack of food, fuel, and clothing. The Scottish Women's Hospitals committee sent a cable advising her withdrawal, but leaving the decision in her hands. Her reply was: 'If there were a disaster none of us would ever be able to forgive ourselves if we had left. We must stand by. If you want us home, get them [the Serbs] out.' Enfeebled as she was, she met the situation courageously. Her plans for the future work of the hospital, should the Serbs be called upon again to fight, were all laid down to the smallest detail, but fortunately, before these plans had been put in operation, the order came for the Serbs to leave for England.

Dr. Inglis's cable home on 14 November announced their departure: 'Everything satisfactory, and all well except myself'—the first intimation which the committee had received of her being ill. She bore the journey home with great fortitude and endurance of physical pain, and on arriving at Newcastle (25 November) refused to allow herself to be carried, but walked down the ship's gangway. Almost to the last her thoughts were of future plans, and in her message to the London committee was a request to them to continue their support of the Serbs, whom she had served so faithfully. One of those present among her family and friends spoke to her of the great work which she had accomplished. She replied: 'Not I, but my unit.' The end came at Newcastle on 26 November. The intrepid spirit met death as calmly as she had faced life. She was buried in the Dean Cemetery, Edinburgh, on 29 November.

[Lady Frances Balfour, *Dr. Elsie Inglis*, 1918; Mrs. Shaw McLaren, *A History of the Scottish Women's Hospitals*, 1919, and *Elsie Inglis*, 1920.]

EDITH PALLISER

published 1927

William Edmund

(1880–1959)

First Baron Ironside

Field-marshal, was born in Edinburgh 6 May 1880, the second child of Surgeon-Major William Ironside of Ironside, Royal Horse Artillery, by his wife, Emma Maria, daughter of William Haggett Richards, of Stapleton House, Martock, Somerset. His father died in January of the following year and his mother, left badly off, frequently took him and his sister to the Continent where living was cheaper. These excursions bore fruit, for Ironside subsequently became a qualified army interpreter in seven languages. Educated at a preparatory school at St. Andrews, Tonbridge School, and the Royal Military Academy, Woolwich, Ironside was commissioned into the Royal Artillery in 1899. He served in the South African war and in 1902 escorted J. C. Smuts to the peace conference at Vereeniging. Then, disguised as a Boer transport driver, he accompanied the German military expedition to South West Africa where his adventures as an intelligence agent suggested the character of Richard Hannay to John Buchan (later Lord Tweedsmuir).

After service in I (Bull's Troop) and Y batteries of the Royal Horse Artillery, Ironside was promoted captain in 1908 and appointed to cavalry and infantry brigade staffs in South Africa. He entered the Staff College in 1913 and in 1914 was sent to Boulogne as staff captain. When the 6th division arrived in France in October, he joined its 'G' staff and was promoted major. He became G.S.O. 1 of the 4th Canadian division in 1916 as a brevet lieutenant-colonel, and in 1917 took part in the battles of Vimy Ridge and Passchendaele. In 1918 he was appointed commandant of the Machine Gun Corps school at Camiers with the rank of temporary colonel. When the Germans broke through on the Somme in March he was sent with all its guns to fill the gap and forming a line beat off several attacks. He was then given command of the 99th Infantry brigade in Haldane's 2nd division, and directed its attacks at Albert and Bapaume.

In September 1918 Ironside went to North Russia as chief of the general staff of the allied forces, and soon took command with the temporary rank of major-general. He moulded a heterogeneous army of many nationalities into an efficient fighting force, and in the following March he became general officer commanding-in-chief of Archangel. Disaffection in Russian units and increasing menace from the Bolshevik forces led to the withdrawal of the expedition in the autumn of 1919. For his services he was promoted substantive major-general. His account of these operations was published in *Archangel 1918–1919* (1953).

In 1920 Ironside went to Hungary as chief of the military mission to Admiral Horthy's government; he was subsequently given command of the Ismid and North Persian forces against possible Turkish and Bolshevik incursions. In 1921, summoned to a conference at Cairo under (Sir) Winston Churchill, Ironside recommended that the Royal Air Force should be made responsible for the defence of Iraq. Flying there to arrange the handover he crashed, broke both legs, and was invalided home. In 1922 he was appointed commandant of the Staff College at Camberley, and in 1926 commander of the 2nd division at Aldershot. In 1928 he went to India to command the Meerut District where his training and tactical doctrine much impressed Sir Philip (later Lord) Chetwode. In 1931 he was promoted lieutenant-general, left India, went on half pay, and was appointed lieutenant of the Tower of London. In 1933 he returned to India as quartermaster-general and in 1935 was promoted general.

Returning to England in 1936, Ironside took over the Eastern Command. Units pitifully under strength, obsolete equipment, and the lack of government policy and tactical doctrine perturbed him. In 1937 he attended the German army manœuvres and met Hitler, Goering, Mussolini, and Badoglio. General Reichenau drank a whisky toast to 'brotherhood with England', adding drunkenly 'but only for two years'. Ironside, like Churchill, was sure that war would come in two or three years, but he was unable to convince the prime minister, Neville Chamberlain, or the secretary of state for war, Leslie (later Lord) Hore-Belisha.

In the autumn of 1938 Ironside was appointed commander-in-chief designate of the Middle East and governor of Gibraltar where he greatly strengthened the fortress. By now he had 'little hope of any active command'. In May 1939 he was appointed inspector-general of overseas forces and made responsible for the higher training of the army and liaison with the dominions and India. But he was not allowed home until July, when Lord Gort, the chief of the imperial general staff, told him that he was to be commander-in-chief of the British expeditionary force. In the meantime he was sent to Warsaw to discover Poland's plans to resist the imminent German invasion. On 3 September Hore-Belisha asked Ironside to become chief of the imperial general staff. Ironside had never served in the War Office in any capacity but felt it his duty to accept. 'I am bitterly disappointed,' ran his diary, 'that I am not to command the Army in the field. . . . I am not suited in temperament to such a job as C.I.G.S., nor have I prepared myself to be such.'

He found a singular lack of preparation: there was no 'imperial' plan; the only plan was to send four divisions to France. The Government, sheltering behind the Maginot line and the French Army, expected a stalemate on the western front, thought the war could be won by bombing and blockade, and saw little need for an expeditionary force. Ironside, on the contrary, maintained that Hitler would use his army and air force in co-operation to force a decision, and that the war would not be won until Hitler was defeated on land. He accordingly planned for armies of twenty divisions in France, twelve in the Middle East, and an imperial reserve of eighteen divisions at home. It would take three years to equip them. The Services worked on separate charters and there was little co-operation between them. Ironside was burdened by many committees; the machinery of government was incapable of quick decisions or even rapid improvisation; moreover his task was aggravated by a minister for war whom he found difficult. Ironside paid several visits to the B.E.F. and the Maginot line and attended conferences with the supreme commander, General Gamelin. The latter was convinced that the decisive battle would be fought on the plains of Belgium; Ironside forecast, correctly, that the German thrust would come through the Ardennes. Both agreed that the allied left wing should advance into Belgium, Ironside with the idea of attacking the German penetration in flank.

When Russia invaded Finland in November 1939 Ironside wanted to send a small force to help the Finns and a larger force to seize the iron-ore field at Gällivare. His plan was delayed by Norwegian and Swedish objections and was cancelled when Finland fell. In April 1940 the Allies decided to seize Narvik, but the Germans got there first. When the convoy dispatched to take Narvik from the Germans was at sea the Government changed the main objective to Trondheim, and Churchill, in spite of Ironside's protests, ordered the rear half to be diverted to Namsos. Both projects failed and the result was an improvised, hasty, but successful evacuation.

In May 1940 the German armoured columns broke through the Ardennes and cut the allied army in two. Ironside hoped to save the B.E.F. by thrusting southwards through the gap between the armour and its supporting columns, and he did his best to persuade the French to co-operate. They failed to attack and Gort's army was evacuated from Dunkirk. At the end of May, Ironside proposed, and the Government agreed, that he should become commander-in-chief of the home forces to prepare against invasion. Once again he had to build from scratch. In July he was succeeded by Sir Alan Brooke (later Viscount Alanbrooke), promoted field-marshal, and in 1941 raised to the peerage. He retired in silence and dignity to his home at Hingham in Norfolk where he devoted himself to his garden and the affairs of the neighbourhood. He became president of the South African Veterans and the Old Contemptibles. Simple, modest, and forthright, his kindness and friendliness made him universally liked and respected.

'Tiny' Ironside was 6 feet 4 inches tall, broad and deep-chested. Forceful, fearless, and outspoken sometimes to the point of indiscretion, he was an intelligent, imaginative, and unconventional soldier, a strong advocate of air co-operation and tank warfare, and essentially a commander. He never intrigued and never refused a job. He played rugby football for Scotland, was an excellent shot, 'plus two' at golf, and a keen follower to hounds. He was appointed C.M.G. (1918), K.C.B. (1919), and G.C.B. (1938), was appointed to the D.S.O. in 1915, and invested with the grand cross of the Legion of Honour in 1940. He received an honorary LL.D. from Aberdeen in 1936.

In 1915 Ironside married Mariot Ysobel, daughter of Charles Cheyne, of the Indian Staff Corps, by whom he had a daughter and a son, Edmund Oslac (born 1924), who succeeded him when he died in London 22 September 1959. Of six portraits, one by Eric Kennington is in the possession of the family; another by Kenneth Hauff is at Tonbridge School, and a third, by C. Corfield, is in the Royal Artillery Mess, Woolwich. The Imperial War Museum has a pastel by Eric Kennington.

[*The Ironside Diaries, 1937–1940*, ed. R. Macleod and D. Kelly, 1962; private information; personal knowledge.]

R. Macleod

published 1971

ISMAY Hastings Lionel

(1887–1965)

Baron Ismay

General, was born at Naini Tal, India, 21 June 1887, younger son of (Sir) Stanley Ismay, a member of the viceroy's legislative council and later chief judge of the Mysore Court, by his wife, Beatrice Ellen, daughter of Colonel Hastings Read. He was educated at Charterhouse and the Royal Military College, Sandhurst. Entering the Indian Army in 1905, he was posted in 1907 to the 21st Prince Albert Victor's Own Cavalry, acquiring the Frontier medal and clasp and becoming adjutant of his regiment. But he felt the need to gain wider military experience, and was thus by a quirk of fate forestalled from serving on any of the main fronts during the war of 1914–18, for he was seconded to the King's African Rifles as captain, and landed at Berbera 9 August 1914; in 1917–19 he was with the Somaliland Indian Contingent, and with the newly formed Camel Corps in 1919–20. All efforts to return to his regiment failed, and he remained in Somaliland until 1920, distinguishing himself in operations against 'the mad Mullah'; he was appointed to the DSO and promoted major, having been temporary lieutenant-colonel in 1919.

Granted a year's leave on medical grounds, he met and married in 1921 Laura Kathleen (died 1978), only daughter of Henry Gordon Clegg, of Wormington Grange, Gloucestershire; they had three daughters. His qualities, already recognized, then took him to the Staff College, Quetta, and they were confirmed in the passing-out report of his commandant, who declared: 'I consider this officer one of the two best, if not the best, of the students who have passed through my hands.' Thereafter Ismay was lost to regimental soldiering; in 1923 he spent a brief period on the staff at Army HQ India, and in 1924 was nominated to the vacancy reserved for an Indian Army officer at the new RAF Staff College, Andover. At the end of 1925 he was appointed assistant secretary to the Committee of Imperial Defence under Sir Maurice (later Lord) Hankey.

Five years at the Committee of Imperial Defence, spent particularly in preparing the substratum of what became the War Book, gave Ismay an exceptional insight into the ways of Whitehall. When his appointment ended in December 1930 his ability had already marked him as potential successor to Hankey, and the recognition of it in the New Year's honours list of 1931 created a problem of protocol: by some failure of communications he was gazetted as both CB in the civil list and CIE in the India Office list: Ismay opted for the former.

The India Office wished to create a Committee of Imperial Defence in Delhi, and Ismay was now pressed to accompany the new viceroy, Lord Willingdon, as military secretary with the organization of an Indian Committee of Imperial Defence—a scheme which eventually proved abortive—among his duties. He was promoted colonel, and although he hoped for command of a cavalry regiment, in 1931 he obediently went east, where he enjoyed a privileged view of the Raj in action. Nevertheless, those two years were a parenthesis and hardly equipped him for the responsibilities, which he took up on his return to the War Office in 1933, of GSO 1 Intelligence Eastern Europe.

Shortly before he left India, Ismay's polo pony slipped while he was playing in the Prince of Wales's tournament; concussion deafened his left ear, but he never allowed this disability to impede a long life of talk and conference. After his return to London there occurred a distressing sequence of deaths in his wife's family, which, however, brought her the inheritance of Wormington and substantial resources. Since Ismay was independent of mind, although a man of devoted loyalties, this independence of means merely increased his value as an objective adviser freed from the restrictions of an officer *de carrière*.

In 1936 Ismay moved into his predestined place as deputy secretary to Hankey at the Committee of Imperial Defence. The succession was not inevitable, for the Treasury and the Foreign Office were eager to take over the Cabinet Office, and it was not without a struggle that the secretaryship of the CID (although not the rest of Hankey's empire) was handed over to Ismay after Hankey's retirement in 1938. Inadequacies of government policy made the months before and immediately after the outbreak of war in 1939 the most frustrating of his life. But in April 1940 Neville Chamberlain appointed (Sir) Winston Churchill as chairman of the Ministerial Co-ordinating Committee, responsible for guiding and directing the chiefs of staff, assisted by 'a suitable central staff under a senior staff officer, who would be an additional member of the chiefs of staff committee'. The man he chose was Ismay, who had been promoted major-general in 1939.

Churchill planned to make a 'garden suburb' by assembling a central staff of his own henchmen. Ismay's first personal contribution to the war effort was to stonewall over this dubious proposal. In consequence, when Churchill became prime minister and minister of defence in May 1940, retaining Ismay as his chief staff officer, the military secretariat which Ismay evolved developed into a machine of unsurpassed quality because those whom he chose to man it—(Sir) Leslie Hollis, (Sir) Ian Jacob, and others who serviced the war administration—were apt for the task and not a prime minister's idiosyncratic miscellany. Moreover, drawn as they were from the staff of the Committee of Imperial Defence or elsewhere in Whitehall, they provided continuity as well as competence.

For the remainder of the war, Ismay's position was unique: none of the other belligerents, neither President Roosevelt's Harry Hopkins, nor Hitler's adjutants, provided an equivalent. Hundreds of Churchill's famous minutes and the replies to them were personally handled by Ismay, who commanded the prime minister's absolute trust. He was the essential link with the chiefs of staff, on whose committee he sat without executive powers of embarrassment. Difficult Allies respected him as much as did difficult colleagues. On delicate missions abroad, amid growing responsibilities for the most secret matters, from 1940 to 1945 Ismay endured strains more continuous than any battle-commander, and sometimes equally intense. Not even Sir Alan Brooke (later Viscount Alanbrooke) was so exposed to the exigencies and exhaustion of intimate work with Churchill by day and by night. Shrewd, resilient, accessible, emollient in diplomacy but of an unbreachable integrity, Ismay created a role as entrepreneur which, in its range and value, surpassed that of his master

Hankey in the previous war. As Ismay himself put it, 'I spent the whole war in the middle of the web.' He became lieutenant-general in 1942 and full general in 1944, and Churchill's 'resignation honours' gave his services the rather curious recognition of his appointment as CH. The next prime minister was not satisfied, and Clement (later Earl) Attlee's final victory list in June 1946 appointed Ismay GCB, and in the following New Year's honours he was created a baron.

Peace did not allow Ismay to 'put up his bright sword'. He retired from the army in December 1946, after largely reorganizing the defence system and setting up the Ministry of Defence. By the following spring he was back in India, as chief of the viceroy's staff and Lord Mountbatten's right-hand man in the days of the 'great divide'. He went there at his own suggestion, although he was anguished by the fear that the coming abandonment of India would be a betrayal of the guardianship to which he and his father had been dedicated, and as his country had also once seemed to be. He was by then a tired man, driven by a sense of duty; but again his performance as a catalyst, a tranquillizer, and a constructive negotiator was exemplary. Trusted by all parties, by his calmness and accumulated wisdom he balanced the mercurial energy of Mountbatten, who more than once dispatched him to London to conduct critical negotiations. Ismay took no pride in the clinical act of partition, although he accepted its draconian necessity, and he declined the grand cross of the Star of India, content merely with the order of release from what he described as the most distasteful assignment of his career.

In the event there was no release. He had hardly been back in England a few weeks when—early in 1948—Attlee appointed him as chairman of the council for the Festival of Britain—a job which, as Ismay himself said, called for strategic planning no less difficult than a military campaign. Shortly after its successful conclusion in September 1951 Churchill returned to power and, by a decision only less idiosyncratic than his subsequent summons of Lord Alexander of Tunis to the Ministry of Defence, made Ismay secretary of state for Commonwealth Relations. In practice the arrangement proved profitable, since Churchill drew heavily on Ismay's own experience of defence matters. It was a natural consequence when, only six months later, Ismay was chosen to be the first secretary-general of NATO and transferred to Paris.

Once more 'the man with the oil-can' went unwillingly; his achievement was brilliant and historic, for all his gifts—clarity of mind, winning charm, intellectual and social dexterity, combined with an unequalled *tact des choses possibles* and a keen appreciation of good press and public relations— were required and applied in the fusion of fourteen nations for a common, self-defensive end. When he retired in April 1957, in his seventieth year, international acclaim recognized his unsparing efforts in providing NATO with an ordered structure and harmony of purpose which could hardly have been anticipated when he took office. He was immediately appointed KG. Other honours had already been bestowed: he was sworn of the Privy Council in 1951, and received honorary degrees from Queen's University, Belfast, Bristol, and Cambridge. He was chairman of the National Institute for the Blind in 1946–52, and president from 1952, as well as being director of various companies and schools, and a deputy-lieutenant for Gloucestershire from 1950.

His retirement was marred by ill health, but in 1960 he was able to publish his self-effacing *Memoirs*. He had already assisted Churchill with *The Second World War* (1948–53). 'Pug' to all the world, he was the personification of honesty, loyalty, and human warmth, with an irresistible smile and that inner core of steel which made his presence at the heart of affairs so effective. An unashamed *bon viveur*, who also enjoyed racing and polo, tennis, and bridge, he nevertheless believed that the best thing in life is to seek to do the State some service. He died 17 December 1965 at Wormington Grange.

Portraits by Anthony Devas, and Allan Gwynne-Jones (1959), and a drawing by Augustus John, are in the possession of the family. A head-and-shoulders study for the full portrait of Ismay in Garter robes, also by Gwynne-Jones (1958), is in the National Portrait Gallery. Cheltenham town hall has a portrait (*c.* 1918) by Mark Birley.

[Sir Ronald Wingate, *Lord Ismay*, 1970; Stephen Roskill, *Hankey, Man of Secrets*, 3 vols. 1970–4; Sir Winston Churchill, *The Second World War*, 6 vols. 1948–53; *The Memoirs of Lord Ismay*, 1960; *The Times*, 20 December 1965; private information.]

RONALD LEWIN

published 1981

JACKSON Henry Bradwardine

(1855–1929)

Sir

Admiral of the fleet and pioneer of wireless telegraphy, was born at Barnsley 21 January 1855, the eldest son of Henry Jackson, farmer, of Cudworth, Yorkshire, by his wife, Jane, daughter of Charles Tee, of Barnsley. He was educated at Chester and at Stubbington House, Fareham, and joined the royal navy at the age of thirteen in December

1868. From the outset Jackson was interested in the more scientific aspects of his work, and at first specialized in navigation. In 1878–1879 he was junior lieutenant on board the *Active* on the African station, and took part in the Zulu War. In 1881 he was appointed to H.M.S. *Vernon*, torpedo-school ship at Portsmouth, and became intensely interested in the mechanism of the torpedo, finally qualifying as a torpedo lieutenant. He served in the *Vernon* for three and a half years. In January 1890 he was promoted to the rank of commander, and in the same year he conceived the idea of employing wireless waves to announce to a capital ship the approach of a friendly torpedo boat. Opportunities to experiment were few and progress was very slow until 1895 when, while in command of the *Defiance*, Jackson became aware of the experiments of Dr. Jagadis Chunder Bose on coherers. Jackson made, and experimented with, many types of coherer, the form finally adopted for his comparatively long distance experiments consisting of a tube of metal filings between two metal plugs. The coherer was tapped by hand and the receiving circuit was a simple loop of wire. With such a receiver Jackson succeeded in effecting communication by electromagnetic radiation from one end of the *Defiance* to the other, the signals transmitted over the length of the ship being sufficiently intense to ring an electric bell of high resistance inserted in the receiving circuit. Tapping the coherer with the bell was the next development, and towards the end of 1896, using the ship's inductance coil, which under favourable conditions gave a spark of two inches, he succeeded in receiving strong signals over distances of several hundreds of yards.

In June 1896 Jackson was promoted to the rank of captain, and in September of the same year he met Signor Guglielmo Marconi at a conference at the War Office. These two pioneers had been working on parallel lines, but whereas Marconi was aiming at long distance wireless communication over land and sea, Jackson's main objective was to improve the efficiency of the communication service of the fleet. In 1897 Jackson was appointed naval attaché in Paris, and in 1899 was given command of the torpedo depot-ship *Vulcan*, in which he continued his wireless experiments. He felt well rewarded for his labours when in 1900 a contract was placed with the Marconi Company for the supply of wireless installations to many ships of the royal navy, an event which was regarded by Jackson's friends as the culmination of his strenuous efforts to introduce this new means of communication into the service.

In 1901 Jackson's scientific work was recognized by his election as a fellow of the Royal Society, and in 1902 he communicated his most important scientific paper to the *Proceedings* of that body. The title of this was *On Some Phenomena Affecting the Transmission of Electric Waves over the*

Surface of the Sea and Earth, and the paper described signalling experiments at sea over distances up to 140 nautical miles. Intervening land of any kind was found to reduce the signalling range between two ships by a distance which varied with the height, thickness, contour, and nature of the land. Jackson observed the disturbing effect of lightning flashes, and particularly noted that whenever any electrical disturbances were present in the atmosphere the travel of the wireless waves was affected, the intensities of received signals being from 30 to 80 per cent. of those obtained in fine weather. He appears to have been the first to observe the mutual interference of two wireless waves of the same wave-length arriving at the same point with varying phase difference. His own words were: 'The phenomenon manifests itself by the gradual weakening and occasionally by the total cessation of signals as the distance between the two ships (one transmitting and the other receiving) increases, up to a certain point, and then reappears as the distance is still further increased.' At that time Jackson could only assign the effect to a want of synchronism in the oscillatory discharge between the spark balls of the transmitter; many years later he remarked that had he had the advantage of cathode ray receivers his conclusions might have been very different.

In 1902 Jackson was appointed assistant director of torpedoes at the Admiralty, and in 1904 captain of the *Vernon*. In February 1905 he was appointed third sea lord of the Admiralty and controller of the navy. He stood then, as always, for the application of science to the practical work of the navy, and it was during his years of control that recommendations were approved for building the first turbine battleship, *Dreadnought*, and the famous *Invincible* class of battle-cruiser. Among other types of warships designed under the general direction of Jackson were the *Frobisher* and *Hawkins* class. He served as controller until 1908, when he was appointed to command the third (afterwards known as the sixth) cruiser squadron in the Mediterranean. In 1910 he represented the Admiralty at the International Conference on Aerial Navigation in Paris, and in 1911 he assumed the direction of the newly created Royal Naval War College at Portsmouth, where he had the task of training the first War Staff officers. In February 1913 he was appointed chief of the War Staff of the Admiralty.

When the European War broke out in August 1914 Jackson had been nominated to be commander-in-chief in the Mediterranean, but instead of taking over that command, he was retained at the Admiralty. Among his other duties were those of president of a sub-committee of the Committee of Imperial Defence which, in co-operation with the War Staff, developed schemes of attack on German colonial possessions. On the resignation of Lord Fisher from the post of first sea lord in May 1915, Mr. Arthur (afterwards Earl of) Balfour, then first lord of the admiralty, selected Jackson to succeed him. It was a period of great anxiety, largely caused by Germany's adoption of ruthless submarine warfare, and Jackson, by reason of his high scientific achievements, his intimate knowledge of the technical services, and his absolute fearlessness in all matters, was obviously well suited for the post. A new mining policy was initiated and an attack on the mole of Zeebrugge was planned, but the latter had to be abandoned owing to the difficulty, at that time, of setting up an effective smoke screen. Means of combating the submarine menace were under constant survey, but the destruction of merchant shipping continued to increase, and in December 1916 Jackson was appointed president of the Royal Naval College at Greenwich and Admiral (afterwards Earl) Jellicoe became first sea lord. During Jackson's period of office as first sea lord the battle of Jutland (31 May 1916) was fought, and he afterwards stated that the evidence which had convinced him that the German high fleet was coming out for action was the result of observations made by a radio direction-finding station, a change of five degrees being shown in the angular position of a German warship. Jackson filled his new post as president of the Royal Naval College with great distinction, and did not vacate it until July 1919, when he was advanced to the rank of admiral of the fleet. From 1917 to 1919 he was first and principal naval aide-de-camp to King George V. In July 1924 he retired from the navy.

In 1920 Jackson was appointed the first chairman of the Radio Research Board of the Department of Scientific and Industrial Research. The task of once more taking up experimental work in wireless telegraphy was most welcome to him. Under his guidance experiments were carried out dealing with the propagation of wireless waves, the nature of atmospherics, radio direction-finding, and precise radio frequency measurements. It was during his tenure of office that methods were developed for determining the height of the Kennelly-Heaviside layer. He gave his personal attention to the work, spending much time in visiting the laboratories and discussing aspects of the investigations with the staff. Under his guidance more than a hundred important papers were published, but his modesty was such that he always disclaimed credit for any of the results obtained. In 1926 the Royal Society awarded him the Hughes medal in recognition of the great merit of his work; although many honours came his way, it is probable that Jackson prized this one the most highly. He was secretary, and later chairman, of the British National Committee on Radio Telegraphy formed in connexion with the International Union for Scientific Radio Telegraphy, and he regularly attended the meetings of the general assemblies of the Union. It is no exaggeration to say that British prestige in the scientific aspects of radio telegraphy owes much to his guidance.

Among the numerous honours which Jackson received were the K.C.V.O. (1906), the K.C.B. (1910), and the G.C.B. (1916). He also received honorary degrees from the universities of Oxford, Cambridge, and Leeds. Of foreign honours he received the grand cross of the Spanish order of naval merit in 1909, the Japanese order of the Rising Sun, and the Russian order of the White Eagle (first class), and he was a grand officer of the legion of honour. He was a member of the Institution of Electrical Engineers and honorary vice-president of the Institution of Naval Architects. He was also vice-president of the Seamen's Hospital Society. He died at his home, Salterns House, Hayling Island, 14 December 1929, and is buried in the neighbouring churchyard.

Jackson married in 1890 Alice Mary Florence, eldest daughter of Samuel Hawksley Burbury, F.R.S.; they had no children. Many of Jackson's early experiments were carried out in co-operation with Burbury's son, H. H. T. Burbury, who was also an enthusiastic investigator in radio telegraphy.

[*The Times*, 16 December 1929; *Proceedings* of the Royal Society, vol. lxx, A, 1901–2, and vol. cxxvii, A, 1930; *Nature*, 11 January 1930; personal knowledge.]

F. E. SMITH

published 1937

JELLICOE John Rushworth

(1859–1935)

First Earl Jellicoe

Admiral of the fleet, was born at Southampton 5 December 1859, the second of the four sons of John Henry Jellicoe, a captain in the Royal Mail Steam Packet Company and later its marine superintendent at Southampton, by his wife, Lucy Henrietta, daughter of John Rushworth Keele, of Southampton. It was natural that the future admiral should elect to follow a sea career; but there were other hereditary incentives; for his family had already contributed seven officers to the Royal Navy, notably on his mother's side. One of her ancestors, Philip Patton, had fought at La Hogue, and her grandfather, Admiral Philip Patton, had served as second-in-command to Lord Keith in the Downs when Napoleon had his camp at Boulogne, and he was second sea lord during the Trafalgar campaign.

Jellicoe spent much of his boyhood among the docks and on the waterfront; and at a very youthful age gained experience of small craft. From the age of six he attended a preparatory school at Southampton, passing at eleven (after a year at a larger school) to Field House, Rottingdean, where he was well grounded in mathematics. In 1872 he received a nomination for the Royal Navy, and in the summer of that year passed second into the *Britannia*, being twelve and a half years old, and four feet six inches high. In the summer of 1874 he passed out top of his term, gaining first class certificates in every subject, with consequent promotion to midshipman. In the autumn he joined the *Newcastle*, his first sea-going ship, an iron sailing frigate with auxiliary steam. As midshipman he had under him broad-shouldered, bearded men, whose agility in making and shortening sail required a combination of knowledge, muscle, and nerve which the youngster was expected to equal or excel. In October the *Newcastle* set sail from Sheerness, and dropped anchor at Plymouth two and a half years later after visiting Gibraltar, Rio de Janeiro, the Falkland Islands, the Cape of Good Hope, St. Helena, Ascension, Bombay, Singapore, Hong-Kong, Nagasaki, and Mauritius. During the long cruise Jellicoe added to his height five inches; and, to his experience of the unexpected always happening at sea, a range remarkable for his years.

In July 1877 Jellicoe joined the battleship *Agincourt* which shortly afterwards sailed to join Vice-Admiral (Sir) Geoffrey Phipps Hornby, at the time under orders to prepare to force the Dardanelles during the Russo-Turkish war. Jellicoe had charge of two steamboats and four cutters; and on arrival at Gallipoli was employed ashore as a dispatch rider. A more daunting experience was the handling of the *Cruiser* (a sailing vessel attached to the fleet for instructional purposes) when the commander-in-chief came on board for inspection and ordered the sloop to take him back to his flagship. At the close of the trip Jellicoe was complimented on his performance, and on his nineteenth birthday obtained a first class certificate in seamanship, and left the *Agincourt* for a period of study at the Royal Naval College, Greenwich.

Here and afterwards in the gunnery and torpedo courses at Portsmouth Jellicoe again obtained first classes, and, as a 'three one-er', was properly entitled to immediate promotion; but for technical reasons this encouragement was denied him, and for six months he served in the *Alexandra*, flagship of the Mediterranean Fleet, as signal sub-lieutenant. In September 1880 he was promoted lieutenant, and returned home through Italy, visiting Rome, and at Florence contracting dysentery. When he recovered he determined to qualify as a gunnery specialist; but before undertaking intensive study ashore for two years or longer it was necessary to complete at least one year's watch-keeping at sea; and in February 1881 Jellicoe returned to the *Agincourt*.

In May 1882, in consequence of the rebellion of Arabi Pasha, the *Agincourt* was ordered to Malta, where she embarked a battalion of infantry; and, despite her low speed and the overcrowding on board, reached Alexandria only thirty-six hours after the bombardment, bringing welcome reinforcements. Jellicoe was sent with a company of seamen to support the turning movement of Sir Garnet Wolseley from Ismailia; and from that base was entrusted with secret dispatches for the commander-in-chief, which, in the disguise of a refugee and amid a horde of verminous natives, he conveyed successfully to Port Said.

After a year of active service Jellicoe was released to qualify as a gunnery specialist. In the theoretical work at Greenwich he defeated all competitors and was awarded the £80 prize; and at Portsmouth he gained first class certificates in gunnery and torpedo. In May 1884, as a full-blown gunnery lieutenant, he was appointed to the staff of the *Excellent* gunnery school and participated in the far-reaching reforms instituted at that time by the dynamic commandant, Captain J. A. (later Lord) Fisher.

In 1885 Admiral Sir Geoffrey Phipps Hornby hoisted his flag in the *Minotaur*. Fisher was appointed his chief of staff, and as his own staff-officer selected the most junior of those who had served under him in the *Excellent*, a very notable testimonial to Jellicoe's merits. The cruise was short, but enabled him to witness the first torpedo attack on a fleet, and the first modern attempt at a tactical fleet action. In September 1885 he was appointed gunnery lieutenant to the *Monarch*, an obsolescent turret ship; and in April 1886, in the same capacity, joined the *Colossus*, the most up-to-date battleship then afloat. At the end of the year he was back again in the *Excellent* as an experimental officer to superintend the gunnery tests of all ships commissioning. The monotony of the work was relieved by experiments which led to the adoption of the 4·7-in. (45-pounder) and 6-in. (90-pounder) guns.

In 1889 the passing of the Naval Defence Act allocated £21,000,000 to the long neglected task of increasing and modernizing the *matériel* of the fleet; and much of the unprecedented labour involved in the provision of ten battleships and forty-two cruisers fell upon Fisher, then director of naval ordnance. To assist him in his task he insisted that Jellicoe should be transferred from the *Excellent* to the Admiralty, although the step was contrary to precedent. Looking back on this period Jellicoe records that he was frequently at work until midnight in his efforts to keep pace with the daily influx of work. In June 1891 he was promoted commander; and in March 1892, in the *Sans Pareil*, commanded by Captain (Sir) A. K. Wilson, joined the Mediterranean Fleet at Malta.

Early in 1893 Admiral Sir George Tryon, then commander-in-chief, asked the captain of the *Sans Pareil* that Jellicoe might come as commander to his flagship, the *Victoria*, then recommissioning at Malta; and when preparations were complete, left for a cruise in the Levant. On 22 June, as he drew near to Tripoli, with his fleet in two lines ahead he prepared to anchor. Before doing so it was necessary to put about. But instead of the customary procedure, he signalled the leading ship of each column to turn inwards towards one another. For this manœuvre Tryon allowed insufficient sea-room; and the *Victoria*, rammed by the *Camperdown*, turned over and sank with the loss of her admiral and nearly 400 men. Jellicoe, who was suffering from a bout of Malta fever, hurried on deck, walked along the port side of the ship as it assumed a horizontal position; and, before the *Victoria* took the final plunge, committed himself to the water. Swimming as strongly as his condition allowed and receiving some assistance from a midshipman, he kept afloat until he was picked up. On his return to England the effects of his immersion declared themselves and he was for a time invalided.

In command of the Mediterranean Fleet Tryon was succeeded by Admiral Sir Michael Culme-Seymour, whose flag flew in the *Ramillies*, a new battleship successfully conforming to the requirements of the age of steel. The utmost care was exercised in the choice of her officers, and for commander the choice of the Admiralty fell upon Jellicoe who, later in life, looked back with pleasure to a commission which lasted three years (October 1893 to December 1896) and of which he retained delightful memories. The other ships of the fleet did their utmost to surpass the flagship in smartness and efficiency; but, thanks to her commander, the *Ramillies* excelled them all. At the close of the commission Jellicoe returned to England and in January 1897 was promoted captain.

After a year's work as a member of the Ordnance Committee Jellicoe set out for the Far East in company with Admiral Sir E. H. Seymour who, flying his flag in the *Centurion* on the China station, chose Jellicoe as his flag captain and chief of staff. The hour of their arrival coincided with a critical conjuncture in the Far East. The utter defeat of China by Japan two years earlier and the seizure by the victor of the key-points on the Gulf of Pe-chi-li led to the intervention of the great powers: the seizure of Port Arthur by Russia, of Kiaochow by Germany, and of Kwang-Chow-wan by France. It was impossible for Great Britain, with her vast interests in the Orient, to stand aside; and she secured from China a lease of Wei-hai-wei for a period co-extensive with the occupation of Port Arthur by Russia. In May 1898 Seymour occupied the place, and Jellicoe busied himself with the conversion of the harbour into a naval base. For the rest it was the duty of the British fleet to keep the peace. All the great powers had squadrons or ships to support their diplomacy in the event of further disputes; and further disputes seemed only too probable. The presence of a strong British fleet, it was hoped, would exercise a stabilizing effect upon the ocean-ways.

243

But it was not at sea that the storm was brewing. On 28 May 1900 a telegram from Peking, requesting a guard for the legations, communicated the first intelligence of the Boxer rising. Seymour, as commander-in-chief of a strictly naval force, was in no position to deal with a military crisis: but appeals for help left him no alternative; and he summoned a conference of international flag officers and invited them to send contingents ashore under his personal command. He selected Jellicoe as his chief of staff; and on 5 June sent him ahead to decide whether to advance by river, road, or railway. Jellicoe reported that the river was choked by sandbanks, the road a broken track, and the railway the only possibility. Assembling all the tugs and lighters in the neighbourhood he sent them to the ships, knowing that small craft only could bring the troops ashore. Signalling by searchlight, he apprised the admiral of the situation; and on 10 June an international naval brigade set out for Peking. The total, representing ten nations, numbered little more than 2,000 men, of whom 915 were British.

The difficulties that were soon to prove insuperable declared themselves at once. The day temperature of 95° sank at night to an icy chillness. The terrain was little better than desert; and the sand-laden wind parched the skin and irritated the throat. The railway was highly vulnerable; and although the imperial army permitted the force to pass the Taku forts and occupy Tientsin, in a few days it openly joined the rebels. Before long the railway was irreparably broken both ahead of the column and in its rear; and a council of war (19 June) decided to leave the railway and retreat by the river bank, towing the wounded in sampans. Serious opposition was encountered; and on 21 June, while leading an attack at Peitsang, Jellicoe received a bullet in the left lung, and fell dangerously wounded. After an injection of morphia he wrote his will on the battlefield and was placed in a sampan to die. But his strong constitution bore him up; moreover, as the last spark of strength flickered out of the expedition, reinforcements from the base had captured the Taku forts (17 June), and brought the exhausted crusaders to the comparative comforts of Tientsin (26 June). From here Jellicoe was removed to Wei-hai-wei to recover from his wound. Some fifteen months later, after a four years' commission, the *Centurion* was relieved by the *Glory* and Jellicoe returned home (September 1901), having accumulated most valuable Far Eastern experience and an insight into the capacities of various nations on active service.

In March 1902 Jellicoe was selected to fill a new post at the Admiralty, that of naval assistant to the controller. As such, his duty was to inspect all new ships under construction, and this took him to Clydeside. While in Scotland he renewed his acquaintance with Sir Charles William Cayzer (later first baronet, of Gartmore, Perthshire), from whom he had previously received hospitality. On this occasion Jellicoe's friendship with Cayzer's second daughter, Florence Gwendoline, ripened into an engagement; and in July 1902 they were married in London. Just over a year later Jellicoe was appointed to command the armoured cruiser *Drake*, and his happy home life was interrupted.

In November 1904 Fisher, who had become first sea lord in the previous October, recalled Jellicoe to the Admiralty, and in February 1905 he was appointed director of naval ordnance and to serve on the committee then assembling to determine the future design of battleships; the existing mixed armament of heavy and medium calibres was considered anachronistic; and the development of long-range firing certainly demanded a radical change. The outcome was the 'all big gun' battleship *Dreadnought*, which rendered all her predecessors obsolete. Jellicoe's duties were of paramount importance: in addition to stimulating the accuracy of long-range gunnery by battle-practice, he conducted a long-delayed reform of revolutionary significance—the transfer of responsibility for the output of naval ordnance from the War Office to the Admiralty. In February 1907 he was promoted rear-admiral; in August he hoisted his flag in the *Albemarle* as second-in-command of the Atlantic Fleet; and in October, on the occasion of the naval review at Spithead, was knighted and invested by King Edward VII with the insignia of the K.C.V.O. He had been appointed C.B. in 1900 and C.V.O. in 1906.

A commission which included a cruise off the coast of Portugal at the time of the assassination of King Carlos and his elder son, and participation in the tercentenary celebrations at Quebec can hardly be described as uneventful. But to a keen naval officer greater significance attached to battle-practice at a range of five miles in contrast with the one-mile maximum of some eleven years earlier when Jellicoe was commander of the *Ramillies*. Still more important for his future was the enforced absence of the commander-in-chief, which for a period put him in charge of the whole fleet. In August 1908, after just a year's sea-time, he returned to England, and in October rejoined the Admiralty as controller and third sea lord.

Jellicoe became responsible for new naval construction at a moment of extreme difficulty. The *Dreadnought* admittedly surpassed all previous battleships; but in promoting a new type Great Britain of necessity had given other nations a better chance of drawing level than they had enjoyed for two and a half centuries. Not only were the Germans intent on seizing this opportunity; but the general election of 1906 brought in a government committed to the curtailment of armaments. When Jellicoe became controller there was a strong probability that by 1912 England would have eighteen dreadnoughts and Germany twenty-one. Jellicoe pointed out that if Britain's shipbuilding capacity might in an emergency enable her to overtake a German lead, the same argument did not apply to heavy ordnance, which could not be constructed against time. It was this hard fact that weighed down the balance and led to the inclusion in the 1909–1910 programme of the eight battleships which restored the lead to Britain. But the adoption of the *Dreadnought* brought another disadvantage. The ships were growing too large for existing docks; and the government was not prepared to face the excessive cost which new docks would entail. Its veto cramped the breadth of the new vessels, which in consequence were not sufficiently proof against under-water attack. The total displacement might compare favourably with that of German ships of the same class: but the German ships, mounting smaller guns and with greater beam, were heavily protected about their vitals; and the greater hitting power of the British ships would be seriously offset if one lucky shell from the enemy found their protection insufficient. The toughness of the German ships required an improvement in British armour-piercing shells; and for these the controller, after experimental firings at a ship, put forward insistent demands. The documented proofs of his foresight clear him of the blame for faulty Cabinet decisions, with which political apologists have tried to saddle him.

Concluding his term of office with the satisfaction of having seen ninety vessels, including twelve battleships, added to the fleet, Jellicoe, in December 1910, with the rank of vice-admiral, hoisted his flag in the *Prince of Wales* as vice-admiral commanding the Atlantic Fleet. The year that followed saw the coronation review of King George V and the Agadir incident. During the latter Jellicoe took his fleet to a south Irish port to be ready for any eventuality. In December 1911 the steamship *Delhi*, with the Princess Royal and her family on board, suffered shipwreck off Cape Spartel, and Jellicoe earned the gratitude of the King for the effective steps taken to rescue them. The same month, to give him experience in handling a squadron of dreadnoughts, he was appointed to command the second division of the Home Fleet, and hoisted his flag in the *Hercules*. The two years of Jellicoe's command afloat passed uneventfully; and in December 1912 he was summoned again to the Admiralty. As second sea lord he became responsible for the discipline and manning of the fleet and all questions affecting officers and men.

Meanwhile the war cloud lowered over Europe; and in June 1914 the tragedy of Serajevo precipitated the crisis. The Admiralty had already ordered a naval mobilization; and at Spithead the King reviewed a fleet which included fifty-seven capital ships. At the close of the exercise the Admiralty cancelled the customary paying off and dispatched the fleet to Scapa Flow. Jellicoe followed overland, ostensibly as second-in-command;

but on 4 August he received a telegram directing him to open a secret envelope which had been handed to him on leaving London. This proved to be his appointment as commander-in-chief, Grand Fleet, with the acting rank of admiral, flying his flag in the *Iron Duke*.

For the distant blockade of the German fleet Scapa Flow was not ill placed; but in August 1914 as a naval base it lacked every requisite. In its desire to avoid action calculated to increase the tension with Germany, the government had refrained from taking the measures necessary for the defence of the place or the maintenance of a fleet there. There were three entrances through which hostile torpedo-craft could gain ingress; and it was not until February 1915 that they were blocked. Jellicoe found it necessary to keep his fleet continually moving; and in August one day only was spent in harbour. When winter came the weather in those latitudes grew dark and tempestuous; and the swirl of waters through the Pentland Firth made return to harbour a hazardous proceeding. Although Jellicoe had a large floating dock towed up to the Cromarty Firth, and although Rosyth was put into full use, there were for some time not sufficient facilities or docks and plant for minor repairs. The fleet was reduced by casualties and damage requiring repairs, for which ships had to be sent south to the Channel ports; and had the Germans been more venturesome they might in January 1915 have challenged Jellicoe's dreadnought strength on practically equal terms. But they preferred to stay snugly in harbour, while the Grand Fleet in the first four months of the war steamed 16,805 miles. The commander-in-chief balanced the rigours of his routine by a personal interest in the welfare of the 60,000 officers and men under his command. Admirals and captains were, in Nelson's phrase, a band of brothers; while the lower deck knew instinctively that Jellicoe thought more of their happiness than of his own.

During 1915 (the year in which he was promoted admiral) Jellicoe strengthened his grip on northern waters. By the middle of the year he had a preponderant margin of dreadnought strength; and, as a base, Scapa was in some degree equipped for repairs and put in a reasonable state of defence. No pains were spared to increase the Grand Fleet's fighting efficiency by evolutions and exercises. But it was no longer necessary to plough the seas as a precaution against torpedo attack; and time could be spent in harbour with comparative immunity. But, as in the days of Hawke, Jervis, Howe, and Nelson, the wearisome, monotonous block-ade continued; and between the outbreak of war and the battle of Jutland the German admiral only five times emerged from harbour. After each modest sally of some hundred miles he hastened home with the men-dacious assurance that he had vainly offered his opponent the chance of battle.

Jellicoe

The King, at the outbreak of war, described the navy as the country's 'sure shield'; and this definition opportunely emphasized the necessarily defensive character of Jellicoe's blockade. So long as the Grand Fleet controlled all sea approaches to and from Germany, the enemy in a naval sense was immobilized. The raids of the German battle-cruisers on British fishing towns and seaside resorts, ethically indefensible and strategically ineffective, were intended to undermine the trust which this country reposed in its sea-governance. In this objective they failed signally, and unless the Germans were content with having built a dreadnought battle fleet to no purpose, it was for them to break Jellicoe's stranglehold; it was for them to assume the offensive. The appointment early in 1916 of Admiral Scheer brought the chances of a collision perceptibly nearer. Not that his plans for reducing the British margin of dreadnought superiority came any nearer success than those of his predecessors, but they did involve him in the meshes of the net which Jellicoe set to catch him. On 31 May, the weather being thick for the time of year, he gave the word to attack a British detached force which Jellicoe had sent in the direction of the Skagerrak. The German battle-cruisers, under Admiral Hipper, were sent on ahead and were sighted at 2.20 p.m. by the British light cruiser *Galatea* wearing the broad pendant of Commodore E. Alexander Sinclair, and the first salvoes of the battle of Jutland were fired when the *Galatea*, in company with the *Phaeton*, opened fire on two enemy destroyers. At 2.35 Hipper's battle-cruisers were sighted, and at 3.48 the two squadrons opened fire on each other.

Although the British battle-cruisers had with them four fast dreadnought battleships, their prime function was that of scouting; and when at 4.33 Scheer himself appeared in Hipper's wake, Beatty put about to join Jellicoe to the northward of the battlefield, drawing the enemy's forces after him. Jellicoe had intercepted the signals from the *Galatea* and other ships, and was making all speed to the south, sending ahead his own battle-cruisers to support those already engaged. But he was in no position to order a 'General Chase', the signal beloved by the navy in sailing days: for he was still some fifty miles away; and from those engaged had received no exact intelligence as to the enemy's position or formation. His own fleet, numbering twenty-four dreadnought battleships, was in sailing order, six lines-ahead disposed abeam. Before he accepted battle he had to deploy his six columns into single line ahead; and before deployment it was essential that he should know at what point on his front the enemy would appear.

At 6.14 the German battle-fleet was reported; not (as was expected) immediately ahead, but to the westward. Jellicoe, with no enemy yet in sight, instantly signalled deployment on his port (or easternmost) wing column. By doing so, he threw a mantle of invisibility over his own fleet, while the glare of the setting sun through the mist made silhouette targets of the enemy. As his six divisions drew into a perfect line ahead he crossed the enemy's T, compelling them to alter course and steer parallel to him. At 6.23 the leading British battleships opened fire, the salvoes of nine dreadnoughts converging on three of their opponents. Outmanœuvred, and outclassed except in *matériel*, Scheer turned and doubled on his tracks. By this time the murky evening was rendered more opaque by the pall of battle-smoke that hung above the combatants. It was thus impossible for Jellicoe to know whether Scheer had actually retreated, or fortuitously disappeared behind the curtain of mist. What he did know was that he had placed the British battle-fleet between the Germans and Germany; and that if they desired to see home again they must re-emerge.

For ten miles Scheer fell back to the inhospitable west. Then pulling his force together he came back in line ahead, hoping to work a passage past, or even through, his opponents, like a snake wriggling through a wire fence. At 7.10 he reappeared; and for the second time reeled backwards under the punishment of Jellicoe's devastating fire. Georg von Hase records that the *Derfflinger* was hit twenty-five times, often by 15-in. shells, and that the British battleships had the range to an inch. [*Kiel and Jutland*, translated by A. Chambers and F. A. Holt, 1921.]

For the second time accepting the necessity of retreat, Scheer ordered his destroyers to veil him with a smoke-screen, and to deliver a massed torpedo attack. In theory he could count on the discharge of 224 of those deadly projectiles; but as Jellicoe instantly launched an effective counter-attack on the enemy flotillas, only thirty-one torpedoes were actually fired, though these might have played havoc with a line of twenty-four ships broadside on. Jellicoe, however, turned his ships individually at an angle of 45° to the eastward of their advance; and the torpedoes thus ran harmlessly between the widened interstices in his line.

Night now sank upon the sea; and Jellicoe, who still stood between the Germans and Germany, took every step that ingenuity could suggest to block their natural avenues of escape. In a land campaign under similar circumstances the enemy would have been compelled to continue the action on the morrow; but in deep waters the entire surface of ocean is a path; and all that Scheer needed was the breadth of one ship where in Indian file the rest could follow. Darkness served him well in this his third and last attempt; and with heavy losses he brought his defeated ships back in dejection to their base. On 1 June Jellicoe found himself alone in German waters. If he had successfully sunk, burnt, or destroyed every vessel brought against him, he could not have been more completely master of the sea.

Jellicoe

The immediate sequel to the action forms an interesting study in popular psychology. Jellicoe signed the Jutland dispatches on 18 June; and upon them any proper appraisal of the action hinged. Before he reached harbour, however, the Germans issued a *communiqué* representing Jutland as a glorious success for their arms; and this preposterous claim the Admiralty published on 2 June; supplementing it with a frank but inadequate statement which disclosed little beyond the serious British losses. The public, finding in the latter no hint of victory, at once conceived the idea that the engagement had been a disaster and were confirmed in their delusion when they discovered that the German losses, both in ships and men, were less heavy than the British. With good cause for annoyance with German publicity and Admiralty reticence, they visited their displeasure on Jellicoe and allowed their resentment to be fanned into flame by undiscerning critics who, not in club-land only, demonstrated what Nelson would have done. But there were two big differences. First, the close blockade, possible in Nelson's day but impossible in Jellicoe's, prevented any general action in home waters in 1805. Secondly, in 1805 Nelson was not even in command of the Grand Fleet. Had he been, he would probably not have taken the risks which he accepted at Trafalgar, where he was covered by the Grand Fleet under Cornwallis. Unhappily the critics of 1916 overlooked these important distinctions; and the mistaken tradition that, if not a defeat, Jutland was at best a drawn battle, for very many years lingered on.

Later events fully established the correctness of Jellicoe's judgement (formed on the battlefield of Jutland) that the Germans would not again risk such an encounter. More serious at the moment was the U-boat assault on British seaborne supplies; and Jellicoe modestly volunteered to serve on a committee to grapple with this baffling problem. It was not, however, until November 1916 that, on appointment as first sea lord, he left the perfect organization of the Grand Fleet for the mass of unsolved problems at headquarters. The merchantmen needing defence were privately owned and were run by private enterprise over which government had no control. The responsibility of the Board of Trade was unsuited to an hour when the vessels were no longer engaged in commerce, but in carrying the supplies on which the life of the nation depended. Some nationalization of the industry was inevitable; but that was for Cabinet action. Taking up his new duties on 4 December Jellicoe went straight to the heart of the problem and made it his first duty to see that the arming of the merchantmen was accelerated. By the end of February 1917 2,899 ships had guns to defend themselves; and depth-charges were daily accumulating. But these measures of protection, with others instituted before he accepted office, drove the Germans in February to unrestricted U-boat warfare; and shipping losses soared in April to the staggering total of 599,000 tons. Britain possessed 3,200 steamers. Of these 1,900 were engaged on war purposes only, leaving 1,300 to stock the country with food and raw material. How long could Britain hold out, if she continued (as in April) to lose ten merchantmen a day?

There is a widespread belief that salvation was found in the convoy system; and that this was evolved by amateurs and imposed from without upon a recalcitrant Admiralty. The first premiss is true; the second is unjust to Jellicoe: for he brought from the Grand Fleet the officers who, under his direction, organized the convoy system. 'The establishment and development of the convoy system', wrote Tirpitz, '(a tremendous achievement on the part of the English) involved years of work.' He was wrong in his time estimate; and yet nearer the truth than those who have claimed for this statesman or that the whole credit for an idea easy to suggest but which only the British Admiralty could implement. It is true that, in the hour of Jellicoe's arrival, the naval staff was opposed to the extension of the convoy system beyond the escort of troopships and other precious freights (which had been convoyed since the outbreak of hostilities): but such opposition (whatever the cause) serves only to emphasize the impossibility of expanding the system in December 1916. In the black days of April 1917 two compensatory factors adjusted the balance. The new Ministry of Shipping (inaugurated in December 1916) began to function, and brought unity of control and direction to the mercantile marine; unrestricted U-boat atrocities brought the United States of America into the war, and so permitted the release, for escort duties, of the tenth cruiser squadron (until then employed in preventing American goods from reaching Germany); the admission into American harbours of armed British merchantmen; and a substantial reinforcement of American escort vessels which were essential for the success of the convoy system. Within a matter of months (to quote Admiral Sims, U.S.N.) 'the whole gigantic enterprise flowed with a precision and regularity which it is hardly likely that any other transportation system has ever achieved'; and the credit, however able the contribution of colleagues and allies, belongs in chief to Jellicoe, whose lifelong sea-experience, administrative gifts, and grasp of technical minutiae were never employed to better advantage.

The tributes paid by the sailors Sims and Tirpitz may be contrasted with the views of the landsman who, in the month after Jellicoe's appointment as first sea lord, became prime minister, and whose impatient temper and utter ignorance of sea-conditions combined to make him chafe at any delay. The peril was indeed extreme; and Jellicoe was doing no more than his duty in demonstrating that there was no infallible panacea for U-boat troubles, and in recommending resort to rationing. But Lloyd George came to believe that the negligence of the Admiralty was proved and that Jellicoe was the embodiment of the maladministration which he denounced [*War Memoirs*, vol. iii, c. xl, 1934]. In July 1917 he translated to a higher political plane the then first lord of the Admiralty, Sir Edward Carson, and put in his place Sir Eric Geddes, the railway king, to teach the Admiralty their business. When, being totally ignorant of naval traditions, customs, and sentiments, Geddes trampled such trifles underfoot, it was Jellicoe's unpleasant task to remind him that the sea lords were his colleagues, not his subordinates; and on Christmas Eve 1917 he found in his office a curt note from Geddes dismissing him from government employ. He carried into the silence of exile the consoling thought that the submarine menace had been mastered and that he had provided the Grand Fleet with the armour-piercing shells which at Jutland would have made the German losses five or six times as heavy. In January 1918 he was raised to the peerage as Viscount Jellicoe, of Scapa. In 1919 he received the thanks of both Houses of Parliament and a grant of £50,000, and was promoted admiral of the fleet.

At the Imperial Conference in March 1917 the Admiralty had been invited by the Dominions to consider the most effective manner in which they could share in the naval defence of the Empire; and when the war ended, this invitation was renewed with a clear hint to utilize Jellicoe's unquestioned status as one of the greatest living sailors. The Admiralty approved; and in February 1919 Jellicoe left Portsmouth for a cruise which included visits to India, Australia, New Zealand, and Canada. The tour lasted a year and involved an immense amount of work of an invaluable but unspectacular kind. The magnitude and secrecy of the recommendations preclude adequate appraisal; but among solid results must be counted the formation of the great naval base at Singapore, and the establishment of the royal Indian navy and of the New Zealand naval division. It was no fault of Jellicoe's if effect was not given to his earnest plea for a strong Pacific Fleet with accumulations of fuel to ensure its mobility. From the personal standpoint the most satisfying aspect of the cruise was the heart-stirring enthusiasm everywhere shown for Jellicoe himself. Such world-wide appreciation and spontaneous tributes of applause could hardly fail to make amends for the censure, contumely, and political persecution from which he had suffered at home.

After six months' leave, Jellicoe, with his household, sailed in August 1920 for New Zealand to take up his duties as governor-general. He held the appointment for four years; and during that time raised the office to a pinnacle of esteem previously unapproached. Unfailing ally of every charitable and philanthropic impulse, wise guide to the most sagacious of his own counsellors, idol of every child in the Dominion, he established between himself and those whom he governed strong ties of personal affection, and left behind him unfading memories of nationwide gratitude. Importuned to stay and reluctant to leave, he re-embarked in November 1924, retiring from the service in December. In June 1925 he was advanced to the rank of Earl Jellicoe.

During the last eleven years of his life Jellicoe patiently shouldered many voluntary tasks. Not only was he chairman of the National Rifle Association and grand president of the British Empire Service League; but he interested himself keenly in the Boy Scout movement and in 1925 became county commissioner for London. On the death of Lord Haig in 1928 the British Legion invited him to fill the vacant presidency. Thinking a soldier to be a more suitable choice, he asked permission to decline. The nomination was then referred to thirteen area conferences, all of which unanimously elected him, and he held office until 1932. In all these causes he laboured strenuously, never sparing himself or allowing himself the rest and recreation which his health demanded and his age condoned. On 9 November 1935 he caught a chill while planting poppies; and two days later attended the Armistice Day service at the Cenotaph. The infection spread to one lung; and on 20 November, fifteen days before his seventy-sixth birthday, he died at his home in Kensington. On 25 November the funeral procession passed through crowded streets to St. Paul's Cathedral, where his body was fittingly laid to rest beside those of Nelson and Collingwood.

Unaided by wealth or social prestige, Jellicoe rose to the head of his profession by sheer merit and force of character. He might have suffered from pride and over-confidence. But the key to his character was self-lessness. A man of deep religious convictions, he never allowed personal considerations to affect his judgement; never spoke of himself; and instead of courting publicity, shunned it. When pilloried by the press and censured by politicians, he answered not a word and allowed no recriminations. In congenial company his shrewd, twinkling eyes radiated friendliness and sympathy; and his countless little acts of kindness to the needy, diffident, and distressed made all who served with him worship 'J. R. J.' with a touching doglike devotion, deepened by their unquestioning trust in his faultless leadership. Those who passed with him through the flame of battle testify to his imperturbable calm, and the lightning speed of his decisions. When, however, he found that ill-informed writers were unjustly attacking the reputations of officers who had served under his command, then and then only would he write to the proper authorities to call attention to the injustice.

In addition to the honours already mentioned, Jellicoe was appointed K.C.B. in 1911, G.C.B. in 1915, and G.C.V.O. in 1916: in the last-named year for his services at Jutland he was appointed to the Order of Merit. He also

John

received the freedom of the City of London and honorary degrees from the universities of Oxford, Cambridge, St. Andrews, and Glasgow. His numerous foreign decorations included the grand cross of the Legion of Honour.

Jellicoe had one son and five daughters, the second of whom died in childhood. He was succeeded as second earl by his son, George Patrick John Rushworth (born 1918), who was awarded the D.S.O. and the M.C. in the war of 1939–1945.

A half-length portrait of Jellicoe, by R. G. Eves, is in the possession of H.M.S. *Excellent* and the United Services Club, and a quarter-length, by the same artist (1935), is in the National Portrait Gallery. A portrait of him is included in Sir A. S. Cope's picture 'Some Sea Officers of the Great War', painted in 1921, in the National Portrait Gallery. A cartoon of him by 'Spy' appeared in *Vanity Fair* 26 December 1906.

[Sir Reginald Bacon, *The Life of John Rushworth Earl Jellicoe*, 1936; Lord Jellicoe, *The Grand Fleet 1914–1916*, 1919, *The Crisis of the Naval War*, 1920, and *The Submarine Peril*, 1934; Sir Julian Corbett, (Official) *History of the Great War. Naval Operations*, vol. iii, 1923; C. E. Fayle, *Seaborne Trade*, vol. iii, 1924; Lord Chatfield, *The Navy and Defence*, 1942.]

GEOFFREY CALLENDER

published 1949

JOHN Caspar

(1903–1984)

Sir

Admiral of the fleet, was born at his parents' home, 18 Fitzroy Street, London W1, 22 March 1903, the second of the five sons (there were no daughters) of Augustus Edwin John, artist, and his wife, Ida, daughter of John Trivett Nettleship, animal painter. Augustus John also had two other sons and four daughters. Caspar John's mother died when he was four. Due to his father's love of gypsies and itinerant life-style during the years preceding World War I, John was not subjected to any form of systematic schooling until the age of nine, when he was sent with his brothers to Dane Court Preparatory School in Parkstone, Dorset. There he won the prize for the best gentleman in the school and a copy of *Jane's Fighting Ships*, and it was this, together with a wish to seek a more orderly existence, that inspired him to join the Royal Navy. In 1916 he entered the

Royal Naval College, Osborne, in the Isle of Wight, at the age of thirteen. He transferred to the RNC, Dartmouth, in 1917 and passed out eighty-third of a hundred in 1920. He became a good long-distance runner and rackets champion: physical fitness being of paramount importance in naval training, he developed a lifelong love of athletics.

His midshipman years were spent aboard the flagship of the Mediterranean Fleet, the *Iron Duke*, against a background of Graeco-Turkish disturbances and the problem of Russian refugees caused by the revolution of 1917. It was at this time (1922–3) that the future of naval aviation was being debated. The issue caught his imagination, and, heeding advice he had previously had from Admiral of the Fleet Lord Fisher to 'Look forward, not backward', decided that this was to be his future. 'I was the angry young man of the day', he later wrote, and questioned the need to clutter up the navy with outdated battleships. He envisaged the role of the aeroplane as broadening the naval horizon, and during his qualifying exams for lieutenant in 1925 (he gained first class certificates in gunnery and torpedo), he applied to train as a pilot in the Fleet Air Arm, then under the dual administration of the navy and Royal Air Force. His request was not welcomed and was considered a grave risk to his promotion prospects. However, after gaining his wings in 1926, he became passionate about flying, and thenceforth devoted his naval career to building up the strength of the Fleet Air Arm, of which he was one of the founding fathers.

In the aircraft carrier *Hermes* he spent the years 1927–9 in the China station during the warring between the communists and Chiang Kai-Shek's nationalist armies. On returning from China he bought his own aeroplane, an open cockpit Avro Avian, and had many flying adventures in France and England.

A loner by nature, he became known for his zeal, clear-headedness, loyalty, and resilience. He had few interests other than the affairs of the navy: his work was his life. Throughout the 1930s he devoted his time to all aspects of naval flying—deck landing, demonstrating, surveying, testing new designs, and night flying—and gradually became involved in the design and production of naval aircraft.

Promotion to lieutenant-commander and commander came in 1933 and 1936 respectively, and, as a result of Italy's war with Abyssinia, he spent 1936 based in the Western Desert outside Alexandria, attached to the carrier *Courageous*. He spent much time practising carrier night flying which was then an innovation. In 1937 he was appointed to the Admiralty's naval air division, where he worked ceaselessly to free the Fleet Air Arm from what he described as 'the folly' of dual control between the navy and RAF. The RAF's hold on the FAA was ended with the 'Inskip award' in July 1937.

John

During the war of 1939–45 he spent eighteen months as second-in-command of the cruiser *York*, patrolling the North Sea, participating in the Norwegian campaign, and transporting arms around the coast of Africa to Egypt for the campaign in the Western Desert. Subsequently he had eighteen months at the Ministry of Aircraft Production (he was promoted to captain in 1941), and in 1943–4 he was in the USA as naval air representative in the British Admiralty delegation in Washington, and naval air attaché at the British embassy. His main task, and one which he considered of supreme importance, was to procure US naval aircraft for the under-equipped FAA and to set up the organization and training of British pilots in Canada and the USA. His meeting with the Russian aircraft designer Igor Sikorski, was in large part responsible for the introduction of the helicopter into its first practical military use by the navy after the war. He spent the last year of the war in home waters in command of two aircraft carriers, *Pretoria Castle*, and, until 1946, *Ocean*, a brand-new light carrier. As captain of *Ocean*, his main concerns were to boost the morale of his men (with the war ended, many longed to return home), and to maintain strict discipline in all flying activities.

In 1947 he attended the Imperial Defence College, London, for a course in world affairs and in 1948 he was given the command of the large and complex naval air station, Lossiemouth. He then returned to the Admiralty, first as deputy chief of naval air equipment and then as director of air organization and training. Although it was not his personal ambition, he excelled at administrative work, and his promotion to rear-admiral in 1951 ushered in his last year at sea, in command of the heavy squadron. In 1952 he was appointed CB. Two years (1952–4) at the Ministry of Supply updating naval aircraft preceded the important administrative post of flag officer (air) Home at Lee-on-Solent, the 'Clapham Junction' of all naval air stations. He was promoted vice-admiral in 1954, was appointed KCB in 1956, and was made a full admiral in 1957, the year he became vice-chief of naval staff to Earl Mountbatten of Burma. This was a period of great uncertainty for the navy, and ranked as one of the most demanding periods of concentrated activity experienced by a naval officer in modern times.

He crowned his career by becoming first sea lord (1960–3), the first ever naval aviator to have done so, and was appointed GCB in 1960. The major issues he dealt with while in office were characteristic of those facing any first sea lord as professional head of the navy but particularly those concerned with plans for the building of a new generation of large aircraft carriers. In 1962 he was promoted admiral of the fleet but later declined a peerage offered to him by Sir Alec Douglas-Home (later Lord Home of the Hirsel).

He embraced a number of widely differing jobs throughout the 1960s and 1970s: member of the government security commission (1964–73), chairman of the Housing Corporation (1964–6), member of the Plowden committee and of the Templer committee (1965), chairman of the Star and Garter Home for disabled servicemen, chairman of the Back Pain Association, and chairman of the tri-service Milocarian Club (athletics). He was made an honorary liveryman of the Fruiterers' Company.

John inherited his parents' good looks. He was tall and slim, with brown eyes and dark bushy eyebrows. His penetrating look and brusque speech, alarming to some, belied a sensitive, moody nature. He loved children, the works of Thomas Hardy, and the music of Claudio Monteverdi. He had the ability to go straight to the point in argument, had a quick wit, and excelled at speech-making. His father painted several oil portraits of him as a child and young man, and there are a number of superb line drawings of him as a child.

He married in 1944 Mary, daughter of Stuart Vanderpump, of New Zealand. They had two daughters and one son. In 1978 he had both his legs amputated because of vascular trouble. His extraordinary courage and his determination to regain some degree of independence gave him the spirit to face life in a wheelchair for six years. His wife was a great support during this difficult time, and together they made their home in the Cornish village of Mousehole, where John became a much loved and familiar figure on the quayside and in the Ship Inn. He died 11 July 1984 at Hayle, Cornwall.

[Rebecca John (daughter), *Caspar John*, 1987; private information; personal knowledge.]

DAVID WILLIAMS

published 1990

JOUBERT DE LA FERTÉ Philip Bennet

(1887–1965)

Sir

Air chief marshal, was born at Darjeeling in India 21 May 1887, the fourth child of a family of four daughters (two of whom died young) and two sons of Colonel Charles Henry Joubert de la Ferté, of the Indian Medical Service, and his wife, Eliza Jane, eldest daughter of Philip Sandys Melville, of the Indian Civil Service. He was of part French descent, for his grandfather had come to England in 1840 and, after being naturalized in 1885, distinguished himself by designing and engraving a four penny Inland Revenue stamp which was to be used for over forty years.

The Joubert children had a sound upbringing, but had a reputation for recklessness. At the age of nine, Philip was sent to school in England, a severe test for a youngster brought up in the East. However, he found solace by reading novels about flying and submarine adventures, books which undoubtedly coloured his future outlook. Since it was impossible to return to India for school holidays, he went to family friends in the country and to an aunt in the south of France. These visits developed in him those self-reliant qualities which were to become evident later, since by the age of eleven he was travelling alone between England and France and was thrown entirely upon his own resources.

It was intended that he should join the army, whereas he himself had a strong desire to join the navy. Parental influence prevailed and he was dispatched to Harrow. He qualified for the Royal Military Academy, Woolwich, at his second attempt and passed out at the lower end of his term, gaining a commission in the Field Gunners in 1907. After five years as a second lieutenant, Joubert regained his desire to fly or to operate a submarine. Quite by chance, his parents had taken a house at Weybridge, adjacent to Brooklands race track. Brooklands soon afterwards became an aerodrome. In 1912 Joubert set out to learn to fly and was given official permission to do so at his own expense. He was soon granted Royal Aero Club certificate No. 280. After a course at the Central Flying School at Upavon, he was attached to the Royal Flying Corps (Military Wing) in March 1913 as a flying officer. He was at last financially independent, and had joined the RFC at a time which favoured his future prospects. He was a fully qualified young army officer, fit and keen to believe in the importance of powered flight, and with the added advantage of being able to speak French.

Joubert was promoted to the rank of temporary captain when war began in 1914, and proceeded to France with No. 3 Squadron. Within a week, flying a Blériot and armed with a pistol, he made aviation history by being one of the two pilots to make the first reconnaissance of enemy lines. He was mentioned in dispatches for the first time two months later—in all he was to be mentioned seven times. He was then recalled to England in 1915 to raise a new squadron. That task completed, he was promoted to the rank of temporary major and given command of No. 15 Squadron in France.

Events moved swiftly as the war developed and he was fortunate to be given command of No. 1 Squadron, in succession to (Sir) (William) Geoffrey Salmond, at a significant time because it covered the battle of

Loos. His younger brother, John Claude, also of No. 1 Squadron and also a pilot, had had the misfortune to be shot down in March 1915 over Holland and remained a prisoner of war for the rest of the war.

Early in 1916 Joubert was invalided out of France with 'trench feet'. When he had recovered he was ordered to form a new squadron, No. 33. Very shortly afterwards he was promoted to the rank of temporary lieutenant-colonel and given command of No. 5 Wing in Egypt. There Joubert's experience and flair for improvization were put to good use since No. 5 Wing's resources were not large and its aircraft were out of date. Joubert left Egypt early in 1917 with many important lessons learned from the fighting in Sinai, particularly in the handling of both air and ground operations. He was appointed to the DSO for his efforts. After only a few months in England in command of No. 21 Wing, he was transferred to No. 14 Wing which he took to Italy after a short stay in France. The move to Italy was an important step in his career since he had now established himself as a leader, a practical airman, a sound administrator, and a good commander in the field—all essential qualities for higher command. These qualities were recognized in 1918 by his appointment to command the RFC in Italy. At this time he was awarded the Order of Saints Maurice and Lazarus, the Cavaliere, and the croce di guerra. Later he was appointed CMG in 1919, CB in 1936, and KCB in 1938.

At the conclusion of the war, he was given command of No. 2 Group at Oxford and received a permanent commission in the Royal Air Force (as the RFC became in April 1918) as a wing commander. No. 2 Group was moved to the Recruits Depot at Uxbridge where Joubert's administrative and leadership qualities were tested to the full because he had both to deal with 1,500 restless and undisciplined Dominion cadets anxious to return home, and to participate in the country's milk distribution during the nationwide railway strike. He emerged from both tests with an enhanced reputation. The following year, 1920, he attended the Army Staff College at Camberley; his happy days there were a welcome respite.

In 1922 he was promoted to group captain and appointed an instructor to the recently formed RAF College at Andover. This period was vital for his subsequent career, for it provided a forum for the formulation of future air policy. On leaving Andover he served as deputy director of personnel and in the directorate of manning at the Air Ministry. In 1926 he became the first RAF instructor at the Imperial Defence College, another milestone. He remained there for three years, being promoted to air commodore when he left. After some nine months in flying training, in which he took every opportunity of modernizing his airmanship, he was posted as commandant of the RAF Staff College, where he remained for three years. This was an admirable post because it enabled him to witness the implementation of the plans made by the Air Council in 1922, and the development of an air policy, broadly conceived and flexible in its application. Above all, Joubert sought to bring the other two Services into closer co-operation. His quick brain infused both a spirit of enthusiasm and a sense of urgency into staff and pupils alike.

In 1933 he was promoted to air vice-marshal and a year later appointed as air officer commanding the Fighting Area of Great Britain—the forerunner of Fighter Command. In this post he devoted much time to studying the air tactics which were gradually evolving from the techniques employed by fighters during the war of 1914–18 to those of the more modern fighters then in service. It was during this period that he took charge of British air defence during the annual air exercises. Promoted to air marshal in 1936, he was appointed for the first time as AOC in C Coastal Command, a post in which he hoped to stay for some time in view of his earlier affection for the sea; but this was not to be, for in 1937 he was sent to India as AOC: the least satisfying of his appointments because the authorities in London were inevitably preoccupied with the dangerous course of events in Europe. Although Joubert made his needs known, he was frustrated by his superiors' inability to face the military facts of life in the Far East where even the nucleus of a modern air force was sadly lacking. Fortunately for Joubert himself, his stay in India was cut short when he was recalled to England at the outbreak of war and appointed air adviser on combined operations. There were, however, more pressing needs for his services elsewhere, and he became assistant chief of air staff with special responsibility for the practical application of radar in the RAF. Much of the ultimate success of the radar war was due to Joubert's realization at this early stage of its great possibilities, both in defence and offence. It was also during this period that he gave his regular broadcasts on the air war; his large audience was evidence of his decided talent in this medium.

In June 1941 he was promoted to air chief marshal and became, for the second time, AOC in C Coastal Command, his own favourite (if not his most successful) command. During the seventeen months he was there, much needed to be done to reduce the very heavy U-boat attacks upon Allied shipping in the Atlantic. The command became better equipped, with more aircraft and superior weapons which enabled tactics to improve. Because Joubert was so well informed about radar, air-to-surface vessel radar became the most effective aid in the anti-submarine war. Joubert also made good use of the civilian scientists available to him to analyse results and to promote greater efficiency with the limited facilities available. These innovations were to have a profound effect upon the Command in the days ahead. It was not a period in his life which was free from criticism and his own outspokenness on the use of air power led to a clash with the Admiralty, which caused him to be moved and appointed inspector general of the RAF, a post he held until his retirement in 1943.

Fortunately for Joubert he was recalled after only a month of retirement to join the staff of Admiral Mountbatten (later Earl Mountbatten of Burma) in the South East Asia Command as the deputy chief of staff (information and civil affairs). Perhaps his most successful venture in this posting was to create a South East Asia Command newspaper which was delivered almost daily to the troops throughout the Command. After the fall of Rangoon, Joubert returned to England for hospital treatment. He finally retired in October 1945.

After some nine months of rest and recuperation he returned as a civilian to the Air Ministry for another year as director of public relations. Joubert permitted himself the luxury of only a short rest before he embarked upon a most successful but exhausting 'coast to coast' lecture tour of the United States talking on his favourite subject, air power. Joubert frequently also gave expression to his thoughts in print and one book, *The Third Service* (1955), provoked considerable controversy amongst the various Services and Ministries. He was by no means universally popular. In appearance Joubert was just under six feet tall, broad in proportion, with a fine complexion, sparkling eyes, and a very healthy look. He had a strong character combined with great charm and an engaging personality.

Joubert first married in 1915 Marjorie Denison, the youngest daughter of Frederick Joseph Hall, of Sheffield; this marriage, of which there were two daughters, was dissolved in 1948, the year in which he married Joan Catherine Cripps, the daughter of Frederick Bucknell. He died at the RAF Hospital, Uxbridge, 21 January 1965.

A portrait by Sir Oswald Birley was destroyed by fire at Joubert's old favourite mess of Headquarters Coastal Command; another portrait, by (Sir) James Gunn (1941), is now in the Imperial War Museum.

[*The Times*, 22 January 1965; *Daily Telegraph*, 22 January 1965; Sir Philip Joubert de la Ferté, *The Fated Sky*, 1952; private information.]

EDWARD CHILTON

published 1981

(1872–1945)

First Baron Keyes

Admiral of the fleet, was born 4 October 1872 at Tundiani on the North-West Frontier of India, the second of the nine children of Colonel (afterwards General Sir) Charles Patton Keyes by his wife, Katherine Jessie, daughter of James Norman, man of business, of Havana and Calcutta, and sister of Field-Marshal Sir H. W. Norman. The family is directly descended from the Norman house of Guiz or Gyse. The chevalier Robert de Guiz entered the service of King John in 1203; his grandson, Sir Anselm de Gyse, was constable of the Tower of London in 1275. Sir Anselm's great-great-grandson, Richard Keyes, was serjeant-at-arms to Richard II, Henry IV, and Henry V; Richard's grandson, Roger Keyes (or Keys), was summoned by Archbishop Chichele to be the architect of All Souls College, Oxford, and became its warden; in 1528 a Richard Keyes was serjeant-at-arms to Henry VIII; his son Thomas Keyes was deputy master of the horse to Queen Elizabeth, and his grandson Thomas settled in Derry where he became sheriff in 1623. For the next two hundred years the Irish estate which he acquired passed from father to son.

Roger Keyes entered the *Britannia* as a naval cadet in July 1885, and two years later was appointed to the *Raleigh*, flagship on the Cape of Good Hope station. In January 1890 he was transferred to the *Turquoise* and saw service boat-cruising for slavers. He was promoted lieutenant in August 1893, and in January 1899 appointed in command of the *Fame*, destroyer, on the China station. For his services during the Boxer rising he was specially promoted to commander in November 1900, and he served next in destroyers and in the intelligence division of the Admiralty. From January 1905 he was for three years naval attaché, Rome, being promoted captain in June 1905, and was then for two years in command of the cruiser *Venus*. In November 1910 he was appointed inspecting captain of submarines, and, in August 1912, commodore in charge of the submarine service.

For the first six months of the war of 1914–18 Keyes was responsible for operating submarines in the North Sea and adjacent waters, being frequently afloat, and flying his broad pennant in a destroyer. On 28 August 1914, when conducting an operation in the Heligoland Bight in conjunction with the Harwich Force under (Sir) Reginald Tyrwhitt, he found himself in the presence of greatly superior enemy forces. The position was restored on the arrival of Sir David (later Earl) Beatty commanding the battle cruiser squadron. For his part in this action, known as the battle of the Heligoland Bight, Keyes, who rescued 220 of the crew of the German cruiser *Mainz*, was mentioned in dispatches. He also in December 1914 received from the Admiralty an appreciation of his services during a seaplane attack on Cuxhaven.

During his six months in command of submarines Keyes had earned the reputation of being a fearless and inspired leader who never missed an opportunity of striking at the enemy. In February 1915 he became chief of staff to (Sir) Sackville Carden in command of the squadron operating off the Dardanelles, and a month later chief of staff to (Sir) John De Robeck when, owing to Carden's ill health, De Robeck assumed command of the Dardanelles operations. In the planning of the naval operations and for the army landings Keyes took a prominent part. The great attempt to force the Narrows on 18 March ended in a severe defeat. By October it was evident that the army could make no headway against the stubborn Turkish defence and General Sir Charles Monro advised evacuation, but Keyes pressed De Robeck to make another attempt to force the Narrows. De Robeck considered the risks involved out of all proportion to the gain even if it attained the highest degree of success which could be expected, but the matter was of such capital importance that he sent Keyes home to lay the plan before the Admiralty. The Government then requested Lord Kitchener to go out in person and report on the situation. As a result of Kitchener's report the operations were abandoned and the army was evacuated. For his services during the campaign Keyes was twice mentioned in dispatches, appointed to the D.S.O., and made a C.M.G. and commander of the French Legion of Honour.

From June 1916 to June 1917 Keyes was in command of the *Centurion*, battleship in the Grand Fleet, and on promotion to rear-admiral was appointed to the fourth battle squadron with his flag in the battleship *Colossus*. In October 1917 he became director of plans at the Admiralty. At this period of the war the German Admiralty was concentrating all its efforts on the submarine campaign, which was showing promise of gaining the victory at sea as the British counter-measures were failing to stem the heavy losses on the trade routes. If the passage of the Straits of Dover and the use of Ostend and Zeebrugge could be denied to the submarines the German campaign would be seriously hampered; and it was to these projects that Keyes turned his attention as soon as he arrived at the Admiralty. By December he had prepared plans for a barrage across the Straits and for blocking the two bases. In January 1918 he was appointed vice-admiral, Dover Patrol, in succession to Sir Reginald Bacon to implement the plans which he had prepared; thus began the most notable period of his naval service.

Keyes

Keyes now proved himself a master of narrow-seas warfare; the officers and men of the patrol were soon aware that a leader had appeared who would make great demands on them, but would never spare himself and would be afloat whenever there was a chance of meeting the enemy. After strengthening the barrage across the Straits and introducing many devices for deterring the German submarines from attempting the passage, Keyes turned his attention to his most cherished project: of blockading Ostend and Zeebrugge. For the defence of the entrances to these ports the Germans had mounted powerful batteries, and unless these batteries were silenced it would not be possible to sink blockships in accurate positions. For Zeebrugge, Keyes's plan may be summarized as follows: under cover of smoke, the old cruiser *Vindictive* and the Mersey ferry-boats, *Daffodil* and *Iris*, were to proceed alongside the mole and land a storming party of marines and bluejackets who would put the German batteries out of action; an old submarine, loaded with explosives, was to be blown up under the viaduct leading to the mole, so as to prevent reinforcements being sent. Meanwhile three old cruisers were to pass down the other side of the mole and sink themselves in the canal entrance, the crews being taken off by coastal craft. At Ostend, where there was no mole, two old cruisers were to be sunk under cover of smoke screens.

This operation, perhaps the most elaborate ever undertaken by the British navy up to that time, demanded the finest seamanship and fighting qualities, and all vessels taking part were manned by volunteers. On 22 April Keyes led his force to sea, and by midnight the *Vindictive* was approaching the mole. Despite heavy casualties, the plan for Zeebrugge was carried out in its entirety, but at Ostend, owing to a buoy having been moved, the blockships did not reach their positions. A second attempt at Ostend, using the *Vindictive* as blockship, also failed.

The Germans cleared the Zeebrugge channel in a few hours, but the audacity of the operation, and the superb courage of all who took part in it, attracted worldwide attention and admiration. Keyes was promoted to K.C.B. on the day after the attack, and he also received the French croix de guerre, and was appointed grand officer of the Legion of Honour and grand cross of the Order of Leopold. Until the end of the war Keyes conducted an unremitting offensive with monitors, destroyers, and coastal craft against the enemy established on the Belgian coast. He was mentioned in dispatches and received the American D.S.M. In December he was appointed K.C.V.O. and in the list of peace awards he was created a baronet and received a grant of £10,000.

In March 1919 Keyes was appointed to command the battle cruiser squadron and after hauling down his flag in 1921 he was transferred to the

Admiralty as deputy chief of the naval staff, having been promoted to vice-admiral in May. One of the chief tasks before him was to arrive at an agreement with the Air Ministry on the administration of the Naval Air Service. It was placed under the dual control of the two departments and the compromise agreement on their respective tasks reached in 1924 remained in force until 1937. In May 1925 Keyes became commander-in-chief, Mediterranean Fleet, a year later being promoted to admiral. He held this appointment for the customary three years and in April 1929 he was appointed commander-in-chief, Portsmouth. In May 1930 he was promoted to admiral of the fleet, and in June to G.C.B. A year later he relinquished his command and in May 1935 he was placed on the retired list.

Even before his retirement Keyes had turned his attention to politics and at a by-election in 1934 he was elected Conservative member of Parliament for North Portsmouth. He had no oratorical gifts, but when he spoke on naval affairs his sincerity, knowledge, and experience won the attention of the House.

When war broke out again in 1939, Keyes was nearly sixty-seven, but he was still young in heart and physique, and he at once sought active service. In the debate of 7 May 1940 in the House of Commons which led to the resignation of Neville Chamberlain he took a prominent part, strongly criticizing the naval staff for mishandling the Norwegian campaign. Three days later he joined King Leopold III of Belgium, whose army was deployed to stem the German westward advance. As liaison officer he was with the King during all the fierce fighting which ended on 27 May when the King asked the Germans for an armistice. When in Parliament and in the press the Belgian King's conduct was sharply criticized Keyes constantly championed his cause.

In June 1940 (Sir) Winston Churchill proposed that units of officers and men should be selected from existing units to be trained as storm troops or 'leopards'. Eventually they emerged as the famous 'Commandos'. Keyes, in July, was made the first director of a new and separate Combined Operations Command for the study of these operations, for which his experience of inshore operations fitted him well. The chief object of study was raids on the enemy coast by bodies of between five and ten thousand men, and also the supervision of the training of the personnel needed for these raids. Keyes thus became the officer responsible for the training and equipment of the first Commandos, but in October 1941 his appointment was terminated. In the months which followed he attacked the Government in the House of Commons for failing to use the Commandos to the best advantage, criticized the workers in the dockyards and shipyards, and pressed for industrial conscription.

In January 1943 Keyes was raised to the peerage as Baron Keyes, of Zeebrugge and of Dover, and in the summer of 1944 he set out on a lecture tour of Canada, the United States, Australia, and New Zealand, under the auspices of the minister of information; at the invitation of the commander-in-chief of the American Pacific Fleet, he was present at the battle of the Philippines in October 1944.

Thus almost to the very end of his life (if only as a spectator) Keyes was in the midst of a hot fight. He died at Buckingham 26 December 1945, and was buried in the Zeebrugge corner of St. James's cemetery at Dover. A plaque, set in the wall of the Nelson chamber of the crypt of St. Paul's Cathedral, commemorates him and his elder son.

Keyes married in 1906 Eva Mary Salvin, daughter of Edward Salvin Bowlby, of Gilston Park, Hertfordshire, and Knoydart, Inverness-shire, by whom he had two sons and three daughters. His elder son, Lieutenant-Colonel Geoffrey Charles Tasker Keyes, Scots Greys, was killed while leading a Commando raid on General Rommel's headquarters in Libya on 18 November 1941, and was posthumously awarded the Victoria Cross. The title passed to Roger George Bowlby (born 1919), Keyes's younger son, then a lieutenant, Royal Navy.

In *Naval Memoirs* (2 vols., 1934–5), *Adventures Ashore and Afloat* (1939), *The Fight for Gallipoli* (1941), and *Amphibious Warfare and Combined Operations* (1943) Keyes put on record his experiences and his conclusions. He received the honorary degrees of D.C.L. from the university of Oxford and LL.D. from Cambridge, Aberdeen, St. Andrews, and Bristol. From 1932 to 1943 he was honorary colonel commandant of the Portsmouth division of the Royal Marines, in whose officers' mess at Eastney there hangs his portrait by P. A. de László. Another portrait by the same artist is in the possession of the family; one by Glyn Philpot is in the Imperial War Museum, where there is also a drawing by Francis Dodd. Keyes is also included in Sir A. S. Cope's group 'Some Sea Officers of the War of 1914–18' in the National Portrait Gallery.

It was Keyes's complete lack of fear and his gift for drawing whole-hearted service from his officers and men which fitted him so well for the inshore operations and narrow-seas warfare with which his name will always be associated. His eagerness to strike at the enemy was not always tempered with good judgement; his plan for a second attempt to force the Dardanelles and some of his plans for utilizing the Commandos, although bold and imaginative, may have held little promise of success or of making a definite contribution to final victory; but had the plans been approved, he would have been in the forefront of the battle.

A place in history is assured for him not only for the planning and execution of the raids on Zeebrugge and Ostend, but also for his conduct of the Dover Command during a critical period of the war of 1914–18.

[Keyes's own writings; *The Times,* 27 December 1945; C. F. Aspinall-Oglander, *Roger Keyes,* 1951; private information; personal knowledge.]

W. M. JAMES

published 1959

KITCHENER Horatio Herbert

(1850–1916)

First Earl Kitchener, of Khartoum and of Broome

Field-marshal, the second son of Lieutenant-Colonel Henry Horatio Kitchener, of Cossington, Leicestershire, and Crotter House, Ballylongford, co. Kerry, by his first wife, Anne Frances, daughter of the Rev. John Chevallier, M.D., vicar of Aspall, Suffolk, was born at Crotter House 24 June 1850. Colonel Kitchener before settling in Ireland had served in the 13th Dragoons and 9th Foot. Owing to the illness of Mrs. Kitchener the family moved, when Herbert was thirteen years old, to Switzerland, where he was educated in a French school and acquired a knowledge of the French language which he never afterwards lost. In 1868 he passed into the Royal Military Academy, Woolwich, and passed out in December 1870, having qualified for a commission in the Royal Engineers. It was at this time, while he was waiting for the gazette, that the French, fired by Gambetta's eloquence, were attempting to create new armies to resist the Germans and to relieve Paris, their regular forces having been almost completely destroyed. Kitchener's parents were living at the time at Dinan, and his affection for France inspired him to offer his services to the army of the Loire. His time with it was short, for he fell ill, but it was remembered by the French Republic, which in 1913 conferred on him the medal commemorative of the campaign. On his return to England he was reprimanded by the commander-in-chief, the Duke of Cambridge, for a breach of discipline, but none the less he received his commission in the Royal Engineers (1871). After a few years of routine service at home, he was lent in 1874 to the Palestine Exploration Fund, and so began a connexion with the East which was to last almost for the remainder of his life. His work in Palestine enabled him to acquire a sound knowledge of the Arabs and of their language, and at the same time his exploration of the Holy Land developed the religious bent in a mind naturally devout.

Kitchener

Kitchener's sympathies were then, and remained throughout his life, with the high church party of the Church of England; and though never either a zealot or a bigot he was always a convinced and professing Christian. In 1878, when Great Britain acquired Cyprus under the Treaty of Berlin, Kitchener was sent to survey the island. The work was broken off for lack of funds, to be resumed in 1880; he spent the interval as vice-consul at Kastamuni in Asia Minor.

In 1882, when the Egyptian army under Arabi Pasha rebelled, Kitchener was naturally eager to join the expedition under Sir Garnet (afterwards Viscount) Wolseley. The high commissioner of Cyprus said that he could not be spared; but, obtaining short leave of absence, he went to Alexandria and was able to take a small and entirely unofficial part in the campaign. He and another officer disguised themselves as Levantines and reconnoitred the route up the Nile valley from Alexandria towards Cairo, this being the first of a long series of such adventures which he was later to undertake. On his return to Cyprus after the enterprise he had some difficulty in placating the high commissioner. At the end of 1882 the survey of Cyprus was nearly completed, and Kitchener then accepted from Sir Henry Evelyn Wood, who had been appointed first British sirdar of the Egyptian army, the offer of the post of second in command of the Egyptian cavalry. In 1883 he devoted two months' leave to a survey of the Sinai Peninsula, which he linked up with his survey of Palestine. In the following year the insurrection of the Sudanese under the Mahdi assumed serious proportions, and Kitchener was sent up the Nile to the frontier of Egypt proper, to endeavour to establish communication with Berber, which was besieged by the Mahdists. Berber surrendered 20 May 1884, and the men on the spot at once realized the gravity of the situation. Kitchener said that it would take 20,000 British troops to crush the Mahdi, but the home government shuddered at the thought of so serious an enterprise. Kitchener's task on the frontier then became that of endeavouring to establish communications with Khartoum, in which General Gordon was shut up, and to confirm the allegiance of wavering Mudirs. This work involved many adventurous rides into the desert, often in disguise. It was not until August that the British government took the step of sending an expedition up the Nile, too late as it proved, to relieve Gordon. Throughout this expedition Kitchener served in Wolseley's intelligence department, and in that capacity guided across the Bayuda desert the ill-fated column under Sir Herbert Stewart. It fell to him to receive the first refugees from Khartoum and to send up the first authoritative report of Gordon's death (26 January 1885). In July 1885 Kitchener resigned his commission in the Egyptian army and returned to England. He was now a brevet lieutenant-colonel with an established reputation as an authority on the habits and customs of the Arabs, Sudanese, and Egyptians, and as a keen, hard-working, and able soldier. After a short spell of leave at home he was nominated, at the request of the Foreign Office, as the British member of a joint English, French, and German commission appointed at the close of 1885 to delimit the territory of the sultan of Zanzibar, a work made necessary by the general scramble of the European powers for territory in Africa, which was then in full course.

On his way home from East Africa in the summer of 1886, Kitchener received the news of his appointment as governor-general of the Eastern Sudan, with head-quarters at Suakin; this post he held till 1888. Here he was in constant conflict with Osman Digna, the local leader of the Dervishes, and on 17 January 1888 he was severely wounded in the jaw in a raid on that chief's head-quarters. For his work at Suakin he was made brevet colonel and aide-de-camp to Queen Victoria. After his recovery he was appointed in September adjutant-general of the Egyptian army, of which Sir Francis (afterwards Baron) Grenfell was then sirdar. In the summer of 1889 the Dervishes threatened an advance down the Nile into Egypt, and a considerable part of the Egyptian army was concentrated to meet them, Kitchener being given the command of the cavalry. On 2 August Grenfell heavily defeated the Dervishes at Toski, a success in which Kitchener's handling of the cavalry had no small part, and all fear of an invasion of Egypt was removed. For his services in this campaign Kitchener received the C.B. Then, at the request of Sir Evelyn Baring (afterwards Earl of Cromer), Kitchener undertook the reorganization of the Egyptian police, and acquired Baring's confidence to such an extent that, when Grenfell resigned the sirdarship (April 1892), Baring pressed for and obtained Kitchener's appointment as his successor. Kitchener had always maintained that the only possible solution of the problem of the Nile valley was to advance into the Sudan and to defeat the Dervishes; and for the next four years he devoted himself to the preparation of the Egyptian army for that task. He attracted to the service of that army a body of young, able, and energetic British officers, before whom he set, both by example and precept, a high standard of keenness and enterprise. With their help he infused a new spirit into the Egyptian Army, the fighting power of which had been materially increased by the formation of battalions of Sudanese. Kitchener's reforms were not always pleasing to the pashas, who intrigued against him with the khedive, but he was now sufficiently acquainted with the methods of Eastern courts to be able to forestall these manœuvres, and he found in Lord Cromer an un-wavering ally. He was created K.C.M.G. in 1894. The preparations for the conquest of the Sudan revived the old controversy as to the rival merits of the desert and the Nile routes, but Kitchener obtained the approval of the home government for his plan of a methodical advance up the river.

In 1896 the River War was inaugurated by an advance on Dongola, the first stage of which was completed by the defeat of a Dervish force at Firket on 7 June. By the end of September Dongola was occupied and the Dervishes had been driven from the province of that name into the Bayuda desert. Kitchener was now promoted major-general and for his services in this campaign was created K.C.B. The winter of 1896–1897 and the following spring were spent in persuading the home government to agree to a further advance, and in making preparations for that end. The plan on which Kitchener had decided was first to move up the Nile and secure Abu Hamed, where the river bends westward to make a great loop round the Korosko desert, and then to build a railway across that desert from Wadi Halfa. The first of these undertakings was entrusted to Major-General Sir Archibald Hunter, who seized Abu Hamed with small loss on 7 August, and thereby created such a panic amongst the Dervishes that, to the general surprise and delight, he was able on 5 September without opposition to occupy Berber, which had been seized by friendly tribesmen on 31 August. These successes brought the reoccupation of Khartoum and the complete reconquest of the Sudan within reach; and the British Cabinet, and Lord Salisbury in particular—converted to reliance on Kitchener's judgement—promised him for the following year the support of British troops and the leadership in the last stage of the enterprise. By the end of January 1898 the greater part of the Egyptian army, with a British brigade under Major-General Sir William Forbes Gatacre, was concentrated south of Berber, near the mouth of the Atbara river. The successor of the Mahdi, the Khalifa Abdullah, now thoroughly alarmed at Omdurman, sent a force of 20,000 men under Mahmud, his leading emir, to recapture Berber; but Mahmud, finding that Kitchener had so far anticipated him on the Atbara as to make a march on Berber impossible without fighting, established his army in a strong zariba on the river. The zariba was stormed by the combined Anglo-Egyptian force on 8 April, Mahmud himself was captured with 4,000 other prisoners, and his army dispersed.

The British government had for some time been aware that a small French expedition under Major Marchand had started from the Congo for the White Nile; and this fact, together with the completeness of the success won on the Atbara, decided the Cabinet to authorize an advance on Omdurman at the next high Nile, and to increase the British force under Kitchener to the strength of a division. By the end of August 8,200 British and 17,000 Egyptian troops were concentrated under Kitchener's command at the head of the Sixth Cataract, about 120 miles north of Omdurman. The greater part of this distance was covered without opposition, and by 1 September the whole force was assembled on the Nile some seven miles north of Omdurman, to find a Dervish army of 50,000 men, under the Khalifa himself, encamped in the plain between it and the Dervish capital. The battle of Omdurman, which took place on 2 September, was fought in two phases. In the first the Dervishes in a determined advance upon the Anglo-Egyptian troops, who were in position on the river bank, were mowed down by artillery, rifle, and machine-gun fire. Kitchener then ordered an advance on Omdurman, and during this movement the Khalifa's reserve attacked the first Egyptian brigade under Colonel (Sir) Hector Archibald Macdonald, and the situation, which was for a time critical, was saved by the steadiness of the brigade and the prompt arrival of support from the British division. Organized resistance then ceased and the Dervish army was dispersed with enormous loss. The Khalifa fled to Kordofan; and on 4 September the British and Egyptian flags were hoisted over the ruins of Gordon's palace in Khartoum, which for twelve years had been Kitchener's goal. The next step was to convince Major Marchand, who with seven French officers and eighty native troops had arrived at Fashoda, that he could not hoist the French flag in the khedive's do-minions. For this purpose Kitchener went with an escort up the White Nile. The interview was conducted with perfect courtesy and the Egyptian flag was hoisted over Fashoda with the customary salute. After a fierce but brief outburst of popular wrath in France, the French government gave way, and the last serious incident with France which preceded the *entente cordiale* was amicably settled.

Kitchener then came home to be received with great enthusiasm. He had wiped out the unpleasant memory of the sacrifice of Gordon, and had removed an outstanding menace to Egypt, at the cost of 60 British and 160 Egyptian lives. He was hailed by Lord Salisbury as not only a distinguished general but a first-class administrator. He was raised to the peerage as Baron Kitchener, of Khartoum, received the thanks of parliament, and was fêted in England, Scotland, and Wales. The first use which he made of his popularity was to raise a fund for the establishment and endowment of a college at Khartoum, which should at once perpetuate Gordon's memory and fulfil one of Gordon's plans for the benefit of the Sudan. He returned as governor-general of the Sudan, with sufficient money for that purpose and with the task of creating a civil administration for the country. Throughout the River War Kitchener's part had been rather that of a brilliant improviser of ways and means than of a commander in the field or of a profound student of war. He had left most of the fighting to Hunter, though he was present himself at the principal actions, and his triumph was one of firmness of purpose and of driving power in the face of great natural difficulties. In the light of the subsequent collapse of Mahdism it is easy to underrate his achievement; but up to the time of the final advance on Omdurman the Dervishes were a name of terror, and it required courage, character, and judgement of a high degree to persuade a government, rendered doubtful and cautious by previous failures, to authorize the successive steps which led to the overthrow of the Khalifa.

The greater part of the year 1899 was devoted to completing the pacification of the Sudan, and to hunting down the Khalifa, who was at large in Kordofan with a dwindling band of followers. This last task was brought to an end by Sir Reginald Wingate, who was destined to be Kitchener's successor as sirdar, on 22 November when the Khalifa was killed in a final stand. Within a month of this event Kitchener was called to other and more important duties.

The critical weeks which followed the outbreak of the South African War in October 1899, culminating in the second week of December in the successive reverses of Stormberg, Magersfontein, and Colenso, made both the government and the public realize that a struggle with the Boers was a serious matter. The decisions, therefore, to send large reinforcements to South Africa and to appoint Lord Roberts to the chief command with Kitchener as his chief of the staff were received with general approval. Kitchener was at Khartoum on 18 December when he received his orders, and, starting at once, was able to join Lord Roberts at Gibraltar on 27 December. During Roberts's command Kitchener rarely performed the functions of chief of the staff. He was employed far more as a second in command and the representative of the commander-in-chief in his absence, so that his duties were executive rather than advisory, and he had very free scope for the employment of his limitless energy and readiness to accept responsibility. His first business was to reorganize the transport, and to make that increase in the number of mounted troops which was needed to give the force the mobility required for the execution of Roberts's plans. When, early in February, the movement for the relief of Kimberley had begun and General Piet Cronje had retreated from Magersfontein, Kitchener was with the leading troops urging on the pursuit, and not at Lord Roberts's side. So when Cronje was forced to stand at Paardeberg, it was Kitchener, with full powers from the commander-in-chief in his pocket, who ordered the attack and directed the operations. The first attack (18 February) on Cronje's laager failed, and failed largely because of Kitchener's faulty tactical dispositions. He had with him only a small personal staff and could not effectively direct the movements of a considerable body of troops scattered over a wide area. Methods applicable to troops in the close formation used in the Sudan against ill-armed natives were not suited to the wide extensions necessary against a determined enemy armed with modern rifles. The attacks were therefore disconnected and were repulsed in succession. Kitchener wished to renew them the next day, but Roberts arrived and decided to blockade the laager instead. There can be no doubt that Kitchener's original decision to attack was right, and it is highly probable that a new and better-arranged attack on the laager on the day following the battle would not only have been successful but would have been less costly than the direct and consequential losses of the blockade, while the time gained might have been of great value. The incident is indeed typical of Kitchener's character and career. His judgement on larger issues was almost always uncannily correct, and he never lacked the courage to put his judgement to the test. His failures were generally due to a lack of knowledge of technical detail, and to a dislike, amounting almost to contempt, of deliberate methods, which he was disposed to regard as red tape. He was accused, but with injustice, of callousness and disregard for the lives of his men. His natural shyness and reserve, accentuated by years of solitary work in the East, made him almost incapable of expressing deep feeling; but he was essentially tender-hearted, and certainly not lacking in consideration for the soldier.

Five days before the surrender of Cronje at Paardeberg (27 February), Kitchener was sent by Roberts to open up railway communications across the Orange river towards Bloemfontein, and was next employed in suppressing a rebellion of the Cape Boers about Priska, and in clearing the southern portion of the Orange Free State. Everywhere he went he endeavoured to infuse the spirit of energy which he had inculcated in Egypt, but found sadly lacking in South Africa, where he said the War was taken 'too much like a game of polo with intervals for afternoon tea'. During Roberts's advance through Pretoria to Koomati Poort, Kitchener varied intervals of office work at head-quarters with expeditions to clear the lines of communication from the Boer raiders, who were becoming increasingly numerous and were usually led by that bold and enterprising leader of guerrillas, Christian De Wet. In one of these Kitchener was all but captured in a night surprise, and had to ride for his life. In November 1900 Roberts's forces had reached the frontiers of Portuguese East Africa; President Kruger had fled, and organized resistance seemed to be at an end. Lord Roberts therefore came home, and Kitchener was left as commander-in-chief to wind up the campaign.

It soon appeared that De Wet had taught the Boers the possibilities of guerrilla warfare, and that the War was far from over. Kitchener met these tactics of the Boers by employing an elaboration of the methods which he had already used in the Orange Free State. Lines of block-houses were established criss-cross through the country, and a series of drives by mounted troops, starting from these barriers, was organized against the guerrillas. This was a slow and wearisome business. Again and again the elusive Boers avoided the mounted columns and broke through the barriers; but gradually, and after many failures, the resistance of the Boers was worn down. One feature in this scheme of subjugation provoked much criticism. The Boers were without any organized systems of supply, and every farm was for them a depot. Flocks and herds were therefore removed, grain was carted away or destroyed, and farms were gutted. This made it necessary to provide for the Boer women and children, who were assembled in concentration camps where sickness soon became prevalent and the rate of mortality was for a time very high. This sickness could not, in fact, be ascribed to any neglect on the part of the British authorities, but the result was that sympathisers with the Boers were provided with apparent grounds for agitation. Moreover, the plan almost certainly had the adverse effect of prolonging the enemy's resistance by relieving the Boers in the field of the responsibility of caring for their dependants. In June 1901 there appeared to be some prospect that the Free State and Transvaal would surrender, but the waverers were rallied by an appeal from Kruger to hold out, and by a series of risings in the Cape Colony, ably led by General Johannes Smuts. But, as in Egypt, Kitchener, having formed his plan, adhered to it, and continued to multiply lines of block-houses, and to organize drives. The end did not come till 31 May 1902, and was then reached largely because of Kitchener's moderating influence upon the terms which Lord Milner, the high commissioner, desired to impose. On his return to England in July Kitchener received a viscountcy, with special remainder, and became one of the original members of the order of merit.

After a few months' rest Kitchener left England in October to take up the post of commander-in-chief in India, breaking his voyage in order to go to Khartoum and open the Gordon Memorial College. The distribution of troops in India had not been varied materially since the reorganization which followed the Mutiny, and the system of military administration was in many ways too much centralized. Kitchener had little difficulty in gaining official acceptance of his plans for removing many of the details of army administration from headquarters to the commands, and for arranging a grouping of the garrisons more in accordance with the existing problems of the defence of India, and better calculated to promote the health and efficiency of the troops. But in his attempts to improve the higher administration of the army in India he encountered serious obstacles. He found in Lord Curzon a masterful viceroy convinced of the necessity of making the civil power predominant, and suspicious of any measures that had the appearance of increasing the authority of the soldier. The existing system provided for a military member of the viceroy's council, independent of the commander-in-chief. He had what amounted to the power of vetoing any proposal of the commander-in-chief which involved expenditure. Kitchener, while recognizing the importance of maintaining the supreme authority of the viceroy, urged the abolition of the system of dual control in a long controversy, in which his arguments prevailed with Mr. (afterwards Viscount) Morley, then secretary-of-state for India. As commander-in-chief he initiated more reforms than any of his predecessors, not excepting even Lord Roberts, who had the advantage of a lifelong knowledge of the Indian army. Kitchener not only succeeded in improving the central administration and the machinery for mobilization, but he also modernized the system of training, and gave a great stimulus to military education by establishing a Staff College in India. It is certain that without the reforms which he instituted India could not have given the Empire the assistance which she furnished during the European War.

On leaving India in September 1909, Kitchener was promoted field-marshal, and after a visit to the battlefields of the Russo-Japanese War, went to Australia and New Zealand to advise the dominion governments as to their organization for defence. He reached England in 1910 in order to receive the field-marshal's baton from the hands of King Edward VII. He then enjoyed some fifteen months of comparative leisure, broken only by his duties as a member of the Committee of Imperial Defence; and he profited by this to visit Turkey and the Sudan and to make a tour through British East Africa. In September 1911 he was appointed British agent and consul-general in Egypt. The prestige of that position had not unnaturally fallen somewhat with the departure of Lord Cromer, but Kitchener almost immediately succeeded in restoring it to its former height. The best tribute to his administration is that, during a period of great unrest in the Near East, when Turkey was engaged in two wars, it was uneventful. He succeeded in keeping Egypt quiet, and was able to devote himself almost entirely to social reforms, and to developing the commerce and resources of the country. The British government showed its gratitude by advising the King to confer on him an earldom, which he received in July 1914. He then returned to England for his annual holiday. When, a month later, war with Germany became imminent, he was on the point of returning to his post, but on 3 August he was recalled from Dover by Mr. Asquith in order to take over the seals of the secretary-of-state for war.

There was no other man then alive who, as head of the War Office, could have commanded so much of the confidence of the public, and that was in itself sufficient reason for Kitchener's appointment; nor was there anyone who had such first-hand knowledge of the military resources of the Empire as a whole. Within recent years he had examined on the spot the military problems of Egypt, India, Australia, New Zealand, Singapore, and East Africa, and from that knowledge the Empire was to reap great benefit. The gaps in his equipment were that he had little experience of the organization of the army at home, and none at all of the methods and machinery of the War Office, or of the system of Cabinet government; but there was more than compensation for these drawbacks in the fact that he entered the War Office fully conscious of the magnitude of the problem before the nation, and of the lamentable deficiencies in the preparations which had been made to meet that problem. Both soldiers and statesmen, in making plans for the event of war with Germany, conceived a struggle in which England should give full naval, but limited military, support to France; and the general conviction was that the complexity of modern international relations, more especially in the realm of finance, made a long war impossible. Of the statesmen and soldiers of Europe Kitchener alone envisaged from the first a war which would last three years, and he alone believed in the possibility of raising and putting in the field large new armies during the War. On entering the War Office he immediately made plans for the expansion of the British army of six regular and fourteen territorial divisions to seventy divisions; and it is not too much to say that this provision not only saved the British Empire from destruction, but Europe from German domination. It is probably true that the expansion of the British army could have been carried through more smoothly and expeditiously by expanding the territorial army than by creating new armies; but Kitchener was not familiar with the effect of Lord Haldane's work upon the territorial army, and his experience in South Africa led him to distrust the influence of county magnates in the formation of new units, while it is also probable that he was to some extent led away by his taste for improvisation. The fact remains that he brought his plans to completion, and in the third year of the War he had seventy divisions either in, or ready for, the field, an achievement which no one in 1914 had believed to be possible. When the public learned in May 1915 that the British forces in France were severely hampered by the lack of high explosive shell, Kitchener was made the target of a bitter attack in a section of the press. The Ministry of Munitions and the systematic mobilization of industry for the manufacture of munitions which resulted therefrom were very necessary additions to the machinery for the conduct of the War; but no arrangements could have made up in the early part of 1915 for the lack of provision for the manufacture of high explosive shells and guns before the War, and until April 1916 the armies in the field were entirely supplied with shell under contracts made by Kitchener in the War Office. Munitions could not be improvised, nor very speedily manufactured, but in all other respects no armies in the field were ever better provided with what was needed both for efficiency and for comfort; this was made possible by Kitchener's immediate anticipation both of the length and of the extent of the War.

The newspaper attacks did not affect the confidence of the public in Kitchener, and the King's action in conferring on him the order of the Garter in June 1915 was widely approved. But at this time the relations of the war minister with some of his colleagues in the Cabinet were becoming strained, and as the difficulties of the war increased these relations did not tend to become more happy. Kitchener had from the first, and retained to the last, the confidence of Mr. Asquith; but, from the formation of the first coalition in May 1915, Mr. Asquith's influence declined, and other members of the government became anxious to know more about the conduct of the War, and to have a more active share in it. Kitchener's fine presence, his European reputation, his command of the French language, and his proved sympathy with France, made him an admirable negotiator. He was instrumental in smoothing over many of the early difficulties of the alliance, notably at the end of August 1914, when the enforced retreat of the British army after the battle of Le Cateau caused grave anxiety both to the French government and to the French commander-in-chief. But these qualities had not much influence with his colleagues in the Cabinet, where his natural reticence, his lack of experience of work in committee, and his inability to throw his ideas into the common stock, raised suspicions, usually groundless, but hard to meet. Nor was his administration of the War Office happy. He did not understand the methods of a government department, and most of the soldiers who were familiar with them had gone to France with the Expeditionary Force. This led to his taking too much work upon himself, and he became at one and the same time the adviser of the Cabinet on strategy and the organizer of an immense expansion of the British army. His methods often lacked system, and not infrequently produced friction; while, for lack of competent advice and of time for due consideration, his conduct of the strategy of the War was more than once open to criticism, though he was often right when others were wrong. Just as he foresaw the length of the War, so he foresaw also that the Germans would march through Belgium north of the Meuse in great strength, and soon after he entered the War Office he pointed out that the British army at Mons would be in an exposed and dangerous position. He deferred, however, to the opinion of the French and British soldiers who had prepared the plans of campaign. But, when the plans for attacking the Dardanelles were under discussion, he allowed himself to be influenced by those who believed that the navy could force the Straits unaided, and he was dragged into the military operations in circumstances which greatly prejudiced their success. Throughout this unfortunate campaign he was torn in divergent directions, on the one hand by his desire with limited means to sustain the British armies in France, and on the other by the need of prosecuting with vigour the attack upon the Straits. Thus there were at times hesitation and doubt when there should have been vigour and decision. When the failure of the Dardanelles campaign was evident, the government, some members of which were not reluctant to be relieved of his presence, sent him to the Near East to report on the possibility and advisability of evacuation. Reluctantly he came to the conclusion that the only course was to abandon the enterprise, and he returned to England at the end of November 1915 to advise the Cabinet to that effect. On his arrival he tendered to the prime minister his resignation, which was at once refused. He was now fully conscious of the defects in the administrative machinery at the War Office; and at the end of the year he brought Major-General Sir William Robertson from France to be chief of the Imperial General Staff, gave him greater powers than former chiefs of the staff had possessed, and authorized him to reorganize the general staff at head-quarters. Thenceforward there was little creaking of the wheels of military administration, though it was many months before the effect of the change could be seen, and Kitchener himself did not live to see it. On the morning of 5 June 1916 he sailed from Scapa Flow in H.M.S. *Hampshire* to visit Russia. The Russian government had long been anxious for his presence and advice; the British government hoped through his influence to revive the waning enthusiasm of the Russian armies, and to establish some method of co-operation between the Allied armies of Eastern and Western Europe. The circumstances of the loss of the *Hampshire* are not absolutely clear, but it appears that the cruiser, when off the Orkneys in bad weather, struck a mine and went down with the loss of all on board save a few of the crew [*The Loss of H.M.S. 'Hampshire'. Official Narrative*, 1926.].

The news of Kitchener's death was received with universal mourning and was treated as a public calamity of the first magnitude; a memorial service was held in St. Paul's Cathedral, where a chapel, in the north-west tower, is dedicated to his memory. Though his countrymen felt deeply the extent of their loss, the great work with which Kitchener's name will always be associated was in a measure completed. At his call and under his inspiration, more than 3,000,000 men had voluntarily joined the colours and had been organized into armies, an achievement without parallel in history. On the very day on which he left for Russia the last of the divisions to which his name was given by the public also sailed from England. He had planned that the British armies in France should be at their greatest strength in the third year of the War, and he hoped that victory would be achieved in that year. He adhered to that plan with the same resolution which had brought him to Khartoum, and had ended the South African War. The British armies in France did reach their highest strength in 1917, and it is at least within the bounds of probability that had he lived he would have prevented some of those divided councils and divergences of purpose which contributed to the prolongation of the War into 1918.

Kitchener never married, and, in accordance with the special remainder, his brother, Colonel Henry Elliott Chevallier Kitchener, succeeded as second Earl.

A portrait of Kitchener was painted by Sir H. von Herkomer in 1891 against a background of Egyptian architecture executed by F. Goodall; this picture was presented to the National Portrait Gallery by Mr. Pandeli Ralli in 1916. There is also in the same gallery a portrait in pastel executed by C. Horsfall in 1899, and presented in 1916 by Sir Lees Knowles. There are other portraits by Sir A. S. Cope (1900) and the Hon. John Collier. A bronze bust by Sir William Goscombe John, is placed in the Gordon Memorial College at Khartoum; another, in marble, by Sir Hamo Thornycroft, was sculptured in 1917. The full-length effigy in marble executed in 1923 for the monument in St. Paul's Cathedral is by W. Read Dick. A statue by John Tweed was erected on the Horse Guards Parade in 1926. (See *Royal Academy Pictures* 1891, 1900, 1917, and 1923.)

[W. S. Churchill, *The River War*, 1899; Sir J. F. Maurice and M. H. Grant, (Official) *History of the War in South Africa, 1899–1902*, 1906–1910; Sir George Arthur, *Life of Lord Kitchener*, 1920.]

FREDERICK MAURICE

published 1927

KNOX (Alfred) Dillwyn

(1884–1943)

Classical scholar and cryptographer, was born 23 July 1884 in Oxford, the fourth of six children (four sons and two daughters) of the Revd Edmund Arbuthnott Knox, a tutor at Merton College (later bishop of Manchester) and his first wife, Ellen Penelope, daughter of Thomas Valpy French, bishop of Lahore. By any standards his family was remarkable, with the evangelical father and Dillwyn's three brothers: 'Evoe', for seventeen years editor of *Punch*, Wilfred, an Anglo-Catholic priest, and Ronald, Roman Catholic priest and translator of the Bible. Ellen Knox died in 1892 but three years later Edmund Knox remarried.

'Dilly', as he was called, went to Summer Fields, Oxford, at the age of eleven and after a year was first in his election to Eton. He went to King's College, Cambridge, in 1903 as a scholar. He obtained a first class in part i

(1906) and a second (division I) in part ii (1907) of the classical tripos. A friend of G. Lytton Strachey and J. Maynard (later Baron) Keynes, he was not an 'Apostle' himself, although his name was put forward for election to the society. He was greatly influenced by Walter Headlam and inspired by his great love and knowledge of Greek literature. When Knox became a fellow of King's in 1909 he inherited the then deceased Headlam's work on Herodas and applied himself to the fragmentary texts of the Herodas papyri in the British Museum. The inconsequential and bawdy mimes proved difficult to unravel but Knox was determined to succeed, exercising on them the scholarship combined with inspired guesswork which was to be his forte in his future career. Like his brothers, he was addicted to puzzles and a devotee of Lewis Carroll (Charles L. Dodgson,). The sort of question he was apt to ask, 'Which way does a clock go round?', was pure Carroll.

Soon after war broke out in 1914 he was asked to join ID 25, the department of naval intelligence known as Room 40, as a cryptographer. By 1917 he had succeeded in breaking much of the German admirals' flag code, detecting, with his ear for metre, lines of poetry in the repeated bigrams of a message, which provided a crib. Instead of returning to Cambridge, he decided to continue working in Room 40, renamed the Government Code and Cipher School. He did, however, finally manage to get the Headlam–Knox Herodas published in 1922. Following German intervention in Spain he solved the Spanish military code and collaborated with the French on Italian naval codes used in Abyssinia.

Immediately before Hitler's invasion of Poland Knox went with A. G. Denniston, the head of GC and CS, to a secret base at Pyry, where he was shown a reconstruction of the Enigma cipher machine, which was used by the Germans. The Polish replica moved the breaking of Enigma on from a theoretical exercise to a practical one and Knox always gave the Poles credit for the part they played. His own section, Intelligence Services Knox (ISK), which worked in 'the Cottage' at Bletchley Park, achieved some notable cryptographic successes, including breaking the Italian naval code which enabled the Matapan signals to be read in March 1941. Although absorbed to the point of stuffing his pipe with sandwiches when obsessed with puzzle-solving, it would be wrong to see Knox's codebreaking as a detached intellectual exercise. It was he who insisted that in order not to compromise Ultra (the breaking of the German high command codes), there should be an immediate press release that aerial reconnaissance had made possible the important naval victory off Cape Matapan in southern Greece (1941). Although ill with cancer, he worked tirelessly on breaking the Abwehr (a German secret service) traffic. A typical short cut was the successful assumption that some indicators set up by the operators in the four machine windows were not random but girls' names or four-letter dirty German words.

Knox worked from his bed to the last, only getting up and dressing in order to receive the CMG (1943) from the Palace emissary appropriately. He died 27 February 1943 at his home, Courn's Wood, near High Wycombe, Buckinghamshire. There is a drawing of him by Gilbert Spencer in the possession of the family.

In 1920 he married his former secretary, Olive, daughter of Lieutenant-Colonel Roddam. They had two sons.

[Penelope Fitzgerald, *The Knox Brothers*, 1977; personal knowledge.]

MAVIS BATEY

published 1993

LAWRENCE Thomas Edward

(1888–1935)

Known as 'Lawrence of Arabia', was born at Tremadoc, North Wales, 15 August 1888, the second in a family of five sons. His father, Thomas Robert Chapman (who had assumed the name of Lawrence), the younger son of an Anglo-Irish landowning family, had followed up a sound classical schooling with an agricultural course and some years of continental travel and mountaineering; he lived on private means permitting of comfort though not luxury; became keenly interested in church architecture and in photography; and was an enthusiastic yachtsman, shot, and (from the early days of the safety bicycle) cyclist. His mother, Sarah Maden, the daughter of a Sunderland engineer, was brought up in the Highlands and afterwards in Skye. Both parents were devout, evangelical members of the Church of England.

Having learnt his letters from hearing his elder brother taught them, Lawrence read newspapers and books at the age of four, began Latin at six, and entered the Oxford High School at eight. From the age of twelve he covered his tuition expenses by scholarships at school and a Welsh exhibition at Jesus College, Oxford. Deep love of literature, archaeology, and architecture, particularly of the Middle Ages, led him to choose as a thesis for the modern history school 'The Influence of the Crusades on European Military Architecture—to the End of the XIIth Century' (published in 1936 as *Crusader Castles*). After bicycle tours throughout England and France he journeyed alone, on foot and without baggage, through Syria,

Palestine, and the southern fringe of Turkey. In 1910 he obtained a first class in history, partly on his thesis, and was awarded a four years' senior demyship for travel by Magdalen College at the instance of D. G. Hogarth, Lawrence's lifelong friend, who in 1911 sent him on the British Museum expedition that was excavating the Hittite city of Carchemish. There, after an interval in Egypt, he returned next year, assisting (Sir) C. Leonard Woolley until the outbreak of war in 1914; of this he wrote, 'it was the best life I ever lived'. He acquired some Arabic, together with the habit of eating Arab food and wearing Arab clothes. From January to March 1914 he and Woolley carried out an archaeological survey of the Negeb and country south of Beersheba for the Palestine Exploration Fund (which in 1915 published their report under the title of *Wilderness of Zin*), joining Captain Stewart Newcombe, who was already surveying that area for the War Office.

On the outbreak of war in 1914 Lawrence, being below standard height (then raised to 5 feet 5 inches) obtained but a sedentary commission in the Geographical Section, General Staff of the War Office. Dispatched to Military Intelligence in Egypt when Turkey joined the central powers, he spent two years in what was later called the Arab Bureau, which became by 1916 the Intelligence Service for the Arab campaign. In the October of that year he accompanied to Jidda (Sir) Ronald Storrs, who had initiated the negotiations which culminated in the Arab Revolt, and presented Lawrence to the Sharif Abdullah, second son of Husain, Grand Sharif of Mecca, and obtained from Husain an introduction to his third son, Faisal, who at that moment was retreating discomfited before a Turkish advance from Medina. Turkish strength in the Hejaz still amounted to nearly 15,000 rifles, 10,000 of which held Medina, 2,500 the railway between Medina and Amman, including the strongly garrisoned port of Aqaba, and 1,200 the port of Wajh. The Arabs in their anxiety pressed for the dispatch to the Hejaz of a British brigade, which Lawrence, on his return to Egypt, opposed as too cumbersome, and was himself dispatched as liaison officer and adviser to Faisal, whose confidence he soon won and whose tribal levies he helped to organize.

The secret of Lawrence's ascendancy, physical, intellectual, and moral, is best explained in his own words: 'Among the Arabs there were no distinctions, traditional or natural, except the unconscious power given a famous shaikh by virtue of his accomplishment: and they taught me that no man could be their leader except he ate the ranks' food, wore their clothes, lived level with them, and yet appeared better in himself.' Preferring to contain rather than to assault or starve the 10,000 Turks in Medina and thus compel the enemy to tie down additional troops to maintain them, Lawrence induced Faisal to threaten their communications by moving north and attacking the Hejaz railway, which thenceforth passed progressively out of effective Turkish control. It was his theory and practice that the Arabs should become 'an influence (as we might be), an idea, a thing invulnerable, intangible, without front or back, drifting about like gas, a vapour, blowing where we listed' ... 'tip and run: not pushes, but strokes ... the smallest force in the quickest time at the farthest place'. After the storming of Wajh Lawrence left Faisal there to establish his headquarters, and rode on into the interior, rousing the northern tribes and passing behind the enemy lines in Syria. Returning, he fell in with a force of the Howaitat tribe, under the celebrated Auda Abu Tayi, with it routed a Turkish battalion near Ma'an, and in August 1917 took and occupied Aqaba for Faisal. Having thus brought the whole Hejaz south of Aqaba, excepting Medina, under Arab-British control, Lawrence was promoted major and was awarded British and French decorations which he subsequently refused.

The climax of Lawrence's campaign began when, hurrying to Egypt to obtain supplies for starving Aqaba, he offered Sir Edmund (later Viscount) Allenby, the newly arrived commander-in-chief, 'to hobble the enemy by his preaching if given stores and arms and a fund of two hundred thousand sovereigns to convince and control his converts', and Allenby briefly replied: 'Well, I will do for you what I can.' Lawrence was given all he asked, and the fund was later increased to half a million pounds; thenceforward he directed Arab levies, now brigaded with the British Expeditionary Force and operating as a mobile right wing. Having defeated the Turks heavily in the model engagement of Tafila, he concentrated upon scientific train-wrecking with such success that Medina became virtually isolated, and the Turks, their rail-guards extended to Aleppo, offered a reward of £20,000 for the capture of 'al Urans, destroyer of engines', in whose protection sixty out of his bodyguard of ninety Arabs lost their lives. Towards the end of 1917, while reconnoitring alone the railway junction of Deraa, Lawrence was seized (but not recognized), forcibly enlisted in the Turkish army, and beaten senseless, but by dawn he had escaped. Next summer he persuaded Faisal to leave Aqaba in favour of Qasr Azrak for the advance upon Damascus. Finally, having broken up the Turkish Fourth Army east of the Jordan, Lawrence led the Arab troops up to Damascus on 1 October 1918, some hours ahead of the British, chivalrously allowing Sharif Nasir to precede his entry; and preserved it against serious threats of reverting to the Turks, until Allenby arrived three days later. 'In the crucial weeks while Allenby's stroke was being prepared ... nearly half of the Turkish forces [some 2,000 sabres and 12,000 rifles] south of Damascus ... were distracted by the Arab forces. With some relatively light assistance from Chaytor's Force these Turkish masses were paralysed by an Arab contingent that counted less than 3,000 men, and of which the actual expeditionary core was barely 600 strong. It would be difficult to find in the whole history of war as extraordinary a case of economy of force in distraction.' The whole payments for the Arab revolt amounted to four millions in gold, of which about half came back in purchases of food and clothing.

His task done, Lawrence retired. 'The East was sucked dry. Never outstay a climax' was his light self-dismissal, behind which, however, pressed heavily the physical toll of the sun, the snow, and the sand, battle, murder, and, never to be redeemed or forgotten, the climax of outrage in Deraa. He reached England on Armistice Day after four years' absence, and having done his utmost (though not to his own satisfaction) for Faisal and the Arab cause at the Peace Conference, settled down to the writing of his adventures. In November 1919 he was elected a research fellow of All Souls College, Oxford, and in 1921 was called by Mr. Churchill as political adviser to the newly formed Middle Eastern Department in the Colonial Office. The partnership was entirely successful. Faisal (whose ejection by the French from Damascus had been the culmination of Lawrence's disillusionment) was made king of Iraq, which was soon to become an independent state: and shortly afterwards the threat to Palestine of an unsettled Arab Transjordan was removed by the appointment of Faisal's elder brother, Abdullah, as its ruling prince on the condition that he, and his future subjects, did not interfere with French-mandated Syria. Feeling that (apart from Syria and Palestine, both already committed to the League of Nations) his 'Arab honour' was satisfied, and that he had gained his 'outlet' from public affairs, Lawrence insisted on his release from the Colonial Office in June 1922, and in August enlisted in the ranks of the Royal Air Force, changing his name to J. H. Ross in order to escape publicity, and again in 1923 to T. E. Shaw. This latter change was legalized by deed poll in 1927. Discharged from the Royal Air Force because his identity became disclosed, he sought refuge in the Tank Corps, but in August 1925 returned to the Royal Air Force. This took him in 1926 to the North-Western Frontier of India whence, in deference to Russian suspicions, he was recalled in 1928. As an aircraftman, neither attaining nor desiring officer's rank, he spent happily the last six years of his service, latterly testing, supervising, and even designing high-speed and power motor-craft at Plymouth, and later on the Solent. His service expired at Bridlington in February 1935, and he was retired at the age of forty-six, sad at leaving his work and comrades in the Royal Air Force. He bicycled to Clouds Hill, his three-roomed cottage at Bovington, Dorset, and remained there, unsettled, and evading the appointments thrust upon him in connexion with the expansion of the Royal Air Force, yet unable to enjoy his unaccustomed leisure which he planned to spend in exploring, by bicycle, the scenery and monuments of England. On 13 May, swerving on his powerful motor-cycle to avoid two boys bicycling abreast, he was violently thrown, and after lingering unconscious for five days, died in Bovington Camp Hospital 19 May 1935. He never married.

Lawrence was slightly but strongly built. His growth had been checked by breaking a leg in his 'teens. His forehead was high; the line of his face vertical and, in proportion to the depth of his head, long. His hair was long and fair and unruly, parted and brushed sideways. He had a straight nose, piercing blue eyes, a firm full mouth, strong square chin, and fine, careful, accomplished hands. He could be the best company in the world, holding his own with Mr. Churchill or Mr. Bernard Shaw: he could also retire within himself in any company. He preferred the society of men to that of women, with very few exceptions, and had friends in all classes. Books gave him almost as much companionship, and he was widely read in French, Latin, and Greek, as well as in English. He was a judge of painting, sculpture, architecture, and craftsmanship of every kind; and had a true appreciation of music, which he trained and gratified on a large collection of carefully tended gramophone records. He preferred neither to smoke nor to drink alcohol, and ate sparingly; but he yielded himself almost voluptuously to the 'dope' of high speed, on the swiftest motor-cycles. At eighty or ninety miles per hour he achieved 'a sense of moulding the hills and dales'.

Unique in kind as were Lawrence's exploits, their chance of historic survival would have been uncertain had he not himself recorded them in his brilliant and arresting *Seven Pillars of Wisdom* (1935) which was twice re-written during the years 1919 and 1920, after the original manuscript had been lost. Into his style, based originally upon *Travels in Arabia Deserta* (1888) by the venerated C. M. Doughty, Lawrence poured the conscious, conscientious devotion of the artist-craftsman which he had lavished upon his maps, his machinery, and his plans for battle. 'Words', he wrote, 'get richer every time they are deliberately used ... but only when deliberately used', and again, more significantly, 'Writing has been my inmost self all my life, and I can never put my full strength into anything else.' Lawrence would not have the book published in his lifetime, but issued in 1926 for subscription about a hundred copies superbly printed and illustrated by the best artists of the day. The loss of £11,000 over this thirty guineas issue was more than covered by his abridged version, *The Revolt in the Desert*, published next year (1927) at thirty shillings: but the surplus was given to charity. Lawrence also organized the re-publication in 1921 (with an admirable introduction) of Doughty's *Arabia Deserta* (the only fruit of his residence at All Souls) and made in 1924 a pseudonymous version, *The Forest Giant*, of *Le Gigantesque* by A. le Corbeaux, and under his own name a prose translation of the Odyssey, commissioned from the United States of America and published in 1932. He wrote a remarkable, if sometimes brutal, picture of his early days in the Royal Air Force, entitled *The Mint*, of which, however, he forbade publication until 1950, although a copyright edition of fifty copies (ten of which were for sale, prohibitively priced) was arranged in America in 1926.

None can begin to realize the unsuspected, the bewildering variety and versatility of Lawrence, before as well as after his Arabian exploits, until he has read *The Letters of T. E. Lawrence*, selected and edited by Mr. David Garnett in 1938. It has indeed been said that he would have survived (as would Edward Fitzgerald without *Omar Khayyam*) if only as a letter-writer. The letters emphasize the strange blend of contrasts and oppositions that made up his elusive, enigmatic, and paradoxical personality. Imperious but retiring, logical yet intuitive, profoundly impressive and provokingly puckish, on equal terms with field-marshals and Cabinet ministers, great writers, mechanics, scholars, and slaves, he bequeathed the example of one who combined physical prowess and courage under the open sky with passionate self-dedication to the testament of the great humanities, which he chose to enjoy in poverty rather than hazard the artificiality and time-wasting servitude of high position; even without his work, without his book, he was a standard and a touchstone of reality in life.

Among the portraits of Lawrence are several by Augustus John, including a painting in the National Portrait Gallery, and a pastel by Eric Kennington at All Souls College, Oxford, made for *Seven Pillars of Wisdom*. The portrait painted by James McBey soon after Lawrence's entry into Damascus hangs in the Imperial War Museum. There is a bronze bust by Eric Kennington in the crypt of St. Paul's Cathedral, and a posthumous effigy, also by Eric Kennington, in St. Martin's church, Wareham.

[*The Times*, 20 May 1935; T. E. Lawrence, *Seven Pillars of Wisdom*, 1935, *Secret Despatches from Arabia*, 1939, *Oriental Assembly*, 1939, and *Men in Print*, 1940; B. H. Liddell Hart, *T. E. Lawrence*, 1934; *The Letters of T. E. Lawrence*, edited by David Garnett, 1938; Charles Edmunds, *T. E. Lawrence*, 1935; R. H. Kiernan, *Lawrence of Arabia*, 1936; Vyvyan Richards, *T. E. Lawrence*, 1939; Clare Sydney Smith, *The Golden Reign*, 1940; Elizabeth W. Duval, *T. E. Lawrence, A Bibliography*, 1938; B. H. Liddell Hart and R. Graves, *T. E. Lawrence to his Biographers*, 1938; Sir Ronald Storrs, *Orientations*, 1937; *T. E. Lawrence, by his Friends*, edited by A. W. Lawrence, 1937; personal knowledge.]

RONALD STORRS

published 1949

Air chief marshal, was born at Mobberley, Cheshire, 11 July 1892, the younger son of the rector, the Rev. Herbert Leigh Mallory, later canon of Chester Cathedral, by his wife, Annie Beridge, daughter of the Rev. John Beridge Jebb, of Walton Lodge, Chesterfield, and rector of Brampton. His elder brother, G. L. Mallory, was lost in the Mount Everest expedition of 1924. Leigh-Mallory was educated at Haileybury and Magdalene College, Cambridge, where he took third class honours in history (1913) and law (1914). In 1914 he was commissioned in the 4th battalion, Lancashire Fusiliers, with which he went to France. In 1916 he was seconded to the Royal Flying Corps. He served in France in Nos. 5 and 15 Squadrons and in command of No. 8 Squadron until the end of the war, being mentioned in dispatches in 1918 and appointed to the D.S.O. in 1919. In the same year he was granted a permanent commission as major, 'aeroplanes', and resigned from the army.

Between the wars Leigh-Mallory underwent courses at the Royal Air Force College and the Imperial Defence College and was an instructor in air subjects at the Army Staff College. He commanded the School of Army Co-operation, served at the Air Ministry as deputy director of staff duties and was senior air staff officer in Iraq. He was promoted air commodore in 1936 and air vice-marshal in 1938. In 1937 he was appointed to command No. 12 (Fighter) Group, a post which he still held on the outbreak of war in 1939. The main responsibility of the group in 1940 was the defence against air attack of the industrial Midlands and the important east-coast shipping route. It took its full share in the Battle of Britain. Leigh-Mallory was mentioned in dispatches and appointed C.B. In December 1940 he was transferred to the command of No. 11 (Fighter) Group, which was then recovering from the Battle of Britain and very much on the defensive. With his usual vigour he proceeded to train it for the offensive—a bold and far-seeing step at that stage of the war. Always quick to appreciate the need for changed tactics, he applied them unhesitatingly. The offensive spirit was manifested in the doctrine of the Fighter Wings, offensive sweeps over enemy territory by large fighter formations in mutual support, intruder sorties into Europe by single day or night fighter aircraft making use of cloud cover for surprise attacks on ground or air targets, and support of light bombers in daylight raids and of amphibious raids against the French coast. His knowledge of the needs of the other Services was invaluable when he directed the air part of the Dieppe operation. Time after time he was able to anticipate the requests for air support which came from the land and sea forces. 'Air co-operation faultless' was one of the messages he received from the Dieppe beaches in August 1942.

In July of that year Leigh-Mallory was promoted to acting air marshal and in November 1942 appointed A.O.C.-in-C., Fighter Command. In the new year he was promoted K.C.B. In his new command his whole effort was again directed to the offensive, anticipating the day when the continent could be invaded. He was early appointed air commander-in-chief designate for the invasion of Europe, and, in conjunction with the naval and army commanders designate, entered whole-heartedly into the planning for this great undertaking, in spite of the weighty pre-occupations of his active command. By the time he was confirmed as air commander-in-chief, Allied Expeditionary Air Force, in December 1943, with the rank of air chief marshal, the air offensive had succeeded beyond all expectation and hardly an enemy aircraft dared show itself near our coast. Despite the widespread military activities on the south coast, not a single enemy reconnaissance aircraft penetrated the defences to discover the preparations for the invasion. Leigh-Mallory was again mentioned in dispatches.

In his new appointment he exercised full command of the Tactical Air Forces of Britain and operational command of those of the United States which were supporting the invasion in western Europe from the United Kingdom. Some idea of the magnitude of his responsibilities may be gauged from the fact that on D-Day he was in operational command of some 9,000 aircraft. The success of this force is historical. The German air force was virtually swept from the skies, and the German armies were practically immobilized by the destruction of their rail and road communications. His handling of a force of unprecedented size, despite the difficulties inherent in such an inter-allied command, was masterly.

Leigh-Mallory's command ceased on 15 October 1944 when the war in Europe seemed as good as won and there was no longer need for detailed co-ordination of the two Allied Tactical Air Forces. On 14 November 1944 he left London by air to take up his new appointment as allied air commander-in-chief, South East Asia Command, at a time when the offensive against Japan was in full swing. The aircraft in which he and his wife were travelling did not arrive at its destination and in June 1945 documents in the wreckage of an aircraft found in the mountains thirty miles west of Grenoble left no doubt that the aircraft was that in which they had been travelling. His untimely death deprived him of the honours which he had so well earned.

He was a great air commander and a born leader: a man of unbounded energy who seemed never to be off duty. He never spared himself or others, was determined to the point of ruthlessness, never losing sight of his objective, and possessed of great self-confidence which sometimes appeared to be self-conceit to those who did not know him well. But beneath this was a genuine solicitude for those working under him and specially for the fighting man. As a group commander he made a point, perhaps after an exhausting spell of duty, of meeting pilots as they came in from patrol, to learn at first hand of their impressions. Then in the mess over a drink he would listen to their suggestions. He inspired loyalty and trust and was particularly popular with the pilots of Fighter Command. His honours included appointment as a chief commander of the American Legion of Merit and to the first class of the Soviet Order of Ushakov, both in 1944.

In 1915 Leigh-Mallory married Doris Jean, daughter of Edmund Stratton Sawyer, by whom he had a son and a daughter. His wife's great natural charm endeared her to all, and Leigh-Mallory himself would have been the first to acknowledge the deep debt which he owed to her in contributing to his success.

The best portrait of Leigh-Mallory is a pastel by William Dring which hangs at Fighter Command headquarters, Bentley Priory, Stanmore. Another by Eric Kennington is in the Imperial War Museum.

[*Burke's Landed Gentry*, 1952; official records; private information; personal knowledge.]

W. B. CALLAWAY

published 1959

LUDLOW-HEWITT Edgar Rainey

(1886–1973)

Sir

Air chief marshal, was born at Eckington, Worcester, 9 June 1886, the second son and second of five children of Thomas Arthur Ludlow-Hewitt, of Clancoole, county Cork, and later vicar of Minety, Wiltshire, and his wife, Edith Annie, daughter of Alfred Ricketts Hudson, of Wick House, Worcestershire. Educated at Radley and Sandhurst, he was commissioned into the Royal Irish Rifles in 1905. He learnt to fly at Upavon a few weeks before the outbreak of World War I, and in August 1914 became a probationary member of the infant Royal Flying Corps. Early in 1915 he was posted to No. 1 Squadron in France, and gained a reputation as an exceptionally able and courageous pilot. He won an MC (1916), was six times mentioned in dispatches, and was rapidly promoted to command No. 3 Squadron. In February 1916 he was promoted wing commander, taking over III Corps Wing at Bertangles. He became a chevalier of the Legion of Honour in 1917, and was appointed to the DSO the following year. By the end of the war, a brigadier at thirty-one, he was marked by Sir H. M. (later Viscount) Trenchard as one of the outstanding brains of the newly created Royal Air Force.

Between the wars, Ludlow—as he was always known—served as commandant of the RAF Staff College, Andover (1926–30), air officer commanding in Iraq (1930–32), director of operations and intelligence, Air Ministry (1933–5), and AOC in India (1935–7). An austere, sombre figure, his intelligence and devotion to duty were widely recognized, but his lack of humour and teetotal dedication to Christian Science did not encourage good fellowship. The tall, lanky figure of Ludlow-Hewitt striding across the tarmac of an airfield was respected, but loved only by those who knew him well. 'Most knowledgeable; very sound on paper; probably more detailed knowledge of service matters than anyone in the RAF', Air Chief Marshal Sir Hugh Pughe Lloyd wrote of him in his diary. 'As a commander a hopeless bungler and fuddler; unable to make up his mind and will change it five times in as many minutes; easily flustered.'

This may be a little ungenerous. But as a commander on the eve of war, Ludlow-Hewitt became the victim of his own intelligence. In 1937 he was recalled from India to become AOC Bomber Command and he became air chief marshal. Since 1918, like almost every senior RAF officer of the period, he had shared that mystical faith in the power of a bomber offensive to win wars held by Viscount Trenchard. Yet in his new post he was quickly forced to terms with the fact that no hard thinking had ever been done about how the bombers were to find their targets; how they were to aim their bombs; how the bombs were to destroy large structures; above all, perhaps, how a credible offensive was to be mounted with the very small force at Bomber Command's disposal. From 1936 onwards, Fighter Command profited greatly from the attention of politicians and scientists—above all Sir Henry Tizard—who addressed themselves determinedly to the problems of creating a workable air defence system for Britain. Perhaps principally because so many politicians and civilians found the concept of a bomber offensive repugnant, no parallel outside stimulus was applied to Bomber Command. Ludlow-Hewitt pressed the Air Ministry in vain for the creation of a Bombing Development Unit. He met Tizard for the first time only in July 1939.

It was Ludlow-Hewitt's thankless task to identify frankly and accurately, on the very edge of the war, the grave shortcomings of his Command. His relentless minutes to the Air Ministry exposed him to the charge of pessimism, even defeatism, yet they were perfectly confirmed by battle experience. He wrote reporting that air-gunners possessed no confidence in their ability to use their equipment. After a generation in which the theory of the 'self-defending bomber formation' had been at the heart of RAF policy, he declared his conviction that fighter escorts would be essential in war. He stated a few weeks before the opening of hostilities that if his force were ordered to undertake an all-out offensive against Germany, the medium bombers—the Blenheims—would be destroyed in three and a half weeks, the heavies—Hampdens, Whitleys, and Wellingtons—would be eliminated in seven and a half weeks. The air staff reluctantly accepted the view that the government had anyway reached for political reasons, that the RAF should not embark on an immediate strategic offensive. In September 1939 Bomber Command began the war with a programme of leaflet-dropping which confirmed Ludlow-Hewitt's worst fears about his command's aircraft navigation, and also carried out operations against the German fleet at sea and in support of the British Expeditionary Force in France. When the first disastrous operations of No. 3 Group's Wellingtons against the German fleet caused heavy casualties, Ludlow-Hewitt flew personally to visit the squadrons, and astonished his men by his own sensitivity to the losses. He was too passionately humanitarian to maintain the confidence of others, and too realistic about the shortcomings of his own force. An officer was needed of less sensitivity and more positive faith in his Command's powers, however ill-founded. In April 1940, before the war began in earnest, Ludlow-Hewitt was removed to become inspector-general of the RAF, a post in which he served with great insight and dedication until 1945. Sir C. F. A. Portal (later Viscount Portal of Hungerford) replaced him at Bomber Command.

Ludlow-Hewitt was appointed CMG (1919), CB (1928), KCB (1933), GBE (1943), and GCB (1946). From 1943 to 1945 he was principal air ADC to the King. In 1945 he became chairman of the board of the new College of Aeronautics, a position he held until 1953. One of the founding fathers of the RAF, an exceptionally thoughtful service officer, he lacked the steel for high command in war.

He married in 1923 Albinia Mary (died 1972), daughter of Major Edward Henry Evans-Lombe, of Marlington Hall, Norwich, and widow of Francis William Talbot Clerke and of Captain Anthony Henry Evelyn Ashley, both of the Coldstream Guards. There were no children of the marriage. Ludlow-Hewitt died at Queen Alexandra's RAF Hospital, Wiltshire, 15 August 1973.

McCarthy

[RAF Museum; C. Webster and N. Frankland, *The Strategic Air Offensive against Germany*, 4 vols., 1961; Max Hastings, *Bomber Command*, 1979; private information.]

MAX HASTINGS

published 1986

MCCARTHY (Emma) Maud

(1858–1949)

Dame

Army matron-in-chief, was born 22 September 1858 at Sydney, New South Wales, Australia, the eldest daughter of William Frederick McCarthy, solicitor, and his wife, Emma Mary à Beckett. She was educated privately and after spending three years in England decided to enter the London Hospital to train as a nurse (1891–3), thereby following a strong philanthropic tendency towards medicine and nursing which had been evinced in her family for generations; one of her ancestors was William Harvey.

On the outbreak of war in South Africa Maud McCarthy, then a sister in Sophia women's ward, was one of the six nurses selected from the London Hospital by Queen Alexandra (then Princess of Wales) to go to South Africa as her own special nursing sisters. The day she left the London Hospital, one of the medical staff wrote with a diamond on the window of her ward sitting-room 'Ichabod'. She served with distinction throughout the war, receiving the Queen's and King's medals, the Royal Red Cross (to which in 1918 she was awarded a bar), and a special decoration from Queen Alexandra on her return to England in 1902. Thereupon she became closely concerned with the formation of Queen Alexandra's Imperial Military Nursing Service (later Queen Alexandra's Royal Army Nursing Corps) in which she served as a matron until 1910 when she became principal matron at the War Office.

On the outbreak of war in 1914 she went to France in the first ship to leave England with members of the British Expeditionary Force. In 1915 she was installed at Abbeville as matron-in-chief of the British armies in France, in charge of the whole area from the Channel to the Mediterranean wherever British, imperial, and American nurses were working. In August 1914 the numbers in her charge were 516; by the time of the armistice they had increased to 5,440 on the lines of communication and a further 954 in casualty clearing stations. They came from Canada,

Australia, New Zealand, South Africa, Portugal, and the United States as well as from the United Kingdom; not all were trained nurses, for some 1,729 were from voluntary aid detachments. To keep this vast body working harmoniously and efficiently called for administrative talent of the highest order. In 1917 and 1918 there were casualties from air raids and in the latter year the influenza epidemic also took its toll. The constant shortage of trained nurses, the continual movements of position, the personal requirements of individuals: all these raised problems which Maud McCarthy solved with tact and skill. It is believed that she was the only head of a department in the British Expeditionary Force who remained in her original post throughout the war—a great tribute to her strength of body, mind, and spirit. She was appointed G.B.E. in 1918 and awarded the Florence Nightingale medal and several foreign decorations. When in August 1919 she sailed for England from Boulogne, whither she had transferred her headquarters the previous year, representatives of the French Government and Medical Service were among those who assembled to do her honour.

In 1920 she was appointed matron-in-chief, Territorial Army Nursing Service, and although she retired five years later the advancement of nursing remained her great interest until she died. She had the highest ideals in her profession and an unselfish, modest character. Her devotion to duty and self-sacrifice were an inspiration to all who worked with her. To her own family she was a tower of strength and in every circumstance they turned for advice and comfort to her home in Chelsea where she died, unmarried, at the age of ninety, 1 April 1949. A pastel by Austin O. Spare is in the Imperial War Museum.

[Sir W. G. Macpherson, (Official) *History of the Great War. Medical Services, General History*, vol. ii, 1923; *The Times*, 8 April 1949; private information.]

HELEN S. GILLESPIE

published 1959

MCCUDDEN James Thomas Byford

(1895–1918)

Airman, was born at Gillingham, Kent, 28 March 1895, the second son of Sergeant-Major William Henry McCudden, Royal Engineers, of Carlow, Ireland, by his wife, Amelia Emma Byford, of Chatham. He was educated at the Royal Engineers' School, Brompton Barracks, Gillingham, joined the Royal Engineers as a bugler in 1910, and became a sapper three years later, but shortly afterwards (April 1913) was transferred to the Royal Flying Corps. After a few weeks at the flying depôt at Farnborough, he was posted as mechanic to No. 3 squadron. He occasionally flew as a passenger. On 1 April 1914 he was appointed first-class air mechanic, and took charge of an aeroplane in which he would often sit, operate the controls, and imagine himself in flight.

On the outbreak of the European War McCudden went to France with No. 3 squadron in August 1914, was promoted corporal in November, and flight-sergeant in April 1915, a post which brought him responsibility for all the engines of his flight. He was now flying occasionally as a gunner, and, by December, as an observer. He had already been recommended for a course of flying, but he could not be spared from his engines until January 1916, when he was sent home to learn to fly. He qualified at Gosport on 16 April 1916, returned to France on 4 July as a sergeant pilot of No. 66 squadron, and flew a Farman Experimental machine, chiefly on offensive patrols and photographic work. He was transferred in August to No. 56 squadron, and brought down his first enemy machine on 6 September. He received his commission on 1 January 1917, returned to England on 23 February in order to instruct in air fighting, was promoted captain on 1 May, and took part in the defence of London against the enemy daylight raids in June and July. He went to France for a 'refresher' fighting course with No. 66 squadron on 11 July, was back in England on 3 August, but was almost at once appointed to No. 56 squadron as a flight-commander, returning to France on the 15th of that month.

From this time until 5 March 1918 McCudden built up his position as the leading British fighting pilot, and enhanced the prestige of his squadron and of his service. His record included fifty-four enemy aeroplanes, of which forty-two were definitely destroyed, nineteen of them in the British lines. On two occasions he destroyed four two-seater machines in one day, the second time completing his work in ninety minutes. On 13 January 1918 he shot down three aeroplanes in twenty minutes. His success was made on the Scout Experimental 5 machine, and his feeling for engines enabled him to get the best out of his machines. He was a dashing patrol leader, always eager to attack, but never hesitating to break off a fight if his judgement so prompted. McCudden's outstanding success, however, was in single-handed attacks against enemy two-seater machines, which would cross the lines at great heights on rapid reconnaissance work. He studied their habits, the psychology of their pilots, and their weak spots. He stalked them with great patience, and seldom failed to bring his enemy down when once he got to grips. He wept when he left his squadron for England on 5 March 1918 and, whilst he was instructing at home, was thinking always of what he was missing in France.

On 9 July 1918 McCudden was promoted major, and he set out the same day for France in high spirits, in order to take command of the famous No. 60 squadron. He was leaving the aerodrome at Auxi-le-Château on his way to the front when his engine was heard to stop. He turned to land again, but his machine side-slipped into the ground and he was killed.

McCudden was gay, modest, intensely loyal, and of a great courage tempered by almost faultless judgement. He admired his enemy and loved his friends. He had two brothers who were pilots in the Flying Corps: both were killed. McCudden was awarded the croix de guerre (1916), the military medal (1916), the military cross and bar (1917), the distinguished service order and bar (1917 and 1918), and the Victoria cross (1918).

[J. T. B. McCudden, *Five Years in the Royal Flying Corps*, 1918; official records; personal knowledge.]

HENRY ALBERT JONES

published 1927

MAITLAND   Edward Maitland

(1880–1921)

Air commodore and airship and parachute pioneer, was born in London 21 February 1880, the elder son of Arthur Gee, farmer and later barrister-at-law and JP, of Shudy Camps Park, Cambridgeshire, and his wife Margaretha Marianne Maitland. Arthur Gee and his family assumed the name of Maitland in 1903. Educated at Haileybury and Trinity College, Cambridge, Edward Maitland volunteered for service in the South African war while he was still an undergraduate. Commissioned in the Essex Regiment, he served in South Africa during 1901–2, receiving the Queen's medal with four clasps. Without resuming residence in Cambridge he took a BA (ordinary) in 1906, obtaining a third class.

Remaining in the army, in 1907 Maitland took up ballooning. The following year, with two companions, he made a record 1,171-mile voyage to Russia. He also made his first descent from a balloon by parachute. After service at the Balloon School in Farnborough, he commanded the airship company in the short-lived air battalion of the Royal Engineers (1911–12), and then, on the formation of the Royal Flying Corps, was given command of No. 1 Squadron (Airships). In 1913, when all British airships came under naval control, he transferred to the Royal Naval Air Service. In the same year he made his first parachute jump from an airship.

Maitland

In October 1914 Maitland was sent to Belgium in charge of an RNAS balloon detachment for artillery spotting. He became impressed with the superiority of the French and Belgian kite-balloons over his own spherical type, reported accordingly to the Admiralty, and was promptly recalled to initiate kite-balloon training at Roehampton in March 1915. From this he moved on to command the airship station at Wormwood Scrubs, and then went to the Admiralty to help in airship design and allocation. During this period he made a parachute descent from a balloon at 10,500 feet to investigate 'swinging'. In 1916, as a wing captain, he was appointed to command the airship station in Pulham, Norfolk, where Zeppelin imitations—rigid airships of a greatly improved type—were later to be based.

In June 1917 Maitland was appointed to the DSO for 'extremely valuable and gallant work in connection with airships and parachutes'. Shortly afterwards he returned to the Admiralty as captain-superintendent, lighter-than-air, to take charge of the airships headquarters staff. In this post he helped to build up the airship service into a major weapon in the war at sea. RNAS non-rigid airships, able to stay aloft for many hours and send down reports by wireless, did important work on patrol and convoy escort, many times directing British destroyers into contact with the enemy's U-boats. Further recognition followed with appointment in 1919 as CMG, and the award of the AFC (1919) and the United States DSM (1917).

July 1919 saw what was probably Maitland's greatest moment, when the naval rigid airship R34, with Maitland as chief observer, crossed the Atlantic successfully in both directions. The following month he received a permanent commission in the Royal Air Force, soon afterwards being promoted air commodore. With the transfer in October of all rigid airships from the Royal Navy to the RAF, Maitland continued at the Air Ministry his work on airship development and operations, but with civil uses now in view.

In 1921 Maitland's previously brilliant career ended in misfortune and tragedy. He was in command of the airship station in Howden, Yorkshire, when on 21 January the R34 struck some high ground and was buffeted in strong winds off the Yorkshire coast, later breaking up. In May the Air Ministry decided to disband the RAF's airship arm. The newly constructed R38, the largest airship yet built, had been sold to the USA in 1919, but was still based in Howden for training and trials. When on 24 August 1921 she broke up over the Humber on a final exercise in sharp turns, Maitland, on board but not in command, died with forty-two others. He was unmarried.

[Papers in the Air Historical Branch, Ministry of Defence; E. M. Maitland, *The Log of HMA R34*, 1920; *The Times*, 25 August 1921; Sir Walter Raleigh, *The War in the Air*, vol. i, 1922; Robin Higham, *The British Rigid Airship, 1908–31*, 1961; D. H. Robinson, *Giants in the Sky*, 1973.]

DENIS RICHARDS

published 1993

MARTEL Giffard Le Quesne

(1889–1958)

Sir

Lieutenant-general, was born in Millbrook, Southampton, 10 October 1889, the only son of (Sir) Charles Philip Martel, later chief superintendent of ordnance factories, and his wife, Lilian Mary, daughter of W. H. Mackintosh, M.D. He was educated at Wellington College, where he won the Wellesley scholarship awarded annually to the top boy on the modern side, and represented the school in gymnastics. In 1908 he entered the Royal Military Academy, Woolwich, and the next year was commissioned in the Royal Engineers. In 1912 and 1913 he won the welterweight championship not only of the army but of the combined Services; after the war he won the army championship (1920) and the imperial Services championship (1921 and 1922).

In August 1914 Martel went to France where for two years he carried out the normal duties of a field company officer, attaining command of his unit in the second year. In the summer of 1916 he was sent home temporarily to design a practice battlefield, based on the trench-front in France, in the secret area at Thetford, in Norfolk, where the crews for the newly produced tanks were being trained. This had a far-reaching effect on his career: early in October, three weeks after the tanks had made their début on the battlefield in France, he was chosen for the key appointment of brigade-major in the small headquarters of the new arm at Bermicourt. There were only three other members, apart from the commander, (Sir) Hugh Elles; but in the following May, as the result of enlargements, Martel became G.S.O. 2 and was promoted from captain to major.

In November 1916 Martel wrote a paper entitled 'A Tank Army' (reprinted in *Our Armoured Forces*, 1945) which showed his long-range vision at a time when the tank was generally regarded as no more than a limited aid to the infantry assault, and when no tank could move at more than four miles an hour. His paper forecast the creation of 'tank armies' and their domination of future great wars. He proposed that they should be organized and operate like fleets at sea, with 'destroyer', 'battle', and 'torpedo' tanks, carrying with them in 'supply' tanks their requirements for an extensive operation. His forecast overlooked some basic differences between the conditions of sea and land warfare, and was only fulfilled in part, but it was of great value in lifting thought out of the rut of trench warfare. The extent to which Martel overshot the mark of potentiality was less than that by which the general run of military thought fell short.

In a more immediate way he contributed much to the performance of the Tank Corps in 1917–18 by his activity and boldness in reconnaissance. He was continually up at the front and lived up there with unit representatives during the preparatory period before offensives were launched. There is a vivid pen portrait of him in a private record written by Sir Evan Charteris. He described 'Q' Martel as a man:

> Of a desperate bravery, who was, however, supposed to have an exact instinct for the falling place of shells and to be a very safe guide. He was a small, loose-limbed man, a natural bruiser, and winner of the army boxing, with a deep hoarse laugh which ... had a most peculiar note of good-humoured ferocity in it. Tales which made the ordinary mortal's flesh creep produced from him regular salvos of this notable laughter ... On leave, his idea of recreation was to shut himself up in a mobile workshop of his own and work at a lathe. At the front, his idea of pleasure was to get into a shelled area and dodge about to avoid the bursts.

After the war, during which he was appointed to the D.S.O. and awarded the M.C., Martel returned to duty with the Royal Engineers, and remained with them when the Royal Tank Corps was formed on a permanent basis in 1923, a choice for which he was later criticized by some of his comrades in the wartime Tank Corps and by others who joined it after its creation. But he continued to take a very active interest in the development of tanks and armoured warfare, writing much on the subject as well as conducting experimental work—initially in the problems of tank-bridging. Shortly before the armistice in November 1918 he had been sent home to command a tank-bridging battalion of the Royal Engineers which had been formed at Christchurch in Hampshire, and after the war this was converted into an experimental establishment. One product of this period was the Martel box girder bridge, which became the standard girder bridge of the army, in place of the more expensive and less adaptable tubular girder bridge.

In 1921 Martel went to the Staff College and after graduating was appointed in 1923 to the directorate of fortifications and works at the War Office, where he remained until the summer of 1926. Meanwhile he had become convinced of the need for small and inconspicuous armoured and tracked vehicles to aid, and operate with, the infantry. Finding little official encouragement, he designed and built such a machine in the garage of his own house at Camberley, which he completed and demonstrated in 1925. At first called the 'one-man tank' and then the tankette, a small number were ordered for the original Experimental Mechanized Force of 1927. It became the prototype both of the light tank and also of the machine-gun carrier.

In 1926 Martel himself was given command of the first field company R.E. to be mechanized, and with it took part in the trials of the Experimental Force during the next two years. In this period he devised a 'stepping-stone' bridge, made up of timber crates spaced at short intervals, which a tank pressed down into the bed of the stream as it ran across them—a device of which the Russians made use during their 1943 advance and later. He also devised a 'mat bridge' composed of a chain of timber panels, or rafts, which were pushed across the stream and over which vehicles could cross so long as they kept moving—an idea which was revived in the Normandy landings of 1944.

His numerous articles in the military journals during the twenties made a wide impression, especially abroad. Guderian, the creator of the German armoured forces, refers to Martel in his memoirs as one of the three men who 'principally' excited his interest in such forces and describes Martel as one of those three 'who became the pioneers of a new type of warfare on the largest scale'. In 1929 Martel went out to India where in 1930 he became an instructor at the Quetta Staff College, remaining until 1933. There followed in 1935 a year's course at the Imperial Defence College. In 1931 he published a book entitled *In the Wake of the Tank*, and an enlarged edition in 1935, but he did not otherwise write so much in this decade as in the previous one.

Much of his technical inventive work had been done at his own expense and with little or no aid from official quarters. He was not given an opportunity to take a hand in directing tank development and production until 1936, by which time Britain had lost her former lead in this field. Then, as assistant director of mechanization, and from January 1938 as deputy director, he strove vigorously to make up the lost years. In the autumn of 1937 the new secretary of state for war, Leslie (later Lord) Hore-Belisha, considered making him master-general of the ordnance, although he was still only a colonel. Martel's own diffidence about such a big jump over the heads of his seniors was one of the factors which led to a different decision. At the beginning of 1939 he left the War Office on promotion to command a motorized division—the 50th Northumbrian, of the Territorial Army.

Martel

After the German break-through on the Meuse in May 1940 which was followed by the Panzer forces' drive to the Channel, Martel's division, which had been in France since January, was rushed to the scene. He was put in charge of the improvised counter-attack delivered at Arras on 21 May by two of his battalions and all the serviceable tanks of the 1st Army Tank brigade. This stroke hit the flank of Rommel's Panzer division, causing disorder, and the news so alarmed the German higher command that their drive was nearly suspended. The shock effect, out of all proportion to the small size of the force, enhanced Martel's reputation, but his conduct of the operation and its faulty co-ordination led to much sharp criticism from the tank officers taking part, who felt that his powers as a commander and tactician did not match his gifts as a technician.

After the fall of France there was growing pressure for the appointment of a single chief of the armoured forces in Britain. (Sir) Winston Churchill himself supported the proposal and wished to see the post given to (Sir) Percy Hobart. Although the Army Council reluctantly agreed to the appointment of a single head of the armoured forces, they were unwilling to meet Hobart's conditions and felt that of the few armoured experts available Martel was likely to be the most amenable: in December 1940 he was appointed commander of the Royal Armoured Corps, under the commander-in-chief Home Forces.

This soon brought Martel into conflict with Hobart, and the tension between these two old friends became severe. It was sharpened when Churchill created what he called a 'tank parliament' where the various armoured division commanders and other experts could meet and express their differing points of view. Martel disliked the arrangement as interfering with his authority and showing a lack of confidence in himself. Moreover, like many champion boxers he was basically a gentle and conciliatory man, anxious to please as well as to avoid trouble, and in his over-tactful efforts to reconcile differing views and interests, particularly of cavalrymen and tankmen, he eventually lost the confidence of both.

In September 1942 he went to India and Burma on a lengthy tour and while he was away his post was abolished. On return he was sent to Moscow as head of the military mission: another frustrating post. He returned to London in February 1944 and a fortnight later lost an eye in the bombing of the Army and Navy Club. He was placed on retired pay in 1945. In the general election of that year he stood unsuccessfully as a Conservative candidate for the Barnard Castle division of Durham. In the same year he published *Our Armoured Forces* which aroused wide interest, but also considerable criticism. In subsequent years he wrote several more books, dealing with his experiences in Russia and expressing a strongly anti-Communist view; his writings always received more attention, and circulation, in Russia than they did at home. Although his career ended in a series of disappointments, Martel deserves recognition for the mark he made on the development of modern warfare. He was appointed C.B. (1940), K.B.E. (1943), and K.C.B. (1944). He had been promoted lieutenant-general in 1942.

In 1922 he married Maud, daughter of Donald Fraser MacKenzie, of Collingwood Grange, Camberley, by whom he had a son and a daughter, the latter killed tragically in 1941 in a riding accident. Martel died in Camberley 3 September 1958.

[Sir Giffard Martel, *An Outspoken Soldier*, 1949; private information; personal knowledge.]

B. H. LIDDELL HART

published 1971

MAURICE Frederick Barton

(1871–1951)

Sir

Major-general, was born in Dublin 19 January 1871, the eldest son of (Major-General Sir) John Frederick Maurice, and grandson of Frederick Denison Maurice. He was educated at St. Paul's School and the Royal Military College, Sandhurst, from which he was commissioned in 1892 in the Derbyshire Regiment (later renamed the Sherwood Foresters). While a subaltern he served as aide-de-camp to his father and with his battalion in the Tirah campaign of 1897–8. He took part in the South African war as special service officer and as D.A.A.G., and was mentioned in dispatches and promoted brevet major at the age of twenty-nine. On his return to England he graduated at the Staff College and held a number of staff appointments including service at the War Office in the directorate of staff duties under Sir Douglas (later Earl) Haig.

In 1913 Maurice went as instructor to the Staff College where his father had been professor of military history over twenty years earlier. For the first nine months Sir William Robertson was commandant, and a close friendship began which had a marked influence on Maurice's subsequent career. When war broke out in 1914 he went to France with the head-quarters of the 3rd division, and during the retreat from Mons was promoted to be head of the general staff of the division. Officers who were serving with him have recorded his coolness in action and the clarity and speed with which he dictated orders.

At the end of January 1915 Robertson became chief of the general staff, British Expeditionary Force, and a few months later he selected Maurice to take charge of the operations section at G.H.Q. Maurice thoroughly understood his chief's method of work and served him admirably throughout 1915. He was appointed C.B. and promoted to brevet colonel. When Robertson became chief of the imperial general staff in December 1915 he took Maurice with him to the War Office as director of military operations with the rank of major-general, and they continued in the complete accord which had marked their association in France. For his services Maurice was appointed K.C.M.G. in January 1918. In February Robertson relinquished his appointment and Maurice did the same on 21 April.

Shortly afterwards Maurice brought his military career to an abrupt end by writing a letter to the London newspapers in which he accused Lloyd George's government of deceiving Parliament and the country about the strength of the British Army on the western front, the extension of the British line there, and other matters. Robertson and Maurice had for long been at loggerheads with the prime minister whom they distrusted both as a man and as an amateur strategist. They consistently maintained that the western front was the decisive theatre but Lloyd George, shocked by the terrible casualties in Haig's battles, was ever seeking some more effective and less costly strategy and was strongly attracted by the eastern policy of defeating Germany by 'knocking away the props'. He had no confidence in his military advisers and he would gladly have dismissed Haig had he felt strong enough to do so.

The Cabinet had underrated Robertson's warnings of the impending German attack in the west, and had not acted upon his recommendations for reinforcing Haig and raising more men for the army. When the Germans broke through our lines in March and drove us back almost to the Channel ports, the Government was charged with having contributed to these disasters by failing to strengthen the army in France with drafts which were available at home. Lloyd George defended himself and his ministers by stating on 9 April 1918 that on 1 January 1918 Haig's army was 'considerably stronger' than it had been on 1 January 1917. Maurice's letter, published on 7 May, gave the direct lie to this and other statements made by the Government.

The military reverses in France had alarmed the whole nation and this indictment came at a time when the general direction of the war had, for some months, been under severe criticism in Parliament and the press. Formidable forces existed which were ready to combine against Lloyd

George, and, as he himself recorded, the controversy which ensued threatened the life of his Government. The debate on the Maurice letter took place on 9 May and in it Lloyd George defended himself successfully and by a majority of almost three to one defeated the Opposition motion which amounted to a vote of censure. He reaffirmed his statement of 9 April and a further statement made by J. I. Macpherson (later Lord Strathcarron), the under-secretary for war, on 18 April with regard to the strength of Haig's army. These, he said, were based upon figures supplied to him by the War Office, which indeed was true.

The figures on which Lloyd George had based his statement of 9 April were his own analysis of a War Office statistical return. Maurice considered that Lloyd George had deceived the House of Commons both by misuse of the statistics of the non-combatants as distinguished from the combatant strength of the army and by implying that there had been no diminution between January and March 1918. This was the foundation of the main charge of his letter. On 18 April Maurice's department provided material for the answer by Macpherson to a question in the House on the point of combatant as distinct from non-combatant forces. But in these figures the strength of the army in Italy was inadvertently included in that of the army in France. A return from the adjutant-general's department of 7 May showed a decrease in the fighting forces in France in January 1918 as compared with the position in 1917 of some 95,000, of which some 70,000 were infantry. It now seems certain that these figures were known to Lloyd George before the debate of 9 May, but that he chose to ignore them. A copy of the return was sent by the War Office to 10 Downing Street where on the morning of 9 May Philip Kerr (later the Marquess of Lothian), the prime minister's secretary, on noting the discrepancy, made inquiries of the deputy director of military operations. Only then was it that the mistake in the figures provided on 18 April was discovered. Kerr was informed before luncheon on the 9th. Nevertheless in that afternoon's debate Lloyd George relied upon the incorrect figures. After the debate he was officially informed by Macpherson and Lord Milner of the mistake, of which he already knew, but he took no action to correct it, saying that he could not be held responsible for an error made by General Maurice's department.

Although Maurice was still technically in charge of his department on 18 April his successor was already in the War Office and Maurice himself knew nothing of the question and answer until Lloyd George repeated the inaccurate figures during the debate of 9 May. He knew that the prime minister, although informed of the mistake after the debate, took no action to put the matter right. It was not apparently until December 1919 that he learned that correct figures had been supplied to the prime minister before the debate. Many years later, after both Lloyd George and

Maurice were dead, Lord Beaverbrook published an extract from a diary kept by Miss Frances Stevenson, later Lloyd George's second wife, which recorded the burning by (Sir) J. T. Davies of a paper from the D.M.O. found forgotten in a dispatch box. Much publicity was given to the 'burnt paper' and it was supposed Lloyd George had never received the revised figures; but further evidence suggests that this was another copy of the adjutant-general's return which had been sent to the secretary of the War Cabinet.

Whether Maurice hoped to bring the Government down when he wrote his letter must remain one of the enigmas of history. Beyond a shadow of doubt he was not a party to any intrigue, military or political, to oust Lloyd George. Whether he was right or wrong in what he did, there can be no difference of opinion regarding his supreme moral courage and sense of duty. His action was instigated by a sincere belief confirmed by a visit to France that the morale of the troops was in danger of being undermined by attempts to shift responsibility for the March disaster on to the shoulders of the military leaders and by the conviction that a plot was being hatched to remove Haig. To the end of his life Maurice believed that he had saved Haig, whose only reaction at the time was a characteristic disapproval of conduct which he regarded as mistaken and improper.

Before Maurice's letter appeared in the press, he wrote to his daughter Nancy, who was then seventeen, telling her with moving sincerity that he fully realized what the consequences might be for himself and his family. He ended: 'I am persuaded that I am doing what is right, and once that is so, nothing else matters to a man. That is I believe what Christ meant when he told us to forsake father and mother and children for his sake.'

The Maurice debate had a lasting importance in political history, far transcending the immediate issue. It marked a turning-point in Lloyd George's career, for his triumph left him in a position of undisputed authority. But in the sequel the debate had, as Lloyd George put it, 'a disruptive effect upon the fortunes of the Liberal Party', by bringing about the emphatic cleavage between his followers and those of Asquith.

In writing the letter Maurice had committed a grave breach of discipline which could not be condoned or overlooked by the Army Council however much the members may have appreciated his motives. He was at once retired from the army, and was refused a court martial or inquiry.

He tackled the problem of earning his living with courage and enterprise. He turned to teaching and writing and in both he achieved considerable success. From 1922 to 1933 he was principal of the Working Men's College, which his grandfather had helped to found in 1854. In 1927 he was appointed professor of military studies at London University, and a year later he became chairman of the adult education committee of the Board of Education. He became D.Lit., London, in 1930. From 1933 to 1944 he was principal of the East London College (later Queen Mary College), university of London, where he was not only highly successful in maintaining the academic standards but also made a great contribution to the development of the social life of both staff and students. He became a fellow of Queen Mary College in 1946 and was a member of the university senate. He was made an honorary LL.D. of Cambridge in 1926, was Lees Knowles lecturer at Trinity College in 1925–6, and was elected an honorary fellow of King's College in 1944 in recognition of the good relations he established between the colleges when Queen Mary College was moved to Cambridge in the war.

Maurice published a number of admirable historical studies including books on the *Russo-Turkish War 1877* (1905) and Robert E. Lee (1925). He wrote a life of his father, and collaborated with Sir George Arthur in a biography of Lord Wolseley (1924). He also wrote biographies of Lord Haldane (2 vols. 1937–9) and Lord Rawlinson (1928). Among his other books are *Governments and War* (1926), *British Strategy* (1929, based on a series of lectures), *The 16th Foot* (1931), a *History of the Scots Guards* (2 vols., 1934), and *The Armistices of 1918* (1943). *Forty Days in 1914* (1919) is a particularly good study of the B.E.F. in the opening campaign of the war; *The Last Four Months* (1919) is hardly on the same level. He was for a time military correspondent to the *Daily Chronicle* and the *Daily News*, and was a contributor to many magazines and reviews and also to the *Cambridge Modern History*.

Maurice took a deep interest in the British Legion and was indefatigable in his work for the welfare of ex-servicemen. He became its honorary treasurer in 1930 and was president in 1932–47. In September 1938 he flew to Berlin and offered the services of the Legion to Hitler for duty in the plebiscite areas of Czechoslovakia, with the result that a contingent of 1,200 ex-servicemen was assembled before the plebiscite was called off. A year later, three days before Great Britain entered the war, he broadcast to the soldiers of the German Army on behalf of the Legion, appealing to them not to bring about another fight with England by attacking Poland. He was colonel of his regiment from 1935 to 1941; was a commander of the Legion of Honour and of the Order of the Crown of Belgium, and had the Russian Order of St. Stanislas and the French croix de guerre.

In appearance Maurice was tall and fair, a little bent, with a round face and a boxer's flattened-out nose. He had a rather abrupt manner and he spoke and wrote with great clarity and conciseness. Those with whom he served were impressed by his efficiency, loyalty, and capacity for friendship. He loved poetry and when he was incapacitated by illness in his last years he would recite aloud favourite passages from Tennyson, Wordsworth, and Kipling. As a soldier his talents were those of a staff officer rather than

Monash

a commander. He inherited a family tradition of high idealism and readiness to sacrifice personal interests to the cause of truth, and the letter which ended his military career was in that tradition.

He married in 1899 Helen Margaret (died 1942), daughter of Frederick Howard Marsh, later professor of surgery at Cambridge and master of Downing College and sister of (Sir) Edward Marsh. They had one son and four daughters, one of whom, Joan Violet Robinson, became professor of economics at Cambridge in 1965. Maurice died at his home in Cambridge 19 May 1951. A portrait by Henry Lamb is in Queen Mary College.

[*The Times*, 21 May 1951; *Westminster Gazette, passim*, 1922; *Spectator*, 2, 16, 23 November and 7 December 1956; Sir Frederick Maurice, *Intrigues of the War* (preface by the Marquess of Crewe), 1922; David Lloyd George, *War Memoirs*, vol. v, 1936; Sir Edward Spears, *Prelude to Victory*, 1939; Lord Beaverbrook, *Men and Power*, 1956; S. W. Roskill, *Hankey, Man of Secrets*, vol. i, 1970; private information; personal knowledge.]

JOHN KENNEDY

published 1971

MONASH John

(1865–1931)

Sir

Australian general, was born of Jewish parentage in Melbourne 27 June 1865, the only son of Louis Monash, of St. James's Park, Hawthorn, Melbourne, by his wife, Bertha Manasse; his parents were born and married in Germany. He was educated at Scotch College and at the university, Melbourne, where he graduated in arts, engineering, and laws. He was Argus scholar with honours in engineering.

Monash began practice as a civil engineer in 1884, specializing in rail, road, bridge, and water-supply design and construction. From his earliest student days he had been a keen and enthusiastic member of the Australian Citizen Forces and in 1887 secured his first commission as a lieutenant with promotion to captain in 1895 and major in 1897. In this connexion his power of lucid exposition was noticed by (Sir) Ian Hamilton and other officers visiting Australia. From 1900 he concentrated on reinforced concrete construction and introduced his methods into Victoria, Tasmania, and South Australia. In 1901 he was given command of the North Melbourne Artillery. In 1905 he had been promoted lieutenant-colonel in the Citizen Forces and by 1913 had achieved his full colonelcy. He also served as an officer of the Intelligence Corps from 1907 to 1914. His progress in the engineering world had by then brought him to the presidency of the Victorian Institute of Engineers, which he held for two years.

On the outbreak of war in 1914 Monash was appointed chief censor for Australia but only held the post for a month as his services were required in a more active field of operations. He was put in command of the 4th Infantry brigade and accompanied it to Gallipoli in April 1915, and was promoted brigadier-general in July. During this campaign his brigade was engaged in defence of a sector which came to be named after him, Monash Valley, and later it was employed in the fighting at Suvla Bay. Towards the end of the year Gallipoli was evacuated and Monash was mentioned in dispatches three times for his services in the campaign.

Monash was then given command of the 3rd Australian division in July 1916 with the rank of major-general, and after training the division in England he proceeded with it to France (November 1916) where it took part in the battles of Messines (June 1917) and Passchendaele (October 1917), the third battle of Ypres (1917), and the defence of Amiens (1918). His great and obvious capacity, especially in the higher commands, was soon recognized and he succeeded General William (later Lord) Birdwood in command of the Australian Army Corps in France, assuming the command in May 1918 with the rank of lieutenant-general.

Monash's great *forte* was planning, and to this objective he brought to bear all his training and experience as a brilliant engineer. His plans for battle were blueprints of the most detailed construction complete to the last detail, and so well were his great qualities recognized and appreciated that it fell to him with the Australian Army Corps successfully to withstand the last offensive of the enemy in the late spring of 1918 and to launch the great Allied offensive of August 1918. To his masterly organization and his brilliance as a corps commander the Allies owed much for the success of the offensive and his great achievements with the corps during the ensuing battles earned for him recognition as one of the ablest corps commanders in the British army. After the armistice was signed he was appointed director-general of the Department of Repatriation and Demobilization of the Australian Imperial Forces in Europe, Africa, and Asia, and for his untiring devotion to this new field of service was mentioned in dispatches eight times. On his return to Australia he became a member of the Council of Defence. He was promoted full general in 1930 and retired from the army in the same year.

Monash's great organizing ability was still further recognized in a new field, when in 1920 he was appointed chairman of the Victorian

Government State Electricity Commission set up by act of parliament. He accepted the invitation in 1923 to become vice-chancellor of Melbourne University and in the following year became president of the Australasian Association for the Advancement of Science, a post which he occupied for two years. In 1931 he acted as official representative of the Commonwealth of Australia at the inauguration of New Delhi, India; and at this time was director and chairman of several Indian and Commonwealth companies.

Monash was appointed C.B. in 1915, K.C.B. in 1918, and G.C.M.G. in 1919. In 1920 he published his book entitled *The Australian Victories in France in 1918* which was a tribute to the great merits of the Australian soldier in the field. In addition he published numerous scientific papers on engineering subjects which had been presented to Australian scientific societies, and also his presidential addresses. In 1920 Melbourne University conferred upon him the honorary degree of doctor of engineering, the first time such a degree was granted by an Australian university. He also received honorary degrees from the universities of Oxford (D.C.L.), Cambridge (LL.D.), and Melbourne (LL.D.).

Monash was without doubt the most prominent Australian soldier of the war of 1914–1918 and when he died at his home, Toorak, Melbourne, 8 October 1931 he was given a state funeral by the city, and many fine eulogies were paid to him. He married in 1891 Victoria (died 1920), youngest daughter of Moton Moss, of Melbourne, and had a daughter.

Portraits of Monash by Sir John Longstaff (1918) and by James Quinn are at the Australian War Memorial at Canberra where there is also a bust by Paul Montford. At the National Gallery, Melbourne, there is a portrait by I. M. Cohen.

[*The Times*, 9 October 1931; *Argus* (Melbourne), 9 October 1931; Fred Johns, *An Australian Biographical Dictionary*, 1934; *Australian Encyclopædia*, 1926; *War Letters of General Monash*, edited by F. M. Cutlack, 1934; Sir J. E. Edmonds, (Official) *History of the Great War. Military Operations. France and Belgium, 1918*, vols. ii–v, 1937–1947; C. F. Aspinall-Oglander, (Official) *History of the Great War. Military Operations. Gallipoli*, vols. i and ii, 1929–1932; C. E. W. Bean, *Official History of Australia in the War of 1914–1918*, 12 vols., 1922–1942.]

C. V. Owen

published 1949

MONTGOMERY Bernard Law

(1887–1976)

First Viscount Montgomery of Alamein

Field marshal, was born in St. Mark's vicarage, Kennington Oval, 17 November 1887, the third of the six sons and fourth of the nine children of the Revd Henry Hutchinson Montgomery, son of Sir Robert Montgomery, lieutenant-governor of the Punjab, and his wife, Maud, third daughter of Canon (later Dean) Frederic William Farrar, author of *Eric, or Little by Little* (1858). Their family was to grow up in Tasmania where Henry Montgomery became bishop in 1889.

A self-willed larrikin of fourteen, at odds with a mother as determined as he was, Bernard went with a brother as a day-boy to St. Paul's School, when the Montgomerys finally returned from Hobart in 1902, to live frugally in Chiswick; but high-spirited family holidays—there were eight children by now (a daughter died young and a son later died as a schoolboy)—were spent at New Park, the property at Moville, Donegal, which the bishop had inherited from his father.

Good at games and eager to lead, Bernard was 'very happy' at St. Paul's and at nineteen (and 5ft. 7ins.) 'the Monkey' eventually managed to pass, not very impressively (seventy-second out of 177), into Sandhurst. Lucky to be allowed to continue there after a cruel jape, he failed to pass out high enough (he was thirty-sixth) to make the coveted Indian Army; instead, he was commissioned, 19 September 1908, into the Royal Warwickshire Regiment with which he had no previous connection. Entirely dependent upon his pay and never having tasted alcohol, he was posted in December to the 1st battalion, then on the North-West Frontier at Peshawar. He rode hard at everything, his chosen profession and the study of Urdu and Pushtu. He always wanted to win, whether an argument or a steeplechase. Wilful and opinionated, he was continually straining at the leash.

Returning to England by 1913 in time to play hockey for the army and to pass out top of the musketry course at Hythe, Lieutenant B. L. Montgomery was acting adjutant when the 1st Warwickshire Regiment was mobilized at Shorncliffe in August 1914, and he crossed to Boulogne 23 August with the 10th brigade in the 4th division. Scarcely twenty-four hours after disembarkation they were under fire at Le Cateau. A notably fearless young officer, Montgomery was reported missing, gravely wounded and left for dead at Meteren, but survived in hospital at Woolwich to learn that he had been appointed, 13 October 1914, as a temporary captain of twenty-seven, to the DSO—the Military Cross was not instituted until December—for his bearing at the first battle of Ypres.

There followed early in the New Year a formative posting to Lancashire as brigade-major, 112th (later 104th) brigade, which enabled him not only to survive (which his return to a battalion would have rendered most improbable) but to begin to take on responsibilities and to uncover that flair for training which characterized his whole career. He pierced impatiently into the heart of matters to discover the most straightforward tactical solution to be used by the new armies which Lord Kitchener was raising to succeed the original British Expeditionary Force. Montgomery's written orders tingled with clarity; he was becoming highly professional.

His dedication soon inspired trust; he was brigade-major, 104th brigade on the Somme, January 1916; GSO 2, 33rd division (at Arras again), 1917; then, from July 1917, GSO 2 of IX Corps at Passchendaele; thereafter, from 16 July 1918, until the war ended, GSO 1, 47th (London) division. Then, at Cologne, with the connivance of Sir William Robertson, he contrived to get himself selected for the Staff College at Camberley for January 1920. A brevet-major (3 June 1918), he had been mentioned in dispatches six times, wounded thrice, and awarded the French croix de guerre.

He came to ponder his experiences deeply only after he had left Camberley. In 1921 he was posted to Cork as brigade-major, 17th (the largest) Infantry brigade, in a war to him 'far worse' than the one he had survived. During the next few years in England, under sympathetic leadership, he became determined that costly mistakes should not be perpetrated again: there should be no more 'useless' carnage under remote generals and their cosy staffs; future battles were to be fought with decent economy and orchestrated artillery—metal saving flesh. Hence it was important to have accurate information, good communication and wireless, and the use of aircraft; there was also a need for sound understanding between effectively trained officers and an informed soldiery. All these considerations underlined the importance of training to which Montgomery now devoted his single-minded bachelor career. He was brigade-major, 8th Infantry brigade at Devonport, then GSO 2, 49th West Riding Territorial division at York where he lived in the same friendly mess as (Sir) F. W. de Guingand, his future chief of staff. In March 1925 he went back to his regiment at Shorncliffe, but the turning point, Montgomery himself believed, was his posting in January 1926 to the Staff College, this time as an instructor, alongside Alan Brooke (later Viscount Alanbrooke), (Sir) Bernard Paget, and (Sir) Richard O'Connor. Their pupils included Harold Alexander (later Earl Alexander of Tunis), (Sir) Miles Dempsey, (Sir) Oliver Leese, (Sir) Richard McCreery, (Sir) Archibald Nye, Brian Robertson (later Lord Robertson of Oakridge), (Sir) Gerald Templer, and A. F. ('John')

Harding (later Lord Harding of Petherton). Montgomery was an inspired teacher, unforgettably clear-headed.

To everybody's surprise he married, 27 July 1927, Elizabeth, widow of Captain Oswald Armitage Carver, a sapper officer killed at Gallipoli, the sister of P. B. S. Hobart, and the daughter of Robert Thompson Hobart, Indian Civil Service, of Tunbridge Wells. She had two sons at preparatory school. They had met on successive skiing holidays in Switzerland. The marriage, which opened new horizons to the monastic, dogmatic soldier, was intensely happy.

Contentment did not attenuate a marked independence of spirit and not infrequent clashes with authority. Set to revise, as secretary of a War Office committee, the manual of *Infantry Training* in 1929, Montgomery, by his own account, published his personal version ignoring amendments; 'exploitation' was a significant omission. Three years followed while he fulfilled a natural ambition, the command of his own first regiment, in Jerusalem, Alexandria, and Poona. His seniors noted 'a certain high-handedness' as a possible handicap to future advancement.

In 1934 he succeeded Paget as chief instructor at Quetta, where he remained until 1937, experiencing the earthquake in May 1935. Then, at the instigation of A. P. (later Earl) Wavell, he was posted May 1937 to Portsmouth to command 9th brigade. Tragedy struck. After ten enjoyable years of their marriage, 'Betty' Montgomery died of septicaemia (19 October 1937) after an insect bite on the beach at Burnham-on-Sea. Montgomery, left a widower with a young son, was utterly desolate. He hid himself in the army and was never the same man again: he had lost his firm base.

Lonely wilfulness could land him in trouble. War Department land at Southsea was let without reference to authority for an August fairground, the rent being spent on garrison amenities. The solitary brigadier found himself for a while 'dicky on the perch', but Wavell (at Southern Command) was never a man to waste eccentric talent, and a successful career was resumed in October 1938 with Montgomery's promotion to Palestine to command the 8th Infantry division from Haifa. O'Connor's 7th division was stationed to his south. Their grip was soon felt: terrorism was dealt with rigorously and the civilian administration regained confidence. By now evidently a most promising major-general, Montgomery was told that, should war break out in Europe, he might expect to command the 3rd division in the proposed expeditionary force. At this moment he was suddenly struck by a feverish illness affecting the lung which had been penetrated in 1914. Taken on board at Port Said on a stretcher, he forced himself to walk confidently ashore at Tilbury and proceeded to badger the military secretary until on 28 August 1939 he received the command he had been promised.

With Brooke, his Corps commander in II Corps, and with Alexander, he was one of the few to emerge from the inglorious campaign in Belgium with an enhanced reputation. However, before the fighting began Brooke had to protect him—not for the last time—from the consequences of acting off his own bat. In this instance, he had issued a tactless ordinance about brothels, which had started an outcry.

Highly trained and diligently rehearsed, Montgomery's 'Third Division worked like clockwork', the Corps commander noted, from the Dyle and Louvain back to Dunkirk where he and Alexander were responsible for the rearguard. Montgomery was appointed CB (1940).

The 3rd division was the first to be re-equipped in England but in July 1940 Montgomery left it to succeed Sir Claude Auchinleck (promoted to Southern Command) as commander, V Corps. Cheerfully disobedient, he held that the way to repel the expected invasion was not on the beaches but by counter-attack after the enemy had landed; yet the army still lacked mobility and he himself had had to beg the prime minister at Brighton that summer for buses for his own division. Brooke, the only soldier Montgomery genuinely respected, and who was to become his surrogate conscience, besought him (3 August 1940) not to let him down 'by doing anything silly'.

In April, having lost all his worldly goods in an enemy bombing raid on Portsmouth in January, Montgomery moved from V Corps to XII Corps, and thence to command South-Eastern Army (17 November 1941). It was from this spell in England that, by his own reckoning, his 'real influence on the training of the army began' and with it the growth of the legend (which reached the Middle East) of the abstemious, dedicated widower, the ruthless oddity who made physical fitness a fetish and declared war on 'dead wood', wives, and complacency. Once the threat of invasion abated (and Montgomery spotted this sooner than most) the army in England had to be made ready for aggressive warfare in all weathers overseas, and this he set about achieving in a series of formidable exercises.

In mid-1942 planning for a Canadian raid on Dieppe was put in train and Montgomery was involved (although in later years he was inclined to be reticent on this score). He felt that since secrecy had been forfeited, another venue should be sought. The raid took place on 19 August 1942; Montgomery had left the United Kingdom nine days earlier.

He had been told to be ready to succeed Alexander (who had been sent to Cairo to succeed Auchinleck as C-in-C Middle East) in command of First Army, which was to invade French North Africa (Operation Torch) under General Eisenhower's overall command. Then, when W. H. E. Gott was killed, Montgomery was dispatched to take his place at El Alamein, in command of Eighth Army. Placing his son David in the care of his friends the Reynolds, he reached Cairo on 12 August. He knew in his bones that he was stepping into history.

Disregarding instructions, he took over in the Western Desert two days early and at once set about imposing his strong will. He was unprepossessing in appearance, skinny, sharp-faced 'like a Parson Jack Russell terrier', and his English knees were still white, but he knew exactly what he wanted: an abrupt change of 'atmosphere', the end of 'bellyaching' (the discussion of orders rather than their execution) and of looking over one's shoulder. There was to be no withdrawal. Eighth Army would fight and die at the Alamein position where the enemy had been halted by Auchinleck's resolution in July. De Guingand was promoted from brigadier general staff to chief of staff, to free the army commander from detail. New corps commanders and a new brigadier Royal Artillery were summoned from England, the 44th division was ordered up imperiously from the delta, and the army headquarters was set down by the sea alongside the desert air force. The armour was rehearsed in its defensive role, dug in or hull down.

Montgomery quickly imposed his personal authority as he quickened the pulse of his new command. In a crisis of confidence among men far from home he provided reassurance and certainty. His army (or enough of it) soon became convinced, as they saw him darting about in unexpected headgear, that, despite his sartorial eccentricity, he knew what he was up to, talked sense (in an odd but readily quotable vocabulary), would deliver the goods, and, above all, not waste their lives. It was a new and exciting technique of command. The model defensive battle (from 31 August) at Alam Halfa, in which the air force played a substantial role, furnished Montgomery with the mastery and Eighth Army with the morale demanded in the major offensive battle to follow. Although he himself came to exaggerate the uniqueness and novelty of his own contribution and to maintain that everything went according to preconceived plan, the unfamiliar sight of Rommel's forces on their way back (3 September) through the minefields they had penetrated with such difficulty heartened Eighth Army enormously and hardened belief in 'Monty' and his self-assurance.

There was political pressure on him to resume battle, partly because the Martuba airfields in the North African bulge had to be regained by mid-November to allow for air cover for the last convoy leaving Alexandria to replenish Malta's almost exhausted aviation fuel, and partly because the departure of 'Torch' in early November would have been hazarded had news reached England of any apathy. With Alexander's imperturbable backing, Montgomery took his own time to mount his offensive. He had to learn to master the new American Sherman tanks and anti-tank guns, to improve the training (especially in dealing with minefields), and to institute deception measures for what was inevitably frontal attack on the strong enemy defences at El Alamein between the sea and the virtually impassable Qattara depression. These requirements, together with the state of the moon and of Eighth Army's readiness, set the date for 23 October. By then, of course, the enemy defences were deeper and stronger.

His design (Operation Lightfoot) was to feint in the south whilst cutting corridors through the northern Axis positions in a moonlit operation with massed artillery support, to hold off the German armour during the 'crumbling' operations which would ensue, and in this 'dogfight', lasting perhaps twelve days, to hold the initiative so as to deprive the enemy armour of firm bases from which to manœuvre or within which to re-furbish.

By 23 October the desert air force had conclusively won the air battle and thereafter successfully devoted its full attention to the close support of the land forces, which had already been so effective at Alam Halfa. By 25 October Eighth Army had gained a bridgehead in the northern Axis positions, which was slowly developed into a salient increasingly menacing the coastal road. With controlled flexibility Montgomery alternated the direction of his thrusts—until, fearful of his ultimate line of advance, the main German forces were congregated, not without severe losses, in the northern sector about Sidi Abd al Rahman. Maintaining his apparent thrust line, Montgomery, who, by shrewd regrouping since 26 October had been accumulating reserves as steadily as the returning Rommel had been forced to commit his, early on 2 November cut through south of the main German concentrations into the preponderantly Italian positions (Operation Supercharge). A quickly improvised Axis anti-tank screen prevented immediate breakthrough but on 4 November this was forced back and the overextended Axis defences crumpled. Those with vehicles could attempt retreat; for the rest, mainly Italian, surrender was the only option. Eighth Army's casualties were 13,500.

It was a considerable victory. With air supremacy and, on the ground, unparalleled numerical superiority in armour and artillery, Montgomery could call on resources denied to his predecessors. But he used them (and a remarkable flow of intelligence) in a unique revelation of determination and skill to enforce the attrition. It was 'a killing match'.

He could be criticized—there were willing critics of, for example, the way he used his armour and the cumbersome arrangements of corps commands with which he began. This was strange indeed in a general who made tidiness a shibboleth. Yet Montgomery retained throughout those twelve days in that chaotic man-made dust storm a clinical control of the mine-filled battlefield, a serenity and balance in his own deployments, and, above all, an intense unswerving determination which dominated the situation and compelled both his own troops and their adversary to submit to his unremitting will. By insisting when it was all over that it had all gone according to plan, he did not do justice (a curious sacrifice) to his own generalship, his trained skill, and his power to improvise in an emergency.

A compulsive student of the military art, he could pierce with fierce concentration into the essence of a battlefield. This talent for simplification could be pressed to excess, as the nuances or rougher edges became subsumed in an overriding certainty. Personal vanity nourished in him a deliberate (and infectious) self-assurance. Within a self-compelled taut serenity lay genuine physical bravery: he made himself ignore danger. There was always too a didactic note: lessons must be drawn from all that was happening. To this educational concern was added a capacity to inspire, an unexpectedly Messianic quality. He had the gift of seeing into the hearts of men, of sensing what was worrying them; they must be convinced (despite a spinsterly voice) that what he and they were going to do together was the best recipe, and it must be readily, memorably explicable. Therefore every battle must be seen to go according to plan, in order to persuade and inspire men to undertake it and sustain their morale for future campaigns.

A caustic critic of others, he was far too intelligent not to know that matters do not go according to plan, but he was often too vain to admit this publicly, too much wrapped up in what he was doing to unravel the problems fully afterwards. In convincing others (or some of them), he came to convince himself too.

He became a full general and was appointed KCB (11 November 1942). The tight control of the battlefield was momentarily relaxed. Montgomery would argue that the sluggish pursuit was ensuring that the Rommel bogey laid at Alamein should never return—to disturb the assiduously nourished morale which had made the victory possible. Eighth Army did not think itself as slow as the outside world found it: it throve on carefully planned success, the build-up which avoided the unnecessary casualty, the assured maintenance before the next hammer-blow by orchestrated artillery, air, infantry, and armour. The brilliant improvisation which cut off the retreating Italians at Beda Fomm in February 1941 was not in Montgomery's repertoire: he wanted Rommel finally expelled from El Agheila, his original springboard. In the event he was unable to cut Rommel off at Benghazi, El Agheila, or Buerat. He personally superintended from his 'Tac HQ' the drive on Tripoli (Eighth Army's perennial target) which he reached on 23 January 1943 because storms in Benghazi had made his maintenance more tenuous than he liked. On the way he prepared a training pamphlet on *High Command in War* which could scarcely have enhanced his popularity outside Eighth Army; neither did the 'teach-in' in Tripoli and the parades there for Churchill's benefit.

Knowing that Rommel, having savaged the Americans at Kasserine in mid-February, would turn on Eighth Army before it was fully ready to tackle the Mareth Line, Montgomery hastened up his tanks by transporter and gave himself time to arrange his anti-tank guns for another model defensive battle at Medenine (6 March). At Mareth an uncharacteristic attack on the coastal flank was repulsed (20 March), but Montgomery cut his losses, swiftly reinforced his attacking forces on his left, and forced the Axis switch-line (27 March) west of the hills before El Hamma. The Akarit position remained to be stormed (6–7 April). A day or so later Eighth Army's armoured cars made contact with tanks of US II Corps on the Gabes–Gafsa road, and Eighth Army's private war was over.

When he arrived in Sfax (10 April 1943) Montgomery tactlessly insisted that as payment of a bet made in Tripoli with General Walter Bedell Smith, Eisenhower's chief of staff, he should receive a Flying Fortress aircraft with its American crew, for his personal use: an early sign that he was to be a difficult ally to work with. Despite his quite remarkable understanding of his own soldiers and his staff, he made no attempt to comprehend American sensibilities.

He was now anxious for the speedy termination of the North African campaign to release his troops and staff to prepare for the invasion of Sicily. He overestimated the ease of the problem and was rebuffed at Enfidaville: even Eighth Army could not move mountains; but he swiftly recognized that, by switching some of his troops and commanders to First Army, Tunis might rapidly be captured.

Meanwhile he had emphatically rejected the plans proposed for the capture of Sicily, and insisted that his army and the Americans (under General George S. Patton) should invade the south-east corner, side by side, a proposal eventually adopted although not without argument and friction. He became increasingly offhand with Alexander, his old pupil, whose headquarters was to co-ordinate the invasion, and, although in the event the campaign took only thirty-eight days, his selfishness in insisting upon Eighth Army's priorities led to further wrangling. But, as at Enfidaville, he could make himself realize better ways of accomplishing military purposes, and to Patton's surprise he deliberately yielded the capture of Messina to him.

Before Sicily was invaded (10 July 1943) he had taken some leave in London where he found himself a popular hero, an enjoyable discovery which made him less and less amenable to subordination or advice. He had come to regard himself as the greatest fighting commander alive. He was ready to lay down the military law and he had no hesitation in criticizing anyone. His hold on his soldiers remained secure and he took great trouble about them, but senior officers of other services and nations became increasingly critical of his unbridled self-importance.

He was thus disconcerted to learn at Taormina in August that in the invasion of Italy his was to be a minor role, since Eisenhower planned to employ forces at Salerno under General Mark Clark quite separately from Eighth Army, which was allocated the secondary task of getting across the straits of Messina and then switching from Reggio to the heel of Italy, to secure the Foggia airfields and the ports of Taranto and Brindisi. The task was over-elaborately performed (3 September 1943) and did little to take pressure off the Allied forces at Salerno.

When it became evident that the Germans (with more than twenty divisions) proposed to hold a line as far south in Italy as they were able, Montgomery was faced with a slow slog up the Adriatic coast until checked at the end of 1943, after an expensive battle, at the Sangro. From the start he was highly critical of the campaign: no master plan; no operational grip; and administratively, 'a dog's breakfast'.

He was therefore overjoyed at Christmas in Vasto to be posted to England to command 21st Army Group in the cross-Channel invasion of France.

As with the Sicilian campaign, his decisive contribution to the Normandy invasion was his insistence upon the invasion plan he himself had proposed. On his way back to the United Kingdom Churchill at Marrakesh showed him the draft plans, which Montgomery sulkily criticized. He was authorized by Eisenhower, the new supreme commander for Operation Overlord, to undertake the initial role of C-in-C of the ground forces, and he insisted upon a widening of the frontage, an increase in the invading forces, two armies to go in side by side, and the consequent postponement of the proposed D-Day until early June to allow additional landing craft to become available. From the first, the British on the left were to go for Caen and the airfield country beyond, the Americans for the Cotentin peninsula to gain the port of Cherbourg. To decisiveness he added inspiration. Having secured the major decisions he required from the navy and air forces and General Omar Bradley, the American army commander, he set about enthusing not only those who would actually take part in the invasion, the troops on the ground, but also the populace who would sustain them. Detailed planning, once the major decisions had been agreed (in a surprisingly short time considering their importance), was left to the staff to get on with: they were more grateful for what they inherited than Montgomery would show himself to be. Instead, he occupied himself in an astonishing revivalist campaign in which he toured the country addressing not only troops but railwaymen, dockers, factory workers, and the City. Since the darker days of 1940 there can scarcely have been a more enthusiastically united nation as the weeks before D-Day lessened: people came to believe that the invasion would happen, and were convinced of victory at last. The whistle-stop tour was interrupted for Montgomery to give a quite remarkable exposition of his assault plans on 15 May at St. Paul's School, Hammersmith (his temporary headquarters before moving close to Portsmouth to be ready for D-Day) to a spellbound senior audience which included the King, the prime minister, J. C. Smuts, Sir Alan Brooke, and Eisenhower, the supreme commander.

With complete air supremacy, the landings of 6 June, though fiercely opposed, were very successful and a firm bridgehead was established fairly rapidly. The danger was stalemate, and Montgomery, whilst the deception plan was still holding enemy reinforcements in the Pas de Calais, managed to sustain the initiative in Normandy by forcing Rommel to commit more and more of his Panzer divisions to plugging holes against expensive British thrusts in the Caen sector until such time as the Americans, having secured Cherbourg, could turn south, then wheel to drive the enemy against the Seine. He was criticized for the slowness of his progress by an impatient supreme commander awaiting more rapid results, by the air marshals anxious to secure their promised airfields, and by the prime minister and the press, especially the American press. From the serenity of his 'Tac HQ' at Creuilly, or later at Bray, with his young liaison officers keeping him well informed of the battlefield (as Ultra did of his enemy), Montgomery's confidence never wavered and he carried with him that of his troops. He was supported by the sturdy loyalty of Dempsey at British Second Army and Bradley at American First Army who both well understood his overall purpose and saw him daily. It was an anxious period, more anxious the further removed one was from Normandy, and there were cries for Montgomery's head. The American break out which he had patiently awaited eventually started on 25 July, the British and Canadian forces having successfully tied down enough of the German Panzers on the further flank; Montgomery's balanced arrangements paid off when, through Hitler's intervention, the enemy launched a desperate counter-offensive on 7 August at Mortain directed towards the coast at Avranches, to cut the Americans in two. But Bradley kept his nerve: the American right was ordered to wheel north whilst the Canadians thrust south to create 'the Falaise pocket'. Fighting was intense and casualties very heavy indeed, and though the enemy left many dead, many escaped to cross the Seine to fight again. However, Montgomery's determination and sustained initiative, together with the punishment meted out by the air forces, resulted in Allied victory and German losses of 400,000—half of them prisoners.

It had always been the intention as Montgomery himself well knew, that around 1 September, once Eisenhower's headquarters were established in France and there were two Army Groups each of two armies under his overall command, the supreme commander would assume direct control of the ground forces himself. Montgomery however was so sure that he had the military answer, just proven by substantial success, that in his heart of hearts he never genuinely accepted the simple political fact: had the Americans considered him the best available commander of ground forces (they did not), it was still impossible, once the restricting emergencies of Normandy had been successfully surmounted, for a British general, however distinguished, to continue in overall command when, through manpower shortages, the British contribution—at first roughly equal—was shrinking and the American effort becoming daily more preponderant.

Normandy was followed by an unseemly period of patronizing, querulous, and insubordinate disagreement about how the campaign should develop and whose ideas should prevail, until eventually a long-suffering Eisenhower was girding himself to demand Montgomery's dismissal when de Guingand intervened and prevailed upon the supreme commander to hold his hand and Montgomery his tongue.

Meanwhile Montgomery had become a field marshal (30 August 1944) and 21st Army Group had reached Brussels and Antwerp. He wanted the Allied advance to be concentrated in a powerful thrust of some forty divisions (which he hoped to command) north-east to cut off the Ruhr. Eisenhower however preferred to advance to the Rhine on a broader front and refused to give Montgomery priority in fuel supply by rationing American advances further south.

As the Allied front broadened, so distance widened the difference of opinion. Whereas it appeared to Montgomery's staff that the first priority was to get the Schelde river open to nourish further advances (especially after the uncovenanted capture of Antwerp on 4 September), Montgomery himself persuaded Eisenhower that this might be delayed (or conducted *pari passu*) whilst an operation was mounted to advance into Germany by vaulting the great Dutch rivers with airborne troops. Eisenhower released his strategic reserve to Montgomery. The subsequent operation (Arnhem, 17 September) was neither well planned nor well conducted. Communications were erratic, the intelligence was untuned, and Montgomery paid the penalty for acting impulsively and out of character in the first and only defeat of his military career. He hoped (it may be supposed) that had he succeeded, the whole Allied *Schwerpunkt* would be dragged north-east, but in his desire to have his own way, the war over, and the sites of the missiles assailing London cut off from their supply, he underestimated both the extent of German recovery and the marked reluctance of American generals to return under his governance. Defeat at Arnhem cost him his bargaining arm and thereafter the northern flank ceased to figure importantly in SHAEF's priorities.

Montgomery bounced back into the forefront when, on 16 December 1944, a surprise German offensive in the Ardennes drove a wedge between the strung-out American divisions. He was called upon to command those north of the new German salient. He rose to the opportunity, and sorted out the front with his former clarity and verve, but the manner of his coming (as if 'to cleanse the temple') and the cocksureness of his subsequent press conference (7 January) left much bitterness, and once the campaign was successfully resumed he was kept increasingly out on a limb. American speed in crossing the Rhine at Remagen (First Army) and Oppenheim (Third Army) was in sharp contrast to the deliberation with which Montgomery prepared to cross at Wesel. Having forfeited his infallibility at Arnhem, he reverted to his proven ways, overinsurance which might lose pace but made for certainty.

The argument about having a ground forces commander (as distinct from Eisenhower's direct command from SHAEF in Versailles) was inextricably entangled with the personality—and nationality—of Montgomery himself. Montgomery even volunteered, how genuinely it is difficult to guess, to serve under Bradley. But this was difficult to envisage, and Churchill's clumsy intervention was too late in the day to bring back Alexander from Italy in the role Montgomery himself objected to. The dispute spilled over into contention over control of US Ninth Army and whether it should be comprised within Bradley's left or Montgomery's right wing. Montgomery's trouble was that he could not achieve his aims without considerable American support; his own forces were by now inadequate for a 'master plan' finishing in Berlin. He was not therefore brought back into the middle of matters but left with the limited role of closing off the entrances to Scandinavia before the Russians reached them. His troops reached Wismar on 2 May 1945 and two days later the German forces in north-west Germany, Holland, and Denmark were surrendered to him on Lüneberg heath.

All his life Montgomery's methods and personality provoked controversy and animosities. By cutting himself off from SHAEF which he visited but once and maintaining, instead, a running correspondence with the War Office, from his sanctuary in 'Tac HQ', he was encouraged by the chief of the imperial general staff and P. J. Grigg, the secretary of state, in an anti-American bias which hindered his getting on with the job. His was not the only way to win the war, and he paid all too little recognition to American resourcefulness, Bradley's dour professionalism, or Patton's outstanding talent for exploitation.

Montgomery—perhaps uniquely—knew how to handle large amounts of military equipment without becoming overwhelmed by them and to inspire large bodies of men (and not just his own fellow countrymen) for military purposes. It was easy to deride his strut, his preoccupation with personal publicity, his two-badged beret, his evangelical messages to his troops; but, whatever one's distaste for 'Montification', he was not 'just a PR general'. He was a very professional soldier, and citizen soldiers at the sharp end felt 'safe' in his hands, a belief their families came to share. It was not just a prolonged stunt: his care for his men was deep-seated. He might rile military clubland by the frankness of his 'ungentlemanly' self-aggrandizement; yet there is not much room for 'nice' men in war. In the dread trade, to which his life was dedicated, of killing considerable numbers of enemy in the most economical way possible, he exhibited a clinical concentration on the essential with morals taking a major share in the calculations. His talents and his behaviour were evidently best fitted to circumscribed command in which he got his own way—he was at his best in the Western Desert commanding Eighth Army in whom he instilled his own especial arrogance, the army of the film *Desert Victory*. As an army group commander, which eventually entailed working loyally alongside allies, he was less well placed. One is tempted to conclude that he had got beyond his ceiling—it was his own view that each officer has his ceiling—yet any account of his command in Normandy would go a long way to challenge that evaluation.

Most awkward to serve alongside, impossible to serve over, he was an excellent man to serve under, especially on his staff. The staff he had mostly inherited from Auchinleck he retained until the war ended. He was indulgent to the young aides-de-camp and liaison officers whom he picked, trusted, and trained.

His sense of fairness and especially of truth were not as other men's. In his convictions he was ruthless, even baleful, yet his insensitively arrogant self-confidence was combined with an indiscreet, mischievous, schoolboyish sense of humour which buoyed up the spirits of those far from home. Above all, he trusted those who worked with him to get on with the job, treating them as experienced professionals. His competence as a general, his economy in the use of his troops, the clarity of his commands, and, quintessentially, his decisiveness made a profound impression. One felt that he would get the war over, so that 'we could all pack up and go home again'. Until that happened, he won ready allegiance.

Montgomery became C-in-C of the British forces of occupation and the British member of the Allied Control Council in Berlin. Having secured what he believed mattered most—the establishment of order, the restoration of communications, the demobilization of the German armed forces, the reopening of the mines, and the sowing of the harvest—he left the fuller implementation to able subordinates: Sir Ronald (later Lord) Weeks and then Brian Robertson in Berlin, and Gerald Templer in the British zone.

In 1945 he was advanced to GCB. Honours were now showered upon him by nations, cities, and universities. He was granted a peerage in the New Year honours of 1946. He took the title Viscount Montgomery of Alamein, of Hindhead, in the county of Surrey. In December 1946 he was installed as a Knight of the Garter. All these were accolades which he enjoyed to the full.

Accounts of his campaigns (ghost-written in the main by 'David' Belchem and issued ostensibly as training manuals for the Rhine Army) were soon published generally: *El Alamein to the River Sangro* (1948) and *Normandy to the Baltic* (1947). Bedell Smith remarked that he now knew that Montgomery's battles had always gone according to plan 'from end to beginning'.

In June 1946 Montgomery, discarding de Guingand like yesterday's shirt, succeeded Alanbrooke ('Brookie'), the only man he recognized as a better soldier, as chief of the imperial general staff. It was a virtually unavoidable succession but the appointment brought out some of his less admirable qualities. He was too set in his ways. He clashed again with Lord Tedder, who was now chief of the air staff: a lack of rapport dating from Alamein. He got on well with C. R. (later Earl) Attlee and Ernest Bevin, and in the War Office itself was soon on nickname terms with Emanuel ('Manny') (later Lord) Shinwell, but he became increasingly at odds with the less convincing A. V. Alexander (later Earl Alexander of Hillsborough) at the Ministry of Defence. After two uncomfortable years for everybody, Montgomery was eased out of Whitehall to become chairman of the Western Union commanders-in-chief, a stop-gap appointment until he became, in March 1951, deputy supreme commander to Eisenhower, commanding the Allied forces of NATO in Europe. He continued to serve as a sort of inspector-general under three other successive supreme commanders until he retired in September 1958. He took the task seriously and, given his limitations, was thought to have performed it well. He had adjusted to the anti-climax with surprising willingness.

The first drafts of his *Memoirs* were in his own clear pencilled handwriting: they were published with too few changes in 1958 and were so much in character that no opinions were altered by them. Publication ended an uneasy friendship with Eisenhower, by then president of the United States. Hackles were also raised in Italy. The book sold well everywhere.

Montgomery lived in active retirement, amidst mementoes and portraits, in a reconstructed mill at Isington on the river Wey near Alton in Hampshire. Tidiness and punctuality were the order of the day. He was a thoughtful and generous host, himself as abstemious as ever. He remained very fit and was to travel widely (though rarely without raising controversy). He wrote in the press about his visits to the USSR (1959), China, and South Africa and published an account of them in *Three Continents* (1962). He was an occasional broadcaster and lecturer and sometimes spoke in the House of Lords, with all his old vigour and habitual reiteration; but he was not well enough to act as pallbearer at Churchill's funeral in 1965. Four years later, however, he performed that office for Field Marshal Alexander and later in the year carried the Sword of State at the opening of Parliament (although in the following year he had to yield it to another). He also had to abandon going to the annual Alamein reunions in London. He used to spend Christmas with the Griggs at the mill and he also enjoyed his seaside arguments with Basil Liddell Hart. His own *History of Warfare* (1968) was mostly by other hands and he recommended his surviving friends to read only those sections he specified as written by himself, but the preface made it clear that his interests were well maintained and was revealing about the commentaries which had impressed him. He continued to be a good correspondent and remained the eager listener he had always been, and he brooded, as he always had, on what he had heard or read. He had come to believe his own legend and to wrap himself in memories which excluded the inconvenient. He died full of years on 25 March 1976 and was succeeded as viscount by his son David Bernard (born 1928). The funeral service was in St. George's chapel, Windsor, and he was buried in a country churchyard at Binstead, Hampshire, a mile from his home.

A statue by Oscar Nemon outside the Ministry of Defence in Whitehall was unveiled by the Queen Mother on 6 June 1980, the anniversary of D-Day.

Montgomery's formidable military skills were best exhibited in the defensive battle, yet it fell to him to mastermind and infuse the two great frontal assaults which heralded the Axis defeats in North Africa and in western Europe, two victories most needed in this country, which forced him, warts and all, into the company of the great captains: the best British field commander, it has been held, since Wellington himself.

[*The Times*, 25 and 26 March 1976; Nigel Hamilton, *Monty, the Making of a General, 1887–1942*, 1981, *Monty, the Master of the Battlefield, 1942–1944*, 1983, and *Monty, the Field Marshal, 1944–1976*, 1986; Ronald Lewin, *Montgomery as Military Commander*, 1971; C. J. C. Malony, *The Mediterranean and the Middle East* (vol. v of the official war history), 1973, pp. 510–13; Michael Howard, *The Causes of Wars*, 1983, pp. 208–

23; Correlli Barnett, *The Desert Generals*, 2nd edn., 1983; Max Hastings, *Overlord*, 1984; Stephen Russell F. Weigley, *Eisenhower's Lieutenants*, 1981; Brian Montgomery, *A Field Marshal in the Family*, 1973; Goronwy Rees, *A Bundle of Sensations*, 1960, pp. 113–51; T. E. B. Howarth (ed.), *Monty at Close Quarters*, 1985; private information; personal knowledge.]

E. T. WILLIAMS

published 1986

MOUNTBATTEN Louis Francis Albert Victor Nicholas

(1900–1979)

First Earl Mountbatten of Burma

Admiral of the fleet, was born at Frogmore House, Windsor, 25 June 1900 as Prince Louis of Battenberg, the younger son and youngest of the four children of Prince Louis Alexander of Battenberg (later Louis Mountbatten, Marquess of Milford Haven, admiral of the fleet), and his wife, Princess Victoria Alberta Elizabeth Marie Irene, daughter of Louis IV of Hesse-Darmstadt. Prince Louis Alexander, himself head of a cadet branch of the house of Hesse-Darmstadt, was brother-in-law to Queen Victoria's daughter, Princess Beatrice; his wife was Victoria's granddaughter. By both father and mother, therefore, Prince Louis was closely connected with the British royal family. One of his sisters married King Gustav VI of Sweden and the other Prince Andrew of Greece.

Prince Louis, 'Dickie' as he was known from childhood, was educated as befitted the son of a senior naval officer—a conventional upbringing varied by holidays with his German relations or with his aunt, the tsarina, in Russia. At Locker's Park School in Hertfordshire he was praised for his industry, enthusiasm, sense of humour, and modesty—the first two at least being characteristics conspicuous throughout his life. From there in May 1913 he entered the naval training college of Osborne as fifteenth out of eighty-three, a respectable if unglamorous position which he more or less maintained during his eighteen months there. Towards the end of his stay his father, now first sea lord, was hounded from office because of his German ancestry. This affected young Prince Louis deeply, though a contemporary recalls him remarking nonchalantly: 'It doesn't really matter very much. Of course I shall take his place.' Certainly his passionate ambition owed something to his desire to avenge his father's disgrace.

In November 1914 Prince Louis moved on to Dartmouth. Though he never shone athletically, nor impressed himself markedly on his contemporaries, his last years of education showed increasing confidence and ability, and at Keyham, the Royal Naval College at Devonport where he did his final course, he came first out of seventy-two. In July 1916 he was assigned as a midshipman to the *Lion*, the flagship of Admiral Sir David (later Earl) Beatty. His flag captain, (Sir) Roger Backhouse, described him as 'a very promising young officer' but his immediate superior felt he lacked the brilliance of his elder brother George—a judgement which Prince Louis himself frequently echoed. The *Lion* saw action in the eight months Prince Louis was aboard but suffered no damage, and by the time he transferred to the *Queen Elizabeth* in February 1917 the prospects of a major naval battle seemed remote. Prince Louis served briefly aboard the submarine K6—'the happiest month I've ever spent in the service'—and visited the western front, but his time on the *Queen Elizabeth* was uneventful and he was delighted to be posted in July 1918 as first lieutenant on one of the P-boats, small torpedo boats designed primarily for anti-submarine warfare. It was while he was on the *Queen Elizabeth* that his father, in common with other members of the royal family, abandoned his German title and was created Marquess of Milford Haven, with the family name of Mountbatten. His younger son was known henceforth as Lord Louis Mountbatten.

At the end of 1919 Mountbatten was one of a group of naval officers sent to widen their intellectual horizons at Cambridge. During his year at Christ's College (of which he became an honorary fellow in 1946) he acquired a taste for public affairs, regularly attending the Union and achieving the distinction, remarkable for someone in his position, of being elected to the committee. Through his close friend Peter Murphy, he also opened his mind to radical opinions—'We all thought him rather left-wing', said the then president of the Union, (Sir) Geoffrey Shakespeare.

While still at Cambridge, Mountbatten was invited by his cousin, the Prince of Wales, to attend him on the forthcoming tour of Australasia in the *Renown*. Mountbatten's roles were those of unofficial diarist, dogsbody, and, above all, companion to his sometimes moody and disobliging cousin. These he performed admirably—'you will never know', wrote the Prince to Lord Milford Haven, 'what very great friends we have become, what he has meant and been to me on this trip.' His reward was to be invited to join the next royal tour to India and Japan in the winter of 1921–2; a journey that doubly marked his life in that in India he learnt to play polo and became engaged to Edwina Cynthia Annette (died 1960), daughter of Wilfrid William Ashley (later Baron Mount Temple).

Mountbatten

Edwina Ashley was descended from the third Viscount Palmerston and the Earls of Shaftesbury, while her maternal grandfather was the immensely rich Sir Ernest Cassel, friend and financial adviser to King Edward VII. At Cassel's death in 1921 his granddaughter inherited some £2.3 million, and eventually also a palace on Park Lane, Classiebawn Castle in Ireland, and the Broadlands estate at Romsey in Hampshire. The marriage of two powerful and fiercely competitive characters was never wholly harmonious and sometimes caused unhappiness to both partners. On the whole, however, it worked well and they established a formidable partnership at several stages of their lives. They had two daughters.

Early in 1923 Mountbatten joined the *Revenge*. For the next fifteen years his popular image was that of a playboy. Fast cars, speedboats, polo, were his delights; above all the last, about which he wrote the classic *Introduction to Polo* (1931) by 'Marco'. Yet nobody who knew his work could doubt his essential seriousness. 'This officer's heart and soul is in the Navy', reported the captain of the *Revenge*, 'No outside interests are ever allowed to interfere with his duties.' His professionalism was proved beyond doubt when he selected signals as his speciality and passed out top of the course in July 1925. As assistant fleet wireless officer (1927–8) and fleet wireless officer (1931–3) in the Mediterranean, and at the signals school at Portsmouth in between, he won a reputation for energy, efficiency, and inventiveness. He raised the standard of signalling in the Mediterranean Fleet to new heights and was known, respected, and almost always liked by everyone under his command.

In 1932 Mountbatten was promoted commander and in April 1934 took over the *Daring*, a new destroyer of 1,375 tons. After only a few months, however, he had to exchange her for an older and markedly inferior destroyer, the *Wishart*. Undiscomfited, he set to work to make his ship the most efficient in the Mediterranean Fleet. He succeeded and *Wishart* was Cock of the Fleet in the regatta of 1935. It was at this time that he perfected the 'Mountbatten station-keeping gear', an ingenious device which was adopted by the Admiralty for use in destroyers but which never really proved itself in wartime.

Enthusiastically recommended for promotion, Mountbatten returned to the Naval Air Division of the Admiralty. He was prominent in the campaign to recapture the Fleet Air Arm from the Royal Air Force, lobbying (Sir) Winston Churchill, Sir Samuel Hoare (later Viscount Templewood), and A. Duff Cooper (later Viscount Norwich) with a freedom unusual among junior officers. He vigorously applauded the latter's resignation over the Munich agreement and maintained a working relationship with Anthony Eden (later the Earl of Avon) and the fourth Marquess of Salisbury in their opposition to appeasement. More practically he was instrumental in drawing the Admiralty's attention to the merits of the Oerlikon gun, the adoption of which he urged vigorously for more than two years. It was during this period that he also succeeded in launching the Royal Naval Film Corporation, an organization designed to secure the latest films for British sailors at sea.

The abdication crisis caused him much distress but left him personally unscathed. Some time earlier he had hopefully prepared for the Prince of Wales a list of eligible Protestant princesses, but by the time of the accession he had little influence left. He had been King Edward VIII's personal naval aide-de-camp and in February 1937 King George VI appointed him to the same position, simultaneously appointing him to the GCVO.

Since the autumn of 1938 Mountbatten had been contributing ideas to the construction at Newcastle of a new destroyer, the *Kelly*. In June 1939 he took over as captain and *Kelly* was commissioned by the outbreak of war. On 20 September she was joined by her sister ship *Kingston*, and Mountbatten became captain (D) of the fifth destroyer flotilla.

Mountbatten was not markedly successful as a wartime destroyer captain. In surprisingly few months at sea he almost capsized in a high sea, collided with another destroyer, and was mined once, torpedoed twice, and finally sunk by enemy aircraft. In most of these incidents he could plead circumstances beyond his control, but the consensus of professional opinion is that he lacked 'sea-sense', the quality that ensures a ship is doing the right thing in the right place at the right time. Nevertheless he acted with immense panache and courage, and displayed such qualities of leadership that when *Kelly* was recommissioned after several months refitting, an embarrassingly large number of her former crew clamoured to rejoin. When he took his flotilla into Namsos in March 1940 to evacuate (Sir) Adrian Carton de Wiart and several thousand Allied troops, he conducted the operation with cool determination. The return of *Kelly* to port in May, after ninety-one hours in tow under almost constant bombardment and with a fifty-foot hole in the port side, was an epic of fortitude and seamanship. It was feats like this that caught Churchill's imagination and thus altered the course of Mountbatten's career.

In the spring of 1941 the *Kelly* was dispatched to the Mediterranean. Placed in an impossible position, Admiral Sir A. B. Cunningham (later Viscount Cunningham of Hyndhope) in May decided to support the army in Crete even though there was no possibility of air cover. The *Kashmir* and the *Kelly* were attacked by dive-bombers on 23 May and soon sunk. More than half the crew of *Kelly* was lost and Mountbatten only escaped by swimming from under the ship as it turned turtle. The survivors were machine-gunned in the water but were picked up by the *Kipling*. The *Kelly* lived on in *In Which We Serve*, a skilful propaganda film by (Sir) Noël

Coward, which was based in detail on the achievements of Lord Louis Mountbatten and his ship. Mountbatten was now appointed to command the aircraft-carrier *Illustrious*, which had been severely damaged and sent for repair to the United States. In October he flew to America to take over his ship and pay a round of visits. He established many useful contacts and made a considerable impression on the American leadership: '... he has been a great help to all of us, and I mean literally ALL', wrote Admiral Starke to Sir A. Dudley Pound. Before the *Illustrious* was ready, however, Mountbatten was called home by Churchill to take charge of Combined Operations. His predecessor, Sir Roger (later Lord) Keyes, had fallen foul of the chiefs of staff and Mountbatten was initially appointed only as 'chief adviser'. In April 1942, however, he became chief of Combined Operations with the acting rank of vice-admiral, lieutenant-general, and air marshal and with *de facto* membership of the chiefs of staff committee. This phenomenally rapid promotion earned him some unpopularity, but on the whole the chiefs of staff gave him full support.

'You are to give no thought for the defensive. Your whole attention is to be concentrated on the offensive', Churchill told him. Mountbatten's duties fell into two main parts: to organize raids against the European coast designed to raise morale, harass the Germans, and achieve limited military objectives; and to prepare for an eventual invasion. The first responsibility, more dramatic though less important, gave rise to a multitude of raids involving only a handful of men and a few more complex operations such as the costly but successful attack on the dry dock at St. Nazaire. Combined Operations were responsible for planning such forays, but their execution was handed over to the designated force commander, a system which led sometimes to confusion.

The ill results of divided responsibilities were particularly apparent in the Dieppe operation of August 1942. Dieppe taught the Allies valuable lessons for the eventual invasion and misled the Germans about their intentions, but the price paid in lives and material was exceedingly, probably disproportionately, high. For this Mountbatten, ultimately responsible for planning the operation, must accept some responsibility. Nevertheless the errors which both British and German analysts subsequently condemned—the adoption of frontal rather than flank assault, the selection of relatively inexperienced Canadian troops for the assault, the abandonment of any previous air bombardment, and the failure to provide the support of capital ships—were all taken against his advice or over his head. Certainly he was not guilty of the blunders which Lord Beaverbrook and some later commentators attributed to him.

When it came to preparation for invasion, Mountbatten's energy, enthusiasm, and receptivity to new ideas showed to great advantage. His principal contribution was to see clearly what is now obvious but was then not generally recognized, that successful landings on a fortified enemy coast called for an immense range of specialized equipment and skills. To secure an armada of landing craft of different shapes and sizes, and to train the crews to operate them, involved a diversion of resources, both British and American, which was vigorously opposed in many quarters. The genesis of such devices as Mulberry (the floating port) and Pluto (pipe line under the ocean) is often hard to establish, but the zeal with which Mountbatten and his staff supported their development was a major factor in their success. Mountbatten surrounded himself with a team of talented if sometimes maverick advisers—Professor J. D. Bernal, Geoffrey Pyke, Solly (later Lord) Zuckerman—and was ready to listen to anything they suggested. Sometimes this led him into wasteful extravagances—as in his championship of the iceberg/aircraft carrier Habbakuk—but there were more good ideas than bad. His contribution to D-Day was recognized in the tribute paid him by the Allied leaders shortly after the invasion: '... we realize that much of ... the success of this venture has its origins in developments effected by you and your staff.'

His contribution to the higher strategy is less easy to establish. He himself always claimed responsibility for the selection of Normandy as the invasion site rather than the Pas de Calais. Certainly when Operation Sledgehammer, the plan for a limited re-entry into the Continent in 1942, was debated by the chiefs of staff, Mountbatten was alone in arguing for the Cherbourg peninsula. His consistent support of Normandy may have contributed to the change of heart when the venue of the invasion proper was decided. In general, however, Sir Alan Brooke (later Viscount Alanbrooke) and the other chiefs of staff resented Mountbatten's ventures outside the field of his immediate interests and he usually confined himself to matters directly concerned with Combined Operations.

His headquarters, COHQ, indeed the whole of his command, was sometimes criticized for its lavishness in personnel and encouragement of extravagant ideas. Mountbatten was never economical, and waste there undoubtedly was. Nevertheless he built up at great speed an organization of remarkable complexity and effectiveness. By April 1943 Combined Operations Command included 2,600 landing-craft and over 50,000 men. He almost killed himself in the process for in July 1942 he was told by his doctors that he would die unless he worked less intensely. A man with less imagination who played safe could never have done as much. It was Alan Brooke, initially unenthusiastic about his elevation, who concluded: 'His appointment as Chief of Combined Operations ... was excellent, and he played a remarkable part as the driving force and main-spring of this organization. Without his energy and drive it would never have reached the high standard it achieved.'

Mountbatten arrived at the Quebec conference in August 1943 as chief of Combined Operations; he left as acting admiral and supreme commander designate, South East Asia. 'He is young, enthusiastic and triphibious', Churchill telegraphed C. R. (later Earl) Attlee, but though the Americans welcomed the appointment enthusiastically, he was only selected after half a dozen candidates had been eliminated for various reasons.

He took over a command where everything had gone wrong. The British and Indian army, ravaged by disease and soundly beaten by the Japanese, had been chased out of Burma. A feeble attempt at counter-attack in the Arakan peninsula had ended in disaster. Morale was low, air support inadequate, communications within India slow and uncertain. There seemed little to oppose the Japanese if they decided to resume their assault. Yet before Mountbatten could concentrate on his official adversaries he had to resolve the anomalies within his own Command.

Most conspicuous of these was General Stilwell. As well as being deputy supreme commander, Stilwell was chief of staff to Chiang Kai-shek and his twin roles inevitably involved conflicts of interest and loyalty. A superb leader of troops in the field but cantankerous, anglophobe, and narrow-minded, Stilwell would have been a difficult colleague in any circumstances. In South East Asia, where his preoccupation was to reopen the road through north Burma to China, he proved almost impossible to work with. But Mountbatten also found his relationship difficult with his own, British, commanders-in-chief, in particular the naval commander, Sir James Somerville. Partly this arose from differences of temperament; more important it demonstrated a fundamental difference of opinion about the supreme commander's role. Mountbatten, encouraged by Churchill and members of his own entourage, believed that he should operate on the MacArthur model, with his own planning staff, consulting his commanders-in-chief but ultimately instructing them on future operations. Somerville, General Sir G. J. Giffard, and Air Marshal Sir R. E. C. Peirse, on the other hand, envisaged him as a chairman of committee, operating like Eisenhower and working through the planning staffs of the commanders-in-chief. The chiefs of staff in London proved reluctant to rule categorically on the issue but Mountbatten eventually abandoned his central planning staff and the situation was further eased when Somerville was replaced by Admiral Sir Bruce Fraser (later Lord Fraser of North Cape).

Mountbatten defined the three principal problems facing him as being those of monsoon, malaria, and morale. His determination that Allied troops must fight through the monsoon, though of greater psychological than military significance, undoubtedly assisted the eventual victories of the Fourteenth Army. In 1943, for every casualty evacuated because of wounds, there were 120 sick, and Mountbatten, by his emphasis on hygiene and improved medical techniques, can claim much credit for the vast improvement over the next year. But it was in the transformation of the soldiers' morale that he made his greatest contribution. By publicity, propaganda, and the impact of his personality, he restored their pride in themselves and gave them confidence that they could defeat the Japanese.

Deciding what campaign they were to fight proved difficult. Mountbatten, with Churchill's enthusiastic backing, envisaged a bold amphibious strategy which would bypass the Burmese jungles and strike through the Andaman Islands to Rangoon or, more ambitious still, through northern Sumatra towards Singapore. The Americans, however, who would have provided the material resources for such adventures, nicknamed South East Asia Command (SEAC) 'Save England's Asiatic Colonies' and were suspicious of any operation which seemed designed to this end. They felt that the solitary justification for the Burma campaign was to restore land communications with China. The ambitious projects with which Mountbatten had left London withered as his few landing-craft were withdrawn. A mission he dispatched to London and Washington returned empty-handed. 'You might send out the waxwork which I hear Madame Tussauds has made', wrote Mountbatten bitterly to his friend (Sir) Charles Lambe, 'it could have my Admiral's uniform and sit at my desk . . . as well as I could.'

It was the Japanese who saved him from so ignoble a role. In spring 1944 they attacked in Arakan and across the Imphal plain into India. The Allied capacity to supply troops by air and their new-found determination to stand firm, even when cut off, turned potential disaster into almost total victory. Mountbatten himself played a major role, being personally responsible at a crucial moment for the switch of two divisions by air from Arakan to Imphal and the diversion of the necessary American aircraft from the supply routes to China. Imphal confirmed Mountbatten's faith in the commander of the Fourteenth Army, General W. J. (later Viscount) Slim and led to his final loss of confidence in the commander-in-chief, General Giffard, whom he now dismissed. The battle cost the Japanese 7,000 dead; much hard fighting lay ahead but the Fourteenth Army was on the march that would end at Rangoon.

Mountbatten still hoped to avoid the reconquest of Burma by land. In April 1944 he transferred his headquarters from Delhi to Kandy in Ceylon, reaffirming his faith in a maritime strategy. He himself believed the next move should be a powerful sea and air strike against Rangoon; Churchill still hankered after the more ambitious attack on northern Sumatra; the chiefs of staff felt the British effort should be switched to support the American offensive in the Pacific. In the end shortage of resources dictated the course of events. Mountbatten was able to launch a small seaborne invasion to support the Fourteenth Army's advance, but it was Slim's men who bore the brunt of the fighting and reached Rangoon just before the monsoon broke in April 1945.

Giffard had been replaced as supreme commander by Sir Oliver Leese. Mountbatten's original enthusiasm for Leese did not endure; the latter soon fell out with his supreme commander and proved unpopular with the other commanders-in-chief. A climax came in May 1945 when Leese informed Slim that he was to be relieved from command of the Fourteenth Army because he was tired out and anyway had no experience in maritime operations. Mountbatten's role in this curious transaction remains slightly obscure; Leese definitely went too far, but there may have been some ambiguity about his instructions. In the event Leese's action was disavowed in London and he himself was dismissed and Slim appointed in his place.

The next phase of the campaign—an invasion by sea of the Malay peninsula—should have been the apotheosis of Mountbatten's command. When he went to the Potsdam conference in July 1945, however, he was told of the existence of the atom bomb. He realized at once that this was likely to rob him of his victory and, sure enough, the Japanese surrender reduced Operation Zipper to an unopposed landing. This was perhaps just as well; faulty intelligence meant that one of the two landings was made on unsuitable beaches and was quickly bogged down. The invasion would have succeeded but the cost might have been high.

On 12 September 1945, Mountbatten received the formal surrender of the Japanese at Singapore. Not long afterwards he was created a viscount. The honour was deserved. His role had been crucial. 'We did it together', Slim said to him on his deathbed, and the two men, in many ways so different, had indeed complemented each other admirably and proved the joint architects of victory in South East Asia.

Mountbatten's work in SEAC did not end with the Japanese surrender; indeed in some ways it grew still more onerous. His Command was now extended to include South Vietnam and the Netherlands East Indies: 1½ million square miles containing 128 million inhabitants, ¾ million armed and potentially truculent Japanese, and 123,000 Allied prisoners, many in urgent need of medical attention. Mountbatten had to rescue the prisoners, disarm the Japanese, and restore the various territories to stability so that civil government could resume. This last function proved most difficult, since the Japanese had swept away the old colonial regimes and new nationalist movements had grown up to fill the vacuum.

Mountbatten's instincts told him that such movements were inevitable and even desirable. Every effort, he felt, should be made to take account of their justified aspirations. His disposition to sympathize with the radical nationalists sometimes led him into naïvely optimistic assessment of their readiness to compromise with the former colonialist regimes—as proved to be the case with the communist Chinese in Malaya—but the course of subsequent history suggests that he often saw the situation more clearly than the so-called 'realists' who criticized him.

Even before the end of the war he had had a foretaste of the problems that lay ahead. Aung San, head of the pro-Japanese Burmese National Army, defected with all his troops. Mountbatten was anxious to accept his co-operation and cajoled the somewhat reluctant chiefs of staff into agreeing on military grounds. Inevitably, this gave Aung San a stronger position than the traditionalists thought desirable when the time came to form Burma's post-war government. Mountbatten felt that, though left wing and fiercely nationalistic, Aung San was honourable, basically reasonable, and ready to accept the concept of an independent Burma within the British Commonwealth; '... with proper treatment', judged Slim, 'Aung San would have proved a Burmese Smuts'. The governor, Sir Reginald Dorman-Smith, conceded Aung San was the most popular man in Burma but considered him a dangerous Marxist revolutionary. When Aung San was accused of war crimes committed during the Japanese occupation, Dorman-Smith wished to arrest and try him. This Mountbatten forestalled; but the hand-over to civil government in April 1946 and the murder of Aung San the following year meant that the supreme commander's view of his character was never properly tested.

In Malaya the problem was more immediately one of law and order. Confronted by the threat of a politically-motivated general strike, the authorities proposed to arrest all the leaders. 'Naturally I ordered them to cancel these orders', wrote Mountbatten, 'as I could not imagine anything more disastrous than to make martyrs of these men.' Reluctantly he agreed that in certain circumstances Chinese trouble-makers might be deported, but rescinded that approval when it was proposed to deport certain detainees who had not had time to profit by his warnings. His critics maintained that sterner action in 1945–6 could have prevented, or at least mitigated the future troubles in Malaya, but Mountbatten was convinced that the prosperity of Malaya and Singapore depended on the co-operation of Malay and Chinese, and was determined to countenance nothing that might divide the two communities.

In Vietnam and Indonesia Mountbatten's problem was to balance nationalist aspirations against the demands of Britain's Allies for support in the recovery of their colonies. He was better disposed to the French than the Dutch, and though he complained when General (Sir) Douglas Gracey exceeded his instructions and suppressed the Viet Minh—'General Gracey has saved French Indo-China', Leclerc told him—the reproof was more formal than real. In Indonesia Mountbatten believed that Dutch intransigence was the principal factor preventing a peaceful settlement. Misled by Dutch intelligence, he had no suspicion of the force of nationalist sentiment until Lady Mountbatten returned from her brave foray to rescue Allied prisoners of war. His forces could not avoid conflict with the Indonesian nationalists but Mountbatten sought to limit their commitment, with the result that both Dutch and Indonesians believed the British were favouring the other side. He did, however, contrive to keep open the possibility of political settlement; only after the departure of the British forces did full-scale civil war become inevitable.

Mountbatten left South East Asia in mid-1946 with the reputation of a liberal committed to decolonization. Though he had no thought beyond his return to the navy, with the now substantive rank of rear-admiral, his reputation influenced the Labour government when they were looking for a successor to Viscount (later Earl) Wavell who could resuscitate the faltering negotiations for Indian independence. On 18 December 1946 he was invited to become India's last viceroy. That year he had been created first Viscount Mountbatten of Burma.

Mountbatten longed to go to sea again, but this was a challenge no man of ambition and public spirit could reject. His reluctance enabled him to extract favourable terms from the government, and though the plenipotentiary powers to which he was often to refer are not specifically set out in any document, he enjoyed far greater freedom of action than his immediate predecessors. His original insistence that he would go only on the invitation of the Indian leaders was soon abandoned but it was on his initiative that a terminal date of June 1948 was fixed, by which time the British would definitely have left India.

Mountbatten's directive was that he should strive to implement the recommendations of the Cabinet mission of 1946, led by Sir R. Stafford Cripps which maintained the principle of a united India. By the time he arrived, however, this objective had been tacitly abandoned by every major politician of the sub-continent with the important exception of M. K. Gandhi. The viceroy dutifully tried to persuade all concerned of the benefits of unity but his efforts foundered on the intransigence of the Muslim leader Mahomed Ali Jinnah. His problem thereafter was to find some formula which would reconcile the desire of the Hindus for a central India from which a few peripheral and wholly Muslim areas would secede, with Jinnah's aspiration to secure a greater Pakistan including all the Punjab and as much as possible of Bengal. In this task he was supported by

Wavell's staff from the Indian Civil Service, reinforced by General H. L. (later Lord) Ismay and Sir Eric Miéville. He himself contributed immense energy, charm and persuasiveness, negotiating skills, agility of mind, and endless optimism.

He quickly concluded that not only was time not on his side but that the urgency was desperate. The run-down of the British military and civil presence, coupled with swelling inter-communal hatred, were intensely dangerous. 'The situation is everywhere electric, and I get the feeling that the mine may go up at any moment', wrote Ismay to his wife on 25 March 1947, the day after Mountbatten was sworn in as viceroy. This conviction that every moment counted dictated Mountbatten's activities over the next five months. He threw himself into a hectic series of interviews with the various political leaders. With Jawaharlal Nehru he established an immediate and lasting rapport which was to assume great importance in the future. With V. J. Patel, in whom he identified a major power in Indian politics, his initial relationship was less easy, but they soon enjoyed mutual confidence. Gandhi fascinated and delighted him, but he shrewdly concluded that he was likely to be pushed to one side in the forthcoming negotiations. With Jinnah alone did he fail; the full blast of his charm did not thaw or even moderate the chill intractability of the Muslim leader.

Nevertheless negotiations advanced so rapidly that by 2 May Ismay was taking to London a plan which Mountbatten believed all the principal parties would accept. Only when the British Cabinet had already approved the plan did he realize that he had gravely underestimated Nehru's objections to any proposal that left room for the 'Balkanization' of India. With extraordinary speed a new draft was produced, which provided for India's membership of the Commonwealth, and put less emphasis on the right of the individual components of British India to reject India or Pakistan and opt for independence. After what Mountbatten described as 'the worst 24 hours of my life', the plan was accepted by all parties on 3 June. He was convinced that any relaxation of the feverish pace would risk destroying the fragile basis of understanding. Independence, he announced, was to be granted in only ten weeks, on 15 August 1947.

Before this date the institutions of British India had to be carved in two. Mountbatten initially hoped to retain a unified army but quickly realized this would be impossible and concentrated instead on ensuring rough justice in the division of the assets. To have given satisfaction to everyone would have been impossible, but at the time few people accused him of partiality. He tackled the problems, wrote Michael Edwardes in a book not generally sympathetic to the last viceroy, 'with a speed and brilliance which it is difficult to believe would have been exercised by any other man'.

Mountbatten

The princely states posed a particularly complex problem, since with the end of British rule paramountcy lapsed and there was in theory nothing to stop the princes opting for self-rule. This would have made a geographical nonsense of India and, to a lesser extent, Pakistan; as well as creating a plethora of independent states, many incapable of sustaining such a role. Mountbatten at first attached little importance to the question, but once he was fully aware of it, used every trick to get the rulers to accept accession. Some indeed felt that he was using improper influence on loyal subjects of the Crown, but it is hard to see that any other course would in the long run have contributed to their prosperity. Indeed the two states which Mountbatten failed to shepherd into the fold of India or Pakistan—Hyderabad and Kashmir—were those which were subsequently to cause most trouble.

Most provinces, like the princely states, clearly belonged either to India or to Pakistan. In the Punjab and Bengal, however, partition was necessary. This posed horrifying problems, since millions of Hindus and Muslims would find themselves on the wrong side of whatever frontier was established. The Punjab was likely to prove most troublesome, because 14 per cent of its population consisted of Sikhs, who were warlike, fanatically anti-Muslim, and determined that their homelands should remain inviolate. Partition was not Mountbatten's direct responsibility, since Sir Cyril (later Viscount) Radcliffe was appointed to divide the two provinces. Popular opinion, however, found it hard to accept that he was not involved, and even today it is sometimes suggested he may have helped shape Radcliffe's final conclusions.

Mountbatten had hoped that independence day would see him installed as governor-general of both new dominions; able to act, in Churchill's phrase, as 'moderator' during their inevitable differences. Nehru was ready for such a transmogrification but Jinnah, after some months of apparent indecision, concluded that he himself must be Pakistan's first head of state. Mountbatten was uncertain whether the last viceroy of a united India should now reappear as governor-general of a part of it, but the Indian government pressed him to accept and in London both Attlee and George VI felt the appointment was desirable. With some misgivings, Mountbatten gave way. Independence day in both Pakistan and India was a triumph, tumultuous millions applauding his progress and demonstrating that, for the moment at least, he enjoyed a place in the pantheon with their national leaders. 'No other living man could have got the thing through', wrote Lord Killearn to Ismay; '. . . it has been a job supremely well done.'

The euphoria quickly faded. Though Bengal remained calm, thanks largely to Gandhi's personal intervention, the Punjab exploded. Vast movements of population across the new frontier exacerbated the already inflamed communal hatred, and massacres on an appalling scale developed. The largely British-officered Boundary Force was taxed far beyond its powers and Delhi itself was engulfed in the violence. Mountbatten was called back from holiday to help master the emergency, and brought desperately needed energy and organizational skills to the despondent government. 'I've never been through such a time in my life', he wrote on 28 September, 'The War, the Viceroyalty were jokes, for we have been dealing with life and death in our own city.' Gradually order was restored and by November 1947 Mountbatten felt the situation was stable enough to permit him to attend the wedding of Princess Elizabeth and his nephew Philip Mountbatten in London. He was created first Earl Mountbatten of Burma, with special remainder to his daughter Patricia.

Estimates vary widely, but the best-documented assessments agree that between 200,000 and 250,000 people lost their lives in the communal riots. Those who criticize Mountbatten's viceroyalty do so most often on the grounds that these massacres could have been averted, or at least mitigated, if partition had not been hurried through. Mountbatten's champions maintain that delay would only have made things worse and allowed the disorders to spread further. It is impossible to state conclusively what *might* have happened if independence had been postponed by a few months, or even years, but it is noteworthy that the closer people were to the problem, the more they support Mountbatten's policy. Almost every senior member of the British administration in India and of the Indian government has recorded his conviction that security was deteriorating so fast and the maintenance of non-communal forces of law and order proving so difficult, that a far greater catastrophe would have ensued if there had been further delay.

Mountbatten as governor-general was a servant of the Indian government and, as Ismay put it, 'it is only natural that they ... should regard themselves as having proprietary rights over you'. Mountbatten accepted this role and fought doughtily for India's interests. He did not wholly abandon impartiality, however. When in January 1948 the Indian government withheld from Pakistan the 55 million crores of rupees owing after the division of assets, the governor-general argued that such conduct was dishonourable as well as unwise. He recruited Gandhi as his ally, and together they forced a change of policy on the reluctant Indian ministers. It was one of Gandhi's final contributions to Indian history. On 30 January he was assassinated by a Hindu extremist. Mountbatten mourned him sincerely. 'What a remarkable old boy he was', he wrote to a friend, 'I think history will link him with Buddha and Mahomet.'

His stand over the division of assets did the governor-general little good in Pakistan where he was believed to be an inveterate enemy and, by persuading Radcliffe to award Gurdaspur to India, to have secured that country access to Kashmir. When, in October 1947, Pathan tribesmen invaded the Vale of Kashmir, Mountbatten approved and helped organize military intervention by India. He insisted, however, that the state must first accede and that, as soon as possible, a plebiscite should establish the wishes of the Kashmiri people. When war between India and Pakistan seemed imminent he was instrumental in persuading Nehru that the matter should be referred to the United Nations.

The other problem that bedevilled Mountbatten was that of Hyderabad. He constituted himself, in effect, chief negotiator for the Indian government and almost brought off a deal that would have secured reasonably generous terms for the Nizam. Muslim extremists in Hyderabad, however, defeated his efforts, and the dispute grumbled on. Mountbatten protested when he found contingency plans existed for the invasion of Hyderabad and his presence was undoubtedly a main factor in inhibiting the Indian take-over that quickly followed his departure.

On 21 June 1948 the Mountbattens left India. In his final address, Nehru referred to the vast crowds that had attended their last appearances and 'wondered how it was that an Englishman and Englishwoman could become so popular in India during this brief period'. Even his harshest critics could not deny that Mountbatten had won the love and trust of the people and got the relationship between India and her former ruler off to a far better start than had seemed possible fifteen months before.

At last Mountbatten was free to return to sea. Reverting to his substantive rank of rear-admiral he took command of the first cruiser squadron in the Mediterranean. To assume this relatively lowly position after the splendours of supreme command and viceroyalty could not have been easy, but with goodwill all round it was achieved successfully. He was 'as great a subordinate as he is a leader', reported the commander-in-chief, Admiral Sir Arthur Power. He brought his squadron up to a high level of efficiency, though not concealing the fact that he felt obsolescent material and undermanning diminished its real effectiveness. After his previous jobs, this command was something of a holiday, and he revelled in the opportunities to play his beloved polo and take up skin-diving. In Malta he stuck to his inconspicuous role, but abroad he was fêted by the rulers of the countries his squadron visited. 'I suppose I oughtn't to get a kick out of being treated like a Viceroy', he confessed after one particularly successful visit, 'but I'd have been less than human if I hadn't been affected by the treatment I received at Trieste.' He was never less, nor more than human.

Mountbatten was promoted vice-admiral in 1949 and in June 1950 returned to the Admiralty as fourth sea lord. He was at first disappointed, since he had set his heart on being second sea lord, responsible for personnel, and found himself instead concerned with supplies and transport. In fact the post proved excellent for his career. He flung himself into the work with characteristic zeal, cleared up many anomalies and outdated practices, and acquired a range of information which was to stand him in good stead when he became first sea lord. On the whole he confined himself to the duties of his department, but when the Persians nationalized Anglo-Iranian Oil in 1951, he could not resist making his opinions known. He felt that it was futile to oppose strong nationalist movements of this kind and that Britain would do better to work with them. He converted the first lord to his point of view but conspicuously failed to impress the bellicose foreign secretary, Herbert Morrison (later Lord Morrison of Lambeth).

The next step was command of a major fleet and in June 1952 he was appointed to the Mediterranean, being promoted to admiral the following year. St. Vincent remarked that naval command in the Mediterranean 'required an officer of splendour', and this Mountbatten certainly provided. He was not a great operational commander like Andrew Cunningham, but he knew his ships and personnel, maintained the fleet at the highest level of peacetime efficiency, and was immensely popular with the men. When 'Cassandra' of the *Daily Mirror* arrived to report on Mountbatten's position, he kept aloof for four days, then came to the flagship with the news that the commander-in-chief was 'O.K. with the sailors'. But it was on the representational side that Mountbatten excelled. He loved showing the flag and, given half a chance, would act as honorary ambassador into the bargain. Sometimes he overdid it, and in September 1952 the first lord, at the instance of the prime minister, wrote to urge him 'to take the greatest care to keep out of political discussions'.

His diplomatic as well as administrative skills were taxed when in January 1953 he was appointed supreme Allied commander of a new NATO Mediterranean Command (SACMED). Under him were the Mediterranean fleets of Britain, France, Italy, Greece, and Turkey, but not the most powerful single unit in the area, the American Sixth Fleet. He was required to set up an integrated international naval/air headquarters in Malta and managed this formidable organizational task with great efficiency. The smoothing over of national susceptibilities and the reconciliation of his British with his NATO role proved taxing, but his worst difficulty lay with the other NATO headquarters in the Mediterranean, CINCSOUTH, at Naples under the American Admiral R. B. Carney. There were real problems of demarcation, but as had happened with Somerville in South East Asia, these were made far worse by a clash of personalities. When Carney was replaced in the autumn of 1953, the differences melted away and the two commands began to co-operate.

In October 1954, when he became first sea lord, Mountbatten achieved what he had always held to be his ultimate ambition. It did not come easily. A formidable body of senior naval opinion distrusted him and was at first opposed to his appointment, and it was not until the conviction hardened that the navy was losing the Whitehall battle against the other services that opinion rallied behind him. 'The Navy wants badly a man and a leader', wrote Andrew Cunningham, who had formerly been Mountbatten's opponent. 'You have the ability and the drive and it is you that the Navy wants.' Churchill, still unreconciled to Mountbatten's role in India, held out longer, but in the end he too gave way.

Since the war the navy had become the Cinderella of the fighting Services, and morale was low. Under Mountbatten's leadership, the Admiralty's voice in Whitehall became louder and more articulate. By setting up the 'Way Ahead' committee, he initiated an overdue rethinking of the shore establishments which were absorbing an undue proportion of the navy's resources. He scrapped plans for the construction of a heavy missile-carrying cruiser and instead concentrated on destroyers carrying the Sea Slug missile: 'Once we can obtain Government agreement to the fact that we are the mobile large scale rocket carriers of the future then everything else will fall into place.' The Reserve Fleet was cut severely and expenditure diverted from the already excellent communications system to relatively underdeveloped fields such as radar. Probably his most important single contribution, however, was to establish an excellent relationship with the notoriously prickly Admiral Rickover, which was to lead to Britain acquiring US technology for its nuclear submarines and, eventually, to the adoption of the Polaris missile as the core of its nuclear deterrent.

In July 1956 Nasser nationalized the Suez canal. Mountbatten was asked what military steps could be taken to restore the situation. He said that the Mediterranean Fleet with the Royal Marine commandos aboard could be at Port Said within three days and take the port and its hinterland. Eden rejected the proposal since he wished to reoccupy the whole canal zone, and it is unlikely anyway that the other chiefs of staff would have approved a plan that might have left lightly armed British forces exposed to tank attack and with inadequate air cover. As plans for full-scale invasion were prepared, Mountbatten became more and more uneasy about the contemplated action. To the chiefs of staff he consistently said that political implications should be considered and more thought given to the long-term future of the Middle East. His views were reflected in the chiefs' recommendations to the government, a point that caused considerable irritation to Anthony Eden, who insisted that politics should be left to the politicians. In August Mountbatten drafted a letter of resignation to the prime minister but, without too much difficulty, was dissuaded from sending it by the first lord, Viscount Cilcennin. He was, however, instrumental in substituting the invasion plan of General Sir Charles Keightley for that previously approved by the Cabinet, a move that saved the lives of many hundreds of civilians. On 2 November, when the invasion fleet had already sailed, Mountbatten made a written appeal to Eden to accept the United Nations resolution and 'turn back the assault convoy before it is too late'. His appeal was ignored. Mountbatten again offered his resignation to the first lord and again was told that it was his duty to stay on. He was promoted admiral of the fleet in October 1956.

With Harold Macmillan (later the Earl of Stockton) succeeding Eden as prime minister in January 1957, Duncan Sandys (later Lord Duncan-Sandys) was appointed minister of defence with a mandate to rationalize the armed services and impose sweeping economies. There were many embittered battles before Sandys's first defence white paper appeared in the summer of 1957. The thirteenth and final draft contained the ominous words: 'the role of the Navy in Global War is somewhat uncertain'. In the event, however, the navy suffered relatively lightly, losing only one-sixth of its personnel over the next five years, as opposed to the army's 45 per cent and the air force's 35 per cent. The role of the navy east of Suez was enshrined as an accepted dogma of defence policy.

In July 1959 Mountbatten took over as chief of defence staff (CDS). He was the second incumbent, Sir William Dickson having been appointed in 1958, with Mountbatten's support but against the fierce opposition of Field-Marshal Sir Gerald Templer. Dickson's role was little more than that of permanent chairman of the chiefs of staff committee but Sandys tried to increase the CDS's powers. He was defeated, and the defence white paper of 1958 made only modest changes to the existing system. Mountbatten made the principal objective of his time as CDS the integration of the three Services, not to the extent achieved by the Canadians of one homogenized fighting force, but abolishing the independent ministries and setting up a common list for all senior officers. During his first two years, however, he had to remain content with the creation of a director of defence plans to unify the work of the three planning departments and the acceptance of the principle of unified command in the Far and Middle East. Then, at the end of 1962, Macmillan agreed that another attempt should be made to impose unification on the reluctant Services. 'Pray take no notice of any obstructions', he told the minister of defence, 'You should approach this . . . with dashing, slashing methods. Anyone who raises any objection can go.'

At Mountbatten's suggestion Lord Ismay and Sir E. Ian Jacob were asked to report. While not accepting all Mountbatten's recommendations—which involved a sweeping increase in the powers of the CDS—their report went a long way towards realizing the concept of a unified Ministry of Defence. The reforms, which were finally promulgated in 1964, acknowledged the supreme authority of the secretary of state for defence and strengthened the central role of the CDS. To Mountbatten this was an important first step, but only a step. He believed that so long as separate departments survived, with differing interests and loyalties, it would be impossible to use limited resources to the best advantage. Admiralty, War Office, Air Ministry—not to mention Ministry of Aviation—should be abolished. Ministers should be responsible, not for the navy or the air force, but for communications or supplies. 'We cannot, in my opinion, afford to stand pat', he wrote to Harold Wilson (later Lord Wilson of Rievaulx) when the latter became prime minister in October 1964, 'and must move on to, or at least towards the ultimate aim of a functional, closely knit, smoothly working machine.' 'Functionalization' was the objective which he repeatedly pressed on the new minister of defence, Denis Healey. Healey was well disposed in principle, but felt that other reforms enjoyed higher priority. Though Mountbatten appealed to Wilson he got little satisfaction, and the machinery which he left behind him at his retirement was in his eyes only an unsatisfactory half-way house.

Even for this he paid a high price in popularity. His ideas were for the most part repugnant to the chiefs of staff, who suspected him of seeking personal aggrandizement and doubted the propriety of his methods. Relations tended to be worst with the chiefs of air staff. The latter believed that Mountbatten, though ostensibly above inter-Service rivalries, in fact remained devoted to the interests of the navy. It is hard entirely to slough off a lifetime's loyalties, but Mountbatten *tried* to be impartial. He did not always succeed. On the long-drawn-out battle over the merits of aircraft-carriers and island bases, he espoused the former. When he urged the first sea lord to work out some compromise which would accommodate both points of view, Sir Caspar John retorted that only a month before Mountbatten had advised him: 'Don't compromise—fight him to the death!' Similarly in the conflict between the TSR 2, sponsored by the air force, and the navy's Buccaneer, Mountbatten believed strongly that the former, though potentially the better plane, was too expensive to be practicable and would take too long to develop. He lobbied the minister of defence and urged his right-hand man, Solly Zuckerman, to argue the case against the TSR 2—'You know why I can't help you in Public. It is *not* moral cowardice but fear that my usefulness as Chairman would be seriously impaired.'

The question of the British nuclear deterrent also involved inter-Service rivalries. Mountbatten believed that an independent deterrent was essential, arguing to Harold Wilson that it would 'dispel in Russian minds the thought that they will escape scot-free if by any chance the Americans decide to hold back release of a strategic nuclear response to an attack'. He was instrumental in persuading the incoming Labour government not to adopt unilateral nuclear disarmament. In this he had the support of the three chiefs of staff. But there was controversy over what weapon best suited Britain's needs. From long before he became CDS, Mountbatten had privately preferred the submarine-launched Polaris missile to any of the airborne missiles favoured by the air force. Though not himself present at the meeting at Nassau between Macmillan and President John F. Kennedy at which Polaris was offered and accepted in exchange for the cancelled Skybolt missile, he had already urged this solution and had made plans accordingly.

Though he defended the nuclear deterrent, he was wholly opposed to the accumulation of unnecessary stockpiles or the development of new weapons designed to kill more effectively people who would be dead anyway if the existing armouries were employed. At NATO in July 1963 he pleaded that 'it was madness to hold further tests when all men of goodwill were about to try and bring about test-banning'. He conceded that tactical nuclear weapons added to the efficacy of the deterrent, but argued that their numbers should be limited and their use subject to stringent control. To use *any* nuclear weapon, however small or 'clean', would, he insisted, lead to general nuclear war. He opposed the 'mixed manned multilateral force' not just as being military nonsense, but because there were more than enough strategic nuclear weapons already. What were needed, he told the NATO commanders in his valedictory address, were more 'highly mobile, well-equipped, self-supporting and balanced "Fire Brigade" forces, with first-class communications, able to converge quickly on the enemy force'.

Mountbatten's original tenure of office as CDS had been for three years. Macmillan pressed him to lengthen this by a further two years to July 1964. Mountbatten was initially reluctant but changed his mind after the death of his wife in 1960. Subsequently he agreed to a further extension to July 1965, in order to see through the first phase of defence reorganization. Wilson would have happily sanctioned yet another year but Healey established that there would be considerable resentment at such a move on the part of the other Service leaders and felt anyway that he would never be fully master of the Ministry of Defence while this potent relic from the past remained in office. Whether Mountbatten would have stayed on if pressed to do so is in any case doubtful; he was tired and stale, and had a multiplicity of interests to pursue outside.

His last few months as CDS were in fact spent partly abroad leading a mission on Commonwealth immigration. The main purpose of this exercise was to explain British policy and persuade Commonwealth governments to control illegal immigration at source. The mission was a success; indeed Mountbatten found that he was largely preaching to the converted, since only in Jamaica did the policy he was expounding meet with serious opposition. He presented the mission's report on 13 June 1965 and the following month took his formal farewell of the Ministry of Defence.

Retirement did not mean inactivity; indeed he was still officially enjoying his retirement leave when the prime minister invited him to go to Rhodesia as governor to forestall a declaration of independence by the white settler population. Mountbatten had little hesitation in refusing: 'Nothing could be worse for the cause you have at heart than to think that a tired out widower of 65 could recapture the youth, strength and enthusiasm of twenty years ago.' However, he accepted a later suggestion that he should fly briefly to Rhodesia in November 1965 to invest the governor, Sir Humphrey Gibbs, with a decoration on behalf of the Queen and generally to offer moral support. At the last minute the project was deferred and never revived.

The following year the home secretary asked him to undertake an enquiry into prison security, in view of a number of recent sensational escapes. Mountbatten agreed, provided it could be a one-man report prepared with the help of three assessors. The report was complete within two months and most of the recommendations were carried out. The two most important, however—the appointment of an inspector-general responsible to the home secretary to head the prison service and the building of a separate maximum security gaol for prisoners whose escape would be particularly damaging—were never implemented. For the latter proposal Mountbatten was much criticized by liberal reformers who felt the step a retrograde one; this Mountbatten contested, arguing that, isolated within a completely secure outer perimeter, the dangerous criminal could be allowed more freedom than would otherwise be the case.

Mountbatten was associated with 179 organizations, ranging alphabetically from the Admiralty Dramatic Society to the Zoological Society. In some of these his role was formal, in many more it was not. In time and effort the United World Colleges, a network of international schools modelled on the Gordonstoun of Kurt Hahn, received the largest share. Mountbatten worked indefatigably to whip up support and raise funds for the schools, lobbying the leaders of every country he visited. The electronics industry, also, engaged his attention and he was an active first chairman of the National Electronic Research Council. In 1965 he was installed as governor of the Isle of Wight and conscientiously visited the island seven or eight times a year, in 1974 becoming the first lord lieutenant when the island was raised to the status of a shire. A role which gave him still greater pleasure was that of colonel of the Life Guards, to which he was also appointed in 1965. He took his duties at Trooping the Colour very seriously and for weeks beforehand would ride around the Hampshire lanes near Broadlands in hacking jacket and Life Guards helmet.

His personal life was equally crowded. The years 1966 and 1967 were much occupied with the filming of the thirteen-part television series *The Life and Times of Lord Mountbatten*, every detail of which absorbed him and whose sale he promoted energetically all over the world. He devoted much time to running the family estates and putting his massive archive in order, involving himself enthusiastically in the opening of Broadlands to the public, which took place in 1978. He never lost his interest in naval affairs or in high strategy. One of his last major speeches was delivered at Strasburg in May 1979, when he pleaded eloquently for arms control: 'As a military man who has given half a century of active service I say in all sincerity that the nuclear arms race has no military purpose. Wars cannot be fought with nuclear weapons. Their existence only adds to our perils because of the illusions which they have generated.'

Some of his happiest hours were spent on tour with the royal family in their official yacht *Britannia*. He derived particular pleasure from his friendship with the Prince of Wales, who treated him as 'honorary grandfather' and attached great value to his counsel. When Princess Anne married, the certificate gave as her surname 'Mountbatten-Windsor'. This was the culmination of a long battle Mountbatten had waged to ensure that his family name, adopted by Prince Philip, should be preserved among his nephew's descendants. He took an intense interest in all the royal houses of Europe, and was a source of advice on every subject. Harold Wilson once called him 'the shop-steward of royalty' and Mountbatten rejoiced in the description.

Every summer he enjoyed a family holiday at his Irish home in county Sligo, Classiebawn Castle. Over the years the size of his police escort increased but the Irish authorities were insistent that the cancellation of his holiday would be a victory for the Irish Republican Army. On 27 August 1979 a family party went out in a fishing boat, to collect lobster-pots set the previous day. A bomb exploded when the boat was half a mile from Mullaghmoor harbour. Mountbatten was killed instantly, as was his grandson Nicholas and a local Irish boy. His daughter's mother-in-law, Doreen Lady Brabourne, died shortly afterwards. His funeral took place in Westminster Abbey and he was buried in Romsey Abbey. He had begun his preparations for the ceremony more than ten years before and was responsible for planning every detail, down to the lunch to be eaten by the mourners on the train from Waterloo to Romsey.

Mountbatten

Mountbatten was a giant of a man, and his weaknesses were appropriately gigantic. His vanity was monstrous, his ambition unbridled. The truth, in his hands, was swiftly converted from what it was to what it should have been. But such frailties were far outweighed by his qualities. His energy was prodigious, as was his moral and physical courage. He was endlessly resilient in the face of disaster. No intellectual, he possessed a powerfully analytical intelligence; he could rapidly master a complex brief, spot the essential and argue it persuasively. His flexibility of mind was extraordinary, as was his tolerance—he accepted all comers for what they were, not measured against some scale of predetermined values. He had style and panache, commanding the loyal devotion of those who served him. To his opponents in Whitehall he was 'tricky Dickie', devious and unscrupulous. To his family and close friends he was a man of wisdom and generosity. He adored his two daughters, Patricia and Pamela, and his ten grandchildren. However pressing his preoccupations he would make time to comfort, encourage, or advise them. Almost always the advice was good.

Among Mountbatten's honours were MVO (1920), KCVO (1922), GCVO (1937), DSO (1941), CB (1943), KCB (1945), KG (1946), PC (1947), GCSI (1947), GCIE (1947), GCB (1955), OM (1965), and FRS (1966). He had an honorary DCL from Oxford (1946), and honorary LL Ds from Cambridge (1946), Leeds (1950), Edinburgh (1954), Southampton (1955), London (1960), and Sussex (1963). He was honorary DSc of Delhi and Patna (1948).

Mountbatten was much painted. His head, by John Ulbricht, is held by the National Portrait Gallery, while portraits by Philip de László, Brenda Bury, Derek Hill, and Carlos Sancha are in the possession of the family. His state portrait by Edward Halliday hangs in the former viceroy's house, New Delhi, and by Da Cruz in the Victoria Memorial Building, Calcutta. A memorial statue by Franta Belsky was erected in 1983 on Foreign Office Green in London.

On Mountbatten's death the title passed to his elder daughter, Patricia Edwina Victoria Knatchbull (born 1924), who became Countess Mountbatten of Burma.

[Philip Ziegler, *Mountbatten*, 1985; family papers.]

PHILIP ZIEGLER

published 1986

NEWALL Cyril Louis Norton

(1886–1963)

First Baron Newall

Marshal of the Royal Air Force, was born 15 February 1886 at Mussoorie, United Provinces, India, the only son and the second child of Captain (later Lieutenant-Colonel) William Potter Newall, Indian Army, and his wife, Edith Gwendoline Caroline Norton. He was educated at Bedford School and proceeded by way of the Royal Military College, Sandhurst, to a commission in the Royal Warwickshire Regiment at the age of nineteen. After moving with his regiment to India he followed his father's footsteps into the Indian Army, being received into the 2nd battalion King Edward's Own Gurkha Rifles in 1909. Like many young army officers of that day he met his first experience of active service amid the mountains of the North-West Frontier. Inspired by a flying demonstration in India, he learned to fly while on leave in Britain in 1911, and was awarded Royal Aero Club certificate No. 144.

He received further training at the Central Flying School in 1913 on a special posting from India and returned to Britain in 1914 to join the Royal Flying Corps. Newall served with that corps throughout the war of 1914–18 and in 1919 became a wing commander in the newly formed Royal Air Force during the reorganization that year. In the great and dangerous days of the RFC Newall saw service as a pilot and as a squadron and formation commander. His last posting was to command the elements of the RFC designated to attack German targets from bases in the Nancy area, a development largely occasioned by German air raids on London in 1917. In this last appointment he came under the immediate control of Brigadier-General (later Viscount) Trenchard, who was posted in May 1918 to the command of what was to become the Independent Force. In the course of his Royal Flying Corps service, Newall was awarded that rather rare and much prized distinction, the Albert medal, for an act of conspicuous gallantry in dealing with a fire in a bomb store.

The first fifteen years of the Royal Air Force in peacetime, although significant in shaping its future development, were also years of struggle and frustration; its future survival was repeatedly a matter of serious doubt and the new Service was retarded and distorted by financial restrictions. Newall was lucky in that during this period he held three key appointments. From 1922 to 1925 he commanded the School of Technical Training at Halton, a star feature of the peacetime pattern of the Royal Air Force producing airmen apprentices of the highest technical skills. Between 1926 and 1931 he was in charge of the operations and intelligence elements of the Air Staff and, for the last year of the appointment, ranked as a member of the Air Council. Between 1931 and 1934 he commanded the Royal Air Force in the Middle East with his headquarters in Cairo and with a vast range of responsibilities throughout Africa. Early in 1935 Newall rejoined the Air Council as the newly created air member for supply and organization, a post he held for some two and a half years and which embodied responsibility for the organization of the expanding Royal Air Force, for meeting its needs for airfields and quarters, and for supplying it with warlike and non-warlike stores of all kinds. The problems which confronted Newall were of a kind unusual or even unprecedented in time of peace. Between 1935 and the outbreak of war in 1939 expenditure on the Royal Air Force was increased by a factor of more than ten but the problems which arose were not those of scale only. They were complicated by the change from slow biplanes to fast monoplanes with enclosed cockpits, retractable undercarriages, and variable-pitch propellers. It was also necessary to construct and equip new aircraft factories and to deal with the problems of the light-alloy industry and with other specialized needs.

In September 1937 Newall was appointed to succeed Sir Edward Ellington as chief of air staff, a position which with that of secretary of state constituted the two appointments most vital to the future of the Service. His qualifications for the appointment were impressive. He had seen active service, he had held an important overseas command, he had served as deputy chief of air staff, and he had presided for three years over the physical development of the Royal Air Force. No one could have been endowed with a better understanding of the problems. Above all, he had the personal qualities required. He was chief of air staff for three years and few men can have faced a time of greater stress. When Austria was overwhelmed in March 1938 Newall put forward his views on the implications to British security with clarity and force. The Munich crisis, involving as it did partial mobilization, brought the Royal Air Force close to the brink of war. After the crisis was over Newall called his staff together and with great prescience told them exactly what would be the responsibilities facing the Service in 1939. Tensions mounted and in September 1939 Britain was at war again. For the Royal Air Force all the work of the last four years was soon to be put to the test. The problems of the first year of the war were many and arduous: there was the issue of whether fighters should be sent to France; and, when France was overrun, Britain's air defence problems multiplied; there was the threat of invasion; and, finally, the crucial and desperately close issue of the Battle of Britain. It was a heavy burden for Newall to carry.

By September 1940 the Luftwaffe's daylight assaults on Britain had given way to the nightly blitz on London and other big cities. This, too, brought many, although less extreme, problems. In the development of the air war something like a natural break had been reached. It was therefore a suitable moment for Newall to hand over as chief of air staff to Sir Charles Portal (later Viscount Portal of Hungerford). Earlier in the month in which he retired Newall had been promoted to the rank of marshal of the Royal Air Force.

Newall had occupied a position of crucial responsibility, but he, the Air Ministry, and the various secretaries of state, faced some criticism. Alternative views about air policy covering matters of detail as well as of policy came from both Churchill and Attlee, and behind the scenes there were some individual critics as well. Some, but by no means all, of the criticism was apposite. This detracts nothing from the fact that over a period of three years and in most difficult circumstances Newall had proved himself a distinguished leader of the Royal Air Force. Newall was appointed governor-general of New Zealand in 1941 and remained in that office for five years, which included the period when New Zealand was exposed to the threat of Japanese attack. He and his wife worked devotedly to sustain the New Zealand war effort at every level and at the end of their mission they were given a warm and gracious tribute from the prime minister of New Zealand, Peter Fraser.

In appearance Newall was slim and slightly over average height. Although an airman, he looked every inch a soldier. He was always immaculately dressed. In times of stress, and in those days this was the normal state, his composure and cheerfulness were beyond praise. His courtesy and kindness to everyone who came into contact with him were a model.

For his services during the war of 1914–18 Newall was appointed CMG and CBE and received decorations from France, Italy, and Belgium. He was appointed GCB in 1938 and GCMG in 1940 and in that year he was also admitted to the Order of Merit. He was created a baron in 1946.

In 1922 Newall married May Dulcie Weddell (died 1924). In 1925 he married Olive Tennyson Foster, the only daughter of Mrs Francis Storer Eaton of Boston, Massachusetts. There were three children of Newall's second marriage, one son and two daughters. Newall died 30 November 1963 at his home in London and was succeeded by his son, Francis (born 1930).

Portraits of Newall by W. G. de Glehn (1931) and by (Sir) Oswald Birley (1941) are in the possession of the family. There are also two portraits by R. G. Eves (1940), one in the Imperial War Museum and the other in the National Portrait Gallery.

[Denis Richards, *Royal Air Force 1939–1945*, vol. i, 1953; *The Times*, 2 December 1963; private information.]

M. J. DEAN

published 1981

O'CONNOR Richard Nugent

(1889–1981)

Sir

General, was born in Srinagar, Kashmir, India, 21 August 1889, the only child of Maurice Nugent O'Connor, a major in the Royal Irish Fusiliers, and his wife, Lilian, daughter of Sir John Morris of Killundine, Argyll. After education at Wellington College and the Royal Military College, Sandhurst, O'Connor was commissioned into the Scottish Rifles (Cameronians) in 1909. In 1914, as signals officer of 22nd brigade in the 7th division, he fought in the first battle of Ypres, in the battles of Neuve Chapelle and Loos in 1915 (he was awarded the MC), and in the battle of the Somme in 1916. In 1917 he was given command, as a lieutenant-colonel, of the 2nd battalion of the Honourable Artillery Company, and with them he took part in the third battle of Ypres (Passchendaele). Subsequently he went with them to Italy. He was appointed to the DSO (1917), gaining a bar (1918). He was mentioned in dispatches nine times.

O'Connor attended the Staff College at Camberley during 1920, and later was an instructor there, and held staff appointments. In 1935 he attended the Imperial Defence College and then was posted to command the Peshawar brigade on the North-West Frontier of India. In 1938 he was promoted to major-general, and appointed to command the 7th division, responsible for operations against Arab terrorists in southern Palestine, and to the post of military governor of Jerusalem. He was there when war broke out in September 1939. In June 1940 O'Connor, promoted temporary lieutenant-general, was appointed to command the Western Desert Force in Egypt.

Sir A. P. (later Earl) Wavell, commander-in-chief Middle East, instructed O'Connor secretly to plan the destruction of the Italian Tenth Army in Egypt. O'Connor's attack, launched on 9 December 1940, was brilliantly successful. Early in 1941 he received reports of an Italian withdrawal from Benghazi towards Tripolitania, and obtained authority to try and cut it off by a direct move across the desert to the Gulf of Sirte. His forces succeeded in forestalling the Italian withdrawal at Beda Fomm on 6 February, 25,000 Italians surrendering with 100 guns and an equal number of tanks. In two months O'Connor's force had advanced 350 miles, capturing 130,000 prisoners, nearly 400 tanks, and 845 guns at a cost to itself of 500 killed, 1,373 wounded, and 55 missing, a victory on which his reputation was to rest. O'Connor was then sent to Cairo to command British troops in Egypt, being replaced by Sir Henry Maitland (later Lord) Wilson and later by (Sir) Philip Neame, who faced the Germans under Rommel. When the latter's attack at the end of March 1941 threw Neame's force into confusion, Wavell sent O'Connor up from Cairo, intending that he should replace Neame, but O'Connor persuaded Wavell to leave Neame in command with himself as an adviser. Benghazi had to be abandoned and the decision was taken to withdraw from Cyrenaica. O'Connor and Neame were both captured and sent to Italy. When Italy surrendered in September 1943, an Italian general helped them get away before the Germans arrived. With the help of Italian partisans they finally reached the Eighth Army's lines, and O'Connor returned to Britain.

In January 1944 O'Connor assumed command of VIII Corps, which, after the landing in Normandy in June, was intended to effect the break-out from the beach-head. It was met by fierce opposition from the German forces in the area of Caen. Two major attacks failed to achieve a break-out, causing recriminations at many levels. VIII Corps was then switched to the western end of Second Army's sector and, from 28 July to 4 August, drove a deep wedge south to Vire on the boundary with US First Army.

O'Connor was given only a subsidiary role in the fighting which followed the liberation of Belgium, and was disappointed when, in December, Sir B. L. Montgomery (later Viscount Montgomery of Alamein) informed him that he was to go to Calcutta to take over India's Eastern Command, a post which involved no responsibility for operations. Soon after he arrived there, he was transferred to command North West Army in India and promoted general in April 1945.

In the following year, when Montgomery had become chief of the imperial general staff, O'Connor was recalled to become his colleague on the Army Council as adjutant-general. He spent much time visiting overseas commands to discuss an orderly demobilization, and proffered his resignation in summer 1947 rather than agree to an Army Council decision to reduce the numbers returning from the Far East, owing to a shortage of shipping. He was held to his offer on the grounds that he was not up to the job, an accusation he greatly resented. He retired on 30 January 1948.

In 1935 O'Connor married Jean, daughter of Sir Walter Charteris Ross of Cromarty. They acquired a house at Rosemarkie, from which O'Connor played a full part in Scottish public life. He was colonel of the Cameronians from 1951 to 1954, and in the following year became lord lieutenant of Ross and Cromarty, a post he held until 1964, in which year he was lord high commissioner of the general assembly of the Church of Scotland. He was appointed CB (1940), KCB (1941), GCB (1947), and KT (1971). He became an honorary DCL (St Andrews, 1947), was a member of the Legion of Honour, and held the croix de guerre with palm. His wife died in 1959. In 1963 he married Dorothy, widow of Brigadier Hugh Russell and daughter of Walter Summers, a steel merchant, of Dublin. In 1978 they moved from Rosemarkie to London, where O'Connor died 17 June 1981. He had no children, the son of his first wife by a previous marriage taking the surname of O'Connor by deed poll in 1944.

[I. S. O. Playfair, *The Mediterranean and the Middle East* (official history), vols. i (1954) and ii (1956); Barrie Pitt, *The Crucible of War*, 1980; Max Hastings, *Overlord*, 1984; O'Connor's personal papers at King's College, London; private information.]

MICHAEL CARVER

published 1990

PARK Keith Rodney

(1892–1975)

Sir

Air chief marshal, was born in Thames, New Zealand, 15 June 1892, the youngest son in the family of three sons and seven daughters of James Park, director of the Thames School of Mines and later professor of mining at the University of Otago, Dunedin, and his first wife, Frances, daughter of Captain W. Rogers, of Surrey. He was educated at King's College, Auckland, Selwyn Collegiate School, the Otago Boys' High School in Dunedin, and Otago University where he studied mining. After a shore job as a clerk in Dunedin with the Union Steamship Company, he managed to get to sea as a purser but the outbreak of war in 1914 gave his adventurous spirit its first great opportunity. In December of that year he volunteered as a gunner and he fought with the New Zealand Expeditionary Force at Gallipoli where distinguished conduct in the field gained him a commission (1915) in the NZ Artillery and he decided to become a regular soldier. He next saw service in France and was so severely wounded (for the second time) on the Somme that he was relegated to Woolwich as artillery officer instructor.

Vigorous and energetic by temperament, he decided it would be better to be airborne than chairbound and so volunteered for the Royal Flying Corps where, between 1917 and 1919, he served with Nos. 8 and 38 (Reserve) Squadrons and ended in command of No. 48 Squadron. When the Royal Air Force replaced the RFC in 1918 he was promoted captain. He gained the MC and bar in 1917, the croix de guerre in 1918, and the DFC in 1919.

Between the wars he was chief instructor in the Oxford University Air Squadron and commanded Northolt and Hornchurch fighter stations, organized flying pageants at Hendon, served as air attaché at Buenos Aires, became an ADC to the King at his coronation in 1937, passed the Imperial Defence College course that year, became officer commanding at Tangmere in 1938, and, as an air commodore later that year, was senior staff officer at HQ, RAF Fighter Command.

In April 1940 he was appointed air officer commanding No. 11 Fighter Group and in July was promoted air vice-marshal. As such he was responsible for much of the protective fighter patrolling during the operations preceding and accompanying the withdrawal from Dunkirk. Here he regularly flew his own Hurricane to get a direct view of the operation and himself took part in the final patrol. He later described Dunkirk as 'a most exciting time' and was convinced that the evacuation could not have succeeded without the fighter protection given by his Group over Calais, Boulogne, and Cherbourg as well as Dunkirk itself. And he believed that the air-fighting over France and Dunkirk gave British fighter squadrons their first real experience of battle, an experience to prove invaluable very soon afterwards.

In his view the Battle of Britain lasted from July till October 1940 and divided into two main phases, the first—the fight for the airfields—ending on 7 September. His own Group had the most extensive and vital area to protect, from Southampton to Norwich, and virtually had to defend London against attack by all the nearest approaches. Although his working day began at 0730 hours in the operations room at Northolt, deep underground, where he was able to see plotted the incoming waves of German aircraft and to order relevant counter-measures, he was no remote figure to his men: at 1730 hours he would set off in his own Hurricane and visit all his fighter stations to see how his pilots, ground-service staff, and squadrons were faring. In general, he found that their morale resembled his own and they all believed, rightly, that they had to defeat the *Luftwaffe* if invasion by sea was not to be inevitable.

Park's strategy, approved by Air Marshal Sir Hugh (later Lord) Dowding, was to place his squadrons where radar helped to predict enemy attack, and to have them intercept and break up the enemy formations before they could reach and bomb their objectives. At no stage did he have at his disposal more than twenty-five squadrons along the south coast and they often had to be serviced by men who had almost no time to eat and were working on the frontiers of exhaustion. Park appreciated their dedication as he did that of his pilots, and of the indispensable WAAF he said: 'Those girls—by God, they were stout-hearted girls.'

Unfortunately, (Sir) Trafford Leigh-Mallory, air officer commanding No. 12 Fighter Group in the midlands, believed in a different strategy: he preferred to concentrate larger 'wing' formations (groups of five to seven squadrons) against the bombing assaults. Eventually the Air Council transferred both Dowding and Park to other posts, in order to resolve the dispute. By that time, however, in Park's view the Battle of Britain had already been won by 7 September when the Germans gave up trying to eliminate the fighter stations and switched to the mass bombing of London. The old dispute was scarcely relevant any more and Park, if at all given to regret (which is unlikely), could have consoled himself that the main battle had been fought and won while he commanded the largest and most important fighter group—in the same period he had flown about 100 hours, mostly in his own fighter, an example as well as an inspiring leader.

Meanwhile, after a brief interlude as air officer commanding No. 23 Group Training Command, he was appointed in January 1942 air officer commanding Egypt, and in the following July moved to become air officer commanding Malta. According to Park himself, the Malta operations were a smaller version of the Battle of Britain itself, except that he found the island's defences in a bad way to begin with, he had a much smaller force to manœuvre, and food and fuel supplies were so sparse that often the pilots had to trust to luck that their engines had been serviced, engine tests being impossible because of fuel shortage. Under Park, however, drive and improvisation were always inspired. He resorted unrepentantly to his earlier strategy of leaving the ground as quickly as possible, swift interception, and early attack. During his time, Malta endured the impact of just under 1,300 tons of bombs but he made sure the island was no 'bomb-sponge' but a fortress which tied up superior enemy forces and made a vital contribution to the campaigns of Eisenhower in Tunisia and of Sir Bernard Montgomery (later Viscount Montgomery of Alamein) in the Western Desert and at Alamein. Simultaneously he conducted a private war with the *Luftwaffe* in Sicily and Sardinia. Having crippled the Germans over Malta, he attacked their massed force of 700 fighters and bombers in Sicily. And when the fighters ceased to come up against him in the air he defied the experts by equipping his Spitfires and Beaufighters with a pair each of 250-pound bombs to deal with them on the ground.

He also set about sinking Rommel's supply convoys to Benghazi, as soon as they set out from Brindisi and Taranto; and he bombed Benghazi itself, Sfax, Tunis, Bizerta, and Tripoli. He also introduced the use of intruder Mosquitoes by day and by night to disrupt and destroy the convoys on land behind Rommel's forward positions. Here his ability to inspire and communicate a fiery zeal at all levels paid off: his men sometimes did two raids in a single night on airfields and installations in Sardinia where the Germans tried to build up a torpedo-bomber force against the Allied armada for the invasion of Tunisia, and he thus eliminated in advance what could have been a serious danger.

After a similar energetic and invaluable contribution to the invasion of Sicily he became, in January 1944, air officer commander in chief in the RAF, Middle East. But the main weight of the German war had now moved to Europe and so he was sent as acting air chief marshal, to become Allied air commander, South-East Asia, in February 1945. Here he made an essential contribution to the reconquest of Burma and to the successful conclusion of the war in the Far East.

Tall and lean of stature, he combined stamina, personal courage, power to organize and improvise, personal modesty, and a natural easy command over men, all these in a rare degree.

He retired in 1946, with the rank of air chief marshal, and in 1947 Oxford University conferred on him an honorary DCL. He was appointed CB in 1940, KCB in 1945, and GCB in 1946. In 1942 he was appointed CBE.

In 1918 he married Dorothy Margarita, daughter of Lt.-Col. Woodbine Parish, CMG, CBE, director of Buenos Aires Great Southern Railway. She died in 1971. There were two sons of the marriage, of whom one was killed on active service in 1951. His retired years were spent in Remuera, Auckland, New Zealand, where, so long as he was able, he indulged in his favourite recreation, sailing. He died in hospital in Auckland, New Zealand, 5 February 1975.

[Alan W. Mitchell, *New Zealanders in the Air War*, 1945; Field-Marshal Michael Carver (ed.), *The War Lords*, 1976; Sir Basil Liddell Hart, *Short History of the Second World War*, 1970; *The Times*, 7 February 1975.]

D. M. DAVIN

published 1986

(1886–1970)

Pasha, founder of the Arab Legion, was born at Ashtead, Surrey, 12 June 1886, the only son of Lieutenant-Colonel Walter Ancell Peake, DSO, of Burrough-on-the-Hill, Leicestershire, by his wife, Grace Elizabeth Ann Fenwicke. He was intended for the navy, and was educated at Stubbington House, Fareham, where he showed little aptitude; he eventually gained entrance to the Royal Military College, Sandhurst, and was commissioned in the Duke of Wellington's Regiment in 1906. Later that year he was posted to India, and, while disliking the social duties then a prominent feature of Indian army life, he hunted, studied the local languages with enthusiasm, and developed a certain ingenuity, acumen, and resolution of his own.

Early in 1914 he was seconded to the Egyptian Army at his own request, and was sent to join the 4th Infantry battalion in the Sudan; although his applications for front-line duty on the outbreak of war were ignored, in 1916 when the Darfur rebellion broke out he transferred to the Camel Corps under (Sir) Hubert Huddleston, and took command of No. 5 company, having been promoted captain in 1915. Due for home leave that year, Peake asked to go instead to Salonika for action against the Bulgarians, and was temporarily posted to No. 17 Squadron, Royal Flying Corps, as observer and later adjutant. Although he outstayed his leave, he was saved from court martial by the sense of humour of General (later Field-Marshal Lord) Milne, who merely sent him back to Darfur with a reprimand. However, on the last lap of the journey south he was thrown from his camel and severely dislocated his neck: he spent several months in hospital before a specialist told him that his case was incurable. Later, walking in the hospital gardens and unable to raise his head from his chest, Peake crashed blindly into a tree: the jolt restored his neck to normal with no subsequent ill effect. He had no sooner returned to his unit after convalescence, however, than he developed a liver abscess and was sent home on sick leave. On the return voyage his ship was torpedoed near Alexandria: Peake jumped overboard with a bottle of beer and a packet of sandwiches and was picked up none the worse.

Early in 1918 he was sent to Sinai and took command of a company of the Egyptian Camel Corps, in the British section of the Northern Arab Army; in April they joined T. E. Lawrence with Sharif Faisal's army at Aqaba. Lawrence's task in the final phase of the Egyptian Expeditionary Force's campaign under Sir Edmund (later Viscount) Allenby—especially after many of Allenby's troops were withdrawn to meet the German offensive in Europe of March 1918—was to cut off and contain the large numbers of Turks defending the Hejaz railway and garrisoning the towns from Medina to Damascus. The Egyptian Camel Corps gave invaluable assistance to Lawrence's guerrilla campaign northwards, even if Peake had cause to complain that his men were reluctant to get themselves killed; they had a vital role to play against those Turkish positions inaccessible to armoured cars, and 'The Peake Demolition Co. Ltd.' became adept as sappers, developing the 'tulip' technique for blowing up stretches of railway; their last job before the decisive battle at Megiddo was to cut the Dera'a–Damascus railway in order to disrupt Turkish communications and hinder their retreat. Demobilization soon followed, and Peake returned to HQ in Cairo.

When hostilities ended in 1918, the Trans-Jordanians set up quaint pockets of autonomous government in every town. To each of these a British officer of one kind or another was posted, as representative of the British high commissioner in Palestine. Most of the area was under Occupied Enemy Territory Administration and also formed part of Faisal's Kingdom of Damascus, while the far south still belonged to his father, Husain, Grand Sharif of Mecca; boundaries were undefined, funds and a tax system non-existent, and civil administration was chaotic. The desert nomads, whom the Turks had made little attempt to control, regarded it as a heaven-sent opportunity to raid the sown, according to age-old custom, and the cultivators of the sown retaliated; the first task was to establish law and security. Peake was sent to administer Aqaba and its environs, and within a year his impartiality had gained the respect and affection of both tribesmen and villagers.

But in 1919 British troops were withdrawn from Trans-Jordan as well as from Syria, following the treaty of Versailles, and Peake returned to his old command of the Egyptian Camel Corps in Palestine with responsibility for policing the eastern frontier south of the Dead Sea. On the establishment of the British mandate in Palestine in 1920, the Camel Corps was disbanded; Peake accepted a position in the Palestine Police, and was posted to supervise internal security in Amman; he found morale and efficiency at a low ebb, and the gendarmerie unpaid, having evidently inherited all the vices and few of the virtues of the Turkish regime. The high commissioner for Palestine, Sir Herbert (later Viscount) Samuel, authorized Peake to raise a force of 105 men and officers: the Arab Legion thus came into being, October 1920. At first there was much opposition from the tribesmen, who saw a threat to their traditional way of life, the villagers were afraid of reprisal and reluctant to join, and Peake was obliged to scrape together a few Egyptian and Sudanese ex-servicemen. However, recruitment slowly increased, although uniforms were 'war surplus' (Peake was later to design the uniforms himself), and the soldiers of the new 'Arab Army' were, to their shame, the only men in the area without weapons until Peake managed to find some old German rifles.

Peake attended the Cairo conference of 1921, at which (Sir) Winston Churchill, Lawrence, and Samuel were also present among many others; while it was in progress, news came that Sharif Abdullah, Husain's second son, had reached Amman to raise a force against the French who had ejected Faisal from Syria. At Lawrence's instigation, Churchill went to meet Abdullah, and persuaded him to accept the emirate of Trans-Jordan under British protection, on condition that he would try to prevent his subjects from troubling the French. The Arab Legion was to be increased to a thousand men, and funds were promised; enlistment gradually became more competitive as the Legion's prestige grew, although arms remained a difficulty; for example, there were ex-Turkish cavalrymen who insisted on swords, and Peake finally obtained from the Cairo Ordnance Depot a 'job lot' which turned out to be part of the Napoleonic army's equipment abandoned in 1801.

Later in 1921 Lawrence toured the country with Peake in an old 'Tin Lizzie' Ford; their esteem and liking was mutual, and Lawrence—a frequent visitor—gave Peake much advice on general policies, and methods of controlling tribal raiding and the threat of incursions from Arabia. Both men foresaw the end of direct British rule, and realized the potency of the Arab awakening.

Peake's early problems arose from the strong anti-French feeling stirred up by Arab officials exiled from Damascus: the French did not hesitate to accuse him of aiding these refugees, many of whom had secured posts in Abdullah's Government and who in turn accused Britain of having handed over Syria to the French. The Balfour Declaration of 1917 was a further cause of friction, and aroused general distrust and fear of Zionism among even the local sheikhs; Peake narrowly escaped death at the hands of a mob enraged by the arrest of an Arab agent, whom Peake had handed over to the Palestinian authorities without being aware of the man's identity. However, Abdullah himself showed unfailing good humour, common sense, and much respect and affection for Peake who consulted him almost daily. A spell of home leave in 1923 was interrupted by a fierce but brief uprising against unfair taxation by corrupt ministers, but another crisis was already on the horizon in 1922: raids by the fanatical Ikhwan from central Arabia, massacring all Muslims who did not belong to their own Wahhabi sect, and slowly increasing in range and ferocity until by 1924 they came within ten miles of Amman. Harry St. John Philby, at that time chief British representative, was the first to tell Peake of the imminent danger, and a desert outpost of the Arab Legion was set up to give early warning, although its purpose was defeated owing to the lack of wireless equipment. However, in 1924, with the help of the RAF, a decisive victory was gained over a large force of Ikhwan, who thereafter left Trans-Jordan in peace.

In 1926 the British Government asked Abdullah to take over the south from Ma'an to Aqaba, as a result of Ibn Saud's invasion of the Hejaz; Peake successfully persuaded—by ingenious if unorthodox methods—the inhabitants of those wild and inaccessible mountains to accept the presence of law and order, and the following year an additional three hundred men were recruited to police the area. However, in 1927 Ibn Saud's Wahhabis were again menacing the south, and a detachment of the Trans-Jordan Frontier Force was sent from Palestine to guard the frontier; the Arab Legion was reduced accordingly, but in 1930 (Sir) John Glubb—Glubb Pasha, who was to succeed Peake as the Legion's commander—came as peacemaker and lawgiver to the border tribes, with a small unit of Bedouins. The decade from 1927 brought peace and prosperity to the Middle East, and within a few years of Trans-Jordan's having been one of the most lawless and dangerous countries, tourists began to visit places such as Petra and Jerash in safety. Peake and the Arab Legion, which he had raised and trained from scratch, established law and order, a peaceful community was able to extend the area of cultivation, and the Government could conduct a regular administration. But the years 1936–9 were more difficult, when the Palestinian rebellion put the Legion's loyalty to a severe test; many Trans-Jordanians were sympathetic to the cause of the Palestine Arabs, and had Palestinian family connections. Six hundred extra men were drafted in to protect the oil pipeline against sabotage and to forestall the movement of rebels through the north of the country.

Peake Pasha built the Arab Legion on a firm foundation, establishing a tradition of loyalty and efficient discipline which withstood many shocks from both within and without the kingdom; a stern disciplinarian whose military style was almost Victorian, he believed that it was good policy to appear angry. His character was always unexpected, and his courage legendary; he learned to fly at the age of forty-four, and when on tour the warning code-word 'thundercloud' would precede him from one police post to another. Nevertheless, his men of the Arab Legion were utterly devoted to him for his honesty and kindness, his almost motherly fondness and consideration for their well-being. In height he was above average, upright, with a rubicund complexion set off, in later life, by white hair and moustache, while his piercing blue eyes seemed to read the very soul of a miscreant; for years after he left Trans-Jordan, men would say, 'May Allah remember him for good! His heart was true and simple.'

Peake retired in 1939, having held the British local rank of lieutenant-colonel since 1921; in the Arab Legion he held successively the ranks of brigadier (1920–2), major-general (1922–6), and general or pasha from 1926. He was awarded the Sudan medal with two clasps (1916), and was appointed OBE (1923), CBE (1926), and commander of the Order of St. John of Jerusalem (1934); he was also appointed CMG (1939) in recognition of his services to Trans-Jordan, and held several Middle Eastern decorations and medals. In 1937 Peake married Elspeth Maclean, younger daughter of Norman Ritchie, of St. Boswells, Roxburghshire; she bore him a daughter, and died in 1967. They retired to his wife's Scottish home, where he served in Civil Defence from 1939, and was acting inspector of constabulary with the local rank of lieutenant-colonel (1942–51); he wrote *A History of Jordan and its Tribes* (1958) and *Change at St. Boswells* (1961), a history of the village. He died at Kelso 30 March 1970. A portrait of him by the American artist Mollie Guyon (1953) is privately owned.

[C. S. Jarvis, *Arab Command*, 1942; J. B. Glubb, *The Story of the Arab Legion*, 1948; T. E. Lawrence, *Seven Pillars of Wisdom*, 1926; *The Times*, 1 and 6 April 1970; personal knowledge.]

JOHN BAGOT GLUBB

published 1981

<hr>

PHILLIPS Tom Spencer Vaughan

(1888–1941)

Sir

Admiral, the son of Captain (later Colonel) T. V. W. Phillips, R.A., and his wife, Louisa May Adeline, daughter of Admiral (Sir) Algernon F. R. de Horsey, was born at Pendennis Castle, Falmouth, 19 February 1888. He became a naval cadet in 1903, midshipman in 1904, sub-lieutenant in 1907, gaining first class certificates in all examinations, and lieutenant in July 1908. He joined the navigating branch and in the war of 1914–18 was navigator first of the cruiser *Bacchante* at the Dardanelles and later of the newer cruiser *Lancaster* in the Far East, and was thus far removed—much to his chagrin—from further active participation in the war. He made his mark, however, for he was granted the acting rank of commander in an unexpected vacancy and was executive officer of his ship from April 1917 onwards. In 1918 he was made acting captain and commanded the *Lancaster* for three months, transferring, still as acting captain, in 1919 to the cruiser

Euryalus and bringing her home. In June 1919 he joined the Staff College, and after qualifying served for three years under the British naval representative at the headquarters of the League of Nations, being promoted commander in June 1921; and for two years in the plans division of the Admiralty naval staff. In July 1925, after eight months in command of the sloop *Verbena* on the Africa station, he was appointed to the operational staff, Mediterranean, the chief of staff being (Sir) Dudley Pound. Phillips served in that capacity until May 1928, being promoted captain in June 1927.

From September 1928 he commanded the sixth destroyer flotilla until April 1930, when he returned to the plans division as assistant director for over two years. He commanded the *Hawkins*, flagship of the East Indies squadron, from September 1932 to January 1935. In August 1935 he became director of plans, Admiralty, and held that important post, throughout the international naval conference of 1935–6, until April 1938. He was then appointed to command the Home Fleet destroyer flotillas as commodore and, from January 1939, as rear-admiral. In May 1939 Pound, when nominated first sea lord and chief of the naval staff, knowing Phillips's personality and abilities, chose him for the post (hitherto invariably held by a much more senior admiral) of deputy chief—later styled vice-chief—of the naval staff. The choice proved well justified, and Phillips, clear-headed and indefatigable as ever, quickly won the full confidence not only of his brother officers of the staff but also of (Sir) Winston Churchill, who took office as first lord on the outbreak of war; on Churchill's recommendation, he was granted the acting rank of vice-admiral on 7 February 1940. Churchill in the third volume of his history of *The Second World War* (1950) styled Phillips 'our trusted vice-chief of the naval staff'; but the accord between the two men had dwindled. Phillips found himself on more than one occasion a convinced opponent of the policy, or action, upon which the prime minister was set; and he would make no compromise on matters of strategy. Churchill records in his second volume (1949) that in September 1940 Phillips demurred to the suggestion of retaliatory bombing of German cities. Early in 1941 he expressed and maintained the view that to divert forces from Cyrenaica to Greece would be unsound and probably disastrous. That diversion took place in March, and from that time, according to his own statement to an intimate, Phillips's personal contact with the prime minister practically ceased.

In May 1941 he was given the 'dormant' appointment of commander-in-chief of the Eastern Fleet—the formation of which in substantial strength he had himself first suggested when the high probability that Hitler would attack Russia was realized—but continued in the onerous post of vice-chief of the naval staff. He was relieved in that capacity in October 1941 and at once took up his new command, with the acting rank of admiral—thus receiving for the second time acting promotion through two ranks. He sailed for the Far East in the battleship *Prince of Wales*, picking up on the way the only other capital ship of his so-called 'fleet', the old battle cruiser *Repulse*. The aircraft carrier *Indomitable* was to have been of his force, but she had been delayed by an accident and was not available, while commitments elsewhere had prevented the defences of Malaya from being brought up to adequate strength, a measure which he had strongly urged while in office at the Admiralty.

The ships arrived at Singapore on 2 December, and on 8 December, without declaration of war, the Japanese attacks on Malaya began with an amphibious assault at the northern frontier. The admiral was thus faced with a problem as difficult as any that occur in war. The air fighter force in Malaya was small and it was by no means certain that its support could be made available to his ships in need. He was faced with the tragic dilemma of either having to take his ships to the scene of invasion in the face of strong land-based enemy air forces, despite the uncertainty of his own air support, or the apparently pusillanimous course of remaining inactive while an enemy army was landing on British soil only 400 miles away. He did not hesitate. He decided that, given the fighter support for which he asked, and provided he could achieve surprise, he should be able to cut the enemy's supply-line by sea and destroy their reinforcements; and he sailed the same evening. The next morning, 9 December, he learned that fighter support could not be provided, and that strong Japanese bomber forces were believed to be already based in Indo-China. He decided to carry on, however, provided his ships were not sighted by enemy reconnaissance; but later in the day the weather cleared, and when Japanese aircraft were sighted from his flagship so that the chance of surprise had gone, it became clear that to carry out his original plan would not only be ineffective but would expose his ships, the only substantial allied naval force left in the Pacific, to certain disablement if not destruction. At 8.15 p.m. he altered course to return to Singapore. From that intention he was diverted by a report—which afterwards proved to be unfounded—that the enemy was landing at Kuantan, only 140 miles north of Singapore. His detour thither actually had the effect of evading the Japanese striking force which was seeking his ships the next morning, but by pure chance it sighted them on its return flight to its Indo-Chinese base. The *Prince of Wales* and *Repulse* were then attacked with bombs and torpedoes by large numbers of Japanese aircraft and were both sunk less than two hours after the first attack. Phillips was not amongst the 1,285 officers and men who were saved from his flagship.

Phillips was appointed C.B. in 1937 and promoted K.C.B. in 1941. He married in 1919 Gladys Metcalfe, daughter of Captain F. G. Griffith-Griffin,

D.C.L.I., and widow of J. H. Brownrigg. There was one son of the marriage who also entered the Royal Navy.

[Admiralty records; S. W. Roskill, (Official) *History of the Second World War. The War at Sea*, vol. i, 1954; Russell Grenfell, *Main Fleet to Singapore*, 1951; private information; personal knowledge.]

H. G. THURSFIELD

published 1959

PLUMER Herbert Charles Onslow

(1857–1932)

First Viscount Plumer, of Messines

Field-marshal, was born at Torquay 13 March 1857, the elder son of Hall Plumer, of Malpas Lodge, Torquay, by his wife, Louisa Alice Hudson, daughter of Henry Turnley, of Kensington. He came from an old York-shire family and was a great-grandson of Sir Thomas Plumer, master of the Rolls. He was educated at Eton, and in the autumn of 1876 he passed direct into the 65th Foot (1st York and Lancaster Regiment) at Lucknow. At the unusually early age of twenty-two Plumer found himself adjutant: he was promoted captain in 1882. The Afghan war passed the 65th by, and after proceeding to Aden the battalion embarked for home in February 1884. Nevertheless, Plumer was to undergo a sharp baptism of fire in the Sudan campaign, for *en route* the 65th were summoned to Trinkitat near Suakin, where a force under Sir Gerald Graham had assembled to retrieve Osman Digna's massacre of the *gendarmerie* commanded by General Valentine Baker at El Teb on 5 February, and to rescue the Egyptian garrison of Tokar. Although too late to do this, the battalion won the fierce fight with hosts of Arabs at El Teb on 29 February, and a fortnight later (13 March) the still fiercer struggle at Tamai, where the 2nd brigade square was pene-trated by the Arabs. In both battles the 65th were hotly engaged and suffered considerably. Plumer was mentioned in dispatches and received the third class Medjidie. Shortly afterwards the battalion resumed its voyage and went to Dover. Next year Plumer passed into the Staff College and in 1890 was appointed deputy-assistant-adjutant-general at Jersey in the days when that appointment covered war-training as well as admin-istration. On its termination in 1893 he joined the 84th Foot in Natal, having been promoted major in January of that year.

363

Plumer

Plumer now entered upon a period in which he was to found his reputation. After the defeat of the Jameson Raid (2 January 1896), he was one of the imperial officers sent to disarm the troops of the British South Africa Company and secure their ammunition before they could attempt a rescue of the imprisoned raiders. The mission was successful, and the best of the company's troops were withdrawn. But the severe outbreak of rinderpest, and the company's preventive measures, unsettled the Matabele, who broke out into rebellion under Lobengula and within a few days murdered over 200 settlers and their families. An irregular relief force consisting eventually of 750 men and 1,100 horses was hastily got together at Kimberley and Mafeking under the command of Plumer with the local rank of lieutenant-colonel, until Sir Robert Martin should arrive to take command in the area. Prompt action by Plumer, who had to train his irregulars and equip them while marching up to the front in Rhodesia, saved the settlers, and after seven months of continual marching and fighting, the Matabele were cowed and surrendered to Cecil Rhodes as a result of the famous meeting where he met them almost single-handed.

The Matabele relief force was now broken up, and Plumer, receiving many encomiums and a brevet lieutenant-colonelcy, returned home at the end of 1896. In a staff appointment at Aldershot he worked from 1897 until the summer of 1899 when, on the approach of war in South Africa, he was hastily dispatched with a number of officers to raise an irregular mounted infantry corps, the Rhodesian Horse, at Bulawayo, while other officers raised a similar force in Bechuanaland, both under Colonel (afterwards Lord) Baden-Powell. These two forces were to protect British territory until imperial troops could arrive. But the Boers, waiting for the grass to grow on the veld for their horses, gave a breathing space to Plumer, who had received an enthusiastic welcome from his veterans. On 3 October the corps was sufficiently trained to go to its war stations; on the 11th war was declared, and the Boer armies invaded British territory, but their western strategy was disarranged by the magnets of Rhodes at Kimberley and the little force under Baden-Powell at Mafeking. Plumer was now in command of all the local forces in the west, north of Kimberley, and many guerrilla engagements followed until in May 1900 he was able to join hands with the southern Mafeking relief force under (Sir) Bryan Mahon, and, Mafeking having been relieved, Plumer commanded the northernmost of the three columns that advanced on Pretoria from the west under General Sir Archibald Hunter. In the great 'De Wet hunt' which followed it was Plumer's column which hung on his heels day and night for 800 miles until, after a six weeks' ride, the guerrilla chief was compelled to bring his remnant back to the starting point. Plumer was appointed C.B., and in March 1902, now a brevet-colonel and brigadier-general, he came home on leave and was posted to a brigade at Aldershot; but being promoted major-general at the early age of forty-five, he was transferred to the Colchester district, and then after a few months he was appointed in 1903, on Lord Roberts's recommendation, to be quartermaster-general in the newly formed Army Council. The new secretary of state for war, H. O. Arnold-Forster, an enthusiastic if theoretical army reformer, wanted to provide a very short service army and to weld this country's too numerous un-correlated military forces into a military organization that would earn her a place in the military opinion of the continent. Although his scheme was not generally acceptable to military thought, Plumer believed that it could be made to work, but when R. B. (afterwards Viscount) Haldane superseded Arnold-Forster, a new, and, as is now known, a better scheme, was carried into effect. But it was a severe and undeserved blow when Haldane, conceiving by some odd misunderstanding that Plumer would not support his plans, reconstituted the Army Council without him in December 1905. Nevertheless, he found fortune return to him when in 1906 he was appointed K.C.B. and placed in command of a fighting division (the 5th) in Ireland, where he remained until 1909. In 1908 he was promoted lieutenant-general and two and a half years later was appointed commander-in-chief at York.

At the Christmas following the outbreak of war in 1914, Plumer was appointed to the command of the II Corps in France, and in May 1915 to that of the Second Army. For two not very exciting years he held the fateful Ypres salient, training young troops and drafts and perfecting communications in complete harmony with Sir Douglas Haig. For long the British had sat in the low land with the enemy on the high land, and Haig had wished to seize the higher ground as far as the Dutch coast. The move had begun in 1916 with the protracted, costly, but not unsuccessful battle of the Somme, followed early in 1917 by the battle of Arras and Lens. To the north lay the Second Army under Plumer, who, knowing what was to come, was making far-sighted preparations against the Messines and Wytschaete Plateau. After the collapse in April 1917 of General Nivelle's offensive, an Allied conference held in Paris in May decided that the offensive must continue. On asking Plumer when he could attack, Haig promptly received the reply 'the 7th of June', and in effect at 3.10 a.m. on that day Plumer's offensive began with immense cannonades. By evening Messines and Wytschaete were carried and by next morning the Oostaverne line as well. All night the troops worked at consolidation in readiness for the counter-attack of three German divisions; but the plateau was carried and the battle was over, with a considerable number of prisoners and many guns captured, at a cost of one-fifth of the expected casualties. It was a triumph of wise preparation, and from all sides congratulations poured in upon the 'little man' whose hair had gone snow-white during the two anxious years just past.

Plumer had now shown that he and his staff could arrange and his troops carry out; and he and Sir Hubert Gough were told to continue as soon as possible the attack on the high ground running from near Messines to the far side of Passchendaele, beyond which the Fourth Army under Sir Henry Rawlinson had been collected. The great series of operations which began on 21 July cannot be described here, but the two commanders, acting in perfect unison, fought eight great battles with immense results despite the foulest weather. On 13 November the Passchendaele high ground was at last secured; but in the meantime the prospects of the Allies had suffered a grievous change. With the disappearance of Russia, the eastern German army was coming west, and in the late autumn the Italian defeat at Caporetto (24 October) had to be retrieved at all costs.

On 7 November Plumer and his chief of the general staff, General (Sir) C. H. Harington, were ordered to Italy to take over an Allied force of six French and five British divisions, behind which the Italian army was to reform. On 3 December they had taken over the line which it was essential to make good, and were holding the Montello section which ran from Lake Garda to the Piave. As Allied divisions struggled into position, the situation was saved, and by Plumer's regrouping (with the cordial acquiescence of the Italians), by his robust common sense, and by the sturdy lesser fighting of the Allies, it was possible to bring back the Second Army to France after four months' absence.

Plumer and his staff reached Cassel on 13 March. On the 21st Gough's attenuated line was attacked and broken through. That very afternoon Haig sent for Plumer, showed him all the facts, and asked what he could do to help. The Second Army had fourteen fairly good divisions and at once Plumer said, placing his hand on his younger chief's shoulder, without even consulting Harington (who was present): 'I will give you twelve divisions in return for tired ones'. Haig said: 'That means giving up Passchendaele'. 'Not a bit of it', replied Plumer.

Haig's gratitude was great. But after the British had weathered the first storm, a second fell on Plumer himself. With the twelve good divisions gone south and their places taken by the tired ones, filled up with new officers and men, Messines and Wytschaete went, and finally Passchendaele itself. Yet in spite of almost desperate crises, Plumer calmly held the Ypres salient until, with the enemy exhausted and starving, the assault died down. It was the last German effort in the north, and it only remained for the Allies to make their victorious effort, when the British were restored and the Americans ready.

In the pursuit of the German army the Second Army took its full share in supporting the Fourth Army and the group under the command of the King of the Belgians. Almost every day before the armistice Plumer's troops secured considerable captures of the enemy, and a month later his corps had crossed the Rhine, making a triumphant march through Cologne. Plumer was appointed to command the occupied territory and, although Germany was in great economic distress, Plumer was not the man to allow nonsense. As the industrial trouble spread, he put down internal riot and German strikes ruthlessly. At the same time by a telegram to the prime minister (8 March) he secured the immediate dispatch of food to the starving Germans. In 1919 he was raised to the peerage as Baron Plumer, of Messines and of Bilton, Yorkshire. He also received the thanks of parliament, a grant of £30,000, and was promoted field-marshal.

Even before peace had been signed, Plumer entered upon the third period of his life, the nine years as proconsul. It opened with his appointment as governor of a disturbed and, for a while, unhappy Malta, where famine and the fourteen points were breeding trouble, the former among the people, the latter among politicians. There had been severe riots and some rioters had been killed. When Plumer landed in June 1919 he found a large crowd awaiting him and a guard of 300 men from the navy. He at once ordered it to be reduced to twenty men. Seeing laurel wreaths on the ground, he asked the reason, and hearing that two rioters had been killed at that spot, he ordered their immediate removal, and proceeded with the formalities. The people were impressed, for it was clear that Plumer was a man who knew his own mind; and it was not long before they were to have ample evidence that their well-being and the removal of just grievances was the governor's first care. Plumer made great efforts to understand the people racially and historically, and he saw how little ground there was for Italian claims. The favourable impression which he had thus made was confirmed by the address delivered by this Anglican general to the clergy of the island (1924) when, in accordance with custom, they waited on him with candles at the palace on Candlemas Day. He showed sympathy, emphasizing how religion must be part of the people's lives and how the clergy were essential to their well-being, but there was also some scolding for indifference and neglect.

It was during Plumer's governorship that in 1921 the first representative government of Malta was introduced, and the legislative assembly was inaugurated by the Prince of Wales. When Plumer left in 1924, the manifestations of esteem and affection were very great.

But civil affairs were not the only questions to which Plumer had to attend. Harington was commanding the Allied garrison in the Dardanelles and Constantinople with a small British contingent when in 1922 the Turks under Mustapha Kemal fell upon the Greeks in Asia Minor and seriously threatened the British garrison at Chanak. Plumer was by chance on his way to Constantinople in the admiral's yacht to meet his old chief of the general staff. Just as in 1918 he offered all his men to Haig, so did he come to the help of Harington, sending from Malta every man on whom he could lay hands.

In August 1925 Plumer accepted the office of high commissioner in Palestine, to which Transjordan was added in 1928, and again his personality helped considerably in making Jewish settlers and Arabs realize that, while sympathetically hearing their troubles, he would allow no disorder. The work was strenuous, especially when carried on with his thoroughness, and the years of war having taken their toll, in July 1928 he resigned, and was raised to the degree of a viscount in 1929.

Plumer died in London 16 July 1932, and was buried in Westminster Abbey. He married in 1884 his second cousin, Annie Constance (died 1941), younger daughter of George Goss, of Park Crescent, London, and was succeeded as second viscount by his only son, Thomas Hall Rokeby Plumer (1890–1944). Of his three daughters, who all survived him, the eldest became principal of St. Anne's Society, Oxford. His many honours included the G.C.M.G. (1916), G.C.V.O. (1917), G.C.B. (1918), and G.B.E. (1924). Cricket ever commanded his great enthusiasm and he was elected president of the Marylebone Cricket Club in 1929.

To ambition of service Plumer added energy and enterprise in military matters, and there were inherent in him those characteristics of good faith and robust common sense for which he was noted and which were responsible for his marked gift of endearing himself to all who came into contact with him, from general to private soldier.

A portrait of Plumer by René de l'Hôpital is in the possession of the family. He figures in J. S. Sargent's picture, 'Some General Officers of the Great War', painted in 1922, which hangs in the National Portrait Gallery. A cartoon of him by 'Spy' appeared in *Vanity Fair* 13 November 1902. He is also included in the cartoon 'A General Group' by 'Spy' which appeared in *Vanity Fair* 29 November 1900.

[Sir Charles Harington, *Plumer of Messines*, 1935; Sir J. E. Edmonds, (Official) *History of the Great War. Military Operations. France and Belgium, 1914–1916*, 1922–1931, and Cyril Falls, 1917, 1940; private information; personal knowledge.]

GEORGE MACMUNN

published 1949

Charles Frederick Algernon

(1893–1971)

Viscount Portal of Hungerford

Marshal of the Royal Air Force, was born 21 May 1893 at Eddington House, near Hungerford, Berkshire, the first child of Edward Robert Portal, country gentleman and former barrister, and his second wife, Ellinor Kate Hill, daughter of Captain Charles West Hill, governor of Winchester prison. There were already two young sons from E. R. Portal's earlier marriage, and later he had four more sons by his second wife. There were no daughters.

The Portals were of Huguenot descent. Their long line of ancestors in southern France had flourished until Louis XIV's persecution, to avoid which two young Portal brothers fled abroad. Apparently they were shipped from Bordeaux in empty wine casks. In England the elder later established a family whose most distinguished member, until Portal of Hungerford, was the eighteenth-century silversmith and dramatist Abraham Portal. The younger founded a family which grew rich on the manufacture of banknote-paper; its most distinguished member in recent times was Viscount Portal, chairman of Portals Ltd. and the initiator of prefabricated houses.

Charles Portal was reared in a leisured but unluxurious household. E. R. Portal had inherited enough from a family wine business in Northampton to give up the law at thirty and devote himself to country life. The Eddington House estate comprised 400 acres, half of which he himself farmed; but most of his time was given to shooting, fishing, riding, hunting (as master of the Craven Hounds), and to his duties as landlord, JP, and major in the Berkshire Yeomanry. The world in which his seven sons grew up was one of manly sport and strict attention to duty. They were taught above all to be honourable, brave, active, well mannered, and considerate. Friendly competitiveness was encouraged, any trace of boasting or ostentation abhorred. Virility and patriotism were family hallmarks, and of the six sons who reached manhood, five opted from youth for a Service career. (Of these the most distinguished was Admiral Sir Reginald Portal, who died in 1983.) Only Charles Portal had no intention of entering the armed forces.

As a boy Portal (known to relatives and friends by his nickname Peter) soon excelled at shooting, fishing, ferreting, and ball games. At fourteen he took up hawking, which long remained an enthusiasm. By sixteen he was an acknowledged expert on this, writing paid articles for *The Field*.

Portal

Portal's education was that of his class: governess, preparatory school, public school. The public school was Winchester, where despite the hours he spent with the hawks he kept there he did well in both work and games. In October 1912 he went up to Christ Church, Oxford, as his father had done, to take a pass degree and subsequently qualify as a barrister of the Inner Temple. Though he spent most of his time hawking, beagling, and motor-cycle racing—he rode victoriously for Oxford against Cambridge in May 1914—he also passed his examinations. Had he gone into the law he would undoubtedly have made a great judge; but August 1914 dictated other courses.

On 6 August, hearing of a call for dispatch-riders, Portal enlisted in the motor-cyclist section of the Royal Engineers. Eight days later he was a corporal in France, about to begin almost incessant riding as the British Expeditionary Force advanced to Mons and retreated to the Marne. His tiredness became such that he once fell asleep on his machine and crashed into the back of the staff car carrying Sir Douglas (later Earl) Haig. But his courage and devotion to duty were quickly recognized. On 26 September he was commissioned, on 8 October he was mentioned in a dispatch of Sir John French (later Earl of Ypres), by late November he was commanding all the riders in HQ Signals Company, 1st Corps.

Staff duties and a stable front made dispatch-riding less appealing, and Portal soon applied for secondment to the Royal Flying Corps as an air observer. In July 1915 he joined No. 3 Squadron, a reconnaissance and artillery observation unit. He had two days' ground training, and on his third day—never having been in the air before—flew on reconnaissance over the enemy lines.

In August 1915 Portal nearly killed himself on home leave when the front fork of his motor cycle broke; his lingual artery was severed, but a passing doctor saved his life. He was back in France within six weeks. At the end of 1915 he left No. 3 Squadron to train as a pilot, graduated flying officer RFC in April 1916, and joined No. 60 Squadron (fighter-reconnaissance) in time for the Somme offensive. In mid-July, less than three months after he had qualified as a pilot, he was promoted temporary captain and returned to No. 3 Squadron as a flight commander. Back on tactical reconnaissance and artillery observation, he made 326 operational flights in the next eleven months. His outstanding service during the five months of the Somme offensive resulted in a recommendation for an immediate award of the MC 'for conspicuous skill and gallantry' (gazetted 19 January 1917).

On 14 June 1917 Portal was promoted temporary major and given command of No. 16 Squadron (reconnaissance and artillery observation). A month later he was appointed to the DSO, also given for his earlier work on the Somme. During the autumn his squadron was required to bomb by night behind the battle front. Its RE 8s, far from easy to fly, had not been designed to carry bombs, and there was apprehension when the order came through. Portal quenched all doubts by personal example. He took off by night alone, with a 112 lb. bomb slung under each wing, and then landed with the bombs still on. He paused, repeated the flight—and then repeated it again. Very soon No. 16 Squadron was skilled in night bombing, with Portal continuing to set an example. One night in January 1918 he made five raids beyond the enemy lines; later, during the German spring offensive, when his squadron was working for the Canadian Corps of the First Army, he flew over the enemy lines for three and a quarter hours one day, sending down calls for action against hostile batteries, and then during the ensuing night flew a bombing mission in driving snow.

Promotion to temporary lieutenant-colonel followed on 17 June 1918 when Portal was sent home to command No. 24 (Training) Wing at Grantham. A few weeks later he was awarded a bar to his DSO. The recommendation, emanating from the Canadian Corps, stated that 'whenever difficult or dangerous work has had to be carried out, this officer has done it himself'.

Portal's fighting war was now over. He had flown over 900 operational sorties and successfully registered more than 250 artillery shoots. A lieutenant-colonel with three decorations and twice mentioned in dispatches, he was still only twenty-five. Such a man was not to be lost to the new Royal Air Force, and Sir Hugh (later Viscount) Trenchard, who had marked him out in France, made sure that he was not. At the end of July 1919 he was appointed to a permanent commission in the rank of major (shortly, squadron leader).

For the next three and a half years Portal was an outstanding chief flying instructor at the newly established RAF Cadet College, Cranwell. He left in April 1922 to attend the first course at the new RAF Staff College, Andover. Posted next to operations and intelligence in the Air Ministry, he came into close contact with Trenchard, by then chief of the air staff, who initiated him into many aspects of RAF work and policy. Trenchard's high opinion of him was seen in Portal's promotion to wing commander in July 1925 and his nomination to attend the senior officers' war course at the Royal Naval College, Greenwich, where the other students were mostly admirals.

After Greenwich came command in March 1927 of No. 7 Squadron. It had experienced troubles before Portal took over, but his efficiency and enthusiasm soon had their effect. That summer, while based at Worthy Down, the squadron won the long-distance bomber event, entitling it to lead the bomber fly-past at the Hendon display; and in September 1927, and again in 1928, an aircraft of No. 7 Squadron won the annual competition for bombing accuracy. The bomb-aimer—lying on his stomach—was in both years the squadron commander, Portal. Another impressive feat at this time was Portal's disproof of an army assertion during manœuvres that tanks moving by night could not be spotted from the air. Patrolling during an evening of blinding rain and poor visibility, he picked out an armoured force with the aid of an Aldis lamp, and was still over it when dawn came nine hours later.

In 1929 Portal was chosen to attend the recently founded Imperial Defence College, after which he toured the RAF stations in India. On his return in 1931 he was promoted group captain and again appointed to the air staff. This time he was deputy director of plans, a post which brought him into close contact with the other Services. His main concerns were with Singapore (where he pleaded for aircraft as opposed to more heavy guns), with the 'air versus gun' controversy as it also related to other bases and the home ports, with questions of future RAF equipment, and with briefs for the British representatives at the disarmament conference. In this work he made a reputation for the speed at which he could produce a concise and convincing paper, and for his skill and fair-mindedness as a negotiator.

In February 1934 Portal received his first big command—over the British forces in Aden. There he brilliantly justified the decision to make the Air Ministry responsible for the defence of the settlement and the tribal protectorate. Soon after he arrived Quteibi tribesmen in the protectorate plundered some passing caravans, and order had to be restored. When the tribe refused to pay a fine and hand over the culprits Portal took action, not by punitive bombing, but by instituting an air blockade which, by threatening attack, kept the Quteibis from their fields and villages. After two months' incessant patrolling by his aircraft the tribesmen gave in, agreed to terms, and returned to good behaviour. This classic, and almost bloodless, demonstration of 'air control' over unadministered territory brought Portal further prestige and, on 1 January 1935, promotion to air commodore.

In the quieter months which then preceded the Abyssinian crisis Portal took up one of the Aden pastimes—sailing. Characteristically he won his first race and headed the table of successes in his first season. On one occasion he beat a naval commander first in his own yacht, and then, when they changed boats, in the commander's.

By the later summer of 1935 Mussolini's designs on Abyssinia were clear, and Portal was at full stretch preparing to repel any attack on Aden and receive reinforcements. With the arrival of these the post of commander,

British forces in Aden, was upgraded, and Portal returned home—to a place on the directing staff of the Imperial Defence College. There he preached inter-Service collaboration rather than any purely 'air' doctrine, and made friendships in the other Services which stood him in good stead later.

Portal left the IDC in July 1937 on promotion to air vice-marshal and appointment as director of organization in the Air Ministry. The RAF was then in the midst of expansion schemes to counter the danger from Hitler's Germany. To determine and meet the Service's rapidly shifting requirements for organization, accommodation, equipment, and trained manpower was a vast and vital task to which Portal now sacrificed all leisure interests. Among the developments which owed much to his work were the creation of Maintenance Command, the organization of the London balloon barrage and Balloon Command, progress with camouflage, the provision of high octane fuel, and the framing of mobilization procedures and administrative plans to support operational projects. The development of the reserve forces and the creation of special units for operational flying training (previously done in the squadrons) were other achievements. The most difficult task of all was finding and developing, with the airfields board and the directorate of works, all the airfields and depot sites needed under the successive expansion schemes. During Portal's eighteen months at organization over thirty new main airfield stations were in fact begun or completed and many satellite sites acquired—work without which victory in the Battle of Britain would hardly have been possible. It was recognized by his appointment as CB in the New Year's honours of 1939.

On 1 February 1939 Portal became air member for personnel. This gave him a seat on the Air Council and responsibility for providing the RAF with its totals of skilled officers and men. To match requirements exactly when these were constantly changing was a formidable task, and when war came in September the RAF still had grave deficiencies in many trades. Had it not been for Portal, however, these would have been much worse. He insisted, for instance, that problems of manning should be considered before expansion schemes were adopted, not afterwards; he recruited air gunners, instead of wastefully using volunteer ground tradesmen in this role; he helped to create a new technical branch of officers; to make women more readily available for work on operational stations, he helped to free the women's RAF companies from the Auxiliary Territorial Service and create instead the Women's Auxiliary Air Force. Above all he played a major part, when war came, in initiating two vital elements in the expansion of aircrew training. The first was a big new initial training organization to deal solely with aircrew training which could be done on the ground. The second, in which he was concerned from the earlier pre-war proposals, was the Commonwealth air training scheme approved in December 1939, and subsequently augmented. This scheme ensured, throughout the rest of the war, aircrew training facilities in safe areas and a wonderful flow of well-trained crews.

Portal was promoted temporary air marshal at the outbreak of war and remained at personnel. But a summons to a major operational post was bound to come and on 4 April 1940 he was appointed to Bomber Command. He had been there less than a week when the Germans invaded Norway. Once the enemy was established there it became Portal's task to attack German ships and German-occupied Norwegian airfields. But attack on warships only confirmed that the British bombers of the time could not operate safely by day without fighter escort; and not much could be achieved by trying to attack airfields at night or under cloud cover across the width of the North Sea—as Portal vainly pointed out to the air staff. His bombers obtained successes by laying mines on the German sea routes, but in general his force of some 240 aircraft was far too small, and too distant, to have any effect on the campaign.

On 10 May 1940 Portal's tasks changed abruptly when the Germans invaded France and the Low Countries. He was now required to use his 'medium' bombers—the Blenheims—against the advancing columns and their communications. This was at once revealed as suicidal work, and only Portal's rapid insistence on fighter cover saved the Blenheims from annihilation. Any delays imposed on the invaders were of the slightest—though in the Dunkirk period even slight delays had value. Little more success was achieved by Portal's 'heavy' bombers—the Wellingtons, Whitleys, and Hampdens. These were required to operate by night against the invaders' communications and—after much Anglo-French controversy—against oil plants, marshalling yards, and aircraft factories in Germany. Attack on German industrial targets was an extension of the war strongly urged by Portal. His small forces, inadequately equipped for accurate navigation and bombing on moonless nights, did little damage—much less than was thought at the time—but at least they suffered few losses, and they carried the war to the enemy's homeland.

Portal's reputation in no way suffered from the Allied failures in Norway and France, and his firm leadership was recognized by his appointment in July 1940 as KCB. In the weeks which followed, Sir Charles Portal—as he now became known—commended himself greatly to the prime minister by the energy he put into preparations to resist a German invasion and by the effective use of his force against enemy invasion ports and barge concentrations. His desire for offensive action against objectives in Germany, and his stimulation of research into better methods of navigation, also appealed to (Sir) Winston Churchill, as did his readiness to attack targets in Berlin immediately after the first German bombs fell on London. These attacks on Berlin in fact did negligible damage, but they had a profound effect on the Battle of Britain then raging. They caused Hitler to direct the *Luftwaffe* prematurely against London, and so took the weight of its attack from Fighter Command's vital sector stations.

While stimulating technical improvements to make the British night bombing more effective, Portal now also began to press for the selection of targets which would be easier to find and hit. Thus far the targets had been precise ones, for both military and humanitarian reasons. Portal urged that German industrial areas, rather than particular plants or factories, should be his prime objective. This was not yet the official policy; but on 4 October 1940 Portal left Bomber Command to succeed, three weeks later, Sir Cyril (later Lord) Newall as chief of the air staff. In a matter of weeks 'area bombing' was initiated, and Bomber Command began its long assault on the German industrial towns.

Promoted acting air chief marshal on his new appointment, Portal had now risen to be head of his Service. The 'accepted star of the Royal Air Force' (in Churchill's words), he drove himself relentlessly throughout the rest of the war. His leadership was never remotely challenged; and he survived strains in dealing with the prime minister which seriously impaired the health or temper of more than one of his colleagues.

As CAS Portal fought his war almost entirely in Whitehall and at the great Anglo-American conferences. He concerned himself not with the day-to-day supervision of the RAF but, in essence, with the settling of strategic plans, priorities, and allocations. This he did both on the RAF level and, in conjunction with the prime minister and his fellow chiefs of staff, on the inter-Service and later inter-Allied levels. The work of determining first British, and then Anglo-American, higher strategy and military policy was particularly arduous. At the end of the war Portal reckoned that he had attended nearly 2,000 chiefs of staff meetings, 'each taking 1½ to 2 hours or more, and needing perhaps 3 or 4 hours of reading beforehand'.

Portal's first battle as CAS was for the retention of Coastal Command. In the autumn of 1940 A. V. Alexander (later Earl Alexander of Hillsborough) and Lord Beaverbrook led a campaign for its transfer to the Admiralty. In Portal's view the shipping protection problem of that time arose not from faulty organization but from the general shortage of aircraft, and he worked out a compromise with the chief of naval staff, Sir A. Dudley Pound by which Coastal Command would be strengthened and formally placed under the Admiralty's 'operational control'. (It already was so in practice, but the phrase was a guarantee.) Thanks to this,

Alexander and Beaverbrook were worsted. Later, in 1942, Portal had to fight a similar battle against Sir Alan Brooke (later Viscount Alanbrooke), who was demanding a very large and virtually separate air force for army support. Together with naval demands at the time, it would have absorbed almost the entire British output of operational aircraft. Again Portal succeeded in satisfying the demand in another way—by demonstrating, through the forces of Sir Arthur (later Lord) Tedder in North Africa, that where the army was actively engaged it could by that time rely on a powerful RAF presence and constantly improving techniques of air support. In resisting such demands Portal preserved both his own Service and the principle of centralized higher control of air power to avoid waste of resources and give maximum flexibility of application. This in itself was a notable contribution to victory.

Portal's other internal battles included several with the prime minister, none of which diminished their mutual liking and respect. Apart from those on strategic issues, the most serious was that over the position of Tedder in the Middle East in the autumn of 1941. Churchill had had little confidence in Tedder's appointment, and was moving towards dismissing him. Portal, convinced of Tedder's outstanding abilities, skilfully averted this by sending out his able and devoted vice-chief of air staff, Sir Wilfrid Freeman, who was also an admirer of Tedder, on a mission of enquiry, and by concerting with the secretary of state for air, Sir Archibald Sinclair (later Viscount Thurso), a joint resignation should the prime minister insist on having his way.

Portal's contributions to the higher strategy and direction of the war were mostly made within the framework of written exchanges with the prime minister (two or three times a week) and meetings with his fellow chiefs of staff, American as well as British. On a few detailed issues his views did not prevail, but in general they did. They were extremely consistent. He steadfastly upheld the basic strategy which he had agreed with his fellow British chiefs of staff, and which he later helped to persuade the Americans to accept—the strategy which brought victory. The essentials of this were the primacy of the war in Europe and North Africa over the war in the Far East; the building up of US armaments and forces and the maintenance of sea communications; and the waging of a bombing offensive against Germany to the point where her capacity to resist invasion by the Allied armies would be fatally weakened. This strategy Portal helped to defend successfully against all attempts to change it, or weaken it by diversions. He overcame Churchill's periodic waverings about the bombing offensive and, in conjunction with Brooke, frustrated the prime minister's proposals for invasions of Norway and Sumatra. He firmly resisted the American Admiral King's inclination in 1942–3 to switch the greater effort to the Pacific. He and Brooke also played a major part in convincing the Americans that the return to France would have to wait until 1944.

It was naturally, however, in the bombing offensive against Germany that Portal's most distinctive contribution lay. After the fall of France the War Cabinet and the chiefs of staff, knowing that years must elapse before the British army could return to the Continent, pinned their faith on a bombing offensive as the only immediate means, with a blockade, of putting direct pressure on the Germans. On becoming chief of the air staff in October 1940 Portal had to make this strategy work; and his first contribution, as indicated above, was for reasons of practicality to introduce night attack on industrial areas instead of precise targets. During 1941, however, it became apparent that much of the British bombing was still ineffective. This crisis Portal met by stimulating the efforts to produce new night navigational and bombing aids and more powerful bombs, and by advocating incendiary attack by selected crews before the arrival of the main bomber stream. He also appointed to Bomber Command a man whose experience, abilities, and character fitted him exceptionally well for the task in hand—Sir Arthur Harris.

The entry of the Americans into the war gave Portal the chance to concert, with General Arnold, the Anglo-American day and night air offensive which ultimately brought decisive results. During 1942, however, the USAAF bombers, purely a daylight force, were unable successfully to penetrate Germany, and voices were raised—especially Churchill's—urging them to go over to attack by night. But Portal, who after the early operations himself felt uneasy, was more aware than Churchill of the difficulties of conversion, and threw all his weight behind the American air leaders in their desire to persist with daylight operations. He helped to still Churchill's criticisms; and eventually long-range fighters, especially the Mustangs backed by Portal, supplied the cover which enabled the Americans to win their daylight battle over Germany. Throughout it was obvious to Portal that a day and night offensive, if it could be achieved, would be vastly more effective than one solely by night: the strain on the defences, the choice of targets, the moral and material effects would be immeasurably greater.

Until the immediate bombing campaign in preparation for the Allied landings in Normandy, Portal was the designated agent of the combined chiefs of staff for the superior control of the strategic air forces of both countries. With the approach of the invasion, 'direction' of these was vested in General Eisenhower—an arrangement which Portal accepted because in practice it would be exercised by Tedder, Eisenhower's deputy. With the establishment and advance of the Allied armies, control reverted in November 1944 to Portal in conjunction with Arnold—working in practice through their deputies.

During the winter months of 1944–5 the primary target systems chosen met strong opposition from Harris. With the development of night navigation and bombing aids Portal was convinced that Bomber Command could now operate effectively against precise targets, notably oil plants, which became the first priority. Harris, distrustful from past experience of 'panacea' targets, would have preferred, for reasons both of effect and operational safety, to complete as his primary task the destruction of his listed German industrial towns. Portal's patience in dealing with Harris was criticized in the British official history, but he was convinced that Harris, while arguing against his orders, had no intention of disobeying them. In point of fact area attacks continued until almost the last month of the war, but attack on more precise targets took precedence when operational conditions permitted.

The strategic air offensive has come under strong criticism since the war, particularly from humanitarians and naval historians. There is no doubt, however, that though its course was long, arduous, and bloody, it finally worked. The Germans were forced to put an enormous effort into defending their homeland; their production suffered and their communications were disrupted; their air force became almost purely defensive and was finally withering away for lack of fuel. Exactly as the chiefs of staff had hoped, Germany's capacity to resist an armed invasion was fatally weakened. Once the possibility of a return to the Continent dawned in 1942, this was always Portal's main intention. In promoting the bombing offensive he did not, like Harris, believe that it could virtually win the war without a serious invasion. If the Germans surrendered before the invasion so much the better; but essentially his concept was first to make the invasion possible, and then to speed, by both tactical and strategic operations, the advance of the Allied armies.

The close involvement of Portal with the strategic air offensive did not mean that he ignored the needs of the army and the navy for direct air support. As supplies of aircraft increased and technical developments were pressed forward, the U-boats were duly mastered and the Allied armies fought under an overwhelming Allied air superiority. Portal was essentially a co-operator: he was determined that the ground and maritime forces should have adequate air support, but equally determined not to sacrifice to this end the embryonic strategic air offensive with all its wide potentialities. It is not only as a proponent of that offensive but also as a great all-round airman and clear-brained strategist co-operating in the closest way with his colleagues at the head of the other British and American Services that Portal qualifies as one of the prime architects of the Allied victory.

The opinions entertained of Portal's ability by his wartime colleagues were extraordinarily high. Harris summed up his lifelong admiration in the words 'anything you could do, Peter Portal could do better'. Churchill remarked to Lord Moran 'Portal has everything'. Eisenhower, while president, told Lord Plowden that he regarded Portal as the greatest British war leader, 'greater even than Churchill'. Lord Ismay told an enquirer that in his opinion Portal was the best of the wartime military leaders 'quite easily'.

During the war Portal had received several honours in addition to his knighthood. They were the Order of Polonia Restituta (1st class), the GCB (June 1942), the Order of St. Olaf (Grand Cross), and the Czechoslovakian Order of the White Lion. In January 1944 he was promoted marshal of the Royal Air Force. At the end of the war a spate of further honours descended upon him. In August 1945, on the recommendation of the departing prime minister, he received a barony, under the title of Baron Portal of Hungerford; and in the New Year's honours of 1946 he became first Viscount Portal of Hungerford and was at the same time admitted to the Order of Merit. Later in 1946 he was awarded the French Legion of Honour (Grand Cross) and croix de guerre with palm, the Distinguished Service Medal (by the president of the USA), and the Grand Cross of the Order of George I (by the King of the Hellenes); and in December King George VI appointed him a Knight of the Garter. In 1947 he was made Knight Grand Cross of the Order of the Netherlands Lion and in 1948 Belgium honoured him with the Order of Crown with palm and croix de guerre 1940. In 1941 Portal had been made an honorary Student of Christ Church, Oxford, and in 1945–7 further honours came in the form of the freedom of the City of London and honorary doctorates from eight universities. In 1951 he was also appointed deputy lieutenant in the county of Sussex.

Once the war was over Portal determined to lay down his office, and he did so at the end of 1945. His intention was to relax, to establish a family home, and to take up a City directorship or two. But he had retired only a few days when the prime minister, C. R. (later Earl) Attlee, pressed him to accept another important post. The government had decided to develop the uses of atomic energy, and Attlee wanted Portal to head the organization to be responsible for producing fissile material.

Portal had no wish at all to do this, but he was one of the few leading figures in the country conversant with the broader aspects of the wartime atomic energy developments. Moreover, almost his last action on the chiefs of staff committee had been to recommend the creation of a British nuclear deterrent force and the building of two atomic piles for the production of plutonium. In these circumstances his patriotism overcame his longing for a rest, and in March 1946 he became controller of production in the highly secret atomic energy directorate of the Ministry of Supply. This was an untidy assignment, for the production organization had yet to be created, and its purposes were still undefined, but the necessary research would mostly have to emanate from the Ministry's Atomic Energy Research Establishment at Harwell, which was functioning separately under (Sir) John Cockcroft, and was not to be within Portal's province. Fortunately Portal and Cockcroft got on well; and in January 1950 the organizational structure was tidied up when Portal was appointed controller of atomic energy and given superior direction over all branches of the atomic energy organization, including Harwell.

The official history of British atomic energy takes the view that Portal was not a very effective head of the atomic energy project except in preserving priorities at the government level and in dealing with the chiefs of staff. Undoubtedly the main work lay in the research achievements of Cockcroft's teams at Harwell; the creation of a production organization by Christopher Hinton (later Lord Hinton of Bankside) and his teams (resulting in the uranium factory at Risley, the graphite piles at Windscale, and the diffusion plant at Copenhurst); and the development under W. G. (later Lord) Penney of the weapons establishments at Fort Halstead and Aldermaston, culminating in the fabrication of the British atomic bomb. These were astonishing achievements in the short space of six years, and though they emanated mainly from the genius of his subordinates it would seem only logical to accord Portal, as co-ordinator generalissimo, some share of the credit. It was Portal, too, who precipitated the government's decision that the bomb should actually be made. When he was appointed the decision went only as far as producing fissile material; but in January 1947 Portal, knowing his views coincided with those of the chiefs of staff, asked for a definite decision that the appropriate research should be undertaken and atomic weapons developed. He got it by showing how this could be done economically, and in the utmost secrecy, by a small specially created organization within the Ministry of Supply headed by Penney and responsible to himself.

With the production of the bomb a certainty Portal felt free to resign in August 1951. Firmly declining Churchill's invitation to become minister of defence if the Conservatives won the forthcoming general election, he added instead to his directorates. He was already on the board of Barclays Bank DCO, Barclays Bank Ltd., Commercial Union Assurance, and the Ford Motor Company Ltd., and was later to take on directorships of Portals Ltd. and the Whitbread Investment Trust. In October 1951 he became a director of the British Aluminium Co. Ltd., and in 1953 its chairman. This involved him in 1958 in a battle—one of the few in his life which he did not win—to resist a take-over bid from the American-backed Tube Investments Ltd. Much greater success attended his subsequent work as director and for a time (1959–64) chairman of the British Match Corporation, and as chairman, from its inception in 1960 until 1968, of the British Aircraft Corporation.

BAC was a difficult assignment undertaken, like atomic energy, only from patriotic motives. The Corporation involved the association, but not amalgamation, of three of the largest manufacturers of airframes. The marriage was virtually dictated by the government, which promised a rational division of orders for new enterprises. A national figure was needed as impartial non-executive chairman, and Portal reluctantly agreed to serve. In the event, he much enjoyed the work and his happy relationship with the deputy chairman and managing director, Sir George Edwards. He and Edwards lost two or three battles to retain projects which governments decided to cancel—notably the TSR 2—but Concorde was preserved and several successful aircraft including the Jaguar strike/trainer developed. Portal was able to retain the goodwill of the various components of the Corporation, to achieve an increasing degree of integration, and to report satisfactory profits—no mean feat for the aircraft industry.

Otherwise, Portal's main interests after the war were in voluntary work and in reconstructing an elegant house at West Ashling, near Chichester, and tending its gardens. The charitable causes with which he was closely associated were the RAF Benevolent Fund, the RAF Escaping Society, the King Edward VII Hospital at Midhurst, the Nuffield Trust for the forces of the Crown, and the Dominion Students Hall Trust (providing accommodation in London for overseas students). He remained an active sportsman—fishing, shooting, and deerstalking in particular—and was president of the MCC in 1958–9. He spoke very infrequently in the House of Lords, where he sat on the cross-benches.

In appearance, Portal was tall and dark, with a large beaked nose and deep facial lines. In his sixties he lost much of his hair and his angular look. His main characteristics were intelligence, integrity, self-control, courage, great powers of endurance, a strong sense of discipline and duty, modesty, a quiet charm of manner, fundamental simplicity, and a deep inner reserve. This last quality was sometimes misunderstood, or resented, by subordinates who expected to be on more intimate terms with their chief. Portal's charm, wit, and sense of fun were not always displayed. They emerged most readily when he had people to convince or entertain, speeches to make, or a few hours to spend with genuine friends.

In 1919 he married Joan Margaret, daughter of a leading Norfolk landowner, Sir Charles Glynne Earle Welby, fifth baronet, CB, and of Lady

Welby, a sister of the Marquess of Bristol. Their only son died at birth in 1921. They subsequently had two daughters. After some months' illness from cancer, stoically borne, Portal died at West Ashling House 22 April 1971. As a special privilege in 1945 a remainder of the barony had been granted through the daughters, and that title was inherited by the elder, Rosemary Ann (born 1923).

A statue of Portal by Oscar Nemon was erected in 1975 on the lawns of the Ministry of Defence, facing the Thames Embankment. There are portraits by Sir Oswald Birley (Christ Church, Oxford), Augustus John (National Museum of Wales), Eric Kennington (Imperial War Museum), and F. Egerton Cooper (RAF Museum).

[Air Ministry and Cabinet papers in the Public Record Office; the Portal papers at Christ Church, Oxford; family papers at West Ashling House; Denis Richards, *Portal of Hungerford*, 1977 (for March 1978); M. M. Gowing, *Independence and Deterrence: Britain and Atomic Energy, 1945–52*, 2 vols., 1974; private information; personal knowledge.]

DENIS RICHARDS

published 1986

POUND (Alfred) Dudley (Pickman Rogers)

(1877–1943)

Sir

Admiral of the fleet, was born at Park View, Wroxall, Isle of Wight, 29 August 1877, the eldest child of Alfred John Pound, barrister, by his wife, Elizabeth Pickman, daughter of Richard Saltonstall Rogers, of Boston, Massachusetts. As a boy, being fond of riding, he wished to join the cavalry, but the sight of a cutter coming under full sail alongside the pier at Stokes Bay in charge of a midshipman turned his thoughts to the Royal Navy, and he entered the *Britannia* as a cadet in January 1891. He therefore refused the offer made by an uncle to find him an opening in the firm of Pierpont Morgan.

From his early days Pound was marked out as likely to go far; he passed his sub-lieutenant's courses with distinction after serving as midshipman in the Channel squadron, in China, and in the old training squadron under sail. The next twelve years were occupied with the ordinary career of a promising naval officer: he commanded torpedo boat 58 at the diamond jubilee naval review, served in the *Opossum* under Roger (later Lord) Keyes with whom then began a close association and friendship lasting for more than forty years; after eighteen months in the *Magnificent* (1898–9), Pound qualified as a specialist torpedo officer, and early in 1902 he was appointed torpedo lieutenant in the *Grafton*. Hopes of leave at the end of this appointment were dashed by an order to begin a course in wireless telegraphy prior to joining (1905) the *King Edward VII*, flagship of Sir William May, and the first big ship to have a considerable amount of electric gear. Although this was a source of great anxiety to Pound, he nevertheless demonstrated that it was possible to go through a battle-practice without any misfires. What perhaps was of greater importance in Pound's career was that he was then shipmates with (Sir) William Fisher, for on Fisher being promoted to commander in the summer of 1906, Pound became first lieutenant, and, although not yet qualified in length of service, was ordered to ship the additional 'half stripe' at once.

An uneventful commission as first lieutenant of the *Queen* in the Mediterranean (1907–8), was followed by a term of service at the Admiralty on the torpedo side of the naval ordnance department, and in June 1909 Pound was promoted commander. Two years later he was appointed to the *Superb* (1911–13) whence he went to the new Naval Staff College as instructor, but after being there a year, he accepted, against the advice of the admiral in charge of the college, an offer from Fisher to go as his commander in the *St. Vincent*. He was therefore at sea when war broke out; in December he was promoted captain, and after a few months at the Admiralty as second naval assistant to the first sea lord, he went again to sea as flag captain in the *Colossus*. In that ship he took part in the battle of Jutland and was commended for his services.

Two years' service in the *Colossus* was ended by a recall to the Admiralty which gave to Pound's career a direction towards high politics. The first lord realized that in the pressure of work at the Admiralty there was no officer whose duty it was to foresee and think out problems, and Pound was selected to form a staff. These few men, known as section 15 of the operations division, starting with no office save the bedroom in the Admiralty of the director of operations, founded a branch which eventually expanded into the plans division under an admiral. At the end of 1917 Pound was transferred to be director of operations (home), whence in the autumn of 1920 he was appointed to command the *Repulse* in the battle cruiser squadron. It was a short interval at sea, for in 1922 he returned to his own plans division as director, and as Admiralty representative he attended the Lausanne conference on the Graeco-Turkish crisis, where he was introduced to the manifold international and political issues with which he was to be so closely connected in the future. Three years later he went to the Mediterranean as chief of staff to Keyes, now commander-in-chief, and in March 1926 he was promoted to flag rank; after two years in the Admiralty as assistant chief of naval staff he was appointed in May 1929 to command the battle cruiser squadron. Having been present at the conference on disarmament in 1932 for six months he became second sea lord in August.

In September 1935 Pound was nominated as commander-in-chief, Mediterranean, in succession to Fisher. Fisher not only knew the Mediterranean like the palm of his hand, but he was deeply versed in international affairs and problems of strategy and supply. Pound was therefore not at all surprised when he was informed that the Admiralty did not think it desirable to make a change at the height of the Abyssinian crisis. The sequel illustrates the generosity in Pound's character. Hearing that a relief was required for Fisher's chief of staff, Pound, although now a full admiral, volunteered for the post. The offer was accepted and he remained chief of staff until in March 1936 the situation had eased sufficiently to allow Fisher to return home and Pound to succeed him.

During the three years in which Pound held the command in chief in the Mediterranean, he set himself to perfect the training of the fleet for war. As flag captain in the *Colossus* he had evolved a series of tactical drills and exercises in order to make the most of the short time that each ship had available for exercises at Scapa Flow. He had enlarged these as chief of staff to Keyes, and now, as commander-in-chief, he perfected them. It was a labour of love, for never was Pound so happy as when he was on the bridge training the fleet to meet every emergency, insisting on captains handling their ships boldly, demanding instantaneous action by a squadron or ship ordered to take up a new station, and training officers to use their initiative and not to wait for orders. Towards the end of his command, he was offered the alternative of going as commander-in-chief, Portsmouth, which would probably be a three-year appointment, or of staying on for an additional command of the Mediterranean Fleet with nothing to follow. Without hesitation he chose the latter, and was looking to another year afloat when the resignation of the first sea lord, Sir Roger Backhouse, brought Pound home to England in his place. He entered into office in June 1939 and on 31 July he was promoted admiral of the fleet.

Of Pound's fitness for this most responsible work the only ground for doubt was his age. He was now sixty-two. Nevertheless he displayed a toughness of body and a fortitude of mind which rose superior to the intense and dreadful strain which fell upon him for four years. He came to office single-handed, for his predecessor died in July, and the deputy chief of the naval staff, Sir Andrew Cunningham (subsequently Viscount Cunningham of Hyndhope), had been sent to take Pound's place in the Mediterranean, so that the help he might have received from their experience was withdrawn from him. The imminence of hostilities doubled the claims of committees on his time, and consultation with other members of departments and boards rose in a similar measure of frequency. The situation had been foreseen, and it had been decided that, immediately upon the outbreak of war, a deputy should be appointed so that the first sea lord should be free to concentrate entirely on plans and operations; but it was not until the summer of 1942 that the makeshift arrangement which had superseded this wise decision was set aside, and a deputy first sea lord appointed. The change came too late to give Pound's health the relief which it needed.

The history of Pound's achievements as first sea lord is the history of the war at sea, together with that on land and in the air, during these four years. It was not a period of unchequered success; that is a favour of fortune which comes to few in operations of such magnitude. It fell to him to organize the naval strategy which brought about, in the Mediterranean, the victory of Cape Matapan, the evacuation of the British forces from Greece and Crete, the retention of Malta as a base, the unheralded landing in North Africa in November 1942, the recovery of control of the sea in the Mediterranean, and the final landing of the allied forces in Sicily. In the Atlantic his strategy led to the scuttling of the *Admiral Graf Spee* and the sinking of the *Bismarck*, while the defeat of the submarine menace, the creation of the Western Approaches Command under Sir Percy Noble, and the establishment of the naval and air headquarters at Liverpool, contributed in no small degree to turning the battle of the Atlantic in favour of the Allies.

In view of the success of these operations, criticism could only fasten itself on three points. The campaign in Norway in the spring of 1940 was held to have shown Pound and the Admiralty as lacking in offensive spirit. The plan of campaign centred on the capture of Trondheim which Pound, with considerable hesitation, agreed should be effected by a direct fleet attack. As a prelude to this assault, landings were made at Namsos and Aandalsnes, which were initially so successful that Pound considered the risks involved in subjecting the fleet to air attack were no longer justified. The plan of campaign was therefore changed by the chiefs of staff and its success entrusted to the land forces only. When heavy air attack brought about an early collapse of the campaign, there was strong criticism of this lack of naval action. Pound took the unpopular but correct view that the security of sea communications was more important than the hazarding of valuable ships in what could not become a major theatre of war.

Eighteen months later another disaster befell British naval arms. It was a principle firmly held by the Admiralty that the naval resources of the country would not permit the dispersion of the navy in three separate areas at once; for that reason the Far East station had been weakened in order to maintain due strength in the Atlantic and the Mediterranean. But political considerations decided, notwithstanding a warning from Pound, that the *Prince of Wales*, fast battleship, should join the *Repulse*, battle cruiser, and proceed to the Far East, in the hope that this strength, added to the United States fleet in the Pacific, would deter the Japanese from declaring war. The hope was not fulfilled, and when the ships were lost by air attack off the coast of Malaya, criticism, based on various familiar principles of strategy, made itself widely heard.

More noisy, but as the event proved, less substantial, was the outcry which followed the escape of the German cruisers *Scharnhorst* and *Gneisenau* from Brest, where they had remained after the sinking of the *Bismarck*. The upshot showed the critics to be no less hasty than those Englishmen who burnt Lord Hawke in effigy on the day when he destroyed the French fleet in Quiberon Bay.

In January 1943 Pound stated confidently at Casablanca that the worst of the war was over, for the Allies had found the measure of the submarine menace. But he was destined to have no share in the final victory which he foresaw. The death of his wife in July was a heavy blow, and it was only will power which carried him, in company with the prime minister, to the conference at Quebec. Early in September he told (Sir) Winston Churchill at Washington that he must resign, and he returned to England, bade farewell to the Admiralty and to the Fleet, and on Trafalgar Day (21 October) he died in a London hospital. After a funeral service in Westminster Abbey, his ashes were scattered at sea.

Not being well-to-do, Pound declined the peerage which was offered to him early in 1943; but on the fourth anniversary of the outbreak of war he was appointed to the Order of Merit. In 1911 he had received the bronze medal of the Royal Humane Society for great courage in attempting to rescue men who had been overcome by poisonous fumes in the hold of the *Superb*. He was appointed C.B. in 1919, K.C.B. in 1933, G.C.V.O. in 1937, and G.C.B. in 1939. His death prevented him from receiving the high honours which would undoubtedly have been conferred upon him on the cessation of hostilities.

As a personality, Pound had the reputation of being reserved and rather unbending. On duty, much of this arose from his expectation that others would set themselves the extremely high standard which he set himself. He picked his senior officers on the naval staff with skill and gave them his complete confidence: his personal staff served him at all times with devotion and affection. Off duty he had a keen sense of humour and in a wide circle of friends showed himself an excellent raconteur. His love of sport in all forms, but especially shooting, was most marked, and his verve as a

driver of motor-cars led occasionally to remonstrances addressed to the
first sea lord from the chief commissioner of police.

In 1908 Pound married Bessie Caroline, daughter of John Livesay
Whitehead, physician, of Ventnor, Isle of Wight, whose help to him was
constant, and who did much for the wives and families of the men under
his command. He was survived by two sons, the elder a naval officer of
distinction, the younger an officer in the Royal Marines, and one daughter.

A portrait of Pound by (Sir) Oswald Birley is in the Greenwich Collection at the Royal Naval College, Greenwich.

[Admiralty records; Winston S. Churchill, *The Second World War*, vols. i–v, 1948–
52; T. K. Derry, (Official) *History of the Second World War. The Campaign in
Norway*, 1952; S. W. Roskill, (Official) *History of the Second World War. The
War at Sea*, vols. i and ii, 1954–6; private information; personal knowledge.]

R. V. Brockman

published 1959

RAMSAY Bertram Home

(1883–1945)

Sir

Admiral, of the Ramsays of Balmain, was born at Hampton Court Palace
20 January 1883, the third son of Captain (later Brigadier-General) William
Alexander Ramsay, 4th (Queen's Own) Hussars, by his wife, Susan,
daughter of William Minchiner, of Clontarf, county Dublin. He joined the
Britannia in 1898. His parents were in India, and the boy spent his holidays
with relatives and friends, but from the age of twelve he practically
managed his own life, and after he had become midshipman in 1899, with
the help of a small allowance from his father, he supported himself, thus
gaining independence and self-confidence. He was not physically a big
boy, nor did he grow to be a big man, but he showed a natural bent for
games and sport, was a keen athlete and a good runner, devoted to horses
and later in life became a keen polo player and a bold rider to hounds. He
was also a keen fisherman, an average good shot, and an enthusiastic
golfer.

Passing out of the *Britannia* in 1899 Ramsay joined the *Crescent*, flagship
of the North America and West Indies station, in which he spent the whole
of his time as a midshipman. Later in life, Ramsay often remarked on his
good fortune in starting his sea service in such a happy gunroom on such a

pleasant station. In his seamanship examination he gained the coveted first class certificate in 1902 and was promoted sub-lieutenant; in his next courses he gained first class certificates in gunnery and torpedo, third class in navigation, and second class in pilotage. After spending a few weeks on manœuvres in the *Greyhound*, he was appointed to the *Hyacinth*, flagship on the East Indies station.

This commission was memorable in that it brought to Ramsay his first experience of both active service, in the Somaliland expedition of 1903–4, and combined operations, for a detachment of 125 men of the 1st battalion of the Hampshire Regiment fought alongside the navy. He landed with the naval brigade and took part in the battle of Illig; and for his services he was mentioned in dispatches. Promoted to lieutenant in December 1904, he returned home and spent eighteen months as watchkeeper in the *Terrible*, *Good Hope*, and *Renown*. In September 1906 he was appointed to the *Dreadnought*, and thus served in the first commission of that historic ship. He served in her as watchkeeper for over two years, and then joined the signal school at the Royal Naval Barracks at Portsmouth, in order to qualify as a signal officer. He was next successively flag lieutenant to Sir Colin Keppel, commanding the Atlantic Fleet battle squadron (flag in the *Albemarle*) from 1909 to 1910, and to Sir Douglas Gamble, commanding the sixth cruiser squadron, Mediterranean Fleet (flag in the *Bacchante* and *Good Hope*). He then joined the staff of the signal school from 1912 to 1913 with a short spell at sea in the manœuvres of 1912.

Until this time Ramsay's career had been typical of any promising young officer specializing in signals, but with his appointment in February 1913 to the War College at Portsmouth, came a change which was to affect his career. His was the second course to qualify as staff officers, and thus he was one of the earliest naval officers to gain experience of the newly established staff system. Save for a short spell of sea service in the *Euryalus* for the 1913 manœuvres, he served at the War College until January 1914, when having qualified as a 'war staff officer' he joined the *Orion* on the staff of Sir Robert Arbuthnot, rear-admiral of the second battle squadron. Being now a 'senior lieutenant', he became lieutenant-commander when that rank was instituted in March 1914. In July he rejoined Gamble, now commanding the fourth battle squadron in the *Dreadnought*, and thus on the outbreak of war found himself in the Grand Fleet. In February 1915, however, he came ashore to join the new signal section of the Admiralty war staff.

In August 1915 Ramsay received his first command, the *M. 25*, a small monitor. Thus began his association with the Dover Patrol, and for the next two years he spent most of his time off the Belgian coast, supporting the left flank of the armies, a fresh experience of combined operations, expanded by contact with the wing of the Royal Naval Air Service then operating from Dunkirk. He was promoted commander in June 1916 and reappointed to his ship, but in October 1917 he transferred to command the famous fighting destroyer *Broke*, also in the Dover Patrol. In this ship he took part in the Ostend operations, for which service he was mentioned in dispatches, and in December 1918 he was appointed M.V.O., after having had the honour of conveying King George V to his visit to the armies in France after the armistice. For war services he was also made an officer of the Order of the Crown of Italy (1917), chevalier of the Legion of Honour (1918), and he received the Belgian croix de guerre (1919).

In February 1919 Ramsay joined the *New Zealand* as flag commander on the staff of Lord Jellicoe on his tour to the Dominions. On his return he was appointed commander of the *Emperor of India* in 1920, and of the *Benbow* in 1921, both in the Mediterranean Fleet, and in June 1923 he was promoted captain.

After passing the senior officers' war and tactical courses, Ramsay was appointed to command the *Weymouth*, carrying out a trooping trip to China in 1924. Next year he assumed command of the *Danae* in the first cruiser squadron, Mediterranean Fleet, and in the two years before going on to serve on the instructional staff of the Royal Naval War College, he brought his ship to a remarkable state of efficiency. He resumed sea service in 1929 as flag captain and chief of staff to Sir Arthur Waistell, vice-admiral commanding the China station (flag in the *Kent*, which Ramsay commanded for two years), and then returned to instructional duty as the naval officer on the staff of the Imperial Defence College. His military colleague was the future Viscount Alanbrooke and his air colleague the future Lord Douglas of Kirtleside. In November 1933 he assumed command of the *Royal Sovereign* in the Mediterranean Fleet and was still serving in her when he was promoted to flag rank in May 1935.

It was no matter for surprise that the first appointment which Ramsay received as rear-admiral was as chief of staff to the commander-in-chief of the Home Fleet, for he was known as a thoroughly efficient executive officer and a staff officer of great brilliance and wide experience. The commander-in-chief in this appointment, one of the two most important sea-going commands, was to be Sir Roger Backhouse. Those who knew both men had misgivings. Backhouse was of the old school of naval officers, a strong individualist with an infinite capacity for hard work, and a profound believer in centralization, who practised what he believed. Ramsay, one of the leading exponents of the modern school, believed heart and soul in the staff system with its decentralization of detail and control from the top of essentials only. He was under no illusions over difficulties ahead, but he relied on his old friendship with Backhouse (they had been shipmates in the *Dreadnought*), and on his conviction that with a commander-in-chief's responsibilities on his shoulders, Backhouse would be forced to decentralize on his chief of staff.

Ramsay joined the *Nelson* in August 1935. For a time all went well, but unhappily this did not last, and within a few months the situation was becoming intolerable. Backhouse thought that his chief of staff was trying to run the fleet for him; Ramsay believed that his commander-in-chief deliberately excluded him from all responsibility and would neither ask nor brook advice or assistance. In such a clash of personalities, Ramsay was not the man to sit back and accept the situation philosophically. Moreover, he believed that his commander-in-chief was overworking to the point of danger in trying to do everything single-handed, and that it was his clear duty to make way for some other officer with whom Backhouse could work more easily. Accordingly he asked to be relieved, and he left the *Nelson* in December 1935, and twelve days later he was placed on half pay. He was not again employed, although he carried out two senior officers' courses and was in fact offered an appointment afloat on foreign service. Believing that this was but a prelude to retirement he refused it. He was appointed C.B. in 1936, was placed on the retired list in 1938 on reaching the top of the rear-admirals' list, and promoted vice-admiral in January 1939.

Ramsay's naval career seemed to have come to an end. In many ways a reserved man he never allowed anyone, not even his wife, to know how heavily he felt his retirement, and it was not until after his death that his papers showed how deeply he had been hurt by what he believed to have been an injustice. Meanwhile life ashore had some compensations. In 1929 he had married Helen Margaret, daughter of Colonel Charles Thomson Menzies, of Kames, Duns, Berwickshire, and two sons were born to them. In the close society of his wife and young family he found much happiness and in 1938 they bought Bughtrig, Coldstream, Berwickshire, and there they settled down to country pursuits.

This peaceful life, however, was not to last for long. As the shadows of war lengthened, so did naval preparations increase. With his experience in the Dover Patrol in 1914–18, Ramsay was an obvious choice for the post of flag officer-in-charge, Dover, whenever that command should be established. At the Munich crisis in 1938 he did a period of duty on the staff of the commander-in-chief, the Nore, and he made all preparations for the naval headquarters and establishments at Dover. He hoisted his vice-admiral's flag, as flag officer-in-charge, Dover, on 24 August 1939. So the outbreak of war found him at his post and commanding waters very familiar to him. Familiar too must have been the early tasks which came his way: the denial of passage through the Straits of Dover to submarines; defence against possible destroyer raids; protection of cross-Channel military traffic, and other repetitions of 1914–18. A new development which caused him anxiety was the aircraft-carried magnetic mine, but time brought a counter to that weapon.

With the German assault on France and the Low Countries, Dover at once became a centre of great activity, but the climax came when, with the collapse of France, Ramsay was ordered to bring the British soldiers home from Dunkirk. This operation will doubtless remain a classic of improvisation, and may well go down in naval history under its original code name 'Dynamo'. With his forces increased by every destroyer which could be spared and every small craft and every ship which could be found to reach Dover, Ramsay, with a staff multiplied for the occasion, turned to his task. The *Luftwaffe* attacked in strength to intercept and prevent the work of embarkation and transport. Despite the splendid efforts of the limited numbers of Royal Air Force fighters, inevitable losses and casualties took place. Nevertheless, night and day the work went forward, and the numbers of soldiers coming out of the port of Dunkirk and off the adjacent beaches rose steadily. Operation Dynamo lasted from 6.57 p.m. 26 May until 2.23 p.m. 4 June. Between these dates 338,226 officers and men of the British and allied armies had been lifted from the continent and brought to England. On the completion of this great achievement, Ramsay reported on the operation to the King in person, and was rewarded by the honour of the K.C.B. at His Majesty's hands.

Ramsay returned to a Dover where his problems were multiplied tenfold by an enemy in possession of the French coastline. For nearly two more years he strove to maintain control of the waters under his command in the face of air attack, the assaults of hostile small craft, and cross-Channel bombardment. Throughout the autumn months of 1940 Dover was in the forefront of our precautions against invasion. Those were anxious days, but Ramsay started with the great advantage of four years' rest and refreshment behind him, and he remained fresh, fit, and imperturbable. Despite losses, our coastwise traffic was kept going. At the end of 1940 he was mentioned in dispatches for his services.

Ramsay left Dover 29 April 1942 to take up an appointment as flag officer, Expeditionary Force, working with General Eisenhower, who had arrived in London to become commanding general, European theatre of operations. The possibility of invading France in 1943 was under active consideration, and Ramsay began to plan for it; but in process of time the project was postponed in favour of an early landing on the coast of North Africa with subsequent operations in the Mediterranean. Under the command of General Eisenhower, now allied commander-in-chief, Ramsay began the detailed planning of this new operation as naval commander-in-chief, Expeditionary Force. It soon became evident that considerable naval forces, with several flag officers commanding the various units, were going to be involved. Objections were raised to so great a force being put under an acting admiral on the retired list who had never actually flown his flag in command at sea. It was therefore decided to bring Sir Andrew Cunningham (subsequently Viscount Cunningham of Hyndhope) back from the United States to take over the naval command, whilst Ramsay was to serve under him as his deputy. This was in accordance with Ramsay's own personal views and wishes, and he did valuable service during the operation as the rear link between the expedition and the British and United States authorities. In connexion with the North African landings he was again mentioned in dispatches in April 1943.

Victory having been achieved in North Africa, it was decided to invade Sicily. Ramsay became the naval commander, Eastern Task Force, in command of the British landing operations, whilst Vice-Admiral Hewitt, United States Navy, commanded the Western Task Force, both under the command of Sir Andrew Cunningham, and the supreme command of General Eisenhower. This was the first large-scale landing on hostile beaches with the enemy present in strength. On both British and American fronts the assault was entirely successful and the subsequent 'build-up' equally effective, in spite of the weather, which deteriorated rapidly and, for the Mediterranean in high summer, unexpectedly. Nevertheless, the stout-hearted decision was taken by the supreme commander to continue the attack, and keen anxiety must it have cost; but the bold decision was justified by steady improvement in the weather. For his success in these operations in the Mediterranean Ramsay was appointed K.B.E. at the end of 1943.

Ramsay returned to London and in December 1943 was appointed allied naval commander-in-chief of the Expeditionary Force. A combined naval, military, and air staff had been working at full pressure on the proposed invasion of France in the spring of 1944. Ramsay's experience in the Mediterranean stood him in good stead during the working out of the campaign; before it came to maturity, to his deep satisfaction he was restored to the active list as vice-admiral and on the following day promoted admiral. His headquarters were originally at Norfolk House, St. James's Square, but in April he moved to battle headquarters at Southwick Park, near Portsmouth, while supreme headquarters were in a near-by wood, as were also those of the 21st Army Group with Sir Bernard Montgomery (later Viscount Montgomery of Alamein) as commander-in-chief. The air commander-in-chief, Sir Trafford Leigh-Mallory, had his headquarters at Stanmore; but he maintained a strong liaison link at naval headquarters. It was at Southwick Park that General Eisenhower made his historic decisions, first to postpone the invasion for twenty-four hours, and later, in spite of unfavourable weather reports but on the strength of a prophesied improvement, to launch the assault for dawn, 6 June 1944; and it was at Southwick Park that Ramsay came gradually to realize that this, the greatest of all combined operations, had achieved success at a mere fraction of the cost in casualties which had been anticipated. However, he knew all too well that the future of the allied military operations hinged on the establishment of their 'build-up', and he brought all his powers to bear on the task of moving the vast quantities of men and material across the Channel with speed and safety. The millionth soldier landed in France twenty-eight days after D-Day, a month over four years since Ramsay had brought the last allied soldier to England from Dunkirk.

During the operation Ramsay spent every day that he could spare from headquarters off the British and American beaches, dealing direct with his task force and assault force commanders. He never spared himself but remained fit and cheerful both in good conditions and in bad. With the advance of the allied armies he transferred his headquarters first to Granville, opposite Jersey, then to St. Germain-en-Laye outside Paris. The most spectacular part of Ramsay's work was now over, but much remained to be done, of which the most eventful was the assault on Walcheren Island, the prelude to the opening of Antwerp. In addition there was the constant work of protecting the cross-Channel traffic against submarines, small craft, and mines, and the opening up of ports as they fell into the hands of the Allies.

On 2 January 1945 Ramsay left his headquarters on a flight to Brussels in order to attend a conference at 21st Army Group headquarters. He took off from the airfield at Toussus-le-Noble in an aircraft allocated to his personal use. It crashed on taking off and Ramsay was killed instantaneously. He was buried at St. Germain-en-Laye. Although he was not to see the day of victory, he died knowing that victory could not be long delayed, and he must have been aware of his considerable contribution to that end; but he doubtless would have had greater pleasure had he known of the measure of affection and admiration in which his memory is held by all who served under his command.

In November 1944 Ramsay was awarded the Russian Order of Ushakov (first class), a rare distinction, and he was posthumously admitted to the American Legion of Merit with the degree of chief commander; he was promoted grand officer of the Legion of Honour, the insignia of this rank being given to his widow in Paris in June 1945.

Rawlinson

A lifelike portrait of Ramsay was posthumously painted by (Sir) Oswald Birley for the Greenwich Collection at the Royal Naval College, Greenwich.

[Private information; personal knowledge.]

G. E. CREASY

published 1959

Sir Henry Seymour

(1864–1925)

Second baronet and Baron Rawlinson, of Trent

General, the elder son of Sir Henry Creswicke Rawlinson, first baronet, by his wife, Louisa, daughter of Henry Seymour, of Knoyle House, Wiltshire, and of Trent Manor, Dorset, was born at Trent Manor 20 February 1864. He was educated at Eton and Sandhurst, and on his twentieth birthday (1884) was gazetted to the King's Royal Rifles, joining the fourth battalion of that regiment in India. In 1886, thanks to the friendship between his father and Sir Frederick (afterwards Lord) Roberts, then commander-in-chief in India, the latter appointed him to be one of his aides-de-camp. Rawlinson accompanied Roberts to Burma, and there, in the guerrilla warfare which followed the capture of Mandalay by (Sir) Harry N. D. Prendergast, saw his first active service, being attached to the mounted infantry of the Rifle Brigade, and earning the Burma medal and a mention in dispatches.

In 1889 Rawlinson was called home by the serious illness of his mother, who died in October, her death making him heir-presumptive to the Seymour property of Trent Manor. In the following year (1890) he married Meredith, daughter of Coleridge John Kennard, of Fernhill, Hampshire. In order to be near his father he resigned his appointment on Lord Roberts's staff, and on his promotion to captain in 1891 obtained a transfer to the Coldstream Guards, being gazetted captain in that regiment in July 1892. In the following year he passed into the Staff College, Camberley, amongst his fellow students there being J. H. G. (afterwards Viscount) Byng and (Sir) Henry Wilson; the latter he had already met in Burma. After passing through the Staff College Rawlinson was appointed brigade-major at Aldershot in November 1895. In the previous spring his father, to whom he had been devoted, died, and he succeeded to the baronetcy.

In the winter of 1897 Rawlinson took his wife to Egypt for her health, and he was in Cairo when (Lord) Kitchener was preparing for his advance to Omdurman. Kitchener offered him an appointment on his staff, which was eagerly accepted, and in that capacity Rawlinson served at the battles of Atbara and Omdurman. He was mentioned in dispatches and promised the brevet of lieutenant-colonel on promotion to major. He received his majority in the Coldstream Guards in January 1899, and the next day was gazetted brevet lieutenant-colonel, at the age of thirty-five.

In the autumn of that year, when the crisis in South Africa came to a head and Sir George White was sent out to Natal with reinforcements, Rawlinson was given an appointment on his staff and was with him throughout the siege of Ladysmith. It was at Rawlinson's suggestion that the naval guns which played such an important part in the defence were brought up from Durban just before the Boers completed the investment. On the relief of Ladysmith Rawlinson was appointed assistant adjutant-general on Lord Roberts's staff, and joined him in March 1900 at Bloemfontein. In November of that year, when all the chief Boer towns had been occupied and the War seemed to be drawing to a close, he accompanied Lord Roberts to England. But it was soon discovered that the British had been too optimistic, and within three weeks of coming to England he had sailed again for South Africa, to join Lord Kitchener in Pretoria. Within a month Kitchener appointed him to the command of a mobile column, and in that capacity he served until the end of the War in May 1902, proving himself one of the most energetic and successful of the younger commanders. For his services in the South African War, during which he had been five times mentioned in dispatches, he was made C.B., and in June 1902 a brevet-colonel.

After eight months' service at the War Office, Rawlinson was in December 1903 promoted brigadier-general and made commandant of the Staff College, and there for three years his experience of staff work in peace and in war enabled him to make the course of instruction more practical than it had been. On leaving the Staff College he was given the command of a brigade at Aldershot, which he gave up on promotion to major-general in May 1909. In June of the following year he was made commander of the 3rd division and spent four happy and strenuous years in its training. His time of command came to an end in May 1914, and to his distress there was no place for him in the Expeditionary Force which went to France in the following August. But he had not long to wait, for in the third week of September he was given command of the 4th division, then on the Aisne, and thence early in October he was sent to Belgium to take command of the 7th division and the 3rd cavalry division, which were landing at Ostend and Zeebrugge to attempt the relief of Antwerp.

Antwerp fell before Rawlinson's force was ready for action, and he then had the difficult task of covering the right flank of the retreating Belgian army and of retiring on Ypres to join the British army, which was moving into Flanders from the Aisne. He reached Ypres on 14 October. There his command soon became involved in the struggle for the defence of the Channel ports. His 7th division was absorbed in the I Corps, under Sir Douglas Haig, and the 3rd cavalry division joined the Cavalry Corps. On this break up of his command Rawlinson returned to England in order to bring out the 8th division, destined with the 7th division to form the IV Corps, under his command. Towards the end of the year the IV Corps went into the line on the Neuve Chapelle front, and on 10 March took a leading part in the battle of Neuve Chapelle. Throughout 1915 Rawlinson commanded the IV Corps, leading it in the battles of Aubers Ridge, Festubert, and Loos. His experiences of those battles made him a strong advocate of the method of attack with limited objectives; but that method was not then generally accepted, and fate decided that he should be the protagonist in the first of the prolonged battles which were the outstanding feature of trench warfare on the Western front.

In December 1915 when Sir Charles Carmichael Monro left France to recommend and organize the evacuation of the Gallipoli Peninsula, Rawlinson was given temporary command of the First Army, and early in the next year he was promoted lieutenant-general and chosen to command the newly created Fourth Army. This army was given the task of preparing for the counter-offensive on the Somme, which was to disengage Verdun. Rawlinson strongly advocated that the battle of the Somme should be begun with limited attacks, but he was overruled and set himself loyally to carry out Haig's plan, which aimed at breaking through the German first and second systems of defence at one blow. The attempt to do this on 1 July failed, only the attacks of the French on the British right and of the right of Rawlinson's army succeeding. Haig's plan then became one of exploiting the success of the right and of gradually forcing the Germans back from the Somme ridges.

By the end of the first week of July Rawlinson had driven the Germans from their first defensive system. He then proposed to attack the second system by night with four divisions. A night attack on this scale had never before been attempted in war, and Haig at first hesitated to accept the risk of such a novel experiment; but, won over by Rawlinson's insistence and by the perfection of his arrangements, Haig in the end consented, and the attack was successfully made on 14 July. Unfortunately in the interval the Germans had been reinforced, and it is at least probable that if the attack had been made 48 hours earlier, as Rawlinson had wished, the results would have been far greater. The battle dragged on until the middle of November, when bad weather and mutual exhaustion brought it to a close. In the following January Rawlinson was promoted general.

During the early months of 1917 the British Fourth Army was occupied in extending its front in order to set free the French troops required for the operations planned by the new French commander-in-chief, General Nivelle. The Fourth Army was thus too much extended to take full advantage of the German retreat to the Hindenburg line, which began in March 1917; it thus took no part in the battles of Arras and Messines. In July, when Haig was preparing to attack the Germans at Ypres, he chose Rawlinson to take charge of the secret preparations for a combined naval and military attack on the Belgian coast; but this, owing to the failure of the Ypres attack to make sufficient progress, came to nothing. In November 1917, towards the close of the battle of Passchendaele, Rawlinson took over the command of the British left, and he was in that position when in February 1918 he was appointed British military representative on the Supreme War Council in succession to his old friend Sir Henry Wilson, who had been recalled to the War Office. From that position he was removed at the end of March 1918 to take command of the remnants of the British Fifth Army, which had been shattered in the great German attack launched on 21 March. These he reconstituted as the Fourth Army, while fully occupied with the defence of Amiens. The last German effort to drive the British from that vital railway junction ended with the recapture by the Fourth Army of Villers-Brettoneux on 25 April, and Rawlinson was then left a period of comparative leisure in which to fill the gaps in his army and perfect its training.

A part of this training consisted of practice in co-operation between infantry and the latest pattern of 'tank'. A test of this carried out on 4 July in an attack on a small scale on Hamel was completely successful, and Rawlinson then prepared to apply his methods on a larger scale. His plans being approved by Haig and Foch, he attacked astride the Somme on the Amiens front on 8 August and at once gained the most important success which up till then had been won by the British army. General Ludendorff has, indeed, described that day, 8 August, as 'the black day in the history of the German army'. Following on this victory Haig extended the front of battle northwards from the Somme, and while the Third and First Armies on his left were pressing back the Germans, Rawlinson's Fourth Army crossed the Somme, captured Peronne (31 August), and by the middle of September had driven the Germans into the shelter of the Hindenburg line. The attack of the Fourth Army, reinforced by an American Corps of two divisions, on those formidable defences began on 29 September, when the St. Quentin canal was crossed, and by 8 October the army had forced its way through the Hindenburg system. Nine days later it attacked in the battle of the Selle the Germans who had made a stand behind that river. On 4 November the army again attacked, forced its way across the Sambre canal, and drove the enemy through the Mormal forest. When the Armistice became effective on 11 November, the Fourth Army had reached a point south-east of Maubeuge, a few miles west of Beaumont, having, since 8 August, fought and won four great battles and eighteen actions, as the result of which the enemy had been driven back 60 miles with the loss of 79,743 prisoners and 1,108 guns. It had engaged 24 British, Australian, Canadian, and American divisions against 67 German divisions; but it had suffered 122,427 casualties.

After the Armistice the Fourth Army remained in occupation in Belgium, and on its dissolution Rawlinson came home in March 1919, to be appointed, at the end of July, to carry out the evacuation of Northern Russia by the Allied forces. On his way to Archangel he received the news that he had been accorded the thanks of both Houses of Parliament, with a grant of £30,000, and had been created a baron. He was back in England in October 1919, having successfully accomplished his mission, and after a short period of command at Aldershot he was, in November 1920, appointed commander-in-chief in India.

The major problems which Rawlinson set himself to solve in India were: (1) the reorganization of army head-quarters and of its relation with the military member of the viceroy's council, a question which had been the subject of long and bitter dispute between Lord Curzon and Lord Kitchener; (2) the reorganization of the Indian army and the improvement of its equipment, consistently with the urgent demand for economy; (3) the introduction of the process of Indianization; and (4), most important of all, the application of a new policy on the North-West Frontier. Rawlinson's father had been one of the earliest advocates of the policy of opening up Baluchistan, as successfully initiated by Sir Robert Groves Sandeman; and despite considerable, and at times somewhat acrimonious, opposition Rawlinson applied the same policy to Waziristan, opening up the country by constructing roads and establishing an important military station at Razmak in the midst of the Waziris. That policy has since stood the test of disturbed conditions on the Frontier. The other items of his programme he carried through with equal success, and he could claim in 1925 that while the military budget had been reduced from 82 crores of rupees in 1921 to 56 crores in 1925, the British garrison from 75,300 to 57,000 men and the Indian army from 159,000 to 140,000, the general standard of efficiency had been raised. He achieved the difficult task of gaining the admiration and affection of the army while making these reductions, and the even more difficult task of winning the respect of the legislative assembly. A fine horseman and brilliant polo player, Rawlinson exercised a healthy influence upon the development of the game both at home and in India. It was after taking part in a hard game of polo on his sixty-first birthday and soon after making 21 runs at cricket against the boys of the new Dehra Dun military school, that he was taken ill at Delhi, and died of the after effects of an operation 28 March 1925. His body was brought home and buried at Trent. He had no children, and on his death the barony became extinct. He was succeeded as third baronet by his brother Alfred (born 1867).

There are portraits of Lord Rawlinson by Oswald Birley in the possession of Lady Rawlinson and at the Staff College, Camberley. He figures in J. S. Sargent's group 'Some General Officers of the Great War' (painted in 1922), in the National Portrait Gallery, and there is a portrait of him by Sir William Orpen in the Imperial War Museum.

[Sir J. F. Maurice and M. H. Grant, (Official) *History of the War in South Africa, 1899–1902*, 1906–1910; Sir J. E. Edmonds, (Official) *History of the Great War. Military Operations. France and Belgium, 1914–1918*, 1922–1935; Sir F. Maurice, *Life of Lord Rawlinson of Trent*, 1928.]

FREDERICK MAURICE

published 1937

RICHMOND Herbert William

(1871–1946)

Sir

Admiral, and master of Downing College, Cambridge, was born at Beavor Lodge, Hammersmith, 15 September 1871, the third child and second son of the artist (Sir) William Blake Richmond. He passed into the *Britannia* in 1885; two years later he went to sea as a midshipman in the *Nelson*, flagship of the commander-in-chief on the Australia station, a twin-screw battleship which nevertheless frequently made long cruises under sail alone. In 1894 he was one of the few lieutenants selected to qualify as torpedo officers, and he later served in that capacity in several battleships, including two years in the *Majestic*, flagship of the Channel squadron, whence he was promoted commander in 1903 and appointed to the naval ordnance department at the Admiralty—a record of service which shows that, as a technical officer, he was in the first rank.

After a year in that department he became executive officer of the *Crescent*, flagship of the commander-in-chief on the Cape of Good Hope station, for nearly three years before returning to the Admiralty where he became naval assistant to the second sea lord. He was promoted captain in 1908 and in 1909 appointed to command for nearly two years the most famous ship in the navy of that day, the *Dreadnought*, then flagship of Sir William May, commander-in-chief of the Home Fleet. These appointments left him little leisure for any intensive prosecution of the historical and strategical studies to which his attention had been increasingly given for some years; but in his next command—that of the cruiser attached to the torpedo school—he found time to edit the Navy Records Society's volume on *The Loss of the Minorca* (1913), to deliver a series of lectures on naval history at the Naval War College, and to complete a book, begun in 1907, on *The Navy in the War of 1739–48*, which, however, was not published until 1920. When the naval war staff was created in 1912, Richmond was one of the officers named as original members of it, and the following year he became assistant director of the operations division of the war staff at the Admiralty.

On the outbreak of war in 1914, however, Richmond, in common with the rest of the staff, was denied participation in anything but the clerical and mechanical part of its work, and he chafed at his exclusion from any of the useful tasks for which he felt himself—and indeed was—well qualified. It was a relief to him when he left the Admiralty in May 1915 to become liaison officer with the Italian naval command, a post which he held for four months before returning home to command the old battleship *Commonwealth* in the third battle squadron. In April 1917 he was appointed to command the battleship *Conqueror* in the Grand Fleet, where he was warmly welcomed by Sir David (later Earl) Beatty, the commander-in-chief. But in April 1918, he was selected, with the latter's strong approval, as director of the newly formed training and staff duties division of the naval staff at the Admiralty. Richmond's ideas were in advance of his time, however, and practically all of his recommendations were vetoed; he was glad after a few months of frustration to return to the Grand Fleet, in command of the battleship *Erin*.

In 1920 he was promoted to flag rank, and appointed to command the re-established Naval War College to which flag officers and captains were sent to study the higher direction of war; in the conduct of its studies he was at last given a free hand. He profited by the long vacations between war courses to resume work for the Navy Records Society, editing volumes iii and iv of the *Spencer Papers* which Sir Julian Corbett had had to relinquish when he undertook the naval history of the war of 1914–18.

In 1923 Richmond was appointed commander-in-chief of the East Indies station. On his return to England at the end of 1925, he would have welcomed active employment at sea or responsible work at the Admiralty; but he found himself in strong disagreement with the views of those in office at the Admiralty on the principles which ought to guide British policy in the negotiations which, from 1921 to 1936, were carried on at several international conferences designed to secure limitation of naval expenditure. Richmond complied with a request that he should not make the task of the Admiralty more difficult by public denunciation of the policy to which it was committed; nevertheless he was excluded from all higher commands, by reason of what were regarded as his heterodox views.

In 1926, however, the Imperial Defence College was founded, and he was so obviously the officer best fitted to inaugurate it that not even the Admiralty disapproval which he had drawn upon himself could exclude him. All problems of national and imperial defence and strategy came under investigation by the college, and it is noteworthy that his views on naval limitation, which had been the cause earlier of the Admiralty refusal to employ him, and were to be so again, were there freely expressed without any objection to them being raised. His term as commandant was brought to an end only by the standing rule which prescribed two years as its duration.

Having been chosen to guide the best brains of all three Services, it was not unreasonable in him to hope that he might then expect high command in his own. He had been promoted vice-admiral in 1925 and admiral in 1929. But the disapproval of the Admiralty had not been relaxed. It was reinforced when, on the eve of the naval conference of 1930, Richmond contributed two articles to *The Times* (21 and 22 November 1929) on the subject of naval reduction, which, although designed to assist the Admiralty in attaining the object at which it was aiming, brought him a formal letter of reprimand from their lordships; and he was refused further employment in terms which aroused his keen, but very justifiable, resentment. In April 1931, twelve months before the date on which he would have been subject to compulsory retirement under the standing regulations, he retired at his own request, and thereafter devoted himself to the task of awakening his countrymen to the importance, for a right understanding of the country's needs, of the study of naval history.

'And so it came about', wrote Dr. G. M. Trevelyan, 'that Richmond's greatest service to this country was his work as a naval historian, in which he was not impeded.' In 1931 he published *The Navy in India, 1763–83*, the fruit of researches in the archives of Ceylon and Pondicherry eight years earlier, and a reasoned argument on the theme of naval limitation under the title *Economy and Naval Security*. He also delivered a series of lectures at University College, London, and the Lees Knowles lectures at Trinity College, Cambridge, for that year, published in 1932 in book form under the title *Imperial Defence and Capture at Sea in War*. In 1933 he published a treatise on *Naval Training*, and the following year a more important work on *Sea Power in the Modern World*. In that year he was elected to the Vere Harmsworth chair of imperial and naval history at Cambridge in succession to J. Holland Rose—a great compliment to his eminence as a historian, for under the statutory age limit he could hold it for no more than two years—and he was made a professorial fellow of Jesus College. The academic world proved to be completely congenial to him, and in its turn took him to its heart. At the close of his two years' tenure of the chair, he was elected to the mastership of Downing College, which had just fallen vacant.

He had thus ten more years of happy and valuable academic activity, not confined to Cambridge alone. He was always ready to lecture or write in support of logic and clear thought in defence policy, and he delivered lectures in Paris—where he was made an associate member of the Académie de la Marine—as well as in his own country. On the outbreak of war in 1939 he became chairman of the university joint recruiting board; he welcomed the establishment in his own college of the Cambridge naval division, and he started a series of lectures on foreign affairs and the progress of the war for the junior combination room, afterwards continued and extended as the 'Richmond lectures'. But still his chief enthusiasm was to impress on his countrymen the importance, deduced from every phase of British history, of sea power and of a British strategy based on it. In 1941 he published, in the Cambridge 'Current Problems' series, a booklet surveying British strategy from the days of Queen Elizabeth I; in 1943 he took the same theme for the Ford's lectures which he delivered at Oxford, and these he afterwards expanded into his greatest book, *Statesmen and Sea Power*, published in 1946 only a few weeks before his death. A volume left in manuscript was edited by E. A. Hughes and published in 1953 under the title *The Navy as an Instrument of Policy, 1558–1727*.

Richmond was appointed C.B. in 1921 and promoted K.C.B. in 1926. He was elected F.B.A. in 1937 and was a fellow of the Royal Historical Society. On the establishment in 1934 of the National Maritime Museum at Greenwich he was appointed one of the trustees. He received the honorary degree of D.C.L. from Oxford in 1939.

He married in 1907 Florence Elsa, second daughter of Sir (Thomas) Hugh Bell, second baronet, of Rounton Grange, and had one son and four daughters. He had a serious illness in 1940, which compelled him thereafter to give up all strenuous physical activity. He died suddenly at the Master's Lodge, Downing College, 15 December 1946. There are two portraits of Richmond at Downing College, one in full-dress admiral's uniform by W. G. de Glehn, and the other, in his academic dress, by R. F. Lamb.

[G. M. Trevelyan in *Proceedings* of the British Academy, vol. xxxii, 1946; Richmond's own papers and journals (now in the National Maritime Museum), and published works; personal knowledge.]

H. G. THURSFIELD

published 1959

ROBERTS Frederick Sleigh

(1832–1914)

First Earl Roberts, of Kandahar, Pretoria, and Waterford

Field-marshal, the younger son of General Sir Abraham Roberts by his wife, Isabella, widow of Major Hamilton Maxwell, and daughter of Abraham Bunbury, of Kilfeacle, co. Tipperary, was born at Cawnpore 30 September 1832. Roberts was one of many distinguished soldiers whom Ireland has sent to the service of the Empire, his family having long been settled in county Waterford. He was brought home from India at the age of two; when thirteen he was sent to Eton; and after one year there he passed second into Sandhurst at the age of fourteen, joining in January 1847. His father, however, wished Frederick to follow his own example and enter the East India Company's service. Accordingly, after waiting some time for a vacancy, he went to the training college at Addiscombe, from which he was gazetted on 12 December 1851 to the Bengal Artillery.

Roberts landed in India in April 1852 and in the same year joined his father, who was in command at Peshawar, to serve both as aide-de-camp and as battery officer. He obtained an introduction to the problems of the North-West Frontier and to the character and customs of the tribesmen of the Himalaya, under his father, who had much experience of active service in India and was for a time in command of a brigade of native levies in Kabul, which he left a few months before the disastrous retreat from Kabul in January 1842. In 1854 Roberts gained the distinction, coveted by every young gunner, of the Horse Artillery jacket. He was serving in the Bengal Horse Artillery when, in May 1857, news reached Peshawar of the outbreak of the Mutiny at Meerut. A mobile column was formed in the Punjab, and Roberts became staff officer to its first commander, (Sir) Neville Bowles Chamberlain, and to the latter's successor, John Nicholson, who won his unbounded admiration and devotion. In June he joined the staff of the force on the ridge before Delhi, and there again during the last stage of the siege did double duty as a staff officer and battery officer. In the rough and tumble fighting around Delhi he had a number of narrow escapes, and was incapacitated for a month by a blow on his spine from a bullet, which was stopped from doing more deadly mischief by the leather pouch which he was wearing. Soon after the fall of Delhi he took part in the second relief of Lucknow under Sir Colin Campbell, by whom he was chosen to guide the force attempting the relief from the Alumbagh to the Dilkusha palace. Roberts was then attached to the cavalry division of the force under (Sir) James Hope Grant, and it was with it, in a cavalry charge at Khudaganj in January 1858, that he won the Victoria Cross for saving the life of a sowar and capturing one of the mutineers' standards. He remained with Hope Grant, and served on the staff during the British siege of Lucknow, at which his great military contemporary, Major (afterwards Viscount) Wolseley, then commanding a company of the 90th Light Infantry, was also present. In April 1858 Roberts's health broke down, and he was succeeded in his staff appointment by the man whose place he was later to take as commander-in-chief of the British army. During a year of convalescence in England (1859) he met and married Miss Nora Henrietta Bews (died 1920), daughter of Captain John Bews, who had retired from the 73rd regiment. So began a married life of mutual devotion and comradeship.

Roberts returned to India in 1859 with his wife, and in the following year was promoted captain, receiving at the same time a brevet majority for his work in the Mutiny. In 1863 he had a short experience of active service on the North-West Frontier in the Umbeyla campaign against the Sitana fanatics, and five years later he went with Sir Robert Napier (afterwards Baron Napier of Magdala) to Abyssinia, as assistant quartermaster-general of the expeditionary force. He spent the campaign at the base, with the organization and control of which he was charged, and gained experience in the work of the quartermaster-general's department in which he was beginning to be recognized as an expert. As a reward for his services, Napier sent him to England with dispatches, and he was made a brevet lieutenant-colonel. In 1871 another of the perennial troubles of the Frontier resulted in an expedition against the Lushais. Here again the main problem was the organization of transport in a country presenting great natural difficulties; and for his work in overcoming them Roberts received the C.B. He had now made his name as a staff officer and was recognized as one of the leading figures in the quartermaster-general's department at the head-quarters of the army in India. In January 1875 he was promoted brevet colonel and became quartermaster-general with the temporary rank of major-general. In this position he came face to face with what was then one of the major problems of imperial defence. Russia's advance through Central Asia was continuous: she had seized Samarkand in 1868, occupied Khiva in 1873, and was making friendly advances to Shere Ali, the ameer of Afghanistan. The danger to India if Afghanistan became a dependency of Russia was obvious. The problem was how best to counter Russia's policy. One school maintained that the right answer was to make the Indus the northern frontier of India and to tell the Russians that any encroachment, territorial or political, in Afghanistan, would mean war with England. This policy would, it was argued, both relieve the Indian tax-payer and bring England's chief weapon, her sea power, into play. The other school argued that Afghanistan left without direct support would inevitably succumb to Russia, and that no pressure elsewhere would make India safe if Russia gained the control of the passes of the Himalaya. The policy of this school became known as the 'forward' policy and aimed at controlling the tribes and securing the passes. Roberts was from the first one of its foremost advocates. He gained the ear of Lord Lytton, who became viceroy in 1876, and of his successors; and the forward policy became, and still is, the defensive policy of India.

In March 1878 Roberts was appointed to the command of the Punjab frontier force, in which position he at once became one of the chief agents of the policy which he had advocated. A few months later the ameer refused to receive a political mission headed by Roberts's old chief and friend, Sir Neville Chamberlain, and welcomed the Russian envoy. Three columns were at once formed for the invasion of Afghanistan, one to move from Quetta to Kandahar, one to demonstrate in the Khyber Pass, and the third under Roberts to occupy the Kurram and Khost valleys and thence threaten Kabul. In November Roberts moved up the Kurram and found a large Afghan force holding the Peiwar Kotal. Roberts turned the Afghan position by a skilful night march and routed the Afghans, who abandoned their guns and baggage, the loss to the British column being less than a hundred killed and wounded. Shere Ali at once fled to Turkestan, and his successor, Yakub Khan, signed on 26 May 1879 the Treaty of Gandamuk, which conceded all that the British government had demanded. At the end of 1878 Roberts was promoted major-general, and he received the K.C.B. and the thanks of parliament for the victory at the Peiwar Kotal. Roberts, who knew the Afghans well, was not satisfied that the British position in Afghanistan was secure, and his doubts were soon justified. In July 1879 a political mission led by Sir Louis Cavagnari went to Kabul, and in

September Cavagnari with his staff and escort was treacherously murdered. Roberts at once returned to the Kurram, and led his force, which had been strengthened, on towards Kabul. No opposition was met until at Charasia, twelve miles south of Kabul, an Afghan army was found in position. On 6 October Roberts, aided by an attack against the Afghan left, gallantly and skilfully led by Major (afterwards Sir George) White, turned the enemy's right and again routed them with trifling loss to his own force. He then occupied Kabul without further fighting. After arranging for the administration of the capital, he transferred his force in November to the cantonments of Sherpur in its vicinity, and here he was suddenly attacked on 11 December by masses of Afghans. After enduring a short siege he repulsed decisively a great assault on his lines (23 December), and this repulse broke the Afghan resistance. In the summer of 1880 Abdur Rahman was recognized by the British government as ameer, the war appeared to be at an end, and orders were issued for the return of the troops to India. Suddenly a fresh storm broke. In July a force of Afghans, which gathered reinforcements as it advanced, invaded Western Afghanistan from Herat, and on 27 July attacked and defeated a British brigade at Maiwand, nearly half the brigade being killed or wounded, while the Afghans captured large quantities of arms and ammunition. The small garrison of Kandahar appeared to be in danger, and Roberts at once proposed that he should lead a column from Kabul to its relief. Roberts had brought his transport to a high state of perfection, and he started from Kabul on 9 August with a picked body of 10,000 men. In the first fourteen days he covered 225 miles through difficult country, but encountered no opposition. He then learned that Kandahar was in no immediate danger and he completed the remaining 88 miles to Kandahar, which he entered on 31 August, at a more leisurely pace. On 1 September he met and defeated the Afghans outside Kandahar, and the pacification of Afghanistan was completed without further difficulty. The march to Kandahar and its triumphant conclusion appealed irresistibly to a public gravely perturbed by the disaster of Maiwand and racked with anxiety as to the fate of Kandahar. Roberts became at once a popular hero. He received the G.C.B. and a baronetcy, and was made commander-in-chief of the Madras army. The march to Kandahar was made possible by Roberts's prompt and bold decision, his careful forethought, the sound organization of his transport, and by the confidence in his leadership with which he inspired his men; but, as he always maintained, it was not as a military feat to be compared with his advance on Kabul in the previous year. The actions of the Peiwar Kotal and Charasia established his reputation amongst soldiers as a tactician; as an organiser of transport in a mountainous country he was without an equal; while his neat figure, fine horsemanship, charm of manner, and constant care for the lives and welfare of his men, won from them a devotion which was not the least of the causes of his success. The name 'Bobs' became one to conjure with in India.

In the autumn of 1880 Roberts came to England for a rest, and was received with all honour. As a firm believer in the forward policy he strongly advocated the retention of Kandahar, but was unable to persuade Mr. Gladstone's government to agree. While he was in England the news came home of the disaster of Majuba Hill (27 February 1881). He was at once sent to South Africa, but on reaching Cape Town he learned that Sir Henry Evelyn Wood had already arranged peace with the Boers. He therefore came straight back to England, and left for India again in the autumn of 1881 to take up his command in Madras. Four years later, when Sir Donald Stewart vacated the chief command in India, Roberts was universally recognized to be his natural successor. He continued to be the commander-in-chief until the spring of 1893. During the seven years in which he was the supreme military authority in India, his chief pre-occupation was Russia's advance to the frontier of Afghanistan, and he regarded the threat of the invasion of India by Russia as the chief military problem of the British Empire. He revised the schemes for the defence of the North-West Frontier, and was engaged in a constant struggle to win from the Indian Treasury money for the improvement of communications leading into the Himalaya, and for the provision of adequate transport. He also devoted himself particularly to the improvement of the shooting, both of the infantry and of the artillery, and established a system of field-training which caused the India of his day to be recognized as the most practical school of training for the British army. He was not in agreement with the military reformers at home, and in particular was opposed to the intro-duction of the short-service system, which, at first, undoubtedly affected the efficiency of the British troops in India. The problems of India required the army to be in a state of instant readiness for war, while a frontier expedition did not involve losses so heavy that they could not be quickly replaced by drafts from home. The need for a reserve was not therefore obvious to one who had passed his military life in India, but later ex-perience caused Roberts to revise his judgement of the reforms which Viscount Cardwell had initiated and Wolseley brought to completion. On 1 January 1892 Roberts was created Baron Roberts, of Kandahar, and early in the following year he left India for good amidst demonstrations of aff-ection and respect such as have rarely been won by a soldier.

In England he had two years to wait for an appointment suited to one of his rank and reputation, and he devoted these to writing his reminiscences. His *Forty-one Years in India* (1897) is at once a stirring story, simply told, and a demonstration of the generous and frank character of its author. In May

1895 he was made field-marshal, and in the same year he became commander-in-chief in Ireland. In his new command he again set himself to improve the shooting and the field-training of the soldier, while Dublin society was soon convinced that the reputation which he had gained in Simla as a charming host was well deserved.

When, in October 1899, the British government's disputes with the Boers culminated in war, few anticipated a serious campaign requiring the services of a British field-marshal, and Sir Redvers Buller's long experience of South Africa marked him as the leader of the expedition to the Cape. In December the news that Sir George White was shut up in Ladysmith was followed quickly by reports of reverses to Sir William Gatacre at Stormberg, to Lord Methuen at Magersfontein, and to Buller's main force at Colenso. The country was deeply stirred, and heard with relief on 17 December that Mr. Balfour's government had appointed Roberts to the supreme command in South Africa with Lord Kitchener as his chief of staff. Roberts left England in his sixty-eighth year, carrying with him the confidence and affection of his countrymen, as well as their sympathy for the loss of his only son, Lieutenant Frederick Roberts, mortally wounded a few days before in a gallant attempt to save some of Buller's guns at Colenso. Lieutenant Roberts died before the Victoria Cross, for which he had been recommended, could be awarded him.

Up to the time of Lord Roberts's arrival at the Cape (10 January) two fundamental mistakes had been made in the conduct of the campaign. Reliance had been placed mainly upon the British infantry, and offers of mounted troops both from South Africa and from the Dominions were treated coldly; the consequent lack of mobility in dealing with enemy forces in which every man was mounted was a fatal handicap. Further, the provision of transport was so limited as to tie the lines of advance to the few railways. This indicated clearly to the Boers the general nature of the British plan. Roberts at once encouraged local levies of mounted men, greatly increased the number of mounted infantry, and, profiting by his long experience of transport difficulties in India, with the help of Kitchener completely remodelled the transport system. He also saw at once that the situation demanded the earliest possible invasion of the Free State from the Cape Colony, and, while reinforcements from England were on the way to him, prepared his plans with the utmost secrecy. To these plans he resolutely adhered, despite urgent calls for relief from Kimberley, the failure of Buller's third attempt to relieve Ladysmith and his despairing suggestion that he should abandon it, despite also the first flicker of revolt in Cape Colony. Disposing his troops so as to indicate a direct advance on Bloemfontein from Naauwpoort, he transferred them rapidly to the Modder river on the road to Kimberley, and on 11 February began a movement round the left flank of the force with which General Piet Cronje was at once besieging Kimberley and opposing Methuen. On 15 February the cavalry division of Major-General (afterwards Earl) French at Klip Drift, on the Modder, galloped through a gap in the Boer lines and rode on into Kimberley. Cronje, finding his communications with Bloemfontein threatened, began a retreat along the Modder. Roberts's infantry hung on to the Boer rear-guard, and on 17 February French, returning in haste from Kimberley, prevented Cronje from crossing the Modder. On the 18th the Boer laager at Paardeberg Drift was attacked by the British infantry divisions under (Sir) Thomas Kelly-Kenny and Kitchener, but this attack was repulsed with 1,270 casualties. Roberts, who had been detained at Jacobsdal by a slight illness, arrived the next day and decided not to renew the attack but to engage in a siege of the laager. Within a week the Boer position in the bed of the river had become desperate, and on 27 February, the anniversary of Majuba, Cronje surrendered with 4,000 men. The effect of Roberts's manœuvre was immediate. The Free State commandos left Natal to defend their own country, and Ladysmith was relieved on 28 February. Deficiency of transport and supplies, due largely to a successful raid by General Christian De Wet upon a large transport column, made an immediate advance on Bloemfontein impossible, and the Free Staters gathered a force to oppose Roberts's farther advance. At Poplar Grove on 7 March they succeeded in evading serious attack, but three days later they stood at Driefontein and were severely handled. This proved to be the last attempt of the Boers to offer battle in the Free State, and Bloemfontein was occupied on 13 March without opposition. After a pause in the Free State capital in order to restore railway communications and get up supplies, Roberts began an advance on Pretoria at the beginning of May. Moving on a broad front and turning the flanks of the Boers whenever they attempted to stand, he reached Kroonstad on 12 May; here a further halt was necessary, to enable the railways to be repaired. During this halt the news arrived that Buller had cleared Natal of Boers, and that Sir Archibald Hunter and Colonel (Sir) Bryan Mahon, moving north from Kimberley, had, in conjunction with a force under Colonel (afterwards Lord) Plumer, coming south from Rhodesia, relieved Mafeking, the last of the besieged garrisons.

The advance from Kroonstad was begun on 22 May and the Vaal was crossed two days later. On 31 May Roberts entered Johannesburg and, after overcoming a feeble resistance, occupied Pretoria on 5 June. On 12 June the main Boer force under General Louis Botha was defeated at Diamond Hill, and it appeared that organized resistance was at an end. President Kruger had removed his government to Machadodorp on the Delagoa railway, and there held some 4,000 British prisoners of war. An advance eastwards to Komati Poort, on the frontier of Portuguese East Africa, seemed all that was needed to complete the subjugation of the Transvaal, and this task was made easier by the junction of Buller's force advancing from Natal with Roberts's main body in the Transvaal in the first week of July. It was true that De Wet and the Free State leaders had been actively engaged in guerrilla warfare in their own country, but at the end of July a large body of Free Staters was surrounded on the border of Basutoland, and their commander, Prinsloo, surrendered with 4,000 men. Before this Roberts had begun his final advance, and on 28 July captured Machadodorp after some stiff fighting. Buller, pursuing the retreating Boers, occupied Lydenberg (6 September), French seized Barberton (13 September), and Major-General (Sir) Ian Hamilton entered Komati Poort (24 September). There was then no Boer town of importance which was not in British hands. Kruger fled to Lourenço Marques and on 11 October left Africa on board a Dutch vessel. The formal annexation of the Transvaal on 25 October, following that of the Free State (28 May), created the general impression that the War was at an end. Roberts was needed at home to succeed Wolseley as commander-in-chief, and he came back to England just in time to be received by Queen Victoria, one of the last of her acts being to reward him with the Garter and an earldom.

Roberts's generalship had changed a dark and doubtful situation in South Africa, with a rapidity which was almost startling, into one which, when he left that country, seemed brilliant. He had achieved the apparently impossible in converting the slow, lumbering columns of the early days of the War into bodies of troops which could manœuvre as swiftly as could their active enemy, and above all, he had at once struck his blow in the right direction. He is open to the criticism that he did not complete his task. Influenced by his desire to save the lives of his men, and probably also by his experience of the effect of turning movements on Asiatics, he continually manœuvred the Boers out of their positions, and rarely brought them to battle. Possibly he underrated the stubbornness of the Boer character, and attached too much importance to the occupation of their towns. If so, he was not alone in holding such opinions; and though he left to Kitchener a legacy far more burdensome than he had anticipated, the issue, when he handed over the command in South Africa, was never in doubt as it had been when he took it up.

His period of service as commander-in-chief of the British army was disappointing. He reached England with an unrivalled reputation, and the public, which the events of the War had at last made aware of the defects of the British military system and training, expected great things from him. In his own special sphere of training troops for war Roberts certainly effected important reforms, and under him a new spirit of keenness and earnestness pervaded the army. A service dress was introduced, and shooting and field-training became of greater importance than pipe-clay and ceremonial, but his endeavours to reform the military system were ineffective. He found himself confronted with an intricate organization, with which, owing to his long service in India, he was little acquainted. As commander-in-chief he had no organized general staff to support him, and he did not know how to set about getting one.

The royal commission on the South African War (1903) pointed out the anomalies in the position of the commander-in-chief, and its report was followed in the autumn of 1903 by the appointment of a commission, under the chairmanship of Viscount Esher, on the organization of the War Office. This commission recommended the abolition of the office of commander-in-chief and the creation of an Army Council. Its findings were accepted by Mr. Balfour's government, and in February 1904 Lord Roberts left the War Office. He continued for a time to be a member of the Committee of Imperial Defence which Mr. Balfour had instituted, but he found himself in disagreement with the government's policy of defence, and in an article in the *Nineteenth Century* (December 1904) he advocated national service for home defence. In November 1905 he resigned, and for the next ten years devoted himself to the cause of national service, becoming in 1905 president of the National Service League. Mr. Balfour's government having been succeeded in 1905 by that of Sir Henry Campbell-Bannerman, Mr. (afterwards Viscount) Haldane, the new minister for war, brought in important measures of army reform which included the formation of the territorial force and the officers' training corps; but Lord Roberts, while agreeing that these were great steps forward, insisted on their inadequacy. The weakness of his own scheme was that what was needed was not a great army for home defence but an increase in the number of troops which could be employed abroad, while there was grave danger that the drastic change which he advocated in the constitution of the military system would injure for many years the efficiency of the voluntary regular army at a time when British relations with Germany were becoming more and more strained. Mr. Haldane had therefore no difficulty in finding, in the War Office, hostile critics of Lord Roberts's proposal; while in 1910 Sir Ian Hamilton, at that time adjutant-general, published a volume on *Compulsory Service* in which he strongly advocated the voluntary system. To this Lord Roberts replied, with the help of two anonymous contributors, in his book *Fallacies and Facts* (1911). Though the controversy continued, Mr. Haldane persevered with his plans; and it was not until the European War had raged for nearly two years that compulsory service became the law of the land. But Lord Roberts's campaign, begun at the age of seventy-two and continued into his eighty-second year, did much to awaken the country to a sense of the dangers with which it was confronted in 1914.

On the outbreak of war with Germany Mr. Asquith summoned Lord Roberts to the first war council which settled the destination of the original British expeditionary force; and when India dispatched an expedition to France the King made Roberts its colonel-in-chief. Feeling that he must go and hearten the men of the country which had been so long his military home, he left for France on 11 November 1914, caught a chill at once, and died at St. Omer on 14 November, as he would have wished, in the midst of an army on active service. His body was brought back to England, and he was buried with due pomp in St. Paul's Cathedral.

Roberts had six children, of whom three died in infancy. His title devolved by special remainder upon his elder surviving daughter, Lady Aileen Mary Roberts; his second daughter, Lady Ada Edwina Stewart, who is the heir presumptive to the title, married in 1913 Colonel Henry Frederick Elliott Lewin, of the Royal Artillery, and has one son.

A portrait of Roberts by W. W. Ouless was painted for the Royal Artillery in 1882. A bust painting by G. F. Watts, executed in 1898, is in the National Portrait Gallery. A portrait by J. S. Sargent, painted in 1904, is in the possession of Lady Roberts, who owns another by P. A. de Laszló; a second portrait by Laszló is at Eton College. Another portrait, by C. W. Furse, belongs to Lady Hudson. A statue of Roberts by Harry Bates (1894) is in Calcutta; there is a copy in Glasgow, and another, without the pedestal, on the Horse Guards Parade, Whitehall. Busts in bronze by C. W. Roberts and Sir Hamo Thornycroft are both dated 1915, and one by W. R. Colton was exhibited in 1916. There is a bust by John Tweed in St. Paul's Cathedral (*Royal Academy Pictures*, 1882, 1894, 1915, 1916).

[Lord Roberts, *Forty-one Years in India*, 1897; *Letters written during the Indian Mutiny, by Fred. Roberts, afterwards Field-Marshal Earl Roberts*, 1924; H. Hensman, *The Afghan War of 1879–1880*, 1881; *The Anglo-Afghan War 1878–1880*, Official Account, 1881; Sir J. F. Maurice and M. H. Grant, (Official) *History of the War in South Africa 1899–1902*, 1906–1910.]

Frederick Maurice

published 1927

(1860–1933)

First baronet

Field-marshal, the eldest son of Thomas Charles Robertson, a villager of Welbourn, Lincolnshire, by his wife, Ann Rosamund Johnson, was born at Welbourn 29 January 1860. He was educated at a private school. In November 1877, giving his birthday as 16 January, he enlisted in the 16th Lancers, and being a strong, well-grown lad he quickly became adept in the many exercises then required of a lancer. He set earnestly to work to educate himself, paying a comrade a few pence an hour to read to him while he was cleaning his kit, and so he gained promotion quickly. He says in his autobiography that, while in the ranks, he was 'crimed' three times, once because a deserter whom he was escorting escaped, once because a horse which he was leading broke loose, and the third time because one of a party in his charge got drunk and was unhorsed. Despite these setbacks he was promoted troop-sergeant-major in 1885, when he had over seven years' service. Then, encouraged by his officers and by the rector of Welbourn, he set to work on the examination for a commission, which he passed in 1887, and in 1888 he was gazetted second-lieutenant in the 3rd Dragoon Guards, then serving in India.

Despite every economy a subaltern's pay in those days could not be made to cover the expenses of an officer in a cavalry regiment, and in order to eke it out Robertson took up the study of native languages, awards being offered to those who passed the examinations. He discovered that he had a gift for languages and in a few years he qualified in Urdu, Hindi, Persian, Pushtu, Punjabi, and Gurkhali. He did most of his work in the hot weather, when there were few military duties and most people slept in the middle of the day. His achievements as a linguist brought him to the notice of army headquarters and in 1892 he was appointed a junior officer of the Intelligence department at Simla. There he was chiefly concerned with the problems of the North-West Frontier. The advance of Russia towards India was a dominating factor in the military situation and Robertson was sent to explore the routes leading into India from the Pamirs. His reports were of such value that when in 1894 Umra Khan raised the tribes of Chitral and besieged the British garrison in the state's capital, forcing us to send relief, he was appointed to the Intelligence staff of the force.

In this little campaign Robertson was severely wounded, was mentioned in dispatches, and awarded the D.S.O. While in hospital he was promoted captain and when he recovered from his wound he began to work for the

Staff College. He qualified for admission—being the first ranker to do so—in 1896 and was nominated by the commander-in-chief in India for one of the vacancies at his disposal. At the Staff College he was much influenced by Lieutenant-Colonel G. F. R. Henderson, the professor of strategy and tactics. When he passed out of the college there was need in the Intelligence department of the War Office for an officer who knew the North-West Frontier of India and Robertson, after a short period of probation, was appointed staff captain in the colonial section of that department. He was serving in it when President Kruger precipitated war in South Africa by invading the Cape Colony and Natal. On his appointment as commander-in-chief in South Africa, after the 'black week' of December 1899, Lord Roberts chose Henderson to be director of his Intelligence department and Henderson chose Robertson to serve under him. There was under the staff system which then prevailed, and of which Robertson was critical, little scope for an Intelligence department at headquarters, and in October 1900, after the occupation of Pretoria, he was sent back to the War Office, having in the meantime been promoted major. In the *Gazette* of November 1901 he was mentioned in dispatches and awarded the brevet of lieutenant-colonel.

Back in the Intelligence department, Robertson was appointed head of the foreign section, which he found to be ill equipped and badly organized, and with the full support of his chief, Sir William Nicholson, he set about remedying these defects. As part of this process he spent some months in each year in visiting the principal foreign countries which were the charge of his section. He was promoted colonel in 1903 and thus caught up with and even passed most of his contemporaries, who had entered the army in the normal way, through the military colleges. He was appointed C.B. in 1905 and, in order that he might complete the reorganization of the foreign section, his appointment was extended for two years, to January 1907, when he was placed for a short time on half pay, using his leisure to translate German and Austrian military hand-books for his old section.

In May 1907 Robertson was appointed assistant quartermaster-general of the Aldershot Command and at the end of the year he became brigadier-general, general staff of the same command, under General Sir Horace Smith-Dorrien. R. B. Haldane's reform of the army was then in full development, the general staff was in being, an expeditionary force had been formed, and the creation of the Territorial army was in progress. This clearly indicated that the main task of the army was to prepare for the possibility of war on the continent of Europe. Robertson and his chief devoted themselves to making the training at Aldershot as realistic as possible, and in this Robertson's practical mind and his prolonged study of the army of Great Britain's most probable enemy proved to be of real value. His reputation in the army grew rapidly. None the less it came as a surprise to him and to the army in general when in June 1910 Nicholson, then chief of the imperial general staff, selected him for promotion to major-general and appointed him commandant of the Staff College; a ranker officer in that position was indeed a novelty. Shortly before this the King, on the occasion of a visit to the Aldershot Command, appointed Robertson a C.V.O.

At the Staff College Robertson applied to his students the same methods which he had used at Aldershot and set himself to make the study of war there less theoretical and more practical. He endeavoured to reproduce in his exercises the strain which falls upon a staff in times of crisis in war, then an entirely new development in training. He told the students 'direct your studies to a special and definite end—that of fighting the most probable and most formidable adversary for the time being'. His sound judgement and critical mind—he had an uncanny knack of spotting at once the weak points in a plan—deeply impressed his students and when he left the Staff College in October 1913 in order to become director of military training at the War Office, he was given a great ovation. Twice during his time as commandant he was in attendance on the King at army manoeuvres and on the second occasion, in June 1913, he was appointed K.C.V.O. His long study of the problems which war with Germany would involve had led him to the conclusion that the enemy would invade Belgium in force with the object of turning the left of the Allied line and that the natural place of the British would be where this blow would fall. 'Hope for the best, prepare for the worst' was one of his favourite maxims, and while at the Staff College he made his students study how to conduct a retreat from an enemy in superior force. The last army manoeuvres which as director of military training he planned in 1914, were arranged to deal with the same problem, and this study bore fruit when in August 1914 British troops were retreating from Mons. On mobilization he was appointed quartermaster-general at general headquarters in France. He did not share the optimism of the general staffs at French and British headquarters and agreed with Kitchener that the British area of concentration in France was dangerously advanced. When the German invasion of Belgium developed he had plans ready for the transfer of British bases from the Channel to the Atlantic coast, before the troops had fired a shot, and it was thanks to this foresight that he succeeded in keeping the army supplied during the long retreat. His handling of this difficult task inspired confidence in his ability and energy and when in January 1915 the health of Sir Archibald Murray, chief of the general staff at general headquarters, broke down, he was welcomed as his successor. He was appointed K.C.B. later that year.

The Allies in the West, having defeated the German attempts to reach Paris and the Channel ports, had to determine their strategy for 1915. French military and public opinion was eager to drive the enemy out of France and was convinced that this was possible. No French commander-in-chief who proposed a defensive strategy could have held his position. The Germans had transferred large forces from the northern to the eastern front and were driving back the Russians, who had come gallantly to the aid of France and Britain in the crisis of 1914. Robertson held that the first essential was to make the co-operation of the Allied forces effective and that therefore the British had no alternative but to aid the offensive campaign of the French to the utmost of their power, in accordance with the instructions of the British government to the commander-in-chief in France. Further he regarded it as very important that the British should drive the Germans farther away from the Channel ports and from Paris, before they brought back troops from the East. Realizing that Britain had not the power to conduct more than one offensive campaign at a time, he was opposed to the plans for attacking the Gallipoli peninsula. He had studied this operation when in charge of the foreign section, and had come to the conclusion that success was doubtful because it was not easy to provide artillery support for landings and he was sceptical of the opinion of the Admiralty that improvements in naval ordnance had overcome this difficulty. So began the prolonged controversy between 'Westerners' and 'Easterners', in which Robertson was a convinced 'Westerner'.

As the summer of 1915 wore on and British commitments grew, Robertson became anxious about the conduct of the war and sent to the War Office a memorandum in which he urged the setting up of an organization for the control and direction of Allied strategy. As a result of this General Joffre called in November 1915 the first conference of Allied commanders and chiefs of staff to consider the Allied campaign for 1916. This Robertson welcomed as a useful beginning. He was no less anxious to improve British arrangements for the control of military operations, and when in the autumn Kitchener told him that he wanted him to come to the War Office as chief of the imperial general staff he prepared for him a memorandum setting out the conditions upon which he was prepared to accept this appointment.

Robertson pointed out that the War Office was responsible for campaigns in France and the Dardanelles, India conducted the campaign in Mesopotamia without the resources to do this effectively, the Foreign Office was responsible for operations against the Senussi in Western Egypt, and the Colonial Office for the campaign in West Africa, a division of responsibility fatal to efficiency. He urged the setting up of a small war council charged with the co-ordination of policy and strategy in every theatre of war in which Great Britain was concerned; that the chief of the imperial general staff should be the responsible military adviser of this council and should issue its instructions to commanders-in-chief, and be in direct touch with these commanders without the intervention of the army council. He also asked for a reorganization of the general staff at the War Office in order to enable it to operate as the general headquarters of the Empire. Kitchener was at first disposed to consider these proposals to be an undue curtailment of the authority of the secretary of state for war, but after a personal interview he accepted them and Robertson became chief of the imperial general staff in succession to Murray in December 1915.

Before he re-entered the War Office Robertson had been asked by the government for his views on the situation in the Gallipoli peninsula and had strongly supported the proposal to evacuate Suvla Bay. This operation was completed before he assumed office and his first act as chief of the imperial general staff was to urge that Helles should also be evacuated. When this was done he created in Egypt a general reserve composed of the troops released from the Dardanelles. This he used to provide reinforcements for the campaign of 1916 in France, a very necessary step in view of the German attack on Verdun. Murray, who had become commander-in-chief in Egypt, materially increased the available reserve by occupying the wells in the Sinai peninsula, a more economical defence against attack from the East than was provided by lining the Suez Canal. This released further reinforcements for Mesopotamia, where Robertson selected General Sir F. S. Maude for the chief command.

The new arrangement began smoothly. Kitchener and Robertson, who was promoted general in June 1916, worked well together and when, on Kitchener's death that same month, Lloyd George became secretary of state for war, he expressed his agreement with the reorganization of the higher command. The successful evacuation of the Gallipoli peninsula, the ending of the campaigns in West Africa and Western Egypt, the occupation of the Sinai peninsula and, early in 1917, when Robertson was appointed G.C.B., the defeat of the Turks at Kut-el-Amara, followed by the occupation of Bagdad, materially improved the British military situation. But against this had to be set the disastrous defeats of the Russians, the heavy cost of the battles of the Somme, the exhaustion of the French army, the over-running of Serbia and Rumania, and growing doubts as to the possibility of breaking through the German lines in the West. These led in December 1916 to the fall of Asquith and the accession of Lloyd George as prime minister.

Lloyd George, horrified by the long casualty lists of the Somme battles, was determined to secure greater political control of Allied strategy and to find an easier road to victory than was provided by assaults on German trenches. He was essentially an opportunist, and Robertson a firm believer in principles; the prime minister liked to form his conclusions after personal discussions; Robertson distrusted his powers of argument with statesmen and preferred to present his views in reasoned memoranda, so that from the first there were incompatibilities of temperament between the two. Friction increased when, at a conference of the Allies held in Rome in January 1917, Lloyd George, without consulting Robertson, put forward a plan for an Allied attack on Austria. This plan overlooked the limitations of communication between France and Italy and the superiority in this respect of the centrally placed enemy. The Allied ministers naturally referred it to the chiefs of staff for examination and report.

The French government, like Lloyd George, was alarmed by the losses of the campaigns of 1916 and it too sought greater political control. Joffre was removed and Nivelle took his place. Lloyd George met Nivelle on his return from Italy and, before the report on the Austrian plan was received, approved Nivelle's proposal for a quick break through the German lines in the West, on the understanding that, if this failed, operations would be broken off. To further this plan, the prime minister, again without consulting the chief of the imperial general staff, encouraged the French government to propose that Nivelle should have operational and administrative control of the British army in France. When, to the surprise of Robertson and Haig, this proposal was produced at an Allied conference held at Calais in February 1917, they held it to be dangerous in view of the many British commitments, and a compromise was reached by which Nivelle was given operational control in France for the campaign of 1917.

The failure of Nivelle's campaign, followed by serious mutinies in parts of the French army, produced a crisis which, it was agreed, could only be met by British attacks on a scale sufficient to keep the Germans occupied. The situation was further complicated by the probability of the collapse of Russian resistance, against which could be set the entry into the war of the United States of America. A conference of Allied commanders-in-chief and chiefs of staff held in June computed the rate at which German troops could be transferred from the eastern to the western front and came to the conclusion that between February and July 1918 the enemy might be in a dangerous superiority on the western front. In order to meet this it was agreed that a defensive attitude should be adopted in all secondary theatres of war and that as many men as possible should be transferred to the western front.

Robertson agreed with this recommendation and in order to implement it he prepared plans for the transfer of troops from Egypt and Salonika to the western front and urged the army council to press for a greater allocation of manpower to the army. This brought him again into conflict with the prime minister, who feared that these reinforcements would be used for another costly attack in France. Delay occurred in meeting the army council's request for more men, and Lloyd George returned to his advocacy of an attack on Austria as preferable to Haig's proposal for an offensive campaign on the Ypres front. When the Austrian plan proved to be impracticable the prime minister urged an invasion of Palestine as likely to provide a stimulus to public morale during the difficult period which was foreseen for the spring of 1918.

The heavy defeat of the Italian army at Caporetto in October 1917 and the disappointing results of the Passchendaele campaign brought about a fresh crisis. Lloyd George, who had been for some time in touch with the French prime minister, M. Painlevé, and had secured his agreement, proposed at a conference held at Rapallo the creation of a supreme war council composed of the prime ministers and one other minister from each Ally, provided with a permanent staff and with military representatives to furnish technical advice. Robertson cordially approved of the supreme council as a means of receiving better co-ordination of Allied policy, but he strongly disapproved of the military representatives having power to give technical advice independently of their chiefs of staff, who, he held, having behind them their general staffs organization, and particularly their intelligence services, were alone competent to give their governments responsible advice. Nivelle's failure had shaken confidence in an Allied supreme command and Lloyd George had expressly stated that this was, at the time, impracticable, but Robertson regarded the multiplication of military advice as a sorry alternative.

The differences between the two men came to a head at a meeting of the Supreme War Council held at Versailles from 30 January to 2 February 1918. There Lloyd George obtained approval, despite Robertson's objections, for an offensive campaign in Palestine in the spring. In the event this had to be postponed when the Germans attacked the western front in March. It was also decided to create an Allied general reserve on the western front controlled by the military representatives with Foch as chairman. Robertson had no faith in command by committee and said so, and in fact this committee was never able to get to work. It had become clear that he and the prime minister could not work together and Lloyd George proposed to bring in Sir Henry Wilson as chief of the imperial general staff, offering Robertson the post of military representative at Versailles. This Robertson refused on the ground that the appointment was wrong in principle. In February he left the War Office for the Eastern Command at home.

In the Eastern Command Robertson undertook a reorganization designed to release men for the fighting fronts and after the armistice he was concerned with the disturbances which arose from the dissatisfaction of the troops with the arrangements for demobilization. In this his firmness and tact avoided serious trouble. In June 1918 he became commander-in-chief, Home Forces, and in April 1919 of the British army of occupation on the Rhine. In this year he was appointed G.C.M.G., and for his eminent services during the war received the thanks of parliament and a grant of £10,000 and was created a baronet. In March 1920 he was promoted field-marshal and retired from active employment in the following year. He was appointed G.C.V.O. in 1931 and died in London 12 February 1933.

Robertson wrote two books; the first, an autobiography *From Private to Field-Marshal*, was published in 1921; the second, *Soldiers and Statesmen 1914–1918*, published in two volumes in 1926, was a reasoned account of the advice which he gave to the government. He was appointed in 1916 colonel of the Scots Greys, in 1925 of the 3rd Dragoon Guards, and in 1928 of the Royal Horse Guards. He received many foreign decorations, including that of grand officer of the Legion of Honour.

Robertson married in 1894 Mildred Adelaide, second daughter of Lieutenant-General Charles Thomas Palin, of the Indian Army, and had two sons, the younger of whom died at the age of eighteen, and two daughters. He was succeeded as second baronet by his elder son, Lieutenant-General Sir Brian Hubert Robertson (born 1896).

There is a portrait of Robertson in the Cavalry Club by R. C. Petre, and in the Imperial War Museum by Sir William Orpen; a portrait of him as colonel of the Royal Horse Guards by Mediria is in the possession of his daughter, Mrs. Locket-Agnew; a portrait of him is also included in J. S. Sargent's picture, 'Some General Officers of the Great War', painted in 1922, in the National Portrait Gallery.

[Sir William Robertson, *From Private to Field-Marshal*, 1921, and *Soldiers and Statesmen 1914–1918*, 2 vols., 1926; personal knowledge.]

FREDERICK MAURICE

published 1949

Stephen Wentworth

(1903–1982)

Naval officer and historian, was born 1 August 1903 in London, the second of four sons (there were no daughters) of John Henry Roskill, KC and judge of the Salford Hundred Court of Record, and his wife, Sybil Mary Wentworth, daughter of Ashton Wentworth Dilke, MP for Newcastle upon Tyne. He was educated at the Royal Naval Colleges at Osborne and Dartmouth. In 1921 he was posted as midshipman to his first ship, the cruiser *Durban*, on the China station, where he was fortunate to act as research assistant to Lieutenant-Commander W. Stephen R. (later Lord) King-Hall, who was then writing a book on western civilization and the Far East. Here Roskill first learned how, in his own words, 'unremittingly arduous' was the pursuit of history.

In 1927 he began the 'long' gunnery course at the Royal Naval College, Greenwich, and HMS *Excellent*, gunnery being then the élite branch of the navy. He passed out third in the course. The 1930s saw Roskill steadily climb the peacetime ladder of promotion, serving as gunnery officer in the aircraft carrier *Eagle* (1933–5) and the battleship *Warspite* (1936–9), with a spell as instructor at *Excellent* in 1935–6. While in *Warspite* he showed his mettle as a professional who would stand firm for what he believed to be right, refusing to take over the ship's armaments from the dockyards until numerous defects were remedied. He also pioneered the location of fire control beneath the armour instead of exposed aloft.

In March 1939 he was appointed to the Admiralty staff, where he successfully insisted on the Swiss Oerlikon 20 mm. gun instead of an inferior British design, and opposed the proposal of F. A. Lindemann (later Viscount Cherwell) that anti-aircraft guns should be replaced by rockets. He later advocated that each main armament turret should have its own fire-control radar—a radical innovation later adopted. However, his unflinching advocacy in these matters brought him into disfavour with more conservative seniors, and in 1941 he saw his posting as executive officer in HMNZS *Leander* in the Pacific as a form of rustication. Here he restored a slack ship's company to a high standard of efficiency and training, so enabling *Leander* to survive a Japanese torpedo hit in 1943. Roskill was reappointed to the ship in command as acting captain, and in 1944 confirmed in rank as captain. In the same year he was awarded the DSC.

In 1944 he was posted as chief staff officer for administration and weapons in the Admiralty delegation in Washington; in 1946 was nominated chief British observer at the Bikini atoll atomic bomb tests; and in

1947 appointed deputy director of naval intelligence. Sadly, increasing deafness caused by exposure to gun detonations at *Excellent* denied him the chance of promotion to flag rank, for in 1948 he was pronounced medically unfit for sea service. While the premature ending of his naval life was a keen disappointment, Roskill was now to achieve eminence in a new career as historian. In 1949 he was appointed the official naval historian in the Cabinet Office historical section. Although he had little previous experience as a writer and historian, he brought to his new profession the same seamanlike attention to detail, order, and exactitude that he had shown in his naval service and the same sometimes prickly determination to stand firm for what he believed to be right, even in the face of pressure from the most eminent.

It was thanks to him that the official naval history of World War II covered the entire war at sea, and not merely the Atlantic as once envisaged. The three volumes of *The War at Sea* (vol. i 1954, vol. ii 1957, vol. iii pt. I 1960, pt. II 1961), comprehensive, majestic, invested with a sailor's personal knowledge of the men and events as well as the historian's judgement, were to prove only the opening salvo in a prolific career as a writer. Outstanding among Roskill's contributions to twentieth-century history must be accounted his magisterial biography *Hankey, Man of Secrets* (vol. i 1970, vol. ii 1972, vol. iii 1974), his two volumes on *Naval Policy Between the Wars* (1968 and 1976), *Churchill and the Admirals* (1977), and his final work, *The Last Naval Hero: Admiral of the Fleet Earl Beatty; an Intimate Biography* (1980), a penetrating yet sympathetic assessment of Earl Beatty as man, fleet commander, and first sea lord. Roskill's forte as historian consisted in unrivalled professional understanding of naval matters, combined with scholarly thoroughness, mastery of detail, and ability to plumb the complexities of naval policy and strategy, although it could be said that his concern for detail sometimes tended to obscure the main thrust of his narrative. Roskill had no peer among twentieth-century British naval historians, only the American Arthur Marder rivalling him for depth of learning and sheer industry.

Roskill's distinction as a historian brought him a senior research fellowship at Churchill College, Cambridge, in 1961; and in 1970 he was made a life fellow. He played a major role in the Churchill Archives Centre, and it was owing to his efforts that many important collections of naval papers were deposited there. Despite worsening deafness, Roskill participated to the full in the life of the college; a much loved colleague and a charming and considerate host to his many guests.

In 1971 he was awarded a Litt.D. by Cambridge, elected a fellow of the British Academy, and appointed CBE. In 1975 he was awarded the Chesney gold medal of the Royal United Services Institute, and made an honorary

D.Litt. by Leeds. In 1980 Oxford awarded him an honorary D.Litt., an honour which gave him special delight.

In 1930 he married Elizabeth, daughter of Henry Van den Bergh, margarine manufacturer, from Holland. Her strength of character and devotion to principle matched his own. They had four sons and three daughters. Roskill died 4 November 1982 at his home in Cambridge.

[Personal knowledge.]

CORRELLI BARNETT

published 1990

SALMOND (William) Geoffrey (Hanson)

(1878–1933)

Sir

Air chief marshal, was born at Hougham, Dover, 19 August 1878, the elder son of Major-General Sir William Salmond, R.E., of Whaddon House, Bruton, Somerset, by his wife, Emma Mary, youngest daughter of William Fretwell Hoyle, of Hooton Levet Hall, Yorkshire. He was educated at Wellington College and the Royal Military Academy. He received his first commission in the Royal Artillery in 1898, and served in the Royal Regiment until 1913, seeing during these years active service in South Africa and in China (1900); he graduated at the Staff College in 1914.

Salmond was among the first of the army officers to give his attention to flying, and while a captain received his Royal Aero Club certificate in 1912. In 1913 he was appointed G.S.O. 3 at the Directorate of Military Aeronautics in the War Office; in August 1914 he was promoted major and went to France a few days after the outbreak of war, on the staff of Major-General (Sir) David Henderson, later commanding the Royal Flying Corps. During the early months of the war he devised the method of 'pinpointing' the enemy's guns. In January 1915 he returned to England to raise a new No. 1 Squadron and was back in time to take part with it in the battle of Neuve Chapelle. He commanded it at the capture of Hill 60 and in the battle of Aubers Ridge. In August 1915 he was promoted lieutenant-colonel and recalled to England.

The following November Salmond was given command of the 5th Wing, Royal Flying Corps, in Egypt. In July 1916 he was promoted temporary brigadier-general with command of the Middle East Brigade, Royal Flying Corps, which had developed out of his original force of one

423

wing, an extra squadron, and an aircraft park. He was rapidly gaining a reputation for accomplishing difficult tasks and for inspiring the most unlikely material to do first-class work. The conditions in which the brigade worked were arduous and unpleasant. Operations had to be organized over the deserts of Mesopotamia and among the mountains of Greece. Salmond set himself to deal with every variety of obstacle and made sure, by means of personal visits, that he understood the peculiar troubles of every unit in his brigade. These visits invariably contributed something to efficiency, partly because they led to useful improvements in equipment or methods, and not least because they were essentially friendly and stimulating in character. His knack of maintaining good human relationships, added to the zest and devotion with which he sought practical solutions for the many problems, created in the Middle East Brigade an intense *esprit de corps*. The help given by the Royal Flying Corps in the campaigns was warmly acknowledged by the army commanders in Salonika, East Africa, Egypt, and Palestine. It had consisted of all kinds of tactical support from artillery spotting and reconnaissance to the pursuit of retreating columns and the heavy bombing of Turkish transport behind the front. Salmond applied the principles afterwards developed in the tactical air forces of the war of 1939–1945, in circumstances and with air equipment which demanded the highest spirit and a genius for improvisation and adaptation. He recognized clearly the strategical implications and arranged his principal air bases with so sure an eye that many of them remained in use right up to the rearrangement of 1946 when British forces were removed from Egypt. By the middle of 1917 his brigade was fully organized, well sited, and well served. In August of that year he returned to England in order to take command of a training brigade, but this respite lasted only until the following January. Then he went back to the Middle East, as major-general, to take over the Middle East Command, Royal Flying Corps, a post which he held until 1921. This command was preserved during the interval between the wars; it served the Allied cause well in the war of 1939–1945; and it was the creation of Salmond who, with a prescience and breadth of outlook uncommon among air officers of his day, understood its full significance and possibilities. As a command, it embraced all the territory covered by the earlier brigade, but it also spread itself beyond to the Persian Gulf and India.

While the war was still in progress Salmond laid out a line of air communications between Cairo and South Africa, making a chain of aerodromes which were used later by the flying pioneers and finally adopted by Imperial Airways. After the armistice he remained for three years in the Middle East consolidating the plan of which he was the author and chief engineer.

Salmond returned to England in 1922 as air member for supply and research, Air Council. He was given a permanent commission in the Royal Air Force as air vice-marshal in 1919. In 1927 he took over the command in India; at the end of 1928, when there was a revolution in Afghanistan, he arranged for the evacuation of Europeans from Kabul by air. He was promoted air marshal in 1929. In September 1931 he returned to England in order to become air officer commanding-in-chief Air Defence of Great Britain. He was promoted air chief marshal in January 1933, and became chief of Air Staff on 1 April of the same year.

Salmond was appointed C.B. in 1918, C.M.G. and K.C.M.G. in 1919, and K.C.B. in 1926; he was awarded the D.S.O. in 1917. The honorary degree of LL.D. was conferred upon him by Cambridge University in 1919. He married in 1910 Margaret Mary, eldest daughter of William Carr, of Ditchingham Hall, Norfolk, and had a son and three daughters. He died in London 27 April 1933.

[*The Times*, 28 April 1933; private information.]

E. COLSTON SHEPHERD

published 1949

SCOTT Sir Percy Moreton

(1853–1924)

First baronet

Admiral, the son of Montagu Scott, solicitor, by his wife, Laura Kezia Snelling, was born in Canonbury, North London, 10 July 1853. He was educated at Eastman's Naval Academy, Southsea, and entered the *Britannia* as a naval cadet in September 1866. In December 1867 he was appointed to the *Forte* frigate and sailed in her to the East Indies, where she became flagship of Commodore Sir Leopold Heath. He was rated midshipman in June 1868, and returned to England at the end of a three and a half years' commission in February 1872. After a year's service in the new armoured battleship *Hercules*, having been promoted sub-lieutenant in December 1872, he joined the *Excellent* gunnery school ship in order to complete examinations. When the Ashanti War broke out Scott volunteered for service on the West coast of Africa and was appointed to the *Active*, flagship of (Sir) William Hewett. He arrived too late for active service in the campaign. He remained in the *Active* until April 1877—a memorable commission covering a number of minor operations on the

West coast of Africa. Scott was made lieutenant in November 1875, and recommended in dispatches for services in the Congo expedition of that year. In September 1877, he was appointed to the *Excellent* for a gunnery course, and stayed in the school as junior staff officer until July 1880.

Scott was then appointed gunnery lieutenant of the *Inconstant*, flagship of Lord Clanwilliam's squadron, which was commissioned for a voyage round the world, was detained on the way for service at the Cape during the Boer War, and on the completion of the cruise was sent to the Mediterranean for the Egyptian campaign at Alexandra in 1882. Scott did valuable service in mounting some heavy Egyptian guns for the army, for which he was praised in military dispatches. In November 1882 he was appointed to the *Cambridge* gunnery school at Devonport as senior staff officer, and in April 1883 was again sent to the *Excellent*, where he remained until promoted commander in September 1886. From September 1887 until February 1890 he was commander of the *Edinburgh*, Mediterranean station, and then returned to the *Excellent* for another three years, during which he was very active in converting the gunnery school at Whale Island into a model naval barracks and training establishment. Scott was promoted captain in January 1893, and after two and a half years' service on the ordnance committee at Woolwich, was in command of the *Scylla* in the Mediterranean from May 1896 to July 1899. While in that ship he developed and introduced a number of valuable inventions in signal apparatus and gunnery appliances. By the latter means he became a pioneer in the improvement of gunnery practice in the fleet and established a record for marksmanship and rate of fire in the firing of his ship.

In September 1899 Scott was appointed captain of the *Terrible* for service on the China station; but owing to the trouble impending in South Africa, the ship proceeded via the Cape, and was detained there until March 1900. On the outbreak of the South African War, Scott rendered valuable service by devising land mountings and carriages for the heavy 4.7-inch naval guns which were landed for the defence of Ladysmith and undoubtedly saved the situation. He also mounted on mobile mountings a number of 4.7-inch and 6-inch guns which accompanied the naval brigades attached to the armies. For these very valuable services he received the C.B. (1900). For a short time Scott acted as military commandant at Durban. He reached the China station at the time of the Boxer rebellion, and once again he was able to devise mountings and to land heavy guns, which were used in the international operations against the Boxers. On the conclusion of the land operations Scott devoted himself with ardour to improving the gunnery efficiency of his own ship, and by example that of the whole squadron. The *Terrible* achieved remarkable success in her firings, and as a result Scott's methods were adopted throughout the service, thereby raising the standard of shooting to a far higher level. On returning home in 1902 Scott received a great public welcome, and was awarded the C.V.O. by King Edward VII.

In April 1903 Scott was appointed captain of the *Excellent*, and during the two years until his promotion to flag rank in 1905, made full use of his opportunities for improving the gunnery appliances and training of the fleet. As flag officer he was immediately given the new appointment of inspector of target practice, which he held until July 1907. The duties required him to attend the firing practices of the fleet, report on them, and make suggestions for improvements. Scott showed characteristic energy, inventiveness, and originality of mind in this task, with the result that the efficiency of the firing practice of the fleet was doubled during these two years. The gunlayer's test and battle practice at towed targets were two of the methods which he instituted. In July 1906, on the occasion of the launch of the *Dreadnought*, he was created K.C.V.O. by King Edward. In July 1907 he was given his first and only flag appointment at sea in command of the second cruiser squadron (flagship H.M.S. *Good Hope*) of the Channel fleet, then under the command of Lord Charles Beresford. During the first year the personal relations between the two admirals became badly strained: both were naturally impulsive and critical of higher authority, and after an unfortunate incident in which Scott hoisted what Beresford considered an insubordinate signal, the Admiralty decided to remove the second cruiser squadron from the Channel fleet, and sent it under Scott on a special cruise to South Africa in connexion with the Convention of the Union of that Dominion, and to South America to show the flag. Scott was highly successful in this Imperial mission, and, having been promoted to vice-admiral in December 1908, hauled down his flag in February 1909. He spent the next four years, until promotion to admiral and retirement in March 1913, in developing and pressing for the introduction of various improvements in gunnery apparatus, particularly his invention of the director firing system. In 1910 he was promoted K.C.B., and given an award of £2,000 by the government for his various inventions and appliances, having had a previous award of £8,000 in 1905. He obtained considerable financial advantage from the arrangements which he made with armament firms for the production of his inventions. This enabled him to accept the offer of a baronetcy which was conferred on him in February 1913.

Soon after the outbreak of the European War, Scott was appointed to the Admiralty for special service, and continued on duty until May 1918. His first work was to fit out a fleet of dummy battleships by converting sixteen merchant steamers so as to give them with fair accuracy the appearance of some of the most important units of the British navy. He was then employed on various duties as adviser on the gunnery efficiency of the fleet and on measures for coping with the submarine danger, which, as he had prophesied some months before the War, had become very serious. In September 1915, when the zeppelins had begun their raids over England, he was appointed by Mr. Balfour, then first lord, to undertake the gunnery defence of London against air attack until the army should be ready to take over the work, which it did in the following February. The Anti-Aircraft Corps which Scott created laid the foundations of the elaborate system of anti-aircraft defence which in the end largely defeated the zeppelin danger.

After the War was over Scott wrote a series of letters to *The Times*, reiterating the theory, which he had first propounded in June 1914, that the day of the battleship was over owing to the development of submarines and aircraft; he urged that Great Britain should no longer build battleships, but rely in future on smaller craft and submarines. He died in London 18 October 1924.

Scott was a man of very remarkable inventive power, and his numerous devices, inventions, and methods for improving the gunnery of the fleet, especially after he had obtained the powerful support of his senior, Admiral of the Fleet Lord Fisher, for their adoption in the service, were of immense advantage to the royal navy in the European War. His methods and apparatus for improving gun drill and thereby the rate of loading, and also for training gun layers in accurately and rapidly aligning their weapons, have been adopted in all the navies of the world. The Scott director system for laying and firing numbers of guns from one gunsight was of particular value in the War, and has also been universally adopted. Scott's persistence in pressing his views, and his contempt for officers of the older school, continually brought him into conflict with the authorities, and, although he was popular with the lower deck, his equals and superiors in rank did not always find him easy to work with. He was a fine seaman, but his judgement in tactical matters was frequently at fault; and it is upon his inventive genius and the services which it enabled him to render to his country that his claim to fame principally rests.

Scott was twice married: first, in 1894 to Teresa Roma, daughter of Sir Frederick Dixon-Hartland, baronet, whom he divorced in 1911; secondly, in 1914 to Fanny Vaughan Johnston, daughter of Thomas Ramsay Dennis and formerly wife of Colonel A. P. Welman. He had two sons and a daughter by his first wife. The elder son was lost as a midshipman in the *Defence* at the battle of Jutland (1916). The younger son, Douglas Winchester (born 1907), succeeded as second baronet.

A cartoon of Scott by 'Spy' appeared in *Vanity Fair* 17 September 1903. [Admiralty Records; Sir P. Scott, *Fifty Years in the Royal Navy*, 1919; private information.]

VINCENT W. BADDELEY

published 1937

SLESSOR John Cotesworth

(1897–1979)

Sir

Marshal of the Royal Air Force, was born at Ranikhet in India 3 June 1897, the eldest in the family of three sons and one daughter of Major Arthur Kerr Slessor, of the Sherwood Foresters, and his wife, Adelaide Cotesworth. He was educated at Haileybury, where he later claimed to have been 'rather an idle boy with a capacity for making friends and getting a good deal of fun out of life, but with a marked distaste for hard work'. An attack of poliomyelitis as a child left him lame in both legs, and an army medical board in 1914 rejected him as 'totally unfit for any form of military service'. But a family friend responsible for selecting officers for the Royal Flying Corps enabled him to circumvent regulations. He was commissioned on his eighteenth birthday, and four months later was seeking vainly to engage a Zeppelin night raider over central London.

Posted to No. 17 Squadron in the Middle East, Slessor spent some months bombing and strafing Turks in the Sinai and rebels in the Sudan until in the spring of 1916 he was sent home to England with a wound in the thigh and the MC. After a tour as an instructor at Northolt, he went to France in May 1917 as a flight commander in No. 5 Squadron, with whom he served until June 1918. He returned to England to lead a squadron at the Central Flying School, Upavon, of which he briefly took command in September. The armistice reduced him to his substantive rank of flight-lieutenant in the new Royal Air Force. Following a bitter quarrel with a senior officer, Slessor became sufficiently disenchanted with Service life to request demobilization. But after just two months as a civilian, he accepted a short-service commission early in 1920, and in the spring of 1921 went to India as a flight commander in No. 20 Squadron, flying Bristol fighters. He then served briefly on the air headquarters staff before attending the third course at the new RAF Staff College at Andover. From 1925 to 1928 he commanded No. 4 (Army Co-operation) Squadron at

Farnborough. In 1928 he was posted to the plans branch of the Air Ministry's Directorate of Operations and Intelligence, where he remained until 1931.

This was the decisive period in Slessor's formative years. He was already marked as an officer of exceptional ability, charm, and force of personality. But his thinking and most of his experience had centred upon the role of aircraft in direct support of ground forces. In his years at the Air Ministry, he now became one of the most passionate disciples of Lord Trenchard and his theories of strategic air power as a war-winning weapon. Slessor was one of that select group of officers which included C. F. A. Portal (later Viscount Portal of Hungerford) and (Sir) Ralph Cochrane, who were clearly destined for the highest ranks of the air force. In the years that followed, he served a second tour of duty in India where he almost died in the Quetta earthquake and won a DSO commanding a wing in the Waziristan operations. But he achieved greater distinction for his lecturing as an instructor at the Army Staff College, Camberley, for his authorship of the RAF manual on army co-operation, and for his book *Air Power and Armies*, published in 1936. The book reflected the belief not only of Slessor, but of his generation of senior airmen, in the moral impact of air attack upon civilian populations. He wrote: 'In air operations against production, the weight of attack will inevitably fall upon a vitally important, and not by nature very amenable, section of the community—the industrial workers, whose morale and sticking power cannot be expected to equal that of the disciplined soldier. And we should remember that if the moral effect of air bombardment was serious seventeen years ago, it will be immensely more so under modern conditions.' Here was the core of the strategic theory which would lie at the heart of the British bomber offensive against Germany, and of which Slessor was among the most articulate proponents.

From 1937 to 1940 Slessor held the critical post of director of plans at the Air Ministry. It must be said that in this role he shared his colleagues' delusions about the power of bombers to influence the course of the war even when these were few in number, and were wholly inadequately trained and equipped to carry out the tasks to which the RAF war plans committed them. In a memorandum to the chief of air staff four days after the outbreak of war, Slessor urged an all-out bomber attack on the Germans: 'Although our numerical inferiority in the air is a most important factor, it should not be allowed to obscure other potent considerations. We are now at war with a nation which possesses an impressive façade of armed might, but which, behind that façade, is politically rotten, weak in financial and economic resources, and already heavily engaged on another front [Poland]. The lessons of history prove that victory does not always go to the big battalions. At present we have the initiative. If we seize it now we may gain important results; if we lose it by waiting we shall probably lose more than we gain.' In the two years that followed, the RAF painfully discovered that the difficulties of implementing Trenchard's doctrine were caused not merely by the limits on resources imposed by pre-war politicians, but also by the failure of the Service to match its skills and training to the ends it sought to achieve. Slessor must share responsibility with his generation of airmen for the lamentable shortcomings of the RAF in close support of ground and naval forces and low-level bombing techniques. It is impossible to escape the conclusion that their failure to address themselves to these problems in the same fashion as the pre-war *Luftwaffe* was influenced by the RAF's determination to find a role in war both more decisive than that of mere flying eyes and artillery for the two older Services, and independent of them.

At the end of 1940, Slessor went to the United States to take part in the 'ABC' staff conversations. In April 1941 he returned to take command of No. 5 Group of Bomber Command at perhaps the most frustrating period of the air offensive, when this was the sole means of carrying the war directly to Germany, and yet it had become evident that its impact upon the enemy was very small. In April 1942 he became assistant chief of air staff (policy), and played an important role in the development, alongside the American airmen, of the plans for Operation Pointblank (a combined air offensive against Germany, designed specifically to pave the way for the invasion of north-west Europe, which was approved at the Casablanca conference).

In February 1943 Slessor took on the role for which he is best remembered in World War II, as C-in-C of Coastal Command. He arrived at Northwood at an exceptionally difficult period in the battle of the Atlantic, when sinkings were running at an alarming level. He controlled some sixty squadrons of which thirty-four (430 aircraft) were committed to the anti-submarine war. Even with the vital assistance of Ultra decrypts of U-boat wireless traffic, which contributed decisively to the Atlantic victory, Slessor faced immense problems in extending air cover into the mid-ocean gap where convoy losses had been so heavy. He possessed only two squadrons of very long-range Liberators with the ability to operate at these distances, and the business of co-ordinating operations not only with the Admiralty but with the American and Canadian navies and air forces taxed Slessor to the utmost. He proved himself both an able administrator of large forces, and a sensitive leader and motivator of his Command.

In January 1944, a little to his own disappointment, he was taken from Coastal Command to succeed Sir Arthur (later Lord) Tedder commanding the RAF in the Mediterranean and Middle East, and acting as deputy to

General Ira Eaker of the USAAF, who was C-in-C Allied Air Forces in that theatre. Slessor shared with Eaker the disappointments and frustrations of the Italian campaign, the complexities of support for Yugoslavia, the vain efforts to supply the Warsaw insurgents. In March 1945 he was brought back to London to serve as air member for personnel, a job in which over the next three years he bore responsibility for the demobilization of the huge wartime air force. He served as commandant of the Imperial Defence College until in January 1950 he succeeded Tedder as chief of air staff. The coming of the atomic bomb had provided an entirely new dimension to air power. Both in office and after his retirement in 1953, Slessor was an impassioned advocate of the need for powerful air forces as a deterrent against war. In his retirement, from his home in Somerset he continued to produce a succession of essays, lectures, broadcast talks, and articles, and he also wrote a lively autobiography. He served as a director of Blackburn Aircraft and of the English and Scottish Investment Trust, and also as a governor of Haileybury, Sherborne, and Wellington schools.

Slessor stood foremost among the second rank of airmen of World War II, behind Portal, Tedder, and Sir Arthur Harris. Sir Maurice Dean, among the most prominent civil servants of Slessor's generation at the Air Ministry, wrote of his 'warmth, knowledge, experience and adaptability'. A devoted countryman, he maintained a lifelong devotion to fishing and shooting. His charm and force of personality won him great affection and respect among his contemporaries, although he never achieved the wider celebrity of the top airmen of the war. He shared with his generation the passionate determination to win a place for the air force alongside the two older services in the councils of national defence. His strategic vision, like theirs, was perhaps narrowed by the years of struggle to bring this about. He was appointed air commodore in 1939, air vice-marshal in 1941, air marshal in 1943, air chief marshal in 1946, and marshal of the Royal Air Force in 1950.

For his services during the war of 1914–18 he was awarded the MC (1916), the Belgian Order of Leopold (chevalier), and the Belgian croix de guerre. He was appointed to the DSO in 1937, and was created CB (1942), KCB (1943), and GCB (1948). He was a member of the French Legion of Honour, the Greek Order of Phoenix, the Norwegian Order of St. Olaf, and the Swedish Order of the Sword; he also held the American Legion of Merit and the Yugoslav Partisan Star. He received the gold medal of the Royal United Services Institute in 1936, and the Chesney memorial award in 1965.

In 1923 he married Hermione Grace, daughter of Gerald Seymour Guinness, merchant banker, and widow of Lt.-Col. Herbert Francis George Carter. They had one son and one daughter. She died in 1970. He married in 1971 Marcella Florence, widow of Brigadier Robert Thomas

Priest of the Royal Artillery, and daughter of Christopher Edward Spurgeon, engineer.

There is a portrait of Slessor by Cuthbert Orde in the possession of the Imperial War Museum, on loan to the Royal College of Defence Studies, and another in the possession of Haileybury School.

Slessor died 12 July 1979 at the Princess Alexandra Hospital, Wroughton.

[Sir John Slessor, *The Central Blue*, 1956, *Air Power and Armies*, 1936, *Strategy For The West*, 1954, and *The Great Deterrent*, 1957; Air files of the Public Record Office; private information.]

MAX HASTINGS

published 1986

SLIM William Joseph

(1891–1970)

First Viscount Slim

Field-marshal, younger son of John Slim, an iron merchant of Bristol, and his wife, Charlotte, daughter of Charles Tucker, of Burnham, Somerset, was born in Bristol 6 August 1891. The family moved to Birmingham at the turn of the century and he began his education at St. Philip's Catholic School and went on to King Edward's School where he showed a flair for literature and the clear thinking which remained a distinctive trait. He was not notable at games but was a keen member of the Officers' Training Corps and his great ambition was to be an army officer. But his parents could not afford to send him to Sandhurst or guarantee the allowance then almost essential for young officers. He took a post with the engineering firm of Stewarts & Lloyds and at the same time succeeded in getting himself accepted by the Birmingham University OTC.

In August 1914 Slim was commissioned in Kitchener's army and posted to the Royal Warwickshire Regiment. With the 9th battalion he first saw active service at Cape Helles and in August 1915 was so seriously wounded at Sari Bair that it seemed unlikely he would ever again be fit for active service. He was posted to the 12th (holding) battalion, but in October 1916, although still officially unfit for active service, went with a draft to his old battalion in Mesopotamia where he was again wounded, gained the MC, and was evacuated to India. He had been granted a regular commission, with seniority from 1 June 1915 in the West India Regiment, but in 1919 he transferred to the Indian Army. From November 1917 until January 1920 he was on the staff at army headquarters, India, becoming a GSO 2 and temporary major in November 1918. In March 1920 he was posted to the 1/ 6th Gurkha Rifles; as he had not been applied for by the regiment his reception was not cordial, but his ability was soon recognized and he was appointed adjutant. Efficient and strict, he yet became well liked and respected.

In January 1926 Slim entered the Staff College, Quetta, and although he had not the interest in games and horsemanship which counted there for so much, he soon gained the respect and friendship of his contemporaries and was without doubt the outstanding student of his time. On passing out in 1928 he was appointed to army headquarters, India, as a GSO 2 and received a brevet majority in 1930. In 1934 he became Indian Army instructor at the Staff College, Camberley, where colleagues and students testified to the brilliance which earned him the brevet of lieutenant-colonel in 1935. After attending the 1937 course at the Imperial Defence College he went back to India to command the 2/7th Gurkhas and a little over a year later was sent to command the Senior Officers School at Belgaum, with the rank of brigadier, a few months before the outbreak of war in 1939.

Slim was now given command of the 10th Indian Infantry brigade of 5th Indian division which went to Eritrea in the autumn of 1940. The Italians had occupied Gallabat on the Sudan–Abyssinia border and Slim was sent with a brigade group to retake it and to ensure that the Italians did not advance into the Sudan. Though Gallabat was captured after a hard fight, it was untenable unless the near-by Italian border post, Metemma, could also be taken before the Italians could move up their large reserves. Rather than risk being caught off balance Slim pulled out of Gallabat to positions from which he could prevent the Italians reoccupying it. Subsequent information indicated that the enemy had panicked and would have abandoned Metemma. Of his failure to attack Metemma Slim wrote later 'I could find plenty of excuses for failure, but only one *reason*—myself. When two courses of action were open to me I had not chosen, as a good commander should, the bolder. I had taken counsel of my fears.' Acceptance of blame if things went wrong and praise for his subordinates in victory were characteristic of Slim throughout his career.

Soon after Gallabat he was wounded in a surprise low-flying attack on a vehicle in which he was travelling. On recovering, in May 1941 he was given command, with the rank of major-general, of the 10th Indian division in Iraq and Syria, where he carried out a brief and successful campaign against the Vichy French forces. There followed an advance into Persia where a brisk minor action and much tactful firmness helped to ensure that Persia gave no further trouble during the war.

Much to his disappointment Slim was next recalled to India but his fears of becoming chair bound were dispelled when, on 19 March 1942, Sir A. P. (later Earl) Wavell sent him to Burma to organize a corps headquarters, which carried the rank of lieutenant-general, to take control of the two British-Indian divisions of the army retreating from Rangoon. He brought 'Burcorps' out battered and exhausted but in good heart, and on its disbandment was given command of XV Corps.

Slim's next task was to pull the chestnuts out of the fire in the closing stages of the disastrous Arakan campaign of 1942–3. His handling of this critical situation brought him into conflict with the commander-in-chief Eastern Army, who wished to relieve him of his command; but he had his way, and events vindicated his methods.

By this time Slim had evolved the strategy which was to put an end to the hitherto unbroken success of Japanese infiltration: to cover the approaches to vital areas (at this time Chittagong and Imphal) with well-stocked strongholds which were to stand fast if by-passed, to be supplied by air if necessary, and to cut the supply lines of the infiltrators. The strongholds would thus become backstops against which army or corps reserves would destroy the infiltrators before moving straight into the counter-offensive.

On being given command of the newly formed 14th Army in October 1943 Slim began to build up the administrative organization, including a highly developed air supply system, to underpin his new strategy. At the same time he saw to it that all units in the 14th Army knew what was expected of them. Wherever he went—and he went everywhere—he inspired confidence. In early 1944 the Japanese launched the grand offensive which they hoped would so shatter the Allied forces on the India–Burma border that there would be revolt in India which could be exploited by the so-called Indian National Army. In Arakan the offensive was broken in three weeks and the counter-stroke drove the Japanese from their North Arakan stronghold. At Imphal/Kohima the Japanese 15th Army suffered a disastrous defeat and over 50,000 casualties, of whom more than half were dead, and withdrew in disorder to the Chindwin. These victories earned Slim the CB and KCB and international fame.

During these critical battles Slim was harassed by two unusual command problems. General Stilwell commanding the American–Chinese forces refused to serve under the 11th Army Group, but eventually agreed to take orders from Slim until his own force reached Kamaing within striking distance of his objective of Myitkyina. Fortunately the friendship between Slim and Sir George Giffard, who commanded the 11th Army Group, ensured that this awkward situation caused no trouble. The second problem was presented by Major-General Orde Wingate. Though Slim admired Wingate's gift for leadership his confidence in Long Range Penetration was limited, he felt unsure about Wingate himself, and he strongly disapproved of fragmenting tested formations like 70th division to furnish the Chindit columns which seemed to him a private army working for private purposes. Wingate's attempt to exploit his connection with Churchill was a particular embarrassment. But operation Thursday was an Anglo-American commitment, and on 5 March it was Slim who, at the take-off airfield, authorized the fly-in of the Chindit striking force despite last-minute evidence from air-photographs of Japanese attempts to block the landing-strips.

In the reconquest of Burma, Slim's task was to capture Mandalay and consolidate on the line of the Irrawaddy from there south-westwards to its junction with the Chindwin about 100 miles distant. When on 12 November 1944 11th Army Group was replaced by Allied Land Forces South East Asia (ALFSEA) under Sir Oliver Leese, the 14th Army advance on Mandalay had already begun. Slim had hoped to trap and destroy the reconstituted Japanese 15th Army west of Mandalay on the plain bounded by the Chindwin and Irrawaddy, but by mid December he realized that it had seen its danger and withdrawn across the Irrawaddy. On 17 December he sent ALFSEA a revised plan and the next day gave his corps commanders verbal orders to put it into operation at once. Slim had taken the bit between his teeth and this, added to the fact that earlier he had refused to fly into north Burma to contact the American–Chinese forces advancing under General Sultan, was perhaps the start of a rift between him and the commander-in-chief ALFSEA which had serious repercussions, although events had vindicated Slim's handling of the operations.

The new plan put in motion a great two-pronged battle designed to cut the Japanese communications to their main base at Rangoon, envelop and destroy the 15th and 33rd Japanese Armies in north Burma, and isolate the 28th Japanese Army in Arakan for destruction later. The Japanese life-line was to be cut at Meiktila, some 80 miles south of Mandalay, while the two Japanese armies in north Burma were to be held there by what was to be made to seem the advance of the whole 14th Army on Mandalay; a deception which made full use of the romantic appeal of 'the road to Mandalay'. While XXXIII Corps, headed by a division known by the Japanese to have been in IV Corps, drove eastwards on Mandalay, IV Corps, in wireless silence, moved unostentatiously south and established a bridgehead near the confluence of the Chindwin and Irrawaddy. Thence a motorized and armoured column burst through to Meiktila, there to be supplied and reinforced by air.

Great in conception, brilliant in execution, the manœuvre mystified and misled the Japanese who took the thrust south to be the deception and so concentrated on trying to stop the thrust on Mandalay. Thus they were unable to prevent Meiktila being overrun. Their desperate efforts to retake Meiktila collapsed by the end of March and meanwhile the garrison of Mandalay left to fight to the last were destroyed. The failure to retake Meiktila sealed the fate of the Japanese Burma Area Army whose commander-in-chief described it as 'the master stroke'.

On 1 April 1945 Slim began the drive on Rangoon. One corps, with most of the armour, pursued the remnants of the 15th and 33rd Japanese armies down the Mandalay–Rangoon road while another drove down the Irrawaddy valley against the 28th Japanese Army, the remnants of which got penned in the Pegu Yomas and as planned were destroyed later. On 5 May 1945 the 14th Army linked up with the amphibious force which had landed unopposed in Rangoon two days earlier. So ended the brilliant series of victories which went far to substantiate Lord Mountbatten's view that 'Slim was the finest general the Second World War produced'. Throughout the campaign Slim was invariably at hand at vital moments to help if needed.

The day after Rangoon was taken over by 14th Army Slim was told by the commander-in-chief of ALFSEA that he proposed to make a change in the command of 14th Army for the invasion of Malaya, and offered him Burma Command. Slim refused it and said that as it seemed that the high command had lost confidence in him he would apply to the commander-in-chief in India to be allowed to retire. There was dismay in 14th Army and at GHQ India, and it was not long before the direct intervention of the CIGS, Lord Alanbrooke, resulted in Slim's supercession being cancelled.

He was promoted full general 1 July 1945 and was shortly afterwards himself appointed commander-in-chief ALFSEA, taking up the appointment on 10 August 1945. At the beginning of 1946 he was recalled to England to resuscitate the Imperial Defence College and on completion of his two years as commandant he retired from the army and was appointed deputy chairman of the Railway Executive. This appointment was short-lived for on 1 November 1948 he was recalled to the army to be chief of the imperial general staff and two months later was promoted field-marshal. He visited every British command overseas as well as India, Pakistan, Canada, the United States, Australia, and New Zealand. Before his term had expired he was nominated the next governor-general of Australia. He took office in 1953 and soon established himself in the affections of the Australian people as 'a human being who understands how human beings think'. Lord Casey considered that Australia was very fortunate in having him as governor-general. Slim made it his business to seek out Australia and the Australians and meet them as a man who had something to contribute, and when he relinquished office after an extended term the prime minister of Australia gave it as his opinion that there never had been two people who achieved a greater hold on the affections and regard of the Australian people than had Sir William and Lady Slim.

On leaving Australia in 1960 Slim accepted four active directorships and membership of the board of advice of the National Bank of Australasia. Eleven universities, including Oxford and Cambridge, conferred honorary degrees on him and in 1962 he was master of the Clothworkers' Company. He was a freeman of the City of London and between 1944 and 1960 was colonel of three regiments. In 1963 he was appointed deputy constable and lieutenant-governor of Windsor Castle and became constable and governor the following year, a post which he held until shortly before his death. Before 1939 he published many short stories under the pen-name of Anthony Mills. His book, *Defeat into Victory* (1956), was considered one of the finest published on the war of 1939–45 and sold over a hundred thousand copies. His other two books, *Courage and other Broadcasts* (1957) and *Unofficial History* (1959), a collection of reminiscences many of which had appeared in *Blackwood's*, were also very successful.

His robust appearance and determined jutting chin gave an impression of ruthlessness, but nothing could be further from the truth. Kindly and approachable with a quiet sense of humour so evident in his book, *Unofficial History*, he possessed tremendous fortitude and determination and, in all walks of life, he inspired the confidence given to a great leader. Once a course of action had been decided he carried it through whatever the difficulties: he lived up to his tenet that 'the difficult is what you do today, the impossible takes a little longer'. His humility about his own achievements is exemplified by a remark he made to a friend on learning that he was to be chief of the imperial general staff 'I only hope I can hold it down'.

Slim was appointed CBE (1942), to the DSO (1943), CB and KCB (1944), GBE (1946), GCB (1950), GCMG (1952), GCVO (1954), KG (1959), and was created a viscount in 1960. He married in 1926 Aileen, daughter of the Revd John Anderson Robertson, minister at Corstorphine, Edinburgh. He had one daughter and one son, John Douglas (born 1927), who also entered the army and who succeeded him when he died in London 14 December 1970. After a public funeral with full military honours at St. George's Chapel, Windsor, Slim was cremated privately.

The National Army Museum has a portrait by Leonard Boden. There is also a portrait by T. C. Dugdale.

[Lord Slim's own writings and his record of service; biographical record in the Australian National Library; S. Woodburn Kirby (Official History), *The War Against Japan*, vols. ii–v, 1958–69; Sir Geoffrey Evans, *Slim as Military Commander*,

1969; Ronald Lewin, *Slim: the Standardbearer*, 1976; private information; personal knowledge.]

M. R. ROBERTS

published 1981

STIRLING (Archibald) David

(1915–1990)

Sir

Founder of the Special Air Service Regiment, was born 15 November 1915 at Keir, Stirlingshire, the third son and fourth child in the family of four sons and two daughters of Brigadier-General Archibald Stirling of Keir, of the Scots Guards and later MP for West Perthshire, and his wife Margaret Mary, daughter of Simon Fraser, fifteenth Baron Lovat. His childhood, mostly spent at Keir, was a happy one. He was educated at Ampleforth and, for a brief period, at Trinity College, Cambridge. Soon after leaving Cambridge, without a degree, he decided that he wanted to climb Mount Everest and, with this in mind, spent some time climbing in Switzerland and later in the American and Canadian Rockies. On the outbreak of war in September 1939 he returned from North America to join the Scots Guards Supplementary Reserve, of which he had become a member the previous year.

Early in 1941 the newly raised Guards Commando, for which he volunteered as soon as he had been commissioned and which he found more congenial than ordinary regimental soldiering, sailed for the Middle East as part of Layforce, consisting of three commando units commanded by a friend of his, Brigadier (Sir) Robert Laycock. Later in 1941 Layforce was disbanded, leaving Stirling at a loose end, but at least in a theatre of war. This offered him the opportunity he needed. The war in the desert had by this time settled down into a slogging match between the opposing armies and Stirling turned a fertile mind to the overall strategic situation. What he quickly grasped was the possibility of turning the enemy's flank by sending well-equipped raiding parties through the allegedly impassable Sand Sea to strike at worthwhile targets far behind the enemy's front line.

Gaining access to the commander-in-chief Middle East, General Sir Claude Auchinleck, by what can best be described as shock tactics, Stirling, still to all appearances an unremarkable subaltern of twenty-five, with little or no military experience, managed to win his confidence, convince him of the soundness of his ideas, and gain from him authority to recruit at the end of July 1941 six officers and sixty other ranks, a small-scale raiding force to be known, misleadingly, as L detachment Special Air Service brigade. He was promoted to captain.

Stirling's first operation, in November 1941 by parachute, was a total failure. But he did not let this deter him, and General Auchinleck, greatly to his credit, continued to back him. Fortunately L detachment's next, land-borne, raids, which followed immediately and were carried out with the invaluable help of the Long Range Desert Group, were spectacularly successful. In two weeks ninety enemy aircraft were destroyed on the ground. They were the first of a succession of no less brilliant operations planned and led by Stirling himself, who was quickly promoted to major (January 1942) and then to lieutenant-colonel (July 1942). In their planning he showed remarkable imagination and resourcefulness. In their execution his personal courage and utter determination were unsurpassed. He possessed above all the ultimate quality of a leader, the gift of carrying those he led with him on enterprises that by any rational standards seemed certain to fail and convincing them that under his leadership they were bound to succeed. Stirling was appointed to the DSO in 1942, and also became an officer of the Legion of Honour and of the Order of Orange Nassau.

By the time Stirling was taken prisoner in Tunisia in January 1943 the potential value of the SAS and of his contribution to military thinking had been generally recognized. As he had intended it should, the regiment went on to play an important part in the Mediterranean and later in the European theatres where, without their founder's outstanding leadership, but using his methods, they achieved a series of remarkable successes.

Stirling escaped from prison in Germany four times and was eventually shut up in Colditz. On his return to Great Britain in May 1945, his first thought was to take full advantage of the obvious opportunities for SAS operations offered by the war against Japan. But before he could put his plans into execution, the war in the Far East was over and by the end of 1945 the SAS had been disbanded. In due course the SAS was, however, reconstituted in the shape of one regular and two territorial regiments. With these Stirling, who as founder had been active in securing their reconstitution, remained in continual contact.

After the war Stirling's imagination was captured by Africa and its problems, to which he was thereafter to devote much time and energy. He settled in Southern Rhodesia and in 1947 became president of the newly founded Capricorn Africa Society, set up, largely on his initiative, to help find a solution to Africa's innumerable racial, economic, social, and political problems, which he felt could not safely be ignored. His efforts were overtaken by political events and he returned to Britain in 1961. In 1974 he organized GB75, to run essential services, such as power stations, in the event of a general strike. He then turned to fighting left-wing extremism in trade unions, by backing the Movement for True Industrial Democracy (Truemid).

Six feet six inches tall, with a deceptively vague and casual manner, Stirling had a very strong personality. He was appointed OBE in 1946 and knighted in 1990 by when, half a century on, the full extent of his achievement had finally been recognized. He died in the London Clinic 4 November 1990. He never married.

[Alan Hoe, *David Stirling*, 1992; John Strawson, *A History of the SAS Regiment*, 1984; personal knowledge.]

FITZROY MACLEAN

published 1996

STOCKWELL Hugh Charles

(1903–1986)

Sir

General, was born 16 June 1903 in Jersey, the only son and youngest of three children of Lieutenant-Colonel Hugh Charles Stockwell, OBE, of the Highland Light Infantry, later chief constable of Colchester, and his wife, Gertrude Forrest. He spent his early childhood in India with his parents before attending school at Cothill House in Abingdon, Marlborough College, and the Royal Military College, Sandhurst. Commissioned into the Royal Welch Fusiliers on 1 February 1923, he was one of a small number of postwar officers among the veterans of the war of 1914–18. High spirited, professionally keen, a proficient rugby football, hockey, and cricket player, he was quickly accepted by both groups.

Garrison life in England and Germany palled, however. 'Hughie' Stockwell was seconded to the Royal West African Frontier Force, serving from 1929 to 1935 as a Vickers machine-gun officer, a position which led to an instructor's post at the Small Arms School, Netheravon, in 1935–8. War approached. The Territorial Army was expanding and, without attending the Staff College, in 1938 he was made brigade-major of 158th—the Royal Welch—brigade at Wrexham, an exceptional appointment. However, his reputation as a leader suggested his employment in the 'special companies' formed hastily in April 1940, for independent tasks in the flagging Norwegian campaign. Promoted to lieutenant-colonel, he commanded a group of these units in the operations, and was appointed to the DSO (1940). He was then made commandant of the special forces training centre at Lochailort.

In June 1942 he led the 2nd Royal Welch Fusiliers in the Madagascar landings. He was promoted to brigadier, commanding the 30th East African and then, from January 1943, the 29th Independent Infantry brigade group during the battles for Arakan and northern Burma. For his leadership in lengthy operations, notably his personal influence in maintaining the morale of his soldiers, he was created CBE (1945).

In January 1945 he was appointed commander, 82nd West African division in Burma. This completed a rise from major to major-general in less than five years, and although he was only forty-two years of age he was confirmed as a general officer at the end of the war. Successively commander of the Home Counties District (1946–7) and 44th Territorial division, and the 6th Airborne division (1947–8), he was responsible for the evacuation of the latter and all other British troops from Palestine in 1948. His friendly but firm relationship with the Jewish authorities ensured a peaceful withdrawal despite late attempts to frustrate British demolition of selected facilities. Appointed CB in 1946, he was promoted to KBE in 1949.

An inspired selection placed him next as commandant of the Royal Military Academy, Sandhurst (1948–50). His early choice of a scooter bearing a major-general's two stars to carry him about the grounds characterized him: unpretentious, practical, and approachable, he moved easily between formal occasions, such as the sovereign's parade, to informal association in the training field with instructors and cadets. Unrecognized by two late returning cadets on one occasion, he helped to push them over the wall to avoid detection at the gate.

After two years with the 3rd division, he was promoted to lieutenant-general and command of the land forces in Malaya in 1952, augmenting the policies of General Sir Gerald Templer to counter terrorism. He was active in the expansion of the Royal Malay Regiment at this time. Command of I British Corps followed (1954–6), from which he was withdrawn to lead the land forces in the Port Said and Suez canal operation in the latter part of 1956. In an environment of political and military fumbling, his resistance to impractical commitments spared his forces many difficulties. Following the seizure of the port and its southern approaches, the British forces were subjected to repeated acts of terrorism. Stockwell visited daily the areas most affected, explaining to the soldiers concerned in his friendly and direct way the need for restraint. His withdrawal plan was a model. It ensured the safety of his troops without jeopardizing the United Nations forces who relieved them. Stockwell's talents as an extrovert, practical commander were seen at their best in the politically fraught Port Said operation. He was also able to stimulate laughter in dismal circumstances. As a consequence, the army units involved disengaged in high morale.

Thereafter, as military secretary (1957–9) and adjutant-general (1959–60), in which appointment he was promoted to general in the army (1957), his name is associated with the well-being of officers and men, whose confidence he held absolutely. He was finally selected by the first Viscount Montgomery of Alamein as his successor in the post of deputy supreme allied commander, Europe (1960–4). His first step, wisely, was to become the trusted friend of two American supreme commanders. On this firm basis he gathered considerable influence among the international commanders and staffs. He worked for the creation of strong mobile forces in Europe, advocating the use of tactical nuclear weapons only as a last resort.

Following his retirement in 1964, he was active in the development and maintenance of British waterways, not least as chairman of the Kennet and Avon Canal Trust from 1966 to 1975. Among many connections with the army, he was colonel of the Royal Welch Fusiliers (1952–65), Royal Malay Regiment (1954–9), and Army Air Corps (1957–63), and ADC-general to the queen (1959–62). He was further appointed KCB (1954), GCB (1959), and a grand officer of the Legion of Honour (1958). He was also awarded a bar to his DSO (1957).

Tall and fair, Stockwell had striking features, notably piercing blue eyes above a beaky nose, and an expression daunting when he was angry, but more frequently relieved by an engaging smile. In 1931 he married Joan Rickman, daughter of Charles and Marion Garrard, of independent means, of Kingston Lisle, Berkshire. They had two daughters. Stockwell died 27 November 1986 at the Royal Air Force Hospital, Wroughton.

[Royal Welch Fusilier archives, Regimental Headquarters, Caernarfon; private information; personal knowledge.]

ANTHONY FARRAR-HOCKLEY

published 1996

STUDDERT KENNEDY Geoffrey Anketell

(1883–1929)

Priest and poet, was born 27 June 1883 in Leeds, the seventh child in the family of seven sons and two daughters of the Revd William Studdert Kennedy, vicar of St Mary's, Quarry Hill, Leeds, and his second wife Jeanette Anketell. There were also one son and four daughters of a first marriage. Educated at Leeds Grammar School, he graduated in classics and divinity at Trinity College, Dublin, in 1904, after which he taught for two years at a school in West Kirby in Liverpool. Following a year of ordination training at Ripon Clergy College, he was ordained in 1908 to a curacy at Rugby parish church, moving from there in 1912 to be curate at Leeds parish church. Appointed as vicar of St Paul's, Worcester, in 1914, a year later he became a chaplain to the armed forces and began the wartime ministry among the troops in France and Flanders for which he is most remembered.

His considerable natural gifts as a preacher were combined with a talent for poetry, particularly dialect verse in the manner of the barrack-room ballads of J. Rudyard Kipling. In the carnage and suffering of the trenches his strongly sacramental Christianity was communicated in memorable addresses and in colloquial verse of sometimes powerful simplicity, which brought together the passion of Christ and the doubt, fear, and courage of soldiers caught in the squalid stalemate of the Flanders trenches. Studdert Kennedy preached a suffering God, Christ the revealer, 'pierced to the heart by the sorrow of the sword'. The experience of war made him question both the metaphysical assumption of an impassible God, and the hortatory patriotic moralism of many contemporary churchmen and political leaders. He could contrast sharply (in *Peace Rhymes of a Padre*) the God of glory in Isaiah's vision with the God revealed in the suffering Christ.

> God, I hate this splendid vision—
> all its splendour is a lie...
> And I hate the God of power on
> His hellish heavenly throne...
> Thou hast bid us seek Thy glory,
> in a criminal crucified...
> For the very God of Heaven is not
> Power, but Power of Love.

A bitter poem from the end of the war saw the statesmen meeting at Versailles to agree to a peace treaty as those who crucified Christ anew.

After the war a number of volumes of his collected poems were published, the most notable being *Rough Rhymes of a Padre* (1918), *Peace Rhymes of a Padre* (1920), *Songs of Faith and Doubt* (1922), and *The Unutterable Beauty* (1927).

Given the nickname 'Woodbine Willie' by the troops, he once described his chaplain's ministry as taking 'a box of fags in your haversack and great deal of love in your heart' and laughing and joking with those he was called to serve. 'You can pray with them sometimes; but pray for them always.' Ministering on the front line under fire he showed conspicuous bravery and was awarded the MC for his tending of the wounded under fire during the attack on the Messines ridge. He was slightly built and liked to joke in public about his prominent ears and simian features, though contemporaries were much more likely to be arrested by the large and melancholy brown eyes.

Demobilized in 1919 he was appointed a chaplain to the king. In 1922 he left his Worcester parish to run the church of St Edmund King and Martyr in Lombard Street in the City of London, a non-parochial cure, which left him free for his major postwar work as 'messenger' of the Industrial Christian Fellowship, which had come into being in 1920 as a result of the amalgamation of the Christian Social Union and the Navvy Mission Society. Critical alike of Marxist socialism and capitalism, Studdert Kennedy commanded considerable audiences for his addresses during the ICF's missions and crusades in the years of the depression. He was sure that his Christianity had political consequences, but that it was religion not political panaceas that met human need. Archbishop William Temple, who described him as 'the finest priest I have known', characterized him as evangelical without a trace of Puritanism, and fired by a strong Catholic sacramentalism, with the cross at the heart of it all. The suffering of war and the suffering of the depression were alike uniquely met by the crucified God.

In 1914 he married Emily, daughter of Alfred Catlow, coal merchant; they had three sons. It was on an ICF crusade that Kennedy died in Liverpool 8 March 1929.

[J. K. Mozley (ed.), *G. A. Studdert Kennedy, by his Friends*, 1929; Roy Fuller, '"Woodbine Willie" Lives', in *Owls and Artificers*, 1971; Gerald Studdert-Kennedy, *Dog-Collar Democracy: the Industrial Christian Fellowship, 1919–1929*, 1982; Alan Wilkinson, *The Church of England and the First World War*, 1978; 'Woodbine Willie', (centenary assessment) in *Church Times*, vol. xxiv, part 6, 1983.]

D. G. ROWELL

published 1993

(1872–1960)

Sir

Rear-admiral, was born in Alverstoke, Gosport, 6 September 1872, the son of fleet-paymaster John Thomas Sueter and his wife, Ellen Feild Lightbourn. He entered the *Britannia* in 1886, served as a midshipman in the *Swiftsure*, flagship on the Pacific station, was promoted lieutenant in 1894, and appointed to the *Vernon* to qualify as a torpedo specialist in 1896. He commanded the destroyer *Fame* at the diamond jubilee naval review of 1897, and after a further two years' service on the staff of the *Vernon* was appointed in 1899 to the *Jupiter* for torpedo duties.

In 1902 Sueter received an appointment to the gunboat *Hazard*, at the time commanded by (Sir) Reginald Bacon and recently commissioned as the first parent ship for submarines, of which the Holland boats were just entering for service as the navy's first submarines. While serving in the *Hazard*, Sueter distinguished himself by entering the battery compartment of the submarine A.1, after an explosion caused by a concentration of hydrogen, to assist in the rescue of injured men who would otherwise have been badly burned. This period of service with the early submarines led to a lifelong interest in these vessels, and in 1907 Sueter published one of the first books of real merit on this subject under the title *The Evolution of the Submarine Boat, Mine and Torpedo*.

Sueter was promoted commander in 1903 and appointed in 1904 to the Admiralty to serve as assistant to the director of naval ordnance. He returned to sea in 1906 to command the cruiser *Barham* in the Mediterranean, returning two years later to the naval ordnance department in the Admiralty. He was promoted captain in 1909.

The Admiralty at this time was considering the use of aircraft, especially airships, for reconnaissance duties with the fleet and in 1909 had placed contracts for the construction of a rigid airship to be named *Mayfly*. Sueter took a very keen interest in her construction and contributed many useful suggestions during her building. As a result he was appointed in 1910 to command the cruiser *Hermione* with the additional title of inspecting captain of airships. Unfortunately before her first flight the *Mayfly's* back was broken while she was being manœuvred out of her hangar in a high wind in 1911, an accident which for a time put a stop to further airship development for the navy. In 1912 Sueter was brought back to the Admiralty to take over the new air department and much of the rapid development of the seaplane as a naval aircraft was due to his enthusiasm.

Shortly before the outbreak of war in 1914, and largely on Sueter's suggestions, the naval wing broke away from its parent body, the Royal Flying
Corps, to become the Royal Naval Air Service. For his work on the development of naval flying Sueter was appointed C.B. in 1914.

Sueter was promoted commodore 2nd class shortly after the outbreak
of war and, still as director of the air department, was largely instrumental
in the rapid build-up of the R.N.A.S. to a full war strength. In this he was
encouraged by (Sir) Winston Churchill, the first lord, and by Lord Fisher,
recalled as first sea lord in October 1914. Sueter, who had continued with
some success to press for airship development, was very largely responsible for the design and rapid production of small non-rigid airships designed to search out U-boats operating in British coastal waters. In all,
some 200 of these were built and proved of great value particularly when
convoy was adopted later in the war. Sueter also interested himself in the
development of torpedo-carrying aircraft, and, working with Lieutenant
Douglas Hyde-Thomson, it was he who initiated the design which was
adopted in the navy. An early success when a Turkish supply ship was sunk
by an air-launched torpedo in the sea of Marmara in 1915 not only vindicated Sueter's ingenuity and foresight but proved to be the first step in
the development of one of the navy's most powerful weapons.

In 1915 Sueter turned his inventive mind to new avenues of service for
the R.N.A.S. and advanced the idea of providing armoured cars for the
defence of airfields established abroad. During the early months these cars
did useful work in Flanders and northern France but as the war settled into
its static phase of trench warfare their value declined. Two squadrons of
these armoured cars were sent abroad, one to Russia under Commander
Oliver Locker-Lampson and one to Egypt under the Duke of Westminster.

Sueter's restless brain, not content with the armoured car design,
concentrated on means of giving it a cross-country capability by fitting it
with caterpillar tracks. From this advance it was a short step to the development of the tank.

With the appointment of an officer of flag rank in September 1915 as
fifth sea lord with responsibility for naval aviation, Sueter was made
superintendent of aircraft construction with full responsibility for the
matériel side of all naval aircraft. At the same time he was promoted
commodore 1st class. But in 1917, after some differences of opinion with
the Board of Admiralty, he was sent to southern Italy to command the
R.N.A.S. units there. Later in the year Sueter wrote a letter to King George
V on the subject of recognition of his work, and that of two other officers
associated with him, in initiating the idea of tanks. This was passed to the
Admiralty in the normal manner and roused considerable resentment.
Sueter was informed that he had incurred their lordships' severe

displeasure and relieved of his command. He returned to England in January 1918 and despite his protests no further employment was found for him. He was placed on the retired list early in 1920 and shortly afterwards the Admiralty obtained a special order in Council to promote him to rear-admiral.

Sueter was gifted with a restless brain which he used skilfully and effectively to suggest means of overcoming difficulties, both technical and professional. He was always outspoken, and intolerant of official lethargy in any matter in which he took an interest. It was this intolerance, allied to a headstrong character, which brought to an end a naval career of considerable future promise.

After the war Sueter did much useful work in the development of the Empire air mail postal services, and he received the thanks of three successive postmasters-general for his assistance in organizing these services. In 1921 he was elected an independent member of Parliament for Hertford, remaining a member as a Conservative until the general election of 1945. He was knighted in 1934. In 1928 he wrote *Airmen or Noahs*, largely autobiographical but also attacking current concepts of naval and military warfare and advocating the development of independent air power. It was followed in 1937 by *The Evolution of the Tank*.

Sueter married in 1903 Elinor Mary de Winton (died 1948), only daughter of Sir Andrew Clarke, and had two daughters. He died at his home at Watlington, Oxfordshire, 3 February 1960. A portrait by (Sir) William Russell Flint was exhibited at the Royal Academy in 1928.

[Admiralty records; *The Times*, 5 February 1960.]

P. K. KEMP

published 1971

SYKES Frederick Hugh

(1877–1954)

Sir

Chief of air staff and governor of Bombay, was born in Croydon, Surrey, 23 July 1877. His father, Henry Sykes, who died less than two years later, was a mechanical engineer; his mother, Margaret Sykes, was a distant cousin of her husband. Sykes had 'a somewhat chequered education': five years at a preparatory school on the south coast; then from the age of fifteen two years in Paris learning French in the hope of a diplomatic career. For a time he worked in a general store in order to save money. On returning to London he entered a shipping firm; then spent some time working on tea plantations in Ceylon, eventually making a leisurely return to England via Burma, China, Japan, and the United States.

On the outbreak of the South African war, Sykes booked a passage to Cape Town and joined the Imperial Yeomanry Scouts as a trooper. He was taken prisoner by C. R. De Wet at Roodevaal but was soon released. He was next commissioned in the bodyguard of Lord Roberts and was wounded during a commando raid in 1901. Later in the year he joined the regular army and was gazetted second lieutenant in the 15th Hussars.

He served in India and West Africa, was promoted captain in 1908, and passed the Staff College in 1909. Very early on he was an enthusiast for ballooning. In 1910 he learned to fly and obtained his pilot's certificate (No. 96) in 1911. In 1912 he became commander of the Military Wing of the newly founded Royal Flying Corps. But on the outbreak of war in 1914 he was considered too junior to command the R.F.C. in action abroad, as still only an acting lieutenant-colonel. The command was given to Sir David Henderson, previously director-general of military aeronautics, and Sykes served as his chief of staff. He was succeeded as commander of the Military Wing by Major Hugh (later Marshal of the R.A.F. Viscount) Trenchard. The two men were deeply antipathetic, and a bitter argument during the takeover set the keynote to their relationship for the rest of Sykes's military career.

Trenchard's hostility was soon displayed. In November 1914 Sykes was appointed to command the R.F.C. in place of Henderson who was promoted to command the 1st division. Meanwhile Trenchard had been posted to France to take charge of one of the new operational wings into which the R.F.C. had been divided. As soon as he found that he was to be under Sykes he requested to be transferred to his original regiment. Lord Kitchener intervened to insist upon Henderson and Sykes reverting to their previous posts: an episode not calculated to improve relations.

During the next few months Henderson was on sick leave and Sykes acted as his deputy. According to Trenchard, Henderson came to the conclusion that Sykes was intriguing to replace him. Whatever the truth of it, the upshot was that Henderson developed a deep distrust of Sykes who was sent in May to Gallipoli to report on air requirements there and in July was given command of the Royal Naval Air Service in the Eastern Mediterranean when the Gallipoli campaign was at its height. He remained there until the end, carrying out his task with conspicuous success and being appointed C.M.G. in recognition.

In March 1916 Sykes was made assistant adjutant and quartermaster-general of the 4th Mounted division at Colchester. In June he became assistant adjutant-general at the War Office with the task of organizing the Machine Gun Corps. In February 1917 he was promoted temporary brigadier-general and deputy director of organization at the War Office. At the end of the year he joined the planning staff of the Supreme War Council under Sir Henry Wilson. Meanwhile the Government, on the recommendation of J. C. Smuts, strongly backed by Henderson yet opposed by Trenchard, had decided to create an independent air force with its own Ministry. Nevertheless Trenchard became the first chief of air staff, under Lord Rothermere, the first air minister; both were appointed on 3 January 1918. Henderson was made vice-president of the newly formed Air Council.

Trenchard and Rothermere soon quarrelled and Trenchard tendered his resignation on 19 March but was persuaded to defer it until after the official birth of the Royal Air Force on 1 April. On 13 April Sykes, promoted to major-general, succeeded him: a choice inevitably controversial in these circumstances; Henderson promptly resigned too. The confusion was increased by Rothermere's own resignation which took effect on the 25th. He paid a high tribute to Sykes in his resignation letter as 'this brilliant officer with his singularly luminous mind ... an ideal Chief of Staff of the Royal Air Force'.

Rothermere was succeeded by Sir William (later Viscount) Weir who retained the post until the end of the war. Sykes was chief of staff throughout this significant period and as a convinced supporter of an independent air force did much to establish the new Service. His post-war plans, however, were regarded as too grandiose by Weir's successor, (Sir) Winston Churchill, who from January 1919 held the posts of both war and air minister. He preferred those of Trenchard whom he was consulting behind Sykes's back. In February 1919 Trenchard again became chief of air staff and Sykes was shunted into the post of controller of civil aviation. One of the conditions of this appointment was that he gave up his military commission and thus ended his career in the armed Services.

In 1920 he married Isabel (died 1969), elder daughter of Andrew Bonar Law; they had one son. Sykes resigned from the Air Ministry in April 1922, dissatisfied with the financial treatment of civil aviation. He was offered but refused the governorship of South Australia, and decided to enter politics. At the general election of 1922 he was elected Unionist member for the Hallam division of Sheffield. In May 1923 he conveyed to King George V his father-in-law's letter of resignation from the premiership. He retained his parliamentary seat until 1928 when he was appointed governor of Bombay.

His term of office in India covered a period of unprecedented financial difficulties and political and industrial unrest which Sykes faced with resolution and a patient determination to improve the lot of the common people. He would have wished for greater powers to deal more promptly and effectively with civil disobedience, but was loyal in conforming to the central Government's policy of conciliation. It was not until 1932 that emergency powers were granted; then, with civil disobedience on the decline, Sykes was able to give attention to the social and economic difficulties which he felt to be the real problem of India. When he left Bombay in 1933 he had the satisfaction of knowing that the outlook for the presidency was more hopeful than it had been five years earlier.

Sykes was again in Parliament from 1940 to 1945 as Conservative member for the Central division of Nottingham. He was chairman of government committees on meteorological services (1920–22), and broadcasting (1923), of the Broadcasting Board (1923–7), of the Miners' Welfare Commission (1934–46), of the Royal Empire Society (1938–41), and for many years honorary treasurer of the British Sailors' Society. He was also a director of various public companies. His autobiography, *From Many Angles*, was published in 1942. He died in London 30 September 1954.

Sykes was a person of high intelligence and much charm, although he did not thaw very easily. He was clearly a most capable administrator but his contribution to the formative period of the air force as an independent arm has been obscured by the hostility between him and some of his brother officers, Trenchard especially, whose opinions subsequently became gospel in the Royal Air Force, thereby conditioning much of the Service's historiography.

Sykes was appointed K.C.B. and G.B.E. in 1919, G.C.I.E. in 1928, and G.C.S.I. in 1934. He was sworn of the Privy Council in 1928. His portrait, painted by Sir William Orpen while he was chief of air staff, is at his home, Conock Manor, near Devizes. A bronze bust by L. F. Roslyn is in the Imperial War Museum.

[Sir Walter Raleigh and H. A. Jones, (Official History) *The War in the Air*, 6 vols., 1922–37; Sir F. Sykes, *From Many Angles*, 1942; Robert Blake, *The Unknown Prime Minister*, 1955; Lord Beaverbrook, *Men and Power*, 1956; Andrew Boyle, *Trenchard*, 1962; Sir Philip Joubert de la Ferté, *The Third Service*, 1955; W. J. Reader, *Architect of Air Power: the Life of the First Viscount Weir of Eastwood*, 1968; private information; personal knowledge.]

ROBERT BLAKE

published 1971

SZABO Violette Reine Elizabeth

(1921–1945)

Secret agent, was born in Paris 26 June 1921, the second child and only daughter in the family of five children of Charles George Bushell, a regular soldier, and his wife Reine Blanche Leroy, a dressmaker from Pont-Rémy, Somme, France. He held various jobs in France and England before settling in 1932 in Brixton as a second-hand motor-car dealer. From her mother's family Violette picked up fluent French, spoken with an English accent. She left the LCC school in Stockwell Road, Brixton, at fourteen to work as a shop assistant. She was under five feet five inches tall, but strikingly good-looking, with dark hair and eyes and vivacious manners.

She married in Aldershot, 21 August 1940, Étienne Michel René Szabo, a thirty-year-old Frenchman of Hungarian descent from Marseilles, who had fought in Norway with the French Foreign Legion and elected to join General de Gaulle's nascent Free French forces. He was soon posted to north Africa, and never met their only child, a daughter born 8 June 1941. He died 27 October 1942 from wounds received the previous day in battle.

To revenge him, his widow joined the independent French section of the Special Operations Executive in October 1943. During the usual para-military, parachute, and security training it emerged that she was an admirable shot. She parachuted twice into occupied France, each time as courier to Philippe Liewer, an experienced agent. Her first mission began 5–6 April 1944. They found that the Gestapo had broken up Liewer's former group of saboteur friends between Rouen and Le Havre; they returned to England by light aircraft on 30 April. Between her first and second missions she was commissioned an ensign in the First Aid Nursing Yeomanry.

She and Liewer returned to France 7–8 June 1944 to set up a new group of resisters between Limoges and Périgueux. On 10 June she and two companions, in a motor car, encountered a German roadblock at Salon-la-Tour, some thirty miles south-east of Limoges. Both sides opened fire. Violette, armed only with a sten sub-machine-gun, covered her companions' retreat through standing corn for twenty minutes until she had no more ammunition, and was taken prisoner. She said nothing she should not have done under interrogation.

On 8 August, handcuffed to a neighbour on a train bound for Germany, she crawled round offering water to her fellow prisoners while the train was under attack by the RAF. She was put in Ravensbrück concentration camp, whence she went with two SOE colleagues, Lilian Rolfe and Denise Bloch, on a working party at Torgau. They were then sent on a much fiercer one, some sixty miles eastward, at Klein Königsberg. Even her tremendously high spirits were lowered by its regime. Her companions returned from it hardly able to stand; she was not much sturdier. About 27 January 1945, shortly after their return to Ravensbrück, all three were shot dead.

She was awarded a French croix de guerre in 1944, and a posthumous George Cross in 1946.

[R. J. Minney, *Carve her Name with Pride*, 1956; M. R. D. Foot, *SOE in France*, 1968 edn.; private information.]

M. R. D. Foot

published 1993

TEDDER Arthur William

(1890–1967)

First Baron Tedder

Marshal of the Royal Air Force, was born at Glenguin in the county of Stirling 11 July 1890. He was the younger son of (Sir) Arthur John Tedder, a civil servant in the Inland Revenue who became a commissioner of customs and excise, and his wife, a distant cousin, Emily Charlotte, daughter of William Henry Bryson. The family's ancestry and background were more English than Scottish, and they lived in Scotland only during civil service appointments there. When his father moved back to London, Tedder began his serious education as a day boy at Whitgift Grammar School, Croydon, and went on to Magdalene College, Cambridge. He was placed in the second class of both parts of the historical tripos (1911–12) and was awarded the Prince Consort prize in 1914 for a dissertation on the Navy of the Restoration. He tried for a university tutorship, while his mild interest in his school and college Officers' Training Corps induced him to take a reserve commission in the Dorsetshire Regiment. But as neither civilian nor Service possibilities looked promising he rather half-heartedly applied for the Colonial Service, and finally succeeded in obtaining a cadetship to the administration in Fiji.

He had served only a few months when war broke out. With no great regret Tedder applied immediately for permission to join up, and when the governor showed reluctance to grant him leave he resigned from the Service. His selfless and strenuous efforts to return to his regiment were ironically rewarded, soon after he had put on its uniform, by incapacitation

453

with a minor knee injury, which finally made him unfit for army duty. He thereupon asked for a commission in the Royal Flying Corps and with this third start found his life's work.

After considerable delay he received a wartime course of ground and flying instruction, and in June 1916 he joined No. 25 Squadron in France, where he carried out a tour on bombing and photographic missions. His intelligence and maturity brought him to the notice of Major-General (later Viscount) Trenchard who appointed him, early in 1917, to the command of No. 70 Fighter Squadron. After a year of successful operations he was posted home to a training unit, where he remained until sent to Egypt in 1918. He had become a training expert, and so remained until the end of the war. Between 1916 and 1918 he was three times mentioned in dispatches, and in 1919 he received a permanent commission in the newly formed Royal Air Force, with the rank of squadron-leader. By accepting it he became one of those whose direction in life had been completely changed by the accident of war, and throughout his subsequent career he showed the style of the gifted civilian in uniform, rather than that of the type-cast military man. He had more interest in the theory and organization of air war than in actual flying.

In appearance Tedder had little of the traditional Service officer; with his large dark eyes, prominent ears, kindly and sometimes vague facial expressions, he seemed rather to have strayed from some cloister or quadrangle. In later life he turned this to advantage; in early years it was no help. Resigned to his unexpected career, he continued during the dull post-war years to specialize in training; commanding schools, serving at the Air Ministry, and completing a course at the Imperial Defence College. His interest in the academic side of the military profession grew steadily, and this logically led him to the Royal Air Force Staff College, where he was an instructor and assistant commandant from 1929 to 1931. Leaving with the rank of group captain, for the next two years he commanded the Air Armament School at Eastchurch, and was then posted to the Air Ministry in 1934 as director of training. After two years in this appointment he was nominated as air officer commanding, Far East, and spent the years 1936–8 in Singapore, being promoted to air vice-marshal in 1937.

In 1938 came his first major opportunity to influence future events, when he was summoned back to the Air Ministry to assume the newly created post of director-general of research and development. The British technical preparations for war were at last in full spate, and Tedder threw himself into the complicated work which was fashioning, with desperate urgency, the weapons on which the country's survival would later depend. The new monoplane fighter aircraft, the advanced bomber projects, the development of radar, sophisticated navigation, vastly improved guns, bombs, and rockets, were all under his surveillance, and were pressed forward with all the haste made necessary by the lateness of the political realization of the nation's peril. When war began he continued this work inside the newly established Ministry of Aircraft Production, as deputy member of the air staff for development and production. In 1940 the appointment of the ebullient Lord Beaverbrook to oversee aircraft production inevitably involved Tedder in friction with the minister, and through him with the prime minister, whose first view of Tedder was therefore painted in the colours of an obstinate obstructionist. When the Royal Air Force commander in the Middle East asked for him as his deputy the request was refused, and another senior officer was dispatched, but his aircraft was forced down in Sicily, and Tedder was appointed as the second choice.

In late 1940 the outlook in the Middle East, as elsewhere, was grim in the extreme, and it was no better when Tedder was promoted to commander-in-chief in June 1941. Churchill, dismayed by what he thought was a too conservative estimate by Tedder of the RAF strength which would be available for the relief of Tobruk, tried to remove him, but (Viscount) Portal, chief of air staff, threatened to resign if this was done, and Tedder remained in his post. The detailed history of this campaign is a complicated fabric of triumphs and disasters, of which the common factors are continuous operations on a number of different fronts by an air command almost cut off from the home base of Britain, with continuously inadequate resources. Not until the entry of the United States into the war, in December 1941, could any hope be seen for a change in the balance of power, and not until the battle of El Alamein any definite sign of ultimate victory. Throughout this period Tedder's policy had three main prongs: a first-class administrative and technical backing for his squadrons; a continuous attack on the Mediterranean supply lines of the Axis forces in North Africa; and the creation, through his field commander (Sir) Arthur Coningham, of a Desert Air Force closely responding to the needs of the army. Like other airmen, Tedder was alive to the danger of the generals and admirals who wanted to split the air arm into small sections each directly under land and sea units. Unlike some of these airmen, he also saw that the only way to ensure the best use of centralized air power was first to prove to the other two Services that only centralization could gain an air situation which would make support possible, and then to produce a better and more responsive support. This is what Tedder's Middle East Air Force did: and it was under its shelter that the Eighth Army retreated to and advanced from Alamein. Tedder was promoted air marshal (1941) and air chief marshal (1942).

His style of command, in these difficult times, was diplomatic and unobtrusive. He was never loud or choleric. He developed an unrivalled power to manage his contemporaries, both military and civil, and kept in close touch with his squadrons by modest, almost furtive, unheralded appearances among them, where his informal dress and manner, his dry wit and lucid explanation, had a greater effect than the most fervent of conventional exhortations. He carried a sketch-book with him, and loved to record things he had seen with simple but vivid drawings. His policies, and his gradually reinforced squadrons, finally produced, with the other two Services and later the forces of the United States, a complete victory in North Africa. In February 1943 Tedder became commander-in-chief of Mediterranean Air Command, under General Eisenhower, with responsibility for all Allied air forces in the area. With the Axis surrender in Tunisia, in May 1943, Tedder's reputation reached a high level and Churchill said to him 'I was told you were just a man of nuts and bolts. It was not true.' Throughout the war, Tedder also retained Portal's confidence and support. Tedder's task required the highest diplomatic ability, yet during the most intensive activity of this period he had to endure the loss of his wife in an air crash, having already lost a son in air operations over Berlin. The first exercises in high-level Anglo-American co-operation were inevitably difficult, arduous, and fraught with complications which could swiftly involve London and Washington, but Tedder acquitted himself with such skill as to keep friction to the minimum, and the successful invasion of Sicily and southern Italy, together with the collapse of the Italian war effort, were all completed by the end of 1943, when Eisenhower was withdrawn to England to plan and command the Allied forces for the invasion of France. With him went Tedder as his deputy supreme commander, with authority over not only the air forces assigned to the invasion (Operation Overlord) but with a call on all Allied air forces which could be brought to bear on the battles, whether assigned or not. This was a unique position, above that of any air commander, and the short time available in which to define it ensured that it contained a large element of ambiguity capable of creating great difficulty, particularly with the Americans. 'Overlord' already enjoyed the personal and detailed attentions of Churchill and Roosevelt. Fortunately Eisenhower's strength and diplomacy were fully developed, and Tedder's wisdom and subtlety, and his complete understanding of the supreme commander, were matched by Eisenhower's support and confidence in him.

The development of 'Overlord' is history. Tedder's great contributions were the top management of the largest force of war aircraft ever directed towards a single objective, his technique for the isolation of the battle area from enemy support by air interdiction, and his use of massive heavy-bomber support of major land force offensive actions (the 'Tedder carpet'). As a fringe activity, he was a continuous and vitally important influence in the not entirely uneventful maintenance of good relations between the major Allied commanders in the field, and with the politicians behind them. He had by now perfected a quite outstanding ability to handle people and resolve differences, and before the final German surrender he was able to exercise it fully. His methods, as in his earlier commands, were first intelligent perception, followed by a gentle, almost apologetic dealing with the protagonists, who were imperceptibly led to adopt the courses he put forward as their own inspired solutions. He seldom allowed the iron in his character to show, but it was there. Throughout the campaign in France and Germany he never lost sight of his foremost precept of the centralized application of air power to the campaign, and nothing would induce him to relax it. By this doctrine he could apply the crushing strength of immense air forces to each part of the theatre as required, as in the intensive attacks on the German forces attempting to break through the Ardennes in January 1945.

As the war ended, Tedder, Marshal Zhukov, and the German Field-Marshal Keitel signed an instrument of surrender in Berlin (8 May 1945) to supplement that signed in Eisenhower's HQ in Rheims. There was nothing left to do but pick up the pieces, and in this he was assisted by his second wife. In memory of Wing Commander H. G. Malcolm, VC, who had been killed in North Africa, she had been establishing and supporting the string of Malcolm Clubs which provided comfort and off-duty relaxation for all ranks of the Service and its civilians, and now he was able to give her his full assistance. During the summer of 1945 the 'Overlord' team broke up, and his future remained uncertain until the Japanese surrender halted the British planning for a Far Eastern campaign. Tedder's reputation stood unrivalled among Allied airmen and he was promoted to marshal of the Royal Air Force in September 1945 and appointed chief of the air staff on 1 January 1946, when he was raised to the peerage.

In the military backwash after a great war even so high an office is seldom onerous, and only the problems of adjusting the Service to peace gave him any difficulty, either as chief of the air staff or when, later in his appointment, he also took his seat as chairman of the combined chiefs of staff committee. In 1948 he published his Lees Knowles lectures as *Air Power in War*. At the end of his four years as chief of the air staff in 1949 he duly retired, but was persuaded to go in 1950 to Washington, during the crucial years of the outset of the cold war, to fill the post of chairman of the British Joint Services Mission and United Kingdom representative on the military committee of the newly formed North Atlantic Treaty Alliance. At last, in 1951, he was able to step down from high military office. As might be expected, he had been loaded with honours. His college had elected him an honorary fellow during the war; immediately afterwards he received honorary doctorates of five universities, including Cambridge. He had already been appointed CB (1937), KCB and GCB (January and November 1942). He was awarded three decorations by the President of the United States, and fourteen other foreign medals and orders. In 1950 he became chancellor of Cambridge University and vice-chairman of the board of governors of the British Broadcasting Corporation. He was chairman of the royal commission which reported in 1952 on Dundee's claims for a university. From 1954 to 1960 he was chairman of the Standard Motor Company. In 1966 he published his memoirs, appropriately titled *With Prejudice*.

Tedder first married, in 1915, Rosalinde, daughter of William McIntyre Maclardy, of Sydney, Australia; they had two sons and a daughter. After her death in January 1943 Tedder married in October of the same year Marie de Seton (died 1965), younger daughter of Sir Bruce Seton, Bt., and formerly wife of Captain Ian Reddie Hamilton Black, RN. They had one son. Tedder died in Banstead, Surrey, 3 June 1967. His title passed to his son, John Michael (born 1926), who was then Roscoe professor of chemistry, Queen's College, Dundee.

There is a portrait of Tedder by H. A. Freeth and another by Henry Carr, both the property of the Imperial War Museum.

[*The Times*, 5 June 1967; Roderic Owen, *Tedder*, 1952; Lord Tedder, *With Prejudice*, 1966; Air Historical Branch (RAF); private information; personal knowledge.]

PETER WYKEHAM

published 1981

TEMPLER Gerald Walter Robert

(1898–1979)

Sir

Field-marshal, was born at Colchester, Essex, 11 September 1898, the only child of (Lt.-Col.) Walter Francis Templer, CBE, DL, of the Royal Irish Fusiliers and later of the army pay department, and his wife, Mabel Eileen, daughter of (Major) Robert Johnston, from county Antrim, of the army pay department in India.

After attending private schools in Edinburgh and Weymouth, Templer went to Wellington College, where, as a small boy who was not good at games, his life was made unhappy by bullying. In December 1915 he entered the Royal Military College, Sandhurst, leaving in July 1916 with no distinction. Being then under the age of nineteen, he was not allowed to join a battalion on active service and had to spend a year in Ireland before he joined the 1st battalion Royal Irish Fusiliers in France in November 1917. He accompanied them to Persia, Iraq, and Egypt after the war, returning to Dover in 1922. There he became a noted athlete, gaining his army colours as a hurdler and being chosen as a reserve for the 1924 Olympics team.

Still a platoon commander, he went to Egypt again in 1925, returning on leave that summer to become engaged to Ethel Margery ('Peggie'), daughter of Charles Davie, a retired solicitor. Married in 1926, they were to have a daughter and a son. In 1927 Templer was finally successful in gaining entry to the Staff College. While a student there, he transferred to the Loyal Regiment, on so-called accelerated promotion to captain, joining them in Aldershot in 1930 for a few months before he was posted as general staff officer, 3rd grade, to the 3rd division on Salisbury Plain. There he fell foul of his GSO 1, who wrote an adverse report, recommending his removal from the army. Templer refused to accept it. The general, (Sir) Harry Knox, tore it up and wrote a favourable one. His next appointment was as GSO 2 at Northern Command at York, where his relations with his GSO 1, H. R. L. G. Alexander (later Earl Alexander of Tunis) were cordial.

The year 1935 saw Templer, still a captain, commanding a company, first in the 2nd battalion the Loyals on Salisbury Plain and then, as a brevet major, with the 1st battalion in Palestine, where the Arab population was causing trouble. There were only two battalions in Palestine at that stage and Templer's company was charged with supporting the police in a large area of the north. He revelled in the independence and responsibility this gave him. In retrospect he regarded it as the best job he ever had. His performance gained him both a mention in dispatches and appointment to the DSO (1936), an exceptional award for a company commander.

In 1936 he returned to a staff appointment in England, becoming a Royal Irish Fusilier again when their 2nd battalion was resuscitated in 1937, but never serving with them at regimental duty. In 1938, at last a substantive major and now a brevet lieutenant-colonel, he became a GSO 2 in the military intelligence directorate in the War Office, responsible for preparing plans for intelligence in wartime, including the formation of an Intelligence Corps and for the organization of clandestine operations. His imagination and the thoroughness of his staff work made a major contribution in these fields. When war broke out, he went to GHQ in France as a GSO 1 under the head of intelligence, Major-General (Sir) F. N. Mason-Macfarlane, and acted as his chief of staff when the latter was ordered by Viscount Gort on 16 May 1940 to take command of an *ad hoc* force to link up with the French on the western flank of the British Expeditionary

Force. Returning from France on 27 May, he was charged with raising the
9th battalion of the Royal Sussex Regiment, in November being promoted
to command 210th Infantry brigade at Weymouth under the 3rd division of
B. L. Montgomery (later Viscount Montgomery of Alamein). In May 1941
he went as brigadier general staff to V Corps and in April 1942 was promoted to major-general to command 47th (London) division at Winchester. Five months later he was promoted again to command II Corps
district at Newmarket, at forty-four the youngest lieutenant-general in the
army, but very short of experience in active service command. When it
appeared that his corps was never going to engage in active fighting, he
asked to be allowed to go down in rank to major-general and be given
command of a division in an active theatre of war.

His request was granted, and on 31 July 1943 he took over command of
the 1st division, resting in North Africa. His chance to see action at last
came in October, when he was transferred to the command of 56th division in the British X Corps in the US Fifth Army in Italy. It had just crossed
the Volturno near Capua and was struggling through the rain-soaked hills
on the far side. In the first week of November the division had closed up to
the German positions south of the river Garigliano and was ordered to
throw them off Monte Camino. Conditions of weather and terrain were
severe, and the attack failed, 201st Guards brigade, which had borne the
brunt and suffered heavy casualties, justifiably feeling that the higher
command had underestimated the force needed. Templer was not popular
with the Guards for some time after that. A month later the assault was
renewed in greater strength, notably in artillery support, and was successful, as was the division's crossing of the Garigliano in mid-January.
Attempts to expand the bridgehead did not however get far and were
called off, just as the need to reinforce the landing at Anzio became urgent.
One of Templer's brigades was sent there on 30 January and he followed
with the rest of the division on 12 February 1944. He was heavily involved
in beating off German counter-attacks, at one time also assuming command of 1st division, whose commander was wounded. After four weeks
in the bridgehead, in which it had suffered heavy casualties, 56th division
was relieved and sailed for Egypt to rest and refit, returning to Italy in July.
On the 26th of that month Templer was transferred to the command of
6th Armoured division, which was leading the advance as the Germans
withdrew to Florence. Two weeks later, as he was driving up to the front, a
lorry, in which was a looted piano, pulled off the road to let him pass and
blew up on a mine. Debris struck his back, crushing one vertebra and
damaging two others. In great pain he was removed to hospital, and
returned to England in plaster in September. His short active war service
was at an end.

When he had recovered, he was employed for a time by Special Operations Executive before, in March 1945, being appointed to the staff of his erstwhile instructor at the Staff College, Field-Marshal Montgomery, at 21st Army Group as director of civil affairs and military government in Germany. As the war drew to an end, and when it ended in May, with a staff of only fifty officers he controlled and directed a population, whose economic and social structure had collapsed. He flung himself into the task with all his accustomed energy and directness, one incident becoming notorious. Exasperated by the failure of the mayor of Cologne, Dr Konrad Adenauer, to take practical steps to improve the physical conditions of his city, while he concentrated on political matters, Templer ordered his dismissal. Adenauer bore him no grudge, and, although when he became chancellor he would never meet Templer socially, he would send him a case of the best hock whenever he visited London.

In March 1946 Templer moved to join Montgomery at the War Office, first as director of military intelligence and, in 1948, as vice-chief of the imperial general staff, remaining in that post with Montgomery's successor, Sir W. J. (later Viscount) Slim, until June 1950, when, promoted general at the age of fifty-two, he took over Eastern Command. He had expected this to be his last post, and it might well have been, had not Sir Henry Gurney, high commissioner in Malaya, been ambushed and killed by communist terrorists in October 1951. The suggestion had already been made that a soldier should be appointed to bring both military operations and civil government under one head. The colonial secretary, Oliver Lyttelton (later Viscount Chandos), accepted Slim's recommendation of Templer for the post, having first tried to obtain the services of General Sir Brian Robertson (later Lord Robertson of Oakridge) and then Slim himself.

Templer's success in Malaya, where he arrived in February 1952, was to compensate for all his previous disappointments. The basis of it was the Briggs plan, proposed and initiated by Lieutenant-General Sir Harold Briggs, brought in from retirement as director of operations in April 1950. He had not however been able to obtain the authority and full co-operation from all branches of the administration, including the police, to implement it effectively. Briggs had left in December 1951, and Templer provided all the authority, drive, and imagination that had been lacking. His arrival was not greeted with universal enthusiasm, many fearing that he would concentrate on security to the neglect of political development. But perhaps his greatest contribution to the success of the long struggle against the communists in Malaya was his insistence on rapid progress to independence and the assumption of political responsibility, including that for security, by the Malay, Chinese, and Indian inhabitants of the Federation.

By the summer of 1954 such progress had been made that Templer could recommend that his place be taken by his civilian deputy, Sir Donald MacGillivray, and this was effected in October. The chief of the imperial general staff, Field-Marshal Sir A. F. Harding (later Lord Harding of Petherton), had recommended Templer as his successor, and wished him to spend a year as commander-in-chief of the British Army of the Rhine in order to gain some first-hand experience of NATO before doing so; but this was blocked by the foreign secretary, Sir R. A. Eden (later the Earl of Avon), who objected to such a short tenure at a crucial period of German rearmament, not, as some suggested, because of Templer's brush with Adenauer.

In September 1955 he became the army's professional head as CIGS. At that time the situation in the Middle East was of major concern to the chiefs of staff and to Eden's Conservative administration. In December Templer was sent to try and persuade the young King Hussain that Jordan should join the Baghdad Pact. The pro-Egyptian faction, supported by the Palestinian element, strongly opposed this, forcing a series of political crises, starting while Templer was in Amman, which culminated in March 1956 with the dismissal of the British General (Sir) John Glubb from the Jordanian Arab Legion.

Templer's whole period as CIGS was an unhappy one for him, including, as it did, the fiasco of Suez and the reductions in the size of the army resulting from the decision of Harold Macmillan (later the Earl of Stockton) to work towards the ending of conscription. At heart an imperialist and a dedicated infantryman, Templer regarded with extreme distaste the abandonment of imperial responsibilities and the reductions in infantry which flowed from them. He was never much interested in the defence problems of Europe and had an instinctive dislike of alliances. He was above all a man dedicated to his duty, and he faced the unpleasant task of cutting down the army, reinforced by the knowledge that his subordinates knew that he would be as fair and just in his decisions as he would be relentless and vigorous in seeing that they were executed promptly and obediently. Exacting in his demands on himself, he demanded high standards in others. A martinet in appearance and manner, his displeasure—even his presence—was intimidating.

He became a field-marshal in 1956. He was appointed OBE (1940), CB (1944), CMG (1946), KBE (1949), KCB (1951), GCMG (1953), GCB (1955), and KG (1963). He had honorary doctorates from Oxford and St. Andrews. His other honours were numerous. His principal activity after leaving active duty in 1958 was the foundation and support of the National Army Museum. He was tireless in raising the money and in badgering government departments and other authorities to lend their support to the project, which owed its success mainly to him. He died at his home in Chelsea, London, 25 October 1979.

[John Cloake, *Templer, Tiger of Malaya*, 1985; private information; personal knowledge.]

MICHAEL CARVER

published 1986

TOWNSHEND Charles Vere Ferrers

(1861–1924)

Sir

Major-general, was born 21 February 1861 in Southwark, the eldest son of Charles Thornton Townshend, by his wife, Louisa, daughter of John Graham, of Melbourne, Australia. His father was the eldest son of the Rev. Lord George Townshend, and a great-grandson of the first Marquess Townshend. Although he was for a time heir presumptive to the marquessate, the father lived in humble circumstances, earning his livelihood as a minor railway official. After his death in 1889 Charles Vere Townshend remained until 1916 heir presumptive to the sixth Marquess Townshend.

Townshend's home life was not happy; he was educated at Cranleigh School, Kent, until his relatives obtained a nomination for him to enter the royal navy. This, however, he did not accept, preferring to work for entrance into the Royal Military College, Sandhurst. Eventually, in February 1881 he was gazetted to the Royal Marine Light Infantry. In 1884 he proceeded to Suakin with a battalion of marines, which, shortly afterwards, was attached to the column with which Sir Herbert Stewart advanced up the Nile valley in an endeavour to relieve General Gordon, then besieged in Khartoum. Townshend was thus present at the fierce actions at Abu Klea and Gubat, and when the fall of Khartoum became known, participated in Stewart's retreat across the Bayuda desert. After being mentioned in dispatches for his work in the Sudan, he was transferred to the Indian army in January 1886.

On arrival in India Townshend was first posted to the seventh Madras Infantry, exchanging very soon into the third Sikh Infantry, and finally into the Central India Horse. The facility with which he changed regiments and sought appointments became a characteristic of Townshend's career. In 1891 he had the good fortune to be selected for service in the Himalayas, and was sent to Gilgit, where he assumed command of the first, or Raga

463

Pertab, battalion of the Imperial Kashmir Contingent. Not long afterwards the Hunza-Nagar expedition was organized at Gilgit, and Townshend thus came to take a prominent part in the capture of the hill forts of Nilt and Hunza. After obtaining another mention in dispatches and acting as military governor of Hunza, he returned to his regiment late in 1892, having been promoted to captain's rank earlier in that year. In 1893 he was once more sent to the Himalayas, being selected for the command of Fort Gupis, which stood midway between Gilgit and Chitral. A series of political murders and the subsequent disaffection of Sher Afzul, the usurping ruler of Chitral, led to the dispatch of the political agent, Sir George Scott Robertson, to Chitral, escorted by Townshend and a detachment of troops from Gupis early in 1895. This little force reached Chitral, but was soon driven into the fortified palace of Chitral and there besieged, suffering severe privations during an investment of forty-six days (4 March–20 April). For Townshend, as commander of the garrison, the situation was difficult: the enemy displayed boldness; his own men were apathetic; and the presence of the political agent complicated his position as military commander. In April 1895 Chitral was relieved. For the skill and judgement displayed in its defence, Townshend received the thanks of the government of India, a brevet majority, and the C.B.—a remarkable reward for so young an officer.

On returning to England Townshend found himself a celebrity, and had little difficulty in obtaining a transfer to the Egyptian army. Accordingly in February 1896 he arrived in Cairo to assume command of the twelfth Sudanese battalion. A few weeks later he set out with (Lord) Kitchener's expedition for the reconquest of the Sudan. During that year he took part in the operations for the recovery of Dongola, obtaining another mention and a brevet lieutenant-colonelcy. Throughout 1897 he remained engaged in the Nile valley, and in 1898 commanded his battalion at the battles of the Atbara and of Khartoum, obtaining the D.S.O. for his services. After resigning his appointment in Egypt, Townshend returned to India in 1899, nominally to take up a staff appointment, but, on the outbreak of the war in South Africa, he made every endeavour to be sent to the Cape. This at length he effected, and he arrived at Bloemfontein in March 1900, to act as assistant-adjutant-general on the staff of the military governor of the Orange Free State. The work and surroundings proved uncongenial and Townshend returned home in September 1900, to be reinstated in the British service as a major in the Royal Fusiliers. In spite of his record of service and of his proved military qualities Townshend now antagonized not a few high authorities. Many idiosyncrasies, regarded with amused tolerance in the young officer, proved less becoming in a soldier of standing and distinction. A passion for theatrical society, gifts as an excellent raconteur and entertainer, a constant flow of quips and quotations in French obscured some true merit. A remarkable knowledge of military history was warped by a lack of systematic training and by a self-confidence that often failed to impress. Townshend's abilities were thus, perhaps not unjustly, regarded as unbalanced, and he now went through a period of lean years. Until March 1903 he served at home, growing more dissatisfied with regimental duty. He then exchanged into the battalion of his regiment stationed in India. Promotion to brevet colonel came in January 1904. He returned home in December of that year, and in 1905 acted for a time as military attaché in Paris. But his restlessness was unabated until, in March 1906, he was transferred to the Shropshire Light Infantry and again went to India. There in August 1907 he became assistant-adjutant-general of the ninth division. In February 1908 he was promoted substantive colonel, while a year later he was appointed commander of the Orange River Colony District, a position carrying the rank of brigadier-general. Townshend remained in South Africa until promoted major-general in July 1911, when he returned to England. He had in the meantime become an ardent admirer of the French army and of the future Marshal Foch; so much so that this predilection even coloured the training of his troops. The command of the East Anglian division of the Territorial Force was next given him; but he preferred more active employment, and was gratified when in June 1913 he left for India to assume command of the Jhanzi brigade. A few months later he left this unit for the Rawal Pindi brigade, and he was at Pindi at the time of the outbreak of the European War.

Townshend's persistent efforts to obtain a command at the front were at length satisfied in April 1915 by his appointment to the sixth (Indian) division, that being one of the two divisions operating in Mesopotamia, under the command of Sir John Eccles Nixon. In the ensuing campaign the brunt of the fighting fell upon Townshend's division. His first task was to drive the Turks northwards from Kurna on the Tigris, which was then in full flood. The water was so high that the fortified Turkish position stood out of the marshy flats almost like a string of islands. Townshend accordingly organized a fleet of ancient Tigris barges, known as *bellums*, on which he embarked two brigades, supported by three naval sloops and other odd craft. With this curious armada on 31 May he delivered a frontal attack on the enemy—a seemingly hazardous proceeding, since the Turkish position was guarded by mines and the depth of water was uncertain. Luckily the mines proved ineffective and most of the defenders fled. Emboldened by success Townshend pursued the Turks with a handful of men, embarked on a few naval craft, until he reached Amara (90 miles up the river from Kurna). There the bulk of the Turkish force surrendered before discovering the weakness of the pursuit. Townshend's audacity was thus amply rewarded.

Shortly afterwards Townshend fell ill and was sent to India for treatment. On resuming his command in September, he found his division distributed along the Tigris with the Turks entrenched astride the river in front of Kut el Amara (150 miles above Amara). Difficulties of transport and supply were already hampering the movements of the British troops, who were, moreover, sorely in need of reinforcement; the Turks on the other hand were growing in numbers and boldness. Nevertheless, an advance on Baghdad had been decided upon by higher authority, and Townshend was not unwilling to fall in with the plan. On 27 September he attacked the Turkish position. It was a bold move, involving a night march and a turning movement. Having divided his force Townshend cleverly feinted on the right bank of the river whilst driving home his main attack away from the left bank. The Turks were defeated and Kut was captured (29 September); but the victory could not be effectively followed up owing to the weakness and fatigue of the British forces. Retreating in good order, the Turks took up a fortified position at Ctesiphon, covering Baghdad. The Tigris now grew so shallow that Townshend, depending largely on water transport, found his supply services still further hampered, so that he was compelled to halt at Azizieh (60 miles beyond Kut).

The final move on Baghdad was then ordered. Townshend raised objections to the proposed operations without the assistance of a second division, but deferred to the judgement of his commander-in-chief, Sir John Nixon. Difficulties were minimized by all authorities concerned in the campaign; and a successful preliminary attack on a Turkish advanced post at El Kutuniya encouraged optimism. But the Turks had in the meanwhile been reinforced, before Townshend, on 22 November, could attack their position. Once more he cleverly manœuvred to turn the Turkish left while launching his main attack at a specially selected point in their main line of resistance. This point was taken after fierce fighting, but only at heavy cost. The Turks, now strengthened by some good troops from the Caucasus, counter-attacked the next day. Townshend's resources proved quite inadequate to the task in hand, and the situation, aggravated by the difficulty of navigating the low waters of the Tigris, grew critical.

After a week's fighting and retreating, holding at bay the enemy's greatly superior forces, Townshend led his men back into Kut on 3 December with 1,350 prisoners. It is more than doubtful whether he could have withdrawn farther. After one or two attempts to carry the place by assault the Turks invested it closely. Townshend expected to be relieved, but attempts by Lieutenant-General Aylmer and Major-General Gorringe in January and February proved unavailing. Townshend conducted the defence skilfully, although the fall of Kut had become inevitable when Aylmer failed to break through the Turkish lines in January. The garrison suffered severely, and men were actually dying of starvation when Townshend opened negotiations with the Turks. The surrender of Kut took place on 29 April 1916.

Townshend and his garrison became prisoners of war. The troops fared lamentably in captivity, but Townshend himself was well treated, being interned on Prinkipo Island, near Constantinople. In October 1917 he was created a K.C.B. A year later he was released by the Turks in order that he should plead on their behalf for the best possible terms of surrender. The armistice with Turkey was signed on 30 October 1918, when Townshend returned to England.

After the War Townshend failed to obtain any further military appointment; he therefore retired and took to political life, and was elected to parliament in November 1920, as an independent conservative for the Wrekin division of Shropshire. In the House he occasionally spoke on matters that concerned the East or the ex-service man, but on the whole he proved ineffective, and did not seek re-election. Subsequently, he sought opportunities of acting as negotiator between Great Britain and Turkey in the final settlement of questions arising out of the War; but his services were curtly declined by the government. Undeterred, he proceeded to Angora in June 1922, and was well received by Kemal Pasha, his pro-Turkish sympathies being thereby strengthened. On his return to London he strongly advocated the Turkish case, but failed to find support. He visited Angora again in 1923. His health, however, was failing, and he died in Paris 18 May 1924.

Townshend married in 1898 Alice, daughter of Count Louis Cahen d'Anvers. He left one daughter.

[*The Times*, 19 May 1924; E. Sherson, *Townshend of Chitral and Kut*, 1928; Sir C. V. F. Townshend, *My Campaign in Mesopotamia*, 1920; Army Lists. Portrait, *Royal Academy Pictures*, 1920.]

H. DE WATTEVILLE

published 1937

TRENCHARD Hugh Montague

(1873–1956)

First Viscount Trenchard

Marshal of the Royal Air Force, was born at Taunton 3 February 1873, the second son and third of the six children of Henry Montague Trenchard, a provincial lawyer, and his wife, Georgiana Louisa Catherine Tower, daughter of John McDowall Skene, captain R.N. His father came of an ancient west-country family, among them Sir John Trenchard, once considerable landowners, but latterly dependent on professional earnings. A happy early childhood, from which conventional learning was almost completely absent, ended when he went to a preparatory school and thence to a crammer's for entry to the Royal Navy. However, he failed the Dartmouth entrance, and so was sent to an army crammer, where his strong preference for sports and games, and the absence of any properly balanced studies, produced in him a certain philistinism which subsequently took many years to eradicate. At the age of sixteen, while still a boarder at this school, he learnt that his father's law practice had failed, and bankruptcy followed. This disgrace weighed heavily upon the boy. Maintained at school by the generosity of relatives, he reluctantly worked out a most unhappy period of his life, first failing the Woolwich entrance examination, then twice failing the examination for militia candidates. Finally, in 1893, he just passed, was gazetted as a second lieutenant in the 2nd battalion Royal Scots Fusiliers, and posted at once to his regiment in India.

These formative years had been almost wholly disastrous, and produced a man tense, taciturn, reserved, and half-educated. The five years' garrison and frontier duty he now served slowly eased some of this tension. Trenchard was a large man, tall and strong. He devoted himself to riding, and principally to polo, during most of his leisure hours, finding in the arrangement of teams and tournaments a natural gift for organization, and reading extensively to repair the gaps in his education.

Comparatively uneventful years in India ended with the outbreak of war in South Africa where Trenchard went to rejoin his battalion. He was promoted to the rank of captain, and given the task of raising and training a mounted company. By unorthodox methods, including the incorporation of Australian volunteers, he quickly assembled a small flying column. While commanding this unit he pursued a large Boer raiding party, cornering them at Dwarsvlei in Western Transvaal. During the engagement that followed he was hit in the chest by a bullet, narrowly escaping death. Half-paralysed, with his left lung permanently damaged, he was invalided back to England. Six months of violent self-cure, including winter sports and tennis, miraculously fitted him, in his own opinion at least, for further active service, and he returned to South Africa as a captain in the 12th Mounted Infantry. Until the end of the war he continued to serve with irregular mounted infantry units, gaining a high reputation for daring, initiative, and will-power.

On leave in England at the end of the war he was considering leaving the army when he was offered the post of assistant commandant of the Southern Nigeria Regiment as a brevet major. He accepted and sailed for Nigeria in 1903. For the next seven years he led the life of a soldier and administrator in an unknown country just opening to colonial law and organization. He was twice mentioned in dispatches, appointed to the D.S.O. in 1906, and in 1908 was promoted temporary lieutenant-colonel and became commandant of the regiment. Expeditions, surveys, patrolling, road-building, and occasional clashes with the Ibos of the interior passed the years until in 1910 he fell dangerously ill with an abscess of the liver and was once more invalided home. After a long convalescence, still unfit for tropical duty, he rejoined his old regiment, dropping in rank to major, and served in Ireland for the next two years.

In 1912 he was a thirty-nine-year-old bachelor, and still held the rank of major. Although he had many adventures behind him there was little in his military career or prospects to distinguish him from hundreds of other officers of his age. Once more he thought of retirement. It was then that Captain Eustace Loraine, an old colleague of his Nigeria service, wrote to tell him that he had taken up flying, and enthusiastically advised him to do the same. To Trenchard it seemed as good an idea as any. Obtaining three months' leave, he paid £75 for flying lessons at the Sopwith School at Brooklands. As he began his instruction he learnt that Loraine had been killed in a flying accident, but he passed his tests after two weeks, including one hour and four minutes flying time, and qualified for his pilot's certificate (R. Ae. C. No. 270) on 31 July 1912.

The Royal Flying Corps had formed on the previous 13 May. The new aviator was seconded to it, and posted to the Central Flying School at Upavon. Instead of a pupil's course, his age and military experience sent him at once to the staff, first as an instructor and later as assistant commandant. There he played a leading part in devising the so far unknown techniques of flying instruction, setting the standards of technical knowledge required of pupils while continuing his own training. His age and his fierce reticence made him a figure more respected than loved by the much younger pupils, and it was here that his large frame, ponderous manner, and loud voice first earned him his lifelong nickname of 'Boom'. He was out of his age-group but he had found his *métier*.

By the outbreak of war in 1914 Trenchard was a well-known figure in the Royal Flying Corps, and when senior aviation officers were so scarce he had high hopes of a flying command with the British Expeditionary Force. Instead he was posted as commandant of the Military Wing at Farnborough, responsible for the organization backing the rapidly expanding front-line squadrons. Trenchard found himself called upon to improvise the complete groundwork of a considerable new fighting force. Hardly had he started when a reorganization of the Royal Flying Corps in France gave him command of No. 1 Wing in the First Army Corps and the opportunity to pursue the war from the muddy airfields of the western front. The early months of 1915 found him strongly pressing for the equipment of his squadrons with airborne radio and cameras. The British spring offensives gave him his first opportunity to try out tactical bombing techniques. But his chief concern was always for the morale of his men and for inculcating in them an aggressive fighting spirit: his first rule of war.

In August 1915 he succeeded Sir David Henderson in command of the Royal Flying Corps in France with the temporary rank of brigadier-general. Sir Douglas (later Earl) Haig was his immediate superior; Maurice Baring his improbable but indispensable aide. The advent of the Fokker monoplane curbed his new tactical innovations and forced his squadrons on to the defensive, a state of war intensely distasteful to him. Regretfully restricting his scope, he instituted larger escorts and bigger formations, and so held on until in early 1916 the new British fighters arrived to redress the balance.

In the meantime in London, resolution of the responsibilities and claims of the army and navy in the field of aviation was becoming monthly more difficult, as the air arms grew in size. Trenchard continued to push, wheedle, and inspire his squadrons through the great land battles they supported from time to time, and the fight for air superiority they waged continually. His struggles in France were matched at home by an ever-increasing contest of the two fighting Services for complete control of the new air weapon.

Through the battles of the Somme, Arras, and Messines, third Ypres, and Cambrai, Trenchard's reputation grew with the size and effectiveness of his force. In these campaigns he was able to drive home his greatest precept, and his legacy to the modern Royal Air Force, that only by persistent attack can air mastery be obtained. This he made into an instinctive and a fundamental basis for all air doctrine, which was never questioned by anybody who came under his influence.

In London the Derby committee, the Bailhache committee, and the Air Board each wrestled ineffectively with the problem of controlling inter-Service air priorities. At last the committee under J. C. Smuts finally gained acceptance of its recommendations for an Air Ministry, and a third Service, the Royal Air Force. Although completely convinced of the rightness of this doctrine Trenchard did not want to execute it in the middle of the war. By the end of 1917 he had begun bombing Germany and his squadrons were heavily engaged throughout the length of the British front. He therefore heard with mixed feelings of his appointment, under Lord Rothermere as air minister, to be first chief of the new air staff, in January 1918, at which date he was also appointed K.C.B. Haig parted from him with the utmost reluctance, but it was not long before Trenchard was back in France. Before the day for the formation of the new Royal Air Force, 1 April 1918, could dawn, Trenchard and Rothermere had proved utterly incompatible. Extreme political pliability met unyielding principle, and the new chief of air staff's resignation took effect on 13 April, an event closely followed, under pressure from his own colleagues, by that of the air minister.

Trenchard returned to France in May 1918 at the head of a new concept, an independent bombing force, which after lengthy negotiation was confirmed in October as the Inter-Allied Independent Air Force, subordinate only to Marshal Foch the supreme allied commander, charged with the task of carrying the war directly to Germany by strategic bombing. Although the first squadrons assigned flew a large number of raids against the enemy homeland, the force was not designed to develop its full potential until mid-1919, and so was disbanded before it could show its power. It is sometimes stated, wrongly, that Trenchard was a fanatical advocate of the military value of this force. In fact he had some considerable doubts concerning its strategic worth at that time and place and compared with other war requirements, though none about the details of its training and employment.

For his war services Trenchard received a baronetcy (1919) and a grant of £10,000. Once again he thought of civilian life. But in 1919 (Sir) Winston Churchill became war and air minister and invited Trenchard to return to his briefly held post as chief of air staff. He took office on 15 February and kept it for more than ten years. He now embarked on two tasks, of a size which taxed even his immense energy and application. The first was to create a new permanent fighting Service out of the ruins left by the precipitate disarmament of 1919, and to build strongly and soundly for the future on the slender budgets allowed by the aftermath of world war. Everything was new, and he had to design everything, down to ranks, uniforms, and insignia. The second task was to guard this growing infant from the wicked uncles whose neglect had helped to create it—the two older Services. He was convinced, as of nothing else, that the air weapon could only develop its full potential in an independent Service, and with the war and its immediate dangers over nothing could hold him back from full insistence on this doctrine. If air power was to be shackled to fleets or armies, he declared with a new fluency, it would go down before any opponent who had grasped the lesson that the air was indivisible, and centrally controlled air power the spearhead of national defence.

Thus the chief of air staff of the new Royal Air Force divided his time between building up his young Service and fiercely protecting it from the attempts of the War Office and Admiralty to reabsorb it into the army and navy. These attempts were not long delayed, or easily disposed of, or very scrupulously conducted. First the War Office attacked, in a campaign lasting many months. A useful weapon in Trenchard's defence was his scheme for 'Air Control' of Iraq, whereby small numbers of R.A.F. aircraft and armoured cars kept the peace in an area which had previously needed three times as large a force of soldiers. The outstanding success of this scheme greatly improved his standing, and that of the Air Force, in the eyes of the politicians. By 1925 the army campaign died down, but in the meantime the navy, headed by the first sea lord, Admiral Beatty, developed a continuous, virulent, and wearing assault.

Trenchard fought off these and other attacks, simultaneously consolidating the Royal Air Force by such important foundations as an Apprentice School, a Cadet College, and a Staff College. In all of these the importance of quality above quantity was persistently preached. He received some criticism for this policy from those who would have had all Air Force money devoted to the maximum number of first-line squadrons, but when in the middle thirties government policy permitted the introduction of a phased expansion of the Royal Air Force, this early doctrine ensured that the quality of the whole was unmatched, and able to absorb the further enormous expansions of the war of 1939–45.

His long period as chief of air staff transformed a high reputation into a legend. As a founding father with a long unbroken reign he knew everything there was to know of a force which never exceeded a total of some 30,000 men. His formidable appearance, strong voice, and decisive manner made him a source of affection, admiration, and apprehension to all who worked for him. He was promoted G.C.B. in 1924, became the first marshal of the Royal Air Force in 1927, and in 1930, after his retirement at the end of 1929, he was created a baron. It seemed impossible to imagine the Royal Air Force without him.

He had scarcely time to settle into civilian life before the Government asked him to take office as commissioner for the Metropolitan Police, whose morale and efficiency then gave grounds for concern. He accepted in November 1931, and plunged at once, with characteristic energy, into a programme of reforms and reorganizations. The most important of these were the creation of a Police College and Forensic Laboratory at Hendon and a ten-year engagement scheme for police officers, both designed to improve the qualifications of the higher ranks of the force. Once more his prime concern was for the creation of a high quality individual, by training, selection, and care of the human units of the organization. For this work he was appointed G.C.V.O. in 1935. Inevitably his actions aroused great controversy inside and outside the force, particularly among the more traditional officers. When he gave up the post in 1935 his major reforms were not pressed home by his successor, and many of them lapsed in 1939.

Created a viscount (1936), and once more released from government service, Trenchard joined the board of the United Africa Company, whose Nigerian interests brought him back to ground familiar in his youth. He became chairman in 1936 and held that position until 1953. At the age of sixty-six, with the outbreak of war, he put on uniform again, once more to serve his country, as a kind of roving ambassador of the Air Council, travelling far and wide among the units of the Service, informing, reporting, and inspiring. Completely without ceremony he moved about, greeted everywhere as a universal elder brother to the Royal Air Force. When the war was over, until the end of his life, he continued, in the House of Lords and elsewhere, to support the cause of air power. He was appointed to the Order of Merit in 1951. He was also an honorary LL.D. of Cambridge and D.C.L. of Oxford, an honorary major-general in the army, and colonel of the Royal Scots Fusiliers.

Although his work as police commissioner was memorable, and his early career by no means negligible, Trenchard's fame was established for all time on his work between 1912 and 1929. In these seventeen short years of his forties and fifties he built up and proved in action the principles of air operation; and then created an Air Force which, within his own lifetime, saved his country from certain disaster. He not only created and preserved the third fighting Service and hammered it out in his own image, but he also fathered the doctrine of air power as an independent force, the pre-requisite of successful operations by land and sea. He had the supreme satisfaction of seeing all his prophecies completely, indeed lavishly, fulfilled before his eyes. Although he disliked the label 'Father of the Royal Air Force' he was in fact the progenitor of almost all independent air forces. His character: strong, stern, touched with eccentricity, but basically kind and humane, assured him the love of all who worked for him.

In 1920 Trenchard married Katherine Isabel Salvin (died 1960), daughter of the late Edward Salvin Bowlby, and widow of Captain the Hon. James

Boyle. Her sister was the wife of Lord Keyes. There were two sons, of whom the elder was killed in action in North Africa in 1943. The younger, Thomas (born 1923), succeeded his father when he died in London 10 February 1956. He was buried in Westminster Abbey.

There are portraits by Sir William Orpen and Francis Dodd in the Imperial War Museum; by A. R. Thomson at the Royal Air Force Staff College, Bracknell; by E. Verpilleux at the Royal Air Force College, Cranwell; by Frank Beresford at H.Q. Fighter Command, Bentley Priory; and by Sir Oswald Birley at the Royal Air Force Club. A memorial bronze statue by William McMillan stands in Embankment Gardens, outside the Ministry of Defence.

[*The Times*, 11 February 1956; Andrew Boyle, *Trenchard*, 1962; Sir Walter Raleigh and H. A. Jones, (Official History) *The War in the Air*, 6 vols., 1922–37; private information.]

PETER WYKEHAM

published 1971

TYRWHITT Sir Reginald Yorke

(1870–1951)

First baronet

Admiral of the fleet, was born in Oxford 10 May 1870, the fifth son of the Rev. Richard St. John Tyrwhitt, vicar of St. Mary Magdalen, and the fourth by his second wife Caroline, daughter of John Yorke, of Bewerley Hall, Yorkshire. He entered the *Britannia* in 1883, served in the *Australia* and *Ajax* for the naval manœuvres of 1889 and 1890 respectively, and in 1892 was promoted lieutenant and appointed to the light cruiser *Cleopatra* on the North America station.

In 1896 Tyrwhitt took over the command of the *Hart*, one of the very early destroyers in the navy, and thus began a long and distinguished association with this class of ship. Towards the end of the year he was appointed first lieutenant in the *Surprise*, the commander-in-chief's yacht in the Mediterranean, and followed that with a similar post in the *Indefatigable* on the North America station. He was promoted commander in 1903 and appointed to the *Aurora*, tender to the *Britannia* at Dartmouth. He commanded the destroyer *Waveney* (1904–5) and the scouts *Attentive* (1906) and *Skirmisher* (1907).

In June 1908 Tyrwhitt was promoted captain and, with a long record of destroyer command behind him, was selected in August to command the *Topaze* as captain (D) of the fourth destroyer flotilla at Portsmouth. After holding that command for two years he was made flag captain to Sir Douglas Gamble on the Mediterranean station, commanding successively the *Bacchante* and the *Good Hope*. In 1912 he returned home to command the *Bellona* as captain (D) of the second destroyer flotilla of the Home Fleet, and in 1914 was promoted commodore (T) being then in charge of all destroyer flotillas in the fleet. In addition to his main interest in destroyer tactics, Tyrwhitt was a strong supporter of the introduction of flying in the navy and his encouragement was a considerable factor in the formation of the Royal Naval Air Service.

At the outbreak of war Tyrwhitt was at Harwich, flying his broad pennant in the light cruiser *Amethyst*, with the first and third destroyer flotillas in company. As commodore—and from 1918 rear-admiral—Harwich Force, he served throughout the whole war in that single appointment, an indication of the Admiralty's high appreciation of the skill and leadership with which he led the force throughout the strenuous operations in which it was engaged.

It was as a war leader that Tyrwhitt really blossomed. He had in abundance the four 'aces' which make the great commander: a gift for leadership, a fertile imagination and a creative brain, an eagerness to make full use of the brains and ideas of juniors, and an offensive spirit. His were the first ships to be in action in the war when they sank the German minelayer *Königin Luise* off the Thames estuary on 5 August 1914. Twenty-three days later the Harwich Force was engaged in the Heligoland Bight action, an operation jointly planned by Tyrwhitt and Roger (later Lord) Keyes, commanding the British submarine flotillas. Three German cruisers were sunk in the engagement, and although Tyrwhitt's ship, the *Arethusa*, was severely damaged in the action she returned safely to Sheerness where, Tyrwhitt recorded, (Sir) Winston Churchill 'fairly slobbered over me'. He was awarded the C.B.

There followed the German battle-cruiser raid on Scarborough and Hartlepool on 16 December 1914 when, although the sea was too rough for his destroyers, he was at sea with his light cruisers and only just failed to make contact with the enemy ships. He commanded the covering force in the Heligoland Bight for the naval seaplane raid on the Zeppelin sheds at Cuxhaven on Christmas Day 1914, and in January 1915 his Harwich Force played a notable part together with the battle cruisers of Sir David (later Earl) Beatty at the battle of the Dogger Bank.

On intercepting the 'enemy sighted' signal on 31 May 1916 which heralded the battle of Jutland, Tyrwhitt put to sea with the Harwich Force only to be recalled by signal from the Admiralty. Eventually he was permitted to sail, but arrived on the scene too late to take any part in the action. In the German fleet operation of 19 August 1916, which was to be a bombardment of Sunderland, the ships of the Harwich Force were the only British vessels to sight the German fleet. Scheer, the German commander-in-chief, ordered a withdrawal before the bombardment could take place and it was as the enemy retired that Tyrwhitt sighted them. He was in chase until nightfall, but as his only chance of making an attack on them would be after the moon had risen, he was forced to draw off before bringing them to action. In uninformed circles Tyrwhitt was later criticized for failing to press an attack home, but virtual suicide was no part of his plan and his action in withdrawing was upheld by both Sir John (later Earl) Jellicoe and the Admiralty.

In 1917 and 1918 the Harwich Force engaged in several small-scale actions, mainly off the Dutch coast or in co-operation with the destroyers of the Dover Patrol, and as the covering force for naval air attacks on enemy installations. After the armistice it was Tyrwhitt's Harwich Force which accepted the surrender of the German U-boats.

Tyrwhitt was appointed to the D.S.O. in 1916 and in 1917 promoted K.C.B. He was created a baronet in 1919 and granted £10,000 by Parliament for his services during the war. He received many foreign decorations and an honorary D.C.L. from Oxford (1919).

After the war Tyrwhitt was appointed senior officer at Gibraltar and in 1921 he returned to sea as flag officer commanding third light cruiser squadron in the Mediterranean. He was commanding officer Coast of Scotland and admiral superintendent Rosyth dockyard in 1923–5 and in 1925 was promoted vice-admiral. He was commander-in-chief China station from 1927 to 1929, serving there with great tact and distinction during the threat to the International Settlement at Shanghai during the Chinese civil war. He was promoted admiral on relinquishing command in China and was also promoted G.C.B. In 1930–33 he was commander-in-chief at the Nore, becoming first and principal naval aide-de-camp to the King in 1932. In 1934, being the senior admiral on the list, he was promoted admiral of the fleet when a vacancy occurred. During the war of 1939–45, at the age of seventy, he joined the Home Guard in 1940 and for a short time commanded the 3rd Kent battalion.

Tyrwhitt married in 1903 Angela Mary (died 1958), daughter of Matthew Corbally, of Rathbeale Hall, Swords, county Dublin, and had one son and two daughters. He died at Sandhurst, 30 May 1951, and was succeeded by his son, St. John Reginald Joseph (1905–61), who also entered the navy, becoming second sea lord in 1959. His elder daughter, Dame Mary Tyrwhitt, retired as director of the Women's Royal Army Corps in 1950.

Portraits of Tyrwhitt by Francis Dodd and Glyn Philpot are in the Imperial War Museum. Tyrwhitt also figures in Sir A. S. Cope's 'Some Sea Officers of the War of 1914–18' in the National Portrait Gallery.

[Admiralty records; *The Times*, 31 May 1951.]

P. K. KEMP

published 1971

VEREKER John Standish Surtees Prendergast

(1886–1946)

First Viscount Gort, in the peerage of Ireland sixth and in the peerage of the United Kingdom

Field-marshal, was born in London 10 July 1886, the elder son of John Gage Prendergast Vereker, later fifth Viscount Gort, by his wife, Eleanor, daughter and coheiress of Robert Smith Surtees, the famous novelist, of Hamsterley Hall, county Durham. He was educated at Harrow, being a schoolboy when he succeeded to the family honours in 1902, and at the Royal Military College, Sandhurst. He was gazetted ensign in the Grenadier Guards in 1905.

On the outbreak of war with Germany in August 1914, the month of his promotion to captain, Gort went to France as aide-de-camp to the commander of the I Corps, Sir Douglas (later Earl) Haig. In 1915 he was appointed G.S.O. 3 to the I Corps, and later brigade-major of the 4th (Guards) brigade, which became the 1st Guards brigade. He was present at the battles of Festubert and Loos. In July 1916 he was appointed G.S.O. 2 to the operations branch at G.H.Q. In January 1917 a special sub-section of the operations branch was formed, with Gort as assistant to its chief, to work out details of the campaign for that year, which it was then hoped would include a landing from the sea behind the German front near Middelkerke. This was a landmark in staff organization: the conception of a planning staff without other duties was a novelty. This sub-section of the operations branch was the embryo of the modern planning staff.

Gort was a competent staff officer, but his greatest gift was for leadership. In April 1917 he was appointed to command the 4th battalion, Grenadier Guards, shortly before the arduous offensive in Flanders. On the first day of that offensive, 31 July, in the battle of Pilckem Ridge, he was wounded, but, despite great pain, remained until the captured ground had been consolidated. For his exploits on that occasion he received a bar to the D.S.O. to which he had been appointed earlier in the year. He returned to lead his battalion in a later phase of the offensive. In November he was wounded again in the battle of Cambrai. In March 1918, now commanding the 1st battalion of his regiment, he played a part in stemming the German offensive at Arras. He was awarded a second bar to the D.S.O. Already he had acquired a reputation for the rarest gallantry, complete disregard of personal danger, and the power to keep alive in troops under his command a spirit of endeavour, untamed by loss and strain.

The great day of Gort's career was 27 September 1918. The occasion was an episode in the victorious British offensive, the passage of the Canal du Nord and storm of the Hindenburg line near the village of Flesquières, in which he found himself temporarily in command of the 3rd Guards brigade. The situation with which he was confronted was all too familiar: the brigade was to pass through and capture the third objective, but found that the second had not been fully attained. Gort first led his own battalion up under very heavy fire to its starting line. He was then wounded, but personally directed a tank against an obstacle holding up the advance. The brigade's left flank was completely exposed, but he covered it with one of his battalions, the 1st Welsh Guards. Severely wounded for the second time, he struggled up from the stretcher on which he had been lying and continued to direct the attack. Later on he collapsed, but recovering partially, insisted on waiting until the success signals were seen. It was an extraordinary feat of physical courage and of will, which was fittingly rewarded by the Victoria Cross. In the course of the war he was also awarded the M.C. and was eight times mentioned in dispatches.

Gort attended the Staff College on its reopening in 1919. In 1921, a brevet lieutenant-colonel, he returned as instructor. He then reverted to regimental duty. In 1926 he became chief instructor at the Senior Officers' School at Sheerness, and his promotion to the rank of colonel was antedated to January 1925. He went on to command the Grenadier Guards and regimental district in 1930, became director of military training in India in 1932, and in 1936 went to the Staff College, Camberley, for the third time, now as commandant.

The secretary of state for war, Leslie (later Lord) Hore-Belisha, desired to rejuvenate the higher appointments at the War Office. His eye fell upon Gort, who early in 1937 was still only fifty years of age. He was appointed military secretary to the secretary of state and later in the year chief of the imperial general staff. He was promoted full general, skipping the intermediate rank of lieutenant-general. He was also appointed C.B., and promoted K.C.B. in 1938. Apart from his desire to introduce younger blood into the general staff, Hore-Belisha was attracted by the almost legendary prestige and reputation for bravery attaching to Gort's name, which he knew would create favourable public interest in the army. Yet it must be borne in mind that up to this point Gort had won every step by attainments as well as character. His staff record was excellent. The appointment of commandant of the Staff College was one of the most important which could come the way of an officer of his seniority in view of its influence on the future career of the most promising officers.

This does not necessarily imply that his appointment to chief of the imperial general staff was ideal. Gort might possibly have been better placed in a home command in peace and at the head of an army corps in war than as chief of the imperial general staff in peace with reversion of the post of commander-in-chief of an expeditionary force in the event of war. In fact, this reversion was not immediately settled. Even after Gort's appointment it was not at once decided that the precedent of 1914 should be followed and that on the outbreak of war he should assume the command of the expeditionary force. Sir John Dill had been nominated for this post, and it was only at short notice that the appointment was given to Gort and that Dill became one of his corps commanders.

The force which Gort took to France in September 1939 on the outbreak of war with Germany was stationed on the neutral Belgian frontier and thus out of contact with the enemy. Beginning at a strength of four divisions, it finally reached that of ten (without counting several sent out without artillery for pioneer work). The winter, generally bad, was occupied with training and construction of defences. Meanwhile plans were devised for action in the event of a German invasion of Belgium. The question of an allied advance into Belgium in such a case was one of high policy, which passed over Gort's head in view of his subordination to the French command. 'It was therefore not for me to comment on it', he writes in his dispatches—a phrase hardly to be justified in the circumstances. Either in person or through his chief of the general staff, Gort had actually participated in the discussions. Yet the plan adopted, that of a rapid advance followed by the formation of a front on the Dyle and the Meuse, caused him anxiety. When the time came the advance was carried out with little difficulty. The trouble was to follow.

The main interest of the operations resulting from the German invasion on 10 May 1940 does not attach to the British Expeditionary Force. It was outflanked on its right by the German break-through on the Meuse, and in the last phase on its left also by the collapse of Belgian resistance. It carried out successive withdrawals, while covering the long right flank. The severance of communications with the base ports in Normandy and Brittany made it necessary to switch supplies from Britain to the northern ports, but by 22 May Boulogne and Calais were no longer available. Ostend was inadequate, so supplies had to be concentrated on Dunkirk, but after the 26th could be landed only on the beach because the cranes had been put out of action. Attempts, by combined thrusts from north and south, to break the German corridor which extended to the coast and had split the allied armies in two were ill co-ordinated and ineffective. A temporary and limited success was gained by a British attack south of Arras on 21 May, carried out in small strength. Gort clearly had little faith in this operation and less in the ability of the French to cut through from the south. On the 19th he had felt that 'there might be no other course open' but withdrawal to the Channel ports. Sir Edmund (subsequently Lord) Ironside, chief of the imperial general staff, had on the 20th brought instructions for the whole British force to break through towards Amiens and take station on the left of the French Army. Gort had replied that it could not disengage itself for this operation, and Ironside had agreed to the limited action taken.

Henceforward Gort insisted that the principal effort must come from the south, although again not believing that anything serious would be effected. There he proved right; but the French case was that he should have attacked simultaneously from the north. On 24 May the Government told him that, while it still believed a French break-through possible, he was authorized to withdraw to the coast if he could not co-operate. On 25 May he abandoned preparations to attack southwards and moved the two divisions involved to fill a gap between the British and Belgian armies. 'By doing so', says the official historian, 'he saved the British Expeditionary Force.' On the 26th the Government informed him that a French break-through was no longer likely and he was again authorized to operate towards the coast. By the 30th the force had withdrawn to a perimeter between Nieuport and Dunkirk, and rapid evacuation was in progress. Late on the 31st, under orders which left him no discretion, Gort handed over command of the rear-guard to Major-General Alexander (subsequently Earl Alexander of Tunis) and went aboard a ship for England. So ended tragic events which have been the subject of fierce controversy. Gort had realized that a Belgian collapse was impending. His appreciation of French capabilities was less favourable than that of the British Government, and he felt assured that the line he consistently followed was the only one that could save his troops from destruction. It is now virtually certain that he was correct. In the course of the campaign he was promoted G.C.B. and received the grand cross of the French Legion of Honour.

Although he had not failed, it was decided that the task of reorganizing the army and preparing for apparently inevitable invasion should go to another hand. He was appointed inspector-general to the forces, a disappointing post for a former commander-in-chief. In 1941 he went to Gibraltar as governor and commander-in-chief. British fortunes were low, and the fortress appeared to be in grave danger. Three great achievements stand to the credit of his governorship: hurrying on the work of putting everything vital into the shelter of vast new excavations in the rock; construction on nominally neutral ground of the air landing strip which proved of immense value in subsequent campaigns; and by sheer personal charm and character so improving local Anglo-Spanish relations that all unfriendly incidents ceased, although there had as yet been no amelioration of the British strategic position.

On transfer to Malta in May 1942, Gort took over without repining a task which might have sent his name down into history under a stigma, however unjust that would have been. He was informed that in all probability the island could not hold out for more than six weeks; it might even have to be surrendered without being invaded, a still more pitiful end to the defence. In April, before his arrival, Spitfire aircraft, flown in from carriers, had been destroyed on the ground. Now another flight was due. Gort, aware that the bowsers from which fuel was pumped into the tanks had been destroyed, had experimented at Gibraltar in filling them from cans. At the Maltese airfields the estimated time for getting the aircraft into the air again was forty minutes. He suggested that, carried out as a drill, it could be done much faster and promised the aid of as many troops as could be employed. The army in the main did the refuelling, while the Royal Air Force attended to rearming, as aircraft had to be flown in without cannon. The Spitfires were in the air before hostile dive-bombers, warned by radar, arrived from Sicily; and there was no loss. It was a first step to the salvation of Malta. Almost immediately afterwards the minelayer *Welshman*, with ammunition, was due. Convinced that a determined attack would be made on her and fearing that like some of her predecessors she would be sunk in dock with her cargo, Gort concentrated all available artillery about the Grand Harbour. He set no limit to expenditure of shell, although stocks were perilously low. Spitfires and guns between them played havoc with the attacking aircraft, and the last dive-bombing attack on Malta was routed. Gort also organized the discharging at top speed and the dispersal of the cargoes of merchant shipping. His methods produced remarkable results, but were not fully tested by heavy bombing.

His other great achievement was in rationing. He made, from improvised equipment, kitchens which served a free daily meal to any who needed it. At first 10,000 meals a day were served, but when store cupboards emptied the number rose to some 200,000 out of a population of 270,000. It is not often given to one man, however great his power, to accomplish so much in the survival of a beleaguered fortress of priceless worth. On the lifting of the siege he turned his energies successfully to preparing the island for use as a base for the invasion of Sicily. The Maltese fully realized the debt they owed him. His popularity became extraordinary. Young children habitually recognized him in the streets of Valetta and gave him a military salute. When he left Malta in 1944 it took him several hours to make his way through the throng which had assembled to bid him farewell. The islanders bestowed upon him a sword of honour and his achievement was rewarded by promotion to the rank of field-marshal in 1943.

Gort's next appointment was that of high commissioner and commander-in-chief of Palestine and high commissioner of Trans-Jordan. He ardently looked forward to this experience, although it was expected to be almost as trying as the last. In fact, the bloodshed and confusion which afflicted Palestine were not renewed in his time. A serious illness compelled him to resign in 1945, and he died in London 31 March 1946. It was during this last illness that in 1945 the viscountcy in the peerage of the United Kingdom was conferred upon him.

The outstanding achievement of his service in the war of 1939–45 was his organization of the defence of Malta. It was widely held that in France he hampered himself by undue concern with detail. The criticism may well be valid, yet the same critics might have put the experiments in refuelling aircraft under the same heading. With the garrison and people of Malta he made his gallant and invincible personality felt as strongly as when in command of a unit in the war of 1914–18. As a staff officer he was thorough and capable. In character he was upright and honourable. He regulated his conduct by a strict code of duty. Although somewhat shy in manner, he possessed a personal charm and magnetism which made him a welcome companion.

Gort married in 1911 his cousin, Corinna Katherine, only daughter of George Medlicott Vereker, formerly a captain in the Royal Dublin Fusiliers. The marriage was dissolved in 1925. His only son, Charles Standish, Grenadier Guards, died in 1941, and the elder of his two daughters died in childhood. The United Kingdom viscountcy became extinct with Gort's death and he was succeeded in his Irish titles by his brother, Standish Robert Gage Prendergast (born 1888).

There are portraits of Gort, in the Guards' Club by (Sir) Oswald Birley and White's Club by Henry Carr; and three in the Imperial War Museum, two by R. G. Eves and one by Edward Seago.

[Sir J. E. Edmonds and others, (Official) *History of the Great War. Military Operations, France and Belgium, 1917*, vol. ii, 1948, *1918*, vol. v, 1947; Viscount Gort, *Dispatches, 1939–40*, 1941; L. F. Ellis, (Official) *History of the Second World War. France and Flanders, 1939–40*, 1953; private information; personal knowledge.]

CYRIL FALLS

published 1959

WARBURTON Adrian

(1918–1944)

Photographic reconnaissance pilot, born at Middlesbrough, 10 March 1918, was the younger child of Commander Geoffrey Warburton, R.N., D.S.O., O.B.E., by his wife, Muriel, daughter of Barnard Hankey Davidson, of the Burmese Police Force. He was educated at St. Edward's School, Oxford, and in 1936 was articled to a chartered accountant in London. Living at home at Enfield, in 1937 he joined an armoured territorial unit which he left after little more than a year when he began to learn to fly. Shortly before his twenty-first birthday in 1939 he joined the R.A.F. Volunteer Reserve with a short-service commission. Although at first his progress as a pilot was not above the average, he was given a permanent commission before the end of the year.

In September 1940, while still a pilot officer, Warburton made his first operational photographic reconnaissance flight, from Malta, where he had been posted with No. 431 Flight (then operating with Martin Marylands). From then on his flying career was one of spectacular success. A great individualist, with an exceptional talent for both high-altitude and low-level photography, 'nothing could keep him on the ground'. Soon he was awarded the D.F.C. for his steady record of daring and successful sorties. He was especially notable for his aggressive persistence in the face of danger and for his resourcefulness, as well as for his brilliant flying and accurate photography, and he first became famous as 'the man who had photographed the Italian fleet at Taranto from fifty feet'. Although it was no part of his duties he often attacked the enemy when flying types of aircraft equipped with guns for defence.

During 1941 and 1942, at six-monthly intervals, he was appointed to the D.S.O. and awarded two bars to his D.F.C. For eight months of this time he was attached to No. 2 Photographic Reconnaissance Unit at Heliopolis, but most of his photographic flights were made from Malta which was ideally placed for tracking the Axis convoys between Naples and North Africa.

In August 1942 Warburton attained the acting rank of squadron leader and was put in command of No. 69 Squadron which had succeeded No. 431 Flight at Malta. Before the end of the year he was given the acting rank of wing commander. This promotion coincided with one of his most re-markable adventures: on 15 November he set off from Malta to photograph Bizerta, but did not return and was reported missing. Several days later he reported back to base, when it proved that during the reconnaissance his

Spitfire had been hit, but after crash-landing at the allied-held airfield at Bone he had managed to make his way back to Malta, via Algiers and Gibraltar, flying in three different kinds of aircraft.

In 1943 when the Americans of the United States Air Force's 3rd Reconnaissance Group began to operate from Malta, Warburton befriended them and became their great hero. Fair, slight, and good-looking, he had an impish, inquisitive, and friendly personality, but his normal manner was almost shy—in marked contrast to the ruthless daring in the air which had made him a legendary figure. In October 1943 he was attached to the allied headquarters of photographic reconnaissance in the Mediterranean Area (the Northwest African Photographic Reconnaissance Wing) commanded by Colonel Elliott Roosevelt, and then based at Tunis. He was awarded the American D.F.C. for a particularly daring low-level reconnaissance of the heavily defended coastline of Pantelleria. This was his sixth decoration—he had already received a bar to his D.S.O.—hence the legend of 'six-medal Warburton', although he was more usually known as 'Warby'.

As the result of a serious motor accident near Tunis Warburton was grounded, but after a few weeks in hospital he went to Italy to take command of the newly formed British reconnaissance wing (No. 336). Early in 1944, however, he returned to England and was posted to the special duties list. On 12 April 1944 he took off from Mount Farm, the American photographic reconnaissance base in Oxfordshire, in a Lightning, allegedly to fly to San Severo in Italy. He never arrived, and no information has subsequently come to light to show what happened.

In October 1939 Warburton married Eileen Adelaide Mary, daughter of William Henry Mitchell, chargeman of shipwrights, H.M. dockyard, Portsmouth.

[Air Ministry and U.S. Air Force records; private information; Constance Babington Smith, *Evidence in Camera*, 1958.]

CONSTANCE BABINGTON SMITH

published 1959

WAVELL Archibald Percival

(1883–1950)

First Earl Wavell

Field-marshal, was born 5 May 1883 at Colchester, the only son and second of the three children of Major, afterwards Major-General, Archibald

Graham Wavell by his wife, Lillie, daughter of Richard N. Percival, of Springfields, Bradwall, Cheshire. Although the family had for some generations been soldiers (A. J. B. Wavell was his cousin), it derived from a stock of which traces have been found for four or more centuries in and around the city of Winchester.

Wavell received his education at Winchester, where he was in College, and passed fourth into the Royal Military College, Sandhurst, in 1900. After a six-months' course he was gazetted to the Black Watch in time to see service in South Africa. In 1903 he went to India where his early childhood had been spent, and he took part in the Bazar Valley campaign of 1908. At his first attempt he headed the list of entrants to the Staff College and in 1911, on completing his course, he was sent for a year to the Russian Army. When war broke out in 1914, he was in the War Office, but managed to get overseas. At Ypres in June 1915 he had the misfortune to lose an eye, and was awarded the M.C. In October 1916 he was sent as liaison officer to the army of the Grand Duke Nicholas, which was fighting in Turkey before Erzerum. In June 1917 he went as liaison officer to Palestine and in March 1918, as a brigadier-general, joined the staff of Sir Edmund (later Viscount) Allenby for whom he conceived a great admiration.

The next ten years were divided between the War Office and the staff. During this period Wavell, already well known within the army, became known outside it as an officer untrammelled by convention; and the general public came to associate him with a phrase he used in a lecture: that his ideal infantryman was a cross between a poacher, a gunman, and a cat-burglar. In 1930 he received command of the 6th brigade at Blackdown which had been chosen for experimental purposes; and five years later, after a short period on half-pay (which he spent in writing a report on the Middle East and in rewriting Field Service Regulations), he was appointed to the command of the 2nd division at Aldershot.

By this time his influence in the army had imperceptibly become considerable. He was recognized as an exceptional trainer of troops. Among the younger generals there was a feeling that the older ones had grown lethargic; public interest in the army was at a low ebb. Wavell's views were sought with respect by both old guard and new. Before he had completed his term with the 2nd division, he was appointed in July 1937 to command in Palestine and Trans-Jordan. Soon after his arrival Arab troubles, which had died down since the outbreak of 1936, broke out with fresh ferocity, and were at their height when he was brought home in April 1938 to take over the Southern Command, one of the two most important commands in the country. He had been there little more than a year when he was sent, at the end of July 1939, to form the new command of the Middle East.

Wavell

When war broke out in September, the forces at his disposal were small; when Italy came into the war in June 1940 his command had been reinforced by Dominion and Indian troops, but was menaced by superior forces on several fronts. Bold patrolling by light covering troops in the Western Desert imposed upon Graziani's Italians a caution quite out of proportion to the relative strengths of the two armies. Wavell was able also to delay the Italian advances into the Sudan from Ethiopia; but upon the Somaliland front, where the defection of the French in Jibuti prejudiced the defence, the local commander was forced to give ground. During Wavell's temporary absence in London the decision was taken to evacuate the protectorate rather than lose its small but valuable garrison. The prime minister disapproved of this decision, Wavell defended it, and relations between (Sir) Winston Churchill and Wavell were never very happy thereafter. But Wavell's stock never sank either with his troops or with the public, and it rose with the authorities during and after his remarkable run of success in the winter of 1940–41. He had been keeping a careful eye on the gingerly advance of the Italians in the west, and he detected unsoundness in their dispositions. Containing the threat to the Sudan with an elaborate bluff, he switched the 4th Indian division from that front for use in the Western Desert, and caught the Italians napping at Sidi Barrani on 9 and 10 December. The 4th Indian division returned to the Sudan, while the remainder of the Western Desert army swept up Bardia and Tobruk. By mid-February, the whole of Cyrenaica was in British hands, with 130,000 prisoners, more than 800 field guns, and 400 tanks.

Meanwhile (Sir) Alan Gordon Cunningham's army from Kenya and (Sir) William Platt's in the Sudan were forcing the Italians from Ethiopia back into their remotest mountains; they capitulated in the north in May and in the south some weeks later. Elsewhere, however, the odds against Wavell had mounted. He had been urged to send help on a larger scale to Greece, which since the end of October 1940 had been fighting stoutly and successfully against greatly superior Italian forces in Epirus. Hitherto Britain had contributed only air support with ground defence, anti-aircraft, and medical units; but on 9 January 1941 he was told that the support of Greece must now take precedence of all operations in the Middle East. His first reaction was sharply adverse; but throughout January and February mounting pressure was brought to bear on him to reinforce the Greeks with fighting formations and units. After conversations with the Greeks, in which both the Cabinet and the chiefs of staff were represented by (Sir) Anthony Eden and Sir John Dill, and during which various stipulations which he made were accepted by the Greeks, Wavell agreed to intervention at a moment when the enthusiasm of the Cabinet and chiefs of staff was cooling.

In two respects he had been misled: the Greeks had accepted in the conversations that they would withdraw from their exposed positions to a line on the River Aliakmon more in keeping with the weakness of the joint armies; and Wavell's intelligence had assured him that the German ground forces in North Africa, whose arrival was known to be imminent, would not be able to take the field until mid-April at the earliest. But the Greeks did not shorten their line; and the Germans appeared in strength on the frontiers of Cyrenaica before the end of March. By that time a high proportion of Wavell's army, and much of the best of it, was irrevocably committed in Greece; by the middle of April, both Greece and Cyrenaica had been lost, Tobruk was invested, and vast quantities of fighting troops, military technicians, tanks, and material were in enemy hands.

Stout efforts were made to defend Crete, but it was invaded from the air on 20 May and lost after desperate fighting before the month ended. The Royal Navy and the Royal Air Force in the Middle East had both crippled themselves in these operations. New anxieties had developed; Rashid Ali in Iraq had thrown in his lot with the enemy, and Syria, occupied by Vichy forces, was harbouring Germans and seemed likely to follow the example of Iraq. Wavell was urged to undertake three almost simultaneous operations against Iraq, against Syria, and against Rommel in the desert. He protested that he had not the resources for all three, but was overruled. Although the operation against Iraq was successful by early June, a series of operations against Rommel proved a costly failure by 17 June; in Syria, however, the French asked for an armistice early in July. But at the beginning of the month Wavell had been superseded by Sir Claude Auchinleck, whose place he took as commander-in-chief in India.

At first India was by comparison almost a sinecure; but when, in December 1941, Japan came into the war, Wavell, whose reputation stood high in the United States, was nominated supreme commander of the ill-fated command of the South-West Pacific. The speed, preparedness, and overwhelming strength of the Japanese were in inverse ratio to those of the defence. Wavell was criticized for the loss of the British 18th division in Singapore, which was landed only two days before the capitulation; but he still enjoyed the confidence of his troops, and his resilience as a commander was exemplified by the fact that he gave orders for the eventual recapture of Burma to be studied by his planning staff before its evacuation was complete. Policy dictated that the German war should be won before the Japanese, and Wavell had to fight the Burma war with the minimum of help from home. He had little success, and in June 1943 he was appointed viceroy of India in succession to the Marquess of Linlithgow and in July was raised to the peerage as Viscount Wavell, of Cyrenaica and of Winchester. He had been promoted field-marshal in January of that year.

Wavell entered upon his last public service with his usual willingness to shoulder an unpopular task, although, as he wrote to a friend, 'I fear I have no talent for persuasion'. Hindus and Moslems were at logger-heads and had somehow to be reconciled before India might be granted self-government. Wavell's first act was administrative and characteristic. Bengal was in the grip of famine and the new viceroy relieved a critical situation by an immediate personal reconnaissance followed by extensive military aid. Thereafter he was immersed in politics. In the summer of 1945 he took the initiative by releasing the Congress leaders who had been in jail since the rebellion of 1942. He then set to work with limitless patience to seek some way of securing agreement on the future of India. When the first series of talks broke down in July 1945 he issued a public statement taking the blame on himself. His task was not made easier by the fact that after the general election of 1945 the Labour Government, although de-siring to endow India with self-government, did not lay down a clear-cut policy. A delegation of three Cabinet ministers conferred with the viceroy and with the party leaders for months in Delhi during 1946, but the parties could not agree. Wavell urged the Government to make up its mind what it would do in the absence of Indian agreement. A definite statement of policy was not made until February 1947, when Wavell's replacement by Lord Mountbatten of Burma was simultaneously announced with some abruptness. Wavell was created an earl with the additional title of Viscount Keren, of Eritrea and Winchester, and returned to London untrammelled by heavy responsibility for the first time for ten years.

The last three years of his life were spent in London and in travel. He was able to indulge at leisure the taste in letters which had long been among his most precious relaxations. He became president of the Royal Society of Literature, and of the Kipling, Browning, Poetry, and Virgil societies; he had been chancellor of Aberdeen University since 1945. He was colonel of the Black Watch; and he steeped himself in regimental matters, visiting its allied regiments in Canada and South Africa. He received honorary degrees from the universities of Aberdeen, St. Andrews, Cambridge, London, Oxford, and McGill. He was a commander of the Legion of Honour and received decorations from many countries in-cluding Greece, Ethiopia, Poland, Czechoslovakia, Holland, China, Russia, and the United States. He was appointed C.M.G. (1919), C.B. (1935), K.C.B. (1939), G.C.B. (1941), and G.C.S.I. and G.C.I.E. in 1943, in which year he was sworn of the Privy Council.

In 1950 Wavell showed signs of illness, culminating in jaundice; in May he underwent a severe operation', from which he seemed to be recovering, when he relapsed and died in London 24 May. His body lay in the chapel of St. John at the Tower, of which he had been constable since 1948; on 7 June it was carried up-river in a barge to Westminster, where a service was held; and he was buried that evening by the men of his regiment in the chantry close of his old school at Winchester.

In appearance Wavell was broad and thickset, sturdy and physically tough, with a deep ridge on either side of his mouth. His silences were proverbial, but among intimates he was the most congenial and jovial of company. He delighted in horses and horsemanship, in golf and shooting. He had a prodigious memory and would quote poetry with gusto and at length. His widely popular anthology, *Other Men's Flowers* (1944), consisted entirely of pieces which he had by heart, and showed how catholic was his taste. His *The Palestine Campaigns* (1928) and his biography of his former chief Allenby (produced during years of high pressure and published in two volumes, 1940 and 1943, and in one volume in 1946) were masterly and easy to read. He had delivered the Lees Knowles lectures at Cambridge on 'Generals and Generalship' in 1939; these were published in 1941. He also published essays and lectures on military subjects, which were collected during his lifetime under the title *The Good Soldier* (1948).

As a soldier, for all his misfortunes in the war of 1939–45, his reputation at its end stood as high as those of any of his contemporaries. In none of the eleven campaigns which he fought did he have preponderance in men or in weapons. He left the Middle East, he was relieved of command in Asia, before the arrival of the material and reinforcements with which his successors were to win their country's battles and their own renown. Yet at no time, in public or in private, in print or by the spoken word, did he ever complain or repine.

Wavell married in 1915 Eugénie Marie, daughter of Colonel John Owen Quirk, and had three daughters and one son, Archibald John Arthur (1916–53) who succeeded his father in his titles, which became extinct when he was killed in Kenya, 24 December 1953, in an attack on Mau-Mau terrorists.

A portrait of Wavell by Simon Elwes was in India.

[Lord Wavell, Dispatches from the Somaliland Protectorate, the Middle East, the Western Desert, the Middle East, and the Eastern Theatre based on India (Supplements to the *London Gazette*, 5, 13, 26 June, 3 July, and 18 September 1946); R. J. Collins, *Lord Wavell*, 1947; Winston S. Churchill, *The Second World War*, vols. iii–v, 1950–52; I. S. O. Playfair and others, (Official) *History of the Second World War. The Mediterranean and Middle East*, vols. i and ii, 1954–6; Sir John Kennedy, *The Business of War*, edited by Bernard Fergusson, 1957; private information; personal knowledge.]

BERNARD FERGUSSON

[V. P. Menon, *The Transfer of Power in India*, 1957.]
published 1959

WEMYSS Rosslyn Erskine

(1864–1933)

Baron Wester Wemyss

Admiral of the fleet, was born in London 12 April 1864, the youngest and posthumous son of James Hay Erskine Wemyss, of Wemyss Castle, Fife, by his wife, Millicent Ann Mary, daughter of Lady Augusta Kennedy Erskine, the fourth daughter of the Duke of Clarence (later King William IV) by Mrs. Dorothy Jordan. His paternal grandfather, Rear-Admiral James Erskine Wemyss, was great-great-grandson of David, third Earl of Wemyss, vice-admiral of Scotland, and his own maternal great-grand-father, King William, had been the last holder of the office of lord high admiral of the United Kingdom; thus the naval strain in his ancestry was strong.

Wemyss entered the training ship *Britannia* in 1877 with his third cousins, the Royal Princes Albert Victor (later Duke of Clarence) and George (later King George V). On passing out in 1879 with distinction he was appointed to the *Bacchante* under Captain Lord Charles Thomas Montagu-Douglas-Scott, in which the princes were to spend three years on a memorable cruise round the world. On its termination he was sent to the *North-umberland* in the Channel squadron for eight months, and then was appointed senior midshipman of the *Canada* on the North America and West Indies station in which Prince George was his next junior. While in her he was promoted sub-lieutenant and in August 1884 came home for the normal twelve months' courses at Portsmouth and Greenwich. He then spent eighteen months in the *Hecla*, torpedo depot ship, in the Mediterranean, being promoted lieutenant in her in March 1887. In October of that year he was, naturally from his early associations, selected for service in the royal yacht *Osborne* for two years, after which he became flag-lieutenant in the *Anson* to Rear-Admiral (Sir) R. E. Tracey, second-in-command of the Channel squadron, and left her in March 1890 to spend two years in the *Undaunted* (serving under Captain Lord Charles Beresford) in the Mediterranean. He then returned to the Channel squadron for two years in the *Empress of India*, flagship of Rear-Admiral (Sir) Edward Seymour and after one year as first-lieutenant of the *Astraea*, 2nd class cruiser, in the Mediterranean, resumed royal yacht duty as first-lieutenant of the *Victoria and Albert* in 1896. On completion of this service he was promoted commander in August 1898 in accordance with established custom. He was commander of the cruiser *Niobe*, detached from the Channel squadron for special service at the Cape during the first year of the South African war. He was disappointed in having no opportunity for fighting service ashore, his ship being employed on ancillary duties, including that of transporting Boer prisoners to St. Helena and guarding them there. On return to England at the end of 1900 he was invited by the Duke of York (later King George V) to accompany him as second-in-command of the *Ophir* (a specially commissioned passenger ship) on his tour to the overseas Dominions, which was arranged mainly for the opening of the first parliament of the Commonwealth of Australia. Queen Victoria's death temporarily delayed the preparations for this cruise, but it took place from March to November 1901. Wemyss won golden opinions from all concerned and was specially promoted captain and appointed M.V.O. on its conclusion.

At Christmas 1902 the second Lord Selborne's memorandum launched the new scheme of naval education promoted by Sir John Fisher. Its first and most important part provided for the establishment of a new cadets' college on novel lines and Fisher had already marked down Wemyss as the ideal man to be its first captain. He was accordingly employed at the Admiralty in working out the details of the new organization and of the building of the college in the grounds of Queen Victoria's house at Osborne until August 1903 when he was appointed to its command. The initial and continued success of this remarkable enterprise was largely due to his qualities of energy, resource, and tact, and his buoyant good temper and infectious enthusiasm. He won the respect and admiration of civilian masters, officers, and cadets alike, and the entire approval of the Board in Whitehall.

After two years at Osborne Wemyss was glad to return to the sea as captain of the *Suffolk* in the Mediterranean where Beresford was then commander-in-chief. He paid her off in April 1908 and, after a few months command of the *Albion*, flagship in the Atlantic Fleet, next year was appointed commodore, 2nd class, of the royal naval barracks at Devonport.

Wemyss's service there was interrupted for several months in 1910 while he commanded the *Balmoral Castle* which was commissioned to take the Duke and Duchess of Connaught to South Africa for the opening of the first Union parliament. He had accepted the offer of this command in April when the Prince of Wales had intended to undertake the ceremony, but the death of King Edward VII necessitated a change. King George made him extra naval equerry after his accession and he was appointed C.M.G. after the voyage. In April 1911 he reached flag rank, only twelve and a half years after promotion to commander, and in October 1912 he was appointed for a year rear-admiral in the second battle squadron of the Home Fleet (flag in the *Orion*).

On 1 August 1914, when war became imminent, Wemyss was appointed to the command of the twelfth cruiser squadron (flag in the *Charybdis*) with orders to act in concert with the French Admiral Rouyer in charge of the western patrol in the English Channel for the protection of the transports conveying the British Expeditionary Force to France. Constantly at sea in an old uncomfortable ship without any sign of the enemy, Wemyss found this a tiresome task, and was glad when in September his squadron was sent to Canada to escort the first contingent of 30,000 Canadians to England. This duty was successfully accomplished, although Wemyss himself considered that old slow cruisers were a risky protection to a convoy. He then resumed charge of the western patrol, transferring his flag to the *Euryalus* until February 1915, when he hauled it down on the dispersal of his cruiser force.

Wemyss was at once selected for a new duty as governor of the island of Lemnos and to take charge of a naval base to be created at Mudros for the impending naval and military Dardanelles campaign, although occupying a most anomalous position in foreign territory without staff or detailed orders to guide him. He was required to organize and equip a base for a great army and fleet on an island which had no facilities for landing troops or discharging cargo, no water supply, and no native labour. He set to work at once with great energy and resourcefulness and in a few weeks troops were able to land and assemble for the attack on the Gallipoli peninsula. In March Vice-Admiral (Sir) S. H. Carden, the commander-in-chief, had to give up the command through ill health. His second-in-command, Rear-Admiral (Sir) J. M. De Robeck, was junior to Wemyss, although older, but Wemyss with great public spirit himself proposed that De Robeck should succeed Carden with the acting rank of vice-admiral, remaining himself in charge of Mudros.

In April Wemyss was able to take an active part in the landing operations in command of the first naval squadron, being in charge of the Helles section, with his flag in his former flagship *Euryalus*, and having Lieutenant-General Sir Aylmer Hunter-Weston and his staff on board. Throughout this critical and dangerous work he maintained close co-operation with the military authorities, readily accepted ideas from his own officers, such as the celebrated beaching of the cargo ship *River Clyde*, and helped to maintain the morale of the whole expedition by his indomitable cheerfulness and imperturbability. In August he was mentioned in dispatches for his invaluable services in the Gallipoli landing.

In November, during De Robeck's absence on leave, Wemyss was appointed acting vice-admiral, transferring his flag to the *Lord Nelson*. Commodore (afterwards Admiral Lord) Keyes, De Robeck's chief of staff, had obtained his admiral's leave to go to London to urge one more naval attempt to get through the Straits before the evacuation recommended by General Sir Charles Monro was effected. De Robeck himself did not advise this proposal, but Wemyss enthusiastically pressed it upon the generals on the spot and by telegrams to A. J. Balfour, the first lord. But military opinion was adverse and the Admiralty did not support him. In the actual evacuation of Suvla and Anzac Wemyss, although detesting the decision to effect it, threw himself into the naval direction of the operation with courage and optimistic determination, thereby sustaining the spirits of doubting generals, and deserved a full share of credit for its being carried out almost without loss.

In January 1916 Wemyss was appointed K.C.B. for his Dardanelles service and commander-in-chief of the East Indies and Egypt station. The *Euryalus* was again his flagship and he soon found opportunities of effective co-operation with the military commanders in the defence of Egypt against the Turks and the Senussi rising and in the support of General Sir Archibald Murray's advance to Sinai. He then took his squadron to the Persian Gulf and went himself up the Tigris in a river-gunboat to try to relieve the critical situation in Mesopotamia. In a forlorn hope of saving the garrison of Major-General Sir C. V. F. Townshend at Kut from surrender he attempted to get a food ship through to the town; it failed, but he could not rightly refuse the military appeal for help. He then completed his tour of his station, visiting both India, where he saw the viceroy, Lord Chelmsford, and Ceylon, and, after meeting Rear-Admiral (Sir) W. L. Grant, commander-in-chief, China station, at Penang, he returned to Egypt in August in time to support the advance by General Sir Edmund Allenby into Palestine, and foster the Arab revolt by his patrols in the Red Sea. He established cordial relations with the Emir Feisal and T. E. Lawrence, as well as with the generals. He was made vice-admiral in 1916.

In June 1917 under an agreement between Great Britain, France, and Italy it was decided to appoint a vice-admiral as commander-in-chief of the British ships in the Mediterranean with headquarters at Malta. Wemyss was offered and accepted the appointment, but on returning to London for instructions he was invited by Sir Eric Geddes, who had just succeeded Sir Edward Carson as first lord, to join his Board as second sea lord; that official had hitherto been expected to take the place of the first sea lord in his absence. But on further reflection Geddes decided to leave the second sea lord to carry on his personnel work and in September created a new office of deputy sea lord for Wemyss.

Geddes had been instructed by Lloyd George to proceed at once with the development of the war staff, already inaugurated by Mr. Churchill in 1912 on a much more extensive scale and on the lines of the General Staff of the army. Wemyss had no previous experience of Admiralty administration but entered with zest upon his new duties and arranged for Keyes to join him as director of the new Plans Division. Admiral Sir John Jellicoe, the first sea lord, did not feel justified in handing over responsibilities to his new deputy and his differences with both Geddes and the prime minister led to his being replaced at the end of the year (1917) by Wemyss himself. Thus at the age of fifty-three Wemyss had reached the highest position in the naval service. Throughout 1918 he worked in complete unity with Geddes. He disliked office work but believed thoroughly in devolution of duties to trusted colleagues and subordinates and was able, by co-ordinating the several divisions of the war staff into a team, to inspire all with his own infectious enthusiasm. His success in dealing with the prolonged submarine menace was mainly due to this, and the dramatic exploit of Zeebrugge (April 1918) was an enterprise after his own heart. He was appointed G.C.B. in June 1918 and promoted admiral in 1919.

Wemyss's intimate knowledge of foreign affairs and friendships with the leading French admirals with whom he served in the Allied naval command were of great advantage as the armistice with its international problems drew near, and he represented the Allied navies with conspicuous distinction together with Marshal Foch at the final capitulation of the Germans at Compiègne. His success in securing what he considered to be the minimum of naval terms in the settlement was only obtained after vigorous resistance to the readiness of some members of the War Cabinet to weaken them, and to the blank ignorance of the French generals about the naval conduct of the war. With the new year preparations for the Peace Conference began in Paris and Wemyss was charged with the difficult task of maintaining the naval interests of this country: as at the armistice he succeeded in spite of many obstacles in getting his terms accepted by both the Allied statesmen and the Germans.

At home Wemyss took a leading part in securing substantial increases in the remuneration of the naval service. His new chief in Whitehall was Walter Long, and, much hurt by an anonymous press agitation demanding his replacement by Sir David Beatty and by his exclusion in July from the list of peerages and money awards to the principal war leaders, in that month he asked his leave to resign. Long refused, but a few months later feeling himself out of sympathy with the government's attitude to the revolutionary Russian régime and to the maintenance of this country's naval supremacy, Wemyss decided definitely to resign and left office on 1 November 1919, being specially promoted admiral of the fleet and raised to the peerage as Baron Wester Wemyss, of Wemyss, co. Fife, the title of an ancient Scottish barony in his family. He remained on half pay until he reached the age limit and retired in 1929, having received no further government employment as a governor or ambassador which he felt he had a right to expect, and lived mainly at Wemyss and at Cannes. But he was actively engaged as director of the Cables and Wireless Company and the British Oil Development Company, conducting a successful mission on behalf of the latter to the Middle East in 1927 and to South America on behalf of the former in 1929. He maintained his intense interest in foreign affairs and occasionally expressed his views in the House of Lords and in the press, particularly his hostility to the Turkish treaty of 1920, and to the Washington naval treaty of 1922.

Wester Wemyss much enjoyed his duties as president of the Institution of Naval Architects, which he became in 1928. He received honorary degrees from the universities of Oxford, Cambridge, and St. Andrews, and the freedom of the last named city. His foreign decorations included the grand cordon of the Legion of Honour, the French médaille militaire (conferred by President Millerand at the unveiling of the Armistice monument in 1922), the United States D.S.M., and the highest distinctions of the other Allied countries.

Wester Wemyss possessed the great advantage of a most attractive courageous personality, although with no claim to deep technical knowledge in his profession. Nicknames are said to be some guide to a man's character, and the fact that he was universally known as 'Rosy' since childhood is a tribute to his bright and sunny disposition. He was a man of the world in the best sense of the phrase, with a simple faith in his own star and a cheerful optimism which carried him through many difficulties. A genial and generous host, he made friends readily and won the loyal devotion of his staff and subordinates. He had no opportunity of showing his qualities as a fleet leader, but as a naval statesman he deserved well of his country in maintaining to the full the great traditions of his post in Whitehall. His knowledge of French, much enhanced after his marriage by his wife's foreign connexions, contributed greatly to his intimate friendship with many of the great French officers of his time and made him a popular figure at many international meetings. He published in 1924 *The Navy in the Dardanelles Campaign*, a lively account of his own experiences and views.

Wester Wemyss married in 1903 Victoria, the only daughter of Sir Robert Burnett David Morier, the eminent diplomat, and had one daughter. He died at Cannes 24 May 1933 and was buried in the chapel garden of Wemyss Castle after preliminary services at Cannes and Westminster Abbey, at which naval honours were officially accorded to him.

There is a drawing of Wester Wemyss by Francis Dodd in the Imperial War Museum, and his portrait is in Sir A. S. Cope's 'Some Sea Officers of the Great War', painted in 1921, in the National Portrait Gallery.

[Admiralty records; Sir H. Newbolt, (Official) *History of the War. Naval Operations*, vol. iv, 1928; C. F. Aspinall-Oglander, (Official) *History of the Great War.*

Wilson

Military Operations, Gallipoli, vols. i and ii, 1929–1932; Lady Wester Wemyss, *The Life and Letters of Lord Wester Wemyss*, 1935; private information; personal knowledge.]

VINCENT W. BADDELEY

published 1949

WILSON Sir Henry Hughes

(1864–1922)

Baronet

Field-marshal, the second son of James Wilson, of Currygrane, Edgeworthstown, co. Longford, by his wife, Constance Grace Martha, eldest daughter of James Freeman Hughes, of The Grove, Stillorgan, co. Dublin, was born at Currygrane 5 May 1864. In 1877 he was sent to Marlborough College, where he worked for entrance into the army. Failing twice to gain admission into Woolwich and three times into Sandhurst, in December 1882 he obtained a commission without examination in the Longford Militia (then 6th battalion, Rifle Brigade); through this channel he gained admission into the 18th Royal Irish Regiment, but was immediately transferred to the Rifle Brigade, being gazetted into it in November 1884. The 1st battalion, which he joined in India, proceeded to Burma soon after in order to take part in the troublesome operations for the suppression of armed brigandage. While engaged on this duty in 1886, Wilson received a severe wound over the right eye and, as a result of the injury, returned home late in 1887. Whilst on sick leave he set to work for entrance to the Staff College, and, after passing the entrance examination in 1891, joined the College at Camberley in January 1892. At the Staff College he made no particular mark as a student but he made many friends. Meanwhile he had married, in 1891, Cecil Mary, youngest daughter of George Cecil Gore Wray, J.P., of Ardnamona, co. Donegal.

On leaving Camberley, after having been promoted captain in December 1893, Wilson remained at home until, early in 1894, he received a temporary appointment in the Intelligence Department at the War Office, at the head of which was his friend, another Irishman, Sir John Ardagh. There he was employed in dealing mainly with South African questions. But he did not complete the normal tenure of his appointment, being transferred in 1897, at the instance of the director of the department, as brigade-major to the 3rd Infantry brigade. On the outbreak of the South

African War, Wilson's brigade was sent to the Cape under the command of Major-General (Sir) Neville Lyttelton, as the 4th brigade of the 2nd division. On arrival the troops were ordered to Natal, where the 4th brigade took part in the unfortunate battle of Colenso (15 December 1899). After this failure a deadlock arose until Sir Redvers Buller tried to turn the Boer position by moving westwards and then crossing the Tugela river. The attempt, in which Wilson took a full share, ended in the reverse at Spion Kop (24–25 January 1900). After these operations Lyttelton was promoted to command a division and left the 4th brigade, having formed a high opinion of his brigade-major and conceived a friendship for him which later proved to be greatly to Wilson's advantage.

After the relief of Ladysmith on 1 March the Natal field force, Wilson with it, eventually made its way into the Transvaal. After visiting Pretoria in order to see Lord Roberts, whose only son, killed at Colenso, had been one of Wilson's Irish friends, he was selected for service on the headquarters staff, first as deputy-assistant-quartermaster-general and then as assistant-military-secretary. In the latter capacity he returned to England with Lord Roberts in January 1901. For his South African service he received the D.S.O. in June and was promoted brevet-lieutenant-colonel on 3 December, the day following his attaining the rank of major in his own regiment. This early promotion, combined with the support of such influential patrons, was certain to lead to further advancement.

Anxious to secure a home appointment, Wilson, in February 1902, obtained command of the 9th provisional battalion at Colchester, and held that position for exactly one year. Having thus qualified for fresh staff appointment, he was made a deputy-assistant-adjutant-general in the military training branch of the War Office in April 1903, being advanced to assistant-adjutant-general in the following June. His work was connected with the training of the auxiliary forces, and in that capacity he often accompanied Lord Roberts on official tours. In 1904 there began the reorganization of the War Office and the formation of the new general staff; during the unsettled period which ensued Wilson was busily engaged on tasks that were after his own heart. Largely as the result of these he was promoted brevet-colonel in December 1904, and finally appointed by Sir Neville Lyttelton, now chief of the general staff, to be commandant of the Staff College, with the rank of brigadier-general, in January 1907.

At Camberley Wilson soon displayed many attributes of the successful teacher, and, thanks to a vivid personality, a remarkable facility for public speaking, a never-failing humorous turn of expression, and a penchant for the dramatic, he achieved great popularity among the students, while his reputation as a lecturer spread throughout the army. In addition, he soon made himself the leading exponent of the policy of close co-operation with

France in the event of a continental war. Here he found a virgin field for his talent for lecturing, and he availed himself of the opportunity to the full. More pregnant with fateful consequences was the friendship which at this period he formed with General (afterwards Marshal) Foch, then head of the French École Supérieure de Guerre. As time went on Wilson became more and more possessed by the idea of placing the British army at the disposal of France in the event of war.

In 1910 Wilson was chosen for the post of director of military operations at the War Office, and on leaving Camberley in August of that year he was made the subject of unusual demonstrations of popularity. He had been created a C.B. in 1908. In his new position he rapidly acquired great influence, and concentrated his energies on elaborating schemes for the instant support of France by the entire armed resources of Great Britain in the event of an outbreak of war with Germany. He often visited France, sometimes in company with Sir John French (afterwards Earl of Ypres), and thereby still further committed the British government to the policy of armed support of France. But his plans, admirably worked out in detail, were largely based on two faulty premisses: first, they relegated to a merely secondary place any potential intervention of the British fleet; secondly, they entirely subordinated the action of the British army to French plans, with inadequate advantages to, or regard for, British military needs. Moreover, insufficient thought was paid to many practical details of command. The Franco-German crisis of 1911 passed off, and Wilson accelerated his plans for the warlike action which he now advocated in public utterances, while in the meantime his relations with General Foch grew still more intimate. In November 1913 he was promoted major-general. Then, in the spring of 1914, occurred the Curragh incident, the result of the British government's apparent intention of coercing Ulster by armed force to participate in the grant of Irish Home Rule. The cavalry officers at the Curragh declared that they would resign their commissions rather than take action against Ulster, and the episode led to the resignation of Sir John French, then chief of the Imperial General Staff, and of Sir John Spencer Ewart, the adjutant-general. Throughout the crisis Wilson, as a protestant Irishman, was active behind the scenes in his support of the Ulster cause. The state of tension, both in Ireland and in the general European situation, continued with little abatement until the sequel to the murders at Serajevo in July 1914 led up to the British declaration of war against Germany in support of France on 4 August. Lord Kitchener thereupon became secretary of state for war. Of his views on matters both of strategy and of raising the 'new armies', Wilson strongly and openly disapproved.

The British Expeditionary Force landed in France under the orders of Sir John French, with Sir Archibald Murray as chief, and Wilson in the entirely new position of sub-chief, of the general staff. The whole scheme of mobilization, which Wilson had inspired, worked admirably. On 14 August British head-quarters crossed to France; the troops followed, and on 23 August were attacked by the German First Army at Mons. The French plan of campaign already showed signs of collapse, whilst co-operation between French and British armies proved faulty. The retreat began, General Murray's health broke down, and Wilson became largely responsible for the work of general head-quarters. In spite of an assumed air of light-heartedness he could do little to retrieve the situation; indeed, at one moment he seemed to be filled with such forebodings that he sent instructions to the troops to burn their baggage and retreat at full speed; but both corps commanders, Sir Douglas Haig and Sir Horace Smith-Dorrien, declined to issue such orders. The tide turned at the River Marne on 6 September; the inconclusive battle of the Aisne followed, until, at the beginning of October, the British army was transferred to Flanders. Throughout this period Wilson performed the work of his office interrupted by frequent visits to French head-quarters. The battle of Ypres was next fought to the bitter end (October–November), but it was scarcely possible for the high command to influence the result, except by a display of remarkable tenacity. In November the question arose whether Wilson should not succeed General Murray as chief of staff. The final decision, however, was not taken until 25 January 1915, when Sir William Robertson became chief of staff, while Wilson was appointed chief liaison officer with French head-quarters, receiving the temporary rank of lieutenant-general, the latter distinction being gazetted on 19 February. He now ceased to exercise any direct influence over the course of events in the field, and busied himself with the political conduct of the War. In June he appears to have become less hostile to the formation of the new armies by Lord Kitchener, a fact which smoothed down the acrimony subsisting between the secretary of state and himself. He was created K.C.B. in the spring.

In August 1915 Wilson received from Sir John French the offer of the command of an army corps; it was also intimated to him privately that his refusal of that offer would not be unacceptable to the secretary of state. In the end the IV Army Corps was entrusted to him in December 1915. During his tenure of command throughout 1916, he was not called upon to participate in any noteworthy action, although on 19 May, after taking over some poorly constructed and sited trenches from the French at the northern end of Vimy Ridge, the Germans developed a heavy surprise attack at that point, which drove the British back a considerable distance with some loss. Wilson thereupon made plans to retake the lost ground, but was ordered to desist, as the attempt promised to be too costly. The IV

Corps was gradually denuded of troops for the battle of the Somme, and on 1 December Wilson himself was selected as head of a mission which was to proceed to Russia in order to discuss the supply of war material. After his return in March 1917 he went back to France in order to act as chief liaison officer with French head-quarters, his rank of lieutenant-general being then made permanent. After General Nivelle had been succeeded as commander-in-chief of the French armies by General Pétain on 15 May, the latter informed British head-quarters that he considered Wilson to be a *persona non grata*. Wilson thereupon returned to England.

After a spell of unemployment Wilson, at the instance of Sir William Robertson, was appointed to the Eastern command at home in September 1917, a position which suited him well since it enabled him to reside in London and keep in close touch with military and political authorities alike: it was in these circumstances that Wilson came into close contact with the prime minister, Mr. Lloyd George. Soon afterwards, on 24 October, occurred the serious defeat of the Italian army, initiated by an Austro-German surprise attack at Caporetto. By threatening the complete collapse of Italy, this event produced a grave crisis in the Allied conduct of the War. A conference of the Powers was accordingly summoned at Rapallo, and thither Wilson hastened in an entirely unofficial capacity, in company with the prime minister on 7 November. As prearranged by Mr. Lloyd George and M. Painlevé, the French premier, there was created at this meeting a 'Supreme War Council', designed to co-ordinate the various war policies and military plans of the Allied countries. This council, which was to meet as required, comprised two leading ministers from Great Britain, France, Italy, and the United States respectively, and these statesmen were supported by a group of permanent military representatives who were to work out all military plans on their behalf. One representative was selected by each Power, and, as the chiefs of staff were not eligible, the choice of British representative fell upon Wilson, who might indeed be considered as one of the chief instigators of the creation of the council. He was then given the temporary rank of general. At Versailles, the seat of the new council, Wilson and the other Allied military representatives set up their offices, surrounded by numerous staffs, on 1 December. For the next ten weeks the military representatives compiled a number of joint notes for the benefit of the council, the fourteenth and last of which alone acquired much importance, since it adumbrated the formation of a general reserve of troops for the entire Western front, inclusive of Italy. The use of this reserve was to be controlled by an executive War Board, of which Wilson was to be the British member. But numerous obstacles at once arose, mainly owing to the disinclination of the various national commanders-in-chief to part with their troops, of which they had all too few; still more, perhaps, owing to the difficulties involved in the command of such a body. The consequent discussions dragged on for many weeks, indeed long after Wilson had left Versailles for London.

For some time it had been apparent that Mr. Lloyd George preferred Wilson's facile personality and his pungent modes of expression to the uncompromising attitude and blunt opinions of Sir William Robertson, then chief of the Imperial General Staff. Supported by Lord Milner alone in the Cabinet, Mr. Lloyd George finally decided that Wilson should supersede Robertson, and the change took place on 18 February 1918. As chief of the Imperial General Staff Wilson found full scope in the political sphere for the exercise of his particular abilities; but he had scarcely settled down in his new office when, on 21 March, the Germans launched their great onslaught against the British Fifth Army. The offensive, although long expected, fell at a point which had not been foreseen by the Versailles Council. Heavily outnumbered, the British gave ground until it seemed as though the Allied front might break. The general reserve, as proposed by the Supreme War Council, not having come into existence, it was clear that some drastic remedy was needed to save the situation. Wilson hastened to France, whither Lord Milner had already proceeded, and on 26 March, after a conference of Allied statesmen and commanders at Doullens, north of Amiens, it was decided to confer the control of the combined Allied armies on General Foch. As the direction of the military operations of the Allies now virtually passed into Foch's hands, Wilson's work became merged in the results of the numerous committees and conferences which grew to be synonymous with the higher conduct of the War. In France the next three months continued to be full of anxiety, as the Germans, after being checked before Amiens, renewed their attacks at other points. At length on 18 July the tide turned, the Allied advance began, and the Germans slowly gave way until they were eventually compelled to accept the Allied terms of armistice on 11 November.

The months which elapsed between the Armistice and the signing of the Peace Treaty at Versailles on 28 June 1919, were spent by Wilson mostly in Paris. During that time he began to drift away somewhat from his close association with Mr. Lloyd George. Eventually he made no secret of his dissatisfaction both with the terms of peace and with the whole management of the political situation by the Allied statesmen. He opposed any British participation in the League of Nations, expressed himself against a pro-Greek policy in Asia Minor, and was an advocate of strong British rule in the East generally; whilst he continued to urge the enforcement of rigorous measures in Ireland. In July 1919 he was promoted field-marshal, and in August was created a baronet, receiving the thanks of parliament and a grant of £10,000.

Affairs in Poland, at Constantinople, and in Mesopotamia occupied Wilson in his official capacity very fully during the next two and a half years. He persisted in recommending vigorous measures, not hesitating to advise military action in each minor crisis as it arose; but the main objects of his deepest antipathy remained the Bolshevik governors of Russia and still more the leaders of Sinn Fein in Ireland; against the latter he never ceased to recommend a system of drastic coercion. Throughout 1921 the breach which was growing between Wilson and Mr. Lloyd George widened, and he became ever more preoccupied with Irish affairs and with the intricacies of party politics. Eventually, on 21 February 1922, he was elected unopposed as conservative member of parliament for North Down (Ireland). At the same time he took leave of the War Office on completing his four years as chief of the Imperial General Staff, Mr. Lloyd George having declined to extend his tenure of that office, and retired from the army.

In the House of Commons Wilson delivered a maiden speech, on 15 March, in the debate concerning the state of the army. The subject had long been a favourite theme with him; his manner and delivery were perfectly suited to the occasion. He was loudly applauded, and although strongly attacked by the labour party in opposition, was welcomed as a great accession to the conservative party and as an opponent of Mr. Lloyd George. In May he visited Northern Ireland, and made public speeches on the Irish problem in a manner which could not fail to arouse violent hostility in the ranks of Sinn Fein. The leaders of that movement thereafter regarded Wilson as an implacable enemy, and fears began to be entertained in London for his personal safety. That these were justified was proved when in the following month he was assassinated by two Sinn Feiners on the doorstep of his London house, No. 36 Eaton Place (22 June). Rumour was prevalent to the effect that his murder was the outcome of an organized conspiracy. But that was never proved, even at the trial of his murderers. He was granted a public funeral and buried in the crypt of St. Paul's Cathedral.

Opinions as to Wilson's talents and as to his place among the great figures of the European War have varied greatly. Even before 1914 some of his own colleagues had looked with growing distrust on his rapid advancement to highly responsible positions. Many saw in him a very great soldier; in that respect his personality and his facility for public speaking served him well; while a whimsical turn of expression and never-failing geniality brought him many friends and admirers. Others were concerned at his perpetual avoidance of responsibility, his lack of any real experience of military command, and his love of intrigue. The publication of his diaries in 1927, full of violently expressed prejudices and mistaken opinions, was followed by the appearance of further literature which went a long way to shatter belief in the superiority of his military talents. It was recognized that he was at heart a politician rather than a soldier.

Wilson left no child, and the baronetcy became extinct on his death. He received honorary degrees from the universities of Oxford and Cambridge and from Trinity College, Dublin; he was colonel of the Royal Irish Rifles (1915) and a colonel commandant of the Rifle Brigade (1919).

There is a portrait of Wilson by Sir William Orpen in the Imperial War Museum, South Kensington; another, by Oswald Birley, appears in *Royal Academy Pictures*, 1922; he also figures in J. S. Sargent's picture 'Some General Officers of the Great War', which hangs in the National Portrait Gallery.

[*The Times*, 23 June 1922; Sir J. E. Edmonds, (Official) *History of the Great War. Military Operations. France and Belgium, 1914–1916* and *1918*, 1922–1935; Sir C. E. Callwell, *Field-Marshal Sir Henry Wilson, his life and diaries*, 2 vols., 1927; Sir Andrew Macphail, *Three Persons*, 1929; John Charteris, *At G.H.Q.*, 1931; Army Lists; personal knowledge.]

H. DE WATTEVILLE

published 1937

WILSON Henry Maitland

(1881–1964)

First Baron Wilson

Field-marshal, was born 5 September 1881, the eldest of the three sons of Captain Arthur Maitland Wilson, OBE, of Stowlangtoft Hall, Suffolk, and his wife, (Harriet Maude) Isabella, daughter of Colonel Sir Nigel Robert Fitzhardinge Kingscote, GCVO, KCB, of Kingscote, Gloucestershire. Wilson went to Eton and Sandhurst and on 10 March 1900 was commissioned into the Rifle Brigade, with which he had family connections: his uncle, later Lieutenant-General Sir Henry Fuller Maitland, was to become colonel commandant of the 2nd battalion. He joined the 2nd battalion himself in South Africa, after the relief of Ladysmith (28 February 1900), and served with it to the end of the South African war, moving with it to Cairo in 1902.

Intense loyalty as a Rifleman to his regiment and a continuing devotion to Eton were to become two prominent strands in Wilson's life. When he became a general it was rare to find an officer on his personal staff who was not wearing black buttons and he took an abiding interest in all regimental matters, above all during his later years as colonel commandant. He was to be president of the Old Etonian Association in 1948–9 and chairman of the committee for fourteen years, from 1950 to 1964. A strand no less prominent was his enthusiasm for field sports, particularly where horses were concerned, though the physical bulk which caused him to be known from very early on as 'Jumbo', and contributed usefully to an impressive presence, did not make him an easy man to mount.

For his service in South Africa Wilson received the Queen's and King's medals, each with two clasps, and was one of the very few senior officers to be seen wearing Boer War medals in World War II.

In 1907 he went with the 2nd battalion for the first time to India, was promoted captain in 1908, served with the 3rd battalion in Bordon and Tipperary, and was posted in 1911 as adjutant to the Oxford University OTC. As such he had much to do with the generous flow of good young officers into the 'Greenjackets' (that is, the Rifle Brigade and 60th Rifles) when war broke out in 1914.

His own service in World War I, which kept him continuously in France from 1915, was wholly on the staff, almost certainly because he was too good a staff officer to be allowed back to the regimental duty he much preferred. He went out as brigade major in the 16th (Irish) division (General Sir James Steele was in later years to recall him as the best brigade major he ever knew) and was successively GSO 2 of 41st division on the Somme and of XIX Corps in the third battle of Ypres before going, in October 1917, as GSO 1 to the New Zealand division, with which he stayed till the end. He then went to Camberley, in 1919, in the hand-picked group which made up the first post-war Staff Course.

He had been appointed to the DSO in 1917 and was mentioned three times in dispatches. He was promoted major on 1 September 1915 and brevet lieutenant-colonel on 1 January 1919.

After a spell at Sandhurst Wilson returned to the regiment (the first time for twelve years) as second-in-command of the 2nd battalion at Aldershot and then, before taking command of the 1st battalion on the North-West Frontier, spent three years as chief umpire to the 2nd division under Strickland, when the GOC-in-C was a professionally exacting officer in General Sir Philip (later Lord) Chetwode. This played a significant part in Wilson's own professional development and made him fairly widely known.

After three years in India, in which he spent time cultivating tribesmen as well as in shooting, racing, and pig-sticking, and three more as an instructor in the rank of colonel at Camberley, he had to endure nine months on half pay before taking over the 16th Infantry brigade, in January

1934, from Brigadier A. P. (later Earl) Wavell. This was a time of experiment in mechanization and the working out of a role for motorized infantry operating with armour. The concept of the Motor Battalion—a type of unit in which Riflemen were before long to distinguish themselves—was now emerging.

Promoted major-general on 30 April 1935, at a time when commands were hard to come by, Maitland Wilson was again on half pay, this time for nearly two years, until taking over the 2nd division again from his old friend Wavell, in August 1937.

In the summer of 1939, in a threatening international situation, Wilson was appointed GOC-in-C, British Troops in Egypt, in the rank of lieutenant-general, and left England on 15 June (noting that it was Ascot Gold Cup day) to spend the next eight years, covering all of World War II, overseas. He was always, until very near the end of that time, to be found somewhere around the Mediterranean.

Wilson was already high in the confidence of Anthony Eden (later the Earl of Avon), secretary of state for war: they had served together as Greenjackets in World War I. He was soon to win the confidence of Winston Churchill and, unlike some other senior commanders who were less fortunate, was never thereafter to lose it. The operations of the Army of the Nile (as it came to be called) under Wilson's command, with Wavell in the position of C-in-C Middle East, resulted in spectacular successes in the Western Desert of Egypt and Libya against dramatically superior Italian forces—operations in which the action of motorized infantry working with tanks was prominent. After the capture of Tobruk, while Lieutenant-General Sir Richard O'Connor carried on the desert campaign to further successes, Wilson was appointed by Wavell as military governor of Cyrenaica—but not for long. The War Cabinet had decided, with grave misgivings on the part of its military advisers, to send an expeditionary force to help Greece withstand German invasion. The British and Imperial forces available were too weak to be of much help and the opinion was heard in Greece that their arrival would do little more than aggravate a difficult situation. Eden, in Cairo, cabled (21 February 1941) that the expeditionary force required the best commander who could be found and that he, Sir J. G. Dill, CIGS and Wavell all agreed that this was Wilson. His quiet authority was certainly useful in a time of high political sensitivity, while his tactical skill was evident in the conduct of the inevitable withdrawal, which was to end with the evacuation by the British of all mainland Greece and its occupation by the enemy. Wavell met Wilson in Crete and almost at once told him: 'I want you to go to Jerusalem and relieve Baghdad.' Wilson thus found himself GOC British Forces in Palestine and Transjordan. The successful relief of Baghdad, under siege by pro-Axis Iraqis, was followed by the move of British and Imperial forces into Vichy-held Syria and Lebanon, where the use by German aircraft of French airfields had invited a British ultimatum. The inclusion of a Free French contingent in this force was, in spite of the low availability of other troops and political pressure from de Gaulle, almost certainly a mistake. British officers with much experience in the Levant knew that what might be only token resistance from the Vichy side, offered as a matter of professional honour, would almost certainly develop into savage fighting if the Free French came in, which is just what happened. Some tended to blame Wilson (now designated C-in-C Allied Forces in Syria) for an error of judgement but the decision (against which Wavell had argued) was taken in London.

Tension between Winston Churchill and Wavell was growing and in July 1941 the latter was replaced as C-in-C Middle East by General (later Field-Marshal) Sir Claude Auchinleck, with whom the prime minister was going to find it no easier to agree. On 2 July the prime minister urged the new C-in-C to consider Wilson for command in the Western Desert. 'It is much to be regretted', Churchill wrote 'that this advice, subsequently repeated, was not taken.' Auchinleck preferred General Sir Alan G. Cunningham, after his success in Abyssinia, but the appointment did nothing to improve British performance in the field and under Cunningham's successor, General (Sir) N. M. Ritchie, results were even worse and retreat towards the Nile Delta continued. Only when Auchinleck did what the prime minister had latterly been urging and took command himself did the position stabilize, almost in the Delta.

Wilson, who had been made GOC-in-C 9th Army, with his HQ in the Lebanon, had been brought down to Egypt to command troops in the Delta against a possible breakthrough by Rommel. He was then (August 1942) ordered personally by the prime minister, whom he was meeting for the first time, to take over the new command being set up in Persia and Iraq, on the Russians' southern flank and, with its communications and oil, of growing importance. From 23 September 1942 he was to spend eighteen months, based on Baghdad, in complex work more political, administrative, and diplomatic than strictly military: work he was well suited to and did well. The transference of General Alexander (later Lord Alexander of Tunis) from the post of C-in-C Middle East to be deputy C-in-C to Eisenhower in January 1943, to assume direction of the last stages of the campaign by Allied land forces in North Africa, left the position of C-in-C Middle East once more vacant. The prime minister, again in Cairo, had Wilson moved into the post. Since the highest Allied priority in the Mediterranean was the support of Eisenhower's command, Wilson's position was soon to become, in Churchill's hyperbole, that of a general 'with responsibilities but no troops'. On the collapse of Italy later in the year the prime minister saw an opportunity to establish a dominent position in the Eastern Mediterranean before the Germans could prevent it. He cabled Wilson from Washington (9 September 1943): 'This is the time to play high. Improvise and dare.' There was little more that Wilson could do, since virtually all resources were earmarked for the Central Mediterranean, than launch some ill-supported, and in the end unsuccessful and wasteful, small operations in the Dodecanese on Cos, Leros, and Samos. The President consistently refused to allow any forces to be diverted from Eisenhower except for the Far East and would hear of nothing that suggested the slightest possibility of delaying 'Overlord', the operation to open a second front in northwest Europe. On the other hand there was enthusiastic American support for a landing in southern France (Operation 'Anvil', later renamed 'Dragoon'), in which neither Wilson nor the prime minister saw any merit. Wilson would dearly have liked to carry out Churchill's cherished wish to capture Rhodes but the President was adamant. Churchill submitted to his decision but, as he wrote, 'with one of the sharpest pangs I suffered in the war'. The 'bleeding of the Eastern Mediterranean' also brought Churchill into the acutest differences he ever had with Eisenhower, but at the same time it brought him even closer to Wilson, and when Eisenhower was moved from the theatre to take charge of the preparations for 'Overlord', Wilson was from 8 January 1944, on the prime minister's suggestion and with the President's full approval, appointed supreme commander in the Mediterranean in his place. There followed the further operations in Italy, under Alexander's command of the land forces, including the Anzio landing with its disappointingly weak command and slow gains, the steady grind northwards, and the continuing difference of emphasis between the Allies on the relative importance of a landing in the South of France, firmly opposed by Wilson and seen by Churchill only as an extravagant and unnecessary diversion. Churchill, and Wilson with him, would have much preferred strengthening Allied forces in Italy, instead of reducing them, and pressing on up through Austria into Hungary, while exploiting Tito's successes along the Adriatic. Under very strong pressure from the Americans (who harboured hardly justifiable suspicions of British intentions in 'the Balkans') the Riviera landings eventually took place, against almost negligible opposition, and were acclaimed a resounding, if scarcely relevant, success.

Trouble in Greece as the Germans withdrew in the autumn of 1944 required very active Allied intervention but Maitland Wilson was again on the move. Field-Marshal Sir John Dill, head of the Joint Staff Mission in Washington, died there 4 November 1944. The good personal relations he had established and above all Dill's firm friendship with General

Marshall had been of the utmost value to the alliance and it was imperative to put in the best available successor. On 21 November the prime minister communicated to Wilson: 'I can find only one officer with the necessary credentials and qualities, namely, yourself.' Wilson, who had been promoted field-marshal, took up the appointment in January 1945 and held it until it lapsed early in 1947. On 23 April 1947 he left for home.

In this, his last post, he had, first of all, having served in one theatre, to find out about four others. He had also to accustom himself to holding a very high-ranking post with no command responsibilities. He was none the less fully occupied acting as trusted intermediary on military matters between the British prime minister and the President, a position which did not change in essence when Roosevelt was succeeded by Truman. Wilson was present at the Yalta and Potsdam conferences and was kept fully informed on all the delicate manœuvring which led up to Hiroshima and Nagasaki.

An active military career which in nearly half a century had moved from the tough but relatively simple warfare of South Africa to involvement in atomic weapons was now at an end. 'Jumbo' Wilson had always been a dedicated professional soldier but as a staff officer early on had given promise of the flair for diplomacy which was possibly to play a more important part in what he achieved than military talent. He was good with people and particularly good with the young and in his retirement he devoted much time and affectionate attention to army cadets.

He was an impressive figure of a man, whose appearance and manner compelled attention and inspired confidence. He usually spoke little but what he had to say was closely, and even sharply, to the point. He had, it was said, 'shrewd little steely eyes', and when he looked at you closely over those half-moon spectacles it could be uncomfortable. He made no pretence to be an intellectual and was rather better in direct confrontation than on paper. His judgement was on the whole sound, though some of his arrangements for operations in the Dodecanese, admittedly at a time of frustration and some confusion, have been criticized. He was much loved by many people and was held in particularly deep affection and respect by young officers who came close to him in personal service. At the same time he could occasionally be guilty of paying perhaps insufficient attention to personal hardship if he thought he saw an overriding need to disregard it. This could have been the result of occasional lapses in imagination.

In addition to his peerage (1946) Wilson's honours included the GCB (1944; KCB, 1940; CB, 1937); GBE (1941); and a wealth of foreign decorations. When elevated to the peerage he chose as supporters to his coat:

'Dexter, a Rifleman, and Sinister, a Bugler, both of the Rifle Brigade in full dress proper.'

In the House of Lords he sat on the cross-benches, as befitted a field-marshal, but took part freely in defence debates. He was active in the affairs of the Royal United Service Institution, the Mounted Infantry Club, and the South African War Veterans' Association, in which he was particularly interested. He was colonel commandant of the Rifle Brigade from 1939 to 1951 and constable of the Tower of London from 1955 to 1960.

His last appearance in public was at Eton on St. Andrew's Day 1964, when the new Regimental Memorial was dedicated in the Cloisters. On the last day of the year he was taken ill and died peacefully at his home, Wheelwrights, Chilton, Aylesbury, 31 December 1964. He was buried with his family at Stowlangtoft and a memorial service was held in Westminster Abbey. For some years he had lived quietly in the Chilterns and close friends say he seemed a lonely man. Wherever he lived his heart remained in Suffolk.

Wilson married in 1914 Hester Mary, daughter of Philip James Digby Wykeham, of Tythrop House, Oxfordshire, and had a son, Patrick Maitland, born 14 September 1915 (by whom he was succeeded on his death) and a daughter.

There are portraits of Wilson by Maurice Codner (Royal Society of Portrait Painters, 1954), and Simon Elwes (exhibited at the Royal Academy Summer Exhibition, 1972).

[*The Times*, 1 January 1965; Field-Marshal Lord Wilson, *Eight Years Overseas*, 1949; *The Rifle Brigade Chronicle for 1965*, ed. Lieutenant-Colonel U. Verney; private information; personal knowledge.]

J. W. HACKETT

published 1981

WINGATE Orde Charles

(1903–1944)

Major-general, was born at Naini Tal, India, 26 February 1903, the third child and eldest son in a family of seven. Both the Bible and the sword were strongly in the family tradition, as also was service in Eastern lands. His grandfather, William Wingate, who came of a Scottish family long settled in Stirlingshire, had been for ten years a missionary to the Jews in Hungary. His father, Colonel George Wingate, who served for more than

thirty years in the Indian Army, taking part in three frontier expeditions, had established the Central Asian Mission to the tribes on the
North-West Frontier and in Baltistan. His mother, Mary Ethel Stanley,
daughter of Captain Charles Orde Browne, Royal Horse Artillery, came of
a Gloucestershire family, which had a tradition of military service but had
produced also in the preceding generation a distinguished Persian scholar.
Her ancestors included Granville Sharp, the philanthropist.

Both Orde Wingate's father and mother were Plymouth Brethren, and
he was brought up in a strictly puritan household, which was shown by his
deep knowledge and study of the Bible. He was a day boy at Charterhouse,
near which his father had settled on retirement. He went on to the Royal
Military Academy, Woolwich, and was gazetted to a commission in the
Royal Artillery in August 1923. As a boy Wingate had shown proficiency in
swimming, boxing, and rifle-shooting rather than in organized games. He
was keenly interested in observation of wild birds and beasts, and was fond
of music. On joining his battery he became an enthusiastic horseman,
riding boldly and well to hounds, and competing with success in point-to-
point races and show-jumping. In 1926 he qualified as an instructor in
equitation at the army school at Weedon, an exacting test of horsemanship. But he kept his brain active as well as his body, and with the encouragement of his father's cousin, General Sir Reginald Wingate, he
began to learn Arabic at the School of Oriental Studies in London. In the
autumn of 1927 he went to the Sudan to continue his study of that language. His method of reaching the Sudan was typical. He had practically
no means except his pay. He had financed his hunting by his success at
races and horse-shows. He now bought a pedal bicycle, rode it to Brindisi,
where he sold it and with the proceeds took passage in an Italian boat to
Port Sudan. He obtained an appointment in the Sudan Defence Force, in
which he spent five years (1928–33) serving mainly on the Abyssinian
frontier.

Wingate next made an expedition in the Libyan desert in search of the
legendary oasis of Zerzura. He spent five weeks in the desert from the
beginning of February 1933 until early in March. Exploration of the desert
by motor-car was just beginning at this period, but Wingate went on foot,
with camels to carry his gear. His journey produced no results but gave
him valuable experience.

During the voyage home Wingate met his future wife, Lorna Elizabeth Margaret, daughter of Walter Moncrieff Paterson, of Tilliefoure,
Monymusk, Aberdeenshire, whom he married in January 1935. From 1933
to 1936 he served with artillery units in England. Towards the end of 1936
he applied for and obtained a post on the intelligence staff in Palestine,
then in the throes of an Arab rebellion against Jewish immigration.

Influenced by the family tradition, Wingate soon became sympathetic to the Jewish cause and he was impressed by the organization and efficiency of the Jewish settlements. He spent his spare time and leave in visiting these settlements and in learning Hebrew, and became a convinced Zionist. He and his wife became friends of the Jewish leader, Chaim Weizmann. The rebellion dragged on; and presently Wingate obtained permission to organize night squads, mainly of youths from the Jewish settlements, to combat Arab sabotage and terrorism. He showed that such work could be more efficiently carried out by local teams than by the orthodox procedure of regular soldiers. The work was exacting and dangerous but productive of results. Wingate's methods had great success and did much to bring the rebellion to an end. He was appointed to the D.S.O. for his services and was wounded in a skirmish in July 1938. His pro-Jewish sympathies and his uncompromising way of expressing his opinions were not always acceptable to some of his superiors and led to controversy with them. Wingate was never an easy subordinate.

The outbreak of war in 1939 found Wingate serving as a brigade-major with an anti-aircraft unit. He was about to attend a course at the Camberley Staff College in 1940, when he was summoned to the Middle East. Sir Archibald (later Earl) Wavell, under whom he had served for some months in Palestine, had asked for him to organize assistance to the rebels in Abyssinia, as a means of embarrassing the Italians, who had now entered the war. Wingate arrived in Khartoum in the late autumn of 1940. He set to work with restless energy and driving power to collect troops, arms, and camels to make an entry into central Abyssinia. One of his first acts was to fly in at great risk to an improvised landing ground and to contact Colonel Daniel Arthur Sandford (a British officer with a long knowledge of Abyssinia who had gone in previously on foot) and some of the principal rebels. In January 1941 Wingate crossed the frontier with the exiled Emperor Haile Selassie, a small mixed force of Sudanese and Ethiopians, and a handful of British officers and N.C.O.s. Less than four months later, on 5 May 1941, he entered Addis Ababa with the Emperor. By a combination of daring and bluff his small force of under 2,000 men had made its way through the rough mountains of western Abyssinia, capturing or putting to flight many Italian garrisons which greatly outnumbered the force. It was a remarkable achievement, the strain of which told on even Wingate's iron nerve and constitution; and he was in hospital in Cairo for some months.

On recovery, Wingate returned home but was soon recalled East again by Wavell, now commander-in-chief in India, to help in stemming the Japanese invasion of Burma. When Wingate arrived the retreat from Burma had been ordered. There was just time before the complete withdrawal for him to visit the front. He quickly grasped the lie of the country and the enemy's tactics and mentality. He put forward proposals for the formation and training of a 'long range penetration group' to operate behind the Japanese lines in the reconquest of Burma. His theory was based on two new factors in war: the power to supply forces for a long period by air, and the use of portable wireless sets to maintain touch between scattered columns. Wingate's ideas were accepted, and in June 1942 he was made a brigadier and given a mixed force of British, Gurkha, and Burmese (Karens, Kachins, and Chins) to organize and train. His preparations were complete by February 1943; and about the middle of that month his eight columns crossed the Chindwin river and struck against the Japanese rear. For some six weeks the force moved and fought behind the enemy front; and although in the end some of the columns had great difficulty in extricating themselves and returning to the base, Wingate's theories had fully justified themselves. He had received a bar to his D.S.O. for his work in Abyssinia and was now given a second bar.

In August 1943 Wingate accompanied (Sir) Winston Churchill to Quebec where he explained his theories to the war leaders, including Roosevelt and Churchill, both of whom he greatly impressed. He was given a force equivalent to a division to train for the operations for the reconquest of Burma under Admiral Lord Louis Mountbatten (later Earl Mountbatten of Burma), and was promoted major-general. The training of the new force was carried out during the winter of 1943–4, and operations began early in March 1944. A new feature of the operations was that the greater part of the force was landed behind the enemy lines by glider and transport aircraft, only one brigade entering on foot. Three weeks after the original landings Wingate's forces commanded a wide area some 200 miles inside the enemy lines. On 24 March during a tropical storm Wingate was flying over the Naga jungles of north Assam in a bomber on a visit to one of his units. From some cause never ascertained the plane crashed into the jungle and all the occupants were killed. He was buried in the Arlington cemetery, United States.

Orde Wingate was cast in the same mould as Thomas Cochrane (Earl of Dundonald), Charles George ('Chinese') Gordon, T. E. Lawrence (with whom on his mother's side he could claim kinship), and others, who have had a genius for novel and unorthodox methods of warfare and the opportunity and energy to put them into practice. Such men are seldom very tractable subordinates, nor are they always easy to serve. Wingate's dynamic personality won acceptance for his ideas. At a time when Japanese tactics of infiltration had produced a feeling of helplessness in some quarters, he showed that similar tactics could be applied even more effectively and on a wider scale against the Japanese themselves. He was no haphazard marauder; his operations were always most carefully planned, his training thorough, and his administrative preparations as complete as possible. He had undoubtedly a high degree of military genius.

Apart from military affairs, Wingate had read widely and thought deeply on many subjects, on which he had very definite views. He could express himself clearly in speech or on paper. He had a strong personal faith in religion and a real belief in prayer.

Wingate had one son, born in 1944 after his father's death.

[*Geographical Journal*, vol. lxxxiii, 1934; private information; personal knowledge.]

WAVELL

published 1959

WOLSELEY Garnet Joseph

(1833–1913)

First Viscount Wolseley

Field-marshal, the eldest son of Major Garnet Joseph Wolseley, 25th Borderers, by his wife, Frances Anne, daughter of William Smith, of Golden Bridge House, co. Dublin, was born at Golden Bridge House 4 June 1833. His family, a junior branch of the Staffordshire Wolseleys, had obtained land in county Carlow under William III. Major Garnet Wolseley died when his eldest son Garnet was only seven years old, leaving a widow, four sons, and three daughters in somewhat straitened circumstances. Garnet was educated at a day school in Dublin, and at a very early age determined to be a soldier. Eager to improve his education to this end, and unable to afford special tuition, he took service in a surveyor's office in Dublin, and there acquired a sound knowledge of draughtsmanship and surveying, which knowledge was to bring him at an early stage of his career to the notice of his superior officers.

Wolseley's mother was a woman of remarkable character. Intensely religious, with a simple form of Irish Protestantism, she took the Bible as her one guide, and from her Wolseley acquired a profound belief, which lasted until his death, that his life was in God's hands. To this faith he added from the first a keen ambition to make a name for himself, while his parentage made him turn naturally to the army for a career. In after-life he said that the first business of the young officer who wishes to distinguish himself in his profession is to seek to get himself killed, and he did his best to apply that principle to himself. His faith in God's providence made him a fatalist. The resultant of this faith joined to an eager temperament and an ambitious nature was a rare degree of courage.

Wolseley received his commission as second lieutenant in the 12th Foot on 12 March 1852, and at once transferred to the 80th Foot, which was engaged in the second Burma War, in order that he might see active service. He arrived in Calcutta at the end of October 1852 to hear the guns of Fort William firing a salute on the death of the Duke of Wellington. Thus, the soldier destined to create a new phase in the history of the British army began his service just when the great leader of the régime which he was to modernize passed away. A few months later Wolseley, not yet twenty, won his first distinction by leading with judgement and gallantry an assault upon Meeah Toon's stockade, in which at the moment of victory he fell severely wounded in the left thigh. For this service he was mentioned in dispatches, was promoted lieutenant on 16 May 1853, and received the Burma War medal. He was sent home to recover from his wound, and transferred to the 90th Foot in Dublin, where, as the crisis in the Near East which culminated in the Crimean War developed, he grew more and more restless until orders arrived for his battalion to embark. When he landed in the Crimea the siege of Sebastopol was in progress, and his knowledge of surveying was soon of service. In January 1855 he was appointed an assistant engineer and served in that capacity in the trenches, becoming, owing to a run of promotion, captain at the age of twenty-one. In the trenches he first met Charles George Gordon, the common bond of religion drawing the two men together and cementing a close friendship which was to last till Gordon's death. In June 1855 he distinguished himself greatly in the attack on the Quarries, in which he was slightly wounded, the success of the operation being in a great measure due to his personal example and initiative. On 30 August, a few days before the fall of Sebastopol, he was severely wounded by a shell, losing the sight of one eye. On recovery he was appointed to the quartermaster-general's staff and remained with it till the end of the War. For his services he was recommended for a brevet majority, which he could not receive till he had completed (24 March 1858) six years' service. Returning home from the Crimea he was for a short time with the 90th at Aldershot. Then orders came for the battalion to go to China, where risings were threatening the security both of Shanghai and Hong Kong. On its way to the Far East the transport was wrecked, and, owing to the mutiny of the Bengal army, a second vessel took the three companies of the 90th, with which Wolseley travelled, from Chinese waters to Calcutta, where they were landed in 1857. In November of that year he took part in Sir Colin Campbell's first relief of Lucknow, and so distinguished himself in the leading of his company that with it he accomplished what Sir Colin had planned to be undertaken the next day by his pet regiment, the 93rd Highlanders. After the withdrawal from Lucknow, the 90th was shut up with Sir James Outram in the Alumbagh until Sir Colin was able to return on 5 February 1858 for the final capture of Lucknow. This achieved, Wolseley was appointed by Sir Colin quartermaster-general on Sir Hope Grant's staff, and served throughout the campaign of Oudh. He was mentioned five times in dispatches, and at the end of the Mutiny was promoted brevet lieutenant-colonel at the age of twenty-five.

Hardly was the Mutiny over before Wolseley was sent to China, still on Sir Hope Grant's staff, for the campaign which the war in India had postponed. Reaching China in April 1860, he took part in the capture of the Taku Forts and of the Summer Palace at Pekin. During the looting of the treasures of the palace he was observed looking sadly upon a scene which he was powerless to stop, and he paid for such few treasures as he could afford to buy, a very real piece of self-denial to a man with great natural taste for works of art, of which as soon as he had any money he became an ardent and judicious collector. Throughout his life he was strongly opposed to looting, which he regarded as immoral and injurious to discipline, and on the first occasion when he had authority, at the capture of Kumassi (1874), he insisted on King Koffee's treasure being regularly valued and systematically sold. The close of the China campaign, at the end of which he was awarded a substantive majority, marks the end of the first period of Wolseley's career. With less than eight years' service he was a brevet lieutenant-colonel, he had distinguished himself in four campaigns, each very different in character, he had established a reputation for personal courage, cool leading and judgement in action, and had proved himself to be a staff officer of ability. He was marked out as a coming man. But his experiences had done more for him than the laying of the foundation of a successful career. They had taught him to respect profoundly the fighting quality of the British soldier, but also they had taught him the grave defects of organization and training from which the British army suffered. In the Crimean winter and the Indian summer he had marked the suffering and want of efficiency due to lack of preparation and organization. He had noted the evils of a long-service system which provided no reserves to fill the losses due to battle and disease, the weakness of the purchase system, and the lack of inducements to officers to study their profession. He left China resolved to devote himself to the remedying of these evils.

After his four campaigns he was entitled to a period of long leave, which he occupied partly in the writing of his first book, *Narrative of the War with China in 1860* (1862), partly in sketching and painting, in which he had considerable skill, and partly in hunting in Ireland, and it was while enjoying this sport that he was suddenly in 1861 ordered to Canada as assistant quartermaster-general. The American Civil War was then in progress, and the *Trent* incident had decided the British government to increase the forces in Canada. During his period of staff service there he had opportunities of testing his theories of military organization and training, and also of increasing his experience of war by a visit to the United States while the Civil War was in progress.

During that visit Wolseley met Robert Lee and 'Stonewall' Jackson, of whose character, generalship, and ability he expressed unbounded admiration in a vivid article on the War which he wrote for *Blackwood's Magazine* in 1863. The Canadian service also gave him more leisure than his campaigns had allowed him for serious study, particularly of military history. In June 1865 he was promoted full colonel, and not long afterwards was made deputy quartermaster-general in Canada. Two years later, during a period of leave, he married Louisa, daughter of Mr. Alexander Erskine; and since he was a man capable of great devotion and very responsive to all that is best in woman's influence, his wife filled during the remainder of his life the place in his mind which his mother had occupied. How large that place was and how much Lady Wolseley's keen wit and shrewd observation influenced and aided her husband are shown in *The Letters of Lord and Lady Wolseley, 1870–1911*, edited by Sir George Arthur (1922).

In 1869 Wolseley increased his reputation by publishing *The Soldier's Pocket Book*, a manual of military organization and tactics, the keynote of which is preparation for war in time of peace. At that time the official manuals and regulations were almost solely concerned with peacetime drill and administration, and Wolseley's book, which ran through many editions, was the forerunner of the modern field service regulations. The next year he obtained his first chance of displaying his ability as a commander. During his period of service in Canada, the Fenians had been giving constant trouble by raids from the United States into Canada, and by their endeavours to enlist the sympathy of the French Canadians. These disturbances culminated at the end of 1869 in the rebellion of Louis Riel, the direct cause of which was the transfer of the Hudson Bay Territory to the Canadian government. Riel proclaimed a republic of the North West and established himself at Fort Garry. It was necessary to send an expedition, known as the Red River expedition (August–September 1870) against him, and Wolseley was chosen to command it. The problem was chiefly one of organization, and consisted in transporting a little force of 1,200 men with all their stores some 600 miles from Lake Superior to Fort Garry mainly by river. For this Wolseley relied largely on the services of the Canadian voyageurs, and he was completely successful, receiving the K.C.M.G. and C.B. for his services. In May 1871 he was brought home to the War Office as assistant adjutant-general, and was from the first an ardent supporter of the reforms which Mr. (afterwards Viscount) Cardwell, then secretary of state for war, was inaugurating. He became the military leader of the reformers and was deeply involved in the fierce struggle which resulted in the establishment of short service, the creation of an army reserve, the abolition of purchase, and the amalgamation of the regular army, auxiliary forces, and reserve under the commander-in-chief.

While this struggle was still in progress, the outrages of King Koffee of Ashanti brought about the first Ashanti War (1873–1874), and Wolseley was sent out in command of the expedition. He took with him a band of men most of whom were to serve with him for the remainder of his career. This band, which became known as the 'Wolseley ring', was the target of much unreasoning jealousy. He had made a practice of noting down the names of soldiers of ability and character, who were keen students of their profession, wherever he met them, and these were the only passports to his favour. The men whom he selected were little known even in the army at the time when he chose them, and included those known later as Sir Evelyn Wood, Sir Henry Brackenbury, Sir Redvers Buller, Sir George Pomeroy Colley, Sir William Butler, and Sir Frederick Maurice. The last of these he picked out for the sole reason that he (Maurice) had beaten him in a competition for a prize offered by the second Duke of Wellington for an essay on the lessons of the Franco-Prussian War. Wolseley's essay, entitled *Field Manœuvres*, was published in *Essays written for the Wellington Prize* (1872). Wolseley landed at Cape Coast Castle in October 1873. The chief difficulties to be overcome were those of country and a pestilent climate. He made his plans so as to keep British troops as short a time as possible in the country. These reached him early in January 1874, and on the 21st of that month he had defeated King Koffee at Amoaful; the capital, Kumassi, was occupied four days later. For this swift success he received the thanks of parliament, was promoted major-general, created G.C.M.G. and K.C.B., and given a grant of £25,000.

These rewards may seem excessive in relation to the scope of the expedition, but Wolseley had come to be regarded by the government as a political asset. The Franco-Prussian War had opened men's eyes to the immense importance of military organization, and there were loud outcries about British unpreparedness. Strangely enough, the man who was the leader of the military reformers was used to show that all was well. Wolseley became a popular hero. 'All Sir Garnet' was the slang equivalent of the day for 'all correct', and George Grossmith made himself up as Wolseley to sing 'The Modern Major-General' in *The Pirates of Penzance*. After a short spell at the War Office as inspector-general of the auxiliary forces, Wolseley was sent in 1875 as administrator and general commanding to Natal, where difficulties had arisen between the colonists and the Kaffirs. He settled these difficulties with tact and judgement. On his return home he became a member of the council of India at the India Office, and in 1878 was promoted lieutenant-general. In that year Lord Beaconsfield acquired Cyprus from the Turks and sent Wolseley to take over the island and to be its first administrator. While he was there the Zulu War broke out, and after the disaster of Isandhlwana (22 January 1879) he was chosen by the government to restore the situation. Before he landed, Lord Chelmsford had defeated the Zulus at Ulundi (4 July), and Wolseley's military tasks consisted in the pursuit and capture of the Zulu king, Cetywayo, and the defeat of Sekukuni, a native chief who had long harried the Boers. The problem of civil administration in South Africa had few attractions for Wolseley, and he was anxious to be rid of them as soon as possible. His instructions from the government separated him from Sir Bartle Frere, who, until his arrival, had in preparation a scheme for the federation of South Africa, with results that were not altogether happy. After establishing an administration in Zululand which was not unjustly criticized, and granting to the Transvaal the constitution of a Crown colony in accordance with the orders of the government, Wolseley returned home to the more congenial duties of quartermaster-general at the War Office.

Wolseley then entered with increased power and authority into the struggle for army reform, and for the completion of the Cardwell programme. This threw him at once into violent opposition to the second Duke of Cambridge, then commander-in-chief. The Duke had a profound knowledge of the personnel of the army, and was very popular in the service, but he believed that drill and discipline were the chief, if not the only, means to military efficiency, and held that long service was essential to discipline. He had not the imagination to enable him to envisage the requirements of modern war, and was satisfied with troops who made a fine show on parade. Wolseley made preparation for war the first principle of his policy, and in order to further that, obtained, after a fight for each item on his programme, an extension of the intelligence department, the preparation of plans for mobilization, the completion of the territorialization of the army, the encouragement of professional study, the simplification of equipment, and a gradual development of training for field warfare. His keenness, his intense belief that he was right, his impatience of opposition, and his quick temper often caused him to make enemies unnecessarily, and placed him in an unfavourable light. The Queen and the Duke of Cambridge, though both later changed their opinions, were disposed to regard him as a pushing upstart. Lord Beaconsfield, who had a high appreciation of Wolseley's qualities, did not think that they were altogether wrong, and he wrote to the Queen in 1879: 'It is quite true that Wolseley is an egotist and a braggart. So was Nelson. ... Men of action when eminently successful in early life are generally boastful and full of themselves. It is not limited to military and naval heroes' [Monypenny and Buckle, *Life of Disraeli*, vi, 435]. Amongst the very conservative class to which most of the officers of the army belonged, a class which he did not always trouble to conciliate, Wolseley figured as an iconoclast who cared nothing for regimental history or tradition. This was far from the truth. No man had a greater belief in the value of regimental esprit de corps, but he believed in it as a thing which made for proficiency, and not as a thing to delight nursemaids. He could get little money for his plans, and in order to provide clothing economically for the reservists on mobilization, dress had to be made uniform; he was therefore driven to abolish the cherished facings of line regiments, an innovation for which he was roundly abused. This is but one example of the kind of struggle which went on throughout Wolseley's periods of service in the War Office. He won, because all the arguments were on his side; but the struggle wore him out.

In 1882 Wolseley became adjutant-general, the official then responsible for the military training, and while in this office his campaign for reform was interrupted by his last two and most famous expeditions. In 1882 Arabi Pasha headed a rebellion of the Egyptian army, and on France's refusal to intervene, the British government took the law into its own hands and sent Wolseley to enforce it. After a futile naval bombardment of Alexandria, which Wolseley condemned, there followed a short and brilliant military campaign. Wolseley left England on 15 August, and after a feint at Alexandria, swiftly and secretly transferred his troops down the Suez Canal to Ismailia. A sharp action at Kassassin brought him before Arabi's fortified lines at Tel-el-Kebir, and these were carried on 13 September by a night attack, a more daring enterprise at that date than it sounds to-day. Arabi's force was routed, and Cairo promptly occupied. For this achievement Wolseley was promoted general, received the thanks of parliament, a grant of £30,000, and was created Baron Wolseley, of Cairo and Wolseley. Eighteen months after his return from Egypt Wolseley saw his friend Charles Gordon off to Khartoum (January 1884), and as soon as the extent of the Mahdi's rising became evident, urged upon a reluctant government the necessity for a relief expedition. He did not prevail in time, and in the Nile campaign he led what was from the first a forlorn hope. It has been said that Wolseley in his choice of the route for the advance to Khartoum was prejudiced by his experiences on the Red River, and he certainly used that experience to the fullest extent, for he had 800 special boats built and employed some 400 Canadian voyageurs in their navigation. Whether the rival school which advocated the Suakin-Berber route across the desert was right can never now be determined, but it is certain that (Lord) Kitchener, who served under Wolseley in the Nile campaign, chose in different circumstances to follow the Nile, and that Gordon himself strongly advocated the same route. As it was, Wolseley's steamers, after the Mahdi's followers had been defeated in a number of engagements, reached Khartoum (28 January 1885) just too late, but it is at least probable that a somewhat earlier arrival would merely have hastened Gordon's death. With this expedition, for which he was created viscount, and knight of Saint Patrick, Wolseley's long series of campaigns ended, and he returned to complete his work as an army reformer.

In October 1890 he was made commander-in-chief in Ireland, an appointment which gave him opportunity for experiment in modernizing the system of military training, and at the same time left him more leisure to indulge his tastes. Though he disliked society functions, he was a delightful host and greatly enjoyed the conversation of men and women of wit, with whom he was well able to hold his own. In furnishing Kilmainham Hospital he was able to give scope to his ardour as a collector of bric-à-brac, and there too he found time both for reading and writing. He again became a fairly constant contributor to the magazines, and in 1894 wrote for the *Pall Mall Magazine* a series of articles on *The Decline and Fall of Napoleon*, which were republished in book form (1895). He also began to write a work for which he had long been collecting material—the *Life of Marlborough*. Of this he only completed two volumes (published 1894), for in 1895, on the resignation of the Duke of Cambridge, he was appointed commander-in-chief. His struggles for reform now entered upon a new phase. He had won his battle within the army, and he now became engaged in an almost continuous effort to get ministers to give him the means to make the army efficient in war. He found his powers more cramped than he had expected. One of the Duke of Cambridge's chief efforts had been to preserve the prerogative of the Crown, particularly as regards army patronage, and in this he had received the full support of Queen Victoria. Ministers, on the other hand, were anxious to make their control complete, and they had the political sagacity to see that this would be best achieved by curbing the power of the commander-in-chief and giving the secretary of state for war a number of military advisers. Thus, Wolseley found himself not supreme but *primus inter pares*, a position which added to his difficulties in preparing for the South African War, which he foresaw, and for the great European struggle which he anticipated. In those days it was difficult to get the government to spend money upon stores and preparations which made no show in time of peace. But Wolseley so far won his way that, when the South African War broke out, for the first time in our military history brigades and divisions, which had been trained as such in time of peace, were swiftly mobilized and dispatched with adequate equipment to the theatre of war. It had taken Wolseley forty years to get the lessons of the Crimean War applied. The struggle with the Boers taught the army the defects in its training, and the truth of all that Wolseley had been preaching for years. Thereafter the training and preparation which enabled Great Britain in 1914 to place in the field an incomparable expeditionary force went forward without controversy.

But the long struggle for efficiency had worn out the protagonist. Wolseley retired in 1899. In 1903 he published *The Story of a Soldier's Life*, an interesting but not very adequate account of his life down to the Ashanti expedition. Thereafter his brain began to fail rapidly, and he died at Mentone 25 March 1913, to be buried with fitting pomp in St. Paul's Cathedral. Lady Wolseley survived her husband seven years, and the title devolved by special remainder upon their only daughter.

As a commander in the field, Wolseley never endured the supreme test of war against an equal adversary, and of his generalship it is only possible to say that everything he was asked to do he did well. His real title to fame is that he recreated the British army, which had fallen into inanition and inefficiency after the Napoleonic wars. It is he who laid the foundations upon which were built up, both the expeditionary force which saved France in 1914, and the great national army which brought victory to the Allies in 1918.

A whole-length portrait of Lord Wolseley standing by his charger, painted by Albert Besnard in 1880, was presented to the National Portrait Gallery by Lady Wolseley in 1917; a bronze bust by Sir J. E. Boehm, modelled in 1883, was also given to the Gallery by Lady Wolseley in 1919. An equestrian statue for Trafalgar Square was designed by Sir W. Goscombe John in 1918.

[Viscount Wolseley, *The Story of a Soldier's Life*, 2 vols., 1903, and *Narrative of the War with China*, 1862; C. R. Low, *A Memoir of Lieutenant-General Sir Garnet Wolseley*, 2 vols., 1878; G. L. Huyshe, *The Red River Expedition*, 1871; Sir Henry Brackenbury, *Narrative of the Ashantee War*, 2 vols., 1874; J. F. Maurice, *The Military History of the Campaign of 1882 in Egypt*, 1888; H. E. Colvile, *The History of the Sudan Campaign*, 2 parts, 1890; Sir F. Maurice and Sir George Arthur, *The Life of Lord Wolseley*, 1924.]

FREDERICK MAURICE

published 1927

(1902–1964)

French resistance organizer, was born in London 17 June 1902, the eldest son of John Yeo-Thomas and his wife, Daisy Ethel Burrows. The Yeo-Thomas family, which had connections with the Welsh coal-mining industry, had established itself in Dieppe in the middle of the nineteenth century. 'Tommy' was sent to the Dieppe Naval College where he early learned to defend his British nationality. Later he went to the Lycée Condorcet in Paris until war broke out in 1914. In spite of all his father's efforts to prevent it, he was determined to take part in the war and was accepted as a dispatch rider when the United States joined in. In 1920 he joined the Poles against the Bolsheviks; was captured and sentenced to death; but managed to escape by strangling his guard the night before his execution was due.

Returning to France, Yeo-Thomas eventually settled down to study accountancy. There followed a variety of employments until in 1932 he became secretary to the fashion house of Molyneux. When war broke out in 1939 he at once tried to enlist, but the two years he had added to his age in the first war now told against him. Eventually he managed to join the Royal Air Force with the rank of sergeant. He completed radar training and was in one of the last boats to leave France when that country fell. In October 1941 he was commissioned and sent as intelligence officer to the 308 Polish Squadron at Baginton. But he was determined to return to occupied France and eventually, in February 1942, with the help of a well-known newspaper and a member of Parliament, he was taken into Special Operations Executive. Here he became responsible for planning in the RF French section which worked in close association with General de Gaulle's Bureau Central de Renseignements et d'Action. It was at this time that he was given the *nom de guerre* 'the White Rabbit'.

After the fall of France small groups of resisters had sprung up all over the country, but they were uncoordinated, ignorant of each other's identities, purposes, or often, whereabouts. It was essential that these efforts should in some way be knit together to work towards the same end. In February 1943 Yeo-Thomas and André Dewavrin, known as Colonel Passy, the head of BCRA, were parachuted into France to join Pierre Brossolette to investigate the potential of resistance groups in the occupied zone. They succeeded in uniting the various groups in allegiance to de Gaulle, pooling their resources to organize a secret army which would spring into action on D-Day. From this mission the three men safely returned in April. But in

June the leader and a number of other members of the Conseil National de la Résistance were arrested and its work seriously disrupted. To help restore the situation Yeo-Thomas and Brossolette in September returned to France where movement and meeting together had become much more difficult. In November Yeo-Thomas, concealed inside a hearse, slipped through the controls, and was picked up by Lysander. Brossolette remained behind. In England Yeo-Thomas's urgent demands for supplies for his organization took him finally to the prime minister, Winston Churchill. This interview produced a considerable increase in aircraft for RF section and consequently in weapons and supplies for the resisters in France.

When in February 1944 Yeo-Thomas heard of Brossolette's capture, he arranged to be parachuted into France yet again in order to replace him and also to try to organize his escape. Another visit by one so well known to the Germans as 'Shelley' was courting disaster, which did indeed befall Yeo-Thomas. He was arrested in Paris and his long period of torture and imprisonment began: in Fresnes, Compiègnes, Buchenwald, and Rehmsdorf. Throughout his appalling tortures he said nothing of any value to the enemy. Despite several bold but unsuccessful attempts, he maintained his resolution to escape. At Buchenwald, in September 1944, when Allied agents were being liquidated, he persuaded the head of the typhus experimental station to allow three agents to exchange identity with three Frenchmen who were already dying. Yeo-Thomas, Harry Peulevé, and a Frenchman were selected, Yeo-Thomas, in his new identity, was transferred to Rehmsdorf as a hospital orderly. When the camp was evacuated in April 1945 before the advancing Allies he organized an escape from the train when men were engaged in burying those who had died on the journey. Yeo-Thomas was among the ten who succeeded in getting away. Starving, desperately weak from dysentery and other illnesses, he was captured by German troops, posed as an escaping French Air Force prisoner of war, and was sent to the Grunhainigen Stalag. He again organized an escape with ten others who refused to leave him when he collapsed and finally helped him to reach the advancing American forces.

Yeo-Thomas was among the most outstanding workers behind enemy lines whom Britain produced. He was stocky, well built, athletic (he had boxed in his youth), and his blue eyes had a direct and fearless look. His sense of humour revealed itself in a ready smile which, on occasions, broke into open laughter. His character was exactly suited to his task. He was fearless, quick-witted, and resourceful, and his endurance under hardship was supreme. He received the George Cross, the Military Cross and bar, the Polish Cross of Merit, the croix de guerre, and was a commander of the Legion of Honour.

Yeo-Thomas

Battered and permanently injured in health, he returned to Britain to be cared for devotedly by Barbara Yeo-Thomas, formerly Barbara Joan Dean. A marriage had ended before war broke out, two children remaining in France with their mother.

After helping to bring to trial several Nazi war criminals Yeo-Thomas returned to Molyneux in 1946 but in 1948 ill health forced him to resign. After a period of recuperation he was appointed in 1950 as representative in Paris of the Federation of British Industries. There, in its different way, he still worked for Anglo-French rapprochement. But his sufferings had taken their toll and he died in Paris 26 February 1964.

[Bruce Marshall, *The White Rabbit*, 1952; M. R. D. Foot, *S.O.E. in France*, 2nd impression, with amendments, 1968; private information; personal knowledge.]

JAMES HUTCHISON

published 1981